17th Annual Meeting of the Special Interest Group on Discourse and Dialogue (SIGDIAL 2016)

Los Angeles, California, USA

13 - 15 September 2016

ISBN: 978-1-5108-3014-1

Printed from e-media with permission by:

Curran Associates, Inc.
57 Morehouse Lane
Red Hook, NY 12571

Some format issues inherent in the e-media version may also appear in this print version.

Copyright© (2016) by the Association for Computational Linguistics
All rights reserved.

Printed by Curran Associates, Inc. (2016)

For permission requests, please contact the Association for Computational Linguistics
at the address below.

Association for Computational Linguistics
209 N. Eighth Street
Stroudsburg, Pennsylvania 18360

Phone: 1-570-476-8006
Fax: 1-570-476-0860

acl@aclweb.org

Additional copies of this publication are available from:

Curran Associates, Inc.
57 Morehouse Lane
Red Hook, NY 12571 USA
Phone: 845-758-0400
Fax: 845-758-2633
Email: curran@proceedings.com
Web: www.proceedings.com

17th Annual Meeting of the
Special Interest Group on Discourse and
Dialogue

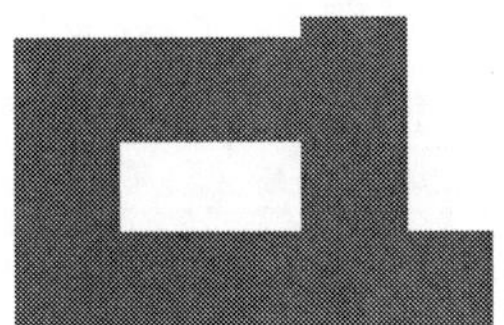 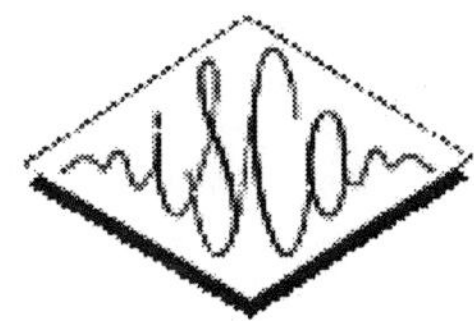 

Proceedings of the Conference

13-15 September 2016
Los Angeles, USA

In cooperation with: Association for Computational Linguistics (ACL)
International Speech Communication Association (ISCA)
Association for the Advancement of Artificial Intelligence (AAAI)

We thank our sponsors:

Microsoft Research   Xerox and PARC   Intel
Facebook   Amazon Alexa   Educational Testing Service
Honda Research Institute   Yahoo!   Interactions

Introduction

We are excited to welcome you to this year's SIGDIAL Conference, the 17th Annual Meeting of the Special Interest Group on Discourse and Dialogue. We are pleased to hold the conference this year in Los Angeles, USA, on September 13-15th, in close proximity to both INTERSPEECH 2016 and YRRSDS 2016, the Young Researchers' Roundtable on Spoken Dialog Systems.

The SIGDIAL conference remains positioned as a premier publication venue for research under the broad umbrella of discourse and dialogue. This year, the program includes oral presentations, poster sessions, and one demo session. SIGDIAL 2016 also hosts a special session entitled "The Future Directions of Dialogue-Based Intelligent Personal Assistants", organized by Yoichi Matsuyama and Alexandros Papangelis.

We received 100 complete submissions this year, which included 65 long papers, 30 short papers and 5 demo descriptions—from a broad, international set of authors. Additionally, 5 papers were submitted and then withdrawn. All papers received at least 3 reviews. We carefully considered both the numeric ratings and the tenor of the comments, both as written in the reviews, and as submitted in the discussion period, in making our selection for the program. Overall, the members of the Program Committee did an excellent job in reviewing the submitted papers. We thank them for the important role their reviews have played in selecting the accepted papers and for helping to maintain the high quality of the program. In line with the SIGDIAL tradition, our aim has been to create a balanced program that accommodates as many favorably rated papers as possible.

This year's SIGDIAL conference runs 2.5 days as it did in 2015, with the special session being held on the first day. Of the 65 long paper submissions: 19 were accepted as oral presentations and 15 were accepted for poster presentations. Of the 30 short paper submissions, 7 were accepted for poster presentation, for a total of 22 accepted posters. All 5 demonstration papers were accepted.

We enthusiastically thank the two keynote speakers, Susan Brennan (NSF/Stony Brook, USA) and Louis-Philippe Morency (CMU, USA), for their inspiring talks on cognitive science and human communication dynamics.

We offer our thanks to Pierre Lison, Mentoring Chair for SIGDIAL 2016, for his dedicated work on coordinating the mentoring process. The goal of mentoring is to assist authors of papers that contain important ideas but lack clarity. Mentors work with the authors to improve English language usage or paper organization. This year, 3 of the accepted papers were mentored. We thank the Program Committee members who served as mentors: Kristina Striegnitz, Helena Moniz and Stefan Ultes.

We extend special thanks to our Local co-Chairs, Ron Artstein and Alesia Gainer, and their team of student volunteers. We know SIGDIAL 2016 would not have been possible without Ron and Alesia, who invested so much effort in arranging the conference venue and accommodations, handling registration, making banquet arrangements, and handling numerous other preparations for the conference. The student volunteers for on-site assistance also deserve our appreciation.

Ethan Selfridge, Sponsorships Chair, has earned our appreciation for recruiting and liaising with our conference sponsors, many of whom continue to contribute year after year. Sponsorships support valuable aspects of the program, such as the invited speakers and conference banquet. In recognition of this, we gratefully acknowledge the support of our sponsors: (Platinum level) Microsoft Research, Xerox and PARC, Intel, (Gold level) Facebook, (Silver level) Amazon Alexa, Interactions, Educational Testing Service, Honda Research Institute, and Yahoo!. At the same time, we thank Priscilla Rasmussen at the ACL for tirelessly handling the financial aspects of sponsorship for SIGDIAL 2016, and for securing our ISBN.

We also thank the SIGdial board, especially officers Amanda Stent, Jason Williams and Kristiina Jokinen for their advice and support from beginning to end.

Finally, we thank all the authors of the papers in this volume, and all the conference participants for making this stimulating event a valuable opportunity for growth in the research areas of discourse and dialogue.

Raquel Fernández and Wolfgang Minker
General Co-Chairs

Giuseppe Carenini and Ryuichiro Higashinaka
Program Co-Chairs

SIGDIAL 2016

General Co-Chairs:

Raquel Fernández, University of Amsterdam, Netherlands
Wolfgang Minker, Ulm University, Germany

Technical Program Co-Chairs:

Giuseppe Carenini, University of British Columbia, Canada
Ryuichiro Higashinaka, Nippon Telegraph and Telephone Corporation, Japan

Local Chairs:

Ron Artstein, University of Southern California, USA
Alesia Gainer, University of Southern California, USA

Mentoring Chair:

Pierre Lison, University of Oslo, Norway

Sponsorship Chair:

Ethan Selfridge, Interactions, USA

SIGdial Officers:

President: Amanda Stent, Bloomberg LP, United States
Vice President: Jason D. Williams, Microsoft Research, United States
Secretary-Treasurer: Kristiina Jokinen, University of Helsinki, Finland

Program Committee:

Stergos Afantenos, University of Toulouse, France
Jan Alexandersson, DFKI GmbH, Germany
Masahiro Araki, Kyoto Institute of Technology, Japan
Ron Artstein, University of Southern California, USA
Rafael E. Banchs, Institute for Infocomm Research, Singapore
Timo Baumann, Universität Hamburg, Germany
Frédéric Béchet, Aix Marseille Université - LIF/CNRS, France
Steve Beet, Aculab plc, UK
José Miguel Benedí, Universitat Politècnica de València, Spain
Nicole Beringer, 3SOFT GmbH, Germany
Timothy Bickmore, Massachusetts Institute of Technology, USA
Nate Blaylock, Nuance Communications, Canada
Dan Bohus, Microsoft Research, USA
Johan Boye, KTH, Sweden
Kristy Boyer, North Carolina State University, USA
Nick Campbell, Trinity College Dublin, Ireland
Christophe Cerisara, CNRS, France
Joyce Chai, Michigan State University, USA
Christian Chiarcos, Goethe-Universitat Frankfurt am Main, Germany
Mark Core, University of Southern California, USA
Paul Crook, Microsoft, USA

Heriberto Cuayáhuitl, Heriot-Watt University, Edinburgh, UK
Xiaodong Cui, IBM T. J. Watson Research Center, USA
Nina Dethlefs, University of Hull, UK
David DeVault, University of Southern California, USA
Laurence Devillers, LIMSI, France
Giuseppe Di Fabbrizio, Amazon.com, USA
Jens Edlund, KTH Speech Music and Hearing, Sweden
Jacob Eisenstein, Georgia Institute of Technology, USA
Keelan Evanini, Educational Testing Service, USA
Mauro Falcone, Fondazione Ugo Bordoni, Italy
Kotaro Funakoshi, Honda Research Institute Japan
Milica Gašić, Cambridge University, UK
Kallirroi Georgila, University of Southern California, USA
Jonathan Ginzburg, Université Paris-Diderot, France
Nancy Green, University of North Carolina Greensboro, USA
Curry Guinn, University of North Carolina at Wilmington, USA
Joakim Gustafson, KTH, Sweden
Thomas Hain, University of Sheffield, UK
Dilek Hakkani-Tür, Microsoft Research, USA
Mark Hasegawa-Johnson, University of Illinois at Urbana-Champaign, USA
Larry Heck, Google, USA
Peter Heeman, Oregon Health and Sciences University, USA
Keikichi Hirose, University of Tokyo, Japan
Anna Hjalmarsson, KTH, Sweden
David Janiszek, Université Paris Descartes, France
Yangfeng Ji, Georgia Tech, USA
Kristiina Jokinen, University of Helsinki, Finland
Arne Jönsson, Linköping University, Sweden
Pamela Jordan, University of Pittsburgh, USA
Shafiq Joty, Qatar Computing Research Institute, Qatar
Tatsuya Kawahara, Kyoto University, Japan
Simon Keizer, Heriot-Watt University, Edinburgh, UK
Dongho Kim, Yonsei University, Korea
Norihide Kitaoka, Nagoya University, Japan
Kazunori Komatani, Osaka University, Japan
Stefan Kopp, Bielefeld University, Germany
Romain Laroche, Orange Labs, France
Staffan Larsson, University of Gothenburg, Sweden
Alex Lascarides, University of Edinburgh, UK
Sungjin Lee, Language Technologies Institute, Carnegie Mellon University, USA
Kornel Laskowski, Carnegie Mellon University, USA
Fabrice Lefevre, University of Avignon, France
James Lester, North Carolina State University, USA
Diane Litman, University of Pittsburgh, USA
Eduardo Lleida Solano, University of Zaragoza, Spain
Ramón López-Cózar, University of Granada, Spain
Matthew Marge, U.S. Army Research Laboratory, USA
Ricard Marxer, University of Sheffield, UK
Michael McTear, University of Ulster, Northern Ireland
Yashar Mehdad, Yahoo! Inc, USA
Raveesh Meena, KTH, Sweden

Helena Moniz, INESC-ID and FLUL, Universidade de Lisboa, Portugal
Teruhisa Misu, Honda Research Institute USA, USA
Satoshi Nakamura, Nara Institutes of Science and Technology, Japan
Mikio Nakano, Honda Research Institute Japan, Japan
Raymond Ng, University of British Columbia, Canada
Vincent Ng, University of Texas at Dallas, USA
Douglas O'Shaughnessy, INRS-EMT (University of Quebec), Canada
Aasish Pappu, Yahoo! Inc, USA
Olivier Pietquin, University Lille1, France
Paul Piwek, The Open University, UK
Andrei Popescu-Belis, Idiap Research Institute, Switzerland
Matthew Purver, Queen Mary, University of London, UK
Rashmi Prasad, University of Wisconsin-Milwaukee, USA
Norbert Reithinger, DFKI GmbH, Germany
Giuseppe Riccardi, University of Trento, Italy
Carolyn Rosé, Carnegie Mellon University, USA
Sophie Rosset, LIMSI, France
Alexander Rudnicky, Carnegie Mellon University, USA
Kenji Sagae, University of Southern California, USA
Sakriani Sakti, Nara Institutes of Science and Technology, Japan
Niko Schenk, Goethe-Universität Frankfurt am Main
Alexander Schmitt, Daimler R&D, Germany
David Schlangen, Bielefeld University, Germany
Gabriel Skantze, KTH Speech Music and Hearing, Sweden
Manfred Stede, University of Potsdam, Germany
Georg Stemmer, Intel Corp., Germany
Matthew Stone, Rutgers, The State University of New Jersey, USA
Svetlana Stoyanchev, Interactions, USA
Kristina Striegnitz, Union College, USA
Björn Schuller, Imperial College London, UK
Reid Swanson, University of Southern California, USA
Marc Swerts, Tilburg University, Netherlands
Antonio Teixeira, University of Aveiro, Portugal
Joel Tetreault, Grammarly, USA
Takenobu Tokunaga, Tokyo Institute of Technology, Japan
David Traum, University of Southern California, USA
Gökhan Tür, Microsoft Research, USA
Stefan Ultes, Cambridge University, UK
David Vandyke, Cambridge University, UK
Hsin-Min Wang, Academia Sinica, Taiwan
Nigel Ward, University of Texas at El Paso, USA
Jason Williams, Microsoft Research, USA
Kai Yu, Shanghai Jiao Tong University, China
Jian Zhang, Dongguan University of Technology and the Hong Kong University of Science and
Technology, China

Invited Speakers:

Susan Brennan, NSF-Stony Brook University, United States
Louis-Philippe Morency, Carnegie Mellon University, United States

Student Volunteers:

Jacqueline Brixey
Carla Gordon
Anya Hee
Cassidy Henry
Siddharth Jain
Ramesh Manuvinakurike
Setareh Nasihati Gilani
Maike Paetzel
Eli Pincus
Satheesh Prabu Ravi

Table of Contents

Conference Program

Tuesday September 13, 2016

13:45–15:00   **Oral Session 1: Dialogue state tracking & Spoken language understanding**

13:45–14:10   *Towards End-to-End Learning for Dialog State Tracking and Management using Deep Reinforcement Learning*
Tiancheng Zhao and Maxine Eskenazi

14:10–14:35   *Task Lineages: Dialog State Tracking for Flexible Interaction*
Sungjin Lee and Amanda Stent

14:35–15:00   *Joint Online Spoken Language Understanding and Language Modeling With Recurrent Neural Networks*
Bing Liu and Ian Lane

15:30–16:20   **Oral Session 2: Corpus creation**

15:30–15:55   *Creating and Characterizing a Diverse Corpus of Sarcasm in Dialogue*
Shereen Oraby, Vrindavan Harrison, Lena Reed, Ernesto Hernandez, Ellen Riloff and Marilyn Walker

15:55–16:20   *The SENSEI Annotated Corpus: Human Summaries of Reader Comment Conversations in On-line News*
Emma Barker, Monica Lestari Paramita, Ahmet Aker, Emina Kurtic, Mark Hepple and Robert Gaizauskas

16:50–18:20   **Special Session: The Future Directions of Dialogue-Based Intelligent Personal Assistants**

Special Session - The Future Directions of Dialogue-Based Intelligent Personal Assistants
Yoichi Matsuyama and Alexandros Papangelis

09:00–10:00   Keynote I

Keynote - More than meets the ear: Processes that shape dialogue
Susan Brennan

10:10–11:10   Poster Session 1

A Wizard-of-Oz Study on A Non-Task-Oriented Dialog Systems That Reacts to User Engagement
Zhou Yu, Leah Nicolich-Henkin, Alan W Black and Alexander Rudnicky

Classifying Emotions in Customer Support Dialogues in Social Media
Jonathan Herzig, Guy Feigenblat, Michal Shmueli-Scheuer, David Konopnicki, Anat Rafaeli, Daniel Altman and David Spivak

Cultural Communication Idiosyncrasies in Human-Computer Interaction
Juliana Miehle, Koichiro Yoshino, Louisa Pragst, Stefan Ultes, Satoshi Nakamura and Wolfgang Minker

Using phone features to improve dialogue state tracking generalisation to unseen states
Iñigo Casanueva, Thomas Hain, Mauro Nicolao and Phil Green

Character Identification on Multiparty Conversation: Identifying Mentions of Characters in TV Shows
Yu-Hsin Chen and Jinho D. Choi

Policy Networks with Two-Stage Training for Dialogue Systems
Mehdi Fatemi, Layla El Asri, Hannes Schulz, Jing He and Kaheer Suleman

Language Portability for Dialogue Systems: Translating a Question-Answering System from English into Tamil
Satheesh Ravi and Ron Artstein

15:20–16:20   Demo Session

Talking with ERICA, an autonomous android
Koji Inoue, Pierrick Milhorat, Divesh Lala, Tianyu Zhao and Tatsuya Kawahara

Rapid Prototyping of Form-driven Dialogue Systems Using an Open-source Framework
Svetlana Stoyanchev, Pierre Lison and Srinivas Bangalore

LVCSR System on a Hybrid GPU-CPU Embedded Platform for Real-Time Dialog Applications
Alexei V. Ivanov, Patrick L. Lange and David Suendermann-Oeft

Socially-Aware Animated Intelligent Personal Assistant Agent
Yoichi Matsuyama, Arjun Bhardwaj, Ran Zhao, Oscar Romeo, Sushma Akoju and Justine Cassell

Selection method of an appropriate response in chat-oriented dialogue systems
Hideaki Mori and Masahiro Araki

16:20–17:35   Oral session 4: Incremental processing

16:20–16:45   *Real-Time Understanding of Complex Discriminative Scene Descriptions*
Ramesh Manuvinakurike, Casey Kennington, David DeVault and David Schlangen

16:45–17:10   *Supporting Spoken Assistant Systems with a Graphical User Interface that Signals Incremental Understanding and Prediction State*
Casey Kennington and David Schlangen

17:10–17:35   *Toward incremental dialogue act segmentation in fast-paced interactive dialogue systems*
Ramesh Manuvinakurike, Maike Paetzel, Cheng Qu, David Schlangen and David DeVault

09:00–10:00   Keynote II

Keynote - Modeling Human Communication Dynamics
Louis-Philippe Morency

10:10–11:10   Poster Session 3

On the Evaluation of Dialogue Systems with Next Utterance Classification
Ryan Lowe, Iulian Vlad Serban, Michael Noseworthy, Laurent Charlin and Joelle
Pineau

Towards Using Conversations with Spoken Dialogue Systems in the Automated Assessment of Non-Native Speakers of English
Diane Litman, Steve Young, Mark Gales, Kate Knill, Karen Ottewell, Rogier van
Dalen and David Vandyke

Measuring the Similarity of Sentential Arguments in Dialogue
Amita Misra, Brian Ecker and Marilyn Walker

Investigating Fluidity for Human-Robot Interaction with Real-time, Real-world Grounding Strategies
Julian Hough and David Schlangen

Do Characters Abuse More Than Words?
Yashar Mehdad and Joel Tetreault

Towards a dialogue system that supports rich visualizations of data
Abhinav Kumar, Jillian Aurisano, Barbara Di Eugenio, Andrew Johnson, Alberto
Gonzalez and Jason Leigh

Analyzing the Effect of Entrainment on Dialogue Acts
Masahiro Mizukami, Koichiro Yoshino, Graham Neubig, David Traum and Satoshi
Nakamura

Towards an Entertaining Natural Language Generation System: Linguistic Peculiarities of Japanese Fictional Characters
Chiaki Miyazaki, Toru Hirano, Ryuichiro Higashinaka and Yoshihiro Matsuo

11:10–12:25   Oral Session 5: Semantics: Learning and Inference

11:10–11:35   *Reference Resolution in Situated Dialogue with Learned Semantics*
Xiaolong Li and Kristy Boyer

11:35–12:00   *Training an adaptive dialogue policy for interactive learning of visually grounded word meanings*
Yanchao Yu, Arash Eshghi and Oliver Lemon

12:00–12:25   *Learning Fine-Grained Knowledge about Contingent Relations between Everyday Events*
Elahe Rahimtoroghi, Ernesto Hernandez and Marilyn Walker

14:00–15:15   Oral Session 6: Conversational phenomena and strategies

14:00–14:25   *When do we laugh?*
Ye Tian, Chiara Mazzocconi and Jonathan Ginzburg

14:25–14:50   *Small Talk Improves User Impressions of Interview Dialogue Systems*
Takahiro Kobori, Mikio Nakano and Tomoaki Nakamura

14:50–15:15   *Automatic Recognition of Conversational Strategies in the Service of a Socially-Aware Dialog System*
Ran Zhao, Tanmay Sinha, Alan Black and Justine Cassell

15:45–16:35   Oral Session 7: Non-task-oriented dialogue systems

15:45–16:10   *Neural Utterance Ranking Model for Conversational Dialogue Systems*
Michimasa Inaba and Kenichi Takahashi

16:10–16:35   *Strategy and Policy Learning for Non-Task-Oriented Conversational Systems*
Zhou Yu, Ziyu Xu, Alan W Black and Alexander Rudnicky

Towards End-to-End Learning for Dialog State Tracking and Management using Deep Reinforcement Learning

Tiancheng Zhao and Maxine Eskenazi
Language Technologies Institute
Carnegie Mellon University
{tianchez, max+}@cs.cmu.edu

Abstract

This paper presents an end-to-end framework for task-oriented dialog systems using a variant of Deep Recurrent Q-Networks (DRQN). The model is able to interface with a relational database and jointly learn policies for both language understanding and dialog strategy. Moreover, we propose a hybrid algorithm that combines the strength of reinforcement learning and supervised learning to achieve faster learning speed. We evaluated the proposed model on a 20 Question Game conversational game simulator. Results show that the proposed method outperforms the modular-based baseline and learns a distributed representation of the latent dialog state.

1 Introduction

Task-oriented dialog systems have been an important branch of spoken dialog system (SDS) research (Raux et al., 2005; Young, 2006; Bohus and Rudnicky, 2003). The SDS agent has to achieve some predefined targets (e.g. booking a flight) through natural language interaction with the users. The typical structure of a task-oriented dialog system is outlined in Figure 1 (Young, 2006). This pipeline consists of several independently-developed modules: natural language understanding (the NLU) maps the user utterances to some semantic representation. This information is further processed by the dialog state tracker (DST), which accumulates the input of the turn along with the dialog history. The DST outputs the current dialog state and the dialog policy selects the next system action based on the dialog state. Then natural language generation (NLG) maps the selected action to its surface form which

is sent to the TTS (Text-to-Speech). This process repeats until the agent's goal is satisfied.

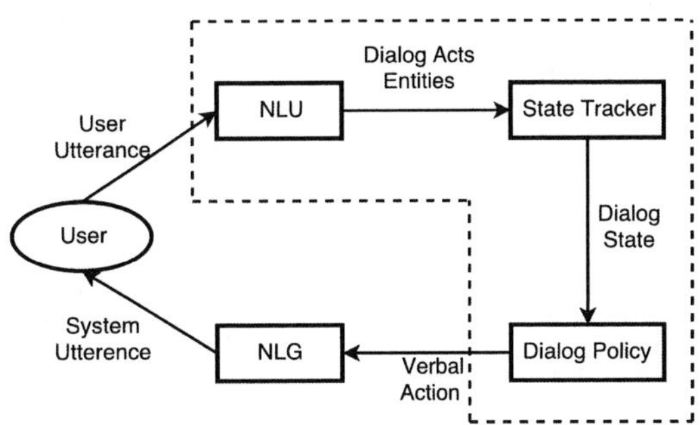

Figure 1: Conventional pipeline of an SDS. The proposed model replaces the modules in the dotted-line box with one end-to-end model.

The conventional SDS pipeline has limitations. The first issue is the *credit assignment problem*. Developers usually only get feedback from the end users, who inform them about system performance quality. Determining the source of the error requires tedious error analysis in each module because errors from upstream modules can propagate to the rest of the pipeline. The second limitation is *process interdependence*, which makes online adaptation challenging. For example, when one module (e.g. NLU) is retrained with new data, all the others (e.g DM) that depend on it become sub-optimal due to the fact that they were trained on the output distributions of the older version of the module. Although the ideal solution is to retrain the entire pipeline to ensure global optimality, this requires significant human effort.

Due to these limitations, the goal of this study is to develop an end-to-end framework for task-oriented SDS that replaces 3 important modules: the NLU, the DST and the dialog policy with a single module that can be jointly optimized. Developing such a model for task-oriented dialog sys-

1

Proceedings of the SIGDIAL 2016 Conference, pages 1–10,
Los Angeles, USA, 13-15 September 2016. ©2016 Association for Computational Linguistics

tems faces several challenges. The foremost challenge is that a task-oriented system must learn a strategic dialog policy that can achieve the goal of a given task which is beyond the ability of standard supervised learning (Li et al., 2014). The second challenge is that often a task-oriented agent needs to interface with structured external databases, which have symbolic query formats (e.g. SQL query). In order to find answers to the users' requests from the databases, the agent must formulate a valid database query. This is difficult for conventional neural network models which do not provide intermediate symbolic representations.

This paper describes a deep reinforcement learning based end-to-end framework for both dialog state tracking and dialog policy that addresses the above-mentioned issues. We evaluated the proposed approach on a conversational game simulator that requires both language understanding and strategic planning. Our studies yield promising results 1) in jointly learning policies for state tracking and dialog strategies that are superior to a modular-based baseline, 2) in efficiently incorporating various types of labelled data and 3) in learning dialog state representations.

Section 2 of the paper discusses related work; Section 3 reviews the basics of deep reinforcement learning; Section 4 describes the proposed framework; Section 5 gives experimental results and model analysis; and Section 6 concludes.

2 Related Work

Dialog State Tracking: The process of constantly representing the state of the dialog is called dialog state tracking (DST). Most industrial systems use rule-based heuristics to update the dialog state by selecting a high-confidence output from the NLU (Williams et al., 2013). Numerous advanced statistical methods have been proposed to exploit the correlation between turns to make the system more robust given the uncertainty of the automatic speech recognition (ASR) and the NLU (Bohus and Rudnicky, 2006; Thomson and Young, 2010). The Dialog State Tracking Challenge (DSTC) (Williams et al., 2013) formalizes the problem as a supervised sequential labelling task where the state tracker estimates the true slot values based on a sequence of NLU outputs. In practice the output of the state tracker is used by a different dialog policy, so that the distribution in the training data and in the live data are mis-

matched (Williams et al., 2013). Therefore one of the basic assumptions of DSTC is that the state tracker's performance will translate to better dialog policy performance. Lee (2014) showed positive results following this assumption by showing a positive correlation between end-to-end dialog performance and state tracking performance.

Reinforcement Learning (RL): RL has been a popular approach for learning the optimal dialog policy of a task-oriented dialog system (Singh et al., 2002; Williams and Young, 2007; Georgila and Traum, 2011; Lee and Eskenazi, 2012). A dialog policy is formulated as a Partially Observable Markov Decision Process (POMDP) which models the uncertainty existing in both the users' goals and the outputs of the ASR and the NLU. Williams (2007) showed that POMDP-based systems perform significantly better than rule-based systems especially when the ASR word error rate (WER) is high. Other work has explored methods that improve the amount of training data needed for a POMDP-based dialog manager. Gašić (2010) utilized Gaussian Process RL algorithms and greatly reduced the data needed for training. Existing applications of RL to dialog management assume a given dialog state representation. Instead, our approach learns its own dialog state representation from the raw dialogs along with a dialog policy in an end-to-end fashion.

End-to-End SDSs: There have been many attempts to develop end-to-end chat-oriented dialog systems that can directly map from the history of a conversation to the next system response (Vinyals and Le, 2015; Serban et al., 2015; Shang et al., 2015). These methods train sequence-to-sequence models (Sutskever et al., 2014) on large human-human conversation corpora. The resulting models are able to do basic chatting with users. The work in this paper differs from them by focusing on building a task-oriented system that can interface with structured databases and provide real information to users.

Recently, Wen el al. (2016) introduced a network-based end-to-end trainable tasked-oriented dialog system. Their approach treated a dialog system as a mapping problem between the dialog history and the system response. They learned this mapping via a novel variant of the encoder-decoder model. The main differences between our models and theirs are that ours has the advantage of learning a strategic plan using

RL and jointly optimizing state tracking beyond standard supervised learning.

3 Deep Reinforcement Learning

Before describing the proposed algorithms, we briefly review deep reinforcement learning (RL). RL models are based on the Markov Decision Process (MDP). An MDP is a tuple (S, A, P, γ, R), where S is a set of states; A is a set of actions; P defines the transition probability $P(s'|s, a)$; R defines the expected immediate reward $R(s, a)$; and $\gamma \in [0, 1)$ is the discounting factor. The goal of reinforcement learning is to find the optimal policy π^*, such that the expected cumulative return is maximized (Sutton and Barto, 1998). MDPs assume full observability of the internal states of the world, which is rarely true for real-world applications. The Partially Observable Markov Decision Process (POMDP) takes the uncertainty in the state variable into account. A POMDP is defined by a tuple $(S, A, P, \gamma, R, O, Z)$. O is a set of observations and Z defines an observation probability $P(o|s, a)$. The other variables are the same as the ones in MDPs. Solving a POMDP usually requires computing the belief state $b(s)$, which is the probability distribution of all possible states, such that $\sum_s b(s) = 1$. It has been shown that the belief state is sufficient for optimal control (Monahan, 1982), so that the objective is to find $\pi^* : b \to a$ that maximizes the expected future return.

3.1 Deep Q-Network

The deep Q-Network (DQN) introduced by Mnih (2015) uses a deep neural network (DNN) to parametrize the Q-value function $Q(s, a; \theta)$ and achieves human-level performance in playing many Atari games. DQN keeps two separate models: a target network θ_i^- and a behavior network θ_i. For every K new samples, DQN uses θ_i^- to compute the target values y^{DQN} and updates the parameters in θ_i. Only after every C updates, the new weights of θ_i are copied over to θ_i^-. Furthermore, DQN utilizes *experience replay* to store all previous experience tuples (s, a, r, s'). Before a new model update, the algorithm samples a mini-batch of experiences of size M from the memory and computes the gradient of the following loss function:

$$\mathcal{L}(\theta_i) = E_{(s,a,r,s')}[(y^{DQN} - Q(s, a; \theta_i))^2] \quad (1)$$

$$y^{DQN} = r + \gamma \max_{a'} Q(s', a'; \theta_i^-) \quad (2)$$

Recently, Hasselt et al. (2015) leveraged the overestimation problem of standard Q-Learning by introducing double DQN and Schaul et al. (2015) improves the convergence speed of DQN via *prioritized experience replay*. We found both modifications useful and included them in our studies.

3.2 Deep Recurrent Q-Network

An extension to DQN is a Deep Recurrent Q-Network (DRQN) which introduces a Long Short-Term Memory (LSTM) layer (Hochreiter and Schmidhuber, 1997) on top of the convolutional layer of the original DQN model (Hausknecht and Stone, 2015) which allows DRQN to solve POMDPs. The recurrent neural network can thus be viewed as an approximation of the belief state that can aggregate information from a sequence of observations. Hausknecht (2015) shows that DRQN performs significantly better than DQN when an agent only observes partial states. A similar model was proposed by Narasimhan and Kulkarni (2015) and learns to play Multi-User Dungeon (MUD) games (Curtis, 1992) with game states hidden in natural language paragraphs.

4 Proposed Model

4.1 Overview

End-to-end learning refers to models that can back-propagate error signals from the end output to the raw inputs. Prior work in end-to-end state tracking (Henderson et al., 2014) learns a sequential classifier that estimates the dialog state based on ASR output without the need of an NLU. Instead of treating state tracking as a standard supervised learning task, we propose to unify dialog state tracking with the dialog policy so that both are treated as actions available to a reinforcement learning agent. Specifically, we learn an optimal policy that either generates a verbal response or modifies the current estimated dialog state based on the new observations. This formulation makes it possible to obtain a state tracker even without the labelled data required for DSTC, as long as the rewards from the users and the databases are available. Furthermore, in cases where dialog state tracking labels are available, the proposed model can incorporate them with minimum modification and greatly accelerate its learning speed. Thus, the following sections describe two models: RL and Hybrid-RL, corresponding to two labelling scenarios: 1) only dialog success labels and 2) dialog

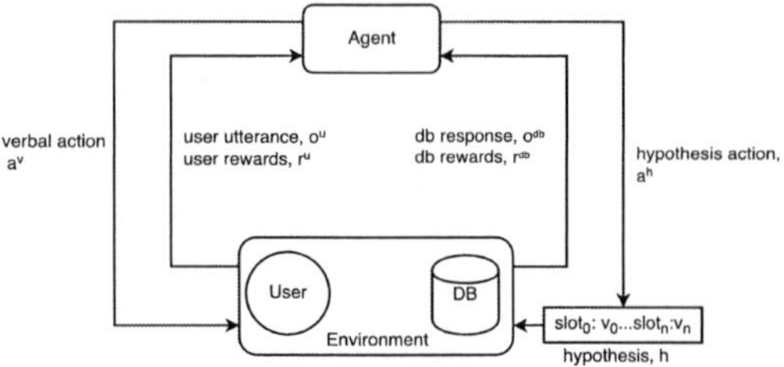

Figure 2: An overview of the proposed end-to-end task-oriented dialog management framework.

success labels with state tracking labels.

4.2 Learning from the Users and Databases

Figure 2 shows an overview of the framework. We consider a task-oriented dialog task, in which there are S slots, each with cardinality $C_i, i \in [0, S)$. The environment consists of a user, E^u and a database E^{db}. The agent can send verbal actions, $a^v \in A^v$ to the user and the user will reply with natural language responses o^u and rewards r^u. In order to interface with the database environment E^{db}, the agent can apply special actions $a^h \in A^h$ that can modify a query hypothesis h. The hypothesis is a slot-filling form that represents the most likely slot values given the observed evidence. Given this hypothesis, h, the database can perform a normal query and give the results as observations, o^{db} and rewards r^{db}.

At each turn t, the agent applies its selected action $a_t \in \{A^v, A^h\}$ and receives the observations from either the user or the database. We can then define the observation o^t of turn t as,

$$o^t = \begin{bmatrix} a_t \\ o_t^u \\ o_t^{db} \end{bmatrix} \tag{3}$$

We then use the LSTM network as the dialog state tracker that is capable of aggregating information over turns and generating a dialog state representation, $b_t = LSTM(o_t, b_{t-1})$, where b_t is an approximation of the belief state at turn t. Finally, the dialog state representation from the LSTM network is the input to $S + 1$ policy networks implemented as Multilayer Perceptrons (MLP). The first policy network approximates the Q-value function for all verbal actions $Q(b_t, a^v)$ while the rest estimate the Q-value function for each slot, $Q(b_t, a^h)$, as shown in Figure 3.

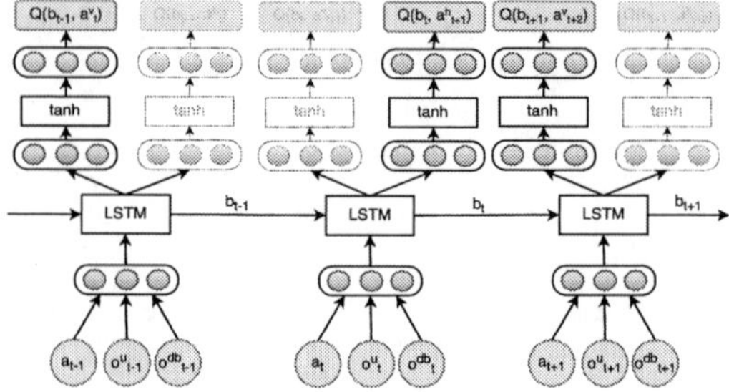

Figure 3: The network takes the observation o_t at turn t. The recurrent unit updates its hidden state based on both the history and the current turn embedding. Then the model outputs the Q-values for all actions. The policy network in grey is masked by the action mask

4.3 Incorporating State Tracking Labels

The pure RL approach described in the previous section could suffer from slow convergence when the cardinality of slots is large. This is due to the nature of reinforcement learning: that it has to try different actions (possible values of a slot) in order to estimate the expected long-term payoff. On the other hand, a supervised classifier can learn much more efficiently. A typical multi-class classification loss function (e.g. categorical cross entropy) assumes that there is a single correct label such that it encourages the probability of the correct label and suppresses the probabilities of the all the wrong ones. Modeling dialog state tracking as a Q-value function has advantages over a local classifier. For instance, take the situation where a user wants to send an email and the state tracker needs to estimate the user's goal from among three possible values: *send*, *edit* and *delete*. In a classification task, all the incorrect labels (*edit*, *delete*) are treated as equally undesirable. However, the cost of mistakenly recognizing the user goal as *delete* is much larger than *edit*, which can only be learned from the future rewards. In order to train the slot-filling policy with both short-term and long-term supervision signals, we decompose the reward function for A^h into two parts:

$$Q^\pi(b, a^h) = \bar{R}(b, a) + \gamma \sum_{b'} P(b'|b, a^h) V^\pi(b') \tag{4}$$

$$\bar{R}(b, a, b') = R(b, a^h) + P(a^h|b) \tag{5}$$

where $P(a^h|b)$ is the conditional probability that the correct label of the slots is a^h given the current belief state. In practice, instead of training a separate model estimating $P(a^h|b)$, we can replace $P(a^h|b)$ by $\mathbb{1}(y = a^h)$ as the sample reward r, where y is the label. Furthermore, a key observation is that although it is expensive to collect data from the user E^u, one can easily sample trajectories of interaction with the database since $P(b'|b, a^h)$ is known. Therefore, we can accelerate learning by generating synthetic experiences, i.e. tuple $(b, a^h, r, b')\forall a^h \in A^h$ and add them to the experience replay buffer. This approach is closely related to the Dyna Q-Learning proposed in (Sutton, 1990). The difference is that Dyna Q-learning uses the estimated environment dynamics to generating experiences, while our method only uses the known transition function (i.e. the dynamics of the database) to generate synthetic samples.

4.4 Implementation Details

We can optimize the network architecture in several ways to improve its efficiency:

Shared State Tracking Policies: it is more efficient to tie the weights of the policy networks for similar slots and use the index of slot as an input. This can reduce the number of parameters that needs to be learned and encourage shared structures. The studies in Section 5 illustrate one example.

Constrained Action Mask: We can constrain the available actions at each turn to force the agent to alternate between verbal response and slot-filling. We define A_{mask} as a function that takes state s and outputs a set of available actions for:

$$A_{mask}(s) = A_h \quad \text{new inputs from the user} \quad (6)$$
$$= A_v \quad \text{otherwise} \quad (7)$$

Reward Shaping based on the Database: the reward signals from the users are usually sparse (at the end of a dialog), the database, however, can provide frequent rewards to the agent. Reward shaping is a technique used to speed up learning. Ng et al. (1999) showed that potential-based reward shaping does not alter the optimal solution; it only impacts the learning speed. The pseudo reward function $F(s, a, s')$ is defined as:

$$\bar{R}(s, a, s') = R(s, a, s') + F(s, a, s') \quad (8)$$
$$F(s, a, s') = \gamma\phi(s') - \phi(s) \quad (9)$$

Let the total number of entities in the database be D and P_{max} be the max potential, the potential $\phi(s)$ is:

$$\phi(s_t) = P_{max}(1 - \frac{d_t}{D}) \quad \text{if } d_t > 0 \quad (10)$$
$$\phi(s_t) = 0 \quad \text{if } d_t = 0 \quad (11)$$

The intuition of this potential function is to encourage the agent to narrow down the possible range of valid entities as quickly as possible. Meanwhile, if no entities are consistent with the current hypothesis, this implies that there are mistakes in previous slot filling, which gives a potential of 0.

5 Experiments

5.1 20Q Game as Task-oriented Dialog

In order to test the proposed framework, we chose the 20 Question Game (20Q). The game rules are as follows: at the beginning of each game, the user thinks of a famous person. Then the agent asks the user a series of Yes/No questions. The user honestly answers, using one of three answers: yes, no or I don't know. In order to have this resemble a dialog, our user can answer with any natural utterance representing one of the three intents. The agent can make guesses at any turn, but a wrong guess results in a negative reward. The goal is to guess the correct person within a maximum number of turns with the least number of wrong guesses. An example game conversation is as follows:

Sys: Is this person male?
User: Yes I think so.
Sys: Is this person an artist?
User: He is not an artist.
...
Sys: I guess this person is Bill Gates.
User: Correct.

We can formulate the game as a slot-filling dialog. Assume the system has $|Q|$ available questions to select from at each turn. The answer to each question becomes a slot and each slot has three possible values: *yes/no/unknown*. Due to the length limit and wrong guess penalty, the optimal policy does not allow the agent to ask all of the questions regardless of the context or guess every person in the database one by one.

5.2 Simulator Construction

We constructed a simulator for 20Q. The simulator has two parts: a database of 100 famous people and a user simulator.

We selected 100 people from Freebase (Bollacker et al., 2008), each of them has 6 attributes: *birthplace, degree, gender, profession and birthday*. We manually designed several Yes/No questions for each attribute that is available to the agent. Each question covers a different set of possible values for a given attribute and thus carries a different discriminative power to pinpoint the person that the user is thinking of. As a result, the agent needs to judiciously select the question, given the context of the game, in order to narrow down the range of valid people. There are 31 questions. Table 1 shows a summary.

Attribute	Q_a	Example Question
Birthday	3	Was he/she born before 1950?
Birthplace	9	Was he/she born in USA?
Degree	4	Does he/she have a PhD?
Gender	2	Is this person male?
Profession	8	Is he/she an artist?
Nationality	5	Is he/she a citizen of an Asian country?

Table 1: Summary of the available questions. Q_a is the number of questions for attribute a.

At the beginning of each game, the simulator will first uniformly sample a person from the database as the person it is thinking of. Also there is a 5% chance that the simulator will consider *unknown* as an attribute and thus it will answer with *unknown* intent for any question related to it. After the game begins, when the agent asks a question, the simulator first determines the answer (*yes, no or unknown*) and replies using natural language. In order to generate realistic natural language with the *yes/no/unknown* intent, we collected utterances from the Switchboard Dialog Act (SWDA) Corpus (Jurafsky et al., 1997). Table 2 presents the mapping from the SWDA dialog acts to *yes/no/unknown*. We further post-processed results and removed irrelevant utterances, which led to 508, 445 and 251 unique utterances with intent respectively *yes/no/unknown*. We keep the frequency counts for each unique expression. Thus at run time, the simulator can sample a response according to the original distribution in the SWDA Corpus.

Intent	SWDA tags
Yes	Agree, Yes answers, Affirmative non-yes answers
No	No answers, Reject, Negative non-no answers
Unknown	Maybe, Other Answer

Table 2: Dialog act mapping from SWDA to *yes/no/unknown*

A game is terminated when one of the four conditions is fulfilled: 1) the agent guesses the correct answer, 2) there are no people in the database consistent with the current hypothesis, 3) the max game length (100 steps) is reached and 4) the max number of guesses is reached (10 guesses). Only if the agent guesses the correct answer (condition 1) treated as a game victory. The win and loss rewards are 30 and -30 and a wrong guess leads to a -5 penalty.

5.3 Training Details

The user environment E^u is the simulator that only accepts verbal actions, either a Yes/No question or a guess, and replies with a natural language utterance. Therefore A^v contains $|Q| + 1$ actions, in which the first $|Q|$ actions are questions and the last action makes a guess, given the results from the database.

The database environment reads in a query hypothesis h and returns a list of people that satisfy the constraints in the query. h has a size of $|Q|$ and each dimension can be one of the three values: *yes/no/unknown*. Since the cardinality for all slots is the same, we only need 1 slot-filling policy network with 3 Q-value outputs for *yes/no/unknown*, to modify the value of the latest asked question, which is the shared policy approach mentioned in Section 4. Thus $A^h = \{yes, no, unknown\}$. For example, considering $Q = 3$ and the hypothesis h is: $[unknown, unknown, unknown]$. If the latest asked question is Q_1 (1-based), then applying action $a^h = yes$ will result in the new hypothesis: $[yes, unknown, unknown]$.

To represent the observation o_t in vectorial form, we use a bag-of-bigrams feature vector to represent a user utterance; a one-hot vector to represent a system action and a single discrete number to represent the number of people satisfying the current hypothesis.

The hyper-parameters of the neural network model are as follows: the size of turn embedding is 30; the size of LSTMs is 256; each policy network has a hidden layer of 128 with $tanh$ activation. We also add a dropout rate of 0.3 for both LSTMs and $tanh$ layer outputs. The network has a total of 470,005 parameters. The network was trained through $RMSProp$ (Tieleman and Hinton, 2012). For hyper-parameters of DRQN, the behavior network was updated every 4 steps and the interval between each target network update C is 1000. ϵ-greedy exploration is used for training, where ϵ is linearly decreased from 1 to 0.1. The reward shaping constant P_{max} is 2 and the discounting factor γ is 0.99. The resulting network was evaluated every 5000 steps and the model was trained up to 120,000 steps. Each evaluation records the agent's performance with a greedy policy for 200 independent episodes.

5.4 Dialog Policy Analysis

We compare the performance of three models: a strong modular baseline, RL and Hybrid-RL. The baseline has an independently trained state tracker and dialog policy. The state tracker is also an LSTM-based classifier that inputs a dialog history and predicts the slot-value of the latest question. The dialog policy is a DRQN that assumes perfect slot-filling during training and simply controls the next verbal action. Thus the essential difference between the baseline and the proposed models is that the state tracker and dialog policy are not trained jointly. Also, since hybrid-RL effectively changes the reward function, the typical average cumulative reward metric is not applicable for performance comparison. Therefore, we directly compare the win rate and average game length in later discussions.

	Win Rate (%)	Avg Turn
Baseline	68.5	12.2
RL	85.6	21.6
Hybrid-RL	90.5	19.22

Table 3: Performance of the three systems

Table 3 shows that both proposed models achieve significantly higher win rate than the baseline by asking more questions before making guesses. Figure 4 illustrates the learning process of the three models. The horizontal axis is the total number of interaction between the agent and either the user or the database. The baseline model has the fastest learning speed but its performance saturated quickly because the dialog policy was not trained together with the state tracker. So the dialog policy is not aware of the uncertainty in slot-filling and the slot-filler does not distinguish between the consequences of different wrong labels (e.g classify *yes* to *no* versus to *unknown*). On the other hand, although RL reaches high performance at the end of the training, it struggles in the early stages and suffers from slow convergence. This is due to that fact that correct slot-filling is a prerequisite for winning 20Q, while the reward signal has a long delayed horizon in the RL approach. Finally, the hybrid-RL approach is able to converge to the optimal solution much faster than RL due to the fact that it efficiently exploits the information in the state tracking label.

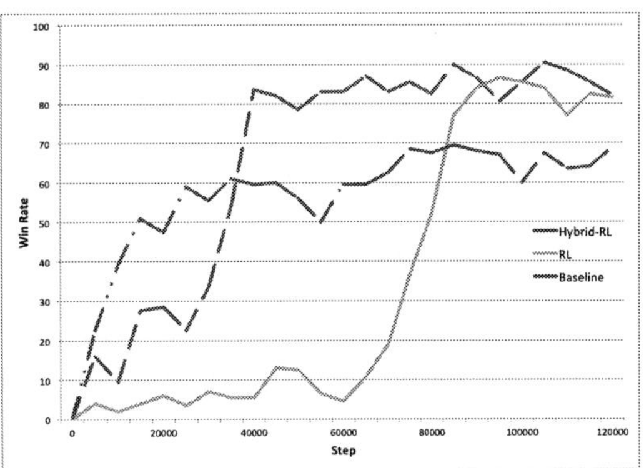

Figure 4: Graphs showing the evolution of the win rate during training.

5.5 State Tracking Analysis

One of the hypotheses is that the RL approach can learn a good state tracker using only dialog success reward signals. We ran the best trained models using a greedy policy and collected 10,000 samples. Table 4 reports the precision and recall of slot filling in these trajectories. The results indi-

	Unknown	Yes	No
Baseline	0.99/0.60	0.96/0.97	0.94/0.95
RL	0.21/0.77	1.00/0.93	0.95/0.51
Hybrid-RL	0.54/0.60	0.98/0.92	0.94/0.93

Table 4: State tracking performance of the three systems. The results are in the format of *precision/recall*

cate that the RL model learns a completely different strategy compared to the baseline. The RL model aims for high precision so that it predicts *unknown* when the input is ambiguous, which is a safer option than predicting *yes/no*, because confusing between *yes* and *no* may potentially lead to a contradiction and a game failure. This is very different from the baseline which does not distinguish between incorrect labels. Therefore, although the baseline achieves better classification metrics, it does not take into account the long-term payoff and performs sub-optimally in terms of overall performance.

5.6 Dialog State Representation Analysis

Tracking the state over multiple turns is crucial because the agent's optimal action depends on the history, e.g. the question it has already asked, the number of guesses it has spent. Furthermore, one of the assumptions is that the output of the LSTM network is an approximation of the belief state in the POMDP. We conducted two studies to test these hypotheses. For both studies, we ran the Hybrid-RL models saved at 20K, 50K and 100K steps against the simulator with a greedy policy and recorded 10,000 samples for each model.

The first study checks whether we can reconstruct an important state feature: the number of guesses the agent has made from the dialog state embedding. We divide the collected 10,000 samples into 80% for training and 20% for testing. We used the LSTM output as input features to a linear regression model with $l2$ regularization. Table 5 shows the correlation of determination r^2 increases for the model that was trained with more data.

Model	20K	50K	100K
r^2	0.05	0.51	0.77

Table 5: r^2 of the linear regression for predicting the number of guesses in the test dataset.

The second study is a retrieval task. The latent state of the 20Q game is the true intent of the users' answers to all the questions that have been asked so far. Therefore, the true state vector, s has a size of 31 and each slot, $s[k], k \in [0, 31)$ is one of the four values: *not yet asked, yes, no, unknown*. Therefore, if the LSTM output b is in fact implicitly learning the distribution over this latent state s, they must be highly correlated for a well-trained model. Therefore, for each $b_i, i \in [0, 10, 000)$,

we find its nearest 5 neighbors based on cosine distance measuring and record their latent states, $N(b_i) : B \to [S]$. Then we compute the empirical probability that each slot of the true state s differs from the retrieved neighbors:

$$p_{\text{diff}}(s[k]) = E_{s_i}\left[\frac{\sum_{n=0}^{4} \mathbb{1}(N(b_i)[n][k] \neq s_i[k])}{5}\right]$$

$$(12)$$

where $\mathbb{1}$ is the indicator function, k is the slot index and n is the neighbor index.

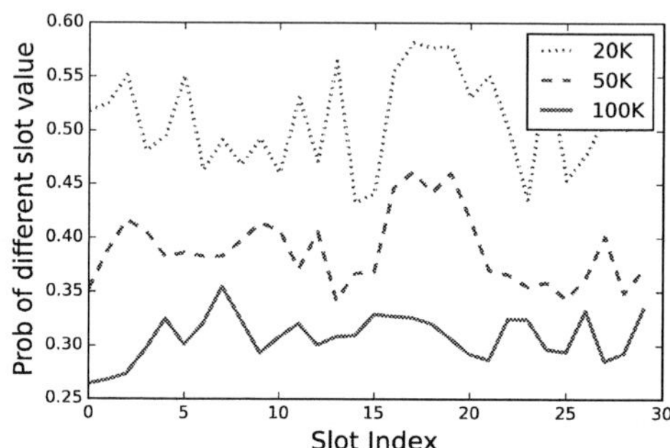

Figure 5: Performance of retrieving similar true dialog states using learned dialog state embedding.

Figure 5 shows that the retrieval error continues to decrease for the model that was trained better, which confirms our assumption that the LSTM output is an approximation of the belief state.

6 Conclusion

This paper identifies the limitations of the conventional SDS pipeline and describes a novel end-to-end framework for a task-oriented dialog system using deep reinforcement learning. We have assessed the model on the 20Q game. The proposed models show superior performance for both natural language understanding and dialog strategy. Furthermore, our analysis confirms our hypotheses that the proposed models implicitly capture essential information in the latent dialog states.

One limitation of the proposed approach is poor scalability due to the large number of samples needed for convergence. So future studies will include developing full-fledged task-orientated dialog systems and exploring methods to improve the sample efficiency. Also, investigating techniques that allow easy integration of domain knowledge so that the system can be more easily debugged and corrected is another important direction.

7 Acknowledgements

This work was funded by NSF grant CNS-1512973. The opinions expressed in this paper do not necessarily reflect those of NSF. We would also like to thank Alan W Black for discussions on this paper.

References

Dan Bohus and Alexander I Rudnicky. 2003. Ravenclaw: Dialog management using hierarchical task decomposition and an expectation agenda.

Dan Bohus and Alex Rudnicky. 2006. A k hypotheses+ otherbelief updating model. In *Proc. of the AAAI Workshop on Statistical and Empirical Methods in Spoken Dialogue Systems*.

Kurt Bollacker, Colin Evans, Praveen Paritosh, Tim Sturge, and Jamie Taylor. 2008. Freebase: a collaboratively created graph database for structuring human knowledge. In *Proceedings of the 2008 ACM SIGMOD international conference on Management of data*, pages 1247–1250. ACM.

Pavel Curtis. 1992. Mudding: Social phenomena in text-based virtual realities. *High noon on the electronic frontier: Conceptual issues in cyberspace*, pages 347–374.

M Gašić, F Jurčíček, Simon Keizer, François Mairesse, Blaise Thomson, Kai Yu, and Steve Young. 2010. Gaussian processes for fast policy optimisation of pomdp-based dialogue managers. In *Proceedings of the 11th Annual Meeting of the Special Interest Group on Discourse and Dialogue*, pages 201–204. Association for Computational Linguistics.

Kallirroi Georgila and David R Traum. 2011. Reinforcement learning of argumentation dialogue policies in negotiation. In *INTERSPEECH*, pages 2073–2076.

Matthew Hausknecht and Peter Stone. 2015. Deep recurrent q-learning for partially observable mdps. *arXiv preprint arXiv:1507.06527*.

Matthew Henderson, Blaise Thomson, and Steve Young. 2014. Word-based dialog state tracking with recurrent neural networks. In *Proceedings of the 15th Annual Meeting of the Special Interest Group on Discourse and Dialogue (SIGDIAL)*, pages 292–299.

Sepp Hochreiter and Jürgen Schmidhuber. 1997. Long short-term memory. *Neural computation*, 9(8):1735–1780.

Dan Jurafsky, Elizabeth Shriberg, and Debra Biasca. 1997. Switchboard swbd-damsl shallow-discourse-function annotation coders manual. *Institute of Cognitive Science Technical Report*, pages 97–102.

Sungjin Lee and Maxine Eskenazi. 2012. Pomdp-based let's go system for spoken dialog challenge. In *Spoken Language Technology Workshop (SLT), 2012 IEEE*, pages 61–66. IEEE.

Sungjin Lee. 2014. Extrinsic evaluation of dialog state tracking and predictive metrics for dialog policy optimization. In *15th Annual Meeting of the Special Interest Group on Discourse and Dialogue*, page 310.

Lihong Li, He He, and Jason D Williams. 2014. Temporal supervised learning for inferring a dialog policy from example conversations. In *Spoken Language Technology Workshop (SLT), 2014 IEEE*, pages 312–317. IEEE.

Volodymyr Mnih, Koray Kavukcuoglu, David Silver, Andrei A Rusu, Joel Veness, Marc G Bellemare, Alex Graves, Martin Riedmiller, Andreas K Fidjeland, Georg Ostrovski, et al. 2015. Human-level control through deep reinforcement learning. *Nature*, 518(7540):529–533.

George E Monahan. 1982. State of the arta survey of partially observable markov decision processes: theory, models, and algorithms. *Management Science*, 28(1):1–16.

Karthik Narasimhan, Tejas Kulkarni, and Regina Barzilay. 2015. Language understanding for text-based games using deep reinforcement learning. *arXiv preprint arXiv:1506.08941*.

Andrew Y Ng, Daishi Harada, and Stuart Russell. 1999. Policy invariance under reward transformations: Theory and application to reward shaping. In *ICML*, volume 99, pages 278–287.

Antoine Raux, Brian Langner, Dan Bohus, Alan W Black, and Maxine Eskenazi. 2005. Lets go public! taking a spoken dialog system to the real world. In *in Proc. of Interspeech 2005*. Citeseer.

Tom Schaul, John Quan, Ioannis Antonoglou, and David Silver. 2015. Prioritized experience replay. *arXiv preprint arXiv:1511.05952*.

Iulian V Serban, Alessandro Sordoni, Yoshua Bengio, Aaron Courville, and Joelle Pineau. 2015. Building end-to-end dialogue systems using generative hierarchical neural network models. *arXiv preprint arXiv:1507.04808*.

Lifeng Shang, Zhengdong Lu, and Hang Li. 2015. Neural responding machine for short-text conversation. *arXiv preprint arXiv:1503.02364*.

Satinder Singh, Diane Litman, Michael Kearns, and Marilyn Walker. 2002. Optimizing dialogue management with reinforcement learning: Experiments with the njfun system. *Journal of Artificial Intelligence Research*, pages 105–133.

Ilya Sutskever, Oriol Vinyals, and Quoc V Le. 2014. Sequence to sequence learning with neural networks. In *Advances in neural information processing systems*, pages 3104–3112.

Richard S Sutton and Andrew G Barto. 1998. *Introduction to reinforcement learning*. MIT Press.

Richard S Sutton. 1990. Integrated architectures for learning, planning, and reacting based on approximating dynamic programming. In *Proceedings of the seventh international conference on machine learning*, pages 216–224.

Blaise Thomson and Steve Young. 2010. Bayesian update of dialogue state: A pomdp framework for spoken dialogue systems. *Computer Speech & Language*, 24(4):562–588.

Tijmen Tieleman and Geoffrey Hinton. 2012. Lecture 6.5-rmsprop: Divide the gradient by a running average of its recent magnitude. *COURSERA: Neural Networks for Machine Learning*, 4:2.

Hado Van Hasselt, Arthur Guez, and David Silver. 2015. Deep reinforcement learning with double q-learning. *arXiv preprint arXiv:1509.06461*.

Oriol Vinyals and Quoc Le. 2015. A neural conversational model. *arXiv preprint arXiv:1506.05869*.

Tsung-Hsien Wen, Milica Gasic, Nikola Mrksic, Lina M Rojas-Barahona, Pei-Hao Su, Stefan Ultes, David Vandyke, and Steve Young. 2016. A network-based end-to-end trainable task-oriented dialogue system. *arXiv preprint arXiv:1604.04562*.

Jason D Williams and Steve Young. 2007. Partially observable markov decision processes for spoken dialog systems. *Computer Speech & Language*, 21(2):393–422.

Jason Williams, Antoine Raux, Deepak Ramachandran, and Alan Black. 2013. The dialog state tracking challenge. In *Proceedings of the SIGDIAL 2013 Conference*, pages 404–413.

Steve J Young. 2006. Using pomdps for dialog management. In *SLT*, pages 8–13.

Task Lineages: Dialog State Tracking for Flexible Interaction

Sungjin Lee and Amanda Stent
Yahoo Research
229 West 43rd Street, New York, NY 10036, USA
{junion, stent}@yahoo-inc.com

Abstract

We consider the gap between user demands for seamless handling of complex interactions, and recent advances in dialog state tracking technologies. We propose a new statistical approach, *Task Lineage-based Dialog State Tracking* (TL-DST), aimed at seamlessly orchestrating multiple tasks with complex goals across multiple domains in continuous interaction. TL-DST consists of three components: (1) task frame parsing, (2) context fetching and (3) task state update (for which TL-DST takes advantage of previous work in dialog state tracking). There is at present very little publicly available multi-task, complex goal dialog data; however, as a proof of concept, we applied TL-DST to the *Dialog State Tracking Challenge* (DSTC) 2 data, resulting in state-of-the-art performance. TL-DST also outperforms the DSTC baseline tracker on a set of pseudo-real datasets involving multiple tasks with complex goals which were synthesized using DSTC3 data.

1 Introduction

The conversational agent era has arrived: every major mobile operating system now comes with a conversational agent, and with the announcements over the past year of messaging-based conversational agent platforms from Microsoft, Google, Facebook and Kik (among others), technology now supports the rapid development and interconnection of all kinds of dialog bots. Despite this progress, most conversational agents can only handle a single task with a simple user goal at any particular moment. There are three significant hurdles to efficient, natural task-oriented interaction with these agents. First, they lack the ability to **share slot values across tasks**. Due to the independent execution of domain-specific task scripts, information sharing across tasks is minimally supported – the user typically has to provide common slot values separately for each task. Second, these agents lack the ability to **express complex constraints on user goals** – the user can rarely communicate in a single utterance goals related to multiple tasks, and can typically not provide multiple preferential constraints such as a boolean expression over slot values (Crook and Lemon, 2010). Third, current conversational agents lack the ability to **interleave discussion of multiple related tasks**. For instance, an agent can help a user find a restaurant, and then a hotel, but the user can't interleave these tasks to manage shared constraints.

The *dialog state tracker* (DST) is the most crucial component for addressing these hurdles. A DST constructs a succinct representation of the current conversation state, based on the previous interaction history, so that the conversational agent may choose the best next action. Recently, researchers have developed numerous DST approaches ranging from handcrafted rule-based methods to data-driven models. In particular, the series of Dialog State Tracking Challenges (DSTC) has served as a common testbed, allowing for a cycle of rigorous comparative analysis and rapid advancement (Williams et al., 2016). A consistent finding across the DSTC series is that the best performing systems are statistical DSTs based on discriminative models. The main focus of recent advances, however, has been largely confined to developing more robust approaches to other conversational agent technologies, such as automated speech recognition (ASR) and spoken language understanding (SLU), in a session-based dialog processing a single task with a relatively simple goal. Session-based, single task, simple goal dialog is easier for dialog system engineers and consistent with 25 years of commercial dialog system development, but does not match users' real-world task needs as communicated with human conversational assistants or recognized in the dialog literature (e.g. (Grosz and Sidner, 1988; Lochbaum, 1998)), and is inconsistent with the mobile-centric, always-on, conversational assistant commercial vision that has emerged over the past few years.

This gap between how humans most effectively converse about complex tasks and what conversa-

Proceedings of the SIGDIAL 2016 Conference, pages 11–21,
Los Angeles, USA, 13-15 September 2016. ©2016 Association for Computational Linguistics

tional agent technology (including DST) permits clearly shows the direction for future research – statistical DST approaches that can seamlessly orchestrate multiple tasks with complex goals across multiple domains in continuous interaction. In this paper, we describe a new approach, *Task Lineage-based Dialog State Tracking* (TL-DST), centered around the concept of a **task lineage**, to lay a framework for incremental developments toward this vision. TL-DST consists of three components: (1) task frame parsing, (2) context fetching and (3) task state update (for which TL-DST takes advantage of previous work in dialog state tracking). As a proof of concept, we conducted a set of experiments using the DSTC2 and DSTC3 data. First, we applied TL-DST to the DSTC2 data which has a great deal of user goal changes, and obtained state-of-the-art performance. Second, in order to test TL-DST on more challenging data, we applied TL-DST to a set of pseudo-real datasets involving multiple interleaved tasks and complex constraints on user goals. To generate the datasets, we fed the DSTC3 data, which includes three different types of tasks in addition to goal changes, to simulation techniques which have been often adopted for the development and evaluation of dialog systems (Schatzmann et al., 2006; Pietquin and Dutoit, 2006; Lee and Eskenazi, 2012). The results of these experiments show that TL-DST can successfully handle complex multi-task interactions, largely outperforming the DSTC baseline tracker.

The rest of this paper is organized as follows. In Section 2 we describe TL-DST. In Section 3 we discuss our experiments. In Section 4 we present a brief summary of related work. We finish with conclusions and future work in Section 5.

2 Task Lineage-based Dialog State Tracking

We start by defining some essential concepts. Following the convention of the DSTC, we represent each utterance produced by the user or agent as a set of **dialog act item**s (DAIs) of the form *dialog-act-type(slot = value)*. A DAI is produced by a SLU; TL-DST may receive input from multiple (domain-specific or general-purpose) SLUs.

Task Schema A task schema is a manually identified set of slots for which values must or may be specified in order to complete the task. For example, the task schema for a restaurant booking task will contain the required slots date/time, location, and restaurant ID, with optional slots cuisine-type, ratings, cost-rating, etc. A task schema governs the configuration of related structures such as task frame and task state.

Task Frame A task frame is a set of DAIs with associated confidence scores and time/sequence information. An augmented DAI has the form $(confidence\ score,\ DAI_{end\ time}^{start\ time})$. Usually task frames come in a collection, called a **task frame parse**, as a result of task frame parsing when there are multiple tasks involved in the user input (see Section 2.1). The following collection of task frames shows an example task frame parse for the user input *"Connection to Manhattan and find me a Thai restaurant, not Italian"*:

$$\left[\begin{array}{ll} \left[\begin{array}{ll} \textbf{Task} & \text{Transit} \\ \textbf{DAIs} & (0.8, \text{inform}(\text{dest}=\text{MH})_{0.7}^{0.1}) \end{array} \right] \\ \left[\begin{array}{ll} \textbf{Task} & \text{Restaurant} \\ \textbf{DAIs} & (0.7, \text{inform}(\text{food}=\text{thai})_{1.2}^{0.9}) \\ & (0.6, \text{deny}(\text{food}=\text{italian})_{1.7}^{1.4}) \end{array} \right] \end{array} \right]$$

Task State A task state includes essential pieces of information to represent the current state of a task under discussion, e.g., the task name, a set of belief estimates for user provided preferential constraints, DB query results, timestamps and a turn index. The following state shows an example restaurant finding task state corresponding to the user input *"Thai restaurant, not Italian"*:

$$\left[\begin{array}{ll} \textbf{Task} & \text{Restaurant} \\ \textbf{Constraints} & (0.7, \text{food} = \text{thai}) \\ & (0.6, \text{food} \neq \text{italian}) \\ \textbf{DB} & [\text{``Thai To Go''}, \text{``Pa de Thai''}] \\ \textbf{Timestamps} & 01/01/2016 : 12\text{-}00\text{-}00 \\ \dots & \dots \end{array} \right]$$

A task state is analogous to a dialog state in typical dialog systems. However, unlike in conventional dialog state tracking, we don't assume a unique value for each slot. Instead, we adopt binary distributions for each constraint. This allows us to circumvent the exponential complexity in the number of values which otherwise would be caused by taking a power set of slot values to handle complex constraints (Crook and Lemon, 2010).

Task Lineage A task lineage is a chronologically ordered list of task states, representing the agent's hypotheses about what tasks were involved at each time point in a conversation. A task lineage can be consulted to provide crucial pieces of information for conversation structure. For instance, the most recent task frames in a lineage can indicate the current focus of conversation. In addition, when the user switches back to a previous task, the agent can trace back the lineage in reverse order to take recency into account. However, conversational agents often cannot determine exactly what the user's task is. For example, there may be ASR or SLU errors, or genuine ambiguities (*"want Thai"* - `food=Thai` and a restaurant finding task or `dest=Thai` and an air travel task?). Thus we maintain a N-best list of possible task lineages. Figure 1 illustrates how task lineages are extended for new user inputs.

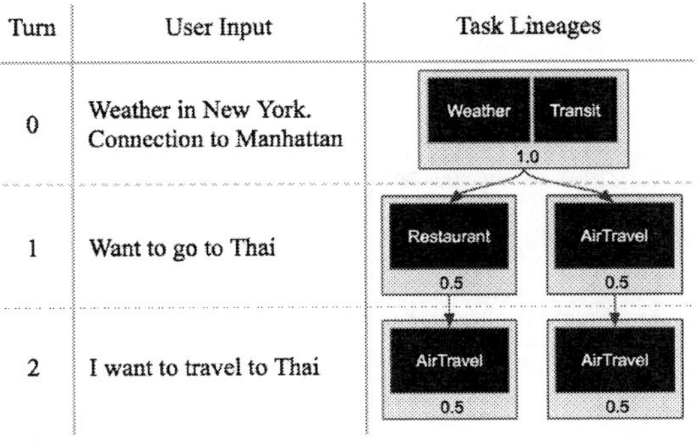

Figure 1: An example illustrating how task lineages are extended as new user inputs come in; this conversation involves multiple tasks (at turn 0) and task ambiguity (at turn 1).

Overall TL-DST Procedure Algorithm 1 describes how the overall TL-DST procedure works. At turn t, given $\widetilde{u}$, a set of DAI sets from one or more SLUs, we perform task frame parsing (see Section 2.1) to generate $\mathcal{H}$, a K-best list of task frame parses with associated belief scores, s^k [1]. Then, in order to generate a set of new task states, $\mathcal{T}$, we consider all possible combinations of the task lineages, $l_{0:t-1}^n$, in the current N-best list of task lineages, $\mathcal{L}_{0:t-1}$, and the parses, $\mathcal{A}^k$, in the K-best list of task frame parses, $\mathcal{H}$. In a task frame parse, there may be multiple task frames, hence the ith frame in the kth parse is denoted by $f^{k,i}$. The main operation in new task state generation is task state update (see Section 2.3) which forms a new task state, $\tau^{n,k,i}$, per task frame, $f^{k,i}$, by applying belief update to the task frame, relevant information in the lineage $l_{0:t-1}^n$ and the agent's output m_t. Task state update is very similar to what is done in typical dialog state tracking except that we need to additionally identify relevant information in the task lineage since a task lineage could be a mix of different tasks. This is the role of context fetching (see Section 2.2). Given a task frame $f^{k,i}$, a task lineage $l_{0:t-1}^n$ and the agent's output m_t, the context fetcher returns a set of relevant information pieces, $c^{n,k,i} \in \mathcal{C}$. Finally we construct a new set of task lineages, $\mathcal{L}_{0:t}$, by extending each current task lineage $l_{0:t-1}^n$ with the newly formed task states, $\forall i, \tau^{n,k,i}$. The belief estimate of a new task lineage is set to the product of that of the source task lineage, s_l^n, and that of the task frame parse, s_h^k. Since the extension process grows the number of task lineages by a factor of K, we perform pruning and belief normalization at the end. Based on a N-best list of task lineages, we can then compute useful quantities for the agent's action selection, such as marginal task beliefs (by adding the be-

---

[1] M sets the maximum number of samples to draw in the stochastic inference in Section 2.1.

Algorithm 1: Overall TL-DST Procedure

Input: $N > 0$, $K > 0$, $M > 0$, $\delta >= 0$
▷ Let $\mathcal{L}_{0:t} = [(l_{0:t}^1, s^1), \dots, (l_{0:t}^N, s^N)]$ be a N-best list of task lineages with scores at turn t
▷ See task_frame_parsing in Section 2.1
▷ See context_fetch in Section 2.2
▷ See task_state_update in Section 2.3
$\mathcal{L}_{0:0} \leftarrow \emptyset$;
$t \leftarrow 1$;
while *True* **do**
  $m_t \leftarrow$ agent_output();
  $\widetilde{u}_t \leftarrow$ user_input();
  $\mathcal{H} \leftarrow$ task_frame_parsing($\widetilde{u}_t, K, M$);
  $\mathcal{C} \leftarrow \{c^{n,k,i} :=$
      context_fetch($l_{0:t-1}^n, f^{k,i}, m_t, \delta$) $|$
      $l_{0:t-1}^n \in \mathcal{L}_{0:t-1}, \mathcal{A}^k \in \mathcal{H}, f^{k,i} \in \mathcal{A}^k\}$;
  $\mathcal{T} \leftarrow \{\tau^{n,k,i} :=$
      task_state_update($c^{n,k,i}, f^{k,i}, m_t$) $|$
      $c^{n,k,i} \in \mathcal{C}, \mathcal{A}^k \in \mathcal{H}, f^{k,i} \in \mathcal{A}^k\}$;
  $\hat{\mathcal{L}}_{0:t} \leftarrow [(l_{0:t-1}^n :: \tau^{n,k,i}, s_l^n \times s_h^k) |$
      $(l_{0:t-1}^n, s_l^n) \in \mathcal{L}_{0:t-1}, \tau^{n,k,i} \in \mathcal{T},$
      $s_h^k \in \mathcal{H}]$;
  $\mathcal{L}_{0:t} \leftarrow$ prune($\hat{\mathcal{L}}_{0:t}, N$);
  $t \leftarrow t + 1$;
end

---

liefs of each task across the lineages) or marginal constraint beliefs (by weighted averaging of the beliefs of each constraint across task states with the task lineage beliefs carrying the weights).

There are a few noteworthy aspects of our TL-DST approach that depart from conventional dialog state tracking approaches. Unlike most methods where the DST keeps on overriding the content of the dialog state (hence losing past states) TL-DST adopts a dynamically growing structure, providing a richer view to later processing. This is particularly important for continuous interaction involving multiple tasks. Interestingly, this is a crucial reason behind advances in deep neural network models using the *attention mechanism* (Bahdanau et al., 2014). Also unlike some approaches that use stack-like data structures for focus management (Larsson and Traum, 2000; Ramachandran and Ratnaparkhi, 2015) where the tracker pops out the tasks above the focused task, losing valuable information such as temporal ordering and partially filled constraints, TL-DST preserves all of the past task states by viewing the focus change as a side effect of generating a new updated task state each time. This allows for flexible task switching among a set of partially fulfilled tasks.

2.1 Task Frame Parsing

In this section we formalize task frame parsing as a structure prediction problem. We use a probabilistic framework that employs a beam search technique using Monte Carlo Markov Chain (MCMC) with simulated annealing (SA) and permits a clean

13

integration of hard constraints to generate legitimate parses with probabilistic reasoning.

Let $d \in \mathcal{D}$ be a domain and $\widetilde{\mathbf{u}}_d$ denote the SLU results from a parser for domain d for observation o, which is a set of confidence score and time information annotated DAIs $\widetilde{u}_d^{i_d}$, $i_d \in \mathcal{I}_d = \{1 \ldots N_d\}$. Let $\mathcal{F} = \{f_d^{i_d, t_d} | d \in \mathcal{D}, i_d \in \mathcal{I}_d, t_d \in \mathcal{T}_d\}$ be a collection of the sets of all possible task frames for each $\widetilde{u}_d$, where $\mathcal{T}_d$ is a set of task schemas defined in domain d. We add a special frame $f_{inactive}$ to $\mathcal{F}$ to which some DAIs may be assigned in order to generate legitimate task frame parses when those DAIs are created by either SLU errors or irrelevant pieces of information (e.g. greetings), or they have conflicting interpretations from different domains. Now we define a task frame parse $\mathcal{A}_{\widetilde{\mathbf{u}}}$ to be a functional assignment of every $\widetilde{u} \in \widetilde{\mathbf{u}} = \bigcup_d \widetilde{\mathbf{u}}_d$ to $\mathcal{F}$ observing the following constraints: 1) one of any two DAIs overlapped in time must be assigned to the inactive frame; 2) $\widetilde{u}_d^{i_d}$ cannot be assigned to any of task frame parses arising from another DAI $\widetilde{u}_{d'}^{i'_{d'}}$ (i.e. $f_{d'}^{i'_{d'}, t_d}$, $\forall t_d$) if the start time of $\widetilde{u}_{d'}^{i'_{d'}}$ is later than that of $\widetilde{u}_d^{i_d}$ (this constraint is necessary to get rid of spurious assignment ambiguities due to symmetry).

At a particular turn, given $\widetilde{\mathbf{u}}$, the aim of task frame parsing is to return a K-best list of assignments $\mathcal{A}_{\widetilde{\mathbf{u}}}^k, k \in \{1, \ldots, K\}$ according to the following conditional log-linear model:

$$p_{\boldsymbol{\theta}}(\mathcal{A}_{\widetilde{\mathbf{u}}} | \widetilde{\mathbf{u}}) = \frac{\exp \boldsymbol{\theta}^T \mathbf{g}(\mathcal{A}_{\widetilde{\mathbf{u}}}, \widetilde{\mathbf{u}})}{\sum_{\mathcal{A}'_{\widetilde{\mathbf{u}}}} \exp \boldsymbol{\theta}^T \mathbf{g}(\mathcal{A}'_{\widetilde{\mathbf{u}}}, \widetilde{\mathbf{u}})} \quad (1)$$

where $\boldsymbol{\theta}$ are the model weights, and $\mathbf{g}$ is a vector-valued feature function. The exact computation of Eq. 1 can become very costly for a complicated user input due to the normalization term. To avoid the exponential time complexity, we adopt a beam search technique (presented below) to yield a K-best list of parses which are used to approximate the sum in the normalization term. Figure 2 presents an example of how the variables in the model are related for different parses.

Parsing Independent assignment of DAIs to task frames may result in parses that violate the rules above. To generate a K-best list of legitimate parses, we adopt a beam search technique using MCMC inference with SA as listed in Algorithm 2. After starting with a heuristically initialized parse, the algorithm draws a sample by randomly moving a single DAI from one task frame to another so as not to produce an illegal parse, until the maximum number of samples M has been reached.

Model Training Having training data consisting of SLU results-parse pairs $(\widetilde{\mathbf{u}}^{(i)}, \mathcal{A}_{\widetilde{\mathbf{u}}}^{(i)})$, we maximize the log-likelihood of the correct parse. Formally,

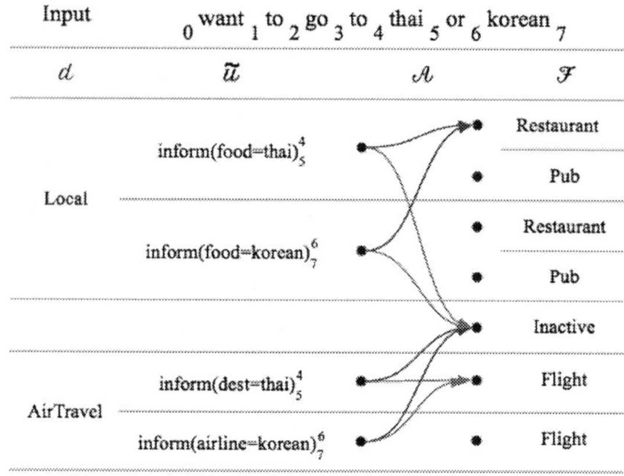

Figure 2: An example illustrating task frame parsing. Here we assume that there are two related domains, *Local* and *AirTravel*, pertinent to the user input *"want to go to Thai or Korean"*. Time information is annotated as word positions in the input.

Algorithm 2: MCMC-SA Beam Parsing

Input: $K > 0$, $M > 0$, $\widetilde{\mathbf{u}}$, $p_{\boldsymbol{\theta}}$ from Eq. 1
Result: $\mathcal{H} = [(\hat{\mathcal{A}}_{\widetilde{\mathbf{u}}}^1, s^1), \ldots, (\hat{\mathcal{A}}_{\widetilde{\mathbf{u}}}^K, s^K)]$, a K-best list of assignments with scores
$\mathcal{A}_{\widetilde{\mathbf{u}}} \leftarrow \text{initialize}(\widetilde{\mathbf{u}})$, $s \leftarrow p_{\boldsymbol{\theta}}(\mathcal{A}_{\widetilde{\mathbf{u}}} | \widetilde{\mathbf{u}})$;
insert_and_sort($\mathcal{H}$, $\mathcal{A}_{\widetilde{\mathbf{u}}}$, s);
$c \leftarrow 0$, acc_rate $\leftarrow 1$;
while $c < M$ **do**
  $\hat{\mathcal{A}}_{\widetilde{\mathbf{u}}}, \hat{s} \leftarrow \text{random\_choice}(\mathcal{H})$;
  $\mathcal{A}_{\widetilde{\mathbf{u}}} \leftarrow \text{sample}(\hat{\mathcal{A}}_{\widetilde{\mathbf{u}}})$, $s \leftarrow p_{\boldsymbol{\theta}}(\mathcal{A}_{\widetilde{\mathbf{u}}} | \widetilde{\mathbf{u}})$;
  if $s > \hat{s}$ *or random(0,1)* $< $ *acc_rate* **then**
    | insert_and_sort($\mathcal{H}$, $\mathcal{A}_{\widetilde{\mathbf{u}}}$, s);
  end
  $c \leftarrow c + 1$, acc_rate $\leftarrow$ acc_rate $- \frac{1}{M}$;
end
return $\mathcal{H}$

---

our training objective is:

$$\mathcal{O}(\boldsymbol{\theta}) = \sum_i \log p_{\boldsymbol{\theta}}(\mathcal{A}_{\widetilde{\mathbf{u}}}^{(i)} | \widetilde{\mathbf{u}}^{(i)}) \quad (2)$$

We optimize the objective by initializing $\boldsymbol{\theta}$ to 0 and applying *AdaGrad* (Duchi et al., 2011) with the following per-feature stochastic gradient:

$$\frac{\partial \mathcal{O}(\boldsymbol{\theta}, \mathcal{A}_{\widetilde{\mathbf{u}}}^{(i)}, \widetilde{\mathbf{u}}^{(i)}, \mathcal{H}^{(i)})}{\partial \theta_j} =$$
$$g_j(\mathcal{A}_{\widetilde{\mathbf{u}}}^{(i)}, \widetilde{\mathbf{u}}^{(i)}) p_{\boldsymbol{\theta}}(\mathcal{A}_{\widetilde{\mathbf{u}}}^{(i)} | \widetilde{\mathbf{u}}^{(i)})$$
$$- \sum_{\hat{\mathcal{A}}_{\widetilde{\mathbf{u}}}^k \in \mathcal{H}^{(i)} : \hat{\mathcal{A}}_{\widetilde{\mathbf{u}}}^k \neq \mathcal{A}_{\widetilde{\mathbf{u}}}^{(i)}} g_j(\hat{\mathcal{A}}_{\widetilde{\mathbf{u}}}^k, \widetilde{\mathbf{u}}^{(i)}) p_{\boldsymbol{\theta}}(\hat{\mathcal{A}}_{\widetilde{\mathbf{u}}}^k | \widetilde{\mathbf{u}}^{(i)})$$

In our experiments we use the features in Table 1, which are all sparse binary features except those marked by †.

- The number of task frames in the parse
- The number of task frames in the parse conjoined with the agent's DA type
- The number of DAIs in the inactive task frame
- The pair of the total number of DAIs and the number of DAIs in the inactive task frame
- All possible pairs of delexicalized agent DAIs and delexicalized user DAIs in the inactive task frame
- All possible pairs of delexicalized user DAIs for each task frame
- The average confidence score of all DAIs assigned to active task frames†
- The average number of DAIs per active task frame†
- The conjunction of the number of DAIs assigned to active task frames and the number of active task frames
- The fraction of the number of gaps to the number of DAIs assigned to active task frames (a gap happens when two DAIs in the same task frame instance have an intermediate DAI in a different task frame instance)
- The entropy of DAI distribution across active task frames †
- The number of active task frames with only one DAI
- An indicator testing if the parse is the same as a heuristically initialized parse
- The degree of deviation of the parse from a heuristically initialized parse in terms of the number of gaps †

Table 1: Features used in model for task frame parsing

2.2 Context Fetching

There are a variety of phenomena in conversation in which context-dependent analysis plays a crucial role, such as ellipsis resolution, reference resolution, cross-task information sharing and task resumption. In order to successfully handle such phenomena, TL-DST must fetch relevant pieces of information from the conversation history. In this section, we mainly focus on modeling the context fetching process for belief update, ellipsis resolution and task resumption, but a similar technique can be used for handling other phenomena. We first formally define the context fetching model and then introduce a set of feature functions that allow the model to capture general patterns of different context-dependent phenomena.

Context Sets At turn t, given a task lineage $l_{0:t-1}$ and context window δ, the context fetcher constructs three context sets:

- $\mathcal{B}(l_{0:t-1})$: A set of δ-latest belief estimates for each constraint that appears in l_t. The δ-latest belief estimate means the latest belief estimate before $t - \delta$.

- $\mathcal{U}(l_{0:t-1})$: A set of all previous SLU results within δ, $\{\tilde{u}_{t-\delta}, \ldots, \tilde{u}_{t-1}\}$.

- $\mathcal{M}(l_{0:t-1})$: A set of all previous agent DAIs within δ, $\{m_{t-\delta}, \ldots, m_{t-1}\}$.

By varying δ, the context fetcher controls the ratio of summarized estimates to raw observations it will use to generate new estimates for the current turn.

Context Fetching Conditioned on the task lineage $l_{0:t-1}$ and the new pieces of information at the current turn such as the task frame f and the agent output m_t, the context fetcher determines which elements from the context sets will be used. We cast the decision problem as a set of binary classifications for each element using logistic regression. For the sake of simplicity, in this work, we focus on the case where δ is 0 which in effect makes the context fetcher use only the latest belief estimates

for each constraint, $\mathcal{B}(l_{0:t-1})$:

$$p_\psi(R(b_{\tau,c}) \mid l_{0:t-1}, f, m_t) = \frac{1}{1 + \exp -\psi^T h(b_{\tau,c}, l_{0:t-1}, f, m_t)}$$

where $b_{\tau,c} \in \mathcal{B}(l_{0:t-1})$ denotes the belief estimate for constraint c at turn τ, R is a binary indicator of fetching decision, ψ are the model weights, and h is a vector-valued feature function.

Model Training As before, we optimize the log-likelihood of the training data using *AdaGrad*. To construct training data, we construct an oracle task lineage based on dialog state labels, SLU labels and SLU results, which allows us to build corresponding context sets and label each element in them by checking if the element appears in the oracle task state. In our experiments we use the features listed in Table 2, which are all sparse binary features except those marked by †.

2.3 Task State Update

In this section, we describe the last component of TL-DST, task state update. A nice property of TL-DST is its ability to exploit alternative methods for dialog state tracking. For instance, by setting a large value to δ for the context fetcher, one can adopt various discriminative models that take advantage of expressive feature functions extracted from a collection of raw observations (Lee, 2013; Henderson et al., 2014c; Williams, 2014). On the other hand, with δ being 0, one can employ a method from a library of generative models which only requires to know the immediately prior belief estimates (Wang and Lemon, 2013; Zilka et al., 2013). Unlike in previous work, instead of predicting a unique goal value for a slot, we perform belief tracking for each individual slot-value constraint to allow complex goals. For the experiments presented here, we chose to use the rule-based algorithm from Zilka et al. (2013) for constraint-level belief tracking. The use of a rule-based algorithm

- A continuation bias feature. This feature indicates if constraint c is present in any of the task states at the previous turn. This feature allows to model the general tendency to continue.
- Adjacency pair features. These features indicate if c comes from the previous turn when the second half of an adjacency pair (e.g. request/inform and confirm/affirm) is present at the current turn.
- Deletion features based on explicit cues. For example, the user informs alternative constraints after the agent's unfulfilment notice (e.g. *canthelp* in the DSTC) or the user chooses an alternative to c at the agent's selection prompt.
- Deletion features based on implicit cues. For instance, the user informs alternative constraints for a slot which is unlikely to admit multiple constraints or after the agent's explicit or implicit confirmation request. For these features we use the confidence score of the user's DAI. †
- Task switching features based on agent-initiative cues. Upon the completion of a task, the agent is likely to resume a previous task, thus the context fetcher needs to retrieve the state of the resumed task. Since our experiments are corpus-based, there is no direct internal signal from the agent action selection module, so these features indirectly capture the agent's initiative on task switching based on which task the agent's action is related to, and indicate if c is present in the agent's action or belongs to the agent's addressed task.
- Task switching features based on user-initiative cues. These features test if c is present in the user's input or belongs to the user's addressed task.

Table 2: Features used in model for context fetching

allows us to focus our analysis only on the new aspects of TL-DST.

We present the formal description of the dialog state tracking algorithm. Let $\Sigma_{t,c}^{+}$ ($\Sigma_{t,c}^{-}$) denote the sum of all the confidence scores associated with *inform* or *affirm* (*deny* or *negate*) for constraint c at turn t. Then the belief estimate of constraint c at turn t, $b_{t,c}$, is defined as follows:

- For informing or affirming,

$$b_{t,c} = b_{\tau,c}(1 - \Sigma_{t,c}^{+}) + \Sigma_{t,c}^{+}$$

- For denying or negating,

$$b_{t,c} = b_{\tau,c}(1 - \Sigma_{t,c}^{-})$$

where $b_{\tau,c}$ is the latest available belief estimate for constraint c fetched from a task state at turn τ.

3 Experiments

In order to validate TL-DST, we conducted a set of corpus-based experiments using the DSTC2 and DSTC3 data. The use of DSTC data makes it possible to compare TL-DST with numerous previously developed methods. We first applied TL-DST on the DSTC2 data. DSTC2 was designed to broaden the scope of dialog state tracking to include user goal changes. TL-DST should be able to process user goal changes without any special handling – it should fetch unchanged goals from the previous task state and incorporate new goals from the user's input to construct a new task state.

However, due to the lack of multi-task conversations in the DSTC2 data, we could not evaluate the performance of task frame parsing. There are also many other aspects of our proposed approach that are hard to investigate without appropriate dialog data. We address this problem by applying simulation techniques to the DSTC3 data. Although there are no DSTC3 dialogs handling multiple task instances in a single conversation, the DSTC3 extended the DSTC2 to include multiple task types, i.e, restaurant, pub and coffee shop finding tasks. This property of the DSTC3 data allows us to generate a set of pseudo-real dialogs involving multiple tasks with complex goals in longer interactions. The generated corpus helped us evaluate additional aspects of TL-DST.

3.1 DSTC2

In the DSTC2, the user is asked to find a restaurant that satisfies a number of constraints such as food type or area. The data was collected from Amazon Mechanical Turkers using dialog systems developed at Cambridge University. The corpus contains 1612 training dialogs, 506 development dialogs and 1117 test dialogs.

Per DSTC2, the dialog state includes three elements – the user's goal (slot values the user has supplied), requested slots (those the user has asked for) and search method. In this work, we focus on tracking the user's goal. Since TL-DST estimates belief for each constraint rather than assigning a distribution over all of the values per slot, we aggregated the constraint-level beliefs for each slot and took the value with the largest belief. We trained the context fetcher on the training data and saved models whenever the performance on the development data was improved. We set the learning rate to 0.1 and used L2 regularization with regularization term 10^{-4}, though the system's performance was largely insensitive to these settings.

Table 3 shows the performance of TL-DST on the test data in accuracy and L2 along with that of other top performing systems in the literature[2]. The result clearly demonstrates the effectiveness of TL-DST, showing higher accuracy and lower L2 than other state-of-the-art systems. This result is

---

[2]In order to make evaluation results comparable, we considered only those systems that used only the provided SLU output, not also ASR information.

particularly interesting in that all of the other systems achieved their best performance through a system combination of various non-linear models such as neural nets, decision trees, or statistical models combined with rules, whereas our system used a lightweight linear model. With the structure among the components of the TL-DST approach, it suffices to use a single linear model to handle sophisticated phenomena such as user goal changes. TL-DST achieved this result without any preprocessing steps such as SLU result correction or the use of lexical features to compensate for relatively poor SLU performance (Kadlec et al., 2014; Zhu et al., 2014). Lastly, we used a generative rule-based model for task state update which is known to be suboptimal for the DSTC2 task. Though it is not the focus of this paper, we expect that one can employ a discriminative model to get further improvements. In particular, there is plenty of room to improve the L2 metric through machine-learned discriminative models.

Entry	Acc.	L2
1-best baseline	0.619	0.738
Sun et al. (2014)	0.735	0.433
Williams (2014)	0.739	0.721
Henderson et al. (2014c)	0.742	**0.387**
Vodolan et al. (2015)†	0.745	0.433
TL-DST†	**0.747**	0.451

Table 3: DSTC2 joint goal tracking results. The post DSTC2 systems are marked by †.

3.2 Complex Interactions

In order to evaluate TL-DST on more challenging data, we generated a set of pseudo-real dialogs from the DSTC3 data that contain multiple tasks with complex user goals (Schatzmann et al., 2006; Pietquin and Dutoit, 2006). First, we constructed a repository of user goals (basically, a dictionary mapping mined goals from DSTC3 to their associated turns in the source dialog logs and labels). Then, we simulated dialogs with complex user goals by merging additional goals and the associated turns to a backbone dialog which was randomly drawn from the original DSTC3 dialogs. We randomly sampled additional goals from the goal repository according to a set of per-slot binary distributions, P_{slot}^{add}. For negative constraint generation, we flipped the polarity of an additional goal according to another set of per-slot binary distributions, P_{slot}^{neg}, and correspondingly altered the dialog act type of the relevant DAIs, e.g, *inform* to *deny*. We iterated the goal addition process up to a configured number of iterations, N^{iter}, to cover cases where more than two constraints exist for a slot. The merge process employs a set of heuristic rules so as to preserve natural discourse segments

(e.g., a subdialog for confirming a value) in the backbone dialog. One can simulate dialogs with different complexities by varying the binary distributions and the number of iterations. After this step, the value for each slot is no longer a single value but a set of constraints.

Finally, to construct a multi-task dialog, we randomly drew a backbone dialog from the corpus and decided whether to sample an additional dialog according to a binary distribution, P^{task}. Then we merged the first turns of each selected dialog to ensure the existence of multiple tasks in a single turn. We arranged the remainder of the selected dialogs in order, so as to simulate task resumption. After this process, the label of a dialog state consists of a list of task state labels. An example pseudo-real dialog might contain: A user searches for an Italian or French restaurant in the north area. (S)he also looks for a coffee shop to go to after lunch that is in a cheap price range and provides internet (See Appendix A for example dialogs).

When two turns from different dialogs have to be merged during the dialog synthesis process, we produce a list of new SLU hypotheses by taking the Cartesian product of the two source SLU hypotheses - confidence scores are also multiplied together. For time information annotation, we use the position of the DAI in the SLU hypothesis instead of the real start and end times detected by the ASR component since the DSTC3 data does not have time information. Due to space limitations, we present evaluation results only for the following dialog corpora generated with three different representative settings:

1. No complex user goals and no multiple tasks: $P_{food}^{add} = 0.0$, $P_{area}^{add} = 0.0$, $P_{pricerange}^{add} = 0.0$, $P_{food}^{neg} = 0.0$, $P_{area}^{neg} = 0.0$, $P_{pricerange}^{neg} = 0.0$, $N^{iter} = 0$, $P^{task} = 0.0$

2. Complex user goals and no multiple tasks: $P_{food}^{add} = 0.5$, $P_{area}^{add} = 0.2$, $P_{pricerange}^{add} = 0.2$, $P_{food}^{neg} = 0.2$, $P_{area}^{neg} = 0.2$, $P_{pricerange}^{neg} = 0.2$, $N^{iter} = 2$, $P^{task} = 0.0$

3. Complex user goals and multiple tasks: $P_{food}^{add} = 0.5$, $P_{area}^{add} = 0.2$, $P_{pricerange}^{add} = 0.2$, $P_{food}^{neg} = 0.2$, $P_{area}^{neg} = 0.2$, $P_{pricerange}^{neg} = 0.2$, $N^{iter} = 2$, $P^{task} = 1.0$

Corpora 2 and 3 were divided into $1,000$ training dialogs, 500 development dialogs and $1,000$ test dialogs. For corpus 1, since we do not generate any new dialogs, we just partitioned the $2,264$ DSTC3 dialogs into 846 training dialogs, 418 development dialogs and $1,000$ test dialogs. We trained the task frame parser and the context fetcher and saved models whenever the performance on the development data was improved. We set the learning rate

Parameters	System	Avg. Acc.	Joint Acc.	L2
No complex user goals and no multiple tasks	baseline	0.837	0.575	0.864
	TL-DST	0.850	0.594	0.737
Complex user goals and no multiple tasks	baseline	0.720	0.315	1.324
	TL-DST	0.819	0.455	0.972
Complex user goals and multiple tasks	baseline	0.411	0.029	1.893
	TL-DST	0.784	0.338	1.208
	TL-DST-OP	0.833	0.466	0.984
	TL-DST-O	0.928	0.607	0.752

Table 4: Evaluation on complex dialogs with simulated data. The exact parameter settings for each simulation condition can be found in the text.

to 0.1 and used L2 regularization with regularization term 10^{-4}.

Table 4 shows how performance varies on different simulation settings. As expected, the performance of the baseline tracker, which is the DSTC3's default tracker, drops sharply as the dialogs get more complicated. On the contrary, the performance of TL-DST decreases more gently. Note that joint goal prediction gets exponentially harder as multiple tasks are involved, since we can get each task wrong if we have any of one task's constraints in another's state. Thus this gentle performance reduction is in fact a significant win.

As noted before, there is an upper bound to achievable performance due to the limitation of the provided SLU results. Thus we also present the performance of the system with different oracles: 1) TL-DST-OP uses oracle task frame parses; 2) TL-DST-O additionally uses an oracle context fetcher. The comparative results suggest that there is much room for improvement in both the task frame parser and the context fetcher. Given the good performance on Avg. Accuracy, despite imperfect joint prediction, a TL-DST based agent should be able to successfully complete the conversation with extra exchanges. This also matches our empirical analysis of the tracker's output; the tracker missed only a couple of constraints in its incorrect joint prediction.

4 Related Work

TL-DST aims to extend conventional approaches for dialog state tracking. A variety of approaches have been proposed, for instance, generative models (Thomson et al., 2010; Wang and Lemon, 2013; Zilka et al., 2013; Sun et al., 2014; Kadlec et al., 2014) and discriminative models (Lee and Eskenazi, 2013; Henderson et al., 2014c; Williams, 2014). The series of DSTCs have played a crucial role in supplying essential resources to the research community such as labeled dialog corpora, baseline systems and a common evaluation framework (Williams et al., 2013; Henderson et al., 2014a; Henderson et al., 2014b). For more information about this line of research, we refer to the recent survey by Williams et al. (2016).

The closest work to our task frame parsing is frame semantic parsing task in NLP (Das, 2014). Differences include that the input here is a collection of potentially conflicting semantic hypotheses from different domain-specific SLUs. Also we are more interested in obtaining a N-best list of parses with well calibrated confidence scores than in getting only a top hypothesis.

Recently there has been growing interest in multidomain and multitask dialog (Crook et al., 2016; Sun et al., 2016; Ramachandran and Ratnaparkhi, 2015; Gašic et al., 2015; Wang et al., 2014; Hakkani-Tür et al., 2012; Nakano et al., 2011). To our knowledge, however, there is no previous work that provides a holistic statistical approach for complex dialog state tracking that can cover the wide range of problems discussed in this paper.

5 Conclusions

In this paper, we have proposed the TL-DST approach toward the goal of seamlessly orchestrating multiple tasks with complex goals across multiple domains in continuous interaction. The proposed method's state-of-the-art performance on common benchmark datasets and purposefully simulated dialog corpora demonstrates the potential capacity of TL-DST. In the future, we want to apply TL-DST to conversational agent platforms for further evaluation with real world multi-domain dialog. There are many opportunities for technical improvements, including: 1) scheduled sampling for context fetcher training to avoid the mismatch between oracles and runtime conditions (Bengio et al., 2015); 2) using discriminative (sequential) models instead of generative rule-based models for task state update; and 3) learning with weak supervision from real time interactions. Future research can include the extension of TL-DST for other conversational phenomena such as reference resolution. It would also be interesting to study the potential impact on other dialog system components of providing more comprehensive state representations to SLU and action selection.

References

Dzmitry Bahdanau, Kyunghyun Cho, and Yoshua Bengio. 2014. Neural machine translation by jointly learning to align and translate. *arXiv preprint arXiv:1409.0473*.

Samy Bengio, Oriol Vinyals, Navdeep Jaitly, and Noam Shazeer. 2015. Scheduled sampling for sequence prediction with recurrent neural networks. In *Advances in Neural Information Processing Systems*, pages 1171–1179.

Paul Crook and Oliver Lemon. 2010. Representing uncertainty about complex user goals in statistical dialogue systems. In *Proceedings of SIGDIAL*.

Paul Crook, Alex Marin, Vipul Agarwal, Khushboo Aggarwal, Tasos Anastasakos, Ravi Bikkula, Daniel Boies, Asli Celikyilmaz, Senthilkumar Chandramohan, Zhaleh Feizollahi, Roman Holenstein, Minwoo Jeong, Omar Khan, Young-Bum Kim, Elizabeth Krawczyk, Xiaohu Liu, Danko Panic, Vasiliy Radostev, Nikhil Ramesh, Jean-Phillipe Robichaud, Alexandre Rochette, Logan Stromberg, and Ruhi Sarikaya. 2016. Task completion platform: A self-serve multi-domain goal oriented dialogue platform. In *Proceedings of NAACL*.

Dipanjan Das. 2014. Statistical models for frame-semantic parsing. In *Proceedings of the ACL*.

John Duchi, Elad Hazan, and Yoram Singer. 2011. Adaptive subgradient methods for online learning and stochastic optimization. *The Journal of Machine Learning Research*, 12:2121–2159.

M Gašic, N Mrkšic, P-H Su, D Vandyke, T-H Wen, and S Young. 2015. Policy committee for adaptation in multi-domain spoken dialogue systems. In *Proceedings of ASRU*.

Barbara J Grosz and Candace L Sidner. 1988. Plans for discourse. Technical report, DTIC Document.

Dilek Z Hakkani-Tür, Gökhan Tür, Larry P Heck, Ashley Fidler, and Asli Celikyilmaz. 2012. A discriminative classification-based approach to information state updates for a multi-domain dialog system. In *Proceedings of INTERSPEECH*.

Matthew Henderson, Blaise Thomson, and Jason Williams. 2014a. The second dialog state tracking challenge. In *Proceedings of SIGDIAL*.

Matthew Henderson, Blaise Thomson, and Jason D Williams. 2014b. The third dialog state tracking challenge. In *Proceedings of SLT*.

Matthew Henderson, Blaise Thomson, and Steve Young. 2014c. Word-based dialog state tracking with recurrent neural networks. In *Proceedings of SIGDIAL*.

Rudolf Kadlec, Miroslav Vodolan, Jindrich Libovicky, Jan Macek, and Jan Kleindienst. 2014. Knowledge-based dialog state tracking. In *Proceedings of SLT*.

Staffan Larsson and David R Traum. 2000. Information state and dialogue management in the TRINDI dialogue move engine toolkit. *Natural Language Engineering*, 6(3&4):323–340.

Sungjin Lee and Maxine Eskenazi. 2012. An unsupervised approach to user simulation: toward self-improving dialog systems. In *Proceedings of SIGDIAL*.

Sungjin Lee and Maxine Eskenazi. 2013. Recipe for building robust spoken dialog state trackers: Dialog state tracking challenge system description. In *Proceedings of SIGDIAL*.

Sungjin Lee. 2013. Structured discriminative model for dialog state tracking. In *Proceedings of SIGDIAL*.

Karen E Lochbaum. 1998. A collaborative planning model of intentional structure. *Computational Linguistics*, 24(4):525–572.

Mikio Nakano, Shun Sato, Kazunori Komatani, Kyoko Matsuyama, Kotaro Funakoshi, and Hiroshi Okuno. 2011. A two-stage domain selection framework for extensible multi-domain spoken dialogue systems. In *Proceedings of SIGDIAL*.

Olivier Pietquin and Thierry Dutoit. 2006. A probabilistic framework for dialog simulation and optimal strategy learning. *Audio, Speech, and Language Processing, IEEE Transactions on*, 14(2):589–599.

Deepak Ramachandran and Adwait Ratnaparkhi. 2015. Belief tracking with stacked relational trees. In *Proceedings of SIGDIAL*.

Jost Schatzmann, Karl Weilhammer, Matt Stuttle, and Steve Young. 2006. A survey of statistical user simulation techniques for reinforcement-learning of dialogue management strategies. *The Knowledge Engineering Review*, 21(02):97–126.

Kai Sun, Lu Chen, Su Zhu, and Kai Yu. 2014. A generalized rule based tracker for dialogue state tracking. In *Proceedings of SLT*.

Ming Sun, Yun-Nung Chen, and Alexander Rudnicky. 2016. An intelligent assistant for high-level task understanding. In *Proceedings of IUI*.

Blaise Thomson, F Jurčíćek, M Gašić, Simon Keizer, François Mairesse, Kai Yu, and Steve Young. 2010. Parameter learning for pomdp spoken dialogue models. In *Proceedings of SLT*.

Miroslav Vodolán, Rudolf Kadlec, and Jan Kleindienst. 2015. Hybrid dialog state tracker. *arXiv preprint arXiv:1510.03710*.

Zhuoran Wang and Oliver Lemon. 2013. A simple and generic belief tracking mechanism for the dialog state tracking challenge: On the believability of observed information. In *Proceedings of SIGDIAL*.

Zhuoran Wang, Hongliang Chen, Guanchun Wang, Hao Tian, Hua Wu, and Haifeng Wang. 2014. Policy learning for domain selection in an extensible multi-domain spoken dialogue system. In *Proceedings of EMNLP*.

Jason Williams, Antoine Raux, Deepak Ramachandran, and Alan Black. 2013. The dialog state tracking challenge. In *Proceedings of SIGDIAL*.

Jason Williams, Antoine Raux, and Matthew Henderson. 2016. The dialog state tracking challenge series: A review. *Dialogue & Discourse*, 7(3):4–33.

Jason D Williams. 2014. Web-style ranking and SLU combination for dialog state tracking. In *Proceedings of SIGDIAL*.

Su Zhu, Lu Chen, Kai Sun, Da Zheng, and Kai Yu. 2014. Semantic parser enhancement for dialogue domain extension with little data. In *Proceedings of SLT*.

Lukas Zilka, David Marek, Matej Korvas, and Filip Jurcicek. 2013. Comparison of bayesian discriminative and generative models for dialogue state tracking. In *Proceedings of SIGDIAL*.

A   Example Simulated Dialogs

The following dialogs show the surface form of simulated complex interactions. The dialog state tracker uses the corresponding SLU results and dialog state annotations to the parts in the labeled DSTC3 logs of which the dialog is composed.

A.1   Dialog 1

System: Thank you for calling the Cambridge Information system. Your call will be recorded for research purposes. You may ask for information about a place to eat, such as a restaurant, a pub, or a cafe. How may I help you?
User: Yes. I'm looking for a seafood or north european restaurant. And I'm looking for a moderately priced coffee shop or in expensive price range.
System: Are you looking for somewhere near a particular venue? For example, Cambridge Contemporary Art, Holy Trinity Church, or Trinity College.
User: In the expensive price range.
System: Loch Fyne, which serves seafood, is an outstanding restaurant. It's in the expensive price range.
User: What's the address?

System: Loch Fyne is located on 37 Trumpington Street. The price for main courses ranges from 9 pounds to 20 pounds.
User: Ah what's the phone number?
System: The phone number of Loch Fyne is 01223902103.
User: And what's the price range?
System: Loch Fyne is in the expensive price range. The price for main courses ranges from 9 pounds to 20 pounds.
User: Ok thanks.
System: For a coffee shop, what kind of price range are you looking for? For example, free, or moderate.
User: Expensive price range.
System: Are you looking for somewhere near a particular venue? For example, Cambridge Contemporary Art, Great Saint Mary's Church, or Primavera.
User: No I'm not.
System: Cafe Eleven, which is in the moderate price range, is an outstanding cafe.
User: Can I get the phone number and the postcode?
System: The phone number of Cafe Eleven is 01223369157. It's in the area with the postcode CB1 1DG.
User: Thank you goodbye.

A.2   Dialog 2

System: Thank you for calling the Cambridge Information system. Your call will be recorded for research purposes. You may ask for information about a place to eat, such as a restaurant, a pub, or a cafe. How may I help you?
User: I'm looking for a cheap Chinese restaurant or a Turkish restaurant. But I don't want a French restaurant. And it should be in the Riverside area. And I would like a cafe.
System: What part of town do you have in mind? For example, something in the Barnwell, Chesterton, or King's Hedges area.
User: Chesterton.
System: There is no restaurant in the Chesterton area in the cheap price range.
User: Cheap Chinese take away restaurant.
System: Would you like a Chesterton area, or you don't care?
User: I don't care.
System: HK Fusion is an outstanding restaurant, it serves chinese food and it's in the cheap price range.
User: Phone number?
System: The phone number of HK Fusion is 01223355909.
User: Address?
System: HK Fusion is on 21 Burleigh Street.
User: Thank you.

System: What type of food would you like? For example, Chinese take away, American, or English.
User: Cafe.
System: What type of food would you like? For example, Greek, Mediterranean, or Middleeastern.
User: I don't care.
System: What kind of price range are you looking for? For example, cheap, or moderate.
User: I don't care.
System: The Cambridge Blue is a great cafe.
User: What is the address and phone number?
System: The Cambridge Blue is on 24 Regent Street and its phone number is 01223369222.
User: Thank you goodbye.

Joint Online Spoken Language Understanding and Language Modeling with Recurrent Neural Networks

Bing Liu
Carnegie Mellon University
Electrical and Computer Engineering
liubing@cmu.edu

Ian Lane
Carnegie Mellon University
Electrical and Computer Engineering
Language Technologies Institute
lane@cmu.edu

Abstract

Speaker intent detection and semantic slot filling are two critical tasks in spoken language understanding (SLU) for dialogue systems. In this paper, we describe a recurrent neural network (RNN) model that jointly performs intent detection, slot filling, and language modeling. The neural network model keeps updating the intent prediction as word in the transcribed utterance arrives and uses it as contextual features in the joint model. Evaluation of the language model and online SLU model is made on the ATIS benchmarking data set. On language modeling task, our joint model achieves 11.8% relative reduction on perplexity comparing to the independent training language model. On SLU tasks, our joint model outperforms the independent task training model by 22.3% on intent detection error rate, with slight degradation on slot filling F1 score. The joint model also shows advantageous performance in the realistic ASR settings with noisy speech input.

1 Introduction

As a critical component in spoken dialogue systems, spoken language understanding (SLU) system interprets the semantic meanings conveyed by speech signals. Major components in SLU systems include identifying speaker's intent and extracting semantic constituents from the natural language query, two tasks that are often referred to as intent detection and slot filling.

Intent detection can be treated as a semantic utterance classification problem, and slot filling can be treated as a sequence labeling task. These two tasks are usually processed separately by different models. For intent detection, a number of standard classifiers can be applied, such as support vector machines (SVMs) (Haffner et al., 2003) and convolutional neural networks (CNNs) (Xu and Sarikaya, 2013). For slot filling, popular approaches include using sequence models such as maximum entropy Markov models (MEMMs) (McCallum et al., 2000), conditional random fields (CRFs) (Raymond and Riccardi, 2007), and recurrent neural networks (RNNs) (Yao et al., 2014; Mesnil et al., 2015).

Recently, neural network based models that jointly perform intent detection and slot filling have been reported. Xu (2013) proposed using CNN based triangular CRF for joint intent detection and slot filling. Guo (2014) proposed using a recursive neural network (RecNN) that learns hierarchical representations of the input text for the joint task. Such joint models simplify SLU systems, as only one model needs to be trained and deployed.

The previously proposed joint SLU models, however, are unsuitable for *online* tasks where it is desired to produce outputs as the input sequence arrives. In speech recognition, instead of receiving the transcribed text at the end of the speech, users typically prefer to see the ongoing transcription while speaking. In spoken language understanding, with real time intent identification and semantic constituents extraction, the downstream systems will be able to perform corresponding search or query while the user dictates. The joint SLU models proposed in previous work typically require intent and slot label predictions to be conditioned on the entire transcribed word sequence. This limits the usage of these models in the online setting.

In this paper, we propose an RNN-based online joint SLU model that performs intent detection and slot filling as the input word arrives. In

Proceedings of the SIGDIAL 2016 Conference, pages 22–30,
Los Angeles, USA, 13-15 September 2016. ©2016 Association for Computational Linguistics

addition, we suggest that the generated intent class and slot labels are useful for next word prediction in online automatic speech recognition (ASR). Therefore, we propose to perform intent detection, slot filling, and language modeling jointly in a conditional RNN model. The proposed joint model can be further extended for belief tracking in dialogue systems when considering the dialogue history beyond the current utterance. Moreover, it can be used as the RNN decoder in an end-to-end trainable sequence-to-sequence speech recognition model (Jaitly et al., 2015).

The remainder of the paper is organized as follows. In section 2, we introduce the background on using RNNs for intent detection, slot filling, and language modeling. In section 3, we describe the proposed joint online SLU-LM model and its variations. Section 4 discusses the experiment setup and results on ATIS benchmarking task, using both text and noisy speech inputs. Section 5 gives the conclusion.

2 Background

2.1 Intent Detection

Intent detection can be treated as a semantic utterance classification problem, where the input to the classification model is a sequence of words and the output is the speaker intent class. Given an utterance with a sequence of words $\mathbf{w} = (w_1, w_2, ..., w_T)$, the goal of intent detection is to assign an intent class c from a pre-defined finite set of intent classes, such that:

$$\hat{c} = \arg\max_{c} P(c|\mathbf{w}) \qquad (1)$$

Recent neural network based intent classification models involve using neural bag-of-words (NBoW) or bag-of-n-grams, where words or n-grams are mapped to high dimensional vector space and then combined component-wise by summation or average before being sent to the classifier. More structured neural network approaches for utterance classification include using recursive neural network (RecNN) (Guo et al., 2014), recurrent neural network (Ravuri and Stolcke, 2015), and convolutional neural network models (Collobert and Weston, 2008; Kim, 2014). Comparing to basic NBoW methods, these models can better capture the structural patterns in the word sequence.

2.2 Slot Filling

A major task in spoken language understanding (SLU) is to extract semantic constituents by searching input text to fill in values for predefined slots in a semantic frame (Mesnil et al., 2015), which is often referred to as slot filling. The slot filling task can also be viewed as assigning an appropriate semantic label to each word in the given input text. In the below example from ATIS (Hemphill et al., 1990) corpus following the popular in/out/begin (IOB) annotation method, *Seattle* and *San Diego* are the from and to locations respectively according to the slot labels, and *tomorrow* is the departure date. Other words in the example utterance that carry no semantic meaning are assigned "O" label.

Utterance	show	flights	from	Seattle	to	San	Diego	tomorrow
Slots	O	O	O	B-fromloc	O	B-toloc	I-toloc	B-depart_date
Intent	Flight							

Figure 1: ATIS corpus sample with intent and slot annotation (IOB format).

Given an utterance consisting of a sequence of words $\mathbf{w} = (w_1, w_2, ..., w_T)$, the goal of slot filling is to find a sequence of semantic labels $\mathbf{s} = (s_1, s_2, ..., s_T)$, one for each word in the utterance, such that:

$$\hat{\mathbf{s}} = \arg\max_{\mathbf{s}} P(\mathbf{s}|\mathbf{w}) \qquad (2)$$

Slot filling is typically treated as a sequence labeling problem. Sequence models including conditional random fields (Raymond and Riccardi, 2007) and RNN models (Yao et al., 2014; Mesnil et al., 2015; Liu and Lane, 2015) are among the most popular methods for sequence labeling tasks.

2.3 RNN Language Model

A language model assigns a probability to a sequence of words $\mathbf{w} = (w_1, w_2, ..., w_T)$ following probability distribution. In language modeling, w_0 and w_{T+1} are added to the word sequence representing the beginning-of-sentence token and end-of-sentence token. Using the chain rule, the likelihood of a word sequence can be factorized as:

$$P(\mathbf{w}) = \prod_{t=1}^{T+1} P(w_t|w_0, w_1, ..., w_{t-1}) \qquad (3)$$

RNN-based language models (Mikolov et al., 2011), and the variant (Sundermeyer et al., 2012)

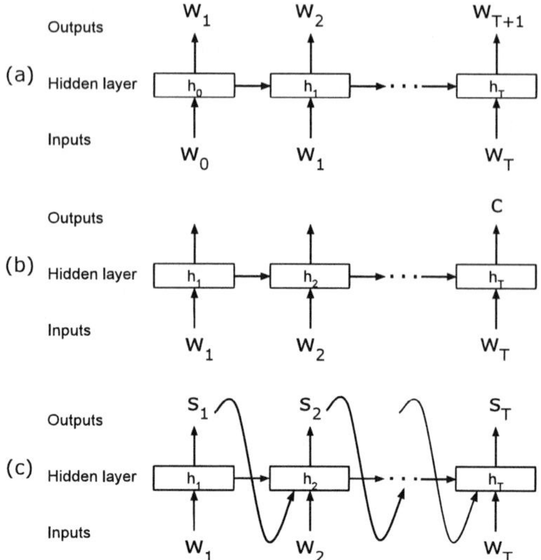

Figure 2: (a) RNN language model. (b) RNN intent detection model. The RNN output at last step is used to predict the intent class. (c) RNN slot filling model. Slot label dependencies are modeled by feeding the output label of the previous time step to the current step hidden state.

using long short-term memory (LSTM) (Hochreiter and Schmidhuber, 1997) have shown superior performance comparing to traditional n-gram based models. In this work, we use an LSTM cell as the basic RNN unit for its stronger capability in capturing long-range dependencies in word sequence.

2.4 RNN for Intent Detection and Slot Filling

As illustrated in Figure 2(b), RNN intent detection model uses the last RNN output to predict the utterance intent class. This last RNN output can be seen as a representation or embedding of the entire utterance. Alternatively, the utterance embedding can be obtained by taking mean of the RNN outputs over the sequence. This utterance embedding is then used as input to the multinomial logistic regression for the intent class prediction.

RNN slot filling model takes word as input and the corresponding slot label as output at each time step. The posterior probability for each slot label is calculated using the softmax function over the RNN output. Slot label dependencies can be modeled by feeding the output label from the previous time step to the current step hidden state (Figure 2(c)). During model training, true label from previous time step can be fed to current hidden

state. During inference, only the predicted label can be used. To bridge the gap between training and inference, scheduled sampling method (Bengio et al., 2015) can be applied. Instead of only using previous true label, using sample from previous predicted label distribution in model training makes the model more robust by forcing it to learn to handle its own prediction mistakes (Liu and Lane, 2015).

3 Method

In this section we describe the joint SLU-LM model in detail. Figure 3 gives an overview of the proposed architecture.

3.1 Model

Let $\mathbf{w} = (w_0, w_1, w_2, ..., w_{T+1})$ represent the input word sequence, with w_0 and w_{T+1} being the beginning-of-sentence ($\langle bos \rangle$) and end-of-sentence ($\langle eos \rangle$) tokens. Let $\mathbf{c} = (c_0, c_1, c_2, ..., c_T)$ be the sequence of intent class outputs at each time step. Similarly, let $\mathbf{s} = (s_0, s_1, s_2, ..., s_T)$ be the slot label sequence, where s_0 is a padded slot label that maps to the beginning-of-sentence token $\langle bos \rangle$.

Referring to the joint SLU-LM model shown in Figure 3, for the intent model, instead of predicting the intent only after seeing the entire utterance as in the independent training intent model (Figure 2(b)), in the joint model we output intent at each time step as input word sequence arrives. The intent generated at the last step is used as the final utterance intent prediction. The intent output from each time step is fed back to the RNN state, and thus the entire intent output history are modeled and can be used as context to other tasks. It is not hard to see that during inference, intent classes that are predicted during the first few time steps are of lower confidence due to the limited information available. We describe the techniques that can be used to ameliorate this effect in section 3.3 below. For the intent model, with both intent and slot label connections to the RNN state, we have:

$$P(c_T|\mathbf{w}) = P(c_T|w_{\leq T}, c_{<T}, s_{<T}) \quad (4)$$

For the slot filling model, at each step t along the input word sequence, we want to model the slot label output s_t as a conditional distribution over the previous intents $c_{<t}$, previous slot labels $s_{<t}$, and the input word sequence up to step t. Using

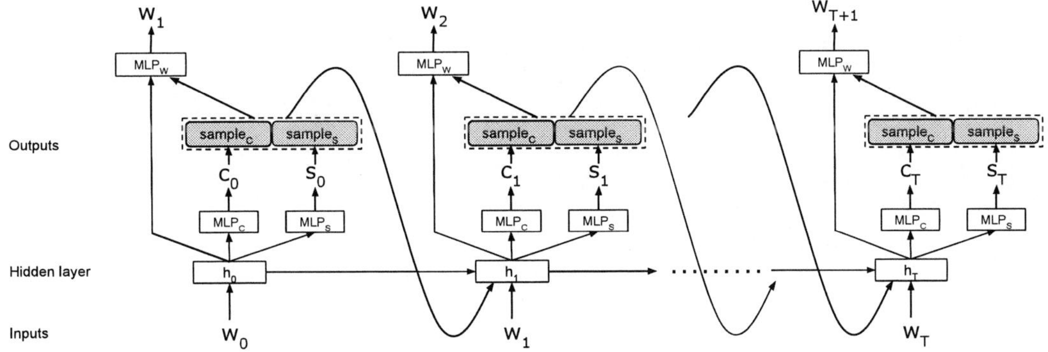

Figure 3: Proposed joint online RNN model for intent detection, slot filling, and next word prediction.

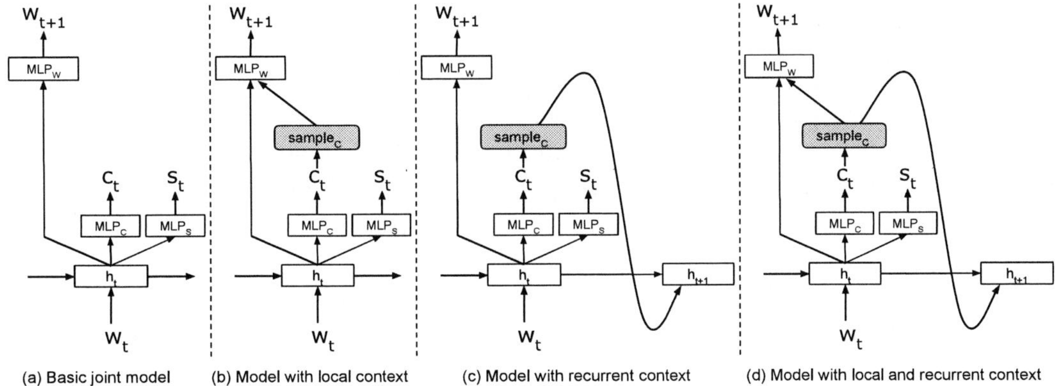

Figure 4: Joint online SLU-LM model variations. (a) Basic joint model with no conditional dependencies on emitted intent classes and slot labels. (b) Joint model with local intent context. Next word prediction is conditioned on the current step intent class. (c) Joint model with recurrent intent context. The entire intent prediction history and variations are captured in the RNN state. (d) Joint model with both local and recurrent intent context.

the chain rule, we have:

$$P(\mathbf{s}|\mathbf{w}) = P(s_0|w_0) \prod_{t=1}^{T} P(s_t|w_{\leq t}, c_{<t}, s_{<t}) \tag{5}$$

For the language model, the next word is modeled as a conditional distribution over the word sequence together with intent and slot label sequence up to current time step. The intent and slot label outputs at current step, together with the intent and slot label history that is encoded in the RNN state, serve as context to the language model.

$$P(\mathbf{w}) = \prod_{t=0}^{T} P(w_{t+1}|w_{\leq t}, c_{\leq t}, s_{\leq t}) \tag{6}$$

3.2 Next Step Prediction

Following the model architecture in Figure 3, at time step t, input to the system is the word at index t of the utterance, and outputs are the intent class, the slot label, and the next word prediction. The RNN state h_t encodes the information of all the words, intents, and slot labels seen previously. The neural network model computes the outputs through the following sequence of steps:

$$h_t = \text{LSTM}(h_{t-1}, [w_t, c_{t-1}, s_{t-1}]) \tag{7}$$
$$P(c_t|w_{\leq t}, c_{<t}, s_{<t}) = \text{IntentDist}(h_t) \tag{8}$$
$$P(s_t|w_{\leq t}, c_{<t}, s_{<t}) = \text{SlotLabelDist}(h_t) \tag{9}$$
$$P(w_{t+1}|w_{\leq t}, c_{\leq t}, s_{\leq t}) = \text{WordDist}(h_t, c_t, s_t) \tag{10}$$

where LSTM is the recurrent neural network function that computes the hidden state h_t at a step using the previous hidden state h_{t-1}, the embeddings of the previous intent output c_{t-1} and slot label output s_{t-1}, and the embedding of current input word w_t. IntentDist, SlotLabelDist, and WordDist are multilayer perceptrons (MLPs) with softmax outputs over intents, slot labels, and words respectively. Each of these three MLPs has its own set of parameters. The intent and slot label distributions are generated by the MLPs with input being the RNN cell output. The next word distribution is produced by conditioning on current step RNN cell output together with the embeddings of the sampled intent and sampled slot label.

3.3 Training

The network is trained to find the parameters θ that minimise the cross-entropy of the predicted and true distributions for intent class, slot label, and next word jointly. The objective function also includes an $L2$ regularization term $R(\theta)$ over the weights and biases of the three MLPs. This equalizes to finding the parameters θ that maximize the below objective function:

$$
\max_{\theta} \sum_{t=0}^{T} \Big[\alpha_c \log P(c^* | w_{\leq t}, c_{<t}, s_{<t}; \theta)
$$
$$
+ \alpha_s \log P(s_t^* | w_{\leq t}, c_{<t}, s_{<t}; \theta)
$$
$$
+ \alpha_w \log P(w_{t+1} | w_{\leq t}, c_{\leq t}, s_{\leq t}; \theta) \Big]
$$
$$
- \lambda R(\theta)
$$

$$(11)$$

where c^* is the true intent class and and s_t^* is the true slot label at time step t. α_c, α_s, and α_w are the linear interpolation weights for the true intent, slot label, and next word probabilities. During model training, c_t can either be the true intent or mixture of true and predicted intent. During inference, however, only predicted intent can be used. Confidence of the predicted intent during the first few time steps is likely to be low due to the limited information available, and the confidence level is likely to increase with the newly arriving words. Conditioning on incorrect intent for next word prediction is not desirable. To mitigate this effect, we propose to use a *schedule* to increase the intent contribution to the context vector along the growing input word sequence. Specifically, during the first k time steps, we disable the intent context completely by setting the values in the intent vector to zeros. From step $k + 1$ till the last step of the input word sequence, we gradually increase the intent context by applying a linearly growing scaling factor η from 0 to 1 to the intent vector.

This scheduled approach is illustrated in Figure 5.

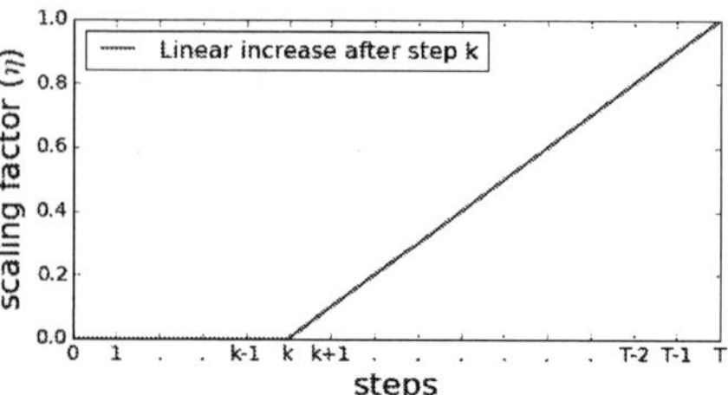

Figure 5: Schedule of increasing intent contribution to the context vector along with the growing input sequence.

3.4 Inference

For online inference, we simply take the greedy path of our conditional model without doing search. The model emits best intent class and slot label at each time step conditioning on all previous emitted symbols:

$$
\hat{c}_t = \arg\max_{c_t} P(c_t | w_{\leq t}, \hat{c}_{<t}, \hat{s}_{<t}) \tag{12}
$$
$$
\hat{s}_t = \arg\max_{s_t} P(s_t | w_{\leq t}, \hat{c}_{<t}, \hat{s}_{<t}) \tag{13}
$$

Many applications can benefit from this greedy inference approach comparing to search based inference methods, especially those running on embedded platforms that without GPUs and with limited computational capacity. Alternatively, one can do left-to-right beam search (Sutskever et al., 2014; Chan et al., 2015) by maintaining a set of β best partial hypotheses at each step. Efficient beam search method for the joint conditional model is left to explore in our future work.

3.5 Model Variations

In additional to the joint RNN model (Figure 3) described above, we also investigate several joint model variations for a fine-grained study of various impacting factors on the joint SLU-LM model performance. Designs of these model variations are illustrated in Figure 4.

Figure 4(a) shows the design of a basic joint SLU-LM model. At each step t, the predictions of intent class, slot label, and next word are based on a shared representation from the LSTM cell output h_t, and there is no conditional dependencies on previous intent class and slot label outputs. The single hidden layer MLP for each task introduces additional discriminative power for different tasks that take common shared representation as input. We use this model as the baseline joint model.

The models in Figure 4(b) to 4(d) extend the basic joint model by introducing conditional dependencies on intent class outputs. Note that the same type of extensions can be made on slot labels as well. For brevity and space concern, these designs are not added in the figure, but we report their performance in the experiment section.

The model in Figure 4(b) extends the basic joint model by conditioning the prediction of next word w_{t+1} on the current step intent class c_t. The intent class serves as context to the language model task. We refer to this design as model with *local intent context*.

The model in Figure 4(c) extends the basic joint model by feeding the intent class back to the RNN state. The history and variations of the predicted intent class from each previous step are monitored by the mode with such class output connections to RNN state. The intent, slot label, and next word predictions in the following step are all dependent on this history of intents. We refer to this design as model with *recurrent intent context*.

The model in Figure 4(d) combines the two types of connections shown in Figure 4(b) and 4(c). At step t, in addition to the *recurrent intent context* ($c_{<t}$), the prediction of word w_{t+1} is also conditioned on the *local intent context* from current step intent class c_t. We refer to this design as model with *local and recurrent intent context*.

4 Experiments

4.1 Data

We used the Airline Travel Information Systems (ATIS) dataset (Hemphill et al., 1990) in our experiment. The ATIS dataset contains audio recordings of people making flight reservations, and it is widely used in spoken language understanding research. We followed the same ATIS corpus[1] setup used in (Mesnil et al., 2015; Xu and Sarikaya, 2013; Tur et al., 2010). The training set contains 4978 utterances from ATIS-2 and ATIS-3 corpora, and test set contains 893 utterances from ATIS-3 NOV93 and DEC94 datasets. We evaluated the system performance on slot filling (127 distinct slot labels) using F1 score, and the performance on

intent detection (18 different intents) using classification error rate.

In order to show the robustness of the proposed joint SLU-LM model, we also performed experiments using automatic speech recognition (ASR) outputs. We managed to retrieve 518 (out of the 893 test utterances) utterance audio files from ATIS-3 NOV93 and DEC94 data sets, and use them as the test set in the ASR settings. To provide a more challenging and realistic evaluation, we used the simulated noisy utterances that were generated by artificially mixing clean speech data with noisy backgrounds following the simulation methods described in the third CHiME Speech Separation and Recognition Challenge (Barker et al., 2015). The average signal-to-noise ratio for the simulated noisy utterances is 9.8dB.

4.2 Training Procedure

We used LSTM cell as the basic RNN unit, following the LSTM design in (Zaremba et al., 2014). The default forget gate bias was set to 1. We used single layer uni-directional LSTM in the proposed joint online SLU-LM model. Deeper models by stacking the LSTM layers are to be explored in future work. Word embeddings of size 300 were randomly initialized and fine-tuned during model training. We conducted mini-batch training (with batch size 16) using Adam optimization method following the suggested parameter setup in (Kingma and Ba, 2014). Maximum norm for gradient clipping was set to 5. During model training, we applied dropout (dropout rate 0.5) to the non-recurrent connections (Zaremba et al., 2014) of RNN and the hidden layers of MLPs, and applied $L2$ regularization ($\lambda = 10^{-4}$) on the parameters of MLPs.

For the evaluation in ASR settings, we used the acoustic model trained on LibriSpeech dataset (Panayotov et al., 2015), and the language model trained on ATIS training corpus. A 2-gram language model was used during decoding. Different N-best rescoring methods were explored by using a 5-gram language model, the independent training RNN language model, and the joint training RNN language model. The ASR outputs were then sent to the joint SLU-LM model for intent detection and slot filling.

---

[1] We thank Gokhan Tur and Puyang Xu for sharing the ATIS dataset.

	Model	Intent Error	F1 Score	LM PPL
1	RecNN (Guo et al., 2014)	4.60	93.22	-
2	RecNN+Viterbi (Guo et al., 2014)	4.60	93.96	-
3	Independent training RNN intent model	2.13	-	-
4	Independent training RNN slot filling model	-	94.91	-
5	Independent training RNN language model	-	-	11.55
6	Basic joint training model	2.02	94.15	11.33
7	Joint model with *local* intent context	1.90	94.22	11.27
8	Joint model with *recurrent* intent context	1.90	94.16	10.21
9	Joint model with *local & recurrent* intent context	1.79	94.18	10.22
10	Joint model with *local* slot label context	1.79	94.14	11.14
11	Joint model with *recurrent* slot label context	1.79	**94.64**	11.19
12	Joint model with *local & recurrent* slot label context	1.68	94.52	11.17
13	Joint model with *local* intent + slot label context	1.90	94.13	11.22
14	Joint model with *recurrent* intent + slot label context	**1.57**	94.47	**10.19**
15	Joint model with *local & recurrent* intent + slot label context	1.68	94.45	10.28

Table 1: ATIS Test set results on intent detection error, slot filling F1 score, and language modeling perplexity. Related *joint* models: **RecNN**: Joint intent detection and slot filling model using recursive neural network (Guo et al., 2014). **RecNN+Viterbi**: Joint intent detection and slot filling model using recursive neural network with Viterbi sequence optimization for slot filling (Guo et al., 2014).

4.3　Results and Discussions

4.3.1　Results with True Text Input

Table 1 summarizes the experiment results of the joint SLU-LM model and its variations using ATIS text corpus as input. Row 3 to row 5 are the independent training model results on intent detection, slot filling, and language modeling. Row 6 gives the results of the basic joint SLU-LM model (Figure 4(a)). The basic joint model uses a shared representation for all the three tasks. It gives slightly better performance on intent detection and next word prediction, with some degradation on slot filling F1 score. If the RNN output h_t is connected to each task output directly via linear projection without using MLP, performance drops for intent classification and slot filling. Thus, we believe the extra discriminative power introduced by the additional model parameters and non-linearity from MLP is useful for the joint model. Row 7 to row 9 of Table 1 illustrate the performance of the joint models with local, recurrent, and local plus recurrent intent context, which correspond to model structures described in Figure 4(b) to 4(d). It is evident that the recurrent intent context helps the next word prediction, reducing the language model perplexity by 9.4% from 11.27 to 10.21. The contribution of local intent context to next word prediction is limited. We believe the advan-

tageous performance of using recurrent context is a result of modeling predicted intent history and intent variations along with the growing word sequence. For intent classification and slot filling, performance of these models with intent context is similar to that of the basic joint model.

Row 10 to row 12 of Table 1 illustrate the performance of the joint model with local, recurrent, and local plus recurrent slot label context. Comparing to the basic joint model, the introduced slot label context (both local and recurrent) leads to a better language modeling performance, but the contribution is not as significant as that from the recurrent intent context. Moreover, the slot label context reduces the intent classification error from 2.02 to 1.68, a 16.8% relative error reduction. From the slot filling F1 scores in row 10 and row 11, it is clear that modeling the slot label dependencies by connecting slot label output to the recurrent state is very useful.

Row 13 to row 15 of Table 1 give the performance of the joint model with both intent and slot label context. Row 15 refers to the model described in Figure 3. As can be seen from the results, the joint model that utilizes two types of recurrent context maintains the benefits of both, namely, the benefit of applying recurrent intent context to language modeling, and the benefit of

ASR Model (with LibriSpeech AM)	WER	Intent Error	F1 Score
2-gram LM decoding	14.51	4.63	84.46
2-gram LM decoding + 5-gram LM rescoring	13.66	5.02	85.08
2-gram LM decoding + Independent training RNN LM rescoring	12.95	4.63	85.43
2-gram LM decoding + Joint training RNN LM rescoring	**12.59**	**4.44**	**86.87**

Table 2: ATIS test set results on ASR word error rate, intent detection error, and slot filling F1 score with noisy speech input.

applying recurrent slot label context to slot filling. Another observation is that once recurrent context is applied, the benefit of adding local context for next word prediction is limited. It might hint that the most useful information for the next word prediction can be well captured in the RNN state, and thus adding explicit dependencies on local intent class and slot label is not very helpful.

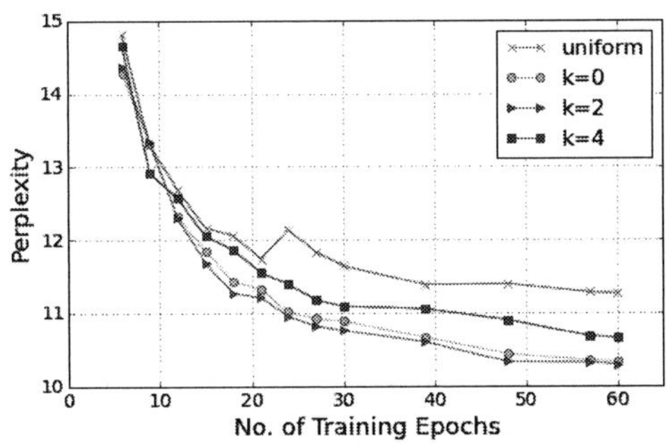

Figure 6: LM perplexity of the joint SLU-LM models with different schedules in adjusting the intent contribution to the context vector.

During the joint model training and inference, we used a schedule to adjust the intent contribution to the context vector by linearly scaling the intent vector with the growing input word sequence after step k. We found this technique to be critical in achieving advantageous language modeling performance. Figure 6 shows test set perplexities along the training epochs for models using different k values, comparing to the model with uniform ($\eta = 1$) intent contribution. With uniform intent contribution across time, the context vector does not bring benefit to the next word prediction, and the language modeling perplexity is similar to that of the basic joint model. By applying the adjusted intent scale ($k = 2$), the perplexity drops from 11.26 (with uniform intent contribution) to 10.29, an 8.6% relative reduction.

4.3.2 Results in ASR Settings

To further evaluate the robustness of the proposed joint SLU-LM model, we experimented with noisy speech input and performed SLU on the rescored ASR outputs. Model performance is evaluated in terms of ASR word error rate (WER), intent classification error, and slot filling F1 score. As shown in Table 2, the model with joint training RNN LM rescoring outperforms the models using 5-gram LM rescoring and independent training RNN LM rescoring on all the three evaluation metrics. Using the rescored ASR outputs (12.59% WER) as input to the joint training SLU model, the intent classification error increased by 2.87%, and slot filling F1 score dropped by 7.77% comparing to the setup using true text input. The performance degradation is expected as we used a more challenging and realistic setup with noisy speech input. These results in Table 2 show that our joint training model outperforms the independent training model consistently on ASR and SLU tasks.

5 Conclusion

In this paper, we propose a conditional RNN model that can be used to jointly perform online spoken language understanding and language modeling. We show that by continuously modeling intent variation and slot label dependencies along with the arrival of new words, the joint training model achieves advantageous performance in intent detection and language modeling with slight degradation on slot filling comparing to the independent training models. On the ATIS benchmarking data set, our joint model produces 11.8% relative reduction on LM perplexity, and 22.3% relative reduction on intent detection error when using true text as input. The joint model also shows consistent performance gain over the independent training models in the more challenging and realistic setup using noisy speech input. Code to reproduce our experiments is available at: http://speech.sv.cmu.edu/software.html

References

Jon Barker, Ricard Marxer, Emmanuel Vincent, and Shinji Watanabe. 2015. The third chime speech separation and recognition challenge: Dataset, task and baselines. In *2015 IEEE Automatic Speech Recognition and Understanding Workshop (ASRU 2015)*.

Samy Bengio, Oriol Vinyals, Navdeep Jaitly, and Noam Shazeer. 2015. Scheduled sampling for sequence prediction with recurrent neural networks. In *Advances in Neural Information Processing Systems*, pages 1171–1179.

William Chan, Navdeep Jaitly, Quoc V Le, and Oriol Vinyals. 2015. Listen, attend and spell. *arXiv preprint arXiv:1508.01211*.

Ronan Collobert and Jason Weston. 2008. A unified architecture for natural language processing: Deep neural networks with multitask learning. In *Proceedings of the 25th international conference on Machine learning*, pages 160–167. ACM.

Daniel Guo, Gokhan Tur, Wen-tau Yih, and Geoffrey Zweig. 2014. Joint semantic utterance classification and slot filling with recursive neural networks. In *Spoken Language Technology Workshop (SLT), 2014 IEEE*, pages 554–559. IEEE.

Patrick Haffner, Gokhan Tur, and Jerry H Wright. 2003. Optimizing svms for complex call classification. In *Acoustics, Speech, and Signal Processing, 2003. Proceedings.(ICASSP'03). 2003 IEEE International Conference on*, volume 1, pages I–632. IEEE.

Charles T Hemphill, John J Godfrey, and George R Doddington. 1990. The atis spoken language systems pilot corpus. In *Proceedings of the DARPA speech and natural language workshop*, pages 96–101.

Sepp Hochreiter and Jürgen Schmidhuber. 1997. Long short-term memory. *Neural computation*, 9(8):1735–1780.

Navdeep Jaitly, Quoc V Le, Oriol Vinyals, Ilya Sutskeyver, and Samy Bengio. 2015. An online sequence-to-sequence model using partial conditioning. *arXiv preprint arXiv:1511.04868*.

Yoon Kim. 2014. Convolutional neural networks for sentence classification. *arXiv preprint arXiv:1408.5882*.

Diederik Kingma and Jimmy Ba. 2014. Adam: A method for stochastic optimization. *arXiv preprint arXiv:1412.6980*.

Bing Liu and Ian Lane. 2015. Recurrent neural network structured output prediction for spoken language understanding. In *Proc. NIPS Workshop on Machine Learning for Spoken Language Understanding and Interactions*.

Andrew McCallum, Dayne Freitag, and Fernando CN Pereira. 2000. Maximum entropy markov models for information extraction and segmentation. In *ICML*, volume 17, pages 591–598.

Grégoire Mesnil, Yann Dauphin, Kaisheng Yao, Yoshua Bengio, Li Deng, Dilek Hakkani-Tur, Xiaodong He, Larry Heck, Gokhan Tur, Dong Yu, et al. 2015. Using recurrent neural networks for slot filling in spoken language understanding. *Audio, Speech, and Language Processing, IEEE/ACM Transactions on*, 23(3):530–539.

Tomáš Mikolov, Stefan Kombrink, Lukáš Burget, Jan Honza Černockỳ, and Sanjeev Khudanpur. 2011. Extensions of recurrent neural network language model. In *Acoustics, Speech and Signal Processing (ICASSP), 2011 IEEE International Conference on*, pages 5528–5531. IEEE.

Vassil Panayotov, Guoguo Chen, Daniel Povey, and Sanjeev Khudanpur. 2015. Librispeech: an asr corpus based on public domain audio books. In *Acoustics, Speech and Signal Processing (ICASSP), 2015 IEEE International Conference on*, pages 5206–5210. IEEE.

Suman Ravuri and Andreas Stolcke. 2015. Recurrent neural network and lstm models for lexical utterance classification. In *Sixteenth Annual Conference of the International Speech Communication Association*.

Christian Raymond and Giuseppe Riccardi. 2007. Generative and discriminative algorithms for spoken language understanding. In *INTERSPEECH*, pages 1605–1608.

Martin Sundermeyer, Ralf Schlüter, and Hermann Ney. 2012. Lstm neural networks for language modeling. In *INTERSPEECH*, pages 194–197.

Ilya Sutskever, Oriol Vinyals, and Quoc V Le. 2014. Sequence to sequence learning with neural networks. In *Advances in neural information processing systems*, pages 3104–3112.

Gokhan Tur, Dilek Hakkani-Tur, and Larry Heck. 2010. What is left to be understood in atis? In *Spoken Language Technology Workshop (SLT), 2010 IEEE*, pages 19–24. IEEE.

Puyang Xu and Ruhi Sarikaya. 2013. Convolutional neural network based triangular crf for joint intent detection and slot filling. In *Automatic Speech Recognition and Understanding (ASRU), 2013 IEEE Workshop on*, pages 78–83. IEEE.

Kaisheng Yao, Baolin Peng, Yu Zhang, Dong Yu, Geoffrey Zweig, and Yangyang Shi. 2014. Spoken language understanding using long short-term memory neural networks. In *Spoken Language Technology Workshop (SLT), 2014 IEEE*, pages 189–194. IEEE.

Wojciech Zaremba, Ilya Sutskever, and Oriol Vinyals. 2014. Recurrent neural network regularization. *arXiv preprint arXiv:1409.2329*.

Creating and Characterizing a Diverse Corpus of Sarcasm in Dialogue

Shereen Oraby[*], **Vrindavan Harrison**[*], **Lena Reed**[*], **Ernesto Hernandez**[*],
Ellen Riloff[†] **and Marilyn Walker**[*]
[*] University of California, Santa Cruz
{soraby,vharriso,lireed,eherna23,mawalker}@ucsc.edu
[†] University of Utah
riloff@cs.utah.edu

Abstract

The use of irony and sarcasm in social media allows us to study them at scale for the first time. However, their diversity has made it difficult to construct a high-quality corpus of sarcasm in dialogue. Here, we describe the process of creating a large-scale, highly-diverse corpus of online debate forums dialogue, and our novel methods for operationalizing classes of sarcasm in the form of rhetorical questions and hyperbole. We show that we can use lexico-syntactic cues to reliably retrieve sarcastic utterances with high accuracy. To demonstrate the properties and quality of our corpus, we conduct supervised learning experiments with simple features, and show that we achieve both higher precision and F than previous work on sarcasm in debate forums dialogue. We apply a weakly-supervised linguistic pattern learner and qualitatively analyze the linguistic differences in each class.

1 Introduction

Irony and sarcasm in dialogue constitute a highly creative use of language signaled by a large range of situational, semantic, pragmatic and lexical cues. Previous work draws attention to the use of both hyperbole and rhetorical questions in conversation as distinct types of lexico-syntactic cues defining diverse classes of sarcasm (Gibbs, 2000).

Theoretical models posit that a single semantic basis underlies sarcasm's diversity of form, namely "a contrast" between expected and experienced events, giving rise to a contrast between what is said and a literal description of the actual situation (Colston and O'Brien, 2000; Partington, 2007). This semantic characterization has not been straightforward to operationalize computationally for sarcasm in dialogue. Riloff et al.

(2013) operationalize this notion for sarcasm in tweets, achieving good results. Joshi et al. (2015) develop several *incongruity* features to capture it, but although they improve performance on tweets, their features do not yield improvements for dialogue.

Previous work on the Internet Argument Corpus (IAC) 1.0 dataset aimed to develop a high-precision classifier for sarcasm in order to bootstrap a much larger corpus (Lukin and Walker, 2013), but was only able to obtain a precision of just 0.62, with a best F of 0.57, not high enough for bootstrapping (Riloff and Wiebe, 2003; Thelen and Riloff, 2002). Justo et al. (2014) experimented with the same corpus, using supervised learning, and achieved a best precision of 0.66 and a best F of 0.70. Joshi et al. (2015)'s *explicit congruity* features achieve precision around 0.70 and best F of 0.64 on a subset of IAC 1.0.

We decided that we need a larger and more diverse corpus of sarcasm in dialogue. It is difficult to efficiently gather sarcastic data, because only about 12% of the utterances in written online debate forums dialogue are sarcastic (Walker et al., 2012a), and it is difficult to achieve high reliability for sarcasm annotation (Filatova, 2012; Swanson et al., 2014; González-Ibáñez et al., 2011; Wallace et al., 2014). Thus, our contributions are:

- We develop a new larger corpus, using several methods that filter non-sarcastic utterances to skew the distribution toward/in favor of sarcastic utterances. We put filtered data out for annotation, and are able to achieve high annotation reliability.

- We present a novel operationalization of both rhetorical questions and hyperbole to develop subcorpora to explore the differences between them and general sarcasm.

- We show that our new corpus is of high quality by applying supervised machine learning with simple features to explore how different

Proceedings of the SIGDIAL 2016 Conference, pages 31–41,
Los Angeles, USA, 13-15 September 2016. ©2016 Association for Computational Linguistics

corpus properties affect classification results. We achieve a highest precision of 0.73 and a highest F of 0.74 on the new corpus with basic n-gram and Word2Vec features, showcasing the quality of the corpus, and improving on previous work.

- We apply a weakly-supervised learner to characterize linguistic patterns in each corpus, and describe the differences across generic sarcasm, rhetorical questions and hyperbole in terms of the patterns learned.

- We show for the first time that it is straightforward to develop very high precision classifiers for NOT-SARCASTIC utterances across our rhetorical questions and hyperbole subtypes, due to the nature of these utterances in debate forum dialogue.

2 Creating a Diverse Sarcasm Corpus

There has been relatively little theoretical work on sarcasm in dialogue that has had access to a large corpus of naturally occurring examples. Gibbs (2000) analyzes a corpus of 62 conversations between friends and argues that a robust theory of verbal irony must account for the large diversity in form. He defines several subtypes, including rhetorical questions and hyperbole:

- **Rhetorical Questions:** asking a question that implies a humorous or critical assertion
- **Hyperbole:** expressing a non-literal meaning by exaggerating the reality of a situation

Other categories of irony defined by Gibbs (2000) include understatements, jocularity, and sarcasm (which he defines as a critical/mocking form of irony). Other work has also tackled jocularity and humor, using different approaches for data aggregation, including filtering by Twitter hashtags, or analyzing laugh-tracks from recordings (Reyes et al., 2012; Bertero and Fung, 2016).

Previous work has not, however, attempted to operationalize these subtypes in any concrete way. Here we describe our methods for creating a corpus for generic sarcasm (Gen) (Sec. 2.1), rhetorical questions (RQ), and hyperbole (Hyp) (Sec. 2.2) using data from the Internet Argument Corpus (IAC 2.0).[1] Table 1 provides examples of SARCASTIC and NOT-SARCASTIC posts from the corpus we create. Table 2 summarizes the final composition of our sarcasm corpus.

Generic Data		
1	S	I love it when you bash people for stating opinions and no facts when you turn around and do the same thing [...] give me a break
2	NS	The attacker is usually armed in spite of gun control laws. All they do is disarm the law abiding. Not to mention the lack of enforcement on criminals.
Rhetorical Questions		
3	S	**Then why do you call a politician who ran such measures liberal?** *OH yes, it's because you're a republican and you're not conservative at all.*
4	NS	**And what would that prove?** *It would certainly show that an animal adapted to survival above the Arctic circle was not adapted to the Arizona desert.*
Hyperbole		
5	S	Thank you for making my point **better than I could ever do!!** It's all about you, right honey? I am woman hear me roar right? LMAO
6	NS	**Again i am astounded** by the fact that you think i will endanger children. it is a topic sunset, so why are you calling me demented and sick.

Table 1: Examples of different types of SARCASTIC (S) and NOT-SARCASTIC (NS) Posts

Dataset	Total Size	Posts Per Class
Generic (Gen)	6,520	3,260
Rhetorical Questions (RQ)	1,702	851
Hyperbole (Hyp)	1,164	582

Table 2: Total number of posts in each subcorpus (each with a 50% split of SARCASTIC and NOT-SARCASTIC posts)

2.1 Generic Dataset (Gen)

We first replicated the pattern-extraction experiments of Lukin and Walker (2013) on their dataset using AutoSlog-TS (Riloff, 1996), a weakly-supervised pattern learner that extracts lexico-syntactic patterns associated with the input data. We set up the learner to extract patterns for both SARCASTIC and NOT-SARCASTIC utterances. Our first discovery is that we can classify NOT-SARCASTIC posts with very high precision, ranging between 80-90%.[2]

Because our main goal is to build a larger, more diverse corpus of sarcasm, we use the high-precision NOT-SARCASTIC patterns extracted by AutoSlog-TS to create a "not-sarcastic" filter. We did this by randomly selecting a new set of 30K posts (restricting to posts with between 10 and 150 words) from IAC 2.0 (Abbott et al., 2016), and applying the high-precision NOT-SARCASTIC

---

[1]The IAC 2.0 is available at https://nlds.soe.ucsc.edu/iac2, and our sarcasm corpus will be released at https://nlds.soe.ucsc.edu/sarcasm2.

[2]We delay a detailed discussion of the characteristics of this NOT-SARCASTIC classifier, and the patterns that we learn, until Sec. 4 where we describe AutoSlog-TS and the linguistic characteristics of the whole corpus.

patterns from AutoSlog-TS to filter out any posts that contain at least one NOT-SARCASTIC cue. We end up filtering out two-thirds of the pool, only keeping posts that did not contain any of our high-precision NOT-SARCASTIC cues. We acknowledge that this may also filter out sarcastic posts, but we expect it to increase the ratio of sarcastic posts in the remaining pool.

We put out the remaining 11,040 posts on Mechanical Turk. As in Lukin and Walker (2013), we present the posts in "quote-response" pairs, where the response post to be annotated is presented in the context of its "dialogic parent", another post earlier in the thread, or a quote from another post earlier in the thread (Walker et al., 2012b). In the task instructions, annotators are presented with a definition of sarcasm, followed by one example of a quote-response pair that clearly contains sarcasm, and one pair that clearly does not. Each task consists of 20 quote-response pairs that follow the instructions. Figure 1 shows the instructions and layout of a single quote-response pair presented to annotators. As in Lukin and Walker (2013) and Walker et al. (2012b), annotators are asked a binary question: *Is any part of the response to this quote sarcastic?*.

To help filter out unreliable annotators, we create a qualifier consisting of a set of 20 manually-selected quote-response pairs (10 that should receive a SARCASTIC label and 10 that should receive a NOT-SARCASTIC label). A Turker must pass the qualifier with a score above 70% to participate in our sarcasm annotations tasks.

Our baseline ratio of sarcasm in online debate forums dialogue is the estimated 12% sarcastic posts in the IAC, which was found previously by Walker et al. by gathering annotations for sarcasm, agreement, emotional language, attacks, and nastiness from a subset of around 20K posts from the IAC across various topics (Walker et al., 2012a). Similarly, in his study of recorded conversation among friends, Gibbs cites 8% sarcastic utterances among all conversational turns (Gibbs, 2000).

We choose a conservative threshold: a post is only added to the sarcastic set if at least 6 out of 9 annotators labeled it sarcastic. Of the 11,040 posts we put out for annotation, we thus obtain 2,220 new posts, giving us a ratio of about 20% sarcasm – significantly higher than our baseline of 12%. We choose this conservative threshold to ensure the quality of our annotations, and we leave aside posts that 5 out of 9 annotators label as sarcastic for future work – noting that we can get even higher ratios of sarcasm by including them (up to 31%). The percentage agreement between

Figure 1: Mechanical Turk Task Layout

each annotator and the majority vote is 80%.

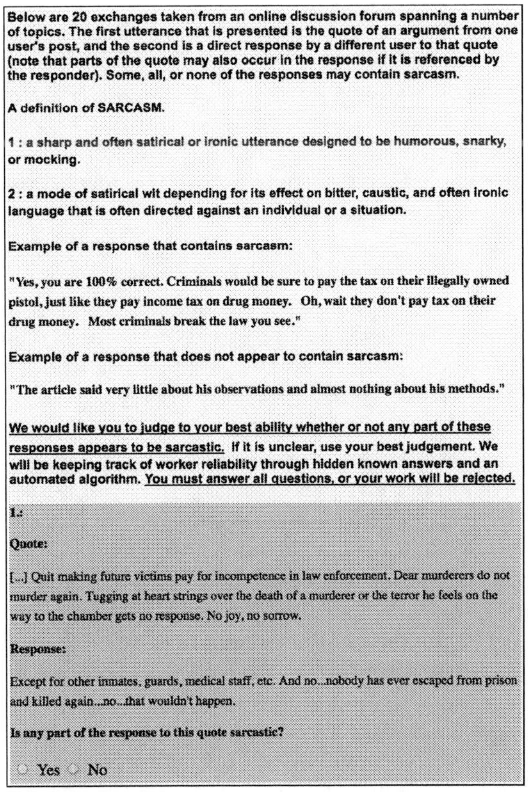

We then expand this set, using only 3 highly-reliable Turkers (based on our first round of annotations), giving them an exclusive sarcasm qualification to do additional HITs. We gain an additional 1,040 posts for each class when using majority agreement (at least 2 out of 3 sarcasm labels) for the additional set (to add to the 2,220 original posts). The average percent agreement with the majority vote is 89% for these three annotators. We supplement our sarcastic data with 2,360 not-sarcastic posts from the original data by (Lukin and Walker, 2013) that follow our 150-word length restriction, and complete the set with 900 posts that were filtered out by our NOT-SARCASTIC filter[3] – resulting in a total of 3,260 posts per class (6,520 total posts).

Rows 1 and 2 of Table 1 show examples of posts that are labeled sarcastic in our final generic sarcasm set. Using our filtering method, we are able to reduce the number of posts annotated from our original 30K to around 11K, achieving a percentage of 20% sarcastic posts, even though we choose

---

[3] We use these unbiased not-sarcastic data sources to avoid using posts coming from the sarcasm-skewed distribution.

to use a conservative threshold of at least 6 out of 9 sarcasm labels. Since the number of posts being annotated is only a third of the original set size, this method reduces annotation effort, time, and cost, and helps us shift the distribution of sarcasm to more efficiently expand our dataset than would otherwise be possible.

2.2 Rhetorical Questions and Hyperbole

The goal of collecting additional corpora for rhetorical questions and hyperbole is to increase the diversity of the corpus, and to allow us to explore the semantic differences between SARCASTIC and NOT-SARCASTIC utterances when particular lexico-syntactic cues are held constant. We hypothesize that identifying surface-level cues that are instantiated in *both* sarcastic and not sarcastic posts will force learning models to find deeper semantic cues to distinguish between the classes.

Using a combination of findings in the theoretical literature, and observations of sarcasm patterns in our generic set, we developed a regex pattern matcher that runs against the 400K unannotated posts in the IAC 2.0 database and retrieves matching posts, only pulling posts that have parent posts and a maximum of 150 words. Table 3 only shows a small subset of the "more successful" regex patterns we defined for each class.

Cue	# Found	# Annot	% Sarc
Hyperbole			
let's all	27	21	62%
i love it when	158	25	56%
oh yeah	397	104	50%
wow	977	153	44%
i'm * shocked|amazed|impressed	120	33	42%
fantastic	257	47	36%
hun/dear*/darling	661	249	32%
you're kidding/joking	132	43	28%
eureka	21	12	17%
Rhetorical Questions and Self-Answering			
oh wait	136	121	87%
oh right	19	11	81%
oh really	62	50	50%
really?	326	151	30%
interesting.	48	27	15%

Table 3: Annotation Counts for a Subset of Cues

Cue annotation experiments. After running a large number of retrieval experiments with our regex pattern matcher, we select batches of the resulting posts that mix different cue classes to put out for annotation, in such a way as to not allow the annotators to determine what regex cues were used. We then successively put out various batches for annotation by 5 of our highly-qualified annotators, in order to determine what percentage of

posts with these cues are sarcastic.

Table 3 summarizes the results for a sample set of cues, showing the number of posts found containing the cue, the subset that we put out for annotation, and the percentage of posts labeled sarcastic in the annotation experiments. For example, for the hyperbolic cue *"wow"*, 977 utterances with the cue were found, 153 were annotated, and 44% of those were found to be sarcastic (i.e. 56% were found to be not-sarcastic). Posts with the cue *"oh wait"* had the highest sarcasm ratio, at 87%. It is the distinction between the sarcastic and not-sarcastic instances that we are specifically interested in. We describe the corpus collection process for each subclass below.

It is important to note that using particular cues (regex) to retrieve sarcastic posts **does not** result in posts whose only cue is the regex pattern. We demonstrate this quantitatively in Sec. 4. Sarcasm is characterized by multiple lexical and morphosyntactic cues: these include the use of intensifiers, elongated words, quotations, false politeness, negative evaluations, emoticons, and tag questions *inter alia*. Table 4 shows how sarcastic utterances often contain combinations of multiple indicators, each playing a role in the overall sarcastic tone of the post.

Sarcastic Utterance
Forgive me if I **doubt** your sincerity, but you seem like **a troll** to me. I **suspect** that you aren't interested in learning about evolution **at all.** Your questions, while they do support your claim to **know almost nothing,** are **pretty** typical of creationist **"prove it to me"** questions.
Wrong again! You **obviously** can't recognize refutation when its printed before you. I haven't made the tag **"you liberals"** derogatory. You liberals have done that to yourselves! **I suppose** you'd rather be called a social reformist! Actually, socialist is closer to a true description.

Table 4: Utterances with Multiple Sarcastic Cues

Rhetorical Questions. There is no previous work on distinguishing sarcastic from non-sarcastic uses of rhetorical questions (RQs). RQs are syntactically formulated as a question, but function as an indirect assertion (Frank, 1990). The polarity of the question implies an assertion of the opposite polarity, e.g. *Can you read?* implies *You can't read.* RQs are prevalent in persuasive discourse, and are frequently used ironically (Schaffer, 2005; Ilie, 1994; Gibbs, 2000). Previous work focuses on their formal semantic properties (Han, 1997), or distinguishing RQs from standard questions (Bhattasali et al., 2015).

We hypothesized that we could find RQs in abundance by searching for questions in the middle of a post, that are followed by a statement, using the assumption that questions followed by a statement are unlikely to be standard information-seeking questions. We test this assumption by randomly extracting 100 potential RQs as per our definition and putting them out on Mechanical Turk to 3 annotators, asking them whether or not the questions (displayed with their following statement) were rhetorical. According to majority vote, 75% of the posts were rhetorical.

We thus use this "middle of post" heuristic to obviate the need to gather manual annotations for RQs, and developed regex patterns to find RQs that were more likely to be sarcastic. A sample of the patterns, number of matches in the corpus, the numbers we had annotated, and the percent that are sarcastic after annotation are summarized in Table 3.

Rhetorical Questions and Self-Answering
So you do not wish to have a logical debate? *Alrighty then. god bless you anyway, brother.*
Prove that? *You can't prove that i've given nothing but insults. i'm defending myself, to mackindale, that's all.* **do you have a problem with how i am defending myself against mackindale?** *Apparently.*

Table 5: Examples of Rhetorical Questions and Self-Answering

We extract 357 posts following the intermediate question-answer pairs heuristic from our generic (Gen) corpus. We then supplement these with posts containing RQ cues from our cue-annotation experiments: posts that received 3 out of 5 sarcastic labels in the experiments were considered sarcastic, and posts that received 2 or fewer sarcastic labels were considered not-sarcastic. Our final rhetorical questions corpus consists of 851 posts per class (1,702 total posts). Table 5 shows some examples of rhetorical questions and self-answering from our corpus.

Hyperbole. Hyperbole (Hyp) has been studied as an independent form of figurative language, that can coincide with ironic intent (McCarthy and Carter, 2004; Cano Mora, 2009), and previous computational work on sarcasm typically includes features to capture hyperbole (Reyes et al., 2013). Kreuz and Roberts (1995) describe a standard frame for hyperbole in English where an adverb modifies an extreme, positive adjective, e.g. *"That was* **absolutely amazing***!"* or *"That was* **simply the most incredible** *dining experience in my entire life."*

Colston and O'Brien (2000) provide a theoretical framework that explains why hyperbole is so strongly associated with sarcasm. Hyperbole exaggerates the literal situation, introducing a discrepancy between the "truth" and what is said, as a matter of degree. A key observation is that this is

a type of contrast (Colston and Keller, 1998; Colston and O'Brien, 2000). In their framework:

- An event or situation evokes a scale;
- An event can be placed on that scale;
- The utterance about the event **contrasts** with actual scale placement.

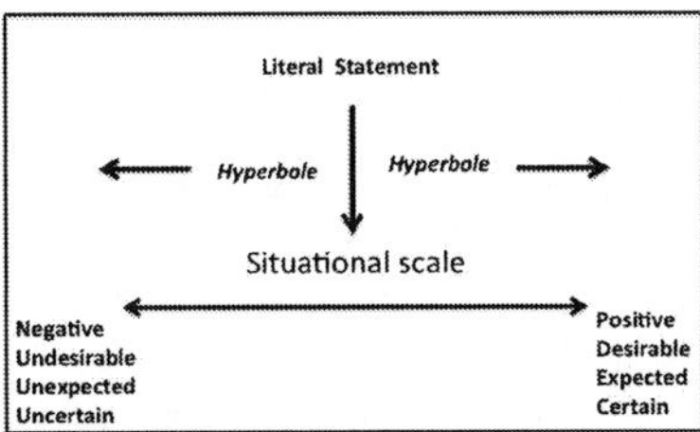

Figure 2: Hyperbole shifts the strength of what is said from literal to extreme negative or positive (Colston and O'Brien, 2000)

Fig. 2 illustrates that the scales that can be evoked range from negative to positive, undesirable to desirable, unexpected to expected and certain to uncertain. Hyperbole moves the strength of an assertion further up or down the scale from the literal meaning, the degree of movement corresponds to the degree of contrast. Depending on what they modify, adverbial intensifiers like *totally, absolutely, incredibly* shift the strength of the assertion to extreme negative or positive.

Hyperbole with Intensifiers
Wow! **I am soooooooo amazed** by your come back skills... another epic fail!
My goodness...**i'm utterly amazed** at the number of men out there that are so willing to decide how a woman should use her own body!
Oh do go on. **I am so impressed** by your 'intellectuall' argument. pfft.
I am very impressed with your ability to copy and paste links now what this proves about what you know about it is still unproven.

Table 6: Examples of Hyperbole and the Effects of Intensifiers

Table 6 shows examples of hyperbole from our corpus, showcasing the effect that intensifiers have in terms of strengthening the emotional evaluation of the response. To construct a balanced corpus of sarcastic and not-sarcastic utterances with hyperbole, we developed a number of patterns based on the literature and our observations of the generic corpus. The patterns, number matches on the whole corpus, the numbers we had annotated and the percent that are sarcastic after annotation are summarized in Table 3. Again, we extract a small subset of examples from our Gen corpus (30 per class), and supplement them with posts that contain our hyperbole cues (considering them sarcastic if they received at least 3/5 sarcastic labels, notsarcastic otherwise). The final hyperbole dataset consists of 582 posts per class (1,164 posts in total).

To recap, Table 2 summarizes the total number of posts for each subset of our final corpus.

3 Learning Experiments

Our primary goal is not to optimize classification results, but to explore how results vary across different subcorpora and corpus properties. We also aim to demonstrate that the quality of our corpus makes it more straightforward to achieve high classification performance. We apply both supervised learning using SVM (from Scikit-Learn (Pedregosa et al., 2011)) and weakly-supervised linguistic pattern learning using AutoSlog-TS (Riloff, 1996). These reveal different aspects of the corpus.

Supervised Learning. We restrict our supervised experiments to a default linear SVM learner with Stochastic Gradient Descent (SGD) training and L2 regularization, available in the SciKit-Learn toolkit (Pedregosa et al., 2011). We use 10-fold cross-validation, and only two types of features: n-grams and Word2Vec word embeddings. We expect Word2Vec to be able to capture semantic generalizations that n-grams do not (Socher et al., 2013; Li et al., 2016). The n-gram features include unigrams, bigrams, and trigrams, including sequences of punctuation (for example, ellipses or "!!!"), and emoticons. We use GoogleNews Word2Vec features (Mikolov et al., 2013).[4]

Table 7 summarizes the results of our supervised learning experiments on our datasets using 10-fold cross validation. The data is balanced evenly between the SARCASTIC and NOT-SARCASTIC classes, and the best F-Measures for each class are shown in bold. The default W2V model, (trained on Google News), gives the best overall F-measure of 0.74 on the Gen corpus for the SARCASTIC class, while n-grams give the best NOT-SARCASTIC F-measure of 0.73. Both of these results are higher F than previously reported for classifying sarcasm in dialogue, and we might expect that feature engineering could yield even greater performance.

---

[4]We test our own custom 300-dimensional embeddings created for the dialogic domain using the Gensim library (Řehůřek and Sojka, 2010), and a very large corpus of user-generated dialogue. While this custom model works well for other tasks on IAC 2.0, it did not work well for sarcasm classification, so we do not discuss it further.

Form	Features	Class	P	R	F
Gen	N-Grams	S	0.73	0.70	0.72
		NS	0.71	0.75	**0.73**
	W2V	S	0.71	0.77	**0.74**
		NS	0.75	0.69	0.72
RQ	N-Grams	S	0.71	0.68	**0.70**
		NS	0.70	0.73	**0.71**
	W2V	S	0.67	0.72	0.69
		NS	0.70	0.64	0.67
Hyp	N-Grams	S	0.68	0.63	**0.65**
		NS	0.66	0.71	**0.68**
	W2V	S	0.57	0.56	0.57
		NS	0.57	0.59	0.58

Table 7: Supervised Learning Results for Generic (Gen: 3,260 posts per class), Rhetorical Questions (RQ: 851 posts per class) and Hyperbole (Hyp: 582 posts per class)

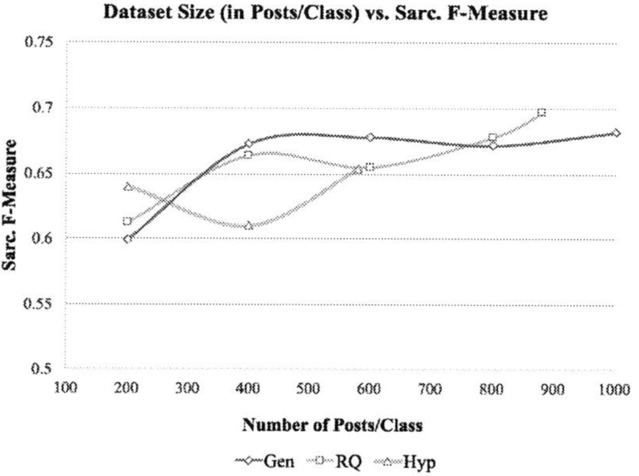

Figure 3: Plot of Dataset size (x-axis) vs Sarc. F-Measure (y-axis) for the three subcorpora, with n-gram features

On the RQ corpus, n-grams provide the best F-measure for SARCASTIC at 0.70 and NOT-SARCASTIC at 0.71. Although W2V performs well, the n-gram model includes features involving repeated punctuation and emoticons, which the W2V model excludes. Punctuation and emoticons are often used as distinctive feature of sarcasm (i.e. *"Oh, really?!?!"*, *[emoticon-rolleyes]*).

For the Hyp corpus, the best F-measure for both the SARCASTIC and NOT-SARCASTIC classes again comes from n-grams, with F-measures of 0.65 and 0.68 respectively. It is interesting to note that the overall results of the Hyp data are lower than those for Gen and RQs, likely due to the smaller size of the Hyp dataset.

To examine the effect of dataset size, we compare F-measure (using the same 10-fold cross-validation setup) for each dataset while holding the number of posts per class constant. Figure 3 shows the performance of each of the Gen, RQ, and Hyp datasets at intervals of 100 posts per class (up to the maximum size of 582 posts per class for Hyp, and 851 posts per class for RQ). From the graph, we can see that as a general trend, the datasets benefit from larger dataset sizes. Interestingly, the results for the RQ dataset are very comparable to those of Gen. The Gen dataset eventually gets the highest sarcastic F-measure (0.74) at its full dataset size of 3,260 posts per class.

Weakly-Supervised Learning. AutoSlog-TS is a weakly supervised pattern learner that only requires training documents labeled broadly as SARCASTIC or NOT-SARCASTIC. AutoSlog-TS uses a set of syntactic templates to define different types of linguistic expressions. The left-hand side of Table 8 lists each pattern template and the right-hand side illustrates a specific lexico-syntactic pattern (**in bold**) that represents an instantiation of each general pattern template for learning sarcastic patterns in our data.[5] In addition to these 17 templates, we added patterns to AutoSlog for adjective-noun, adverb-adjective and adjective-adjective, because these patterns are frequent in hyperbolic sarcastic utterances.

The examples in Table 8 show that Colston's notion of contrast shows up in many learned patterns, and that the source of the contrast is **highly variable**. For example, Row 1 implies a contrast with a set of people who are not *your mother*. Row 5 contrasts what *you were asked* with *what you've (just) done*. Row 10 contrasts *chapter 12* and *chapter 13* (Hirschberg, 1985). Row 11 contrasts *what I am allowed* vs. what *you have to do*.

AutoSlog-TS computes statistics on the strength of association of each pattern with each class, i.e. P(SARCASTIC $\mid p$) and P(NOT-SARCASTIC $\mid p$), along with the pattern's overall frequency. We define two tuning parameters for each class: θ_f, the frequency with which a pattern occurs, θ_p, the probability with which a pattern is associated with the given class. We do a grid-search, testing the performance of our patterns thresholds from $\theta_f = \{2\text{-}6\}$ in intervals of 1, $\theta_p=\{0.60\text{-}0.85\}$ in intervals of 0.05. Once we extract the subset of patterns passing our thresholds, we search for these patterns in the posts in our development set, classifying a post as a given class if it contains $\theta_n=\{1,$

---

⁵The examples are shown as general expressions for readability, but the actual patterns must match the syntactic constraints associated with the pattern template.

	Pattern Template	Example Instantiations
1	<subj> PassVP	Go tell your mother, <**she**> **might be interested** in your fulminations.
2	<subj> ActVP	Oh my goodness. This is a trick called semantics. <**I**> **guess** you got sucked in.
3	<subj> ActVP Dobj	yet <**I**> **do nothing** to prevent the situation
4	<subj> ActInfVP	I guess <**I**> **need to check** what website I am in
5	<subj> PassInfVP	<**You**> **were asked to give** us your explanation of evolution. So far you've just ...
6	<subj> AuxVP Dobj	Fortunately <**you**> **have the ability** to ...
7	<subj> AuxVP Adj	Or do you think that <**nothing**> **is capable** of undermining the institution of marriage?
8	ActVP <dobj>	Oh yes, I **know** <**everything**> that [...]
9	InfVP <dobj>	Good idea except we do not have **to elect** <**him**> to any post... just send him over there.
10	ActInfVP <dobj>	**Try to read** <**chptr 13**> before chptr 12, it will help you out.
11	PassInfVP <dobj>	i love it when people do this. 'you have to prove everything you say, but i **am allowed to** simply **make** <**assertions**> and it's your job to show i'm wrong.'
12	Subj AuxVP <dobj>	So your **answer** [then] **is** <**nothing**>...
13	NP Prep <np>	There are **MILLIONS of** <**people**> saying all sorts of stupid things about the president.
14	ActVP Prep <np>	My pyramidal tinfoil hat is an antenna for knowledge and truth. It reflects idiocy and dumbness into deep space. You still have not **admitted to** <**your error**>
15	PassVP Prep <np>	Likelihood is that they will have to **be left alone for** <**a few months**> [...] Sigh, I wonder if ignorance really is blissful.
16	InfVP Prep <np>	I masquerade as an atheist and a 6-day creationist at the same time to try **to appeal to** <**a wider audience**>.
17	<possessive> NP	O.K. let's play <**your**> **game**.

Table 8: AutoSlog-TS Templates and Example Instantiations

2, 3} of the thresholded patterns. For more detail, see (Riloff, 1996; Oraby et al., 2015).

An advantage of AutoSlog-TS is that it supports systematic exploration of recall and precision tradeoffs, by selecting pattern sets using different parameters. The parameters have to be tuned on a training set, so we divide each dataset into 80% training and 20% test. Figure 4 shows the precision (x-axis) vs. recall (y-axis) tradeoffs on the test set, when optimizing our three parameters for precision. Interestingly, the subcorpora for RQ and Hyp can get higher precision than is possible for Gen. When precision is fixed at 0.75, the recall for RQ is 0.07 and the recall for Hyp is 0.08. This recall is low, but given that each retrieved post provides multiple cues, and that datasets on the web are huge, these P values make it possible to bootstrap these two classes in future.

Prob.	Freq.	Pattern and Text Match	Sample Post
		Sarcastic Example Patterns	
1.00	8	Adv Adv (AH YES)	**Ah yes**, your diversionary tactics.
0.91	11	Adv Adv (THEN AGAIN)	But **then again**, you become what you hate [...]
0.83	36	ActVP Prep <NP> (THANKS FOR)	**Thanks for** missing the point.
0.80	20	ActVP <dobj> (TEACH)	**Teach** the science in class and if that presents a problem [...]
0.80	10	InfVP <dobj> (ANSWER)	I think you need to **answer** the same question [...]
0.79	114	<subj>ActVp (GUESS)	So then I **guess** you could also debate that algebra serves no purpose
0.78	18	ActVP <dobj> (IGNORE)	Excellent **ignore** the issue at hand and give no suggestion
0.74	27	Adv Adv (ONCE AGAIN)	you attempt to **once again** change the subject
0.71	35	Adj Noun (GOOD IDEA)	...especially since you think everything is a **good idea**
		Not-Sarcastic Example Patterns	
0.92	25	Adj Noun (SECOND AMENDMENT)	the nature of the **Second Amendment**
0.90	10	Np Prep <NP> (PROBABILITY OF)	the **probability of** [...] in some organism
0.88	42	ActVP <dobj> (SUPPORT)	I really do not **support** rule by the very, very few
0.84	32	Np Prep <NP> (EVIDENCE FOR)	We have no more **evidence for** one than the other.
0.79	44	Np Prep (THEORY OF)	[...] supports the **theory of** evolution [...]
0.78	64	Np Prep <NP> (NUMBER OF)	minor differences in a limited **number of** primative organisms
0.76	46	Adj Noun (NO EVIDENCE)	And there is **no evidence** of anything other than material processes
0.75	41	Np Prep <NP> (MAJORITY OF)	The **majority of** criminals don't want to deal with trouble.
0.72	25	ActVP <dobj> (EXPLAIN)	[...] it does not **explain** the away the whole shift in the numbers [..]

Table 9: Examples of Characteristic Patterns for Gen using AutoSlog-TS Templates

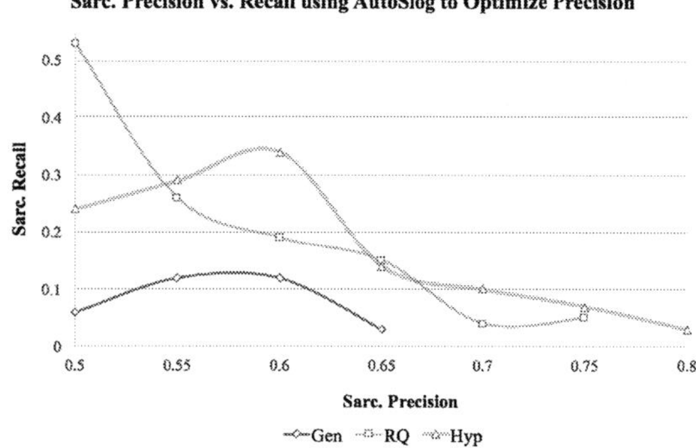

Figure 4: Plot of Precision (x-axis) vs Recall (y-axis) for three subcorpora with AutoSlog-TS parameters, aimed at optimizing precision

4 Linguistic Analysis

Here we aim to provide a linguistic characterization of the differences between the sarcastic and the not-sarcastic classes. We use the AutoSlog-TS pattern learner to generate patterns automatically, and the Stanford dependency parser to examine relationships between arguments (Riloff, 1996; Manning et al., 2014). Table 10 shows the number of sarcastic patterns we extract with AutoSlog-TS, with a frequency of at least 2 and a probability of at least 0.75 for each corpus. We learn many novel lexico-syntactic cue patterns that are not the regex that we search for. We discuss specific novel learned patterns for each class below.

Generic Sarcasm. We first examine the different patterns learned on the Gen dataset. Table 9 show examples of extracted patterns for each class. We observe that the NOT-SARCASTIC patterns appear to capture technical and scientific language, while the SARCASTIC patterns tend to capture subjective language that is not topic-specific. We observe an abundance of adjective and adverb patterns for the sarcastic class, although we do not use adjective and adverb patterns in our regex retrieval method. Instead, such cues co-occur with the cues we search for, expanding our pattern inventory as we show in Table 10.

Dataset	# Sarc Patterns	# NotSarc Patterns
Generic (Gen)	1,316	3,556
Rhetorical Questions (RQ)	671	1,000
Hyperbole (Hyp)	411	527

Table 10: Total number of patterns passing threshold of Freq $\geq$ 2, Prob $\geq$ 0.75

Rhetorical Questions. We notice that while the NOT-SARCASTIC patterns generated for RQs are similar to the topic-specific NOT-SARCASTIC patterns we find in the general dataset, there are some interesting features of the SARCASTIC patterns that are more unique to the RQs.

Many of our sarcastic questions focus specifically on attacks on the mental abilities of the addressee. This generalization is made clear when we extract and analyze the verb, subject, and object arguments using the Stanford dependency parser (Manning et al., 2014) for the *questions* in the RQ dataset. Table 11 shows a few examples of the relations we extract.

Hyperbole. One common pattern for hyperbole

Relation	Rhetorical Question
`realize(you, human)`	Uhm, **you do realize that humans** and chimps are not the same things as dogs, cats, horses, and sharks ... right?
`recognize(you)`	Do **you recognize** that babies grow and live inside women?
`not read(you)`	Are you blind, or **can't you read**?
`get(information)`	Have you ever considered **getting scientific information** from a scientific source?
`have(education)`	And you claim to have an education?
`not have(dummy, problem)`	If these **dummies don't have a problem** with information increasing, but do have a problem with beneficial information increasing, don't you think there is a problem?

Table 11: Attacks on Mental Ability in RQs

involves adverbs and adjectives, as noted above. We did not use this pattern to retrieve hyperbole, but because each hyperbolic sarcastic utterance contains multiple cues, we learn an expanded class of patterns for hyperbole. Table 12 illustrates some of the new adverb adjective patterns that are frequent, high-precision indicators of sarcasm.

We learn a number of verbal patterns that we had not previously associated with hyperbole, as shown in Table 13. Interestingly, many of these instantiate the observations of Cano Mora (2009) on hyperbole and its related semantic fields: creating contrast by exclusion, e.g. *no limit* and *no way*, or by expanding a predicated class, e.g. *everyone knows*. Many of them are also contrastive. Table 12 shows just a few examples, such as *though it in no way* and *so much knowledge*.

Pattern	Freq	Example
`no way`	4	that is a pretty impresive education you are working on (though it in **no way** makes you a shoe in for any political position).
`so much`	17	but nooooooo we are launching missiles on libia thats solves alot .... because we gained **so much** knowledge and learned from our mistakes
`oh dear`	12	**oh dear**, he already added to the gene pool
`how much`	8	you have no idea **how much** of a hippocrit you are, do you
`exactly what`	5	simone, **exactly what** is a gun-loving fool anyway, other than something you...

Table 12: Adverb Adjective Cues in Hyperbole

5   Conclusion and Future Work

We have developed a large scale, highly diverse corpus of sarcasm using a combination of linguistic analysis and crowd-sourced annotation. We use filtering methods to skew the distribution of sarcasm in posts to be annotated to 20-31%, much higher than the estimated 12% distribution of sarcasm in online debate forums. We note that when

Pattern	Freq	Example
`i bet`	9	**i bet** there is a university thesis in there somewhere
`you don't see`	7	**you don't see** us driving in a horse and carriage, do you
`everyone knows`	9	**everyone knows** blacks commit more crime than other races
`I wonder`	5	hmm **i wonder** ware the hot bed for violent christian extremists is
`you trying`	7	if **you are seriously trying** to prove your god by comparing real life things with fictional things, then yes, you have proved your god is fictional

Table 13: Verb Patterns in Hyperbole

using Mechanical Turk for sarcasm annotation, it is possible that the level of agreement signals how lexically-signaled the sarcasm is, so we settle on a conservative threshold (at least 6 out of 9 annotators agreeing that a post is sarcastic) to ensure the quality of our annotations.

We operationalize lexico-syntactic cues prevalent in sarcasm, finding cues that are highly indicative of sarcasm, with ratios up to 87%. Our final corpus consists of data representing generic sarcasm, rhetorical questions, and hyperbole.

We conduct supervised learning experiments to highlight the quality of our corpus, achieving a best F of 0.74 using very simple feature sets. We use weakly-supervised learning to show that we can also achieve high precision (albeit with a low recall) for our rhetorical questions and hyperbole datasets; much higher than the best precision that is possible for the Generic dataset. These high precision values may be used for bootstrapping these two classes in the future.

We also present qualitative analysis of the different characteristics of rhetorical questions and hyperbole in sarcastic acts, and of the distinctions between sarcastic/not-sarcastic cues in generic sarcasm data. Our analysis shows that the forms of sarcasm and its underlying semantic contrast in dialogue are highly diverse.

In future work, we will focus on feature engineering to improve results on the task of sarcasm classification for both our generic data and subclasses. We will also begin to explore evaluation on real-world data distributions, where the ratio of sarcastic/not-sarcastic posts is inherently unbalanced. As we continue our analysis of the generic and fine-grained categories of sarcasm, we aim to better characterize and model the great diversity of sarcasm in dialogue.

Acknowledgments

This work was funded by NSF CISE RI 1302668, under the Robust Intelligence Program.

References

Robert Abbott, Brian Ecker, Pranav Anand, and Marilyn Walker. 2016. Internet argument corpus 2.0: An sql schema for dialogic social media and the corpora to go with it. In *Language Resources and Evaluation Conference, LREC2016*.

Dario Bertero and Pascale Fung. 2016. A long short-term memory framework for detecting humor in dialogues. In *North American Association of Computational Linguistics Conference, NAACL-16*.

Shohini Bhattasali, Jeremy Cytryn, Elana Feldman, and Joonsuk Park. 2015. Automatic identification of rhetorical questions. In *Proc. of the 53rd Annual Meeting of the Association for Computational Linguistics and the 7th International Joint Conference on Natural Language Processing (Short Papers)*.

Laura Cano Mora. 2009. All or nothing: a semantic analysis of hyperbole. *Revista de Lingüística y Lenguas Aplicadas*, pages 25–35.

Herbert L. Colston and Shauna B. Keller. 1998. You'll never believe this: Irony and hyperbole in expressing surprise. *Journal of psycholinguistic research*, 27(4):499–513.

Herbert L. Colston and Jennifer O'Brien. 2000. Contrast and pragmatics in figurative language: Anything understatement can do, irony can do better. *Journal of Pragmatics*, 32(11):1557 – 1583.

Elena Filatova. 2012. Irony and sarcasm: Corpus generation and analysis using crowdsourcing. In *Language Resources and Evaluation Conference, LREC2012*.

Jane Frank. 1990. You call that a rhetorical question?: Forms and functions of rhetorical questions in conversation. *Journal of Pragmatics*, 14(5):723–738.

Raymond W. Gibbs. 2000. Irony in talk among friends. *Metaphor and Symbol*, 15(1):5–27.

Roberto González-Ibáñez, Smaranda Muresan, and Nina Wacholder. 2011. Identifying sarcasm in twitter: a closer look. In *Proc. of the 49th Annual Meeting of the Association for Computational Linguistics*, volume 2, pages 581–586.

Chung-hye Han. 1997. Deriving the interpretation of rhetorical questions. In *The Proc. of the Sixteenth West Coast Conference on Formal Linguistics, WCCFL16*.

Julia Hirschberg. 1985. *A Theory of Scalar Implicature*. Ph.D. thesis, University of Pennsylvania, Computer and Information Science.

Cornelia Ilie. 1994. *What else can I tell you?: a pragmatic study of English rhetorical questions as discursive and argumentative acts*. Acta Universitatis Stockholmiensis: Stockholm studies in English. Almqvist & Wiksell International.

Aditya Joshi, Vinita Sharma, and Pushpak Bhattacharyya. 2015. Harnessing context incongruity for sarcasm detection. In *Proceedings of the 53rd Annual Meeting of the Association for Computational Linguistics*, volume 2, pages 757–762.

Raquel Justo, Thomas Corcoran, Stephanie M Lukin, Marilyn Walker, and M Inés Torres. 2014. Extracting relevant knowledge for the detection of sarcasm and nastiness in the social web. *Knowledge-Based Systems*.

Roger J. Kreuz and Richard M. Roberts. 1995. Two cues for verbal irony: Hyperbole and the ironic tone of voice. *Metaphor and Symbolic Activity*, 10(1):21–31.

Jiwei Li, Xinlei Chen, Eduard Hovy, and Dan Jurafsky. 2016. Visualizing and understanding neural models in nlp. In *North American Association of Computational Linguistics Conference, NAACL-16*.

Stephanie Lukin and Marilyn Walker. 2013. Really? well. apparently bootstrapping improves the performance of sarcasm and nastiness classifiers for online dialogue. *NAACL 2013*, page 30.

Christopher D. Manning, Mihai Surdeanu, John Bauer, Jenny Rose Finkel, Steven Bethard, and David McClosky. 2014. The Stanford CoreNLP natural language processing toolkit. In *ACL (System Demonstrations)*, pages 55–60.

Michael McCarthy and Ronald Carter. 2004. "there's millions of them": hyperbole in everyday conversation. *Journal of Pragmatics*, 36(2):149–184.

Tomas Mikolov, Ilya Sutskever, Kai Chen, Greg S Corrado, and Jeff Dean. 2013. Distributed representations of words and phrases and their compositionality. In *Advances in Neural Information Processing Systems*, pages 3111–3119.

Shereen Oraby, Lena Reed, Ryan Compton, Ellen Riloff, Marilyn Walker, and Steve Whittaker. 2015. And thats a fact: Distinguishing factual and emotional argumentation in online dialogue. *2nd Workshop on Argument Mining, NAACL HLT 2015*, page 116.

Alan Partington. 2007. Irony and reversal of evaluation. *Journal of Pragmatics*, 39(9):1547–1569.

Fabian Pedregosa, Gael Varoquaux, Alexandre Gramfort, Vincent Michel, Bertrand Thirion, Olivier Grisel, Mathieu Blondel, Peter Prettenhofer, Ron Weiss, Vincent Dubourg, Jake Vanderplas, Alexandre Passos, David Cournapeau, Matthieu Brucher, Matthieu Perrot, Edouard Duchesnay. 2011. Scikit-learn: Machine learning in Python. *Journal of Machine Learning Research*, 12:2825–2830.

Radim Řehůřek and Petr Sojka. 2010. Software Framework for Topic Modelling with Large Corpora. In *Proc. of the LREC 2010 Workshop on New Challenges for NLP Frameworks*, pages 45–50.

Antonio Reyes, Paolo Rosso, and Tony Veale. 2013. A multidimensional approach for detecting irony in twitter. *Data Knowl. Eng.*, 47(1):239–268, March.

Antonio Reyes, Paolo Rosso, and Davide Buscaldi. 2012. From humor recognition to irony detection: The figurative language of social media. *Data Knowl. Eng.*, 74:1–12.

Ellen Riloff and Janyce Wiebe. 2003. Learning extraction patterns for subjective expressions. In *Proc. of the 2003 conference on Empirical methods in natural language processing-Volume 10*, pages 105–112. Association for Computational Linguistics.

Ellen Riloff, Ashequl Qadir, Prafulla Surve, Lalindra De Silva, Nathan Gilbert, and Ruihong Huang. 2013. Sarcasm as contrast between a positive sentiment and negative situation. In *Proc. of the 2013 Conference on Empirical Methods in Natural Language Processing (EMNLP 2013)*.

Ellen Riloff. 1996. Automatically generating extraction patterns from untagged text. In *Proceedings of the Thirteenth National Conference on Artificial Intelligence (AAAI-96)*, pages 1044–1049.

Deborah Schaffer. —2005—. Can rhetorical questions function as retorts? : Is the pope catholic? *Journal of Pragmatics*, 37:433–600.

Richard Socher, Alex Perelygin, Jean Wu, Jason Chuang, Christopher D. Manning, Andrew Ng, and Christopher Potts. 2013. Recursive deep models for semantic compositionality over a sentiment treebank. In *Proc. of the 2013 Conference on Empirical Methods in Natural Language Processing*, pages 1631–1642.

Reid Swanson, Stephanie Lukin, Luke Eisenberg, Thomas Chase Corcoran, and Marilyn A Walker. 2014. Getting reliable annotations for sarcasm in online dialogues. In *Language Resources and Evaluation Conference, LREC 2014*.

Michael Thelen and Ellen Riloff. 2002. A bootstrapping method for learning semantic lexicons using extraction pattern contexts. In *Proc. of the ACL-02 Conference on Empirical Methods In Natural Language Processing*, pages 214–221.

Marilyn Walker, Pranav Anand, Robert Abbott, and Jean E. Fox Tree. 2012a. A corpus for research on deliberation and debate. In *Language Resources and Evaluation Conference, LREC2012*, pages 812–817.

Marilyn A. Walker, Pranav Anand, Rob Abbott, Jean E Fox Tree, Craig Martell, and Joseph King. 2012b. That's your evidence?: Classifying stance in online political debate. *Decision Support Systems*, 53(4):719–729.

Byron C. Wallace, Do Kook Choe, Laura Kertz, and Eugene Charniak. 2014. Humans require context to infer ironic intent (so computers probably do, too). In *Proc. of the Association for Computational Linguistics*, pages 512–516.

The SENSEI Annotated Corpus: Human Summaries of Reader Comment Conversations in On-line News

**Emma Barker, Monica Paramita, Ahmet Aker, Emina Kurtic,
Mark Hepple** and **Robert Gaizauskas**
University of Sheffield, UK
`e.barker@ m.paramita@ ahmet.aker@ e.kurtic@`
`m.r.hepple@ r.gaizauskas@ sheffield.ac.uk`

Abstract

Researchers are beginning to explore how to generate summaries of extended argumentative conversations in social media, such as those found in reader comments in on-line news. To date, however, there has been little discussion of what these summaries should be like and a lack of human-authored exemplars, quite likely because writing summaries of this kind of interchange is so difficult. In this paper we propose one type of reader comment summary – the *conversation overview* summary – that aims to capture the key argumentative content of a reader comment conversation. We describe a method we have developed to support humans in authoring conversation overview summaries and present a publicly available corpus – the first of its kind – of news articles plus comment sets, each multiply annotated, according to our method, with conversation overview summaries.

1 Introduction

In the past fifteen years there has been a tremendous growth in on-line news and, associated with it, the new social media phenomenon of on-line reader comments. Virtually all major newspapers and news broadcasters now support a reader comment facility, which allows readers to participate in *multi-party conversations* in which they exchange views and opinion on issues in the news.

One problem with such conversations is that they can rapidly grow to hundreds or even thousands of comments. Few readers have the patience to wade through this much content. One potential solution is to develop methods to summarize comment automatically, allowing readers to gain an overview of the conversation.

In recent years researchers have begun to address the problem of summarising reader comment. Broadly speaking, two main approaches to the problem have been pursued. In the first approach, which might be described as *technology-driven*, researchers have proposed methods to automatically generate summaries of reader comment based on combining existing technologies (Khabiri et al., 2011; Ma et al., 2012; Llewellyn et al., 2014). These authors adopt broadly similar approaches: first reader comments are topically clustered, then comments within clusters are ranked and finally one or more top-ranked comments are selected from each cluster, yielding an extractive summary. A significant weakness of such summaries is that they fail to capture the essential argument-oriented nature of these multi-way conversations, since single comments taken from topically distinct clusters do not reflect the argumentative structure of the conversation.

In the second approach, which might be characterised as *argument-theory-driven*, researchers working on argument mining from social media have articulated various schemes defining argument elements and relations in argumentative discourse and in some cases begun work on computational methods to identify them in text (Ghosh et al., 2014; Habernal et al., 2014; Swanson et al., 2015; Misra et al., 2015). If such elements and relations can be automatically extracted then they could serve as the basis for generating a summary that better reflects the argumentative content of reader comment. Indeed, several of these authors have cited summarization as a motivating application for their work. To the best of our knowledge, however, none have proposed how, given an analysis in terms of their theory, one might produce a summary of a full reader comment set.

Proceedings of the SIGDIAL 2016 Conference, pages 42–52,
Los Angeles, USA, 13-15 September 2016. ©2016 Association for Computational Linguistics

Id	Poster	Reply	Comment
1	A		I can't see how it won't attract rats and other vermin. I know some difficult decisions have to be made with cuts to funding, but this seems like a very poorly thought out idea.
2	B	2 → 1	Plenty of people use compost bins and have no trouble with rats or foxes.
3	C	3 → 2	If they are well-designed and well-managed- which is very easily accomplished. If 75% of this borough composted their waste at home then they could have their bins collected every six-weeks. It's amazing what doesn't need to be put into landfill.
4	D	4 → 1	It won't attract vermin if the rubbish is all in the bins. Is Bury going to provide larger bins for families or provide bins for kitchen and garden waste to cut down the amount that goes to landfill? Many people won't fill the bins in 3 weeks - even when there was 5 of us here, we would have just about managed.
5	E	5 → 1	Expect Bury to be knee deep in rubbish by Christmas it's a lame brained Labour idea and before long it'll be once a month collections. I'm not sure what the rubbish collectors will be doing if there are any. We are moving back to the Middle Ages, expect plague and pestilence.
6	F		Are they completely crazy? What do they want a new Plague?
7	G	7 → 6	Interesting how you suggest that someone else is completely crazy, and then talk about a new plague.
8	H	8 → 7	Do you think this is a good idea? We struggle with fortnightly collection. This is tantamount to a dereliction of duty. What are taxpayers paying for? I doubt anyone knew of this before casting their vote.
9	I	9 → 8	I think it is an excellent idea. We have fortnightly collection, and the bin is usually half full or less[family of 5].. Since 38 of the 51 council seats are held by Labour, it seems that people did vote for this. Does any party offer weekly collections?
10	G	10 → 8	I don't think it's a good idea. But..it won't cause a plague epidemic.

Figure 1: Comments responding to a news article announcing reduced bin collection in Bury. Full article and comments at: `http://gu.com/p/4v2pb/sbl`.

In our view, what has been lacking so far is a discussion of and proposed answer to the fundamental question of what a summary of reader comments should be like and human-generated exemplars of such summaries for real sets of reader comments. A better idea of the target for summarisation and a resource exemplifying it would put the community in a better position to choose methods for summarisation of reader comment and to develop and evaluate their systems.

In this paper we make three principal contributions. First, after a brief discussion of the nature of reader comment we make a proposal about one type of informative reader comment summary that we believe would have wide utility. Second, we present a three stage method for manually creating reference summaries of the sort we propose. This method is significant since the absence to date of human-authored reader comment summaries is no doubt due to the very serious challenge of producing them, something our method alleviates to no small degree. Third, we report the construction and analysis of a corpus of human-authored reference summaries, built using our method – the first publicly available corpus of human-authored reader comment summaries.

2 Summaries of Reader Comments

What should a summary of reader comment contain? As Spärck-Jones (2007) has observed, what a summary should contain is primarily dependent on the nature of the content to be summarised and the use to which the summary is to be put. In this section we first make a number of observations about the character of reader comments and offer a specification for a general informative summary.

2.1 The Character of Reader Comments

Figure 1 shows a fragment of a typical comment stream, taken from reader comment responses to a *Guardian* article announcing the decision by Bury town council to reduce bin collection to once every three weeks. While not illustrating all aspects of reader comment interchanges, it serves as a good example of many of their core features.

Comment sets are typically organised into *threads*. Every comment is in exactly one thread and either initiates a new thread or replies to exactly one comment earlier in a thread. This gives the conversations the formal character of a set of trees, with each thread-initial comment being the root node of a separate tree and all other comments being either intermediate or leaf nodes, whose parent is the comment to which they reply. While threads may be topically cohesive, in practice they rarely are, with the same topic appearing in multiple threads and threads drifting from one topic onto another (see, e.g. comments 5 and 6 in Figure 1 both of which cite plague as a likely outcome of the new policy but are in different threads).

Our view, based on an analysis of scores of comment sets, is that reader comments are primarily argumentative in nature, with readers making *assertions* that either (1) express a *viewpoint* (or *stance*) on an *issue* raised in the original article or by an earlier commenter, or (2) provide *evidence* or grounds for believing a viewpoint or assertion already expressed. Issues are questions on which multiple viewpoints are possible; e.g., the issue of whether reducing bin collection to once every three weeks is a good idea, or whether reducing bin collection will lead to an increase in vermin. Issues are very often implicit, i.e not directly expressed in the comments (e.g., the issue of whether reducing bin collection will lead to an increase in vermin is never explicitly mentioned yet this is clearly what comments 1-4 are addressing). A fuller account of this issue-based framework for analysing reader comment is given in Barker and Gaizauskas (2016).

Aside from argumentative content, reader comments exhibit other features as well. For example, commenters may seek clarification about facts (e.g. comment 4 where the commenter asks *Is Bury going to provide larger bins for families …?*). But these clarifications are typically carried out in the broader context of making an argument, i.e. advancing evidence to support a viewpoint. Comments may also express jokes or emotion, though these too are often in the service of advancing some viewpoint (e.g. sarcasm or as in comments 4 and 6 emotive terms like *lamebrained* and *crazy* clearly indicating the commenters' stances, as well as their emotional attitude).

2.2 A Conversation Overview Summary

Given the fundamentally argumentative nature of reader comments as sketched above, one type of summary of wide potential use is a generic informative summary that aims to provide an overview of the argument in the comments. Ideally, such a summary should:

1. **Identify and articulate the main issues in the comments.** Main issues are those receiving proportionally the most comments. They should be prioritized for inclusion in a space-limited summary.

2. **Characterise opinion on the main issues.** To characterise opinion on an issue typically involves: identifying alternative viewpoints; indicating the grounds given to support viewpoints; aggregating – indicating how opinion was distributed across different issues, viewpoints and

grounds, using quantifiers or qualitative expressions e.g. "the majority discussed x"; indicating where there was consensus or agreement among the comment; indicating where there was disagreement among the comment.

We presented this proposed summary type to a range of reader comment users, including comment readers, posters, journalists and news editors and received very positive feedback via a questionnaire[1]. Based on this, we developed a set of guidelines to inform the process of summary authoring. Whilst clear about what the general nature of the target summary should be, the guidelines avoid being too prescriptive, leaving authors some freedom to include what feels intuitively correct to include in the summary for any given conversation.

3 A Method for Human Authoring of Reader Comment Summaries

To help people write overview summaries of reader comments, we have developed a 4-stage method, which is described below[2]. Summary writers are provided with an interface, which guides annotators through the 4-stage process, presenting texts in a form convenient for annotation, and collecting the annotations. The interface has been designed to be easily configurable for different languages, with versions for English, French and Italian already in issue. Key details of the methodology, guidelines and example annotations follow. Screenshots of the interfaces supporting stages 1 and 3 can be found in the Appendix.

Stage 1: Comment Labeling In this stage, annotators are shown an article in the interface, plus its comments (including the online name of the

---

[1] Further details on the summary specification and the end-user survey on it can be found in SENSEI deliverable D1.2 "Report on Use Case Design and User Requirements" at: `http://www.sensei-conversation.eu/deliverables/`.

[2] The method described here is not unlike the general method of thematic coding widely used in qualitative research, where a researcher manually assigns codes (either pre-specified and/or "discovered" as the coding process unfolds) to textual units, then groups the units by code and finally seeks to gain insights from the data so organised (Saldana, 2015). Our method differs in that: (1) our "codes" are propositional paraphrases of viewpoints expressed in comments rather than the broad thematic codes, commonly used in social science research, and (2) we aim to support an annotator in writing a summary that captures the main things people are saying as opposed to a researcher developing a thesis, though both rely on an understanding of the data that the coding and grouping process promotes.

> 1. Comment: *"Smart machines now collect our highway tolls, check us out at stores, take our blood pressure . . . " And yet unemployment remains low.*
>
>   Label: smart machines now carry out many jobs for us (collect tolls; checkout shopping; take blood pressure), but unemployment stays low.
>
> 2. Comment: *Not compared to the 70s, only relative to the 80s/90s.*
>
>   Label: disagrees with 1; unemployment is not low compared to the 70's; is low relative to the 80's/90's

Figure 2: Two comments with labels (source: `www.theguardian.com/commentisfree/2016/apr/07/robots-replacing-jobs-luddites-economics-labor`).

poster, and reply-to information). Annotators are asked to write a 'label' for each comment, which is a short, free text annotation, capturing its essential content. A label should record the main "points, arguments or propositions" expressed in a comment, in effect providing a mini-summary. Two example labels are shown in Figure 2.

We do not insist on a precise notation for labels, but we advise annotators to:

1. record when a comment agrees or disagrees with something/someone
2. note grounds given in support of a position
3. note jokes, strong feeling, emotional content
4. use common keywords/abbreviations to describe similar content in different comments
5. return regularly to review/revise previous labels, when proceeding through the comments
6. make explicit any implicit content that is important to the meaning, e.g. "unemployment" in the second label of the figure (note: this process can yield labels that are longer than the original comment).

The label annotation process helps annotators to gain a good understanding of key content of the comments, whilst the labels themselves facilitate the grouping task of the next stage.

Stage 2: Label Grouping In stage 2, we ask annotators to sort through the Stage 1 labels, and to group together those which are similar or related. Annotators then provide a "Group Label" to describe the common theme of the group in terms of e.g. topic, propositions, contradicting viewpoints, humour, etc. Annotators may also split the labels in a group into "Sub-Groups" and assign a "Sub-Group Label". This exercise helps annotators to

make better sense of the broad content of the comments, before writing a summary.

The annotation interface re-displays the labels created in Stage 1 in an edit window, so the annotator can cut/paste the labels (each with its comment id and poster name) into their groups, add Group Labels, and so on. Here, annotators work mainly with the label text, but can refer to the source comment text (shown in context in the comment stream) if they so wish. When the annotator feels they have sorted and characterised the data sufficiently, they can proceed to stage 3.

Stage 3: Summary Generation Annotators write summaries based on their Label-Grouping analysis. The interface (Figure 5) displays the Grouping annotation from Stage 2, alongside a text box where the summary is written in two phases. Annotators first write an 'unconstrained summary', with no word-length requirement, and then (with the first summary still visible) write a 'constrained-length summary' of 150–250 words.

Further analysis may take place as a person decides on what sentences to include in the summary. For example, an annotator may:

- develop a group label, e.g. producing a polished or complete sentence;
- carry out further abstraction over the groups, e.g. using a new high-level statement to summarise content from two separate groups;
- exemplify, clarify or provide grounds for a summary sentence, using details from labels or comments within a group, etc.

We encourage the use of phrases such as "many/several/few comments said. . .", "opinion was divided on. . .", "the consensus was. . .", etc, to quantify the proportion of comments/posters addressing various topics/issues, and the strength/polarisation of opinion/feeling on different issues.

Stage 4: Back-Linking In this stage, annotators link sentences of the constrained-length summary back to the groups (or sub-groups) that informed their creation. Such links imply that at least some of the labels in a group (or sub-group) played a part supporting the sentence. The interface displays the summary sentences alongside the Label Grouping from Stage 2, allowing the annotator to select a sentence and a group (or sub-group — the more specific correct option is preferred) to assert a link between them, until all links have been added. Note that while back-links are to groups of *labels*, the labels have associated comment ids, so indirectly summary sentences are linked back to the source comments that support them. This last stage goes beyond the summary creation process, but captures information valuable for system development and evaluation.

4 Corpus Creation

4.1 Annotators and training

We recruited 15 annotators to carry out the summary writing task. They included: final year journalism students, graduates with expertise in language and writing, and academics. The majority of annotators were native English speakers; all had excellent skills in written English. We provided a training session taking 1.5-2 hours for all annotators. This included an introduction to our guidelines for writing summaries.

4.2 Source Data

From an initial collection of 3,362 *Guardian* news articles published in June-July 2014 and associated comment sets, we selected a small subset for use in the summary corpus. Articles were drawn from the *Guardian*-designated topic-domains: politics, sport, health, environment, business, Scotland-news and science. Table 1 shows the summary statistics for the 18 selected sets of source texts (articles and comments). The average article length is 772 words. The comment sets ranged in size from 100 to 1,076 comments. For the annotation task, we selected a subset of each full comment set, by first ordering threads into chronological order (i.e. oldest first), and then selecting the first 100 comments. If the thread containing the 100th comment had further comments, we continued including comments until the last comment in that thread. This produced a collection of reduced comment sets totalling 87,559 words in 1,845 comments. Reduced summary comment sets vary in length from 2,384 words to 8,663 words.

5 Results and Analysis

The SENSEI Social Media Corpus, comprising the full text of the original *Guardian* articles and reader comments as well as all annotations generated in the four stage summary writing method described in Section 3 above – comment labels, groups, summaries and backlinks – is freely available at: `nlp.shef.ac.uk/sensei/`.

5.1 Overview of Corpus Annotations

There were 18 articles and comment sets, of which 15 were double annotated and 3 were triple annotated, giving a total of 39 sets of complete annotations. Annotators took 3.5-6 hours to complete the task for an article and comment set.

Table 2 shows a summary of corpus annotations counts. The corpus includes 3,879 *comment labels*, an average of 99.46 per annotation set (av. 99.46/AS). There are, in total, 329 *group annotations* (av. 8.44/AS) and 218 *subgroups* (av. 5.59/AS). Each of the 547 groups/subgroups has a short *group label* to characterise its content. Such labels range from keywords ("midges", "UK climate", "fining directors", "Air conditioning/fans") to full propositions/questions ("Not fair that SE gets the investment", "Why use the fine on wifi?"). Each of the 39 annotation sets has two summaries, of which the *unconstrained summaries* have average length 321.41 words, and the *constrained summaries*, 237.74 (a 26% decrease). Each summary sentence is back-linked to one or more groups comment labels that informed it.

5.2 Observations

Variation in Grouping There is considerable variation between annotators in use of the option to group/sub-group comment labels. Whilst the average of groups per annotation set was 9.0, for the annotator who grouped the least this was 4.0, and the maximum average 14.5. For sub-groups, the average per annotation set was 5.0. 14 of 15 annotators used the sub-group option in at least one annotation set, and only 5 of the 39 sets included no sub-groups. A closer look shows a divide between annotators who use sub-groups quite frequently (7 having an average of $\geq$6.5/AS) and those who do not (with av. $\leq$2/AS).

Other variations in annotator style include the fact that around a third of them did most of their grouping at the sub-group level (4 of the 6 who frequently used subgroups were amongst those having the lowest average number of groups). Also, whilst a fifth of annotators preferred to use mainly a single level of grouping (i.e. had a high average of groups, and a low average of sub-groups, per annotation set), another fifth of annotators liked to create both a high number of groups and of subgroups, i.e. used a more fine-grained analysis.

We also investigated whether the word-length of a comment set influenced the number of

	Total	Min	Max	Mean
Article and Comment Sets(number)	18	-	-	-
Article, word length	13,898	415	2,021	772.11
Full Comment Set, total word length	318,618	4,918	37,543	17,701
Full Comment Set, total comments	6,968	100	1,076	387.11
Reduced Comment Set (number)	18	-	-	-
Reduced Comment Set, total comments	1,845	100	109	102.5
Reduced Comment Set, total word length	87,559	2,384	8,663	4,864.39
Reduced Comment Set, single comment word length	-	1	547	47.46

Table 1: Summary Statistics for Corpus Source Texts

	Total	Min	Max	Mean
Annotated Comment Set (number)	18	-	-	-
Completed Annotation Sets (number)	39	-	-	-
Stage 1 Labels (number)	3,879	69	109	99.46
Length of Unconstrained Summaries (words)	12,535	131	664	321.41
Length of Constrained Summaries (words)	9,272	152	249	237.74
Number of Groups / Group Labels	329	4	17	8.44
Number of Sub-Groups / Sub-Group Labels	218	0	15	5.59
Number of Labels in Groups	4,050	1	84	12.31
Number of Labels in Sub-groups	1,435	1	27	6.58
Note: Total count, min, max and mean are drawn from across the full set of corpus annotations				

Table 2: Annotation Statistics

groups/subgroups created by the annotators, but surprisingly, there was no obvious correlation.

Reader Comment Summaries We carried out a preliminary qualitative analysis to establish the character of the summaries produced, which shows that they are in general all coherent and grammatical, and that the majority of summary sentences characterise views on issues. Some observations on summary content follow:

1. All summaries contain sentences reporting different *views* on issues. Figure 2 shows two typical summaries, which describe a range of views on two main issues: "whether or not citizens can cope with reductions in bin collection" (Summary 1), and "whether or not new taxes on the rich should be introduced to pay for the NHS" (Summary 2).

2. Summaries frequently indicate points of contention or counter arguments, e.g. sentences *(S2)* and *(S5)* of Summary 2.

3. Summaries often provide examples of the reasons people gave in support of a viewpoint: e.g. *(S2)* of Summary 1 explains that people thought a reduced bin collection would attract vermin because the bins will overflow with rubbish.

4. Annotators often indicate the proportion/amount of comment addressing a particular topic/issue or supporting a particular viewpoint, e.g. see *(S6)* of Summary 2; *(S3)* of Summary 1.

5. While the majority of annotators abstracted across groups of comments to describe views on issues, there were a few outliers who did not. For example, for an article about a heatwave in the UK, the two annotators grouped the same 8 comments, but summarised the content very differently. Annotator 1 generalised over the comments: "A small group of comments discussed how the heat brings about the nuisance of midges and how to deal with them". Annotator 2 listed the points made in successive comments: "One person said how midges were a problem in this weather, another said they should shut the windows or get a screen. One person told an anecdote about the use of a citronella candle . . . another said they were surprised the candle worked as they had been severely bitten after using citronella oil".

6. Very few summary sentences describe a discussion topic without indicating views on it (e.g. "Many comments discuss the disposal of fat").

Analysis revealed that summaries also include examples of: *Background* about, e.g., an event,

Summary 1	Summary 2
(S1) Opinions throughout the comments were divided regarding whether residents could cope with Bury's decision to collect grey household bins every three weeks rather than every two, and the impact this could have on households and the environment. *(S2)* Some argued how the reduction in bin collection would attract vermin as bins overflow with rubbish, while others gave suggestions of how waste could be reduced. *(S3)* The largest group of commenters reflected on how successful (or not) their specific bin collection scheme was at reducing waste and increasing recycling. *(S4)* Throughout the comments there appeared to be some confusion on what waste could be recycled in the grey household bin in Bury. *(S5)* It also appeared unclear if Bury currently provides a food waste bin and if not one commenter suggested that the borough should provide one in the effort to reduce grey bin waste. *(S6)* A large number of comments suggested how residents could reduce the amount of waste going into the grey household bin by improving their recycling behaviour. *(S7)* This led to a deeper discussion regarding the pros and cons of reusable and disposable nappies...	*(S1)* The majority of people agreed that businesses and the rich should pay more tax to fund the NHS, rather than those on low incomes. *(S2)* Some said income tax should be raised for the highest earners and others suggested a 'mansion tax'. *(S3)* Some commenters suggested that the top one percent of earners should pay up to 95 in income tax. *(S4)* Although, there was a debate as to how 'rich' can be defined fairly. *(S5)* Other commenters pointed out that raising taxes would damage the economy and drive the most talented minds and business to different countries with lower taxes. *(S6)* A large proportion of commenters said the government should do more to tackle tax evasion and avoidance by big businesses and the rich. *(S7)* But some said the extent of tax evasion was exaggerated by the press. *(S8)* A strong number of people criticised the coalition for cutting taxes for the rich and placing the burden on lower-paid workers. *(S9)* They said that income tax has been cut for the very rich, while benefits have been slashed and VAT has increased, making life for low-paid workers more difficult. *(S10)* Many criticised the Liberal Democrats for going into a coalition with the Conservatives and failing to keep promises. *(S11)* Many said they had failed to curb Tory excesses and had abandoned their core principles and pledges. *(S12)* A small minority said that the NHS is too expensive and needs reform.

Figure 3: Two human authored summaries of comment sets. These summaries and the source articles and comments are in the SENSEI Corpus available at: `nlp.shef.ac.uk/sensei`.

practice or person, to clarify an aspect of the debate, e.g. see *(S5)* of Summary 1, *Humour*; *Feelings* and *Complaints*, about e.g. commenters and reporters.

5.3 Similarity of Summary Content

We investigated the extent to which summaries of the same set of comments by different annotators have the same summary content, by performing a content comparison assessment on 10 randomly selected summary pairs, using a method similar to the manual evaluation method of DUC 2001 (Lin and Hovy, 2002).

Given summaries A and B, for each sentence s in A, a subject judges the extent to which the meaning of s is evidenced (anywhere) in B, assigning a score on a 5-point scale (5=all meaning evidenced; 1=none is). Any score above 1 requires evidence of *common propositional content* (i.e., a common entity reference alone would not suffice). After A is compared to B, B is compared to A.

Comparison of the 10 random summary pairs required 300 sentence judgements, which were each done twice by two judges and averaged. In these results, 17% of summary sentences received a score of 5 (indicating all meaning evidenced) and 40% a score between 3 and 4.5 (suggesting some or most of their meaning was evidenced). Only 15% of sentences received a score of 1.

Looking at the content overlap per individual summary pair (by averaging the sentence overlap scores for that pair), we find values for the 10 pairs that range from 2.56 up to 3.65 (with overall average 3.06). Scores may be affected by the length of comment sets (as longer sets give more scope for variation and complexity), and we observe that the two lowest scores are for long comment sets.

We assessed the agreement between judges on this task, by comparing their scores for each sentence. Scores differ by 0 in 46% of cases, and by 1 in 33%, giving a combined 79% with 'near agreement'. Scores differ by >2 in only 6% of cases. These results suggest that average sentence similarity is a reliable measure of summary overlap.

6 Related Work

Creating abstractive reference summaries of extended dialogues is hard. A more common approach involves humans assessing source units (e.g., comments in comment streams, turns in email exchanges) based on their perceived importance (aka "salience") for inclusion in an end summary. See, e.g., Khabiri et al.'s (2011) work on comments on YouTube videos; Murray and Carenini's (2008) work on summarizing email discussions. The result is a "gold standard" set of units, each with a value based on multiple human annotations. A system generated extractive summary is then scored against this gold standard. The underlying assumption is that a good summary of length n is one that has a high score when compared against the top-ranked n gold standard units.

Such an approach is straightforward and provides useful feedback for extractive summarization systems. While the gold standard is extractive, the selected content may have an abstractive flavour if annotators are instructed to favour "meta-level" source units that contain overview content. But the comment domain has few obvious examples of meta-level sentences; explicit references to the issues under discussion are few, as are reflective comments that sum up a preceding series of comments. Moreover, extractive approaches to writing comment summaries will almost certainly fall short of indicating aggregation over views and opinion. In sum, this is not an ideal approach to creating reference summaries from comment.

A more abstractive approach to writing summaries of multi-party conversations was used in the creation of the AMI corpus annotations, based on 100 hours of recorded meetings dialogues (Carletta et al., 2006). There are some similarities and differences between the AMI approach and our own. First, AMI summary writers first completed a topic segmentation task to prepare them for the task of writing a summary. While segmentation might appear to resemble our *grouping* stage, these are very different tasks. Key differences are that segmentation was carried on AMI dialogues using a pre-specified list of topic descriptions. This would be difficult to provide for comment summary writers, since we cannot predict everything the comments will talk about. Secondly, the AMI abstractive summaries are linked to dialogue acts (DAs) in their manual extractive summaries (a link is made if a DA is judged to "support" a sentence in the abstractive summary). Similar to our back-links, their links provide indices from the abstractive summary to source text units. However, our back-links are from a summary sentence to *groups* of comment labels that the summary author has judged to have informed his sentence. Finally, the AMI abstractive summaries comprise an overview summary of the meeting, and list "decisions", "problems/issues" and "actions". However, while a very small number of non-scenario corpus summaries included reports of alternative views in a meeting (e.g. on which film to choose for a film club), the AMI scenario summaries include very few examples of differences in opinion.

Misra et al. (2015) have created manual summaries of short dialogue sequences, extracted from different conversations on similar issues on debating websites. They then collected summaries together, and applied the Pyramid method (Nenkova et al., 2007) to identify common, central propositions, which, they describe as "abstract objects" that represent facets of an argument on an issue, e.g. gay marriage. Indeed the task of identifying central propositions across multiple conversations is a key aim in their work and one they point out is central to others working in argumentation mining. They use the Pyramid annotations to provide indices from the central proposition to the summary and underlying comment, with a view to learning how to recognize similar argument facets automatically. Note their task differs from ours in that we aim to generate a summary of a single reader comment conversation, while they aim to identify (and then possibly summarize) all facets of a single argument, gleaned from multiple distinct conversations.

Barker and Gaizauskas (2016) elaborate the issue-viewpoint-evidence framework introduced in Section 2.1 above and show how an argument graph representing an analysis in this framework may be created for a set of comments. They show how the content in a single reference summary, created using the informal label and group method described above, corresponds closely to a subgraph in the more formally specified argument graph for the article and comment set.

7   Concluding Remarks and Future Work

We have presented a proposal for a form of informative summary that aims to capture the key content of multi-party, argument-oriented conversations, such as those found in reader comment. We have developed a method to help humans author such summaries, and used it to build a corpus of reader comment multiply annotated with summaries and other information. We believe the method of labeling and grouping has wide application, i.e. in creating reference summaries of complex, multi-party dialogues in other domains.

The summaries produced correspond closely to the target specification given in Sec. 2.2, and exhibit a high degree of consistency, as shown by the content similarity assessment of Sec. 5.3. Informal feedback from media professionals (at the *Guardian* and elsewhere) suggests that the summaries are viewed very positively as a summary of comments in themselves, and as a target for what an automated system might deliver online.

Our summary corpus has already proved useful in providing insights for system development, and for training and evaluation. We have used group annotations to evaluate a clustering algorithm (Aker et al., 2016a); used back-links to inform the training of a cluster labeling algorithm (Aker et al., 2016b); used the summaries as references in evaluating system outputs (with ROUGE as metric), and to inform human assessors in a task-based system evaluation (Barker et al., 2016).

Even so, there are limitations to the work done which give pointers to further work. The current corpus is limited in size, and would ideally contain annotations for more comment sets, with more annotations per set. One possibility is to break the summary creation method into smaller tasks suitable for crowd-sourcing. Another issue is scalability: annotators can write summaries for $\sim$100 comments, but this is time-consuming and taxing, casting doubt on whether the method could scale to 1000 comments. Results from a pilot suggest annotators find it much easier to work on sets of 30–50 comments, so we are investigating how annotations for smaller subsets of a comment set might be merged into a single annotation.

Many of our annotators found the option to have groups *and* sub-groups useful, but this feature presents problems for some practical uses of the annotations, such as evaluation of some clustering methods. Hence, we have investigated methods to flatten the group-subgroup structure into one level, including the following two methods: (1) simple flattening, where all sub-groups merge into their parent groups (but this loses much of the analysis of some annotators), and (2) promoting subgroups to full group status (which has proved useful for generating useful group labels). More research is needed to establish the most effective flattening to best capture the consensus between annotators.

Finally, there is the open question of how to automatically evaluate system-generated summaries against the reference summaries proposed here. In particular, is ROUGE (Lin, 2004), the most widely used metric for automatic summary evaluation, an appropriate metric for use in this context? ROUGE, which calculates n-gram overlap between system and reference summaries, may not deal well with the abstractive nature of our summaries, and in particular with statements quantifying the distribution of support for various viewpoints. Its utility needs to be established by correlating it with human judgements on system output quality. If it cannot be validated, the challenge arises to develop a metric better suited to this evaluation need.

Acknowledgments

The authors would like to thank the European Commission for supporting this work, carried out as part of the FP7 SENSEI project, grant reference: FP7-ICT-610916. We would also like to thank all the annotators without whose work the SENSEI corpus would not have been created, Jonathan Foster for his help in recruiting annotators and *The Guardian* for allowing us access to their materials. Finally, thanks to our anonymous reviewers whose comments and suggestions have helped us to improve the paper.

References

Ahmet Aker, Emina Kurtic, AR Balamurali, Monica Paramita, Emma Barker, Mark Hepple, and Rob Gaizauskas. 2016a. A graph-based approach to topic clustering for online comments to news. In *Advances in Information Retrieval*, pages 15–29. Springer.

Ahmet Aker, Monica Paramita, Emina Kurtic, Adam Funk, Emma Barker, Mark Hepple, and Rob Gaizauskas. 2016b. Automatic label generation for news comment clusters. In *Proceedings of the 9th International Conference on Natural Language Generation Conference (INLG)*, Edinburgh, UK.

Emma Barker and Robert Gaizauskas. 2016. Summarizing multi-party argumentative conversations in reader comment on news. In *Proceedings of the 3rd Workshop on Argument Mining*, Berlin.

Emma Barker, Monica Paramita, Adam Funk, Emina Kurtic, Ahmet Aker, Jonathan Foster, Mark Hepple, and Robert Gaizauskas. 2016. What's the issue here?: Task-based evaluation of reader comment summarization systems. In *Proceedings of LREC 2016*.

Jean Carletta, Simone Ashby, Sebastien Bourban, Mike Flynn, Mael Guillemot, Thomas Hain, Jaroslav Kadlec, Vasilis Karaiskos, Wessel Kraaij, Melissa Kronenthal, Guillaume Lathoud, Mike Lincoln, Agnes Lisowska, Iain McCowan, Wilfried Post, Dennis Reidsma, and Pierre Wellner. 2006. The AMI meeting corpus: A pre-announcement. In *Proceedings of the Second International Conference on Machine Learning for Multimodal Interaction*, MLMI'05, pages 28–39, Berlin, Heidelberg. Springer-Verlag.

Debanjan Ghosh, Smaranda Muresan, Nina Wacholder, Mark Aakhus, and Matthew Mitsui. 2014. Analyzing argumentative discourse units in online interactions. In *Proc. of the First Workshop on Argumentation Mining*, pages 39–48.

Ivan Habernal, Judith Eckle-Kohler, and Iryna Gurevych. 2014. Argumentation mining on the web from information seeking perspective. In *Proc. of the Workshop on Frontiers and Connections between Argumentation Theory and Natural Language Processing*, pages 26–39.

Elham Khabiri, James Caverlee, and Chiao-Fang Hsu. 2011. Summarizing user-contributed comments. In *Proceedings of The Fifth International AAAI Conference on Weblogs and Social Media (ICWSM-11)*, pages 534–537, Barcelona.

Chin-Yew Lin and Eduard Hovy. 2002. Manual and automatic evaluation of summaries. In *Proceedings of the ACL-02 Workshop on Automatic Summarization - Volume 4*, AS '02, pages 45–51, Stroudsburg, PA, USA. Association for Computational Linguistics.

Chin-Yew Lin. 2004. Rouge: a package for automatic evaluation of summaries. In *Proceedings of the ACL 2004 Workshop on Text Summarization Branches Out*, jul.

Clare Llewellyn, Claire Grover, and Jon Oberlander. 2014. Summarizing newspaper comments. In *Proceedings of the Eighth International Conference on Weblogs and Social Media, ICWSM 2014, Ann Arbor, Michigan, USA, June 1-4, 2014*.

Zongyang Ma, Aixin Sun, Quan Yuan, and Gao Cong. 2012. Topic-driven reader comments summarization. In *Proceedings of the 21st ACM international conference on Information and knowledge management*, CIKM '12, pages 265–274, New York, NY, USA. ACM.

Amita Misra, Pranav Anand, Jean E. Fox Tree, and Marilyn Walker. 2015. Using summarization to discover argument facets in online idealogical dialog. In *Proceedings of the 2015 Conference of the North American Chapter of the Association for Computational Linguistics: Human Language Technologies*, pages 430–440, Denver, Colorado, May–June. Association for Computational Linguistics.

Gabriel Murray and Giuseppe Carenini. 2008. Summarizing spoken and written conversations. In *Proceedings of the Conference on Empirical Methods in Natural Language Processing*, EMNLP '08, pages 773–782, Stroudsburg, PA, USA. Association for Computational Linguistics.

Ani Nenkova, Rebecca Passonneau, and Kathleen McKeown. 2007. The Pyramid method: Incorporating human content selection variation in summarization evaluation. *ACM Trans. Speech Lang. Process.*, 4, May.

Johnny Saldana. 2015. *The Coding Manual for Qualitative Researchers*. Sage Publications Ltd, 3 edition.

Karen Spärck Jones. 2007. Automatic summarising: The state of the art. *Information Processing & Management*, 43(6):1449–1481.

Reid Swanson, Brian Ecker, and Marilyn Walker. 2015. Argument mining: Extracting arguments from online dialogue. In *Proc. of the SIGDIAL 2015 Conference*, pages 217–226. Association for Computational Linguistics.

Comment Number	User Name	Comment Communication	Comment	Comment Label
1	lindalusardi	1	what about having a word with them about ticket prices aswell?	NR - ticket prices (implies too high)
2	Cynic24	2 --> 1	That would be fairly pointless, given that Network Rail don't operate passenger trains!	NR do not set fares / operate trains
3	Cynic24	3 --> 1	The fact that the first post is getting recommends shows that there are some clueless people out there! If you are going to criticise the railways (I do so fairly often), then at least read up on how they actually work! Criticising from from a position of complete ignorance won't gain you any credibility! Passenger trains are not operated by Network Rail (their remit is solely to maintain the railway infrastructure), therefore the ticket prices are nothing to do with them!	NR do not set fares / operate trains
4	lindalusardi	4 --> 2	silly me, of course I forgot that network rail provide their services to rail operators completely free and have nothing whatsoever to do with increasing ticket prices d'oh	NR do not set fares - accepted
5	martin77	5 --> 3	OK so the lady made a mistake , calm down for Heavens sake.	non-topic; calm down
6	Craig Axon	6 --> 2	Average ticket prices are set by the government. The train company then as a leeway to increase or decrease the price from the average set. Ticket prices are determined not by distance, as such, but by the number of people travelling from one particular point to another and so forth. There's more to it but that's the gist of it. Also, most the money made by fares is invested back into the railway infrastructure, so it's a cycle. Only a small amount per £ spent on a ticket goes to train company profits. Most goes to network rail, fuel, train maintenance, staff costs and so forth. It must also be noted that network rail is a not for profit company and many profits either get invested back into the railway or given to the government to find major projects like thameslink and crossrail. The railway is not very transparent which is the problem why most people vent their rage on train companies and network rail.	Ticket prices set by government; NR not-for-profit; system not transparent

Figure 4: Stage 1 interface. The first 4 columns are created automatically from the source reader comments. The last column is a label supplied by the annotator.

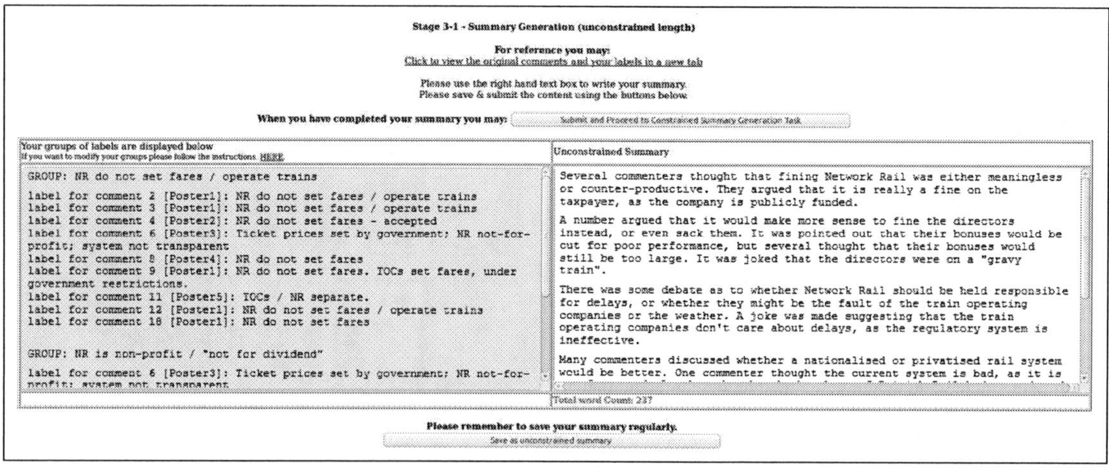

Figure 5: Stage 3 interface. Grouping annotations collected in Stage 2 are shown in the left frame. The summary is authored in the right frame.

Special Session

The Future Directions of Dialogue-Based Intelligent Personal Assistants

Abstract : Today is the era of intelligent personal assistants. All the major tech giants have introduced personal assistants as the front end of their services, including Apple's Siri, Microsoft's Cortana, Facebook's M, and Amazon's Alexa. Several of these companies have also released bot toolkits so that other smaller companies can join the fray. However, while the quality of conversational interactions with intelligent personal assistants is crucial for their success in both business and personal applications, fundamental problems, such as discourse processing, computational pragmatics, user modeling, and collecting and annotating adequate real data, remain unsolved. Furthermore, the intelligent personal assistants of tomorrow raise a whole set of new technical problems.

The special SIGDIAL session "The Future of Dialogue-Based Intelligent Personal Assistants" holds a panel discussion with notable academic and industry players, leading to insights on future directions.

Time Table
- **Introduction (15 minutes)**
  - Overview of the session
  - Introduction of the panels
- **Panel Discussion (75 minutes)**
  - Short position talks
  - Discussion
  - QA and summary

Organizers
- **Yoichi Matsuyama**, Postdoctoral Fellow, Human-Computer Interaction Institute / Language Technologies Institute, Carnegie Mellon University
- **Alexandros Papangelis**, Research Scientist, Toshiba Cambridge Research Laboratory

Advisory Board
- **Justine Cassell**, Associate Dean of the School of Computer Science for Technology Strategy and Impact, Carnegie Mellon University

Panelists
- **Steve Young,** Professor of Information Engineering, Information Engineering Division, University of Cambridge
- **Jeffrey P. Bigham**, Associate Professor, Human-Computer Interaction Institute / Language Technologies Institute, Carnegie Mellon University
- **Thomas Schaaf**, Senior Speech Scientist, Amazon
- **Zhuoran Wang**, CEO, trio.ai

http://articulab.hcii.cs.cmu.edu/sigdial2016/

Los Angeles, USA, 13-15 September 2016. ©2016 Association for Computational Linguistics

Keynote
More than meets the ear: Processes that shape dialogue

Susan E. Brennan
Stony Brook University
Departments of Psychology, Computer Science, and Linguistics
Stony Brook, NY, United States
susan.brennan@stonybrook.edu

Abstract: What is dialogue, anyway—language produced in alternating turns by two or more speakers? A way to collaboratively accomplish a task or transaction with an agent, whether human or computer? An interactive process by which two people entrain and coordinate their behaviors and mental states? A corpus that can be analyzed to answer a research question? The ways in which researchers conceptualize dialogue affect the assumptions and decisions they make about how to design an experiment, collect or code a corpus, or build a system. Often such assumptions are not explicit. Researchers may decide to characterize, stage, control, or entirely ignore such potentially key factors as the task two people are charged with, their identities, their common ground, or the medium in which dialogue is conducted.

Such decisions, especially when left implicit, can affect the products and processes of dialogue in substantial but unanticipated ways; in fact, they can change the results of an experiment. As one example, spoken dialogue experiments often use a simulated partner or confederate in the role of speaker or addressee; just how the confederate is deployed reflects the researcher's explicit theory and implicit assumptions about the nature of dialogue. As another example, sometimes experiments place people in infelicitous situations; this can change the kind of language game people think they're playing. I will cover some implicit assumptions about the nature of dialogue that affect the risks researchers take, and highlight pairs of studies that have found different results, perhaps due to these assumptions.

Speaker's Bio: Susan Brennan is Professor of Psychology in the Cognitive Science Program at Stony Brook University (State University of New York), with joint appointments in the Departments of Linguistics and Computer Science. She received her Ph.D. in Cognitive Psychology from Stanford University with a focus on psycholinguistics; her M.S. is from the MIT Media Lab, where she worked on computer-generated caricature and teleconferencing interfaces; and her B.A. is in cultural anthropology from Cornell University. She has worked in industry at Atari Research, Hewlett-Packard Labs, and Apple Computer. Her research interests span language processing in conversation, joint attention, partner-specific adaptation during interactive dialogue, the production and comprehension of referring expressions, lexical entrainment, discourse functions of prosody and intonation, speech disfluencies, multimodal communication, social/ cognitive neuroscience, natural language and speech interfaces to computers, spoken dialogue systems, and repair in human and human-computer dialogue. She has used eye-tracking both as a method for studying the incremental comprehension and production of spontaneous speech and as a channel in computer-mediated communication. A currently funded project is "Communication in the Global University: A Longitudinal Study of Language Adaptation at Multiple Timescales in Native- and Non-Native Speakers." She is temporarily on leave from Stony Brook University in order to serve as Program Director for NSF's oldest program, the Graduate Research Fellowship Program in the Division of Graduate Education.

Proceedings of the SIGDIAL 2016 Conference, page 54,
Los Angeles, USA, 13-15 September 2016. ©2016 Association for Computational Linguistics

A Wizard-of-Oz Study on A Non-Task-Oriented Dialog Systems That Reacts to User Engagement

Zhou Yu, Leah Nicolich-Henkin, Alan W Black and Alex I. Rudnicky
School of Computer Science
Carnegie Mellon University
{zhouyu, leah.nh, awb, air}@cs.cmu.edu

Abstract

In this paper, we describe a system that reacts to both possible system breakdowns and low user engagement with a set of conversational strategies. These general strategies reduce the number of inappropriate responses and produce better user engagement. We also found that a system that reacts to both possible system breakdowns and low user engagement is rated by both experts and non-experts as having better overall user engagement compared to a system that only reacts to possible system breakdowns. We argue that for non-task-oriented systems we should optimize on both system response appropriateness and user engagement. We also found that apart from making the system response appropriate, funny and provocative responses can also lead to better user engagement. On the other hand, short appropriate responses, such as "Yes" or "No" can lead to decreased user engagement. We will use these findings to further improve our system.

1 Introduction

Non-task-oriented conversational systems do not have a stated goal to work towards. Nevertheless, they are useful for many purposes, such as keeping elderly people company and helping second language learners improve conversation and communication skills. More importantly, they can be combined with task-oriented systems to act as a transition smoother or a rapport builder for complex tasks that require user cooperation. They have potential wide use in education, medical and service domains.

There are a variety of existing methods to generate responses for non-task-oriented systems, such as machine translation (Ritter et al., 2011), retrieval-based response selection (Banchs and Li, 2012), and sequence-to-sequence recurrent neural network (Vinyals and Le, 2015). All aim to improve system coherence, but none of them focus on the experience of the user. Conversation is an interaction that involves two parties, so only improving the system side of the conversation is insufficient. In an extreme case, if the system is always appropriate, but is a boring and passive conversational partner, users would not stay interested in the conversation or come back a second time. Thus we argue that user engagement should be considered a critical part of a functional system. Previous researchers found that users who completed a task with a system but disliked the experience would not come back to use the system a second time. In a non-task-oriented system, the user experience is even more crucial, because the ultimate goal is to keep users in the interaction as long as possible, or have them come back as frequently as possible. Previously systems have not tried to improve user experience, mostly because these systems are text-based, and do not have access to the user's behaviors aside from typed text. In this paper, we define user engagement as the interest to continue the conversation in each turn. We study the construct using a multimodal dialog system that is able to process and produce audio-visual behaviors. Making the system aware of user engagement is considered crucial in creating user stickiness in interaction designs. Better user engagement leads to a better experience, and in turn attracts repeat users. We argue that a good system should not only be coherent and appropriate but should also be engaging.

We describe a multimodal non-task-oriented conversational system that optimizes its performance on both system coherence and user engagement. The system reacts to both user engagement and system generation confidence in real time us-

55

Proceedings of the SIGDIAL 2016 Conference, pages 55–63,
Los Angeles, USA, 13-15 September 2016. ©2016 Association for Computational Linguistics

ing a set of active conversational strategies. System generation confidence is defined as the confidence that the generated response is considered appropriate with respect to the previous user utterance. Although the user engagement metric is produced by an expert in a Wizard-of-Oz setting, it is the first step towards a fully automated engagement reactive system. Previously very little research addressed reactive systems due to the difficulty of modeling the users and the lack of audiovisual data. We also make the audiovisual data along with the annotations available.

2   Related Work

Many experiments have shown that an agent reacting to a user's behavior or internal state leads to better user experience. In an in-car navigation setting, a system that reacts to the user's cognitive load was shown to have better user experience (Kousidis et al., 2014). In a direction giving setting, a system that reacts to user's attention was shown to be preferred (Yu et al., 2015a). In a tutoring setting, a system that reacts to the user's disengagement resulted in better learning gain (Forbes-Riley and Litman, 2012). In task-oriented systems users have a concrete reason to interact with the system. However, in a non-task-oriented setting, user engagement is the sole reason for the user to stay in the conversation, making it an ideal situation for engagement study. In this paper, we focus on making the system reactive to user engagement in real time in an everyday chatting setting.

In human-human conversations, engagement has been studied extensively. Engagement is considered important in designing interactive systems. Some believe engagement is correlated with immersiveness (Lombard and Ditton, 1997). For example, how immersed a user is in the interaction plays a key role in measuring the interaction quality. Some believe engagement is related to the level of psychological presence (i.e. focus) during a certain task (Abadi et al., 2013), for example how long the user is focused on the robot (Moshkina et al., 2014). Some define engagement as "the value a participant in an interaction attributes to the goal of being together with the other participant(s) and of continuing the interaction" (Peters et al., 2005). In this paper, we define engagement as the interest to continue the conversation. Because the goal of a non-task-oriented system is to keep the user interacting with the system voluntar-

ily, making users have the interest to continue is critical.

A lot of conversational strategies have been proposed in previous work to avoid generating incoherent utterances in non-task-oriented conversations, such as introducing topics, (e.g. "Let's talk about favorite foods!" in (Higashinaka et al., 2014)) and asking the user to explain missing words. (Schmidt et al., 2015). In this paper, we propose a set of strategies that actively deal with both user engagement and system response appropriateness.

3   System Design and User Experiment Setting

The base system used is Multimodal TickTock, which generates system responses by retrieving the most similar utterance in a conversation database using a key word matching method (Yu et al., 2015b). It takes spoken utterances from the user as input and produces synthesized speech as output. A cartoon face signals whether it is speaking or not, and can present some basic expressions. This clearly artificial design aims to avoid the uncanny valley dilemma, so that the users do not expect realistic human-like behaviors from the system. It has the capability to collect and extract audio-visual features, such as head and face movement (Baltrusaitis et al., 2012), in real time. These features are not used in this experiment, but will be incorporated as part of automatic engagement recognition in the future.

We designed six strategies based on previous literature to deal with possible system breakdowns and to improve user engagement.

1. **Switch Topics** (switch): propose a new topic other than the current topic, such as "Let's talk about sports."

2. **Initiate activities** (initiation): propose an activity to do together, such as "Do you want to see the latest Star Wars movie together?".

3. **End topics with an open question** (end): close the current topic using an open question, such as "Could you tell me something interesting?".

4. **Tell A Joke** (joke): tell a joke such as: "Politicians and diapers have one thing in common. They should both be changed regularly, and for the same reason.".

5. **Refer Back to A Previously Engaged Topic** (refer back): refer back to the previous engaging topic. We keep a list of utterances that have resulted in high user engagement. This strategy will refer the user back to the most recently engaged turn. For example: "Previously, you said 'I like music', do you want to talk more about that?"

Each strategy has a set of surface forms to choose from in order to avoid repetition. For example, the *switch* strategy has several forms, such as, "How about we talk about sports?" and "Let's talk about sports."

We designed two versions of Multimodal Tick-Tock: REL and REL+ENG. The REL system uses the strategies above to deal with low system generation confidence (system breakdown). The generation confidence is the weighted score of matching key words between the user input and the chosen utterance from the database. The REL+ENG system uses the strategies to deal with low system generation confidence, and in addition reacts to low user engagement. One caveat is that the *refer back* strategy is not available for the REL system. In the REL+ENG system, a trained expert annotates the user's engagement as soon as the user finishes the utterance. A randomly selected strategy triggers whenever the user engagement is 'Strongly Disengaged' or 'Disengaged'. Any non-task-oriented system can adopt the above policy and strategies with minor system adjustments.

For systems that use other response generation methods, the confidence score can be computed using other metrics. For example, a neural network generation system (Vinyals and Le, 2015) can use the posterior probability for the confidence score.

In order to avoid culture and language proficiency confound, all participants in the study are originally from North America. Gender was balanced as well. We had 10 people (6 males) interact with REL and 12 people (7 males) interact with REL+ENG. Participants were all university students and none of them had interacted with a multimodal dialog system before. There are no repeat users in the two groups. We also collected how frequently they use spoken dialog systems, such as Apple Siri, in the after-experiment user survey in the REL+ENG study, and found that 25% of them have used dialog systems frequently. In the future, we hope to collect a more balanced dataset to test this factor's influence.

An example dialog of a user interacting with REL is shown in Table 1. In Turn 5, the system used the *switch* strategy to deal with the fact that it was unable to retrieve a response with similar content to the user's utterance. An example dialog from REL+ENG is shown in Table 2. In Turn 3, the system used the *initiation* strategy to deal with the fact that the user was not engaged in the previous turn. Figure 1 is a snapshot of an example video recording of one of the interactions. The blue box represents the head-tracking results, and the red dots represent face-tracking. Together with the audio-visual recordings, we have also made all the annotations and manual transcriptions available [1].

Figure 1: Screen shot of an example conversation recording

4   Annotations

We annotated each conversational exchange with user engagement and system response appropriateness. One conversational exchange includes one speech segment from the system and the following speech segment from the user. The engagement is a rating based on the user's performance during the entire turn, while the system's appropriateness is a rating with respect to the user's utterance in the previous turn. User engagement is defined as "user's interest to continue the conversation", and the system appropriateness as "the coherence and appropriateness of the system utterance given the context". Table 3 and 4 describe the user engagement annotation scheme and the system appropriateness annotation scheme respectively. For turns when users failed to respond, we label the engagement as 0. We labeled the turns that the system failed to understand the user and asked the user to repeat to be 0 in appropriateness. We exclude all these turns in the analysis

---

[1] www.cmuticktock.org

Turn	Participant	TickTock
1	Your noise is a question mark, I think that's interesting.	Of course, what's your idea?
2	I think it fits you perfectly.	Let me see, his nose is still broke.
3	Do you want me to make your nose broken?	Ah, yes, why did you ask me for this?
4	Because I thought you might mind.	Well, I am not getting into specifics about what doctor treated him, how he was treated.
5	You have not been treated yet. That is in the future.	Let me see, by the way, are you interested in movies?
6	Yes, I watch movies sometimes.	Great.

Table 1: An example conversation in REL

Turn	Participant	TickTock
1	How are you	I think so, any thoughts?
2	How are you doing?	I am fine, how are you, any thought?
3	Any thought?	Let me see, do you want to go to my friends' party tonight?
4	No I have a lot of work to do. I can't go.	Everyday?

Table 2: An example conversation in REL+ENG

in order to avoid adding system failure in the analysis. The inter-annotator agreement between the two experts is high (kappa = 0.73) in appropriateness, but the agreement between the two experts in annotating engagement is relatively lower (kappa =0.43). However, if we collapse the rating for "strongly disengaged" with "disengaged" and "very engaged" with "engaged", our agreement improves (kappa = 0.67).

5 Evaluation

To evaluate the efficacy of the strategies, we also conducted an Amazon Mechanical Turk study to test if a non-expert would agree with the experts about which system elicits better user engagement. We selected video recordings with participants who are not familiar with dialog systems. There are only five participants in the REL dataset and nine participants in the REL+ENG dataset who meet this requirement. In order to balance the two sets, we randomly selected five participants from the nine in the REL+ENG. We picked one video from each dataset to form a A/B comparison study. In total there are 25 pairs, and we recruited three raters for each pair. Nobody rated the same pair twice. We ask them to watch the two videos and then compare them through a set of questions including "Which system resulted in a better user experience?", "Which system would you rather interact with?" and "Which person seemed more enthusiastic about talking to the system". In addition, we also included some factual question related to the video content in order to test if the rater had watched the video, which all of them had. Raters are allowed to watch the two videos multiple times. The limitations of such a comparison

is that some system failures, such as ASR failure, may affect the quality of the conversation, which may be a confound. In the task, we specifically asked the users to overlook these system defects, but they still commented on these issues in their feedback. We will collect more examples in the future to balance the influence of system defects.

6 Quantitative Analysis and Results

In this section, we first discuss whether the designed strategies are useful in avoiding system inappropriateness and improving user engagement. Then, we discuss whether both experts and non-experts who watched the video recordings of the interactions prefer a system that reacts to both low user engagement and system inappropriateness over a system that only reacts to low system appropriateness. In addition, we discuss the relationship between system appropriateness and user engagement. In the end, we discuss the relationship and methods to elicit user engagement and user experience.

6.1 Strategies and System Appropriateness

We found that designed conversational strategies are useful in avoiding system breakdowns. The system randomly selects one of the strategies described in Section 4 whenever its confidence in generating an appropriate answer is extremely low. In Table 5, we show for both REL and REL+ENG, how many times each strategy is triggered to react to low confidence in generating system responses and the distribution of the produced utterances being rated as "Inappropriate", "Interpretable" and "Appropriate". Among them, 63% and 73% of the turns are rated as "Interpretable" or "Appropriate"

Label	Definition	Description
1	Strongly Disengaged	Shows no interest in the conversation, not responding or engaged in other things.
2	Disengaged	Shows little interest to continue the conversation, passively interacts with his conversational partner.
3	Neither Disengaged nor Engaged	Interacts with the conversational partner, showing neither interest nor lack of interest to continue the conversation.
4	Engaged	Shows mild interest to continue the conversation.
5	Strongly Engaged	Shows a lot of interest to continue the conversation and actively contributes to the conversation.

Table 3: Engagement annotation scale and definition.

Label	Definition	Example
Inappropriate (1)	Not coherent with the user utterance	*Participant*: How old are you? *TickTock*: Apple.
Interpretable (2)	Related and can be interpreted	*Participant*: How old are you? *TickTock*: That's too big a question for me to answer.
Appropriate (3)	Coherent with the user utterance	*Participant*: How is the weather today? *TickTock*: Very good.

Table 4: Appropriateness rating scheme.

in REL and REL+ENG respectively. The percentage is higher in REL+ENG than REL mostly due to the introduction of *refer back* strategy, which the REL system could not use because it does not track the user's engagement. Compared to REL, which doesn't react to low system response generation confidence, REL+ENG successfully made 69% of inappropriate turns to be "Interpretable" or "Appropriate".

Each strategy has a different effect on improving the system's appropriateness. Among them, the *refer back* strategy leads to more appropriate responses in general, but happens infrequently, due to its strict trigger condition. It can only be triggered if the user previously had a high engagement utterance. The *initiation* strategy leads to more interpretable responses overall, because utterances like "Do you want to go to my friend's party?" actively seek user consent. Even though it may seem abrupt in some contexts, the transition will usually be considered to be interpretable. The *joke* strategy has a high probability of being inappropriate. However, if the joke fits the context, it may be appropriate. For example,

TickTock: "Let's talk about politics."

User: "I don't know too much about politics."

TickTock: "Let me tell you something, politicians and diapers have one thing in common, they both need to be changed regularly."

However, if the joke is out of the context, it will leave the participant with an impression that Tick-Tock is saying random things.

In the future, we intend to track the topic of the conversation, and design specific jokes with respect to conversation topic. We intend to design additional strategies, such as performing grounding requests on out-of-vocabulary words (Schmidt et al., 2015), to address possible system breakdowns, and we will also implement a policy to control when to use which strategy.

6.2 Strategies and User Engagement

We found that designed conversational strategies are useful in improving user engagement. We created an engagement change metric that measures the difference between the current turn engagement and the previous turn engagement. In Table 6, we list the user engagement change for when each strategy triggered in the REL+ENG dataset. In total, 72% of the time when the system reacts to low user engagement, it leads to positive engagement change. We believe this is because the strategies we designed have an active tone, which can reduce the cognitive load required to actively come up with something to say. In addition, since these strategies are triggered when the user engagement is low, the random chance of them improving user engagement is already high, so the percentage of improving user engagement is even

Strategy	REL				REL+ENG			
	Total	InApp	Inter	App	Total	InApp	Inter	App
switch	46	13(28%)	27(59%)	6(13%)	32	6(19%)	18(56%)	8(25%)
initiation	10	2(20%)	6(60%)	2(20%)	18	0(0%)	8(44%)	10(56%)
end	29	14(48%)	13(45%)	2(17%)	16	6(38%)	8(50%)	2(13%)
joke	10	5(50%)	2(20%)	3(30%)	20	14(70%)	0(0%)	6(30%)
refer back	-	-	-	-	12	0(0%)	6(50%)	6(50%)
Total	95	34(35%)	48(51%)	13(14%)	98	26(27%)	40(41%)	32(33%)

Table 5: System appropriateness distribution when two systems react to possible system breakdowns.

higher.

For each strategy, the chance of improving the user's engagement is different. The *refer back* strategy is the most effective strategy: 75% of the time, it leads to better user engagement. We believe this is because once the system refers back to what the user said before, the user feels that the agent is somewhat intelligent and in turn increases his/her interest to continue the conversation, to find what else the system can do. For the *switch* and *end* strategies, there are examples of them both reducing and increasing user engagement. When we looked at the specific cases where the user engagement decreased, we found that those utterances are rated as inappropriate given the context. This leads us to believe that during the selection of what strategies we should use to react to user's low engagement, we should also consider whether the system utterance would be appropriate. We also examined the turns that did not improve or decreased user engagement and found that they are towards the end of the conversation, when the user lost interest and ended the conversation regardless of what the system said.

Strategy	Total	$\Delta < 0$	$\Delta = 0$	$\Delta > 0$
switch	10	1(10%)	3(30%)	6(60%)
initiation	5	0(0%)	2(40%)	3(60%)
end	3	1(33%)	1(33%)	1(33%)
joke	4	0(0%)	2(50%)	2(50%)
refer back	4	0(0%)	1(25%)	3(75%)
Total	26	2 (6%)	9(22%)	15(72%)

Table 6: User engagement change distribution when system reacts to low user engagement.

6.3 Third-person Preference

In our study, we found that a system that reacts to low user engagement and possible system breakdowns is rated as having better user engagement and experience compared to a system that only reacts to possible system breakdowns. This rating held true for both experts and non-experts. We performed an unbalanced Student's t-test on expert-rated user engagement of turns in REL and REL+ENG and found the engagement ratings are statistically different ($p < 0.05$). REL+ENG has more user engagement (REL: Mean = 3.09 (SD = 0.62); REL+ENG: Mean = 3.51 (SD = 0.78). A t-test on utterances that are not produced by designed strategies shows the two systems are not statistically different in terms of user engagement ($p = 0.13$). This suggests that the difference in user engagement is mostly due to the utterances that are produced by strategies. Experts also rated the interaction for overall user experience and we found that REL+ENG interactions are rated significantly higher than REL system overall ($p < 0.05$).

In REL+ENG, 37% of the strategies were triggered to react to low user engagement and 63% were used to deal with low generation confidence. Among the strategies that were triggered to react to low user engagement, 72% of them lead to user engagement improvement. We believe the ability to react to low user engagement is the reason that REL+ENG has more user engagement than REL. Another reason is that REL+ENG has an extra strategy, *refer back*, which in general performs best in improving user engagement. In the user survey, one of the participants also mentioned that he likes the REL+ENG system because it actively proposes engaging topics.

For non-expert ratings, there are 25 A/B comparison tasks. Each task had three raters, and we used the majority vote of the three raters as the final result. People rate REL+ENG as more engaging in 12 tasks, and REL more engaging in 3 tasks. Ten tasks were rated the same for both systems. For non-experts who watched the videos of the interactions, the REL+ENG system elicited significantly more user engagement than the REL system. This conclusion is also true when the systems are judged on which leads to a better user experience. We examined the three tasks on which the REL system is rated higher than REL+ENG and found that two of them involved the same interaction produced by REL. In that interaction, the user is very actively interpreting the system's utterance and responding with interesting questions. Table 1 shows a part of that interaction.

6.4 System Appropriateness and User Engagement

In the conversations produced using REL, an unbalanced Student's t-test of engagement change between turns that are appropriate and ones that are inappropriate shows that turns that are appropriate (Mean $=-0.01$, (SD=0.84)) have significantly ($p = 0.03$) better engagement change than turns that are inappropriate (Mean = 0.33, (SD=0.92)). Figure 2 shows a box plot of the resulting engagement change from appropriate and inappropriate responses. The figure suggests that having appropriate responses leads to better engagement change overall. However some inappropriate responses lead to positive engagement change as well. The same trend is found in conversations produced by REL+ENG.

We tested the hypothesis with respect to each strategy via an unbalanced Student's t-test. The hypothesis holds for the *switch*, *initiation* and *joke* strategies. It did not hold for the *end* strategy, but this is probably because there were very few examples of *end* being triggered and rated appropriate, making it hard to yield any statistical significance. In addition, across all responses, we find some outliers, where even though the system's response is appropriate the user's engagement decreased. This may happen when the system provides a simple 'yes' or 'no' answer, when the system interrupts the user, or when the user misunderstands the system. Some users are not familiar with synthetic voices and misheard the system, and thus thought the system was inappropriate.

We believe that in the future we can improve our system's turn-taking mechanism and try to tune the system retrieval method to prefer longer responses. This will help to overcome the issue that even appropriate answers can lead to a decrease in user engagement. Since appropriate system responses make users more engaged, are all the pos-

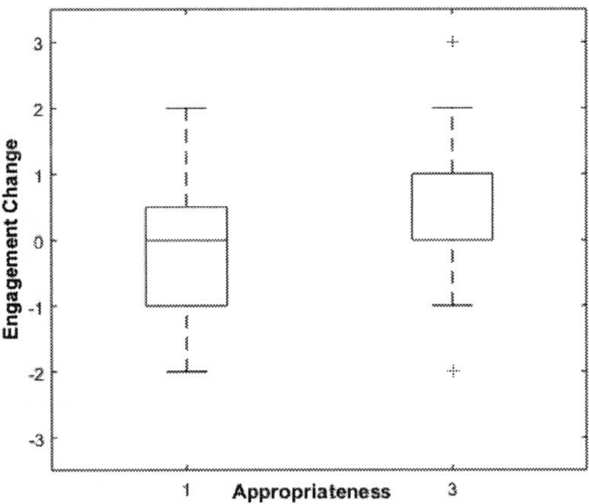

Figure 2: User engagement change with respect to system appropriateness in REL.

itive engagement changes the result of appropriate responses? We performed an unbalanced t-test of the appropriateness values between turns that have positive engagement change (Mean = 1.79 (SD = 0.82)) and turns that have negative engagement change (Mean = 1.53 (SD = 0.67)) and found that they are statistically significant ($p < 0.05$). We examined the recordings of conversations and found that there are other factors that contribute to the engagement change other than the system's appropriateness. For example, funny comments and provocative utterances on the part of the system can also increase user engagement. In Table 1, the system response in Turn 4 is only rated as "Interpretable," and yet it leads to an increase in user engagement. The speaker even smiled when replying to the system. In another interaction, "Don't talk to an idiot, because they will drag you down to the same level and beat you with experience." is rated as "Inappropriate" with respect to the previous user utterance. However the user reacted to it with increased engagement and asked the system: "Are you calling me an idiot, TickTock?". We conclude that being appropriate is important to achieve better user engagement, however it is not the only way.

6.5 User Engagement and User Experience

In the survey after the REL+ENG study, we asked three questions to test the relationships among users' overall interaction engagement, users' positivity towards the agent, and users' overall experience in interacting with the system. We used a five-point Likert scale (1-5). The higher the score is, the more engaged the user is, and the more positive the user is towards the system, the better the user experience the user has. We designed the survey carefully so these three questions are not next to each another, in order to avoid people's tendency to equate these questions. Exact matches between users' rating on their overall engagement (Mean = 2.75 (SD = 0.75)) and their positivity towards the system are found. This is surprising yet possible, since normal users may not differentiate between the two questions: "How engaged you felt during the interaction?" and "How positive you felt towards TickTock during the interaction?". They may internalize that being positive to your partner is the same as being engaged in the conversation. The overall user experience (Mean = 2.83 (SD = 0.71)) is also highly correlated (ρ = 0.92) with both user engagement and user positivity towards the system. Our finding suggests that improving user engagement is critical to eliciting better user experience in an everyday chatting setting. However, our sample size (12) is relatively small, and we plan to include more users in the study in the future.

Another question is whether users really know what "user experience" is. In future studies, we plan to include questions that are more specific such as, "Would you want to interact with the system again?", "Would you invite your friend to interact with the system?" and "Do you think the system is easy to talk to?".

7   Qualitative Results

After the users interacted with REL+ENG, we asked them to fill out a survey. We asked the users what they liked and disliked about the system, and for their suggestions for how to improve the system. A number of participants commented on the visual aspects of the system, mentioning that they liked the cartoon face and that it smiles a lot. Two participants said they liked the system because it actively proposes engaging topics, and tells jokes. This supports our hypothesis that our designed strategies are useful in increasing user engagement. Three users disliked the system because of its incoherence. Two users could not understand the synthesizer very well, which made them unsure whether answers were inappropriate or whether they had simply misunderstood the system. Two participants also complained that the system interrupted them sometimes and one participant mentioned that the system changes topics too often.

One participant suggested displaying subtitles below TickTock's face so that people would be able to comprehend the system's utterances better. Another participant proposed that TickTock should start the conversation with a topic to discuss in order to avoid the cognitive load imposed by the user's coming up with topics. We will consider both suggestions in our future studies.

8   Conclusion and Future Work

We designed and deployed a non-task-oriented conversational system powered with a set of designed strategies that not only reacts to possible system breakdowns but also monitors user engagement in real time in a Wizard-of-Oz implementation. The system reacts to user engagement or system breakdown respectively by randomly selecting one of the designed strategies whenever the user's engagement is low or the system's response generation confidence is low. In the study, our designed strategies are shown to be useful in increasing the system's appropriateness as well as in increasing the user's engagement. We found that appropriateness leads to better user engagement. However not all improved user engagement is elicited by appropriate responses. Sometimes, provocative and funny responses also work.

In a third-person study, experts rated the system that reacts to both low user engagement and low generation confidence as having more overall user engagement than the system that only reacts to low generation confidence. In an Amazon Mechanical Turk study, we found non-experts agreed with experts. We conclude that the improvement gained by reacting to user's engagement is generally recognizable.

One caveat is that due to the lack of a user survey in the REL study, we could not directly compare the self-reported engagement or user experience to determine which system is better. Thus, we plan to ask people to interact with both systems and report which system they like better and which system they think is more engaging.

We will implement an automatic engagement predictor in the real-time system to replace the human in the loop. In addition, a better policy to select strategies based on both user engagement and system response appropriateness will be developed.

References

Mojtaba Khomami Abadi, Jacopo Staiano, Alessandro Cappelletti, Massimo Zancanaro, and Nicu Sebe. 2013. Multimodal engagement classification for affective cinema. In *2013 Humaine Association Conference on Affective Computing and Intelligent Interaction, ACII 2013, Geneva, Switzerland, September 2-5, 2013*, pages 411–416.

Tadas Baltrusaitis, Peter Robinson, and L Morency. 2012. 3D constrained local model for rigid and non-rigid facial tracking. In *Proceedings of International Conference on Computer Vision and Pattern Recognition (CVPR)*, pages 2610–2617. IEEE.

Rafael E Banchs and Haizhou Li. 2012. Iris: a chat-oriented dialogue system based on the vector space model. In *Proceedings of the ACL 2012 System Demonstrations*, pages 37–42. Association for Computational Linguistics.

Katherine Forbes-Riley and Diane J. Litman. 2012. Adapting to multiple affective states in spoken dialogue. In *Proceedings of the SIGDIAL, Seoul National University, Seoul, South Korea*, pages 217–226.

Ryuichiro Higashinaka, Kenji Imamura, Toyomi Meguro, Chiaki Miyazaki, Nozomi Kobayashi, Hiroaki Sugiyama, Toru Hirano, Toshiro Makino, and Yoshihiro Matsuo. 2014. Towards an open-domain conversational system fully based on natural language processing. In *COLING*, pages 928–939.

Spyros Kousidis, Casey Kennington, Timo Baumann, Hendrik Buschmeier, Stefan Kopp, and David Schlangen. 2014. A multimodal in-car dialogue system that tracks the driver's attention. In *Proceedings of the 16th International Conference on Multimodal Interaction*, pages 26–33. ACM.

M Lombard and T Ditton. 1997. At the heart of it all: The concept of presence, journal of computer mediated-communication. *Journal of Computer Mediated Communication*, 3(2).

Lilia Moshkina, Susan Trickett, and J. Gregory Trafton. 2014. Social engagement in public places: A tale of one robot. In *Proceedings of the 2014 ACM/IEEE International Conference on Human-robot Interaction*, HRI '14, pages 382–389, New York, NY, USA. ACM.

Christopher Peters, Catherine Pelachaud, Elisabetta Bevacqua, Maurizio Mancini, and Isabella Poggi. 2005. A model of attention and interest using gaze behavior. In *Intelligent Virtual Agents, 5th International Working Conference, IVA 2005, Kos, Greece, September 12-14, 2005, Proceedings*, pages 229–240.

Alan Ritter, Colin Cherry, and William B Dolan. 2011. Data-driven response generation in social media. In *Proceedings of the conference on empirical methods in natural language processing*, pages 583–593. Association for Computational Linguistics.

Maria Schmidt, Jan Niehues, and Alex Waibel. 2015. Towards an open-domain social dialog system. In *Proceedings of the 6th International Workshop Series on Spoken Dialog Systems*, pages 124–129.

Oriol Vinyals and Quoc Le. 2015. A neural conversational model. ICML Deep Learning Workshop 2015.

Zhou Yu, Dan Bohus, and Eric Horvitz. 2015a. Incremental coordination: Attention-centric speech production in a physically situated conversational agent.

Zhou Yu, Alexandros Papangelis, and Alexander Rudnicky. 2015b. TickTock: A non-goal-oriented multimodal dialog system with engagement awareness. In *Proceedings of the AAAI Spring Symposium*.

Classifying Emotions in Customer Support Dialogues in Social Media

Jonathan Herzig, Guy Feigenblat,
Michal Shmueli-Scheuer,
David Konopnicki
IBM Research - Haifa
Haifa 31905, Israel
{hjon,guyf,shmueli,davidko}@il.ibm.com

Anat Rafaeli, Daniel Altman,
David Spivak
Technion-Israel Institute of Technology
Haifa 32000, Israel
Anatr@ie.technion.ac.il,
altmand@campus.technion.ac.il,
dspivak@campus.technion.ac.il

Abstract

Providing customer support through social media channels is gaining increasing popularity. In such a context, automatic detection and analysis of the emotions expressed by customers is important, as is identification of the emotional techniques (e.g., apology, empathy, etc.) in the responses of customer service agents. Result of such an analysis can help assess the quality of such a service, help and inform agents about desirable responses, and help develop automated service agents for social media interactions. In this paper, we show that, in addition to text based turn features, dialogue features can significantly improve detection of emotions in social media customer service dialogues and help predict emotional techniques used by customer service agents.

1 Introduction

An interesting use case for social media is customer support that can now take place over public social media channels. Using this medium has its advantages as described, for example, in (De-Mers, 2014): Customers appreciate the simplicity and immediacy of social media conversations, the ability to reach real human beings, the transparency, and the feeling that someone listens to them. Businesses also benefit from the publicity of giving good services almost in real-time, online, building an online community of customers and encouraging more brand mentions in social media. A recent study shows that one in five (23%) customers in the U.S. say they have used social media for customer service in 2014, up from 17% in 2012[1]. Obviously, companies hope that such

uses are associated with a positive experience. Yet there are limited tools for assessing this. In this paper, we analyze customer support dialogues using the Twitter platform and show the utility of such analyses.

The particular aspect of such dialogues that we concentrate on is *emotions*. Emotions are a cardinal aspect of inter-personal communication: they are an implicit or explicit part of essentially any communication, and of particular importance in the setting of customer service, as they relate directly to customer satisfaction and experience (Oliver, 2014). Typical emotions expressed by customers in the context of social media service dialogues include anger and frustration, as well as gratitude and more (Gelbrich, 2010). On the other hand, customer service agents also express emotions in service conversations, for example apology or empathy. However, it is important to note that emotions expressed by service agents are typically governed by company policies that specify which emotions should be expressed in which situation (Rafaeli and Sutton, 1987). This is why we talk in this paper about agent emotional *techniques* rather than agent emotions.

Consider, for example, the real (anonymized) Twitter dialogue depicted in Figure 1. In this dialogue, customer disappointment is expressed in the first turn ('Bummer. =/'), followed by customer support empathy ('Uh oh!'). Then in the last two turns both customer and support express gratitude.

The analysis of emotions being expressed in customer support conversations can take two applications: (1) to discern and compute quality of service indicators and (2) to provide real-time clues to customer service agents regarding the cus-

---

[1] `http://about.americanexpress.com/news/docs/2014x/2014-Global-Customer-Service-Barometer-US.pdf`

Proceedings of the SIGDIAL 2016 Conference, pages 64–73,
Los Angeles, USA, 13-15 September 2016. ©2016 Association for Computational Linguistics

Figure 1: Example of customer service dialogue that was initiated by a customer (left side), and the agent responses (right side).

tomer emotion expressed in a conversation. A possible application here is recommending to customer service agents what should be their emotional response (for example, in each situation, should they apologize, should they thank the customer, etc.)

Another interesting trend in customer service, in addition to the use of social media described above, is the automation of various functions of customer interaction. Several companies are developing text-based chat agents, typically accessible through corporate web sites, and partially automatized: In these platforms, a computer program handles simple conversations with customers, and more complicated dialogues are transferred to a human agent. Such partially automated systems are also in use for social media dialogues. The automation in such systems helps save human resources and, with further development based on Artificial Intelligence, more automation in customer service chats is likely to appear. Given the importance of emotions in service dialogues, such systems will benefit from the ability to detect (customer) emotions and will need to guide employees (and machines) regarding the right emotional technique in various situations (e.g., apologizing at the right point).

Thus, our goal, in this paper, is to show that the

functionality of guiding employees regarding appropriate responses can be developed based on the analysis of textual dialogue data. We show first that it is possible to automatically detect emotions being expressed and, second that it is possible to predict the emotional technique that is likely to be used by a human agent in a given situation. This analysis reflects our ultimate goal: To enable a computer system to discern the emotions expressed by human customers, and to develop computerized tools that mimic the emotional technique used by a human customer service agent in a particular situation.

We see the main contributions of this paper as follows: (1) To our knowledge, this is the first research focusing on automatic analysis of emotions expressed in customer service provided through social media. (2) This is the first research using unique dialogue features (e.g., emotions expressed in previous dialogue turns by the agent and customer, time between dialogue turns) to improve emotion detection. (3) This is the first research studying the prediction of the agent emotional techniques to be used in the response to customer turns.

The rest of this paper is organized as follows. We start by reviewing the related work and a description of the data that we collected. Then we formally define the methodology for detection and prediction of emotion expression in dialogues. Finally, we describe our experiments, evaluate the various models, conclude and suggest future directions.

2   Related Work

2.1   Emotion Detection

Approaches to categorical emotion classification often employ machine learning classifiers, and SVM has typically outperformed other classifiers. In (Mohammad, 2012; Roberts et al., 2012; Qadir and Riloff, 2014) a series of binary SVM classifiers (one for each emotion) were trained over datasets from different domains (news headlines, social media). These works utilize unigrams and bigrams among other lexical based features (e.g., utilizing the NRC emotion lexicon (Mohammad and Turney, 2013)) and punctuation based features. In our work, we also used an SVM classifier, however, while these works aim at classifying single posts (i.e., sentence, tweet, etc.) without context, our work utilizes the context while considering dialogues. The work in (Hasegawa et al., 2013) showed how to predict and elicit emotions in online dialogues. Their approach for emotion classification is different from ours, for example they only considered the last turn as informative (we consider the full context of the dialogue), and focused on eliciting emotions, while we focus on predicting the agent emotional technique.

2.2 Emotion Expression Prediction

The works in (Skowron, 2010) and (D'Mello et al., 2009) presented dialogue systems that sense the user emotions, such that the system further optimizes its affect response. Both systems use rule-based approaches to generate responses, however, the authors do not discuss how they developed the rules.

It is worth mentioning the works in (Ritter et al., 2011; Sordoni et al., 2015) that are focused on data-driven response generation in the context of dialogues in social media. These works generated general responses, while we focused on predicting the appropriate emotional response.

2.3 Emotions in Written Customer Service Interactions

In the domain of customer support, several papers studied emotions as part of written interactions. The work in (Gupta et al., 2013), analyzed emotions in textual email communications and the authors focused on prioritizing customer support emails based on detected emotions. In the setting of online customer service (chats), in (Zhang et al., 2011) the authors studied the impact of emotional text on the customer's perception of the service agent. To extract the emotions, the authors used relatively basic features such as emoticons, exclamation marks, all caps, and some internet acronyms (such as 'lol' or 'imho').

Emotion detection is also applied to the domain of call centers (Vidrascu and Devillers, 2005; Morrison et al., 2007) and this differs from our focus since call center data are voice, and, thus, emotion detection is mainly based on paralinguistic aspects rather than on the text. In addition, if the textual part is considered, then the texts are transcripts of calls that are very different from written text (Wallace Chafe, 1987), and even more different from the social media setting where the dialogue is fully public.

3 Data

In this section we describe the data collection process and provide some statistics about the Twitter dialogue dataset we have collected.

3.1 Data Collection

Companies that utilize the Twitter platform as a channel for customer service use a dedicated Twitter account which provides real-time support by monitoring tweets that customers address to it. At the same time corporate support agents reply to these tweets also through the Twitter platform. A customer and an agent, can use the Twitter reply mechanism to discuss until the issue is solved (e.g., a solution is provided, or the customer is directed to another channel), or until the customer is no longer active.

In the present work, we define a dialogue to be a sequence of turns between a specific customer and an agent, where the customer initiates the first turn. Consecutive posts of the same party (customer or agent) uninterrupted by the other party, are considered as a single turn (even if there are several tweets). Given the nature of customer support services, we assume the last turn in the dialogue is an agent turn (e.g., "You're very welcome. :) Hit us back any time you need support"). Thus, we expect an even number of turns in the dialogue. We filtered out dialogues in which more than one customer or one agent are involved. Formally, we define a dialogue to be an ordered list of turns $[t_1, t_2, \cdots, t_n]$ where odd turns are customer turns, and even turns are agent turns, and n is even.

Each turn t_i is a tuple consisting of {*turn number, timestamp, content*} where *turn number* represents the sequential position of the turn in the dialogue, *timestamp* captures the time the message was published on Twitter, and *content* is the textual message.

3.2 Data Statistics

We gathered data for two North America based customer support services Twitter accounts that provide support for customers from North America (so tweets are in English). One service is for general customer care (denoted as *Gen*), and the other is for technical customer support (denoted as *Tech*). We extracted this data from December 2014 until June 2015. Specifically, for each customer that posted a tweet to the customer support accounts, we searched for the previous, if any, turn

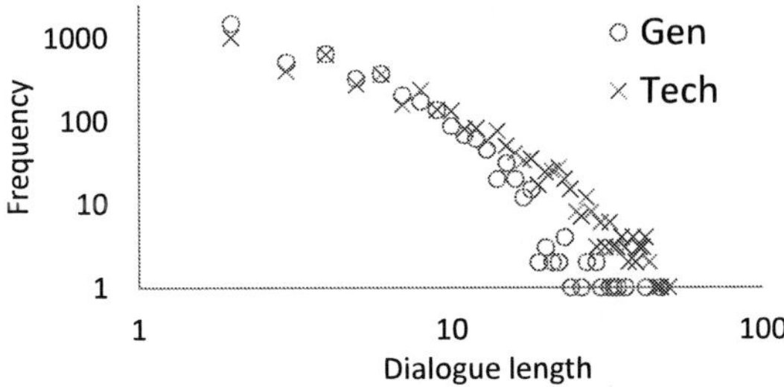

Figure 2: Frequency versus dialogue length for *Gen* and *Tech* on a log-log scale.

	# Dialogues	Mean # turns	AVG word count
Gen	4243	4.83	16.69
Tech	4016	6.81	14.28

Table 1: Descriptive statistics of customer service dialogues extracted from Twitter.

to which it replied. Given this method we traced back previous turns and reconstructed entire dialogues.

Table 1 summarizes some statistics about the collected data, and Figure 2 depicts the frequencies of dialogue lengths which follow a power-law relationship. Table 1 shows differences between the two services; the dialogues in *Tech* tend to be longer (i.e., typically include more turns), with an average of 6.81 turns vs. average of 4.83 turns for *Gen*.

As most of the dialogues include at most 8 turns (88% and 76% for *Gen* and *Tech*, respectively), we removed dialogues longer than 8 turns. In addition, we removed dialogues that contained only 2 turns as these are too short to be meaningful as the customer never replied or provided more details about the issue. After applying these preprocessing steps, we had 1189 dialogues of *Gen* support, and 1224 dialogues of *Tech* support.

4 Methodology

The first objective of our work is to detect emotions expressed in customer turns and the second is to predict the emotional technique in agent turns. We treated these two objectives as two classification tasks. We generated a classifier for each task, where the classification output of one classifier can be part of the input to the other classifier. While both classifiers work at the level of turns, i.e., classify the current turn to emotions ex-

pressed in it, they are inherently different. When detecting emotions in a customer turn, the turn's content is available at classification time (as well as the history of the dialogue) - meaning, the customer has already provided her input and the system must now understand what is the emotion being expressed. Whereas, when predicting the emotional technique for an agent turn, the turn's content is not available during classification time, but only the agent action and the history of the dialogue since the agent did not respond yet. This difference stems from the fact that in order to train an automated service agent to respond based on customer input, the agent's emotional technique needs to be computed before the agent generates its response sentence.

We defined a different set of relevant emotion classes for each party in the dialogue (customer or agent), based on our above survey of research on customer service (e.g., (Gelbrich, 2010)). Relevant customer emotions to be detected are: *Confusion, Frustration, Anger, Sadness, Happiness, Hopefulness, Disappointment, Gratitude,* and *Politeness*. Relevant agent emotional techniques to be predicted are: *Empathy, Gratitude, Apology,* and *Cheerfulness*.

We utilized the context of the dialogue to extract informative features that we refer to as *dialogue features*. Using these features for emotion classification in written dialogues is novel, and as our experimental results show, it improves performance compared to a model based only on features extracted from the turn's text.

4.1 Features

We used the following features in our models.

4.1.1 Dialogue Features

Comprises three contextual feature families: *integral, emotional,* and *temporal*. A feature can be *global*, namely its value is constant across an entire dialogue or it can be a *local*, meaning that its value may change at each turn. In addition, a feature can be *historical* (as will be discussed below).

The *integral* family of features includes three sets of features:

1. *Dialogue topic*: a set of *global* binary features representing the intent of the customer who initiated the support inquiry. Multiple intents can be assigned to a dialogue from a taxonomy of popular topics, which are adapted to the specific service. Examples of topics include *ac-*

count issues, payments, technical problem and more [2]. This feature set captures the notion that customer emotions are influenced by the event that led the customer to contact the customer service (Steunebrink et al., 2009).

2. *Agent essence*: a set of *local* binary features that represent the action used by the agent to address the last customer turn, independently of any emotional technique expressed. We refer to these actions as the *essence* of the agent turn. Multiple essences can be assigned to an agent turn from a predefined taxonomy. For instance, *"asking for more information"* and *"offering a solution"* are possible essences [3]. This feature set captures the notion that customer emotions are influenced by actions of agents (Little et al., 2013).

3. *Turn number*: a *local* categorical feature representing the number of the turn.

The *emotional* family of features includes *Agent emotion* and *Customer emotion*: these two sets of *local* binary features represent emotions predicted for previous turns. Our model generates predictions of emotions for each customer and agent turn, and uses these predictions as features to classify a later customer or agent turn with emotion expression.

The *temporal* family of features includes the following features extracted from the timeline of the dialogue:

1. *Customer/agent response time*: two *local* features that indicate the time elapsed between the timestamp of the last customer/agent turn and the timestamp of the subsequent turn. This is a categorical feature with values *low*, *medium* or *high* (using categorical values yielded better results than using a continuous value).

2. *Median customer/agent response time*: two *local* categorical features defined as the median of the *customer/agent response times* preceding the current turn. The categories are the same as the previous temporal features.

---

[2]Currently this feature is not supported in social media. In other channels, for example, customer support on the phone, the customer is requested to provide a topic before she is connected to a support agent (usually using an IVR system). As this feature is inherent in other customer support channels, we assume that in the future it will also be supported in social media.

[3]We assume that if the agent is human, then this input is known to her e.g., based on company policies. For the automated service agent case, we assume that the dialogue system will manage and provide this input.

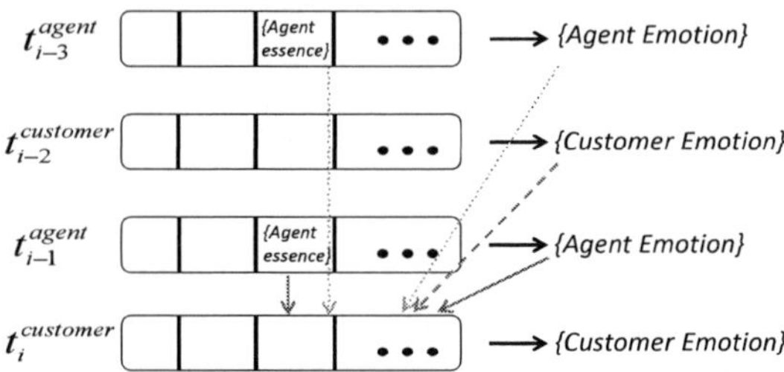

Figure 3: Example for *Historical* features propagation for customer turn, t_i, with $history = 3$. When $history = 1$, the *historical* features are the *agent essence* of turn t_{i-1} and the *agent emotion* predicted for turn t_{i-1} (purple solid line). When $history = 2$, we also add the *customer emotion* detected in turn t_{i-2} (red dashed line). Finally, if we set $history = 3$, then we also add the *agent essence* of turn t_{i-3} and the *agent emotion* predicted for turn t_{i-3} (blue dotted line), so in total we have 5 *historical* features. Notice that the *customer emotion* and *agent essence* features have different values based on their turn number.

3. *Day of week*: a *local* categorical feature indicating the day of the week when the turn was published [Monday - Sunday]. This feature captures the effects of weekend versus weekday influences on emotions (Ryan et al., 2010).

When representing a turn, t_i, as a feature vector, we added some features originating in previous turns $j < i$ to t_i. These features, that are *historical*, include the *emotional* features family and *local integral* features (namely *agent emotions*, *customer emotions* and *agent essence*). We do not include the *turn number* of previous turns, as this is dependent on the turn number of t_i. We denote these features as *historical* features. The value of *history*, that is a parameter of our models, defines the number of sequential turns that precede t_i which propagate *historical* features to t_i.

Figure 3 shows an example of the *historical* features in relation to the classification of customer turn t_i, for *history* size between 1 and 3.

4.1.2 Textual Features

These features are extracted from the text of a customer turn, without considering the context of the dialogue. We use various state-of-the-art text based features that have been shown to be effective for the social media domain (Mohammad, 2012;

Roberts et al., 2012). These features include various n-grams, punctuation and social media features. Namely, *unigrams*, *bigrams*, *NRC lexicon features* (number of terms in a post associated with each affect label in NRC lexicon), and presence of *exclamation marks*, *question marks*, *usernames*, *links*, *happy emoticons*, and *sad emoticons*. We note that these are the features we used in our baseline model detailed below, in the description of our experiments.

4.2 Turn Classification System

For both of the agent and customer turn classification tasks, we implemented two different models which incorporate all of the feature sets we have detailed above. We considered these tasks as multi-label classification tasks. This captures the notion that a party can express multiple emotions (e.g., confusion and anger) in a turn. We chose to use a problem transformation approach which maps the multi-label classification task into several binary classification tasks, one for each emotion class which participates in the multi-label problem (Tsoumakas and Katakis, 2006). For each emotion e, a binary classifier is created using the one-vs.-all approach which classifies a turn as expressing e or not. A test sample is fully classified by aggregating the classification results from all independent binary classifiers. We next define our two modeling approaches.

4.2.1 SVM Dialogue Model

In our first approach we trained an SVM classifier for each emotion class as explained above. The feature vector we used to represent a turn incorporates *dialogue* and *textual features*. The *history* size is also a parameter of this model. Feature extraction for a training/testing feature vector representing a turn t_i, works as follows. *Textual features* are extracted for t_i if it is a customer turn, or for t_{i-1} if it is an agent turn (recall that the system does not have the content of agent turn t_i at classification time). The *temporal* features are also extracted using time lapse values between previous turns as explained above. As discussed above, *agent essence* is assumed to be an input to our module, while *agent emotion* and *customer emotion* features are propagated from classification results of previous turns during testing (or from ground truth labels during training), where the number of previous turns is determined according to the value of *history*. These *historical*

features are also appended to the feature vector of t_i, similarly to (Kim et al., 2010) where this method was used for classifying dialogue acts.

4.2.2 SVM-HMM Dialogue Model

Our second approach to classifying dialogue turns is to use a sequence classification method (SVM-HMM), which classifies a sample sequence into its most probable tag sequence. For instance (Kim et al., 2010; Tavafi et al., 2013) used SVM-HMM and Conditional Random Fields for dialogue act classification. Since emotions expressed in customer and agent turns are different, we treated them as different classification tasks (like in our previous approach) and trained a separate classifier for each emotion. We made the following changes when using SVM-HMM:

(1) We treated the emotion classification problem of turn t_i as a sequence classification problem of the sequence $t_1, t_3, ..., t_i$ (i.e., only customer turns) if t_i is a customer turn and $t_2, t_4, ..., t_i$ (i.e., only agent turns) if it is an agent turn. (2) The SVM-HMM classifier generates models that are isomorphic to a kth-order hidden Markov model. Under this model, dependency in past classification results is captured internally by modeling transition probabilities between emotion states. Thus, we removed historical *customer emotion* (resp. *agent emotion*) feature sets when representing a feature vector for a customer (resp. agent) turn. (3) We note that in our setting we provide classifications in real-time during the progress of the dialogue, so at classification time we have access only to previous turns and global information, and we cannot change classification decisions for past turns. Thus, we tagged a test turn, t_i, by classifying the sequence which ends in t_i. Then, t_i was tagged with its sequence classification result.

5 Experiments

5.1 Experimental Setup

A first step in building a classification model is to obtain ground truth data. For this, we sampled dialogues from our dataset, as detailed in Table 2, based on each data source's dialogue length distribution. This sample included 1056 customer turns and 1056 agent turns in total. The sampled dialogues were tagged using Amazon Mechanical Turk[4]. Each dialogue was tagged by five different Mechanical Turk's master level judges. Each

---

[4] https://www.mturk.com/

Source	# 4 turn dialogues	# 6 turn dialogues	# 8 turn dialogues
Gen	100	66	33
Tech	100	58	38

Table 2: Number of dialogues tagged by judges per source.

judge performed the following tagging tasks given the full dialogue:

1. Emotion tagging: indicate the intensity of emotion expressed in each turn (customer or agent) for each emotion, on a scale of ($[0...5]$), such that 0 defines no emotion, 1 a low emotion intensity and 5 a high emotion intensity. The intraclass correlation (ICC) among the judges was 0.53 which indicates a moderate agreement which is common in this setting (LeBreton and Senter, 2007).

2. Dialogue topic tagging: select one or several topic(s), to represent the customer's intent. The topics are based on a taxonomy of popular customer support topics (Zeithaml et al., 2006): *Account issues, Pricing, Payments, Customer service, Customer experience, Technical problem, Technical question, Order and delivery issues, Behavior of a staff member, Company policy issues* and *General statement*.

3. Agent essence tagging: select one or several of the following for each agent's turn, to describe the agent's action in the specific turn: *Recognizing the issue raised, Asking for more information, Providing an explanation, Offering a solution, General statement* and *Assurance of efforts*. The taxonomy is based on (Zomerdijk and Voss, 2010).

We generated true binary labels from the emotion tagging. For turn t_i, we considered it to express emotion e if $tag(e, t_i) \geq 2$ where $tag(e, t)$ is the average judges' tag value of e in t. This process generated the class sizes detailed in Table 3. Dialogue topic tagging was converted to binary features representing the top-2 selected topics. *Agent essence* feature set representation for each turn was defined analogously. The temporal response time values were translated to *low/medium/high* categorical values according to their relation to the 33-th and 66-th percentiles.

We evaluated our methods by using leave-one-dialogue-out cross-validation (as in (Kim et al., 2010)), over the whole dataset (for the two cus-

Customer		Agent	
Emotion	# of instances	Emotion	# of instances
Happiness	66	Apology	146
Sadness	31	Gratitude	81
Anger	160	Empathy	163
Confusion	68	Cheerfulness	177
Frustration	342		
Disappointment	257		
Gratitude	119		
Hopefulness	30		
Politeness	180		

Table 3: Class size per classification task

tomer service data sources together). Each test dialogue was classified by its order of turns, where each turn type (customer or agent) is classified by its corresponding classifier.

Our baseline in all experiments is an SVM classifier that uses only the *textual features* described above, which do not utilize the dialogue context. This was used as a state-of-the-art single sentence emotion detection approach in many cases, e.g., (Mohammad, 2012; Roberts et al., 2012; Qadir and Riloff, 2014) and more. As described above, agent turn emotion prediction is performed before its content is known. Thus, the baseline representation of an agent turn consisted of *textual features* extracted from its preceding customer turn. We evaluated each emotion's classification performance by using precision (P), recall (R) and F1-score (F). We evaluated the total performance for all emotion classes using *micro* and *macro* averages. We used Liblinear[5] as an SVM implementation and SVM-HMM[6] for sequence classification. Additionally, we used ClearNLP[7] for textual features extraction.

5.2 History Size Impact

Since *history* size is a parameter of our models, we first tested the classification results for all possible *history* sizes (given that that maximum dialogue size in our dataset is 8). For each task and for each possible *history* size, we generated *SVM Dialogue* and *SVM-HMM Dialogue* models and evaluated them as detailed above. We compared the *macro* and *micro* average *F1-score* of our classifiers against the baseline classifier performance. As depicted in Figure 4 both the *SVM Dialogue* and *SVM-HMM Dialogue* models were superior

---

[5]http://liblinear.bwaldvogel.de/
[6]https://www.cs.cornell.edu/people/tj/svm_light/svm_hmm.html
[7]https://github.com/clir/clearnlp

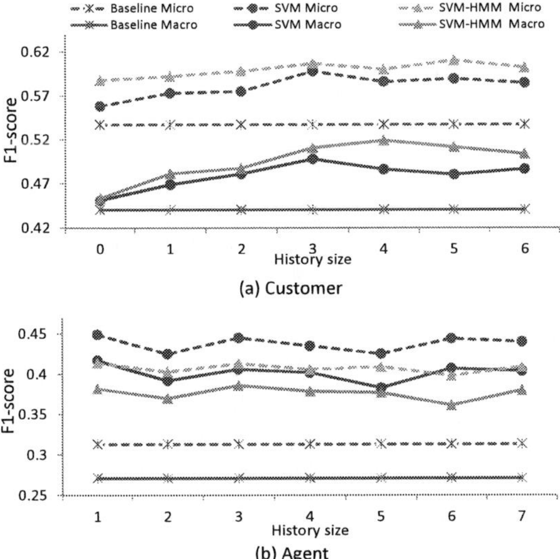

(a) Customer

(b) Agent

Figure 4: Macro and micro average F1-score for various history sizes for customer (a) and agent (b) turn classifiers.

for all history ranges and for both tasks. Examining the customer turns emotion detection performance, we can see in Figure 4(a) that it increases until $history = 3$, and then remains relatively stable for larger *history* sizes. This means that information about the behavior of the customer and agent in past turns is beneficial for detecting customer emotions in a current turn. For assessing the performance of our predictions of agent turns emotion techniques, we first note that we tested with $history > 0$ range, since we assume that the minimal information needed for agent turn classification is the information extracted from the last customer turn. Figure 4(b) shows that overall, performance is highest when $history = 1$, and does not decline much for higher *history* values. This indicates that for agent emotion technique prediction the last customer turn is the most informative one.

In all of our experiments, we used the *Wilcoxon signed-rank test* to validate the statistical significance of our models' *micro* and *macro* average *F1-score* comparing to baseline performance. Additionally, we used *McNemar's test* on the contingency tables aggregated over all emotions. These tests showed that both of our models were significantly different from the baseline model, under a value of 0.001, for both classification tasks and all *history* sizes.

5.3 Detailed Classification Results

Table 4 depicts the detailed classification results for optimal *history* values that obtained maximal *macro F1-score*, namely for customer emotion detection $history = 4$ and for agent emotion technique prediction $history = 1$. The table presents performance for each emotion, for *macro* and *micro* average results over all dialogues, and for each data source (*Gen* or *Tech*) separately. For both classification tasks, both of our models outperformed baseline results for almost all emotions, where average *macro* and *micro* results are statistically significant compared to the baseline, as described above.

For customer turn emotion detection, the *SVM-HMM Dialogue* model performed better than the *SVM Dialogue* model, and reached a *macro* and *micro* average *F1-score* improvements over all dialogues of 17.8% and 11.7%, respectively. Furthermore, the *macro* and *micro* average *F1-score* results of the *SVM-HMM Dialogue* model (0.519 and 0.6, respectively) are satisfying given the moderate ICC score between the judges (0.53). For predicting the agent emotional technique, the *SVM Dialogue* model obtained slightly better results than *SVM-HMM Dialogue* model, and reached a *macro* and *micro* average *F1-score* improvements over all dialogues of 53.9% and 43.5%, respectively. These results emphasize the differences between the *SVM Dialogue* and *SVM-HMM Dialogue* models. Specifically, when *history* size is large, as in customer emotion prediction, *SVM-HMM Dialogue* model, which internally captures dependencies in past classifications, outperforms the simplistic *SVM Dialogue* model. We note that an improvement is also obtained when calculating *macro* and *micro* average performance for each data source separately. This highlights our models' superiority as well as their general applicability and robustness for different data sources.

5.4 Feature Set Contribution Analysis

We examined the contribution of different feature sets in an incremental fashion, using the optimal *history* value detailed above. Based on the families of feature sets that we defined in the Methodology section, we tested the performance of different feature set combinations in our models, added in the following order: *baseline* (textual features), *emotional*, *temporal* and *integral*. Figure 5 depicts

Classification task	Emotion	Baseline			SVM Dialogue Model				SVM-HMM Dialogue Model			
		P	R	F	P	R	F	%	P	R	F	%
Customer emotion detection	Happiness	.556	.379	.450	.622	.424	.505	12.0	**.627**	**.561**	**.592**	31.4
	Sadness	.412	.226	.292	.429	.194	.267	-8.6	**.444**	**.258**	**.327**	12.0
	Anger	.615	.469	.532	**.669**	.569	.615	15.6	.638	**.606**	**.622**	16.9
	Confusion	.200	.147	.169	**.255**	.191	.218	28.9	.254	**.221**	**.236**	39.4
	Frustration	**.667**	.608	.636	.659	.623	.641	.7	.659	**.673**	**.666**	4.7
	Disappointment	.529	.432	.475	.618	**.572**	**.594**	24.9	**.628**	.553	.588	23.7
	Gratitude	.786	.739	.762	**.827**	**.765**	**.795**	4.3	.826	.756	.789	3.6
	Hopefulness	.133	.067	.089	**.286**	.067	.108	21.6	.280	**.233**	**.255**	186.4
	Politeness	.607	.472	.531	**.618**	.494	.549	3.4	.561	**.583**	**.572**	7.7
	Gen - macro	.540	.405	.463	.582	.456	.511	10.3	**.592**	**.514**	**.551**	18.9
	Gen - micro	.685	.527	.596	**.716**	.606	.657	10.2	.691	**.641**	**.665**	11.6
	Tech - macro	.394	.332	.361	**.478**	.356	.408	13.2	.457	**.419**	**.437**	21.3
	Tech - micro	.450	.410	.429	**.482**	.417	.447	4.2	.479	**.469**	**.474**	10.5
	Total - macro	.500	.393	.440	**.554**	.433	.486	10.4	.546	**.494**	**.519**	17.8
	Total - micro	.597	.488	.537	**.637**	.543	.586	9.1	.617	**.583**	**.600**	11.7
Agent emotional technique prediction	Apology	.276	.264	.270	.418	**.423**	**.420**	55.6	**.424**	.380	.400	48.1
	Gratitude	.108	.049	.068	**.326**	**.197**	**.245**	260.3	.200	**.197**	.198	191.2
	Empathy	.287	.240	.261	**.401**	**.390**	**.395**	51.3	**.401**	.349	.373	42.9
	Cheerfulness	.491	.463	.477	**.592**	**.598**	**.594**	24.5	.546	.564	.554	16.1
	Gen - macro	.310	.275	.291	**.488**	**.462**	**.474**	62.9	.450	.433	.441	51.5
	Gen - micro	.342	.281	.308	**.489**	**.468**	**.478**	55.2	.461	.429	.444	44.2
	Tech - macro	.216	.201	.208	**.277**	**.263**	**.269**	29.3	.265	.256	.260	25.0
	Tech - micro	.338	.302	.319	**.425**	**.392**	**.407**	27.6	.379	.366	.372	16.6
	Total - macro	.290	.254	.271	**.434**	**.402**	**.417**	53.9	.393	.372	.382	41.0
	Total - micro	.340	.289	.313	**.463**	**.437**	**.449**	43.5	.427	.403	.414	32.3

Table 4: Detailed performance results for customer and agent classification tasks given optimal *history* size. For brevity, the table presents improvement relative to baseline in percentages only for *F1-score*.

the results for both classification tasks. The x-axis represents specific combination of features sets, and the y-axis represents the *macro* or *micro* average *F1-score* value obtained. Figure 5 shows that adding each feature set improved performance for all models, for both tasks, which indicates the informative value of each feature set. Additionally, the figure suggests that the most informative dialogue feature sets are the *integral* and *emotional*.

6 Conclusions

In this work we studied emotions being expressed in customer service dialogues in the social media. Specifically, we described two classification tasks, one for detecting customer emotions and the other for predicting the emotional technique used by support service agent. We have proposed two different models (*SVM Dialogue* and *SVM-HMM Dialogue* models) for these tasks. We studied the impact of *dialogue features* and dialogue *history* on the quality of the classification and showed improvement in performance for both models and both classification tasks. We also showed the robustness of our models across different data sources. As for future work we plan to work on several aspects: (1) In this work, we showed that it is possible to predict the emotional

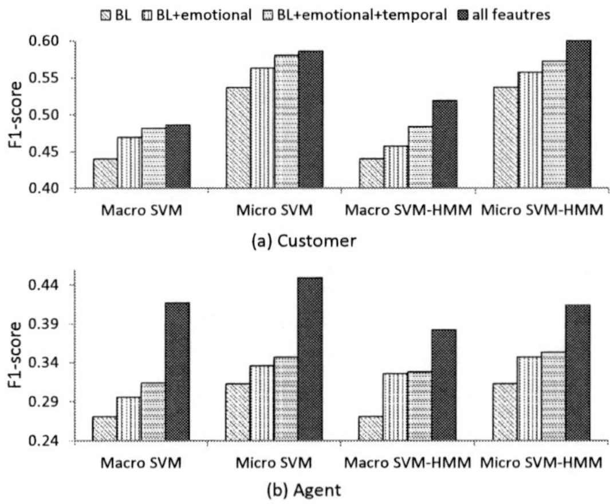

Figure 5: Macro and micro average F1-score for various feature set combinations for customer (a) and agent (b) turn classifiers. BL stands for baseline.

technique. In the future, we plan to run experiments in which the predicted emotional technique is actually applied in the context of new dialogues to measure the effect of such predictions on real support dialogues. (2) Distinguish between dialogues that have positive outcomes (e.g., high customer satisfaction) and others.

References

Jayson DeMers. 2014. 7 reasons you need to be using social media as your customer service portal. *Forbes*.

Sidney D'Mello, Scotty Craig, Karl Fike, and Arthur Graesser. 2009. Responding to learners' cognitive-affective states with supportive and shakeup dialogues. In *Proceedings of HCI*, pages 595–604.

Katja Gelbrich. 2010. Anger, frustration, and helplessness after service failure: coping strategies and effective informational support. *Journal of the Academy of Marketing Science*, 38(5):567–585.

Narendra K. Gupta, Mazin Gilbert, and Giuseppe Di Fabbrizio. 2013. Emotion detection in email customer care. *Computational Intelligence*, 29(3):489–505.

Takayuki Hasegawa, Naoki Yoshinaga Kaji, Nobuhiro and, and Masashi Toyoda. 2013. Predicting and eliciting addressee's emotion in online dialogue. In *ACL (1)*, pages 964–972.

Su Nam Kim, Lawrence Cavedon, and Timothy Baldwin. 2010. Classifying dialogue acts in one-on-one live chats. In *Proceedings of EMNLP*, pages 862–871.

James M LeBreton and Jenell L Senter. 2007. Answers to 20 questions about interrater reliability and interrater agreement. *Organizational Research Methods*.

Laura M Little, Don Kluemper, Debra L Nelson, and Andrew Ward. 2013. More than happy to help? customer-focused emotion management strategies. *Personnel Psychology*, 66(1):261–286.

Saif M Mohammad and Peter D Turney. 2013. Crowdsourcing a word–emotion association lexicon. *Computational Intelligence*, 29(3):436–465.

Saif Mohammad. 2012. Portable features for classifying emotional text. In *Proceedings of NAACL HLT*, pages 587–591.

"Donn Morrison, Ruili Wang, and Liyanage C. De Silva. 2007. Ensemble methods for spoken emotion recognition in call-centres. *Speech Communication*, 49(2):98–112.

Richard L Oliver. 2014. *Satisfaction: A behavioral perspective on the consumer*. Routledge.

Ashequl Qadir and Ellen Riloff. 2014. Learning emotion indicators from tweets: Hashtags, hashtag patterns, and phrases. In *Proceedings of EMNLP*, pages 1203–1209.

Anat Rafaeli and Robert I Sutton. 1987. Expression of emotion as part of the work role. *Academy of management review*, 12(1):23–37.

Alan Ritter, Colin Cherry, and William B. Dolan. 2011. Data-driven response generation in social media. In *Proceedings of EMNLP*.

Kirk Roberts, Michael A Roach, Joseph Johnson, Josh Guthrie, and Sanda M Harabagiu. 2012. Empatweet: Annotating and detecting emotions on twitter. In *LREC*, pages 3806–3813.

Richard M Ryan, Jessey H Bernstein, and Kirk Warren Brown. 2010. Weekends, work, and well-being: Psychological need satisfactions and day of the week effects on mood, vitality, and physical symptoms. *Journal of social and clinical psychology*, 29(1):95–122.

Marcin Skowron. 2010. Affect listeners: Acquisition of affective states by means of conversational systems. In *Development of Multimodal Interfaces: Active Listening and Synchrony*, pages 169–181.

Alessandro Sordoni, Michel Galley, Michael Auli, Chris Brockett, Yangfeng Ji, Meg Mitchell, Jian-Yun Nie, Jianfeng Gao, and Bill Dolan. 2015. A neural network approach to context-sensitive generation of conversational responses. In *In NAACL-HLT*.

B.R. Steunebrink, M.M. Dastani, and J.-J.Ch. Meyer. 2009. The occ model revisited. In *Proceedings of the 4th Workshop on Emotion and Computing*, pages 478–484.

Maryam Tavafi, Yashar Mehdad, Shafiq Joty, Giuseppe Carenini, and Raymond Ng. 2013. Dialogue act recognition in synchronous and asynchronous conversations. In *Proceedings of the SIGDIAL*, pages 117–121.

Grigorios Tsoumakas and Ioannis Katakis. 2006. Multi-label classification: An overview. *Dept. of Informatics, Aristotle University of Thessaloniki, Greece*.

Laurence Vidrascu and Laurence Devillers. 2005. Detection of real-life emotions in call centers. In *INTERSPEECH*, pages 1841–1844.

Deborah Tannen Wallace Chafe. 1987. The relation between written and spoken language. *Annual Review of Anthropology*, pages 383–407.

Valarie A Zeithaml, Mary Jo Bitner, and Dwayne D Gremler. 2006. Services marketing: Integrating customer focus across the firm.

L. Zhang, L. B. Erickson, and H. C. Webb. 2011. Effects of emotional text on online customer service chat. In *Graduate Student Research Conference in Hospitality and Tourism*.

Leonieke G Zomerdijk and Christopher A Voss. 2010. Service design for experience-centric services. *Journal of Service Research*, 13(1):67–82.

Cultural Communication Idiosyncrasies in Human-Computer Interaction

Juliana Miehle[1], Koichiro Yoshino[3], Louisa Pragst[1],
Stefan Ultes[2], Satoshi Nakamura[3], Wolfgang Minker[1]
[1]Institute of Communications Engineering, Ulm University, Germany
[2]Department of Engineering, Cambridge University, UK
[3]Graduate School of Information Science, Nara Institute of Science and Technology, Japan

Abstract

In this work, we investigate whether the cultural idiosyncrasies found in human-human interaction may be transferred to human-computer interaction. With the aim of designing a culture-sensitive dialogue system, we designed a user study creating a dialogue in a domain that has the potential capacity to reveal cultural differences. The dialogue contains different options for the system output according to cultural differences. We conducted a survey among Germans and Japanese to investigate whether the supposed differences may be applied in human-computer interaction. Our results show that there are indeed differences, but not all results are consistent with the cultural models.

1 Introduction

Nowadays, intelligent agents are omnipresent. Furthermore, we live in a globally mobile society in which people of widely different cultural backgrounds live and work together. The number of people who leave their ancestral cultural environment and move to countries with different culture and language is increasing. This spurs the need for culturally sensitive conversation agents. Hence, our aim is to design a culture-aware dialogue system which allows a communication in accordance with the user's cultural idiosyncrasies. By adapting the system's behaviour to the user's cultural background, the conversation agent may appear more familiar and trustworthy.

However, it is unclear whether cultural idiosyncrasies found in human-human interaction (HHI) may be transferred to human-computer interaction (HCI) as it has been shown that there exist clear differences in HHI and HCI (Doran et al., 2003). To investigate this, we designed and conducted a user study with a dialogue in German and

Japanese containing cultural relevant system reactions. In every dialogue turn, the study participants had to indicate their preference concerning the system output. With the findings of the study, we demonstrate whether there are different preferences in communication style in HCI and which concepts of HHI may be applied.

The structure of the remaining paper is as follows: In Section 2, related work is presented. Subsequently, in Section 3, we present the cultural idiosyncrasies which we consider relevant for spoken dialogue systems. In Section 4, we present cultural differences between Germany and Japan supposed by the cultural models for HHI. The concept and the results of our study are presented in Section 5 before concluding in Section 6.

2 Significant Related Work

Brejcha (2015) has described patterns of language and culture in HCI and has shown why these patterns matter and how to exploit them to design a better user interface. Furthermore, Traum (2009) has outlined how cultural aspects may be included in the design of a visual human-like body and the intelligent cognition driving action of the body of a virtual human. Therefore, different cultural models have been examined and the author points out steps for a fuller model of culture. Georgila and Traum (2011) have presented how culture-specific dialogue policies of virtual humans for negotiation and in particular for argumentation and persuasion may be built. A corpus of non-culture specific dialogues is used to build simulated users which are then employed to learn negotiation dialogue policies using Reinforcement Learning. However, only negotiation specific aspects are taken into account while we aim to create an overall culture-sensitive dialogue system which takes into account cultural idiosyncrasies in every decision and adapts not only what is said, but also how it is said to the user's cultural background.

Proceedings of the SIGDIAL 2016 Conference, pages 74–79,
Los Angeles, USA, 13-15 September 2016. ©2016 Association for Computational Linguistics

3 Integrating cultural idiosyncrasies

In a culturally aware intelligent conversation agent, the Dialogue Management (DM) sitting at the core of a dialogue system (Minker et al., 2009) has to be aware of cultural interaction idiosyncrasies to generate culturally appropriate output. Hence, the DM is not only responsible for what is said next, but also for how it is said. This is what makes the difference to generic DM where the two main tasks are to track the dialogue state and to select the next system action, i.e., what is uttered by the system (Ultes and Minker, 2014).

According to various cultural models (Hofstede, 2009; Elliott et al., 2016; Kaplan, 1966; Lewis, 2010; Qingxue, 2003), different cultures prefer different communication styles. There are four dimensions which we consider relevant for DM:

Animation/Emotion The display of emotions and the apparent involvement in a topic can be perceived very differently across cultures. While in some cultures the people are likely to express their emotions, in other cultures this is quite unusual.

Directness/Indirectness Information provided for the user has to be presented suitable so that the user is more likely to accept it. It has to be decided whether the intent is directly expressed (e.g. "Drink more water.") or if an indirect communication style is chosen (e.g. "Drinking more water may help with headaches.") whereby the listener has to deduce the intent from the context.

Identity Orientation Internalised self-perception and certain values influence the decisions of humans which depend on their culture. Hence, arguments addressing these values may be constructed based on the user's culture. In some cultures, the people are individualistically oriented which means that the peoples' personal goals take priority over their allegiance to groups or group goals and decisions are made individualistically. In other cultures, the people are collectivistically oriented which means that there is a greater emphasis on the views, needs, and goals for the group rather than oneself and decisions are often made in relation to obligations to the group (e.g. family).

Thought Patterns and Rhetorical Style Different cultures use different argumentation styles (e.g. linear, parallel, circular and digressive). In a discussion, the way arguments are presented helps to provide necessary information to the user in an appropriate way. Additionally, some cultures have low-context communication whereas other cultures have high-context communication. In low-context communication, there is a low use of non-verbal communication. Therefore, the people need background information and expect messages to be detailed. In contrast, in high-context communication, there is a high use of non-verbal communication and the people do not require, nor do they expect much in-depth background information. Taking these facts into account means that the DM has to make a very detailed decision about how to present the information to the user.

4 Cultural differences

According to the aforementioned cultural models, various cultural differences are expected to exist between Germany and Japan. However, concerning *Animation/Emotion*, both Germans and Japanese are not expected to be emotionally expressive. According to (Elliott et al., 2016), both cultures avoid intensely emotional interactions as they may lead to a loss of self-control. Lewis (2010) affirms the fact that both Germans and Japanese don't like losing their face. Hence, emotionally expressive communication is not a preferred mode and the people try to preserve a friendly appearance.

Regarding *Directness/Indirectness*, Elliot et al. (2016) and Lewis (2010) indeed supposes differences between Germany and Japan in their cultural model. While Germans tend to speak very direct about certain things, Japanese prefer an implicit and indirect communication.

According to (Hofstede, 2009; Elliott et al., 2016; Lewis, 2010; Qingxue, 2003), the *Identity Orientation* is also expected to be different for Germans and Japanese. Germans are supposed to be rather individualistically oriented and the personal goals take priority over the allegiance to groups or group goals. In contrast, Japanese are more collectivistically oriented and often make their decisions in relation to obligations to their family or other groups. They tend to be people-oriented and the self is often subordinated in the interests of harmony.

In terms of *Thought Patterns and Rhetorical Style*, the cultural models also suppose various differences between Germans and Japanese. First of all, Qingxue (2003) states that Germans have a low-context communication while Japanese have a high-context communication. Therefore, Germans need background information and expect messages to be detailed. In contrast, Japanese provide a lot of information through gestures, the use of space, and even silence. Most of the information is not explicitly transmitted in the verbal part of the message. Furthermore, according to (Elliott et al., 2016), the two cultures are expected to use different argumentation styles. For Germans, directness in stating the point, purpose, or conclusion of a communication is the preferred style while for Japanese this is not considered appropriate.

5   Concept and Evaluation

Based on the cultural differences in the dimensions *Directness/Indirectness*, *Identity Orientation* and *Thought Patterns and Rhetorical Style* which have been presented in Section 4, we have designed a study to investigate if these differences may be transferred to HCI. We formulated four hypotheses:

1. Germans choose options with direct communication more often than Japanese do.

2. Japanese choose options with motivation using group oriented arguments more often than Germans do.

3. Germans choose options with background information more often than Japanese do.

4. There are differences in the selection of argumentation styles.

Experimental Setting   For the study, a dialogue in the healthcare domain has been created. This domain has the potential capacity to reveal such differences as very sensitive subjects are covered. For every system output, different variations have been formulated. Each of them has been adapted according to the supposed cultural differences. The participants assumed the role of a caregiver who is caring for their father.

In the beginning of the dialogue, the agent greets the user. The user also greets him and tells him that their father doesn't drink enough. The agent asks how much he usually drinks and the answer is that he drinks only one cup of tea after breakfast. Afterwards, different possibilities for the agent's output are presented. The first one doesn't contain any background information: "You're right, that's not enough. Do you know why your father doesn't drink enough?" In contrast, the other four options include some background information why it is important for an adult to drink at least 1.5 litres of water per day. However, they differ in the argumentation style (parallel, linear, circular, digressive). The user answers that he doesn't know why their father doesn't drink enough. Then, the agent has different proposals how the water-intake may be increased and there are four different options for each proposal how it is presented to the user. The first option contains background information and expresses the content directly. The second option is also direct but doesn't give any background information. For the third and the fourth options an indirect communication style is chosen, whereby one option contains background information and the other doesn't. An example for the different options can be found in Table 1.

Option	Formulation
1	Offer him tea instead of water. It tastes good and is not as bad as soft drinks.
2	Offer him tea instead of water.
3	Offering tea instead of water can help. It tastes good and is not as bad as soft drinks.
4	Offering tea instead of water can help.

Table 1: There are four different options for each proposal how it is presented to the user: (1) direct, background information, (2) direct, no background information, (3) indirect, background information, (4) indirect, no background information.

In the end of the dialogue, the agent tries to motivate the user. Two different kinds of motivation are formulated and presented by the agent. The first one uses individualistically oriented arguments ("You're really doing a great job! It's impressive that you are able to handle all of this.") whereas the second one uses group oriented arguments ("You're really a big help for your family!"). Afterwards, the agent and the user say goodbye and the dialogue ends.

The survey has been conducted on-line. A video for each possible system output has been created using a Spoken Dialogue System with an animated agent. For all recordings, the same system and the same agent have been used. In each dialogue turn, the participants had to watch videos representing the different variants of the system output and decide which one they prefer. An example

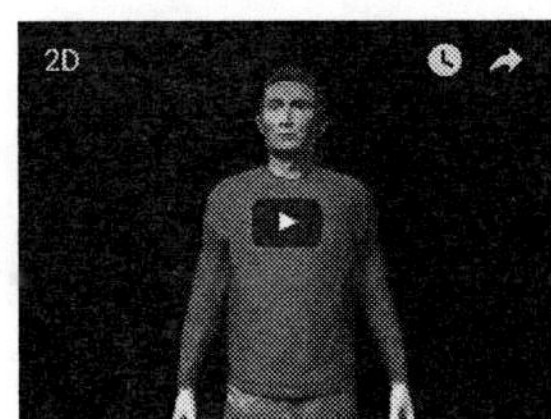

Figure 1: In each dialogue turn, the participants had to watch different videos and decide which one they prefer.

of this web page is shown in Figure 1. During the survey, all descriptions have been provided in English, German and Japanese. The videos have been recorded in English and subtitled in German and Japanese. The translations have been made by German and Japanese native speakers who were instructed to be aware of the linguistic features and details of the cultural differences to assure equivalence in the translations.

The survey Altogether, 65 Germans and 46 Japanese participated in the study. They have been recruited using mailing lists and social networks. The participants are aged between 15 and 62 years. The average age of the Germans is 25.7 years while the average age of the Japanese participants is 27.9 years. The gender distribution of the participants is shown in Table 2. It can be seen that 65 % of the German and only 17 % of the Japanese participants are female.

	German	Japanese
male / female	23 / 42	38 / 8

Table 2: The participants' gender distribution.

Evaluation results The evaluation of the survey confirms our main hypothesis that Germans and Japanese have different preferences in communication style in HCI.

Our first hypotheses says that Germans choose options with direct communication more often than Japanese do. The study contains four questions where the participants have to choose be-

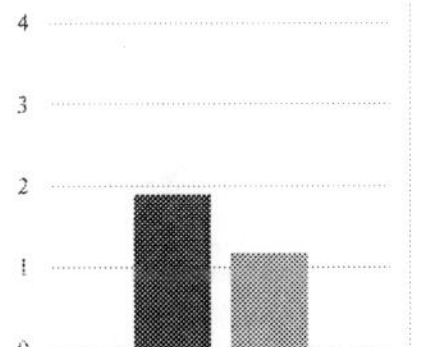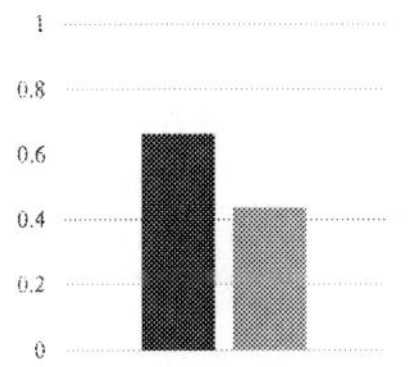

(a) On average, Germans (dark) choose options with direct communication significantly ($p < 0.001$) more often than Japanese (light) do ($M_{Ger} = 1.89$, $M_{Jap} = 1.17$).

(b) On average, Germans (dark) choose options with motivation using group oriented arguments significantly ($p < 0.05$) more often than Japanese (light) do ($M_{Ger} = 0.66$, $M_{Jap} = 0.43$).

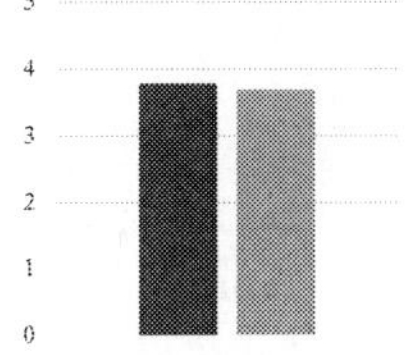

(c) On average, both Germans (dark) and Japanese (light) prefer options with background information ($M_{Ger} = 3.77$, $M_{Jap} = 3.67$). There is no significant difference.

Figure 2: Differences between Germans/Japanese.

tween direct and indirect options. Figure 2a shows the mean of how often Germans (dark grey) and Japanese (light grey) selected the direct option. The German mean is with 1.89 significantly higher than the Japanese mean ($p < 0.001$ using the T-Test) thus confirming our hypothesis.

Our second hypotheses says that Japanese choose options with motivation using group oriented arguments more often than Germans do. The survey includes one system action where the agent motivates the user. Figure 2b shows the mean of how often Germans (dark grey) and Japanese (light grey) selected the motivation with group oriented arguments. It can be seen that the opposite of the hypothesised effect occurred. On average, the Germans chose the option with group oriented arguments more often than the Japanese ($p < 0.05$ using the T-Test). An explanation for this result might be that motivation may be dependent on the topic of the dialogue. In our case, the dialogue is in the healthcare domain and caring for a family member is inherently group oriented. Therefore, it is most likely that motivating using group oriented arguments is more preferred for individualistically oriented people. However, if for someone it is natural to care for a family member because he is group oriented, then motivation using group oriented arguments is not needed and individualistically oriented arguments seem to be favoured.

Our third hypotheses says that Germans choose options with background information more often than Japanese do. The survey comprises five questions where the participants could select between system outputs with and without background information. Figure 2c shows the mean of how often Germans (dark grey) and Japanese (light grey) selected the option with background information. On average, both Germans and Japanese preferred the options with background information. This suggests that there is no non-verbal communication in this kind of HCI which is only based on speech and does not include other modalities (the agent in the videos does not produce any output but the speech). In this case, Japanese tend to miss the non-verbal communication which they use to have in HHI and therefore need verbal background information.

Our last hypotheses says that there are differences in the selection of argumentation styles. The survey contains one system output where the participants have to choose between different argumentation styles. However, no significant difference could be found.

Due to the difference in the gender distribution, it is important to investigate whether this has an effect on the overall results. As can be seen in Figure 3, only for *Thought Patterns and Rhetorical Style*, a significant difference has been found: on average, women chose options with background information more often than men. However, as the majority of both genders and both cultures chose the options with background information ($M_m > 2.5$, $M_w > 2.5$, $M_{Ger} > 2.5$, $M_{Jap} > 2.5$), the difference between the genders is not supposed to effect the result based on the culture.

6 Conclusion and Future Directions

In this work, we presented a study investigating whether cultural communication idiosyncrasies found in HHI may also be observed during HCI in a Spoken Dialogue System context. Therefore, we have created a dialogue with different options for the system output according to the supposed differences. In an on-line survey on the user's preference concerning the different options we have shown that there are indeed differences between Germany and Japan. However, not all results are consistent with the existing cultural models for HHI. This suggests that the communication pat-

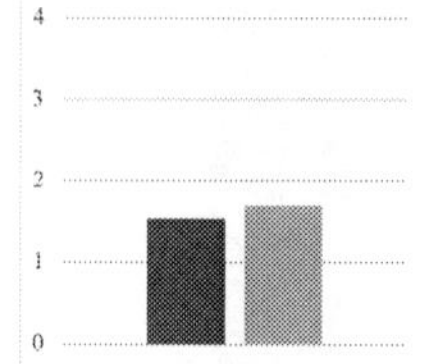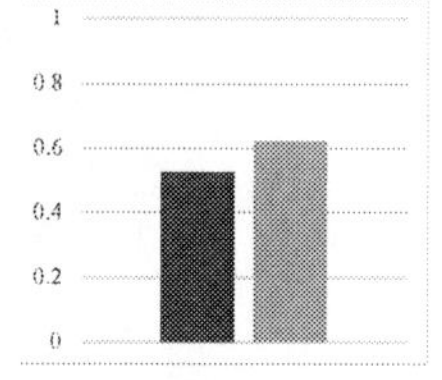

(a) On average, both men (dark) and women (light) prefer options with indirect communication ($M_m = 1.52$, $M_w = 1.68$). There is no significant difference.

(b) On average, both men (dark) and women (light) prefer options with motivation using group oriented arguments ($M_m = 0.52$, $M_w = 0.62$). There is no significant difference.

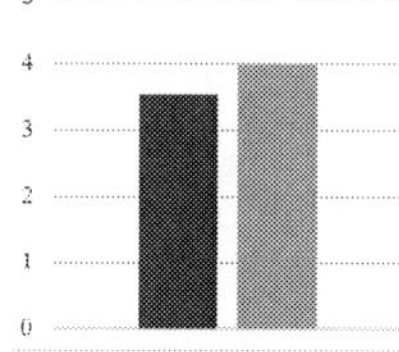

(c) On average, women (light) choose options with background information significantly ($p < 0.05$) more often than men (dark) do ($M_m = 3.52$, $M_w = 3.98$).

Figure 3: Differences between men/women.

terns are not only influenced by the culture, but also by the dialogue domain and the user emotion. Moreover, it is shown that not all cultural idiosyncrasies that occur in HHI may be applied for HCI.

In this work, only one specific dialogue has been considered. To get a more general view and exclude effects which may depend rather on the domain than on the culture, in future work other dialogues from different domains should be examined. Furthermore, we have to identify how the defined cultural idiosyncrasies may be implemented in the Dialogue Management to design a culture-sensitive spoken dialogue system.

Acknowledgements

This work is part of a project that has received funding from the *European Union's Horizon 2020 research and innovation programme* under grant agreement No 645012. This research and development work was also supported by the MIC/SCOPE #152307004.

References

Jan Brejcha. 2015. *Cross-Cultural Human-Computer Interaction and User Experience Design: A Semiotic Perspective*. CRC Press.

Christine Doran, John Aberdeen, Laurie Damianos, and Lynette Hirschman. 2003. Comparing several aspects of human-computer and human-human dialogues. In *Current and new directions in discourse and dialogue*, pages 133–159. Springer.

Candia Elliott, R. Jerry Adams, and Suganya Sockalingam. 2016. Multicultural toolkit: Toolkit for cross-cultural collaboration. Awesome Library. `http://www.awesomelibrary.org/multiculturaltoolkit.html`. Accessed: 2016-05-01.

Kallirroi Georgila and David Traum. 2011. Learning culture-specific dialogue models from non culture-specific data. In *Universal Access in Human-Computer Interaction. Users Diversity*, pages 440–449. Springer.

Geert Hofstede. 2009. *Culture's Consequences: Comparing Values, Behaviors, Institutions and Organizations Across Nations*. Sage.

Robert B. Kaplan. 1966. Cultural thought patterns in inter-cultural education. *Language learning*, 16(1-2):1–20.

Richard D. Lewis. 2010. *When Cultures Collide: Leading Across Cultures*. Brealey.

Wolfgang Minker, Ramón López-Cózar, and Michael F. McTear. 2009. The role of spoken language dialogue interaction in intelligent environments. *Journal of Ambient Intelligence and Smart Environments*, 1(1):31–36.

Liu Qingxue. 2003. Understanding different cultural patterns or orientations between east and west. *Investigationes Linguisticae*, 9:21–30.

David Traum. 2009. Models of culture for virtual human conversation. *Universal Access in Human-Computer Interaction. Applications and Services*, pages 434–440.

Stefan Ultes and Wolfgang Minker. 2014. Managing adaptive spoken dialogue for intelligent environments. *Journal of Ambient Intelligence and Smart Environments*, 6(5):523–539.

Using phone features to improve dialogue state tracking generalisation to unseen states

Iñigo Casanueva, Thomas Hain, Mauro Nicolao, and Phil Green
Department of Computer Science, University of Sheffield, United Kingdom
{i.casanueva, t.hain, m.nicolao, p.green}@sheffield.ac.uk

Abstract

The generalisation of dialogue state tracking to unseen dialogue states can be very challenging. In a slot-based dialogue system, dialogue states lie in discrete space where distances between states cannot be computed. Therefore, the model parameters to track states unseen in the training data can only be estimated from more general statistics, under the assumption that every dialogue state will have the same underlying state tracking behaviour. However, this assumption is not valid. For example, two values, whose associated concepts have different ASR accuracy, may have different state tracking performance. Therefore, if the ASR performance of the concepts related to each value can be estimated, such estimates can be used as general features. The features will help to relate unseen dialogue states to states seen in the training data with similar ASR performance. Furthermore, if two phonetically similar concepts have similar ASR performance, the features extracted from the phonetic structure of the concepts can be used to improve generalisation. In this paper, ASR and phonetic structure-related features are used to improve the dialogue state tracking generalisation to unseen states of an environmental control system developed for dysarthric speakers.

1 Introduction

Dialogue state tracking (DST) (Thomson and Young, 2010) is a key component for spoken interfaces for electronic devices. It maps the dialogue history up to the current dialogue turn (Spoken language understanding (SLU) output, actions taken by the device, etc.) to a probabilistic representation over the set of *dialogue states*[1] called the *belief state* (Young et al., 2013). This representation is the input later used by the dialogue policy to decide the next action to take (Williams and Young, 2007; Gašić and Young, 2014; Geist and Pietquin, 2011). In the Dialogue State Tracking Challenges (DSTC) (Williams et al., 2013; Henderson et al., 2014), it was shown that data driven discriminative models for DST outperform generative models in the context of a slot based dialogue system. However, generalisation to unseen dialogue states (e.g. changing the dialogue domain or extending it) remains an issue. The 3rd DSTC (Henderson et al., 2014b) evaluated state trackers in extended domains, by including dialogue states not seen in the training data in the evaluation data. This challenge showed the difficulty for data-driven approaches to generalise to unseen states, as several machine learned trackers were outperformed by the rule-based baseline. Data driven state trackers with slot-specific models cannot handle unseen states. Therefore, general state trackers track each value independently using general value-specific features (Henderson et al., 2014c; Mrksic et al., 2015). However, dialogue states are by definition in discrete space where similarities cannot be computed. Thus, a general state tracker has to include a general value-tracking model that can combine the statistics of all dialogue states. This strategy assumes that different dialogue states have the same state tracking behaviour, but such assumption is rarely true. For example, two values, whose associated concepts have different ASR accuracy, have differ-

---

[1]In a slot based dialogue system the dialogue states are defined as the set of possible value combinations for each slot. However, in this paper we use *dialogue states* to refer to the set of *slot-value* pairs and *joint dialogue states* to the actual dialogue states.

Proceedings of the SIGDIAL 2016 Conference, pages 80–89,
Los Angeles, USA, 13-15 September 2016. ©2016 Association for Computational Linguistics

ent state tracking performance. A general feature able to define similarities between dialogue states would improve state tracking generalisation to unseen states, as the new values could be tracked using statistics learned from the most similar states seen in the training data.

Dialogue management was shown to improve the performance of spoken control interfaces personalised to dysarthric speakers (Casanueva et al., 2014; Casanueva et al., 2015). For these type of interfaces (e.g. homeService (Christensen et al., 2013; Christensen et al., 2015)), the user interacts with the system using single word commands[2]. Each slot-value in the system has its associated command. It is a reasonable assumption that two dialogue states or values associated to commands with similar ASR accuracy will also have similar DST performance. If the ASR performance of commands can be estimated (e.g. in a held out set of recordings), the measure can be used as a general feature to help the state tracker relate unseen dialogue states to similar states seen in the training data.

However, a held out set of recordings can be costly to obtain. If it is assumed that phonetically similar commands will have similar recognition rates, general features extracted from the phonetic structure of the commands can be used. For example, the ASR can find "problematic phones", i.e. phones or phone sequences that are consistently misrecognised. Therefore, the state tracker can learn to detect such problematic phones and adapt its dialogue state inference to the presence of these phones. If an unseen dialogue state that contains these phone patterns is tracked, the state tracker can infer the probability of that state more efficiently. Using the command phonetic structure as additional feature for state tracking can be interpreted as moving from state tracking in the "command space", where similarities between dialogue states cannot be computed, to state tracking in the "phone space", where those similarities can be estimated.

In this paper, we propose a method to use ASR and phone-related general features to improve the generalisation of a Recurrent Neural Network (RNN) based dialogue state tracker to unseen states. In the next section, state-of-the-art methods for generalised state tracking are de-

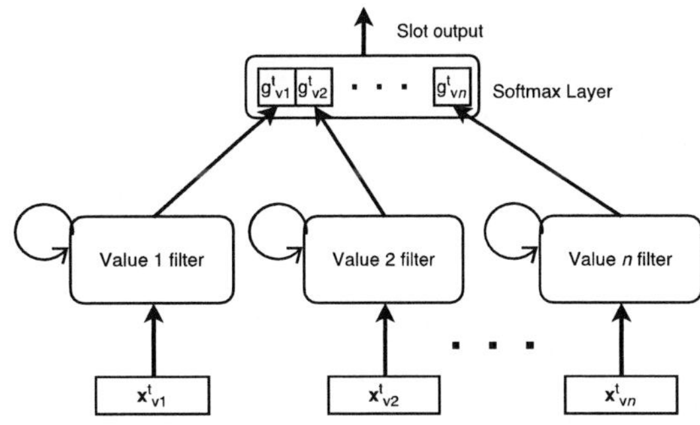

Figure 1: *General DST for a single slot.*

scribed. Following section describes the proposed ASR and phone-related features as well as different approaches to encode variable length phone sequences into fixed length vectors. Section 4 describes the experimental set-up. Sections 5 and 6 present results and conclusions.

2 Generalised dialogue state tracking

In slot-based dialogue state tracking, the *ontology* defines the set of slots S and the set of possible values for each slot V_s. A dialogue state tracker is hence a classifier, where classes correspond to the joint dialogue states. However, slot-based trackers often factorise the joint dialogue state into slots and therefore use a classifier to track each slot independently (Lee, 2013). Then, the set of values for that slot V_s are the classes. The joint dialogue state is computed by multiplication and renormalisation of individual probabilities for each slot. Even if the factorisation of the dialogue state helps to generalise by reducing the number of effective dialogue states or values to track, slot specifically trained state trackers are not able to generalise to unseen values as they learn the specific statistics of each slot and value. State trackers able to generalise to unseen values track the probability of each value independently using value specific general features, such as the confidence score of the concept associated to that value in the SLU output (Henderson et al., 2014d).

2.1 Rule based state tracking

Rule-based state trackers (Wang and Lemon., 2013; Sun et al., 2014b) use slot-value independent rules to infer the probability of each dialogue state. An example is the sum of confidence scores of the concept related to that value or the answers confirming that the value is correct. Rule based methods show a competitive performance when evaluated in new or extended domains, as

---

[2]Severe dysarthric speakers cannot articulate complete sentences.

it was demonstrated in the 3rd DSTC. However, low adaptability can reduce the performance in domains that are challenging for ASR.

2.2 Slot-value independent data-driven state tracking

In the first two DSTC, most of the data driven approaches to dialogue state tracking learned specific statistics for each slot and value (Lee, 2013; Williams, 2014). However, in some cases (Lee and Eskenazi., 2013), parameter tying was used across slot models, thereby assuming that the statistics of two slots can be similar. The 3rd DSTC addressed domain extension, and state trackers able to generalise to unseen dialogue states had to be developed. One of the most successful approaches (Henderson et al., 2014d) combined the output of two RNNs trackers: one represented slot-specific statistics and the other modelled slot-value independent general statistics. Later, (Mrksic et al., 2015) modified this model to be able to track the dialogue state in completely different domains by using only the general part of the model of (Henderson et al., 2014d). The slot-value independent model (shown in Fig. 1) comprises of a set of binary classifiers or *value filters*[3], one for each slot-value pair, with parameters shared across all filters. These filters track each value independently, and the slot s output distribution in each turn is obtained by concatenating the outputs of each value filter g_v^t in $\mathcal{V}_s$, followed by applying a softmax function. The set of filters only differs from each other in two aspects: in the input composed by value specific general features (also called *delexicalized features*); and in the label used during the training. An RNN-based general state tracker[4] updates the probability of each value p_v^t in each turn t as follows:

$$\mathbf{h}_v^t = \sigma(\mathbf{W}_x \mathbf{x}_v^t + \mathbf{W}_h \mathbf{h}_v^{t-1} + \mathbf{b}_h)$$
$$g_v^t = \sigma(\mathbf{w}_g \mathbf{h}_v^t + b_g)$$
$$p_v^t = \frac{\exp(g_v^t)}{\sum_{v' \in V} \exp(g_{v'}^t)} \qquad (1)$$

Where $\mathbf{h}_v^t$ is the hidden state of each filter, $\mathbf{x}_v^t$ are the value specific inputs and $\mathbf{W}_x$, $\mathbf{W}_h$, $\mathbf{b}_h$, $\mathbf{w}_g$ and b_g are the parameters of the model.

---

[3]Addressed as *filters* due to their resemblance with convolutional neural networks filters.

[4]This is a simplified version of the model described in (Mrksic et al., 2015).

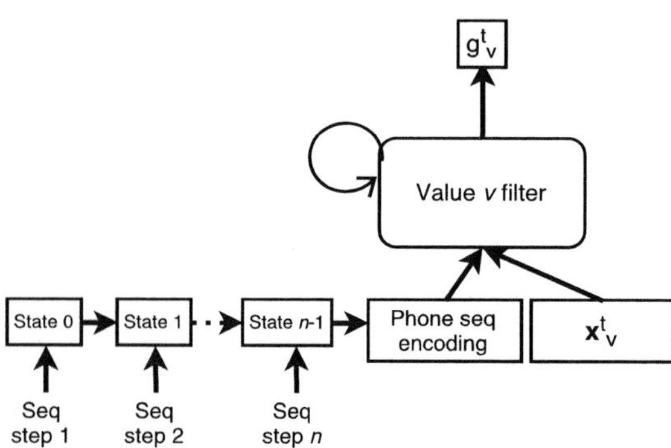

Figure 2: *Joint RNN encoder.*

3 ASR and phone-related general features

The model explained in section 2.2 works with value-specific general features $\mathbf{x}_v^t$ (e.g. the confidence score seen for that particular value in that turn). These features do not help to relate dialogue states with similar state tracking performance, thus the model has to learn the mean statistics from all the states. However, different values have different state tracking performance. Features that can give information about the ASR performance or that can be used to relate the state tracking performance of values seen in the training data to unseen states, should allow to generalise to new dialogue states. In the following section, we introduce various features that can improve generalisation.

3.1 ASR features

In a command-based environmental control system, if recordings of the commands related to the unseen dialogue states are available, they can be used to estimate the ASR performance for the new commands. Then, the value specific features for each filter can be extended by concatenating the ASR accuracy of that specific value. When the tracker faces a value not seen in the training data, it can improve the estimation of the probability of that value by using the statistics learnt form values with similar ASR performance.

3.2 Phone related features

In the previous section, accuracy estimates were proposed to improve general state tracking accuracy. However, these features would have to be inferred from a held out set of word recordings, which may not always be available. In order to avoid this requirement, the phonetic structure of

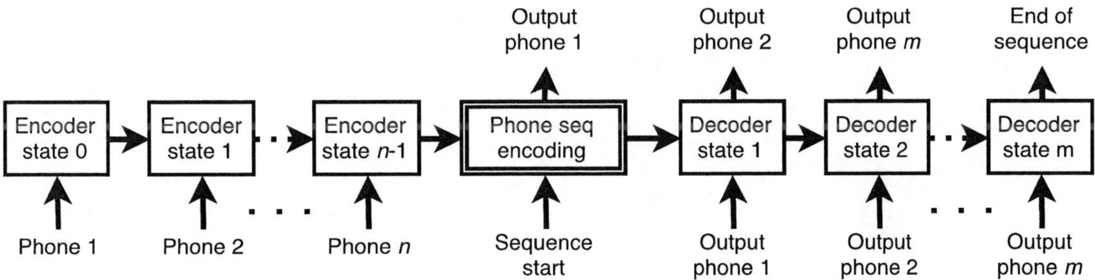

Figure 3: *Seq2seq phone encoder.*

the commands can be used to find similarities between dialogue states with similar ASR performance. The phonetic structure of the commands can be seen as a space composed by subunits of the commands, where similarities between states can be computed.

Phone related features can be extracted in several ways. A deep neural network trained jointly with the ASR can be used to extract a sequence of phone posterior features, one vector per speech frame (Christensen et al., 2013b). Another way is to use a pronunciation dictionary to decompose the output of the ASR into sequences of phones. The later method can be also used to extract a "phonetic fingerprint" of the associated value for each filter. For example, a filter which is tracking the value "RADIO", would have the sequence of phones "r-ey-d-iy-ow" as phonetic fingerprint.

In each dialogue turn, these features are based on sequences of different length. In the case of the ASR phone posteriors, the sequence length is equal to the number of speech frames. When using a pronunciation dictionary, the length is equal to the number of phonemes in the command. However, in each dialogue turn, a fixed length vector should be provided as input of the tracker. Thus, a method to transform these sequences into fixed length vectors is needed. A straightforward method is to compute the mean vector of the sequence, thereby loosing the phone order information. In addition, the number of phones that the sequence has would affect the value of each phone in the mean vector. To compress these sequences in fixed length vectors while maintaining the ordering and the phone length of the sequence, we propose to use a RNN encoder (Cho et al., 2014). We propose two ways to train this encoder, jointly with the model, and with a large pronunciation dictionary.

3.2.1 Joint RNN phone encoder

The state of an RNN is a vector representation of all the previous sequence inputs seen by the model. Therefore, the final state after processing a sequence can be seen as a fixed length encoding of the sequence. If this encoding is put to the filters of the state tracker (Fig. 2), the tracker and the encoder can be trained jointly using backpropagation. We propose to concatenate the encoding of the phonetic sequence in each turn with the value specific features $\mathbf{x}_v^t$ for each filter as shown in Fig. 2. This defines a structure with two stacked RNNs, one encoding the phonetic sequences per turn and the other processing the sequence of dialogue turns.

3.2.2 Seq2seq phone encoder

The need to encode the phone sequences into fixed length "dense" representations which allow to compute similarities, resembles the computing of word embeddings (Mikolov et al., 2013). The difference lies in the fact that word embedding transforms one-hot encodings of words into dense vectors, while in the scope of this work we transform *sequences* of one-hot encodings of phones into dense vectors. Sequence to sequence models (a.k.a. *seq2seq* models, RNN encoder-decoders), can be used to perform such a task. These models consist of two RNNs; an *encoder* which processes the input sequence into a fixed length vector (the final RNN state); and a *decoder*, which "unrolls" the encoded state into an output sequence (Fig. 3). These models have shown state-of-the-art performance in machine translation tasks (Cho et al., 2014), and have been applied to text-based dialogue management with promising results (Lowe et al., 2015; Wen et al., 2016). For the task of generating dense representations of phone sequences, the seq2seq model is trained in a similar way to auto-encoders (Vincent et al., 2008), where in-

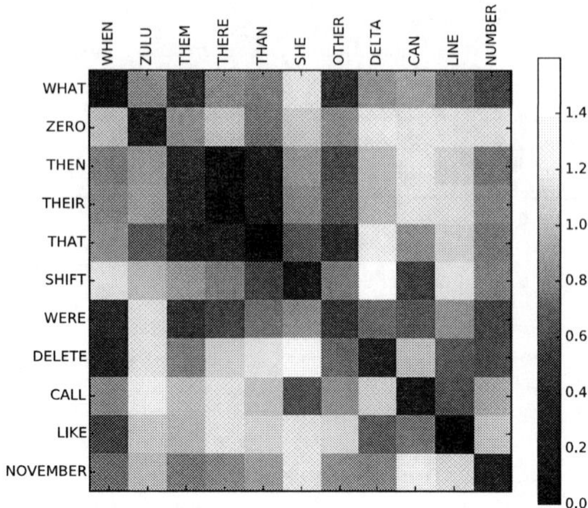

Figure 4: *Cosine distance in the phone encoding space of different words of the UASpeech database.*

put and target sequences are the same, forcing the model to learn to reconstruct the input sequence. The final state of the encoder RNN (the two-line block in Fig. 3) is taken as dense representation of the phone sequence. For this task, the *combilex* pronunciation dictionary (Richmond et al., 2010) is used to train the model. An RNN composed of two layers of 20 LSTM units is able to reconstruct 95% of the phone sequences in an independent evaluation set. This means compressing sequences of one-hot vectors of size 45 (the number of phones in US English) into a vector of size 20. In Fig. 4, the cosine distance between the dense phone representations of two sets of words of the UASpeech database (see sec. 4.1.1) is plotted, illustrating that these encodings are able to effectively relate words with similar phone composition.

4 Experimental setup

The experiments are performed within the context of a voice-enabled control system designed to help speakers with dysarthria to interact with their home devices (Christensen et al., 2013; Casanueva et al., 2016). The user can interact with the system in a mixed initiative way, speaking single-word commands from a total set of 36. As the ASR is configured to recognise single words (Christensen et al., 2012), the SLU operates a direct mapping from the ASR output, an N-Best list of words, to an N-Best list of commands. The dialogue state of the system is factorized into three slots, with

the values of the first slot representing the devices to control (TV, light, bluray...), the second slot its functionalities (channel, volume...) and the third slot the actions that these functionalities can perform (up, two, off...). The slots have 4, 17 and 15 values respectively, and the combination of the values of the three slots compose the joint dialogue state or *goal* (e.g. TV-channel-five, bluray-volume-up). The set of valid[5] joint goals $\mathcal{J}$ has a cardinality of 63, and the belief state for each joint goal j is obtained by multiplying the slot probabilities of each of the individual slot values and normalising:

$$P(j) = \frac{P_{s1}(j_1)P_{s2}(j_2)P_{s3}(j_3)}{\sum_{h\in\mathcal{J}} P_{s1}(h_1)P_{s2}(h_2)P_{s3}(h_3)} \quad (2)$$

where $P_{sx}(j_x)$ is the probability of the value j_x in slot s_x and $j = (j_1, j_2, j_3)$.

4.1 Dialogue corpus

One of the main problems in dialogue management research is the lack of annotated dialogue corpora. The corpora released for the first three DSTCs aimed to mitigate this problem. However, this corpus does not include acoustic data. Hence, features extracted from the acoustics such as phone posteriors cannot be used. A large part of dialogue management research relies on *simulated users* (SU) (Georgila et al., 2006; Schatzmann et al., 2007; Thomson et al., 2012) for collection of the data needed. The dialogue corpus used in the following experiments has been generated with simulated users interacting with a rule based dialogue manager. To simulate data collected from dysarthric speakers, a set of 6 SUs with dysarthria has been created.

To simulate data in two different domains, two environmental control systems are simulated, each controlled with a different vocabulary of 36 commands. 72 commands selected from the set of 155 more frequent words in the UASpeech database (Kim et al., 2008), and split into 2 groups, which are named *domain A* and *domain B*. 1000 dialogues are collected in each domain[6]. To be sure that the methods work independently of the set of commands selected, 3 different vocabularies of 72 words are randomly selected and the results presented in the following section show the mean results for the 3 vocabularies.

---

[5]Many combinations of slot values are not valid sequences, e.g. light-channel-on.

[6]200 extra dialogues are collected in *domain B* for the second set of experiments in section 5.

4.1.1 Simulated dysarthric users

Each SU is composed of a *behaviour simulator* and an *ASR simulator*. The *behaviour simulator* decides on the commands uttered by the SU in each turn. It is rule-based and depending on the machine action, it chooses a command corresponding to the value of a slot or answers a confirmation question. To simulate confusions by the user, it uses a probability of producing a different command, or of providing a value for a different slot than the requested one. The probabilities of confusion vary to simulate different expertise levels with the system. Three different levels are used to generate the corpus to increase its variability.

The *ASR simulator* generates ASR N-best outputs. These N-best lists are sampled from ASR outputs of commands uttered by dysarthric speakers from the UASpeech database, using the ASR model presented in (Christensen et al., 2014). To increase the variability of the data generated, the time scale of each recording is modified to 10% and 20% slower and 10% and 20% faster, generating more ASR outputs to sample from. Phone posterior features are generated as described in (Christensen et al., 2013b) without the principal component analysis (PCA) dimensionality reduction. Six different SUs, corresponding to low- and mid-intelligible speakers, are created from the UASpeech database. ASR accuracy on these users ranges from 32% to 60%.

4.1.2 Rule-based state tracker

One of the trackers used in the DSTCs as baseline (Wang and Lemon., 2013) has been used to collect the corpus. This baseline tracker performed competitively in the 3 DSTCs, proving its capability to generalise to unseen states. The state tracking accuracy of this tracker is also used as the baseline in the following experiments.

4.1.3 Rule-based dialogue policy

The dialogue policy used to collect the corpus follows simple rules to decide the action to take in each turn. For each slot, if the maximum belief of that slot is below a threshold, the system will ask for that slot's value. If the belief is above that threshold but below a second one, it will confirm the value. If the maximum beliefs of all slots are above the second threshold, it will take the action corresponding to the joint goal with the highest probability. The thresholds values are optimised by grid search to maximise the dialogue reward. In addition, the policy implements a stochastic behaviour to induce variability in the collected data; choosing a different action with probability p and requesting the values of the slots in a different order. The corpus is collected using two different policy parameter sets.

4.2 General LSTM-based state tracker

A general dialogue state tracker, based on the model described on section 2.2, has been implemented. Each value filter is composed by a linear feedforward layer of size 20 and a LSTM (Hochreiter and Schmidhuber, 1997) layer of size 30. *Dropout* (Srivastava et al., 2014) regularisation is used in order to reduce overfitting with dropout rate of 0.2 in the input connections and 0.5 in the remaining non-recurrent connections. The models are trained for 60 iterations with stochastic gradient descent. A validation set consisting on 20% of the training data is used to choose the parameter set corresponding to the best iteration. Model combination is also used to avoid overfitting. Every model is trained with 3 different seeds, and 5 different parameter sets are saved for each seed, one for the best iteration in the first 20, and then another for the best iteration in each interval of 10 iterations.

4.2.1 ASR and phone related general features

In each turn t, each value-specific state tracker (filter) takes as input the value-specific input features $\mathbf{x}_v^t$. In this model, these correspond to the confidence score of the command related to the specific value, the confidence scores of the meta-commands such as "yes" or "no" and a one-hot encoding of the last system action. In addition, the models are evaluated concatenating the value specific features $\mathbf{x}_v^t$ with the following ASR and phone related general features $\mathbf{z}_v^t$:

•*ValAcc*: The ASR performance of the command corresponding to the value of the tracker can be used as general feature. In this paper, the accuracy per command is used, defining $\mathbf{z}_v^t$ as the estimated ASR accuracy of the value v.

•*PhSeq*: A weighted sequence of phones is generated form the ASR output (N-best list of commands) as described below. A pronunciation dictionary is used to translate each word into a sequence of one-hot encodings of phones (the size of the one-hot encoding is 45, as the number of phones in US English). Each of these encodings is weighted by the confidence score of that command in the N-best list. This sequence is fed into an RNN as explained in section 3.2.1, and $\mathbf{z}_v^t$ is de-

	Joint	Slot 1	Slot 2	Slot 3	Mean
Baseline	50.51%	81.00%	51.53%	55.72%	62.75%
General	68.87%	87.59%	66.57%	67.68%	73.95%
ValAcc	74.13%	88.90%	72.16%	66.59%	75.88%
PhSeq	68.38%	89.30%	66.20%	67.74%	74.41%
PostSeq	67.92%	89.20%	65.94%	67.61%	74.25%
ValPhEnc	57.93%	77.91%	61.56%	59.31%	66.26%
PhSeq-ValPhEnc	58.56%	79.85%	62.03%	58.97%	66.95%

Table 1: Joint, mean and per slot state tracking accuracy of trackers trained on *domain A* and tested on *domain B* for trackers using different features.

fined as the vector corresponding to the final state of this RNN. The RNN is composed by a single *GRU* (Chung et al., 2014) layer of size 15.

•*PostSeq*: A sequence of vectors (one vector per speech frame) with monophone-state level posterior probabilities are extracted from the output layers of a Deep Neural Network trained on the UASpeech corpus. The extracted vectors contain the posteriors of each of the 3 states (initial, central, and final) for the 45 phones of US English. To reduce the dimensionality of vectors, the posteriors of the each phone states are merged by summing them. To reduce the length of the sequence, the mean of each group of 10 speech frames is taken. This produces a sequence of vectors of size 45 and maximum length of 20, which is fed into an RNN in the same way as *PhSeq* features to obtain $\mathbf{z}_v^t$.

•*ValPhEnc*: For each value filter, $\mathbf{z}_v^t$ is defined as the 20 dimensional encoding of the sequence of phones of the command associated to the value v, extracted from the *seq2seq* model defined in section 3.2.2. The encoder and decoder RNNs of the seq2seq model are composed of two layers of 20 LSTM units and the model is trained on the *combilex* dictionary (Richmond et al., 2010).

Note that two different kinds of features can be distinguished; *value identity* features and *ASR output* features. Value identity features (*ValAcc* and *ValPhEnc*) give information about the value tracked. These features are different for each filter (as each filter has a different associated value), but they do not change over turns (time invariant). ASR output features (*PhSeq* and *PostSeq*), on the other hand, give information about the ASR output observed. They are the same for each filter but change in each dialogue turn.

5 Results

The results presented are the joint state tracking accuracy, the accuracy of each individual slot and the mean accuracy of the 3 slots. This is because it was found that the relation between the mean slot accuracy and the joint accuracy is highly non-linear, due to the high dependency on the ontology of the joint goals, while the costs optimized are related to the mean accuracy of the slots[7]. All the following numbers represent the average results for the models tested with the 6 simulated users described in sec. 4.1.1.

Table 1 presents the accuracy results for the model described in section 4.2, using only value specific general features (*General*) and using the different features described in section 4.2.1. The models are trained on data from *domain A* and evaluated on data from *domain B*. *Baseline* presents the state tracking accuracy for the rule-based state tracker presented in section 4.1.2. It can be seen that the *General* tracker outperforms the baseline by more than 10%, suggesting that the baseline tracker does not perform well in ASR challenging environments. As it is expected, including the accuracy estimates (*ValAcc*) outperforms all the other approaches, especially on the joint goal. Including *PhSeq* features has a slightly worse performance in the joint but outperforms the *General* features in the mean slot accuracy. Comparing the slot by slot results, it can be seen that *PhSeq* features outperform *General* features in slot 1 accuracy by almost 2% while having similar behaviour in the other 2 slots. *PostSeq* features have a performance very similar to *PhSeq*, suggesting that both features carry very similar information. Surprisingly, *ValPhEnc* and *PhSeq-*

---

[7]When joining the slot outputs, the "invalid goals" are discarded as described in section 4. Future work will explore how to join the slot outputs more efficiently.

	Joint	**Slot 1**	**Slot 2**	**Slot 3**	**Mean**
General	68.97%	87.81%	66.91%	67.55%	74.09%
PhSeq	69.27%	89.54%	66.14%	68.24%	74.64%
ValAcc	74.65%	89.62%	72.73%	67.24%	76.53%
ValPhEnc	72.98%	89.88%	72.87%	75.66%	79.47%
PhSeq-ValPhEnc	73.48%	91.61%	74.03%	77.20%	80.95%
ValId	60.83%	86.38%	66.95%	75.08%	76.14%

Table 2: Joint, mean and per-slot state tracking accuracy of trackers when including 200 dialogues from *domain B* in the training data.

ValPhEnc perform much worse than the other features. A detailed examination of the training results showed that, compared to *General* features, these features were performing about 10% better in the validation set (*domain A*) while getting 10% worse results in the test set (*domain B*). This suggests a strong case of overfitting to the training data, probably caused because the vocabulary size (36 words for train and other 36 words for test) is not large enough for the model to find similarities between the phone encoding vectors.

To partially deal with this problem, Table 2 shows the accuracy results when 200 dialogues from *domain B* are included in the training data. Including these dialogues in the training data has a very slight effect with the *General* and *PhSeq* features. *ValPhEnc* features, however, show a large improvement, outperforming *General* features by 4% in the joint goal and more than 5% in the mean slot accuracy. This improvement is seen in all the slots individually. To be sure that the model is not just learning the identities of the words, *ValId* features extend the *General* features including a one-hot encoding of the word identity. As it can be seen, even if the performance in the joint goal is very low the mean slot accuracy improves the performance of *General* features by 2%. However, it is still more than 3% below the *ValPhEnc* features, showing that *ValPhEnc* features are not just learning the value identity, they are effectively correlating the performance of values similar in the phone encoding space. Finally, including the concatenation of *PhSeq* and *ValPhEnc* features, outperforms all the other approaches, even *ValAcc* features for the mean slot accuracy by more than 4%.

6 Conclusions

This paper has shown how the generalisation to unseen states of a dialogue state tracker can be improved by extending the value specific fea-tures with ASR accuracy estimates. Using an RNN encoder jointly trained with the general state tracker to encode phone-related sequential features slightly improved state tracking generalisation. However, when the model was trained using dense representations of phone sequences encoded with a *seq2seq* model, the tracker strongly overfitted to the training data, even if *dropout* regularization and model combination was used. This might be caused by the small variability of the command vocabulary (36 commands in each domain), which was not large enough for the model to find useful correlations between phone encodings. When a small amount of data from the unseen domain was included into the training data, phone encodings greatly boosted performance. This showed that phone encodings are useful as dense representations of the phonetic structure of the command, helping the model correlate state tracking performance of values close in the phonetic encoding space. This method was tested on a single-word command-based environmental control interface, where slot-value accuracies can easily be estimated. In addition, in this domain, the sequences of phonetic features are usually short. However, this method could be adapted to larger spoken dialogue systems by estimating the concept error rate of the SLU output of concepts related to slot-value pairs. Longer phonetic feature sequences could also be used to detect "problematic phones", or correlate sentences with similar phonetic composition, given enough variability of the training dataset to avoid overfitting.

Acknowledgments

The research leading to these results was supported by the University of Sheffield studentship network PIPIN and EPSRC Programme Grant EP/I031022/1 (Natural Speech Technology).

References

I. Casanueva, H. Christensen, T. Hain, and P. Green. 2014. *Adaptive speech recognition and dialogue management for users with speech disorders.* Proceedings of Interspeech.

I. Casanueva, T. Hain, H. Christensen, R. Marxer, and P. Green 2015. *Knowledge transfer between speakers for personalised dialogue management..* 16th Annual Meeting of the Special Interest Group on Discourse and Dialogue

I. Casanueva, T. Hain, and P. Green 2016. *Improving generalisation to new speakers in spoken dialogue state tracking..* Proceedings of Interspeech.

H. Christensen, S. Cunningham, C. Fox, P. Green, and T. Hain. 2012. *A comparative study of adaptive, automatic recognition of disordered speech.* Proceedings of Interspeech.

H. Christensen, I. Casanueva, S. Cunningham, P. Green, and T. Hain. 2013. *homeService: Voice-enabled assistive technology in the home using cloud-based automatic speech recognition.* Proceedings of SLPAT.

H. Christensen, I. Casanueva, S. Cunningham, P. Green, and T. Hain. 2014. *Automatic selection of speakers for improved acoustic modelling: recognition of disordered speech with sparse data.* Proceedings of SLT.

H. Christensen, M. B. Aniol, P. Bell, P. Green, T. Hain, S. King, and P. Swietojanski 2013. *Combining in-domain and out-of-domain speech data for automatic recognition of disordered speech.* proceedings of Interspeech.

H. Christensen, Nicolao, M., Cunningham, S., Deena, S., Green, P., and Hain, T. 2015. *Speech-Enabled Environmental Control in an AAL setting for people with Speech Disorders: a Case Study.* arXiv preprint arXiv:1604.04562.

K. Cho, B. van Merrienboer, C. Gulcehre, D. Bahdanau, F. Bougares, H. Schwenk, and Y. Bengio 2014. *Learning Phrase Representations using RNN Encoder-Decoder for Statistical Machine Translation.* EMNLP.

J. Chung, C. Gulcehre, K. Cho, and Y. Bengio 2014. *Empirical evaluation of gated recurrent neural networks on sequence modeling.* arXiv preprint arXiv:1412.3555.

M. Gašić and S. Young. 2014. *Gaussian Processes for POMDP-based dialogue manager opimisation.* IEEE Transactions on Audio, Speech and Language Processing.

M. Geist and O. Pietquin. 2011. *Managing uncertainty within the KTD framework.* Proceedings of JMLR.

K. Georgila, J. Henderson and O. Lemon. 2006. *User simulation for spoken dialogue systems: learning and evaluation.* proceedings of INTERSPEECH

M. Henderson, B. Thomson, and J. Williams. 2014. *The second dialog state tracking challenge.* 15th Annual Meeting of the Special Interest Group on Discourse and Dialogue

M. Henderson, B. Thomson, and J. Williams. 2014. *The third dialog state tracking challenge.* Spoken Language Technology Workshop (SLT)

M. Henderson, B. Thomson and S. Young. 2014. *Word-Based Dialog State Tracking with Recurrent Neural Networks.* Proceedings of the SIGDIAL 2014 Conference

M. Henderson, B. Thomson and S. Young 2014. *Robust dialog state tracking using delexicalised recurrent neural networks and unsupervised adaptation.* Spoken Language Technology Workshop (SLT)

S. Hochreiter and J. Schmidhuber. 1997. *Long short-term memory..* Neural computation

H. Kim, M. Hasegawa-Johnson, A. Perlman, J. Gunderson, T. Huang, K. Watkin, and S. Frame. 2008. *Dysarthric speech database for universal access research.* Proceedings of Interspeech.

S. Lee and M. Eskenazi. 2013. *Recipe For Building Robust Spoken Dialog State Trackers: Dialog State Tracking Challenge System Description.* Proceedings of the SIGDIAL 2013 Conference

S. Lee 2013. *Structured discriminative model for dialog state tracking.* Proceedings of the SIGDIAL 2013 Conference

R. Lowe, Pow, N., Serban, I., and Pineau, J. 2015. *The ubuntu dialogue corpus: A large dataset for research in unstructured multi-turn dialogue systems.* SIGDial conference

N. Mrksic, D. O. Saghdha, B. Thomson, M. Gai, P. H. Su, D. Vandyke, and S. Young 2015. *Multi-domain dialog state tracking using recurrent neural networks.* arXiv preprint arXiv:1506.07190.

T. Mikolov, I. Sutskever, K. Chen, G. S. Corrado, and J. Dean 2013. *Distributed Representations of Words and Phrases and their Compositionality.* Advances in neural information processing systems.

K. Sun, L. Chen, S. Zhu and K. Yu. 2014. *The SJTU System for Dialog State Tracking Challenge 2.* Proceedings of the SIGDIAL 2014 Conference.

K. Sun, L. Chen, S. Zhu and K. Yu. 2014. *A generalized rule based tracker for dialogue state tracking.* Spoken Language Technology Workshop (SLT).

K. Richmond, R. Clark, and S. Fitt. 2010. *On generating combilex pronunciations via morphological analysis.* Proceedings of Interspeech.

N. Srivastava, G. Hinton, A. Krizhevsky, I. Sutskever and R. Salakhutdinov. 2014. *Dropout: A simple way to prevent neural networks from overfitting*. The Journal of Machine Learning Research

J. Schatzmann, B. Thomson, K. Weilhammer, H. Ye and S. Young. 2006. *Agenda-based user simulation for bootstrapping a POMDP dialogue system*. Human Language Technologies

B. Thomson, and S. Young. 2010. *Bayesian update of dialogue state: A POMDP framework for spoken dialogue systems*. Computer Speech and Language.

B. Thomson, M. Gasic, M. Henderson, P. Tsiakoulis and S. Young. 2012. *N-best error simulation for training spoken dialogue systems*. Spoken Language Technology Workshop (SLT)

P. Vincent, H. Larochelle, Y. Bengio, and P. A. Manzagol 2008. *Extracting and composing robust features with denoising autoencoders*. Proceedings of the 25th international conference on Machine learning

Z. Wang, and O. Lemon. 2013. *A simple and generic belief tracking mechanism for the dialog state tracking challenge: On the believability of observed information*. Proceedings of the SIGDIAL 2013 Conference

J. Williams and S. Young. 2007. *Partially observable Markov decision processes for spoken dialog systems*. Computer Speech and Language.

J. Williams. 2014. *Web-style Ranking and SLU Combination for Dialog State Tracking*. Proceedings of SIGDIAL.

J. Williams, A. Raux, D. Ramachandran, and A. Black. 2013. *The dialog state tracking challenge*. Proceedings of the SIGDIAL 2013 Conference

T. Wen, Gasic, M., Mrksic, N., Rojas-Barahona, L. M., Su, P. H., Ultes, S., and Young, S. 2016. *A Network-based End-to-End Trainable Task-oriented Dialogue System*. arXiv preprint arXiv:1604.04562.

S. Young, M. Gašić, B. Thomson and J. D. Williams. 2013. *POMDP-Based Statistical Spoken Dialog Systems: A Review*. Proceedings of the IEEE.

Character Identification on Multiparty Conversation: Identifying Mentions of Characters in TV Shows

Henry (Yu-Hsin) Chen
Math and Computer Science
Emory University
Atlanta, GA 30322, USA
`henry.chen@emory.edu`

Jinho D. Choi
Math and Computer Science
Emory University
Atlanta, GA 30322, USA
`jinho.choi@emory.edu`

Abstract

This paper introduces a subtask of entity linking, called character identification, that maps mentions in multiparty conversation to their referent characters. Transcripts of TV shows are collected as the sources of our corpus and automatically annotated with mentions by linguistically-motivated rules. These mentions are manually linked to their referents through crowdsourcing. Our corpus comprises 543 scenes from two TV shows, and shows the inter-annotator agreement of $\kappa = 79.96$. For statistical modeling, this task is reformulated as coreference resolution, and experimented with a state-of-the-art system on our corpus. Our best model gives a purity score of 69.21 on average, which is promising given the challenging nature of this task and our corpus.

1 Introduction

Machine comprehension has recently become one of the main targeted challenges in natural language processing (Richardson et al., 2013; Hermann et al., 2015; Hixon et al., 2015). The latest approaches to machine comprehension show lots of promises; however, most of these approaches face difficulties in understanding information scattered across different parts of documents. Reading comprehension in dialogues is particularly hard because speakers take turns to form a conversation such that it often requires connecting mentions from multiple utterances together to derive meaningful inferences.

Coreference resolution is a common choice for making connections between these mentions. However, most of the state-of-the-art coreference resolution systems are not accustomed to handle dialogues well, especially when multiple participants are involved (Clark and Manning, 2015; Peng et al.,

2015; Wiseman et al., 2015). Furthermore, linking mentions to one another may not be good enough for certain tasks such as question answering, which requires to know what specific entities that mentions refer to. This implies that the task needs to be approached from the side of entity linking, which maps each mention to one or more pre-determined entities.

In this paper, we introduce an entity linking task, called character identification, that maps each mention in multiparty conversation to its referent character(s). Mentions can be any nominals referring to humans. At the moment, there is no dialogue corpus available to train statistical models for entity linking using such mentions. Thus, a new corpus is created by collecting transcripts of TV shows and annotating mentions with their referent characters. Our corpus is experimented with a coreference resolution system to show the feasibility of this task by utilizing an existing technology. The contributions of this work include:[1]

- Introducing a subtask of entity linking, called character identification (Section 2).

- Creating a new corpus for character identification with thorough analysis (Section 3).

- Reformulating character identification into a coreference resolution task (Section 4).

- Evaluating our approach to character identification on our corpus (Section 5).

To the best of our knowledge, it is the first time that character identification is experimented on such a large corpus. It is worth pointing out that character identification is just the first step to a bigger task called character mining. Character mining is a task that focuses on extracting information and

---

[1] All our work is publicly available at:
`github.com/emorynlp/character-mining`

90

Proceedings of the SIGDIAL 2016 Conference, pages 90–100,
Los Angeles, USA, 13-15 September 2016. ©2016 Association for Computational Linguistics

constructing knowledge bases associated with particular characters in contexts. The target entities are primarily participants, either spoken or mentioned, in dialogues. The task can be subdivided into three sequential tasks, character identification, attribute extraction, and knowledge base construction. Character mining is expected to facilitate and provide entity-specific knowledge for systems like question answering and dialogue generation. We believe that these tasks altogether are beneficial for machine comprehension on multiparty conversation.

2   Task Description

Character identification is a task of mapping each mention in context to one or more characters in a knowledge base. It is a subtask of entity linking; the main difference is that mentions in character identification can be any nominals indicating characters (e.g., *you*, *mom*, *Ross* in Figure 1), whereas they are mostly related to the Wikipedia entries in entity linking (Ji et al., 2015). Furthermore, character identification allows plural or collective nouns to be mentions such that a mention can be linked to more than one character, and they can either be pre-determined, inferred, or dynamically introduced ; however, a mention is usually linked to one pre-determined entity for entity linking.

The context can be drawn from any kind of document where characters are present (e.g., dialogues, narratives, novels). This paper focuses on context extracted from multiparty conversation, especially from transcripts of TV shows. Entities, mainly the characters in the shows or the speakers in conversations, are predetermined due to the nature of the dialogue data.

Instead of grabbing transcripts from the existing corpora (Janin et al., 2003; Lowe et al., 2015), TV shows are selected because they represent everyday conversation well, nonetheless they can very well be domain-specific depending on the plots and settings. Their contents and exchanges between characters are written for ease of comprehension. Prior knowledge regarding characters is usually not required and can be learned as show proceeds. Moreover, TV shows cover a variety of topics and are carried on over a long period of time by specific groups of people.

The knowledge base can be either pre-populated or populated from the context. For the example in Figure 1, all the speakers can be introduced to the knowledge base without reading the conversation. However, certain characters, mentioned during the conversation but not the speakers, should be dynamically added to the knowledge base (e.g., Ross' mom and dad). This is also true for many real-life scenarios where the participants are known prior to a conversation, but characters outside of these participants are mentioned during the conversation.

Character identification is distinguished from coreference resolution because mentions are linked to global entities in character identification whereas they are linked to one another without considering global entities in coreference resolution. Furthermore, this task is harder than typical entity linking because contexts switch of topics more rapidly in dialogues. In this work, mentions that are either plural or collective nouns are discarded, and the knowledge base does not get populated from the context dynamically. Adding these two aspects will greatly increase the complexity of this task, which we will explore in the future.

3   Corpus

The framework introduced here aims to create a large scale dataset for character identification. This is the first work to establish a robust framework for annotating referent information of characters with a focus on TV show transcripts.

3.1   Data Collection

Transcripts of two TV shows, *Friends*[2] and *The Big Bang Theory*[3] are selected for the data collection. Both shows serve as ideal candidates due to the casual and day-to-day dialogs among their characters. Seasons 1 and 2 of *Friends* (F1 and F2), and Season 1 of *The Big Bang Theory* (B1) are collected. A total of 3 seasons, 63 episodes, and 543 scenes are collected (Table 1).

	Epi	Sce	Spk	UC	SC	WC
F1	24	229	116	5,344	9,168	76,038
F2	22	219	113	9,626	12,368	82,737
B1	17	95	31	2,425	3,302	37,154
Total	63	543	225	17,395	24,838	195,929

Table 1: Composition of our corpus. Epi/Sce/Spk: # of episodes/scenes/speakers. UC/SC/WC: # of utterances/statements/words. Redundant speakers between F1 & F2 are counted only once.

---

[2] friendstranscripts.tk
[3] transcripts.foreverdreaming.org

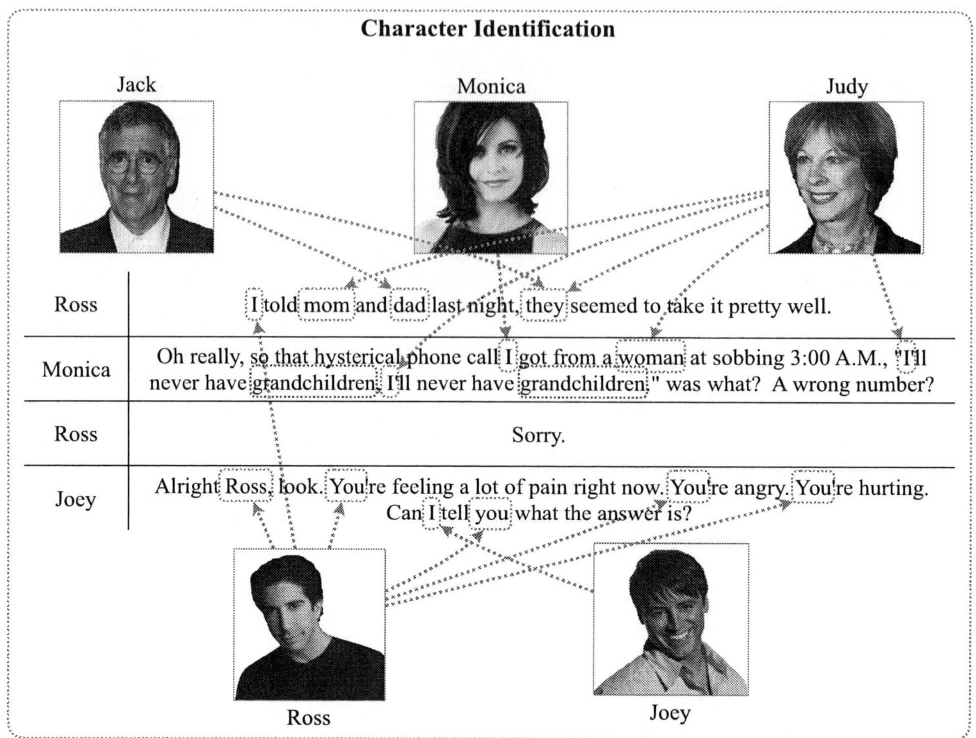

Figure 1: An example of character identification. All three speakers are introduced as characters before the conversation (Ross, Monica, and Joey), and two more characters are introduced during the conversation (Jack and Judy). The goal of this task is to identify each mention as one or more of these characters.

Each season is divided into episodes, and each episode is divided into scenes based on the boundary information provided by the transcripts. Each scene is divided into utterances where each utterance belongs to a speaker (e.g., the scene in Figure 1 includes four utterances). Each utterance consists of one or more sentences that may or may not contain action notes enclosed by parentheses (e.g., *Ross stares at her in surprise*). A sentence with its action note(s) removed is defined as a statement.

3.2 Mention Detection

Given the dataset in Section 3.1, mentions indicating humans are pseudo-annotated by our rule-based mention detector, which utilizes dependency relations, named entities, and a personal noun dictionary provided by the open-source toolkit, NLP4J.[4] Our rules are as follows: a word sequence is considered a mention if [(1)]it is a person named entity, [(2)]it is a pronoun or possessive pronoun excluding *it**, or [(3)]it is in the personal noun dictionary. The dictionary contains 603 common and singular

personal nouns chosen from Freebase[5] and DBpedia.[6] Plural (e.g., *we*, *them*, *boys*) and collective (e.g., *family*, *people*) nouns are discarded but will be included in the next version of the corpus.

	NE	PRP	PNN(%)	All
F1	1,245	7,536	1,464 (24.18)	10,245
F2	1,209	7,568	1,766 (27.28)	10,543
B1	648	3,586	785 (20.05)	5,019
Total	3,102	18,690	4,015 (24.41)	25,807

Table 2: Composition of the detected mentions. NE: named entities, PRP: pronouns, PNN(%): singular personal nouns and its ratio to all nouns.

For quality assurance, 5% of the corpus is sampled and evaluated. A total of 1,584 mentions from the first episode of each season in each show are extracted. If a mention is not identified by the detector, it is considered a "miss". If a detected mention does not refer human character(s), it is considered an "error". Our evaluation shows an F1 score of 95.93, which is satisfactory (Table 3).

---

[4]https://github.com/emorynlp/nlp4j

[5]http://www.freebase.com
[6]http://wiki.dbpedia.org

	Miss	Error	Total	P	R	F
F1	17	19	615	96.82	94.15	94.47
F2	15	3	448	99.31	95.98	97.62
B1	19	14	475	96.93	93.05	94.95
Total	51	36	1,538	97.58	94.34	**95.93**

Table 3: Evaluation of our mention detection. P: precision, R: recall, F: F1 score (in %).

A further investigation on the causes is conducted on the misses and errors of our mention detection. Table 4 shows the proportion of each cause. The majority of them are caused by either negligence of personal common nouns or inclusion of interjection use of pronouns, which are mostly coming from the limitation of our lexicon.

1. Interjection use of pronouns (e.g., *Oh mine*).

2. Personal common nouns not included in the personal noun dictionary.

3. Non-nominals tagged as nouns.

4. Proper nouns not tagged by either the part-of-speech tagger or name entity recognizer.

5. Misspelled pronouns (e.g., *I'm* → *Im*).

6. Analogous phrases referring to characters (e.g, *Mr. I-know-everything*).

Causes of Error and Miss	**%**
Interjection use of pronouns	27%
Common noun misses	27%
Proper noun misses	18%
Non-nominals	14%
Misspelled pronouns	10%
Analogous phrases	4%

Table 4: Proportions of the misses and errors of our mention detection.

3.3 Annotation Scheme

All mentions from Section 3.2 are first double annotated with their referent characters, then adjudicated if there are disagreements between annotators. Both annotation and adjudication tasks were conducted on Amazon Mechanical Turk. Annotation and adjudication of 25,807 mentions took about 8 hours and costed about $450.

Annotation Task

Each mention is annotated with either a main character, an extra character, or one of the followings: collective, unknown, or error. *Collective* indicates the plural use of *you/your*, which cannot be deterministically distinguished from the singular use of those by our mention detector. *Unknown* indicates an unknown character that is not listed as an option or a filler (e.g., *you know*). *Error* indicates an incorrectly identified mention that does not refer to any human character.

Our annotation scheme is designed to provide necessary contextual information and easiness for accurate annotation. The target scene for annotation includes highlighted mentions and selection boxes with options of main characters, extra characters, collective, unknown, and error. The previous and next two scenes from the target scene are also displayed to provide additional contextual information to annotators (Table 5). We found that including these four extra scenes substantially reduced annotation ambiguity. The annotation is done by two annotators, and only scenes with 8-50 mentions detected are used for the annotation; this allows annotators to focus while filtering out the scenes that have insufficient amounts of mentions for annotation.

Adjudication Task

Any scene containing at least one annotation disagreement is put into adjudication. The same template as that for the annotation task is used for the adjudication, except that options for the mentions are modified to display options selected by the previous two annotators. Nonetheless, adjudicators still have the flexibility of choosing any option from the complete list as shown in the annotation task. This task is done by three adjudicators. The resultant annotation is determined by the majority vote of the two annotators from the annotation task and the three adjudicators from this task.

3.4 Inter-Annotator Agreement

Serval preliminary tasks were conducted on Amazon Mechanical Turk to improve the quality of our annotation using a subset of the *Friends* season 1 dataset. Though the result on annotating the subset gave reasonable agreement scores ($F1_p$ in Table 6), the percentage of mentions annotated as *unknown* was noticeably high. Such ambiguity was primarily attributed to the lack of contextual information since these tasks were conducted with a template that did not provide additional scene information other than the target scene itself. The unknown rate decreased considerably in the later tasks (F1, F2,

Friends: Season 1, Episode 1, Scene 1		
	. . .	
Ross:	I_1 told mom$_2$ and dad$_3$ last night, they seemed to take it pretty well.	1. 'I_1' refers to?
Monica:	Oh really, so that hysterical phone call I got from a woman$_4$ at sobbing 3:00 A.M.,	- . . .
	"I_5'll never have grandchildren, I_6'll never have grandchildren." was what?	2. 'mom$_2$' refers to?
Ross:	Sorry.	- . . .
Joey:	Alright Ross$_7$, look. You$_8$'re feeling a lot of pain right now. You$_9$'re angry.	3. 'dad$_3$' refers to?
	You$_{10}$'re hurting. Can I_{11} tell you$_{12}$ what the answer is?	- Main character$_{1..n}$
	. . .	- Extra character$_{1..m}$
Friends: Season 1, Episode 1, Scene 2		- Collective
	. . .	- Unknown
Friends: Season 1, Episode 1, Scene 3		- Error
	. . .	

Table 5: An example of our annotation task conducted. Main character$_{1..n}$ displays the names of all main characters of the show. Extra character$_{1..m}$ displays the names of high frequent, but not main, characters.

and B1) after the previous and the next two scenes were added for context. As a result, our annotation gave the absolute matching score of 82.83% and the Cohen's Kappa score of 79.96% for inter-annotator agreement, and the unknown rate of 11.87% across our corpus, which was a consistent trend across different TV shows included in our corpus.

	Match	**Kappa**	**Col**	**Unk**	**Err**
F1$_p$	83.00	79.94	13.2	33.96	3.95
F1	84.55	80.75	11.2	21.42	3.71
F2	82.22	80.42	13.13	11.69	0.63
B1	81.54	78.73	11.35	7.80	4.99
Avg.	**82.83**	**79.96**	**12.42**	**11.87**	**2.75**

Table 6: Annotation analysis. Match and Kappa show the absolute matching and Cohen's Kappa scores between two annotators (in %). Col/Unk/Err shows the percentage of mentions annotated as collective, unknown, and error, respectively.

One common disagreement in annotation is caused by the ambiguity of speakers that *you/your/yourself* might refer to. Such confusion often occurs during a multiparty conversation when one party attempts to give a general example using personal mentions that refer to no one in specific. For the following example, annotators label the *you*'s as *Rachel* although they should be labeled as *unknown* since *you* indicates a general human being.

> Monica: (to Rachel) You$_1$ do this, and you$_2$
> do that. You$_3$ still end up with nothing.

The case of *you* also results in another ambiguity when it is used as a filler:

> Ross: (to Chandler and Joey)
> You$_1$ know, life is hard.

The referent of *you* here is subjective and can be interpreted differently among individuals. It can refers to Chandler and Joey collectively. It can also be unknown if it refers to a general scenario. Furthermore, it potentially can refers to either Chandler or Joey based on the context. Such use case of *you* is occasionally unclear to human annotators; thus, for the purposes of simplicity and consistency, this work treats them as *unknown* and considers that they do not refer to any speaker.

4 Approach

4.1 Coreference Resolution

Character identification is tackled as a coreference resolution task here, which takes advantage of utilizing existing state-of-the-art systems although it may not result the best for our task since it is more similar to entity linking. Most of the current entity linking systems are accustomed to find entities in Wikipedia (Mihalcea and Csomai, 2007; Ratinov et al., 2011), which are not intuitive to adapt to our task. We are currently developing our own entity linking system, which we hope to release soon.

Our corpus is first reformed into the CoNLL'12 shared task format, then experimented with two of the open source systems. The resultant coreference chains from these system are linked to a specific character by our cluster remapping algorithm.

CoNLL'12 Shared Task

Our corpus is reformatted to adapt the CoNLL'12 shared task on coreference resolution for the compatibility with the existing systems (Pradhan et al., 2012). Each statement is parsed into a constituent tree using the Berkeley Parser (Petrov et al., 2006), and tagged with named entities using the NLP4J tagger (Choi, 2016). The CoNLL format allows speaker information for each statement, which is used by both systems we experiment with. The converted format preserves all necessary annotation for our task.

Stanford Multi-Sieve System

The Stanford multi-pass sieve system (Lee et al., 2013) is used to provide a baseline of how a coreference resolution system performs on our task. The system is composed of multiple sieves of linguistic rules that are in the orders of high-to-low precision and low-to-high recall. Information regarding mentions, such as plurality, gender, and parse tree, is extracted during mention detection and used as global features. Pairwise links between mentions are formed based on defined linguistic rules at each sieve in order to construct coreference chains and mention clusters. Although no machine learning is involved, the system offers efficiency in decoding while yielding reasonable results.

Stanford Entity-Centric System

Another system used in this work is the Stanford entity-centric system (Clark and Manning, 2015). The system takes an ensemble-like statistical approach that utilizes global entity-level features to create feature clusters, and it is stacked with two models. The first model, mention pair model, consists of two tasks, classification and ranking. Logistic classifiers are trained for both tasks to assign probabilities to a mention. The former task considers the likelihood of two mentions are linked. The latter task estimates the potential antecedent of a given mention. The model makes primary suggestions of the coreference clusters and provides additional feature regarding mention pairs. The second model, entity-centric coreference model, aims to produce a final set of coreference clusters through learning from the features and scores of mentions pairs. It operates between pairs of clusters unlike the previous model. Iteratively, it builds up entity-specific mention clusters using agglomerative clustering and imitation learning.

This approach is particularly in alignment with our task, which finds groups of mentions referring to a centralized character. Furthermore, it allows new models to be trained with our corpus. This would give insight on whether our task can be learned by machines and whether a generalized model can be trained to distinguish speakers in all context.

4.2 Coreference Evaluation Metrics

All systems are evaluated with the official CoNLL scorer on three metrics concerning coreference resolution: MUC, B^3, and $CEAF_e$.

MUC

MUC (Vilain et al., 1995) concerns the number of pairwise links needed to be inserted or removed to map system responses to gold keys. The number of links the system and gold shared and minimum numbers of links needed to describe coreference chains of the system and gold are computed. Precision is calculated by dividing the former with the latter that describes the system chains, and recall is calculated by dividing the former with the later that describes the gold chains.

B^3

In stead of evaluating the coreference chains solely on their links, the B^3 (Bagga and Baldwin, 1998) metric computes precision and recall on a mention level. System performance is evaluated by the average of all mention scores. Given a set M that contains mentions denoted as m_i. Coreference chains S_{m_i} and G_{m_i} represent the chains containing mention m_i in system and gold responses. Precision(P) and recall(R) are calculated as below:

$$P(m_i) = \frac{|S_{m_i} \cap G_{m_i}|}{|S_{m_i}|}, \quad R(m_i) = \frac{|S_{m_i} \cap G_{m_i}|}{|G_{m_i}|}$$

$CEAF_e$

$CEAF_e$ (Luo, 2005) metric further points out the drawback of B^3, in which entities can be used more than once during evaluation. As result, both multiple coreference chains of the same entity and chains with mentions of multiple entities are not penalized. To cope with this problem, CEAF evaluates only on the best one-to-one mapping between the system's and gold's entities. Given a system entity S_i and gold entity G_j. An entity-based similarity metric $\phi(S_i, G_j)$ gives the count of common mentions that refer to both S_i and G_j. The alignment with the best total similarity is denoted as $\Phi(g^*)$. Thus precision(P) and recall(R) are measured as below.

$$P = \frac{\Phi(g^*)}{\sum_i \phi(S_i, S_i)}, \quad R = \frac{\Phi(g^*)}{\sum_i \phi(G_i, G_i)}$$

4.3 Cluster Remapping

Since the predicted coreference chains do not directly point to specific characters, a mapping mechanism is needed for linking those chains to certain

TRN	TST	Document: episode				Document: scene			
		MUC	B^3	$CEAF_e$	Avg	MUC	B^3	$CEAF_e$	Avg
Stanford multi-pass sieve	F1+F2+B1	80.73	44.91	27.00	50.88	79.09	62.26	50.22	63.86
Stanford entity-centric	F1+F2+B1	84.44	44.95	19.66	49.68	83.39	69.59	54.48	69.15
F1	F1	90.79	61.25	48.63	66.89	90.16	80.46	69.05	79.89
	F2	92.18	44.40	35.07	57.22	88.49	72.74	59.14	73.46
	B1	94.83	73.46	61.78	76.69	91.55	80.36	66.95	79.62
F1+F2	F1	89.83	67.18	43.98	67.00	90.02	80.48	71.44	80.65
	F2	89.27	55.94	38.55	61.25	89.61	76.76	64.34	76.90
	B1	92.94	75.26	48.61	72.27	92.87	83.55	68.09	81.50
	F1+F2	90.07	63.33	42.44	65.28	89.89	78.75	68.39	79.01
	F1+F2+B1	90.63	**65.64**	43.21	66.49	90.55	**79.84**	**68.53**	**79.64**
B1	B1	93.33	75.83	59.28	76.15	91.79	82.50	69.69	81.33
F1+F2+B1	F1	89.47	64.56	49.63	67.89	90.04	79.63	71.45	80.37
	F2	89.21	57.00	44.31	63.51	89.60	73.78	62.33	75.24
	B1	95.72	72.92	53.87	74.17	92.97	84.23	70.58	82.59
	F1+F2	89.89	62.26	47.92	66.69	89.92	76.95	67.68	78.18
	F1+F2+B1	**91.06**	64.94	**48.26**	**68.09**	**90.59**	78.53	68.37	79.16

Table 7: Coreference resolution results on our corpus. Stanford multi-pass sieve is a rule-based system. Stanford entity-centric uses its pre-trained model. Every other row shows results achieved by the entity-centric system using models trained on the indicated training sets.

characters. The resultant chains from the above systems are mapped to either a character, collective, or unknown. Each coreference chain is reassigned through voting based on the group that majority of the mentions refer to. The referent of each mention is determined by the below rules:

1. If the mention is a proper noun or a named entity that refers to a known character, it is referent to the character.

2. If the mention is a first-person pronoun or possessive pronoun, it is referent to the character of the utterance containing the mention.

3. If the mention is a collective pronoun or possessive pronoun, it is referent to the *collective* group.

If none of these rules apply to any of the mentions in a coreference chain, the chain is mapped to the *unknown* group.

5 Experiments

Both the sieve system and the entity-centric system with its pre-trained model are first evaluated on our corpus. The entity-centric system is further evaluated with new models trained on our corpus. The gold mentions are used for these experiments because we want to focus solely on the performance analysis of these existing systems on our task.

5.1 Data Splits

Our corpus is split into the training, development, and evaluation sets (Table 8). Documents are for-

mulated into two ways, one treating each episode as a document and the other treating each scene as a document, which allows us to conduct experiments with or without the contextual information provided across the previous and next scenes.

	Epi	Sce	Spk	UC	SC	WC
TRN	51	427	189	13,681	19,575	155,789
DEV	5	46	39	1,631	2,313	17,406
TST	7	70	46	2,083	2,950	22,734
Total	63	543	225	17,395	24,838	195,929

Table 8: Data splits. TRN/DEV/TST: training, development, and evaluation sets. See Table 1 for the details about Epi/Sce/Spk/UC/SC/WC.

5.2 Analysis of Coreference Resolution

The results indicate several intriguing trends (Table 7), explained in the following observations.

5.2.1 Multi-pass sieve vs. Entity-centric

These models yield close performance when run out-of-box. It is interesting because both rule-based and statistical models give similar baseline results. This serves as an indicator of how current systems, trained on the CoNLL'12 dataset, do not work as well with day-to-day multiparty conversational data that we attend to solve in this work.

5.2.2 Cross-domain Evaluation

Before looking at the results of the models trained on F1 and F1+F2, we anticipated that these models would give undesirable performance when evaluated on B1. Those models give the average scores

TRN	TST	Document: episode					Document: scene				
		FC	EC	UC	UM	Purity	FC	EC	UC	UM	Purity
Stanford multi-pass sieve		46	53	38.64	16.33	45.97	38	60	22.15	5.97	**64.01**
Stanford entity-centric		36	60	32.59	8.41	38.78	26	60	8.85	1.49	44.12
F1	F1	19	30	30.23	4.20	61.13	21	30	4.94	1.35	54.11
	F2	12	24	40.00	3.15	42.13	17	24	17.91	4.86	51.58
	B1	9	14	0.00	0.00	75.99	14	14	6.25	1.90	70.10
F1+F2	F1	20	30	39.39	7.52	69.92	20	30	10.11	2.72	56.28
	F2	18	24	49.06	8.25	62.54	23	24	7.46	2.12	57.64
	B1	12	14	51.52	12.69	72.16	14	14	10.87	4.56	67.11
	F1+F2	30	46	42.24	7.54	66.65	26	46	9.26	1.83	45.11
	F1+F2+B1	39	60	44.22	8.44	67.67	30	60	7.76	1.35	41.79
B1	B1	11	14	25.00	1.90	80.08	12	14	14.00	5.47	72.83
F1+F2+B1	F1	25	30	21.67	4.06	73.21	20	30	9.41	3.15	51.74
	F2	25	24	29.17	3.64	64.62	25	24	5.80	1.34	58.79
	B1	9	14	20.00	1.31	71.29	15	14	6.67	1.33	69.45
	F1+F2	39	46	24.76	3.78	69.60	29	46	7.62	1.74	44.49
	F1+F2+B1	45	60	23.93	3.27	**69.21**	36	60	6.84	1.39	42.81

Table 9: Character identification results on our corpus using cluster remapping on the coreference resolution system results. FC: found clusters after remapping. EC: expected clusters from gold. UC: percentage of unknown clusters after remapping. UM: percentage of unknown mentions in the unknown clusters to all the mentions.

of 76.69 and 72.27 for B1 on the episode-level, and 79.62 and 79.01 for B1 on the scene-level, respectively. Surprisingly, the models trained on B1 do not yield a better accuracy on the episode-level (76.15), and show an improvement of 1.69 on the scene-level, which is smaller than expected. Thus, it is plausible to take models trained on one show and apply it to another for coreference resolution.

5.2.3 Cross-domain Training

When looking at the models trained on F1+F2+B1, we found that more training instances do not necessarily guarantee a continuous increase of system performance. Although more training data from a single show gives improvements in the results (F1 vs. F1+F2), a similar trend cannot be assumed for the case of the models trained on both shows (F1+F2+B1) when data of another show (B1) is added for training; in fact, most scores show decreases in performance for both episode- and scene-level evaluations. We suppose that this is caused by the introduction of noncontiguous context and content of the additional show. Thus, we deduce that models trained on data from multiple shows are not recommended for the highest performance.

5.2.4 Episode-level vs. Scene-level

We originally foresaw the models trained on the episode-level would outperform the ones trained on the scene-level because the scene-level documents would not provide enough contextual information. However such speculation is not reflected on our evaluation; the results achieved by the scene-level models consistently yield higher accuracy, which is probably because the scene-level documents are much smaller than the episode-level documents so that fewer characters appear within each document.

5.3 Analysis of Character Identification

The resultant coreference chains produced by the systems in Section 4.1 do not point to any specific characters. Thus, our cluster remapping algorithm in Section 4.3 is run on the coreference chains to group multiple chains together and assign them to individual characters. These remapped results provide a better insight of the effective system performance on our task. Table 9 shows the remapped results and the cluster purity scores.

5.3.1 Remapped Clusters

As discussed in Section 5.2.4, the scene-level models consistently outperform the episode-level models for coreference resolution. However, an opposite trend is found for character identification when the coreference chains are mapped to their referent characters. The purity scores of the overall character-mention clusters can be viewed as an effective accuracy score for character identification. The purity scores, or the percentages of recoverable character-mentions clusters, of the remapped clusters for the scene-level models are generally lower than the ones for the episode-level models. Although the percentages of unknown clusters and unknown mentions are considerably higher for the episode-level models, we find these results more reasonable and realistic to the nature of our corpus, since the average percentages of mentions that are annotated as *unknown* are 11.87% for the entire corpus and 14.01% for the evaluation set. The primary cause of lower performance for the scene-level models is the lack of contextual information across scenes. The following example is excerpted from the first utterance in the opening scene of F1:

Monica: There's nothing to tell!
He_1's just some guy_2 I_3 work with!

As the conversation proceeds, there is no clear indication of who He_1 and guy_2 refer to until later scenes introduce the character. As a result, the coreference chains in the scene-level documents are noticeably shorter than those in the episode-level documents. When trying to determine the referent characters, fewer mentions exist in the coreference chains produced by the scene-level models such that there is a higher chance for those chains to be mapped to wrong characters. Thus, the episode-level models are recommended for better performance on character identification.

6 Related Work

There exist few corpora concerning multiparty conversational data. SwitchBoard is a telephone speech corpus with focuses on speaker authentication and recognition (Godfrey et al., 1992). The ICSI Meeting Corpus is a collection of meeting audios and transcript recordings created for research in speech recognition (Janin et al., 2003). The Ubuntu Dialogue Corpus is a recently introduced dialogue corpus that provides task-domain specific conversation with multiple turns (Lowe et al., 2015). All these corpora provide an immense amount of dialogue data. However, the primary purposes of them are aimed to tackle tasks like speaker or speech recognition and next utterance generation. Thus, mention referent information are missing for the purpose of our task.

Entity Linking is a natural language processing task of determining entities and connecting related information in context to them (Ji et al., 2015). Linking can be done on domain-specific information using extracted local context (Olieman et al., 2015). Wikification is a branch of entity linking with an aim of associating concepts to their corresponding Wikipedia pages (Mihalcea and Csomai, 2007). Ratinov et al. (2011) used linked concepts and their relevant Wikipedia articles as features on

disambiguation. Kim et al. (2015) explored dialogue data in the realm of the task in attempt to improve dialogue tracking using Wikification-based information.

Similar to entity linking, coreference resolution is another NLP task that connects mentions to their antecedents (Pradhan et al., 2012). The task focuses on finding pair-wise connection between mentions and forming coreference chains of the pairs. Dialogues have been studied as a particular domain for coreference resolution (Rocha, 1999) due to the complex and context-switching nature of the data. For most of the systems presented for the task, they target on narrations or conversations between two parties, such as tutoring systems (Niraula et al., 2014). Despite their similarity, coreference resolution still differs from character identification since the resolved coreference chains do not directly refer to ant centralized characters.

7 Conclusion

This paper introduces a new task, called character identification, that is a subtask of entity linking. A new corpus is created for the evaluation of this task, which comprises multiparty conversations from TV show transcripts. Our annotation scheme allows to create a large dataset with the personal mentions and their referent characters annotated. The nature of this corpus is analyzed with potential challenges and ambiguities identified for future investigation.

Hence, this work provides baseline approaches and results using the existing coreference resolution systems. Experiments are run on combinations of our corpus in various formats to analyze the applicability of the current systems as well as the model trainability for our task. A cluster remapping algorithm is then proposed to connect the coreference chains to their reference characters or groups.

Character identification is the first step to a machine comprehension task we define as character mining. We are going to extend this task to handle plural and collective nouns, and develop an entity linking system customized for this task. Furthermore, we will explore an automatic way of building a knowledge base containing information about the characters that can be used for more specific tasks such as question answering.

References

Amit Bagga and Breck Baldwin. 1998. Algorithms for scoring coreference chains. In *The first international conference on language resources and evaluation workshop on linguistics coreference*, volume 1, pages 563–566. Citeseer.

Jinho D. Choi. 2016. Dynamic Feature Induction: The Last Gist to the State-of-the-Art. In *Proceedings of the Conference of the North American Chapter of the Association for Computational Linguistics: Human Language Technologies*, NAACL'16.

Kevin Clark and Christopher D. Manning. 2015. Entity-Centric Coreference Resolution with Model Stacking. In *Proceedings of the 53rd Annual Meeting of the Association for Computational Linguistics*, ACL'15, pages 1405–1415.

John J. Godfrey, Edward C. Holliman, and Jane McDaniel. 1992. SWITCHBOARD: Telephone Speech Corpus for Research and Development. In *Proceedings of the IEEE International Conference on Acoustics, Speech and Signal Processing*, ICASSP'92, pages 517–520.

Karl Moritz Hermann, Tomás Kociský, Edward Grefenstette, Lasse Espeholt, Will Kay, Mustafa Suleyman, and Phil Blunsom. 2015. Teaching Machines to Read and Comprehend. In *Annual Conference on Neural Information Processing Systems*, NIPS'15, pages 1693–1701.

Ben Hixon, Peter Clark, and Hannaneh Hajishirzi. 2015. Learning Knowledge Graphs for Question Answering through Conversational Dialog. In *Proceedings of the 2015 Conference of the North American Chapter of the Association for Computational Linguistics: Human Language Technologies*, NAACL'15, pages 851–861.

Adam Janin, Don Baron, Jane Edwards, Dan Ellis, David Gelbart, Nelson Morgan, Barbara Peskin, Thilo Pfau, Elizabeth Shriberg, Andreas Stolcke, and Chuck Wooters. 2003. The ICSI Meeting Corpus. In *Proceedings of IEEE International Conference on Acoustics, Speech, and Signal Processing*, ICASSP'03, pages 364–367.

Heng Ji, Joel Nothman, Ben Hachey, and Radu Florian. 2015. Overview of TAC-KBP2015 Tri-lingual Entity Discovery and Linking. In *Proceedings of Text Analysis Conference*, TAC'15.

Seokhwan Kim, Rafael E. Banchs, and Haizhou Li. 2015. Towards Improving Dialogue Topic Tracking Performances with Wikification of Concept Mentions. In *Proceedings of the 16th Annual Meeting of the Special Interest Group on Discourse and Dialogue*, SIGDIAL'15, pages 124–128.

Heeyoung Lee, Angel Chang, Yves Peirsman, Nathanael Chambers, Mihai Surdeanu, and Dan Jurafsky. 2013. Deterministic Coreference Resolution Based on Entity-centric, Precision-ranked Rules. *Computational Linguistics*, 39(4):885–916.

Ryan Lowe, Nissan Pow, Iulian Serban, and Joelle Pineau. 2015. The Ubuntu Dialogue Corpus: A Large Dataset for Research in Unstructured Multi-Turn Dialogue Systems. In *Proceedings of the 16th Annual Meeting of the Special Interest Group on Discourse and Dialogue*, SIGDIAL'15, pages 285–294.

Xiaoqiang Luo. 2005. On coreference resolution performance metrics. In *Proceedings of the conference on Human Language Technology and Empirical Methods in Natural Language Processing*, pages 25–32. Association for Computational Linguistics.

Rada Mihalcea and Andras Csomai. 2007. Wikify!: Linking Documents to Encyclopedic Knowledge. In *Proceedings of the Sixteenth ACM Conference on Conference on Information and Knowledge Management*, CIKM'07, pages 233–242.

Nobal B. Niraula, Vasile Rus, Rajendra Banjade, Dan Stefanescu, William Baggett, and Brent Morgan. 2014. The DARE Corpus: A Resource for Anaphora Resolution in Dialogue Based Intelligent Tutoring Systems. In *Proceedings of the Ninth International Conference on Language Resources and Evaluation*, LREC'14, pages 3199–3203.

Alex Olieman, Jaap Kamps, Maarten Marx, and Arjan Nusselder. 2015. A Hybrid Approach to Domain-Specific Entity Linking. In *Proceedings of 11th International Conference on Semantic Systems*, SEMANTiCS'15.

Haoruo Peng, Kai-Wei Chang, and Dan Roth. 2015. A Joint Framework for Coreference Resolution and Mention Head Detection. In *Proceedings of the 9th Conference on Computational Natural Language Learning*, CoNLL'15, pages 12–21.

Slav Petrov, Leon Barrett, Romain Thibaux, and Dan Klein. 2006. Learning accurate, compact, and interpretable tree annotation. In *Proceedings of the 21st International Conference on Computational Linguistics and the 44th annual meeting of the Association for Computational Linguistics (COLING-ACL'06)*, pages 433–440.

Sameer Pradhan, Alessandro Moschitti, Nianwen Xue, Olga Uryupina, and Yuchen Zhang. 2012. CoNLL-2012 Shared Task: Modeling Multilingual Unrestricted Coreference in OntoNotes. In *Proceedings of the Sixteenth Conference on Computational Natural Language Learning: Shared Task*, CoNLL'12, pages 1–40.

Lev Ratinov, Dan Roth, Doug Downey, and Mike Anderson. 2011. Local and Global Algorithms for Disambiguation to Wikipedia. In *Proceedings of the 49th Annual Meeting of the Association for Computational Linguistics: Human Language Technologies*, ACL'11, pages 1375–1384.

Matthew Richardson, Christopher J.C. Burges, and Erin Renshaw. 2013. MCTest: A Challenge Dataset for the Open-Domain Machine Comprehension of

Text. In *Proceedings of the 2013 Conference on Empirical Methods in Natural Language Processing*, EMNLP'13, pages 193–203.

Marco Rocha. 1999. Coreference Resolution in Dialogues in English and Portuguese. In *Proceedings of the Workshop on Coreference and Its Applications*, CorefApp'99, pages 53–60.

Marc Vilain, John Burger, John Aberdeen, Dennis Connolly, and Lynette Hirschman. 1995. A model-theoretic coreference scoring scheme. In *Proceedings of the 6th conference on Message understanding*, pages 45–52. Association for Computational Linguistics.

Sam Wiseman, Alexander M. Rush, Stuart Shieber, and Jason Weston. 2015. Learning Anaphoricity and Antecedent Ranking Features for Coreference Resolution. In *Proceedings of the 53rd Annual Meeting of the Association for Computational Linguistics*, ACL'15, pages 1416–1426.

Policy Networks with Two-Stage Training for Dialogue Systems

Mehdi Fatemi   Layla El Asri   Hannes Schulz   Jing He   Kaheer Suleman

Maluuba Research
Le 2000 Peel, Montréal, QC H3A 2W5
`first.last@maluuba.com`

Abstract

In this paper, we propose to use deep policy networks which are trained with an advantage actor-critic method for statistically optimised dialogue systems. First, we show that, on summary state and action spaces, deep Reinforcement Learning (RL) outperforms Gaussian Processes methods. Summary state and action spaces lead to good performance but require pre-engineering effort, RL knowledge, and domain expertise. In order to remove the need to define such summary spaces, we show that deep RL can also be trained efficiently on the original state and action spaces. Dialogue systems based on partially observable Markov decision processes are known to require many dialogues to train, which makes them unappealing for practical deployment. We show that a deep RL method based on an actor-critic architecture can exploit a small amount of data very efficiently. Indeed, with only a few hundred dialogues collected with a handcrafted policy, the actor-critic deep learner is considerably bootstrapped from a combination of supervised and batch RL. In addition, convergence to an optimal policy is significantly sped up compared to other deep RL methods initialized on the data with batch RL. All experiments are performed on a restaurant domain derived from the Dialogue State Tracking Challenge 2 (DSTC2) dataset.

1 Introduction

The statistical optimization of dialogue management in dialogue systems through Reinforcement Learning (RL) has been an active thread of research for more than two decades (Levin et al., 1997; Lemon and Pietquin, 2007; Laroche et al., 2010; Gašić et al., 2012; Daubigney et al., 2012). Dialogue management has been successfully modelled as a Partially Observable Markov Decision Process (POMDP) (Williams and Young, 2007; Gašić et al., 2012), which leads to systems that can learn from data and which are robust to noise. In this context, a dialogue between a user and a dialogue system is framed as a sequential process where, at each turn, the system has to act based on what it has understood so far of the user's utterances.

Unfortunately, POMDP-based dialogue managers have been unfit for online deployment because they typically require several thousands of dialogues for training (Gašić et al., 2010, 2012). Nevertheless, recent work has shown that it is possible to train a POMDP-based dialogue system on just a few hundred dialogues corresponding to online interactions with users (Gašić et al., 2013). However, in order to do so, pre-engineering efforts, prior RL knowledge, and domain expertise must be applied. Indeed, summary state and action spaces must be used and the set of actions must be restricted depending on the current state so that notoriously bad actions are prohibited.

In order to alleviate the need for a summary state space, deep RL (Mnih et al., 2013) has recently been applied to dialogue management (Cuayáhuitl et al., 2015) in the context of negotiations. It was shown that deep RL performed significantly better than other heuristic or supervised approaches. The authors performed learning over a large action space of 70 actions and they also had to use restricted action sets in order to learn efficiently over this space. Besides, deep RL was not compared to other RL methods, which we do in this paper. In (Cuayáhuitl, 2016), a simplistic implementation of deep Q Networks is presented,

Proceedings of the SIGDIAL 2016 Conference, pages 101–110,
Los Angeles, USA, 13-15 September 2016. ©2016 Association for Computational Linguistics

again with no comparison to other RL methods.

In this paper, we propose to efficiently alleviate the need for summary spaces and restricted actions using deep RL. We analyse four deep RL models: Deep Q Networks (DQN) (Mnih et al., 2013), Double DQN (DDQN) (van Hasselt et al., 2015), Deep Advantage Actor-Critic (DA2C) (Sutton et al., 2000) and a version of DA2C initialized with supervised learning (TDA2C)[1] (similar idea to Silver et al. (2016)). All models are trained on a restaurant-seeking domain. We use the Dialogue State Tracking Challenge 2 (DSTC2) dataset to train an agenda-based user simulator (Schatzmann and Young, 2009) for online learning and to perform batch RL and supervised learning.

We first show that, on summary state and action spaces, deep RL converges faster than Gaussian Processes SARSA (GPSARSA) (Gašić et al., 2010). Then we show that deep RL enables us to work on the original state and action spaces. Although GPSARSA has also been tried on original state space (Gašić et al., 2012), it is extremely slow in terms of wall-clock time due to its growing kernel evaluations. Indeed, contrary to methods such as GPSARSA, deep RL performs efficient generalization over the state space and memory requirements do not increase with the number of experiments. On the simple domain specified by DSTC2, we do not need to restrict the actions in order to learn efficiently. In order to remove the need for restricted actions in more complex domains, we advocate for the use of TDA2C and supervised learning as a pre-training step. We show that supervised learning on a small set of dialogues (only 706 dialogues) significantly bootstraps TDA2C and enables us to start learning with a policy that already selects only valid actions, which makes for a safe user experience in deployment. Therefore, we conclude that TDA2C is very appealing for the practical deployment of POMDP-based dialogue systems.

In Section 2 we briefly review POMDP, RL and GPSARSA. The value-based deep RL models investigated in this paper (DQN and DDQN) are described in Section 3. Policy networks and DA2C are discussed in Section 4. We then introduce the two-stage training of DA2C in Section 5. Experimental results are presented in Section 6. Finally, Section 7 concludes the paper and makes suggestions for future research.

____

[1]Teacher DA2C

2 Preliminaries

The reinforcement learning problem consists of an environment (the user) and an agent (the system) (Sutton and Barto, 1998). The environment is described as a set of continuous or discrete states $\mathcal{S}$ and at each state $s \in \mathcal{S}$, the system can perform an action from an action space $\mathcal{A}(s)$. The actions can be continuous, but in our case they are assumed to be discrete and finite. At time t, as a consequence of an action $A_t = a \in \mathcal{A}(s)$, the state transitions from $S_t = s$ to $S_{t+1} = s' \in \mathcal{S}$. In addition, a reward signal $R_{t+1} = R(S_t, A_t, S_{t+1}) \in \mathbb{R}$ provides feedback on the quality of the transition[2]. The agent's task is to maximize at each state the expected discounted sum of rewards received after visiting this state. For this purpose, value functions are computed. The action-state value function Q is defined as:

$$Q^\pi(S_t, A_t) = \mathbb{E}_\pi[R_{t+1} + \gamma R_{t+2} + \gamma^2 R_{t+3} + \ldots$$
$$| S_t = s, A_t = a], \quad (1)$$

where γ is a discount factor in $[0, 1]$. In this equation, the *policy* π specifies the system's behaviour, *i.e.*, it describes the agent's action selection process at each state. A policy can be a deterministic mapping $\pi(s) = a$, which specifies the action a to be selected when state s is met. On the other hand, a stochastic policy provides a probability distribution over the action space at each state:

$$\pi(a|s) = \mathbb{P}[A_t = a|S_t = s]. \quad (2)$$

The agent's goal is to find a policy that maximizes the Q-function at each state.

It is important to note that here the system does not have direct access to the state s. Instead, it sees this state through a *perception* process which typically includes an *Automatic Speech Recognition* (ASR) step, a *Natural Language Understanding* (NLU) step, and a *State Tracking* (ST) step. This perception process injects noise in the state of the system and it has been shown that modelling dialogue management as a POMDP helps to overcome this noise (Williams and Young, 2007; Young et al., 2013).

Within the POMDP framework, the state at time t, S_t, is not directly observable. Instead, the system has access to a noisy observation O_t.[3] A

____

[2]In this paper, upper-case letters are used for random variables, lower-case letters for non-random values (known or unknown), and calligraphic letters for sets.

[3]Here, the representation of the user's goal and the user's utterances.

POMDP is a tuple $(\mathcal{S}, \mathcal{A}, P, R, \mathcal{O}, Z, \gamma, b_0)$ where $\mathcal{S}$ is the state space, $\mathcal{A}$ is the action space, P is the function encoding the transition probability: $P_a(s, s') = \mathbb{P}(S_{t+1} = s' \mid S_t = s, A_t = a)$, R is the reward function, $\mathcal{O}$ is the observation space, Z encodes the observation probabilities $Z_a(s, o) = \mathbb{P}(O_t = o \mid S_t = s, A_t = a)$, γ is a discount factor, and b_0 is an initial belief state. The *belief state* is a distribution over states. Starting from b_0, the state tracker maintains and updates the belief state according to the observations perceived during the dialogue. The dialogue manager then operates on this belief state. Consequently, the value functions as well as the policy of the agent are computed on the belief states B_t:

$$Q^\pi(B_t, A_t) = \mathbb{E}_\pi \left[\sum_{t' \geq t} \gamma^{t'-t} R_{t'+1} \mid B_t, A_t \right]$$
$$\pi(a|b) = \mathbb{P}[A_t = a | B_t = b]. \tag{3}$$

In this paper, we use GPSARSA as a baseline as it has been proved to be a successful algorithm for training POMDP-based dialogue managers (Engel et al., 2005; Gašić et al., 2010). Formally, the Q-function is modelled as a Gaussian process, entirely defined by a mean and a kernel: $Q(B, A) \sim \mathcal{GP}(m, (k(B, A), k(B, A)))$. The mean is usually initialized at 0 and it is then jointly updated with the covariance based on the system's observations (*i.e.*, the visited belief states and actions, and the rewards). In order to avoid intractability in the number of experiments, we use kernel span sparsification (Engel et al., 2005). This technique consists of approximating the kernel on a dictionary of linearly independent belief states. This dictionary is incrementally built during learning. Kernel span sparsification requires setting a threshold on the precision to which the kernel is computed. As discussed in Section 6, this threshold needs to be fine-tuned for a good tradeoff between precision and performance.

3 Value-Based Deep Reinforcement Learning

Broadly speaking, there are two main streams of methodologies in the RL literature: value approximation and policy gradients. As suggested by their names, the former tries to approximate the value function whereas the latter tries to directly approximate the policy. Approximations are necessary for large or continuous belief and action spaces.

Indeed, if the belief space is large or continuous it would not be possible to store a value for each state in a table, so generalization over the state space is necessary. In this context, some of the benefits of deep RL techniques are the following:

- Generalisation over the belief space is efficient and the need for summary spaces is eliminated, normally with considerably less wall-clock training time comparing to GP-SARSA, for example.

- Memory requirements are limited and can be determined in advance unlike with methods such as GPSARSA.

- Deep architectures with several hidden layers can be efficiently used for complex tasks and environments.

3.1 Deep Q Networks

A Deep Q-Network (DQN) is a multi-layer neural network which maps a belief state B_t to the values of the possible actions $A_t \in \mathcal{A}(B_t = b)$ at that state, $Q^\pi(B_t, A_t; w_t)$, where w_t is the weight vector of the neural network. Neural networks for the approximation of value functions have long been investigated (Bertsekas and Tsitsiklis, 1996). However, these methods were previously quite unstable (Mnih et al., 2013). In DQN, Mnih et al. (2013, 2015) proposed two techniques to overcome this instability-namely *experience replay* and the use of a *target network*. In experience replay, all the transitions are put in a finite pool $\mathcal{D}$ (Lin, 1993). Once the pool has reached its predefined maximum size, adding a new transition results in deleting the oldest transition in the pool. During training, a mini-batch of transitions is *uniformly* sampled from the pool, *i.e.* $(B_t, A_t, R_{t+1}, B_{t+1}) \sim U(\mathcal{D})$. This method removes the instability arising from strong correlation between the subsequent transitions of an episode (a dialogue). Additionally, a target network with weight vector w^- is used. This target network is similar to the Q-network except that its weights are only copied every τ steps from the Q-network, and remain fixed during all the other steps. The loss function for the Q-network at iteration t takes the following form:

$$L_t(w_t) = \mathbb{E}_{(B_t, A_t, R_{t+1}, B_{t+1}) \sim U(\mathcal{D})} \Bigg[$$
$$\left(R_{t+1} + \gamma \max_{a'} Q^\pi(B_{t+1}, a'; w_t^-) \right.$$
$$\left. - Q^\pi(B_t, A_t; w_t) \right)^2 \Bigg]. \tag{4}$$

3.2 Double DQN: Overcoming Overestimation and Instability of DQN

The *max* operator in Equation 4 uses the same value network (*i.e.*, the target network) to select actions and evaluate them. This increases the probability of overestimating the value of the state-action pairs (van Hasselt, 2010; van Hasselt et al., 2015). To see this more clearly, the target part of the loss in Equation 4 can be rewritten as follows:

$$R_{t+1} + \gamma Q^\pi(B_{t+1}, \underset{a}{\mathrm{argmax}}\, Q^\pi(B_{t+1}, a; w_t^-); w_t^-).$$

In this equation, the target network is used twice. Decoupling is possible by using the Q-network for action selection as follows (van Hasselt et al., 2015):

$$R_{t+1} + \gamma Q^\pi(B_{t+1}, \underset{a}{\mathrm{argmax}}\, Q^\pi(B_{t+1}, a; w_t); w_t^-).$$

Then, similarly to DQN, the Q-network is trained using experience replay and the target network is updated every τ steps. This new version of DQN, called Double DQN (DDQN), uses the two value networks in a decoupled manner, and alleviates the overestimation issue of DQN. This generally results in a more stable learning process (van Hasselt et al., 2015).

In the following section, we present deep RL models which perform policy search and output a stochastic policy rather than value approximation with a deterministic policy.

4 Policy Networks and Deep Advantage Actor-Critic (DA2C)

A policy network is a parametrized probabilistic mapping between belief and action spaces:

$$\pi_\theta(a|b) = \pi(a|b; \theta) = \mathbb{P}(A_t = a | B_t = b, \theta_t = \theta),$$

where θ is the parameter vector (the weight vector of a neural network).[4] In order to train policy

---

[4]For parametrization, we use w for value networks and θ for policy networks.

networks, policy gradient algorithms have been developed (Williams, 1992; Sutton et al., 2000). Policy gradient algorithms are model-free methods which directly approximate the policy by parametrizing it. The parameters are learnt using a gradient-based optimization method.

We first need to define an objective function J that will lead the search for the parameters θ. This objective function defines policy quality. One way of defining it is to take the average over the rewards received by the agent. Another way is to compute the discounted sum of rewards for each trajectory, given that there is a designated start state. The policy gradient is then computed according to the *Policy Gradient Theorem* (Sutton et al., 2000).

Theorem 1 (Policy Gradient) *For any differentiable policy $\pi_\theta(b, a)$ and for the average reward or the start-state objective function, the policy gradient can be computed as*

$$\nabla_\theta J(\theta) = \mathbb{E}_{\pi_\theta}[\nabla_\theta \log \pi_\theta(a|b) Q^{\pi_\theta}(b, a)]. \tag{5}$$

Policy gradient methods have been used successfully in different domains. Two recent examples are AlphaGo by DeepMind (Silver et al., 2016) and MazeBase by Facebook AI (Sukhbaatar et al., 2016).

One way to exploit Theorem 1 is to parametrize $Q^{\pi_\theta}(b, a)$ separately (with a parameter vector w) and learn the parameter vector during training in a similar way as in DQN. The trained Q-network can then be used for policy evaluation in Equation 5. Such algorithms are known in general as *actor-critic* algorithms, where the Q approximator is the critic and π_θ is the actor (Sutton, 1984; Barto et al., 1990; Bhatnagar et al., 2009). This can be achieved with *two* separate deep neural networks: a *Q-Network* and a *policy network*.

However, a direct use of Equation 5 with Q as critic is known to cause high variance (Williams, 1992). An important property of Equation 5 can be used in order to overcome this issue: subtracting any differentiable function Ba expressed over the belief space from Q^{π_θ} will not change the gradient. A good selection of Ba, which is called the *baseline*, can reduce the variance dramatically (Sutton and Barto, 1998). As a result, Equation 5 may be rewritten as follows:

$$\nabla_\theta J(\theta) = \mathbb{E}_{\pi_\theta}[\nabla_\theta \log \pi_\theta(a|b) Ad(b, a)], \tag{6}$$

where $Ad(b, a) = Q^{\pi_\theta}(b, a) - Ba(b)$ is called the *advantage function*. A good baseline is the value function V^{π_θ}, for which the advantage function becomes $Ad(b, a) = Q^{\pi_\theta}(b, a) - V^{\pi_\theta}(b)$. However, in this setting, we need to train two separate networks to parametrize Q^{π_θ} and V^{π_θ}. A better approach is to use the TD error $\delta = R_{t+1} + \gamma V^{\pi_\theta}(B_{t+1}) - V^{\pi_\theta}(B_t)$ as advantage function. It can be proved that the expected value of the TD error is $Q^{\pi_\theta}(b, a) - V^{\pi_\theta}(b)$. If the TD error is used, only one network is needed, to parametrize $V^{\pi_\theta}(B_t) = V^{\pi_\theta}(B_t; w_t)$. We call this network the *value network*. We can use a DQN-like method to train the value network using both experience replay and a target network. For a transition $B_t = b$, $A_t = a$, $R_{t+1} = r$ and $B_{t+1} = b'$, the advantage function is calculated as in:

$$\delta_t = r + \gamma V^{\pi_\theta}(b'; w_t) - V^{\pi_\theta}(b; w_t). \quad (7)$$

Because the gradient in Equation 6 is weighted by the advantage function, it may become quite large. In fact, the advantage function may act as a large learning rate. This can cause the learning process to become unstable. To avoid this issue, we add L_2 regularization to the policy objective function. We call this method Deep Advantage Actor-Critic (DA2C).

In the next section, we show how this architecture can be used to efficiently exploit a small set of handcrafted data.

5 Two-stage Training of the Policy Network

By definition, the policy network provides a probability distribution over the action space. As a result and in contrast to value-based methods such as DQN, a policy network can also be trained with direct *supervised learning* (Silver et al., 2016). Supervised training of RL agents has been well-studied in the context of Imitation Learning (IL). In IL, an agent learns to reproduce the behaviour of an expert. Supervised learning of the policy was one of the first techniques used to solve this problem (Pomerleau, 1989; Amit and Mataric, 2002). This direct type of imitation learning requires that the learning agent and the expert share the same characteristics. If this condition is not met, IL can be done at the level of the value functions rather than the policy directly (Piot et al., 2015). In this paper, the data that we use (DSTC2) was collected with a dialogue system similar to the one we train

so in our case, the demonstrator and the learner share the same characteristics.

Similarly to Silver et al. (2016), here, we initialize both the policy network and the value network on the data. The policy network is trained by minimising the categorical cross-entropy between the predicted action distribution and the demonstrated actions. The value network is trained directly through RL rather than IL to give more flexibility in the kind of data we can use. Indeed, our goal is to collect a small number of dialogues and learn from them. IL usually assumes that the data corresponds to expert policies. However, dialogues collected with a handcrafted policy or in a Wizard-of-Oz (WoZ) setting often contain both optimal and sub-optimal dialogues and RL can be used to learn from all of these dialogues. Supervised training can also be done on these dialogues as we show in Section 6.

Supervised actor-critic architectures following this idea have been proposed in the past (Benbrahim and Franklin, 1997; Si et al., 2004); the actor works together with a human supervisor to gain competence on its task even if the critic's estimations are poor. For instance, a human can help a robot move by providing the robot with valid actions. We advocate for the same kind of methods for dialogue systems. It is easy to collect a small number of high-quality dialogues and then use supervised learning on this data to teach the system valid actions. This also eliminates the need to define restricted action sets.

In all the methods above, *Adadelta* will be used as the gradient-decent optimiser, which in our experiments works noticeably better than other methods such as *Adagrad*, *Adam*, and *RMSProp*.

6 Experiments

6.1 Comparison of DQN and GPSARSA

6.1.1 Experimental Protocol

In this section, as a first argument in favour of deep RL, we perform a comparison between GPSARSA and DQN on simulated dialogues. We trained an agenda-based user simulator which at each dialogue turn, provides one or several dialogue act(s) in response to the latest machine act (Schatzmann et al., 2007; Schatzmann and Young, 2009). The dataset used for training this user-simulator is the Dialogue State Tracking Challenge 2 (DSTC2) (Henderson et al., 2014) dataset. State tracking is also trained on this dataset. DSTC2 includes

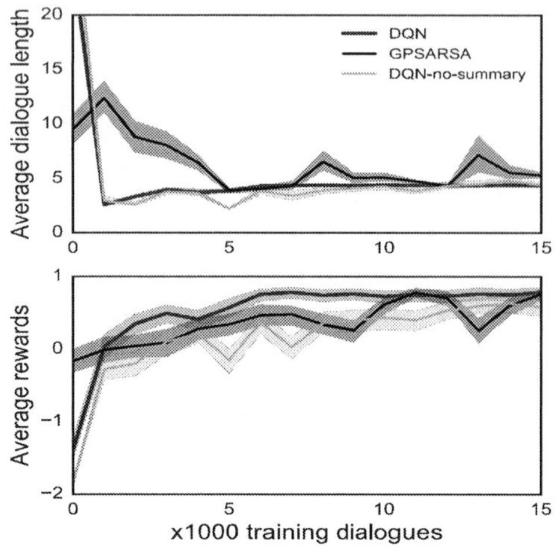 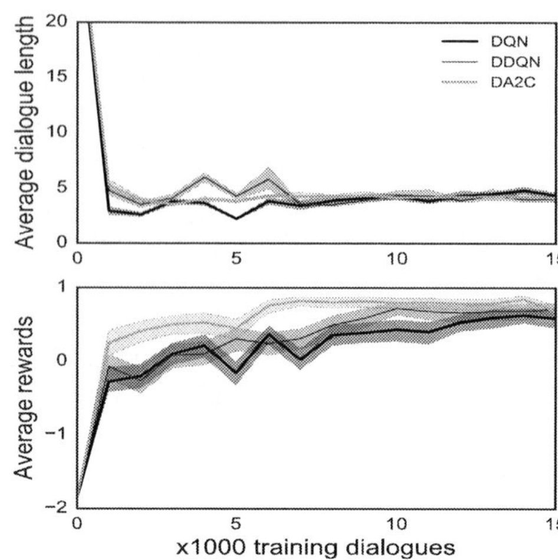

(a) Comparison of GPSARSA on summary spaces and DQN on summary (DQN) and original spaces (DQN-no-summary).

(b) Comparison of DA2C, DQN and DDQN on original spaces.

Figure 1: Comparison of different algorithms on simulated dialogues, without any pre-training.

dialogues with users who are searching for restaurants in Cambridge, UK.

In each dialogue, the user has a goal containing constraint slots and request slots. The constraint and request slots available in DSTC2 are listed in Appendix A. The constraints are the slots that the user has to provide to the system (for instance the user is looking for a specific type of food in a given area) and the requests are the slots that the user must receive from the system (for instance the user wants to know the address and phone number of the restaurant found by the system).

Similarly, the belief state is composed of two parts: constraints and requests. The constraint part includes the probabilities of the top two values for each constraint slot as returned by the state tracker (the value might be empty with a probability zero if the slot has not been mentioned). The request part, on the other hand, includes the probability of each request slot. For instance the constraint part might be [food: (Italian, 0.85) (Indian, 0.1) (Not_mentioned, 0.05)] and the request part might be [area: 0.95] meaning that the user is probably looking for an Italian restaurant and that he wants to know the area of the restaurant found by the system. To compare DQN to GPSARSA, we work on a summary state space (Gašić et al., 2012, 2013). Each constraint is mapped to a one-hot vector, with 1 corresponding to the tuple in the grid vec-

tor $g_c = [(1, 0), (.8, .2), (.6, .2), (.6, .4), (.4, .4)]$ that minimizes the Euclidean distance to the top two probabilities. Similarly, each request slot is mapped to a one-hot vector according to the grid $g_r = [1, .8, .6, .4, 0.]$. The final belief vector, known as the summary state, is defined as the concatenation of the constraint and request one-hot vectors. Each summary state is a binary vector of length 60 (12 one-hot vectors of length 5) and the total number of states is 5^{12}.

We also work on a summary action space and we use the act types listed in Table 1 in Appendix A. We add the necessary slot information as a post processing step. For example, the *request* act means that the system wants to request a slot from the user, *e.g.* request(food). In this case, the selection of the slot is based on min-max probability, *i.e.*, the most ambiguous slot (which is the slot we want to request) is assumed to be the one for which the value with maximum probability has the minimum probability compared to the most certain values of the other slots. Note that this heuristic approach to compute the summary state and action spaces is a requirement to make GPSARSA tractable; it is a serious limitation in general and should be avoided.

As reward, we use a normalized scheme with a reward of +1 if the dialogue finishes successfully before 30 turns,[5] a reward of -1 if the dialogue is not successful after 30 turns, and a reward of -0.03 for each turn. A reward of -1 is also distributed to the system if the user hangs up. In our settings, the user simulator hangs up every time the system proposes a restaurant which does not match at least one of his constraints.

For the deep Q-network, a Multi-Layer Perceptron (MLP) is used with two fully connected hidden layers, each having a *tanh* activation. The output layer has no activation and it provides the value for each of the summary machine acts. The summary machine acts are mapped to original acts using the heuristics explained previously. Both algorithms are trained with 15000 dialogues. GPSARSA is trained with ϵ-*softmax* exploration, which, with probability $1 - \epsilon$, selects an action based on the logistic distribution $\mathbb{P}[a|b] = \frac{e^{Q(b,a)}}{\sum_{a'} e^{Q(b,a')}}$ and, with probability ϵ, selects an action in a uniformly random way. From our experiments, this exploration scheme works best in terms of both convergence rate and variance. For DQN, we use a simple ϵ-*greedy* exploration which, with probability $1 - \epsilon$ (same ϵ as above), uniformly selects an action and, with probability ϵ, selects an action maximizing the Q-function. For both algorithms, ϵ is annealed to less than 0.1 over the course of training.

In a second experiment, we remove both summary state and action spaces for DQN, *i.e.*, we do not perform the Euclidean-distance mapping as before but instead work directly on the probabilities themselves. Additionally, the state is augmented with the probability (returned by the state tracker) of each user act (see Table 2 in Appendix A), the dialogue turn, and the number of results returned by the database (0 if there was no query). Consequently, the state consists of 31 continuous values and two discrete values. The original action space is composed of 11 actions: `offer`[6], `select-area`, `select-food`, `select-pricerange`, `request-area`, `request-food`, `request-pricerange`, `expl-conf-area`, `expl-conf-food`, `expl-conf-pricerange`, `repeat`. There

---

[5]A dialogue is successful if the user retrieves all the request slots for a restaurant matching all the constraints of his goal.

[6]This act consists of proposing a restaurant to the user. In order to be consistent with the DSTC2 dataset, an `offer` always contains the values for all the constraints understood by the system, *e.g.* offer(name = Super Ramen, food = Japanese, price range = cheap).

is no post-processing via min-max selection anymore since the slot is part of the action, *e.g.*, `select-area`.

The policies are evaluated after each 1000 training dialogues on 500 test dialogues without exploration.

6.1.2 Results

Figure 1 illustrates the performance of DQN compared to GPSARSA. In our experiments with GPSARSA we found that it was difficult to find a good tradeoff between precision and efficiency. Indeed, for low precision, the algorithm learned rapidly but did not reach optimal behaviour, whereas higher precision made learning extremely slow but resulted in better end-performance. On summary spaces, DQN outperforms GPSARSA in terms of convergence. Indeed, GPSARSA requires twice as many dialogues to converge. It is also worth mentioning here that the wall-clock training time of GPSARSA is considerably longer than the one of DQN due to kernel evaluation. The second experiment validates the fact that Deep RL can be efficiently trained directly on the belief state returned by the state tracker. Indeed, DQN on the original spaces performs as well as GPSARSA on the summary spaces.

In the next section, we train and compare the deep RL networks previously described on the original state and action spaces.

6.2 Comparison of the Deep RL Methods

6.2.1 Experimental Protocol

Similarly to the previous example, we work on a restaurant domain and use the DSTC2 specifications. We use ϵ-greedy exploration for all four algorithms with ϵ starting at 0.5 and being linearly annealed at a rate of $\lambda = 0.99995$. To speed up the learning process, the actions `select-pricerange`, `select-area`, and `select-food` are excluded from exploration. Note that this set does not depend on the state and is meant for exploration only. All the actions can be performed by the system at any moment.

We derived two datasets from DSTC2. The first dataset contains the 2118 dialogues of DSTC2. We had these dialogues rated by a human expert, based on the quality of dialogue management and on a scale of 0 to 3. The second dataset only contains the dialogues with a rating of 3 (706 dialogues). The underlying assumption is that these dialogues correspond to optimal policies.

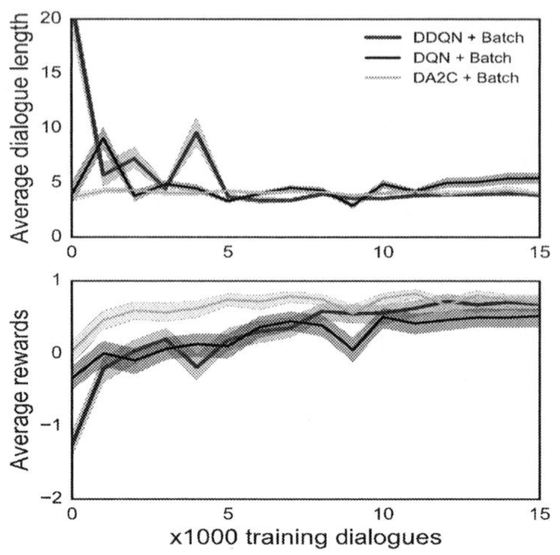

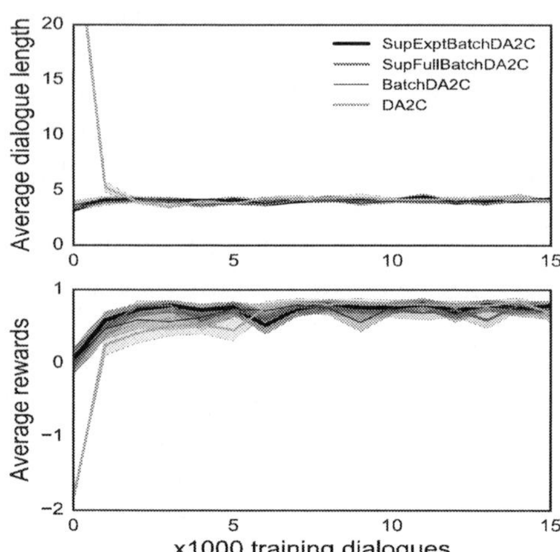

(a) Comparison of DA2C, DQN and DDQN after batch initialization.

(b) Comparison of DA2C and DA2C after batch initialization (batchDA2C), and TDA2C after supervised training on expert (SupExptBatchDA2C) and non-expert data (SupFullBatchDA2C).

Figure 2: Comparison of different algorithms on simulated dialogues, with pre-training.

We compare the convergence rates of the deep RL models in different settings. First, we compare DQN, DDQN and DA2C without any pre-training (Figure 1b). Then, we compare DQN, DDQN and TDA2C with an RL initialization on the DSTC2 dataset (Figure 2a). Finally, we focus on the advantage actor-critic models and compare DA2C, TDA2C, TDA2C with batch initialization on DSTC2, and TDA2C with batch initialization on the expert dialogues (Figure 2b).

6.2.2 Results

As expected, DDQN converges faster than DQN on all experiments. Figure 1b shows that, without any pre-training, DA2C is the one which converges the fastest (6000 dialogues *vs.* 10000 dialogues for the other models). Figure 2a gives consistent results and shows that, with initial training on the 2118 dialogues of DSTC2, TDA2C converges significantly faster than the other models. Figure 2b focuses on DA2C and TDA2C. Compared to batch training, supervised training on DSTC2 speeds up convergence by 2000 dialogues (3000 dialogues *vs.* 5000 dialogues). Interestingly, there does not seem to be much difference between supervised training on the expert data and on DSTC2. The expert data only consists of 706 dialogues out of 2118 dialogues. Our observation is that, in the non-expert data, many

of the dialogue acts chosen by the system were still appropriate, which explains that the system learns acceptable behavior from the entire dataset. This shows that supervised training, even when performed not only on optimal dialogues, makes learning much faster and relieves the need for restricted action sets. Valid actions are learnt from the dialogues and then RL exploits the good and bad dialogues to pursue training towards a high performing policy.

7 Concluding Remarks

In this paper, we used policy networks for dialogue systems and trained them in a two-stage fashion: supervised training and batch reinforcement learning followed by online reinforcement learning. An important feature of policy networks is that they directly provide a probability distribution over the action space, which enables supervised training. We compared the results with other deep reinforcement learning algorithms, namely Deep Q Networks and Double Deep Q Networks. The combination of supervised and reinforcement learning is the main benefit of our method, which paves the way for developing trainable end-to-end dialogue systems. Supervised training on a small dataset considerably bootstraps the learning process and can be used to significantly improve the convergence rate of reinforcement learning in statistically optimised dialogue systems.

References

R. Amit and M. Mataric. 2002. Learning movement sequences from demonstration. In *Proc. Int. Conf. on Development and Learning*. pages 203–208.

A. G. Barto, R. S. Sutton, and C. W. Anderson. 1990. In *Artificial Neural Networks*, chapter Neuronlike Adaptive Elements That Can Solve Difficult Learning Control Problems, pages 81–93.

H. Benbrahim and J. A. Franklin. 1997. Biped dynamic walking using reinforcement learning. *Robotics and Autonomous Systems* 22:283–302.

D. P. Bertsekas and J. Tsitsiklis. 1996. *Neuro-Dynamic Programming*. Athena Scientific.

S. Bhatnagar, R. Sutton, M. Ghavamzadeh, and M. Lee. 2009. Natural Actor-Critic Algorithms. *Automatica* 45(11).

H. Cuayáhuitl. 2016. Simpleds: A simple deep reinforcement learning dialogue system. arXiv:1601.04574v1 [cs.AI].

H. Cuayáhuitl, S. Keizer, and O. Lemon. 2015. Strategic dialogue management via deep reinforcement learning. arXiv:1511.08099 [cs.AI].

L. Daubigney, M. Geist, S. Chandramohan, and O. Pietquin. 2012. A Comprehensive Reinforcement Learning Framework for Dialogue Management Optimisation. *IEEE Journal of Selected Topics in Signal Processing* 6(8):891–902.

Y. Engel, S. Mannor, and R. Meir. 2005. Reinforcement learning with gaussian processes. In *Proc. of ICML*.

M. Gašić, C. Breslin, M. Henderson, D. Kim, M. Szummer, B. Thomson, P. Tsiakoulis, and S.J. Young. 2013. On-line policy optimisation of bayesian spoken dialogue systems via human interaction. In *Proc. of ICASSP*. pages 8367–8371.

M. Gašić, M. Henderson, B. Thomson, P. Tsiak-oulis, and S. Young. 2012. Policy optimisation of POMDP-based dialogue systems without state space compression. In *Proc. of SLT*.

M. Gašić, F. Jurčíček, S. Keizer, F. Mairesse, B. Thomson, K. Yu, and S. Young. 2010. Gaussian processes for fast policy optimisation of POMDP-based dialogue managers. In *Proc. of SIGDIAL*.

M. Henderson, B. Thomson, and J. Williams. 2014. The Second Dialog State Tracking Challenge. In *Proc. of SIGDIAL*.

R. Laroche, G. Putois, and P. Bretier. 2010. Optimising a handcrafted dialogue system design. In *Proc. of Interspeech*.

O. Lemon and O. Pietquin. 2007. Machine learning for spoken dialogue systems. In *Proc. of Interspeech*. pages 2685–2688.

E. Levin, R. Pieraccini, and W. Eckert. 1997. Learning dialogue strategies within the markov decision process framework. In *Proc. of ASRU*.

L-J Lin. 1993. *Reinforcement learning for robots using neural networks*. Ph.D. thesis, Carnegie Mellon University.

V Mnih, K. Kavukcuoglu, D. Silver, A. Graves, I Antonoglou, D. Wierstra, and M. Riedmiller. 2013. Playing Atari with deep reinforcement learning. In *NIPS Deep Learning Workshop*.

V. Mnih, K. Kavukcuoglu, D. Silver, A.A. Rusu, J. Veness, M.G. Bellemare, A. Graves, M. Riedmiller, A.K. Fidjeland, G. Ostrovski, S. Petersen, C. Beattie, A. Sadik, I. Antonoglou, H. King, D. Kumaran, D. Wierstra, S. Legg, and D. Hassabis. 2015. Human-level control through deep reinforcement learning. *Nature* 518(7540):529–533.

B. Piot, M. Geist, and O. Pietquin. 2015. Imitation Learning Applied to Embodied Conversational Agents. In *Proc. of MLIS*.

D. A. Pomerleau. 1989. Alvinn: An autonomous land vehicle in a neural network. In *Proc. of NIPS*. pages 305–313.

J. Schatzmann, B. Thomson, K. Weilhammer, H. Ye, and S. Young. 2007. Agenda-based user simulation for bootstrapping a POMDP dialogue system. In *Proc. of NAACL HLT*. pages 149–152.

J. Schatzmann and S. Young. 2009. The hidden agenda user simulation model. *Proc. of TASLP* 17(4):733–747.

J. Si, A. G. Barto, W. B. Powell, and D. Wunsch. 2004. *Supervised ActorCritic Reinforcement Learning*, pages 359–380.

D. Silver, A. Huang, C.J. Maddison, A. Guez, L. Sifre, G. van den Driessche, J. Schrittwieser,

I. Antonoglou, V. Panneershelvam, M. Lanctot, S. Dieleman, D. Grewe, J. Nham, N. Kalchbrenner, I. Sutskever, T. Lillicrap, M. Leach, K. Kavukcuoglu, T. Graepel, and D. Hassabis. 2016. Mastering the game of go with deep neural networks and tree search. *Nature* 529(7587):484–489.

S. Sukhbaatar, A. Szlam, G. Synnaeve, S. Chintala, and R. Fergus. 2016. Mazebase: A sandbox for learning from games. arxiv.org/pdf/1511.07401 [cs.LG].

R. S. Sutton. 1984. *Temporal credit assignment in reinforcement learning*. Ph.D. thesis, University of Massachusetts at Amherst, Amherst, MA, USA.

R. S. Sutton, D. McAllester, S. Singh, and Y. Mansour. 2000. Policy gradient methods for reinforcement learning with function approximation. In *Proc. of NIPS*. volume 12, pages 1057–1063.

R.S. Sutton and A.G. Barto. 1998. *Reinforcement Learning*. MIT Press.

H. van Hasselt. 2010. Double q-learning. In *Proc. of NIPS*. pages 2613–2621.

H. van Hasselt, A. Guez, and D. Silver. 2015. Deep reinforcement learning with double Q-learning. arXiv:1509.06461v3 [cs.LG].

J.D. Williams and S. Young. 2007. Partially observable markov decision processes for spoken dialog systems. *Proc. of CSL* 21:231–422.

R.J. Williams. 1992. Simple statistical gradient-following algorithms for connectionist reinforcement learning. *Machine Learning* 8:229–256.

S. Young, M. Gasic, B. Thomson, and J. Williams. 2013. POMDP-based statistical spoken dialog systems: A review. *Proc. IEEE* 101(5):1160–1179.

A Specifications of restaurant search in DTSC2

Constraint slots area, type of food, price range.

Request slots area, type of food, address, name, price range, postcode, signature dish, phone number

Table 1: Summary actions.

Action	Description
Cannot help	No restaurant in the database matches the user's constraints.
Confirm Domain	Confirm that the user is looking for a restaurant.
Explicit Confirm	Ask the user to confirm a piece of information.
Offer	Propose a restaurant to the user.
Repeat	Ask the user to repeat.
Request	Request a slot from the user.
Select	Ask the user to select a value between two propositions (*e.g.* select between Italian and Indian).

Table 2: User actions.

Action	Description
Deny	Deny a piece of information.
Null	Say nothing.
Request More	Request more options.
Confirm	Ask the system to confirm a piece of information.
Acknowledge	Acknowledge.
Affirm	Say yes.
Request	Request a slot value.
Inform	Inform the system of a slot value.
Thank you	Thank the system.
Repeat	Ask the system to repeat.
Request Alternatives	Request alternative restaurant options.
Negate	Say no.
Bye	Say goodbye to the system.
Hello	Say hello to the system.
Restart	Ask the system to restart the dialogue.

Language Portability for Dialogue Systems: Translating a Question-Answering System from English into Tamil

Satheesh Ravi[1] and **Ron Artstein**[1,2]

University of Southern California

[1]Department of Computer Science, 941 Bloom Walk, Los Angeles, CA 90089-0781, USA

[2]Institute for Creative Technologies, 12015 Waterfront Drive, Playa Vista CA 90094, USA

`satheesr@usc.edu, artstein@ict.usc.edu`

Abstract

A training and test set for a dialogue system in the form of linked questions and responses is translated from English into Tamil. Accuracy of identifying an appropriate response in Tamil is 79%, compared to the English accuracy of 89%, suggesting that translation can be useful to start up a dialogue system. Machine translation of Tamil inputs into English also results in 79% accuracy. However, machine translation of the English training data into Tamil results in a drop in accuracy to 54% when tested on manually authored Tamil, indicating that there is still a large gap before machine translated dialogue systems can interact with human users.

1 Introduction

Much of the effort in creating a dialogue system is devoted to the collection of training data, to allow the system to process, understand, and react to input coming from real users. If a comparable system is available for a different language, it would be helpful to use some of the existing foreign language resources in order to cut down the development time and cost – an issue known as *language portability*. Recent efforts have shown machine translation to be an effective tool for porting dialogue system resources from French into Italian (Jabaian et al., 2010; Jabaian et al., 2013; Servan et al., 2010); this system used concept-based language understanding, and the findings were that machine translation of the target language inputs yielded better results than using translation to train an understanding component directly for the target language. Here we report similar findings on more challenging data, by exploring a dialogue system with a less structured understanding com-

ponent, using off-the-shelf rather than domain-adapted machine translation, and with languages that are not as closely related.

Question-answering characters are designed to sustain a conversation driven primarily by the user asking questions. Leuski et al. (2006) developed algorithms for training such characters using linked questions and responses in the form of unstructured natural language text. Given a novel user question, the character finds an appropriate response from a list of available responses, and when a direct answer is not available, the character selects an "off-topic" response according to a set policy, ensuring that the conversation remains coherent even with a finite number of responses. The response selection algorithms are language-independent, also allowing the questions and responses to be in separate languages. These algorithms have been incorporated into a tool (Leuski and Traum, 2011) which has been used to create characters for a variety of applications (e.g. Leuski et al., 2006; Artstein et al., 2009; Swartout et al., 2010). To date, most characters created using these principles understood and spoke only English; one fairly limited character spoke Pashto, a language of Afghanistan (Aggarwal et al., 2011).

To test language portability we chose Tamil, a Dravidian language spoken primarily in southern India. Tamil has close to 70 million speakers worldwide (Lewis et al., 2015), is the official language of Tamil Nadu and Puducherry in India (Wasey, 2014), and an official language in Sri Lanka and Singapore. There is active development of language processing tools in Tamil such as stemmers (Thangarasu and Manavalan, 2013), POS taggers (Pandian and Geetha, 2008), constituent and dependency parsers (Saravanan et al., 2003; Ramasamy and Žabokrtský, 2011), sentence generators (Pandian and Geetha, 2009), etc.; commercial systems are also available, such as

Proceedings of the SIGDIAL 2016 Conference, pages 111–116,
Los Angeles, USA, 13-15 September 2016. ©2016 Association for Computational Linguistics

Google Translate[1] between Tamil and English. Information-providing spoken dialogue systems have been developed for Tamil (Janarthanam et al., 2007), but we are not aware of any conversational dialogue systems.

The main questions we want to answer in this paper are: (Q1) How good is a dialogue system created using translation between English and Tamil? (Q2) Is there a difference between manual and machine translation in this regard? (Q3) Can machine translation be used for interaction with users, that is with manually translated test data?

To answer these questions, we translated linked questions and responses from an English question-answering system into Tamil both mechanically and manually, and tested the response selection algorithms on the English and both versions of the Tamil data. We found that translation caused a drop in performance of about 10% on either manually or mechanically translated text, answering a tentative *fair* to Q1 and *no* to Q2. The answer to Q3 is mixed: a similar performance drop of about 10% was found with machine translation on the target language inputs (that is, translating test questions from Tamil into English); a much more severe drop in performance was observed when using machine translation to create a system in the target language (that is, translating the training data from English into Tamil, and testing on manually authored Tamil). The remainder of the paper describes the experiment and results, and concludes with directions for future research.

2 Method

2.1 Materials

Our English data come from the *New Dimensions in Testimony* system, which allows people to ask questions in conversation with a representation of Holocaust Survivor Pinchas Gutter; this system had undergone an extensive process of user testing, so the linked questions and responses contain many actual user questions that are relevant to the domain (Artstein et al., 2015; Traum et al., 2015). The *New Dimensions in Testimony* system has more than 1700 responses, almost 7000 training questions, and 400 test questions, with a many-to-many linking between questions and responses (Traum et al., 2015). To get a dataset that is large enough to yield meaningful results yet small

enough to translate manually, we needed a subset that included questions with multiple links, and answers that were fairly short. We selected all the test questions that had exactly 4 linked responses, and removed all the responses that were more than 200 characters in length; this yielded a test set with 28 questions, 45 responses, and 63 links, with each test question linked to between 1 and 4 responses. We took all the training questions linked to the 45 test responses, resulting in a training set with 441 questions and 1101 links. This sampling procedure was deliberately intended to enable high performance on the English data, in order to provide a wide range of possible performance for the various translated versions.

Automatic translation into Tamil was done using Google Translate, and manual translation was performed by the first author. Thus, each question and response in the training and test datasets has three versions: the original English, and automatic and manual translations into Tamil.

2.2 Tokenization

We use unigrams as tokens for the response classification algorithm; these are expected to work well for Tamil, which has a fairly free word order (Lehmann, 1989). The English text was tokenized using the `word_tokenize` routine from NLTK (Bird et al., 2009). This tokenizer does not work for Tamil characters, so we used a simple tokenizer that separates tokens by whitespace and removes periods, exclamation marks, question marks and quotation marks. The same simple tokenizer was used as a second option for the English text.

2.3 Stemming

Tamil is an agglutinative language where stems can take many affixes (Lehmann, 1989), so we experimented with a stemmer (Rajalingam, 2013).[2] For comparison, we also ran the English experiments with the `SnowballStemmer("english")` routine from NLTK.[3]

2.4 Response ranking

We reimplemented parts of the response ranking algorithms of Leuski et al. (2006), including both the language modeling (LM) and cross-language modeling (CLM) approaches. The LM approach

---

[1] http://translate.google.com

[2] https://github.com/rdamodharan/tamil-stemmer
[3] http://www.nltk.org/howto/stem.html

constructs language models for both questions and responses using the question vocabulary. For each training question S, a language model is estimated as the frequency distribution of tokens in S, smoothed by the distribution of tokens in the entire question corpus (eq. 1). The language model of a novel question Q is estimated as the probability of each token in the vocabulary coinciding with Q (eq. 2). Each available response R is associated with a pseudo-question Q_R made up by the concatenation of all the questions linked to R in the training data. The responses are ranked by the distance between a novel question Q and the associated pseudo-questions Q_R using Kullback-Leibler (KL) divergence (eq. 3).

$$(1) \quad \pi_S(w) = \lambda_\pi \frac{\#_S(w)}{|S|} + (1 - \lambda_\pi) \frac{\sum_{S'} \#_{S'}(w)}{\sum_{S'} |S'|}$$

$$(2) \quad P(w|Q) \cong \frac{\sum_{S'} \pi_{S'}(w) \prod_{q \in \text{tok}(Q)} \pi_{S'}(q)}{\sum_{S'} \prod_{q \in \text{tok}(Q)} \pi_{S'}(q)}$$

$$(3) \quad D(Q||Q_R) = \sum_{w \in V_{S'}} P(w|Q) \log \frac{P(w|Q)}{\pi_{Q_R}(w)}$$

In eq. (1), $\#_S(w)$ is the number of times token w appears in sequence S; $|S|$ is the length of sequence S; the variable S' iterates over all the questions in the corpus, and λ_π is a smoothing parameter. The sum in eq. (2) is over all the questions in the training corpus; the product iterates over the tokens in the question, and thus is an estimate the probability of the question Q given a training question S'. In eq. (3), $V_{S'}$ is the entire question vocabulary.

The CLM approach constructs language models for both questions and responses using the response vocabulary. The language model of a response is estimated in a similar way to eq. (1), but with the smoothing factor using the response corpus (eq. 4). The language model associated with a novel question Q represents the ideal response to Q, and is estimated as the probability of each token in the response vocabulary coinciding with Q in the linked question-response training data (eq. 5); available responses are ranked against this ideal response (eq. 6).

$$(4) \quad \phi_R(w) = \lambda_\phi \frac{\#_R(w)}{|R|} + (1 - \lambda_\phi) \frac{\sum_{R'} \#_{R'}(w)}{\sum_{R'} |R'|}$$

$$(5) \quad P(w|Q) \cong \frac{\sum_j \phi_{R_j}(w) \prod_{q \in \text{tok}(Q)} \pi_{S_j}(q)}{\sum_j \prod_{q \in \text{tok}(Q)} \pi_{S_j}(q)}$$

$$(6) \quad D(Q||R) = \sum_{w \in V_{R'}} P(w|Q) \log \frac{P(w|Q)}{\phi_R(w)}$$

The sum in eq. (5) is over all linked question-response pairs $\{S_j, R_j\}$ in the training data, and the product is an estimate the probability of the question Q given the training question S_j. In eq. (6), $V_{R'}$ is the entire response vocabulary.

We did not implement the parameter learning of Leuski et al. (2006); instead we use a constant smoothing parameter $\lambda_\pi = \lambda_\phi = 0.1$. We also do not use the response threshold parameter, which Leuski et al. (2006) use to determine whether the top-ranked response is good enough. Instead, we just check for the correctness of the top-ranked response.

2.5 Procedure

Our basic tests kept the language and processing options the same for questions and responses. Each dataset (English and the two Tamil translations) was processed with both the LM and CLM approaches, both with and without a stemmer; English was also processed with the two tokenizer options.

Additionally, we processed some cross-language datasets, with questions in Tamil and responses in English, and vice versa. We also performed two tests intended to check whether it is feasible to use machine-translated data with human questions: the manually translated Tamil test questions were machine translated back into English and tested with the original English training data (target language input translation); the manually translated Tamil test questions were also tested with the automatically translated Tamil training questions (creating a target language system).

2.6 Evaluation

We use accuracy as our success measure: the top ranked response to a test question is considered correct if it is identified as a correct response in the linked test data (there are up to 4 correct responses per question). This measure does not take into account non-understanding, that is the classifier's determination that the best response is not good enough (Leuski et al., 2006), since this capability was not implemented; however, since all of our test questions are known to have at least one appropriate response, any non-understanding of a question would necessarily count against accuracy anyway.

Language	Tokenizer / Translation	Stem	Accuracy (%)	
			LM	CLM
English	Simple	–	89	82
		+	89	79
	NLTK	–	89	79
		+	89	79
Tamil	Google	–	79	68
		+	71	64
	Manual	–	79	61
		+	68	57

Table 1: Response accuracy on 28 test questions

Question		Response	Accuracy (%)	
Train	Test		LM	CLM
English	English	Tam (G)	89	82
Tam (G)	Tam (G)	English	79	68
English	Eng (G)	English (NLTK)	79	57
		English (Simple)	64	46
Tam (G)	Tam (M)	English	54	43
		Tam (G)	54	39

Table 2: Accuracy with question and response in different languages (G = Google, M = manual)

3 Results

The results of the experiments with matched question and response languages are reported in Table 1. The LM approach almost invariably produced better results than the CLM approach; this is the opposite of the findings of Leuski et al. (2006), where CLM fared consistently better. In most cases, the errors produced by the CLM approach were a superset of those of the LM approach; the only exceptions were Tamil with stemming.

Accuracy of response selection on the Tamil data is about 10% lower than that of English, or twice the errors (6 errors rather than 3). The errors of automatically translated Tamil are a superset of the English errors; however, manually translated Tamil did get right some of the errors of English.

Some of the errors are due to the complexity of Tamil morphology. For example, the following test question receives a correct response in English but incorrect responses in Tamil:

(7) How do you envision the future?
எதிர்காலம் எவ்வாறு கற்பனை செய்கிறிர்கள்

The correct responses are linked to the following training questions.

(8) Are you hopeful about the future?
நீங்கள் எதிர்காலத்தின் மீது நம்பிக்கையாக இருக்கிறீர்களா

(9) Do you have hope for the future?
உங்களுக்கு எதிர்காலத்தின் மீது நம்பிக்கை இருக்கிறதா

In English the word *future*, common to training and test questions, helps identify the desired responses. In Tamil, however, the word "future" appears in distinct case forms: unmarked எதிர்காலம் *etirkaalam* in the test question, but genitive எதிர்காலத்தின் *etirkaalattin* in the training questions. It looks as though some morphological analysis of the Tamil text would be useful. However, while English appears almost invariant to the use of stemming, Tamil performs markedly worse with a stemmer. In this particular case, the stemmer does not unify the *-am* and *-attin* forms, and leaves both forms intact (these forms involve both a stem alternation *-am/-att* as well as a case morpheme *-in*). We are still not able to say why the stemmer hurts performance, but it appears that our application could benefit from a different level of morphological analysis than provided by the current stemmer.

Table 2 reports the results of the experiments which use different languages for the questions and responses. The top two rows use the same language for training and test questions, and only the response language varies. Accuracy is the same as that of the question language: this is necessarily the case for the LM approach, which does not use any of the response content; but it turned out to be the case even for the CLM approach. The middle two rows show the effect of machine translation on the target language inputs: questions in Tamil (manually translated from English) are automatically translated into English, and tested with the original English system. The performance penalty turns out to be the same as for the Tamil systems with matched training and test data, when using the NLTK tokenizer; the simple tokenizer incurs a larger performance penalty. Finally, the bottom two rows show the effect of using machine translation to create a target language system: manually translated questions in Tamil are tested with a system trained on automatic translation from English into Tamil. Performance drops sharply, likely due to mismatches between automatically and manually translated Tamil; this probably speaks to the quality of present state machine translation from English to Tamil. The result means that at present, off-the-shelf machine translation into Tamil is not quite sufficient for a translated dialogue system to work well with human user questions.

4 Discussion

The experiments demonstrate that translating data in the form of linked questions and responses from one language to another can result in a classifier that works in the target language, though there is a drop in performance. The reasons for the drop are not clear, but it appears that simple tokenization is not as effective for Tamil as it is for English, and the level of morphological analysis provided by the Tamil stemmer is probably not appropriate for the task. We thus need to continue experimenting with Tamil morphology tools. The further drop in performance when mixing automatically and manually translated Tamil is probably due to translation mismatches.

Several questions remain left for future work. One possibility is to improve the machine translation itself, for example by adapting it to the domain. Another alternative is to use both languages together for classification; the fact that the manual Tamil translation identified some responses missed by the English classifier suggests that there may be benefit to this approach. Another direction for future work is identifying bad responses by using the distance between question and response to plot the tradeoff curve between errors and return rates (Artstein, 2011).

In our experiments the LM approach consistently outperforms the CLM approach, contra Leuski et al. (2006). Our data may not be quite natural: while the English data are well tested, our sampling method may introduce biases that affect the results. But even if we achieved full English-like performance using machine translation, the questions that Tamil speakers want to ask will likely be somewhat different than those of English speakers. A translated dialogue system is therefore only an initial step towards tailoring a system to a new population.

Acknowledgments

The original English data come from the *New Dimensions in Testimony* project, a collaboration between the USC Institute for Creative Technologies, the USC Shoah Foundation, and Conscience Display.

The second author was supported in part by the U.S. Army; statements and opinions expressed do not necessarily reflect the position or the policy of the United States Government, and no official endorsement should be inferred.

References

Priti Aggarwal, Kevin Feeley, Fabrizio Morbini, Ron Artstein, Anton Leuski, David Traum, and Julia Kim. 2011. Interactive characters for cultural training of small military units. In *Intelligent Virtual Agents (IVA 2011)*, pages 426–427. Springer, September.

Ron Artstein, Sudeep Gandhe, Jillian Gerten, Anton Leuski, and David Traum. 2009. Semi-formal evaluation of conversational characters. In Orna Grumberg, Michael Kaminski, Shmuel Katz, and Shuly Wintner, editors, *Languages: From Formal to Natural. Essays Dedicated to Nissim Francez on the Occasion of His 65th Birthday*, volume 5533 of *Lecture Notes in Computer Science*, pages 22–35. Springer, May.

Ron Artstein, Anton Leuski, Heather Maio, Tomer Mor-Barak, Carla Gordon, and David Traum. 2015. How many utterances are needed to support time-offset interaction? In *Proc. FLAIRS-28*, pages 144–149, Hollywood, Florida, May.

Ron Artstein. 2011. Error return plots. In *Proceedings of SIGDIAL*, pages 319–324, Portland, Oregon, June.

Steven Bird, Edward Loper, and Ewan Klein. 2009. *Natural Language Processing with Python*. OReilly Media Inc.

Bassam Jabaian, Laurent Besacier, and Fabrice Lefèvre. 2010. Investigating multiple approaches for SLU portability to a new language. In *Proceedings of Interspeech*, pages 2502–2505, Chiba, Japan, September.

Bassam Jabaian, Laurent Besacier, and Fabrice Lefèvre. 2013. Comparison and combination of lightly supervised approaches for language portability of a spoken language understanding system. *IEEE Transactions on Audio, Speech, and Language Processing*, 21(3):636–648, March.

Srinivasan Janarthanam, Udhaykumar Nallasamy, Loganathan Ramasamy, and C. Santhosh Kumar. 2007. Robust dependency parser for natural language dialog systems in Tamil. In *Proceedings of 5th IJCAI Workshop on Knowledge and Reasoning in Practical Dialogue Systems*, pages 1–6, Hyderabad, India, January.

Thomas Lehmann. 1989. *A Grammar of Modern Tamil*. Pondicherry Institute of Linguistics and Culture, Pondicherry, India.

Anton Leuski and David Traum. 2011. NPCEditor: creating virtual human dialogue using information retrieval techniques. *AI Magazine*, 32(2):42–56.

Anton Leuski, Ronakkumar Patel, David Traum, and Brandon Kennedy. 2006. Building effective question answering characters. In *Proceedings of SIGDIAL*, Sydney, Australia, July.

M. Paul Lewis, Gary F. Simons, and Charles D. Fennig. 2015. *Ethnologue: Languages of the World*. SIL International, Dallas, Texas, eighteenth edition. Online version: http://www.ethnologue.com.

S. Lakshmana Pandian and T. V. Geetha. 2008. Morpheme based language model for Tamil part-of-speech tagging. *Polibits*, 38:19–25.

S. Lakshmana Pandian and T. V. Geetha. 2009. Semantic role based Tamil sentence generator. In *International Conference on Asian Language Processing*, pages 80–85, Singapore, December.

Damodharan Rajalingam. 2013. A rule based iterative affix stripping stemming algorithm for Tamil. In *Twelfth International Tamil Internet Conference*, pages 28–34, Kuala Lumpur, Malaysia, August. International Forum for Information Technology in Tamil.

Loganathan Ramasamy and Zdeněk Žabokrtský. 2011. Tamil dependency parsing: Results using rule based and corpus based approaches. In Alexander F. Gelbukh, editor, *Computational Linguistics and Intelligent Text Processing: 12th International Conference, CICLing 2011, Tokyo, Japan, February 20–26, 2011, Proceedings, Part I*, volume 6608 of *Lecture Notes in Computer Science*, pages 82–95. Springer, February.

K. Saravanan, Ranjani Parthasarathi, and T. V. Geetha. 2003. Syntactic parser for Tamil. In *Sixth International Tamil Internet Conference*, pages 28–37, Chennai, India, August. International Forum for Information Technology in Tamil.

Christophe Servan, Nathalie Camelin, Christian Raymond, Frédéric Béchet, and Renato De Mori. 2010. On the use of machine translation for spoken language portability. In *Proceedings of ICASSP*, pages 5330–5333, Dallas, Texas, March.

William Swartout, David Traum, Ron Artstein, Dan Noren, Paul Debevec, Kerry Bronnenkant, Josh Williams, Anton Leuski, Shrikanth Narayanan, Diane Piepol, Chad Lane, Jacquelyn Morie, Priti Aggarwal, Matt Liewer, Jen-Yuan Chiang, Jillian Gerten, Selina Chu, and Kyle White. 2010. Ada and Grace: Toward realistic and engaging virtual museum guides. In *Intelligent Virtual Agents (IVA 2010)*, pages 286–300. Springer, September.

M. Thangarasu and R. Manavalan. 2013. Stemmers for tamil language: Performance analysis. *International Journal of Computer Science and Engineering Technology*, 4(7):902–908, July.

David Traum, Kallirroi Georgila, Ron Artstein, and Anton Leuski. 2015. Evaluating spoken dialogue processing for time-offset interaction. In *Proceedings of SIGDIAL*, pages 199–208, Prague, September.

Akhtarul Wasey. 2014. 50th report of the Commissioner for Linguistic Minorities in India. CLM Report 50/2014, Indian Ministry of Minority Affairs.

Extracting PDTB Discourse Relations from Student Essays

Kate Forbes-Riley and **Fan Zhang** and **Diane Litman**
University of Pittsburgh
Pittsburgh, PA 15260 USA
`katherineforbesriley@gmail.com, faz23@pitt.edu`
`dlitman@pitt.edu`

Abstract

We investigate the manual and automatic annotation of PDTB discourse relations in student essays, a novel domain that is not only learning-based and argumentative, but also noisy with surface errors and deeper coherency issues. We discuss methodological complexities it poses for the task. We present descriptive statistics and compare relation distributions in related corpora. We compare automatic discourse parsing performance to prior work.

1 Introduction

The Penn Discourse Treebank (PDTB) framework (Prasad et al., 2014) has been used to add discourse relation annotation to numerous corpora, including the Wall Street Journal corpus. It differs from other approaches because of its focus on the lexical grounding of discourse relations, such that all discourse relations either are or can be instantiated by a discourse connective (e.g., *however, in other words*). This linkage between lexicon and discourse relation has been shown to yield reliable human annotation across languages (Alsaif and Markert, 2011; Zhou and Xue, 2015; Zeyrek et al., 2013; Sharma et al., 2013; Polkov et al., 2013; Danlos et al., 2012) and as a result has facilitated the increased use of discourse relations in language technology and psycholinguistics research (e.g. (Ghosh et al., 2012; Patterson and Kehler, 2003; Torabi Asr and Demberg, 2013)). Researchers are also working towards automating PDTB annotation, although performance to date is still low, with F1 scores near 30% under the strictest evaluation terms (e.g., (Lin et al., 2014; Xue et al., 2015; Ji and Eisenstein, 2014)).

The purpose of the present study is to investigate the manual and automatic annotation of PDTB relations in a corpus of student essays. This corpus differs markedly from all prior ones to which the PDTB framework has been applied. First, it is both argumentative and learning-based: students are learning about argumentative writing through the essay-writing process. Second it is noisy, displaying not only spelling and grammar errors but also deeper problems of referential and relational coherency. We hypothesized that these differences would shed light on unclear aspects of the PDTB framework, while also challenging an automatic discourse parser. However, if despite their inherent noise, learning-based datasets could be shown able to be reliably annotated for discourse relations, then they could provide language technology and psycholinguistics research a wealth of new applications. For example, interactions between students' discourse relation use and their quality and quantity of learning and affective states could be investigated (c.f. (Litman and Forbes-Riley, 2014)), as could the use of discourse relations for improving automated essay graders and writing tutors (c.f. (Zhang et al., 2016)).

In this paper we discuss methodological complexities posed by applying the PDTB framework to noisy, learning-based, and argumentative data, including a heightened ambiguity between EntRel, Expansion, and Contingency relations. We present descriptive statistics showing how the relation distributions compare to both the PDTB (Prasad et al., 2014) and BioDRB corpus (Prasad et al., 2011), whose texts possess argumentative structure without being noisy or learning-based. Some of these results suggest targets for future learning research. For example, the essays contain 12% fewer explicit connectives, contributing not only to the lowered coherency but also reflecting inexperience with connective use. We then investigate the performance of the Lin et al. (2014) PDTB-trained parser, and find that relaxing the minimal

Proceedings of the SIGDIAL 2016 Conference, pages 117–127,
Los Angeles, USA, 13-15 September 2016. ©2016 Association for Computational Linguistics

argument constraint and predicting only Level-1 senses tempers the negative impact of the noise; the parser yields an end-to-end F1 score of 31% under strictest evaluation terms, similar to other corpora and parsers (Xue et al., 2015). Like this prior work, performance is highest on the first steps of connective identification and argument match. Patterns of errors in the remaining steps indicate training on domain-specific data could help, and also that parser and human find the same relations ambiguous. Overall our results suggest that despite the inherent noise, learning-based datasets can be reliably annotated for discourse relations.

2 Student Essay Data

Most prior PDTB applications have focused on the published news domain, although the Turkish DB (Zeyrek et al., 2013) also used published novels, while the BioDRB (Prasad et al., 2011) used published biomedical research articles.

The present study uses first and second drafts of 47 AP English high school student essays (94 essays, 4271 sentences, 75900 words) (Zhang and Litman, 2015). The first drafts were written after students read the first five cantos of Dante's Inferno, and required explaining why a contemporary should be sent to each of the first six sections of Dante's hell. The second drafts were revisions by the original writers after they received and generated peer feedback as part of the course.

The essays differ markedly from news articles both in possessing an argumentative structure and being learning-based, with the goal that by the second draft they consist of an introduction, intermediate paragraphs developing the reasoning for each contemporary's placement in hell, and a conclusion. Although such over-arching rhetorical structure is deliberately ignored in the PDTB, Prasad et al. (2011) concluded that it still impacts relation distribution after applying the framework to the BioDRB, whose biomedical articles are also argumentative and segmented into introduction, method, results and discussion (IMRAD).

The student essays further differ from all prior PDTB applications in that they are noisy, containing not only grammar and spelling errors but also deeper problems of referential and relational coherency. The noise often does not improve between first and second drafts. A.1-A.4 in the appendix provide essay excerpts illustrating noise variations. As shown, not only are spelling and grammar errors common, but a comparison of A.1 and A.2 (beginning an essay) and A.3 and A.4 (mid-essay) illustrate how the lack or misuse of cohesive devices, along with weakness in or deviation from argumentative structure, creates semantic ambiguity and reduces referential and relational coherence (Sanders and Maat, 2006).

3 Manually Annotating PDTB Relations

Central tenets of the PDTB framework are its focus on the lexical grounding of discourse relations and its neutrality with respect to discourse structure beyond seeking two abstract object arguments for all relations (Prasad et al., 2014). Five relation *types* are annotated: EXPLICIT, IMPLICIT, ALTLEX, ENTREL, NOREL. Four Level-1 *senses* are annotated: COMPARISON, CONTINGENCY, EXPANSION, TEMPORAL. Level-2 and -3 senses are also annotated, along with the relation's two minimal argument spans, and when applicable, the explicit or inserted implicit connective that signals it, as well as its attribution (i.e., speaker).

Annotated essay examples for each relation type and Level-1 sense are in Appendix A.5 and below. In each, the lexical grounding of one relation is <u>underlined</u> (it may be implicit, explicit or alternatively lexicalized), its syntactically bound argument (ARG2) is **bolded**, its non-structural argument (ARG1) is *italicized*, and its type and sense (where applicable) are in parenthesis.

3.1 Method

Prior applications of the PDTB framework have adopted its central tenets and most of its annotation conventions while adapting others to suit language and domain (Prasad et al., 2011; Alsaif and Markert, 2011; Zhou and Xue, 2015; Zeyrek et al., 2013; Sharma et al., 2013; Polkov et al., 2013; Danlos et al., 2012). Prasad et al. (2014) provide a comparative discussion of this prior work. Following this work we too retained PDTB's central tenets and adhered to most of its annotation conventions but modified some to fit our domain, increase reliability, and reduce cost:

a) As in the Hindi DRB (Sharma et al., 2013), our workflow proceeded in one pass through each essay, with each relation annotated for type, argument span, and sense before moving on.

b) As in the BioDRB (Prasad et al., 2011), we did not label attribution, as apart from Dante quotes the student was nearly always the speaker.

c) We only labeled Level-1 senses because our noisy conditions often made finer distinctions ambiguous. We did not adopt the BIoDRB's new argument-oriented senses because it is unclear how they all map to PDTB senses[1].

d) The PDTB's STRUCTURAL ADJACENCY CONSTRAINT requires Implicits to take arguments from adjacent units. This exacerbated annotation difficulty in our noisy conditions by favoring weak relations often ambiguous between Implicit, EntRel, or NoRel over stronger non-adjacent ones. Thus as in the BioDRB we permitted Implicit non-structural arguments in non-adjacent within-paragraph units, even though the automatic parser would not. This case is illustrated in Example 1.

(1) *In the place of the hoarders houses Mary who took in too much and did not relinquish these treasures.* Dante states in Canto seven line forty-seven "Are clerks – yea, popes and cardinals, in whom covetousness hath made its masterpiece". So **Although not understanding why Gods men are housed in this circle she is sentenced to this as she is also a strong believer in God and his ways.** (Implicit/Contingency)

e) The PDTB's MINIMAL ARGUMENT CONSTRAINT requires labeling only the minimal necessary argument text. Because our noisy conditions often made boundaries ambiguous, we did not strictly enforce this. In hard cases a larger unit was labeled with the expectation that minimality could be pursued on a subsequent pass. This case is also illustrated above.

f) Often in the essays relations hold between ungrammatical units, including sentences concatenated without punctuation or syntactically incomplete ones, as illustrated in Example 2. Due to their frequency, we decided to annotate them even if the automatic parser would not.

(2) *The first layer of hell is the vestibule in the entrance of hell* **this is a large open gate symbolizing that is easy to get into.** (EntRel)

The annotation was performed using the PDTB tool from the website. The lists of connectives from the PDTB manual were used to help identify

	Exp	Imp	AltL	EntR	NoR	n/a
Exp	73					8
Imp		56	1	13		
AltL			1			
EntR		2		10		
NoR					0	
n/a	2	1		1		n/a

Table 1: Relation Types in Interannotator Agreement Study (SE in rows; PDTB in cols)

	Comp	Cont	Expn	Temp
Comp	28	1		
Cont		24	2	
Expn	6	4	42	1
Temp		1		21

Table 2: Senses for Agreed Types in Interannotator Agreement Study (SE in rows; PDTB in cols)

and insert implicit connectives. Although these lists are productive, only rarely was a new connective inserted, because the conditions regarding connective classification are still unclear. [2]

3.2 Interannotator Reliability Study

The annotator used here was one of the early developers of the D-LTAG environment that engendered the PDTB framework (Forbes-Riley et al., 2006; Miltsakaki et al., 2003; Forbes et al., 2002), and was thus viewed as an expert. To verify this presumption an inter-annotator agreement study was performed. Four WSJ articles[3] were annotated for the five relation types and the four Level-1 senses and compared with the gold-standard annotations. The student essay (SE) annotator produced 163 relations while the PDTB produced 160, yielding a total of 168 unique relations. 140 agreed for relation type, meaning the type label matched and the argument spans were overlapping, i.e. an exact or partial match. Table 1 shows the type labels across the SE (rows) and PDTB (columns), with the final column/row ("n/a") representing relations identified by only one. Table 2 shows the senses for the 130 agreed types, excluding the 10 EntRels, which take no sense label. For type, agreement is 140/168, or 83%, and for sense it is 115/130, or 89%, with a Kappa of .84.

This level of agreement is on par with prior PDTB annotations. For example in the BioDRB agreement for Explicit and AltLex is 82% (Implicit agreement is not reported), and Kappa for

---

[1]Prasad et al. (2011) state that Continuation and Background map to Expansion and are reformulations of EntRel.

[2]E.g. two common clause subordinators, "by" and "in order to," are annotated in the BioDRB but not the PDTB.

[3]wsj1000, wsj2303, wsj2308, and wsj2314

Type	Count (%)	Comp	Cont	Exp	Tmp	Comp/ Cont	Comp/ Exp	Comp/ Tmp	Cont/ Exp	Cont/ Tmp	Exp/ Tmp
Exp	1657 (33%)	315	626	474	192	1	1	7	1	33	7
Imp	2495 (49%)	186	739	1492	18	2	8	4	36	4	6
AltL	103 (2%)	1	49	51	0	0	0	0	0	0	2
EntR	844 (17%)	-	-	-	-	-	-	-	-	-	-
NoR	0	-	-	-	-	-	-	-	-	-	-
All	5099	502	1414	2017	210	3	9	11	37	37	15
Exp/Imp Senses	4262	12%	34%	48%	6%						

Table 3: Relation Type and Sense Distribution in Student Essays

	Exp	Imp	AltL	EntR	NoR	Comp	Cont	Expn	Tmp
PDTB	45%	40%	2%	13%	0.6%	23%	22%	42%	13%
BioDRB	45%	51%	3%	0%	0.5%	11%	20%	?	17%

Table 4: Comparison Percentages of Types and Senses in PDTB Corpus and BioDRB Corpus

the 31 BioDRB senses is .71 for Explicit and AltLex and .63 for Implicit (Prasad et al., 2011). In the PDTB agreement was only reported for argument spans because some types were developed as the annotation went along. Agreement for partial match arguments is 94.5% and 92.6% for Explicits and Implicits, respectively (Miltsakaki et al., 2004; Prasad et al., 2008), while sense agreement is 94% for Level-1, falling to 84% and 80% for Level-2 and -3, respectively (Prasad et al., 2008).

3.3 Manual Annotation Results

Table 3 shows the distributions of manually annotated discourse relations in the essays. Type counts in the second column are broken down into senses across the remaining columns. As shown, Explicit, Implicit and AltLex can have multiple senses simultaneously. Table 4 compares relation distributions in the PDTB and BioDRB corpora.

Considering first relation type, there are 12% fewer Explicits in the essays than in the PDTB and BioDRB, both of which report 45%. That high school students are less likely to provide explicit markers of their intended discourse relations not only contributes to lowered coherency but also reflects their inexperience with the use of these cohesive devices, and points to an area for future learning-based language technology research. The type counts are recovered across Implicits and EntRels, with the essays containing 49% and 17%, while the PDTB contains only 40% and 13%, respectively. In the BioDRB, the addition of new senses inflated the percentage of Implicits (51%)

by removing EntRels completely. AltLex appears only rarely at 2-3% across all three corpora; however, these are underannotated in the framework, i.e. only when inserting a connective creates semantic redundancy (Prasad et al., 2014). NoRels are even more rare, occurring in the PDTB and BioDRB at rates of 0.5-0.6%, and not at all in the essays. A major reason was our loosening of the structural adjacency requirement (Section 3.1)[4]; most NoRels were replaced by an Implicit with a non-adjacent argument, as in Example 3.

(3) *The people in the second circle are the lustful.* Their punishment is to bang against one an another in Hell for all eternity. The modern day examples would be prostitutes or Jerry Sandusky. <u>Next,</u> **The third circle is for the gluttons.** (Implicit/Expansion)

Other potential NoRels were deemed better classified as indirect EntRels (i.e. set/subset, part/whole, or other bridging inferences) (Prince, 1981). However some ambiguity typically remained since EntRels can be extremely indirect in the essays, which also contributes to their lowered coherency. In Example 4, an encompassing entity extending through time can be inferred from "the world today" and "In Dante."

(4) *There are many types of people in the world today, people with different beliefs.*

---

[4]In the BioDRB, NoRels still occurred in the abstracts and were used to mark duplicate sentences (Prasad et al., 2011).

In Dante, there are different circles for every level of hell. (EntRel)

Considering relation sense, the final row of Table 3 shows the overall percentage of each Level-1 sense for Explicits and Implicits, as computed by totaling all occurrences in every sense combination (e.g., Comp = 315+186+3+9+11 = 524/4262 = 12%). Sense distributions for these types in the PDTB and BioDRB are shown in Table 4.

The essays contain substantially fewer Comparisons than the PDTB (12% versus 23%) but are very similar to the BioDRB, which contains 11%. This suggests Comparisons tend to have less use in argumentative texts, regardless of their level of sophistication. On the other hand, the essays contain substantially more Contingencies (34%) than both the PDTB (22%) and the BioDRB (20%). This may reflect a "sledgehammer" approach to argument construction, and thus a target for learning-based language technology research.

Temporals occur less frequently in the essays than in the PDTB (6% versus 13%) because in the essays most ordering is done in relation to the exposition and so falls under the definition of Expansion, as shown in Example 5. However, the BioDRB contains a much higher proportion of Temporals (17%) that may reflect a more sophisticated use of temporal ordering for argument construction, and another target for learning-based language technology research.

(5) *The fourth level of Hell is the hoarder/ spendthrifts of life. ...* <u>Lastly,</u> **the Wrathful are those who are active while others are passive.** (Explicit/Expansion)

The tendency in the essays to order propositions may also account for the increased proportion of Expansions (48%) as compared to the PDTB (42%). A comparison can't be made here with the BioDRB senses because some map to both Expansion and EntRel (see Footnote 1).

However, the essays' relative proportions of Implicit/Expansion, Implicit/Contingency, and EntRel should be considered fluid, because noise heightened the ambiguity between them. Relation *concurrency* is more common in published texts, i.e. multiple relations holding between two arguments simultaneously (exemplified by "when" and "since," which can convey Contingency and Temporal senses concurrently). Relation *ambiguity* is more common in the essays, however, and particularly between these three relations. EntRels' indirectness is often the cause, exacerbating the ambiguity with Implicit/Expansion even despite the PDTB framework's subdivision of the latter into 10 sub-categories. However, a better explanation of how phrases function as connectives would also help. In Example 6, "In this case" can be inserted but is not listed in the PDTB manual, although other prepositional phrases with abstract objects are, e.g. "as a result," "to this end," etc. If "in this case" is a connective the relation may be an Expansion; else it is probably an EntRel.

(6) *For example an Indian tribe that worships the moon but not God.* **There is no real punishment but the fact that they cannot go to heaven.** (Implicit/Expansion ∨ EntRel?)

The ambiguity between Implicit Expansion and Contingency appears partially rooted in the noise of learning. Students are still acquiring the ability to assert causality through voice and language and so their sentences are not always clearly linked. However the ambiguity also results from argument construction. Thus did the BioDRB researchers recognize a need to distinguish two new classes of Contingency: Claims and Justifications, which hold when one situation is the cause for the truth or validity of a *proposition*, from the PDTB's Reasons and Results, which hold when one situation is the cause of another situation. In our data Claims and Justifications often occur with a modal verb, which can disambiguate cases such as Example 7 but not Example 8, suggesting the ambiguity is a function of both noise and domain.

(7) *A hoarder in life would be myself.* <u>Because</u> **I love ice-cream and keep large amounts in my freezer.** (Implicit/Contingency:Justification)

(8) *The descent into the pit of hell would likely be peppered with many more of the faces of todays celebrities.* <u>Because/In other words</u> **Our world today is easily as corrupt as that in which Dante lived.** Sins are timeless, and, in Dantes view, their corresponding punishments are eternal.(Implicit/Expansion ∨ Contingency?)

Parser/ Train/ Senses	Test/ Senses	Overall E-to-E pMatch	Overall E-to-E eMatch	Conn ID	Arg ID pMatch	Arg ID eMatch	EXP E-to-E pMatch	EXP E-to-E eMatch	NoEXP E-to-E pMatch	noEXP E-to-E eMatch
Lin14 PDTB L1	Essays L1	45%	31%	90%	85%	57%	64%	36%	39%	26%
Lin14 PDTB L2	Essays L1	38%	26%	90%	85%	57%	63%	39%	27%	20%
Lin14 PDTB L2	PDTB L2	38%	21%	94%	81%	40%	81%	-	25%	-
CoN15 PDTB L2	PDTB L2	-	30%	94%	-	49%	-	40%	-	20%
CoN15 PDTB L2	WikiN L2	-	24%	92%	-	46%	-	31%	-	19%

Table 5: Comparison of F1 Scores across Discourse Parsers, Training and Test Sets

4 Automatic Discourse Relations

We used the PDTB-trained Lin et al. discourse parser (Lin et al., 2014) to automatically predict our human-annotated relations. As the first end-to-end free text PDTB discourse parser, it is typically the parser to which novel technical advances are compared (e.g., (Xue et al., 2015; Ji and Eisenstein, 2014)). In its sequential pipeline architecture, all functional occurrences of a predefined set of discourse connectives are identified, and then their two arguments are identified and assigned a sense. Subsequently within each paragraph all remaining unannotated adjacent sentence pairs are labeled as Non-Explicit, and their argument spans are identified and assigned a sense. EntRel, AltLex and NoRel relations are also predicted during this step. Since our essays are only annotated with Level-1 senses, we used the Lin et al. parser[5] in two different ways. First, we used the original parser trained on PDTB Level-2 senses to parse essays in terms of Level-2 senses; we then converted the predicted Level-2 senses to their Level-1 abstractions. Second, we retrained the parser by using only PDTB Level-1 senses; this retrained Lin et al. parser directly predicted Level-1 senses.[6]

Table 5 compares both versions of the Lin et al. parser's performance on the essays predicting Level-1 senses, with the original parser's performance on the PDTB test set predicting Level-2 senses. Also compared are variations of the Lin et al. architecture recently evaluated in the

CoNLL-2015 Shared Task on Shallow Discourse Parsing (Xue et al., 2015) (**CoNNL15**), trained on and predicting a similar set of Level-2 senses. The fourth row compares the best parsers from this task on the PDTB test set, while the fifth row compares them on the task's own blind test set of WikiNews texts. Note the essays can be viewed as a similar blind test set for the Lin et al. parser, in that the WikiNews texts and essays are unpolished and unpublished; however spelling and grammar errors were removed from the WikiNews texts.

As shown, performance is typically assessed in terms of an F1 score. F1s are computed for overall end-to-end performance (**Overall E-to-E**) as well as performance on the first step of connective identification (**Conn ID**) and the second step (with error propagation from the first step) of argument span identification (**Arg ID**). The F1 score for the final step of sense assignment (with error propagation from the first two steps) corresponds to end-to-end performance. End-to-end performance on Explicits (**EXP E-to-E**) is also distinguished from Non-Explicits (**NoEXP E-to-E**), i.e. Implicit, AltLex and EntRel. Further, within each evaluation (except for the first step of ConnID), performance can be evaluated using exact match (**eMatch**), whereby the parser's arguments must exactly match the human's, or using partial match (**pMatch**), whereby the spans may exactly match or overlap. The CoNLL-2015 Shared Task did not report partial match results even though as Lin et al. (2014) note, most disagreements between exact and partial match do not show significant semantic differences (Miltsakaki et al., 2004) and result from small text portions being included or deleted

---

[5]wing.comp.nus.edu.sg/~linzihen/parser

[6]Thanks to Ilija Ilievski of the National University of Singapore for retraining the Lin et. al parser, and running both the original and retrained versions on our essay corpus.

to enforce the minimal argument constraint, whose presumption of deep semantics poses difficulties for parsers. Because noise made determining minimal arguments problematic (Section 3.1), we report exact and partial match results.

Measuring overall end-to-end performance, Table 5 shows that on the essays the Lin et al. parser yielded F1s of 45% with partial match and 31% with exact match when trained on L1, while its F1s when trained on L2 were lower (38% and 26%). On the PDTB test set its F1s were also lower (38% and 21%). The best CoNLL-2015 parser improved upon the Lin et al. parser for exact match both on the PDTB test set and their own blind test set. Because the annotations being predicted were somewhat different in each case, breaking down performance into component steps helps clarify the import of these results.

On the first step of connective identification, Table 5 shows that performance is uniformly high, which is unsurprising since few explicit connectives are ambiguous (Pitler et al., 2008; Lin et al., 2014; Prasad et al., 2011). On the essays the Lin et al. parser yielded a slightly lower F1 of 90%; this was due to grammatical errors that caused it to miss some connectives, and the fact that it did not recognize all the human-annotated connectives, including prepositional phrases such as "in that case" and "after all." On the second step of argument span identification (with error propagation from connective identification but regardless yet of relation type or sense), Table 5 shows that on the essays the Lin et al. parser yielded partial and exact match F1s of 85% and 57%, outperforming all other parsers and corpora. This was almost certainly because the minimal argument constraint was not strictly enforced in the essay annotation due to noise making argument boundaries ambiguous (Section 3.1); the larger argument enabled more exactly and partially matched spans. Whether relaxing the minimal argument constraint could also increase the usefulness of automatic discourse relation annotation in language technology applications is still an open question.

Finally contrasting end-to-end parser performance on Explicits and Non-Explicits as well as Overall, Table 5 shows the performance improvement on the essays is reduced. In particular, the 8-17% increase over other test sets and parsers for exact match argument identification drops once relation type and sense are predicted for those arguments. Overall the L1 trained essay parser only retains a 1-10% increase, while the L2 trained version's increase is less or nonexistent. Thus even relaxing the minimal argument constraint and predicting only Level-1 senses cannot fully temper the negative impact of noise. Interestingly, the L1 trained essay parser performs better on the Non-Explicits but the L2 trained essay parser performs better on the Explicits; this suggests that the greater training specificity helps to counteract the effect of noise when parsing Explicits.

Table 6 illustrates patterns of errors that occur in the final steps of relation type and sense identification, presenting a confusion matrix of the 4216 relations in the essays whose arguments were at least partially matched. Considering first Explicits, Table 6 shows most disagreements involve parser predictions of Explicit/Temporal (9+28+11) for connectives that can take other senses as well, such as "since" in Example 9 as well as "then" used for textual instead of temporal ordering (Section 3.3). In addition, the parser failed to identify a number of explicit connectives signaling Expansion, labeling them instead as Implicit/Contingency (7) or Implicit/Expansion (22), including sentence-initial, comma-delimited "First" and "Next" as well as sentence-final "too" and "as well." Further investigation is needed to determine why.

(9) *He now has to spend eternity in the second circle of hell* <u>since</u> **he ruined his marriage as a "cheetah" and not a Tiger.** (Human: Explicit/Contingency; Parser: Explicit/Temporal)

Considering Non-Explicits, Table 6 shows no AltLex were predicted by the parser, not surprising since AltLex are so syntactically productive and only the first three stemmed terms of the second argument span were used by the Lin et al. parser to identify them. However, in these essays the human annotator had a highly repetitive cue signaling the most commonly occurring AltLex relation, namely various syntactic permutations of "The example is..." as in Examples 10 and 11. Most of the 99 Implicit/Expansions the parser mislabeled as EntRel contained further permutations of this relation, as shown in Example 11. This suggests that training the parser on essay data could improve its performance on AltLex, EntRel, and Implicit/Expansion.

(10) *Their punishment is to "bang" against*

	Exp: Comp	Exp: Cont	Exp: Expn	Exp: Temp	Imp: Comp	Imp: Cont	Imp: Expn	Imp: Temp	EntR	AltL
Exp: Comp	**191**	1	3	9	0	2	3	0	0	0
Exp: Cont	0	**422**	1	28	0	2	3	0	0	0
Exp: Expn	0	0	**253**	11	0	7	22	0	1	0
Exp: Temp	6	2	1	**140**	0	3	2	0	0	0
Imp: Comp	0	1	0	0	**5**	36	108	0	7	0
Imp: Cont	0	3	0	0	7	**119**	524	2	35	0
Imp: Expn	0	0	1	1	16	208	**1017**	1	99	0
Imp: Temp	0	0	0	0	0	4	16	**0**	0	0
EntR	4	3	5	1	1	121	569	0	**99**	0
AltL	0	1	0	0	1	18	59	0	11	**0**

Table 6: 4216 Partially-Matched Argument Relations in Student Essays (Human: rows, Parser: cols)

one an another in Hell for all eternity. **The modern day examples would be prostitutes or Jerry Sandusky.** (Human: AltLex/Expansion; Parser: EntRel)

(11) *The fourth level of Hell is the hoarder / spendthrifts of life.* As an example, **The person that falls into this layer is Christopher Sisley.** (Human: Implicit/Expansion; Parser: EntRel)

Otherwise Table 6 reflects the relation ambiguity that occurred in the human annotation (Section 3.3). That is, the clusters of counts around the diagonal show the parser also had difficulty distinguishing Implicit/Contingency, Implicit/Expansion and EntRel. As illustration, Example 12 shows one of the 208 cases in which the human annotated Expansion and the parser, Contingency. Example 13 shows one of the 524 cases where the human annotated Contingency and the parser, Expansion. Example 14 shows one of the 569 cases where the human annotated EntRel and the parser, Expansion.

(12) *Pretty much any teenage boy you talk to is gluttonous and never stops eating.* **Every meal is large and overindulgence in food happens every day.** (Human: Implicit/Expansion (In other words); Parser: Implicit/Contingency)

(13) *Paul Fields is one who is in this layer of Hell.* **He scorn the name of band kids who have no idea what they are doing.** (Human: Implicit/Contingency (Because); Parser: Implicit/ Expansion)

(14) *The third circle is for the gluttons.* **They are not only gluttons for food but also gluttons for attention.** (Human: EntRel; Parser: Implicit/Expansion)

Finally, inspection of the 883 remaining disagreed relations (5099-4216) whose arguments weren't both at least partially matched shows as expected that the parser disagreed with 55 Implicits whose left argument was non-adjacent (Section 3.1), since it only labeled Implicits between adjacent sentences. As expected the parser also failed to recognize many relations holding between ungrammatical sentences (Section 3.1), although a manual accounting is still necessary to determine exactly how often this occurred.

5 Conclusions

We investigated manual and automatic PDTB discourse relation annotation in high school student AP English essays. In contrast to prior PDTB applications, the essays are learning-based, in that the writers are learning about argumentative writing through the essay-writing process, and they are also noisy, containing errors of spelling, grammar, and deeper cohesive ties. We discussed methodological complexities of noisy learning-based data, including a heightened ambiguity between EntRel, Expansion, and Contingency that the PDTB framework does not yet resolve. Descriptive statistics showed how relation distributions differ from the PDTB (Prasad et al., 2014) and BioDRB (Prasad et al., 2011) corpora, and also suggested possible targets for future learning-based language technology research. Comparison of automatic discourse parser performances showed that relaxing the minimal argument constraint and predicting only Level-1 senses helped counter the negative impact of noise; the Lin et al. parser, when trained on the PDTB's Level 1 senses, gave an overall F1 score of 31% under strictest evaluation terms, similar to other corpora and parsers (Lin et al., 2014; Xue et al., 2015). Performance was highest on connective and argument identification, and dropped precipitously during relation type and sense identification. Patterns of errors occurring in those steps indicate training on essay data would improve the parser's ability to distinguish AltLex, Implicit/Expansion, and EntRel, but distinguishing EntRel, Expansion, and Contingency requires first resolving these ambiguities in the manual case. Our results thus support prior work suggesting benefits to tailoring manual annotations to the target data (Zeyrek et al., 2013) and training domain-specific parsers to predict them (Prasad et al., 2011; Ramesh and Yu, 2010).

We are currently exploring the effectiveness of other available discourse parsers. We also plan to annotate and release a new corpus of student essays[7] that we are currently collecting. In addition, we are starting to explore the relationships between student learning and discourse relations, including not only relation use but also the manual and automatic annotations. For example, there may be an interaction such that more coherent, less ambiguous essays also receive higher grades. We will also investigate ways in which annotated discourse relations in learning-based domains can be used to improve existing educational technologies such as language-based tutors and writing assistants (e.g., (Litman and Forbes-Riley, 2014; Zhang et al., 2016)). Level-1 senses have already been shown to be useful for improving sentiment analysis in product reviews (Yang and Cardie, 2014), and we are seeing improvements when using Level-1 senses to enhance our prior work on classifying writing revisions.

Acknowledgments

This work was funded by the Learning Research and Development Center at the University of Pittsburgh.

References

Amal Alsaif and Katja Markert. 2011. Modelling discourse relations for arabic. In *Proceedings of the Conference on Empirical Methods in Natural Language Processing*, EMNLP '11, pages 736–747, Stroudsburg, PA, USA. Association for Computational Linguistics.

Laurence Danlos, Diego Antolinos-Basso, Chlo Braud, and Charlotte Roze. 2012. Vers le FDTB: French Discourse TreeBank. In *Proceedings of Traitement Automatique des Langues Naturelles (TALN)*, pages 471–478, Grenoble, France.

Katherine Forbes, Eleni Miltsakaki, Rashmi Prasad, Anoop Sarkar, A. Joshi, B. Webber, Aravind Joshi, and Bonnie Webber. 2002. D-LTAG system: Discourse parsing with a lexicalized tree adjoining grammar. *Journal of Logic, Language and Information*, 12:261–279.

Katherine Forbes-Riley, Bonnie Webber, and Aravind Joshi. 2006. Computing discourse semantics: The predicate-argument semantics of discourse connectives in D-LTAG. *Journal of Semantics*, 23(1):55–106.

Sucheta Ghosh, Richard Johansson, Giuseppe Riccardi, and Sara Tonelli. 2012. Improving the recall of a discourse parser by constraint-based postprocessing. In *Proceedings of the Eighth International Conference on Language Resources and Evaluation (LREC'12); Istanbul, Turkey; May 23-25*, pages 2791–2794.

Yangfeng Ji and Jacob Eisenstein. 2014. One vector is not enough: Entity-augmented distributional semantics for discourse relations. *CoRR*, abs/1411.6699.

Ziheng Lin, Hwee Tou Ng, and Min-Yen Kan. 2014. A PDTB-styled end-to-end discourse parser. *Natural Language Engineering*, 20(2):151–184.

Diane Litman and Katherine Forbes-Riley. 2014. Evaluating a spoken dialogue system that detects and adapts to user affective states. In *Proceedings 15th Annual SIGdial Meeting on Discourse and Dialogue (SIGDIAL)*, Philadelpha, PA, June.

Eleni Miltsakaki, Re Creswell, Katherine Forbes, and Aravind Joshi. 2003. Anaphoric arguments of discourse connectives: Semantic properties of antecedents versus non-antecedents. In *In EACL Workshop on Computational Treatment of Anaphora*.

Eleni Miltsakaki, Rashmi Prasad, Aravind Joshi, and Bonnie Webber. 2004. Annotating discourse connectives and their arguments. In *In Proceedings of the HLT/NAACL Workshop on Frontiers in Corpus Annotation*, pages 9–16.

Gary Patterson and Andrew Kehler. 2003. Predicting the presence of discourse connectives. In *EMNLP*, pages 914–923. ACL.

Emily Pitler, Mridhula Raghupathy, Hena Mehta, Ani Nenkova, Alan Lee, and Aravind Joshi. 2008. Easily Identifiable Discourse Relations. In *Coling*, pages 87–90, Manchester, UK, August. Coling 2008 Organizing Committee.

---

[7]The existing essays were collected for another project prior to our PDTB research and unfortunately cannot be freely distributed.

Lucie Polkov, Jiri Mrovsk, Anna Nedoluzhko, Pavlna Jnov, Srka Ziknov, and Eva Hajicov. 2013. Introducing the Prague Discourse TreeBank 1.0. In *International Joint Conference on Natural Language Processing*, pages 91–99, Nagoya, Japan.

Rashmi Prasad, Nikhil Dinesh, Alan Lee, Eleni Miltsakaki, Livio Robaldo, Aravind Joshi, and Bonnie Webber. 2008. The Penn Discourse TreeBank 2.0. In *In Proceedings of LREC*.

Rashmi Prasad, Susan McRoy, Nadya Frid, Aravind K. Joshi, and Hong Yu. 2011. The Biomedical Discourse Relation Bank. *BMC Bioinformatics*, 12:188.

Rashmi Prasad, Bonnie L. Webber, and Aravind K. Joshi. 2014. Reflections on the Penn Discourse Treebank, comparable corpora, and complementary annotation. *Computational Linguistics*, 40(4):921–950.

Ellen F. Prince. 1981. Toward a taxonomy of given-new information. In P. Cole, editor, *Syntax and semantics: Vol. 14. Radical Pragmatics*, pages 223–255. Academic Press, New York.

Balaji Polepalli Ramesh and Hong Yu. 2010. Identifying discourse connectives in biomedical text. In *AMIA Annual Symposium Proceedings*, volume 2010, page 657.

T. Sanders and H. Pander Maat. 2006. Cohesion and coherence: Linguistic approaches. In Keith Brown, editor, *Encyclopedia of Language and Linguistics*, pages 591–595. Elsevier, Amsterdam.

Himanshu Sharma, Praveen Dakwale, Dipti Misra Sharma, Rashmi Prasad, and Aravind K. Joshi. 2013. Assessment of different workflow strategies for annotating discourse relations: A case study with HDRB. In *Computational Linguistics and Intelligent Text Processing - 14th International Conference, CICLing 2013, Samos, Greece, March 24-30, 2013, Proceedings, Part I*, pages 523–532.

Fatemeh Torabi Asr and Vera Demberg. 2013. On the information conveyed by discourse markers. In *Proceedings of the Fourth Annual Workshop on Cognitive Modeling and Computational Linguistics (CMCL)*, pages 84–93, Sofia, Bulgaria, August. Association for Computational Linguistics.

Nianwen Xue, Hwee Tou Ng, Sameer Pradhan, Rashmi Prasad, Christopher Bryant, and Attapol T. Rutherford. 2015. The CoNLL-2015 Shared Task on shallow discourse parsing. In *Proceedings of the Nineteenth Conference on Computational Natural Language Learning: Shared Task*, pages 1–16, Beijing, China, July.

Bishan Yang and Claire Cardie. 2014. Context-aware learning for sentence-level sentiment analysis with posterior regularization. In *Proceedings of the 52nd Annual Meeting of the Association for Computational Linguistics (Volume 1: Long Papers)*, pages 325–335, Baltimore, Maryland, June.

Deniz Zeyrek, Işın Demirşahin, Ayışığı B Sevdik Çallı, and Ruket Çakıcı. 2013. Turkish Discourse Bank: Porting a discourse annotation style to a morphologically rich language. *Dialogue & Discourse*, 4(2):174–184.

Fan Zhang and Diane Litman. 2015. Annotation and classification of argumentative writing revisions. In *Proceedings of the Tenth Workshop on Innovative Use of NLP for Building Educational Applications*, pages 133–143, Denver, Colorado, June. Association for Computational Linguistics.

Fan Zhang, Rebecca Hwa, Diane Litman, and Homa B. Hashemi. 2016. Argrewrite: A web-based revision assistant for argumentative writings. In *Proceedings Conference of the North American Chapter of the Association for Computational Linguistics: Demonstrations (NAACL-HLT)*, San Diego, CA, June.

Yuping Zhou and Nianwen Xue. 2015. The Chinese Discourse Treebank: a chinese corpus annotated with discourse relations. *Language Resources and Evaluation*, 49(2):397–431.

A   Appendix

A.1   Low Noise Start-of-Essay Excerpt

In Dante's Inferno we have read about the first five circles. Each circle has a different punishment for each sin. In this paper I will fit modern day people into each circle.

A.2   High Noise Start-of-Essay Excerpt

The ones who are born to not flesh nor earth, where blessed with the divine grace and the highway of hell based on Dante's representation of Hell. They are watchers; they have seen Dante's struggles on Earth as well as his teachings through his book. They are all-knowing and represent what Dante tried to explain through his interpretations of Hell. Although he was a bit off they have the true story to be told. To make the levels more relatable they have place modern day people to accompany each level.

A.3   Low Noise Mid-Essay Excerpt

As Dante descends into the second circle, he sees "the sinners who make their reason bond thrall under the yoke of their lust" (98). These were the souls of those who made an act of love, but inappropriately and on impulse. This would be a fine level of Hell for all those who cheat on their boyfriends or girlfriends in high school because let's face it; they aren't really in love.

A.4 High Noise Mid-Essay Excerpt

Michael B calls this home as he was lazy and enjoyed himself to much in his life as a person. Within his home he kept the foods that satisfied his sin, indulging in them whenever he could. The reasoning of this was due to his insatiable appetite, which seemed to never end as he continues to do this sin without much notice and without many hurtles to keep him from the craves. Being housed within the circle he would lay in the mud of waste, living in the waste of the sin that he lives with. While Cerberus acts as his actual sin, him wanting more therefore having three heads. This would give him the experience of the sin that Michael housed within him.

A.5 Essay Examples of Relation Annotations

I don't personally know anyone that is over 2012 years old <u>so</u> **I cannot place any modern people into this layer.** (Explicit/Contingency)

<u>Usually when</u> **I get money** *I plan what I am going to use it for and wait until I have that much or spend it immediately on something I probably don't need.* (Explicit/Temporal)

Filled with hatred for many, <u>yet</u> **never acts upon his grim thoughts.** (Explicit/Comparison)

The man who is stuck in this layer is Hue Heffner. <u>Because</u> **He has devoted his entire life for other people's lustful pleasure and his own.** (Implicit/Contingency)

A prime example of this is a woman by the name of Marie, who abandons man after man in search of a thrill, thrusting her body to anyone willing enough. <u>In other words</u> **She leaves one man for the arms of another, just as Francesca fled to Paolo for satisfaction.** (Implicit/Expansion)

Teachers such as Mr. Braverman are externally wrathful and intentionally cause agony to others like Mrs. Pochiba. <u>In contrast</u> **Other English teachers, such as Mrs. Butler, are very quiet and don't let people know that certain things bother her.** (Implicit/Comparison)

The punishment for these people is to bleed forever with worms sucking up the blood at their feet. **The example would be people who would not** <u>choose</u> **a side in the civil war.** (AltLex/Expansion)

He does not believe in Christ, but believes in the religion of scientology. <u>**Due to this,**</u> **he is against the fact that Christ had existed, and had been on Earth.** (AltLex/Contingency)

It may cause you fame and fortune, but what is money if you are greedy? **Although Donald Trump doesn't look at it that way, in God's eyes greed gets you nowhere but the third circle of Hell.** (EntRel/-)

He gives us a better understanding of why certain people are in a certain level of hell. **I will be discussing in the following paragraphs people who deserve to be in each level of hell, in Dante's perspective.** (EntRel/-)

She is young and has not experience a lot of things to be put into a certain level of sin. **The level I'm currently discussing is located in between heaven and hell.** (EntRel/-)

Empirical comparison of dependency conversions
for RST discourse trees

†**Katsuhiko Hayashi, Tsutomu Hirao** and **Masaaki Nagata**
NTT Communication Science Laboratories, NTT Corporation
2-4 Hikaridai, Seika-cho, Soraku-gun, Kyoto, 619-0237 Japan
†hayashi.katsuhiko@lab.ntt.co.jp

Abstract

Two heuristic rules that transform Rhetorical Structure Theory discourse trees into discourse dependency trees (DDTs) have recently been proposed (Hirao et al., 2013; Li et al., 2014), but these rules derive significantly different DDTs because their conversion schemes on *multinuclear* relations are not identical. This paper reveals the difference among DDT formats with respect to the following questions: (1) How complex are the formats from a dependency graph theoretic point of view? (2) Which formats are analyzed more accurately by automatic parsers? (3) Which are more suitable for text summarization task? Experimental results showed that Hirao's conversion rule produces DDTs that are more useful for text summarization, even though it derives more complex dependency structures.

1 Introduction

Recent years have seen an increase in the use of dependency representations throughout various NLP applications. For the discourse analysis of texts, dependency graph representations have also been studied by many researchers (Prasad et al., 2008; Muller et al., 2012; Hirao et al., 2013; Li et al., 2014). In particular, Hirao et al. (2013) proposed a current state-of-the-art text summarization method based on trimming discourse dependency trees (DDTs). Dependency tree representation is the key to the formulation of the tree trimming method (Filippova and Strube, 2008), and dependency-based discourse syntax has further potential to improve the modeling of a wide range of text-based applications.

However, no large-scale corpus exists that is annotated with DDTs since it is expensive to manually construct such a corpus from scratch. Therefore, Hirao et al. (2013) and Li et al. (2014) proposed heuristic rules that automatically transform RST discourse trees (RST-DTs)[1] into DDTs. However, even researchers, who cited these two works in their papers, have ignored their differences, probably because the authors described only abstracts of their conversion methods. To clarify their algorithmic differences, this paper provides pseudocodes where the two different methods can be described in a unified form, showing that they analyze *multinuclear* relations differently on RST-DTs. As we show by example in Section 4, such a slight difference can derive significantly different DDTs.

The main purpose of this paper is to experimentally reveal the differences between dependency formats. By investigating the complexity of their structures from the dependency graph theoretic point of view (Kuhlmann and Nivre, 2006), we prove that the Hirao13 method, which keeps the semantic equivalence of multinuclear discourse units in the dependency structures, introduces much more complex DDTs than Li14, while a simple post-editing method greatly reduces the complexity of DDTs.

This paper also compares the methods with both intrinsic and extrinsic evaluations: (1) Which dependency structures are analyzed more accurately by automatic parsers? and (2) Which structures

---

[1]Mann and Thompson (1988)'s Rhetorical Structure Theory (RST), which is one of the most influential text organization frameworks, represents discourse as a (constituent-style) tree structure. RST was developed as the basis of annotated corpora for the automatic analysis of text syntax, most notably the RST Discourse Treebank (RST-DTB) (Carlson et al., 2003).

Proceedings of the SIGDIAL 2016 Conference, pages 128–136,
Los Angeles, USA, 13-15 September 2016. ©2016 Association for Computational Linguistics

are more suitable to text summarization? We show from experimental results that even though the Hirao13 DDT format reduces performance, as measured by intrinsic evaluations, it is more useful for text summarization. While researchers developing discourse syntactic parsing (Soricut and Marcu, 2003; Hernault et al., 2010; Feng and Hirst, 2012; Joty et al., 2013; Li et al., 2014) have focused excessively on improving accuracies, our experimental results emphasize the importance of extrinsic evaluations since the more accurate parser does not always lead to better performance of text-based applications.

2 Related Work

Mann and Thompson (1988)'s Rhetorical Structure Theory (RST), which is one of the most influential text organization frameworks, represents a discourse structure as a constituent tree. The RST Discourse Treebank (RST-DTB) (Carlson et al., 2003) has played a critical role in automatic discourse analysis (Soricut and Marcu, 2003; Hernault et al., 2010; Feng and Hirst, 2012; Joty et al., 2013), mainly because trees are both easy to formalize and computationally tractable. RST discourse trees (RST-DTs) are also used for modeling many text-based applications, such as text summarization (Marcu, 2000) and anaphora resolution (Cristea et al., 1998).

Hirao et al. (2013) and Li et al. (2014) introduced dependency conversion methods from RST-DTs into DDTs in which a full discourse structure is represented by head-dependent binary relations between elementary discourse units. Hirao et al. (2013) also showed that a text summarization method, based on trimming DDTs, achieves significant improvements against Marcu (2000)'s method using RST-DTs.

On the other hand, some researchers argue that trees are inadequate to account for a full discourse structure (Wolf and Gibson, 2005; Lee et al., 2006; Danlos and others, 2008; Venant et al., 2013). Segmented Discourse Representation Theory (SDRT) (Asher and Lascarides, 2003) represents discourse structures as logical form, and relations function like logical operators on the meaning of their arguments. The annotation in the ANNODIS corpus was conducted based on SDRT (Afantenos et al., 2012). For automatic discourse analysis using the corpus, Muller et al. (2012) adopted dependency tree representation to

simplify discourse parsing. They also presented a method to automatically derive DDTs from SDR structures.

Wolf and Gibson (2005) used a chain-graph for representing discourse structures and annotated 135 articles from the AP Newswire and the Wall Street Journal. The annotated corpus is called the Discourse Graphbank. The graph represents crossed dependency and multiple parentship discourse phenomena, which cannot be represented by tree structures, but whose graph structures become very complex (Egg and Redeker, 2010).

The Penn Discourse Treebank (PDTB) (Prasad et al., 2008) is a large-scale corpus of annotated discourse connectives and their arguments. Its connective-argument structure can also represent complex discourse phenomena like multiple parentship, but its objective is to annotate the discourse relations between individual discourse units, not full discourse structures. Unfortunately, to the best of our knowledge, neither the Discourse Graphbank nor the PDTB has been used for any specific NLP applications.

3 RST Discourse Tree

RST represents a discourse as a tree structure. The leaves of an RST discourse tree (RST-DT) correspond to *Elementary Discourse Units* (EDUs). Adjacent EDUs are linked by rhetorical relations, forming larger discourse units that are also subject to this relation linking. Figure 1 shows part of an RST-DT (wsj-0623), taken from RST-DTB, for this text fragment:

$$
\begin{aligned}
&\big\{ [\text{The fiscal 1989 budget deficit figure came out Friday .}]_{e\text{-}1} \big\}_1, \ \big\{ [\text{It was down a little .}]_{e\text{-}2} \big\}_2, \\
&\big\{ [\text{The next time you hear a Member of Congress moan about the deficit ,}]_{e\text{-}3}, [\text{consider what Congress did Friday .}]_{e\text{-}4} \big\}_3, \ \big\{ [\text{The Senate , 84-6 , voted to increase to \$ 124,000 the ceiling on insured mortgages from the FHA ,}]_{e\text{-}5}, [\text{which lost \$ 4.2 billion in loan defaults last year .}]_{e\text{-}6} \big\}_4, \\
&\big\{ [\text{Then , by voice vote , the Senate voted a pork-barrel bill ,}]_{e\text{-}7}, [\text{approved Thursday by the House ,}]_{e\text{-}8}, [\text{for domestic military construction .}]_{e\text{-}9} \big\}_5, \\
&\big\{ [\text{the Bush request to what the Senators gave themselves :}]_{e\text{-}10} \big\}_6, \cdots
\end{aligned}
$$

where each subscript at the end of square brackets [] corresponds to a leaf unit (EDU) in the tree. EDUs grouped by {} consist of a sentence that is labeled with its index in the text.

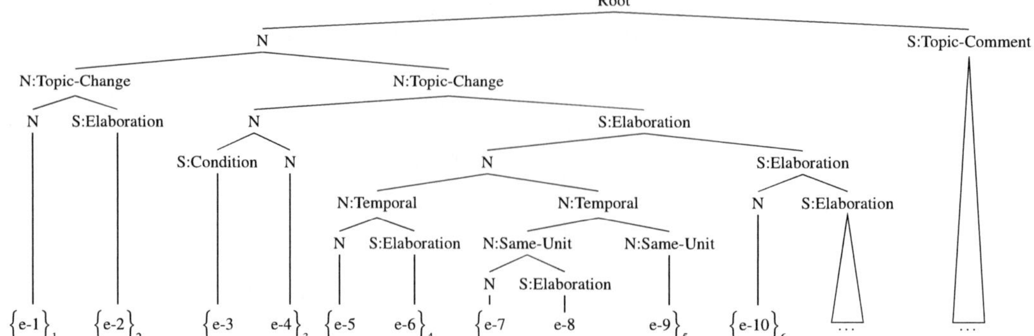

Figure 1: Part of discourse tree (wsj-0623) in RST-DTB: 'S', 'N' and 'e' stand for Satellite, Nucleus and EDU. Each EDU is labeled with its index in the text, and EDUs grouped with {} brackets are in the same sentence.

Each discourse unit in the tree that forms a rhetorical relation is characterized by a rhetorical status: *Nucleus* (N), which represents the most essential piece of information in the relation, or *Satellite* (S), which indicates the supporting information. Rhetorical relations must be either *mononuclear* or *multinuclear*. Mononuclear relations hold between two units with Nucleus and Satellite, whereas multinuclear relations hold among two or more units with Nucleus. Each unit in a multinuclear relation has similar semantic information as the other units. Rhetorical relations can be grouped into classes that share such rhetorical meaning as "Elaboration" and "Condition". In Figure 1, the Satellite unit (covering e-3) and its sibling Nucleus unit (covering e-4) are linked by a mononuclear relation with rhetorical label "Condition", and two Nucleus units (covering e-5, e-6 and e-7, e-8, e-9) are linked by a multinuclear relation with rhetorical label "Temporal".

4 Conversions from RST-DTs to DDTs

Next, this paper discusses text-level dependency syntax, which represents grammatical structure by head-dependent binary relations between EDUs. This section introduces two existing automatic conversion methods from RST-DTs to DDTs: the methods of Li et al. (2014) and Hirao et al. (2013). Additionally, this paper presents a simple post-editing method to reduce the complexity of DDTs. The heart of these conversions closely resembles that of constituent-to-dependency conversions for English sentences (Yamada and Matsumoto, 2003; Johansson and Nugues, 2007; De Marneffe and Manning, 2008), since RST-DTs can be regarded

as Penn Treebank-style constituent trees because EDUs and discourse units respectively correspond to terminal and non-terminal nodes, and a rhetorical relation, like a CFG-rule, forms an edge in the tree.

4.1 Li et al. (2014)'s Method

Algorithm 1 convert-rst-into-dep

Require: RST discourse tree: *rst-dt*
Ensure: discourse dependency tree: *ddt*
1: $ddt \leftarrow \emptyset$
2: **for all** EDU e-j in *rst-dt* **do**
3:    $P \leftarrow \begin{cases} \text{find-My-Top-Node(e-}j) \,\text{// Li14} \\ \text{find-Nearest-S-Ancestor(e-}j) \,\text{// Hirao13} \end{cases}$
4:    **if** isRoot(P) = TRUE **then**
5:      $\ell \leftarrow$ Root
6:      $i \leftarrow 0$
7:    **else**
8:      $\ell \leftarrow$ Label(P)
9:      $P' \leftarrow$ Parent(P)
10:     $i \leftarrow$ find-Head-EDU(P')
11:   **end if**
12:   $j \leftarrow$ Index(e-j)
13:   $ddt \leftarrow ddt \cup (i, \ell, j)$
14: **end for**
15: Return *ddt*

Algorithm 2 find-My-Top-Node(e)

Require: EDU: e
Ensure: C
1: $C \leftarrow e$
2: $P \leftarrow$ Parent(e)
3: **while** LeftmostNucleusChild(P) = C and
     isRoot(P) = FALSE **do**
4:   $C \leftarrow P$
5:   $P \leftarrow$ Parent(P)
6: **end while**
7: **if** isRoot(P) = TRUE **then**
8:   $C \leftarrow P$
9: **end if**
10: Return C

Algorithm 3 find-Head-EDU(P)

Require: non-terminal node: P
Ensure: i
 1: **while** isLeaf(P) = FALSE **do**
 2:   $P \leftarrow$ LeftmostNucleusChild(P)
 3: **end while**
 4: $i \leftarrow$ Index(P)
 5: Return i

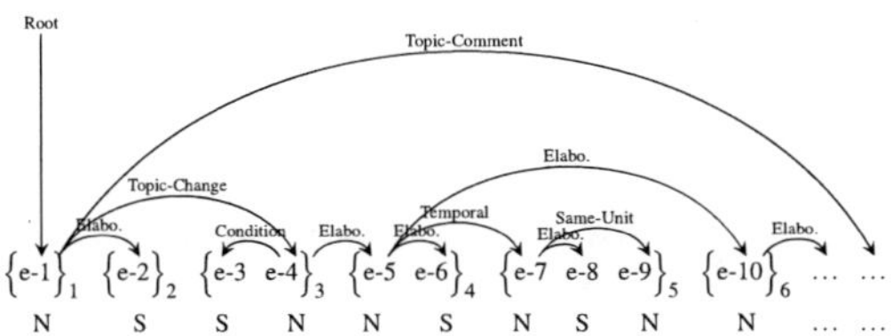

Figure 2: Discourse dependency tree produced by Li's method for RST discourse tree in Figure 1: "Elabo." is short for "Elaboration".

Li et al. (2014)'s dependency conversion method is based on the idea of assigning each discourse unit in an RST-DT a unique head selected among the unit's children. Traversing each non-terminal node in a bottom-up manner, the head-assignment procedure determines the head from its children in the following manner: the head of the leftmost child node with the Nucleus is the head; if no child node is the Nucleus, the head of the leftmost child node is the head.

The procedure was originally introduced by Sagae (2009), and its core idea is identical as the head-assignment rules for Penn Treebank-style constituent trees (Magerman, 1994; Collins, 1999). Li's conversion method uses the procedure to assign a head to each non-terminal node of a right-branching binarized RST-DT (Hernault et al., 2010) and transforms the head-annotated binary tree into a DDT.

Algorithms 1-3 show the dependency conversion method. For brevity, we describe it in a different form from Li's original conversion process[2] cited above. In Algorithm 1, the main routine iteratively processes every EDU in given RST-DT t to directly find its single head rather than transforming head-annotated trees into DDTs. The main process is largely separated into three steps:

1. Algorithm 1 calls Algorithm 2 at line 3, which finds the highest non-terminal

node in t to which current processed EDU e-j must be assigned as the head in Sagae's lexicalization manner. Parent(P) and LeftmostNucleusChild(P) are respectively operations that return the parent node of node P and the leftmost child node with the Nucleus of node P[3].

2. After obtaining node P from Algorithm 2, Algorithm 1 seeks the head EDU that is assigned to the parent node of P. If P is the root node of t, we set ℓ to rhetorical label "Root" and i to a special index 0 of virtual EDU e-0 (lines 5-6 in Algorithm 1). Otherwise, we set $\ell \leftarrow$ Label(P) and $P' \leftarrow$ Parent(P) (lines 8-9 in Algorithm 1), where Label(P) returns the rhetorical label attached to node P[4]. Then Algorithm 1 at line 10 calls Algorithm 3, which iteratively seeks the leftmost child node with the Nucleus in a top-down manner, starting from P', until it reaches terminal node e-i. Operation Index(P) returns the index of EDU P.

3. We attach e-j to head e-i and assign rhetorical label ℓ to the dependency edge. We write (i,ℓ,j) to denote that a dependency edge exists with rhetorical label ℓ from head e-i to modifier e-j.

Assuming that e-j is the e-7 of the RST-DT in Figure 1, Algorithm 2 returns the 'N:Temporal' node (covering e-7, e-8, e-9) since its parent node 'N' has the other 'N:Temporal' node (covering e-5, e-6) as its leftmost Nucleus child. Starting from the parent node 'N', Algorithm 3 iteratively seeks the leftmost Nucleus child in the top-down manner until it reaches the terminal node e-5. Finally, we obtain a dependency edge $(5, \text{Temporal}, 7)$.

The DDT in Figure 2 is produced by this method for the RST-DT in Figure 1. To each EDU, we also assign 'N' or 'S' rhetorical status of its parent node. Li's dependency format is always *projective*, i.e., when all the edges are drawn in the half-plane above the text, no two edges *cross* (Kübler et al., 2009).

4.2 Hirao et al. (2013)'s Method

---

[2]Unlike Li's procedure, our algorithm can take not only binary but also *n*-ary RST-DTs as inputs. To derive the same DDTs as those produced by Li's original method, experiments were performed on right-branching binary RST-DTs.

[3]If P has no Nucleus children, LeftmostNucleusChild(P) returns the leftmost child node.

[4]If P does not have any rhetorical labels, Label(P) returns a special non-rhetorical label: "Span".

Algorithm 4 find-Nearest-S-Ancestor(e)

Require: EDU: e
Ensure: P
 1: $P \leftarrow$ Parent(e)
 2: **while** isNucleus(P) = TRUE and
        isRoot(P) = FALSE **do**
 3:    $P \leftarrow$ Parent(P)
 4: **end while**
 5: Return P

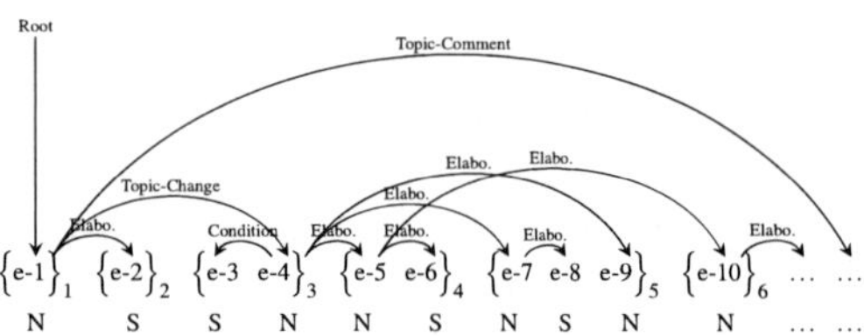

Figure 3: Discourse dependency tree produced by Hirao's method for RST discourse tree in Figure 1.

Hirao et al. (2013) also proposed a dependency conversion method for RST-DTs. The only difference between Li's and Hirao's methods is the process that finds the highest non-terminal node to which each EDU must be assigned as the head. At line 3 of Algorithm 1, Hirao's method calls Algorithm 4, which seeks the nearest Satellite to each EDU on the path from it to the root node of t. Note that this head-assignment manner was originally presented in the Veins Theory (Cristea et al., 1998).

Assuming that e-j is the e-7 in Figure 1, Algorithm 4 returns the 'S:Elaboration' node (covering e-5, e-6, e-7, e-8, e-9, e-10, ...), which is the nearest Satellite on the path from e-7 to the root node. Then, as well as in Li's method, Algorithm 3 iteratively seeks the leftmost child node with the Nucleus, starting from the parent node of the Satellite, until it reaches terminal node e-4. Finally, we obtain a dependency edge $(4, \text{Elaboration}, 7)$.

Figure 3 represents the DDT produced by Hirao's method for the RST-DT in Figure 1. Note that unlike Li's method, Hirao's dependency format is not always projective. The dependency edges made from the mononuclear relations are the same as those in Figure 2, but the difference comes from the treatment of the multinuclear relations. We take as an example the "Temporal" multinuclear relation in Figure 1 that links sentences 4 (e-5 and e-6) and 5 (e-7, e-8, and e-9). The Li14 DDT format links them with a "parent-child" relation, while in the Hirao13 DDT format, they have a "sibling" relation.

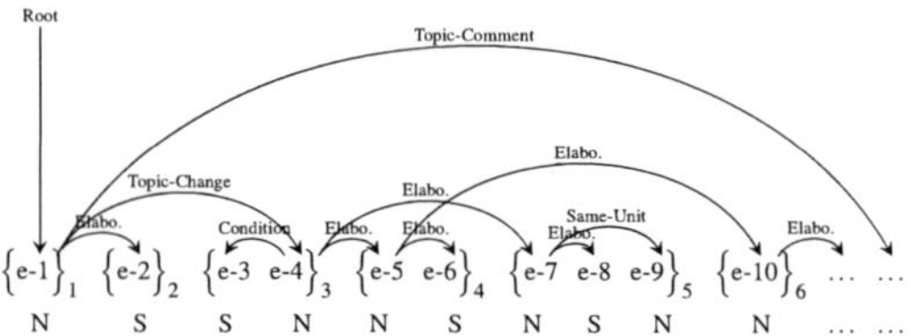

Figure 4: Discourse dependency tree (DDT) obtained by post-editing the DDT in Figure 3.

4.3 Post-editing Algorithm for Multi-rooted Sentence Tree Structures

Unlike Li's method, the dependency structures produced by Hirao's method often lose the single-rooted tree structure of a sentence since Algorithm 4 has no constraints that restrict the EDUs covered by multinuclear relations to find its head outside the sentence. For example, in Figure 3, both EDUs e-7 and e-9 in sentence 5 have the same head e-4 outside the sentence.

Most sentences form a single-rooted subtree in a full-text RST-DT (Joty et al., 2013), and previous studies on sentence-level discourse parsing were based on this insight (Soricut and Marcu, 2003; Sagae, 2009). To reduce the complexity of DDTs, it is reasonable to restrict the tree structure of a sentence to be single-rooted in a full-text DDT.

To revise a multi-rooted dependency tree structure of a sentence to a single-rooted one, we propose a simple post-editing method. Let $\mathscr{L} = \langle \text{e-}x_1, \ldots, \text{e-}x_n \rangle$ be a *multi-root list* consisting of more than two EDUs ($n \geq 2$ and $x_1 < \cdots < x_n$) in identical sentence s, each of which has a head outside s. Next we define the *post-editing* process of multi-root list $\mathscr{L}$; for each EDU e-x_j ($2 \leq j \leq n$), let its head be e-y_j with rhetorical label ℓ_j. Then the post-editing method replaces the dependency edge (y_j, ℓ_j, x_j) by $(x_1, \text{Label}(P), x_j)$, where P is a child node, which covers e-x_j, of the highest node among those that cover only sentence s in the RST-DT.

For the DDT in Figure 3, the post-editing process for multi-root list $\mathscr{L} = \langle \text{e-7}, \text{e-9} \rangle$ replaces the edge $(4, \text{Temporal}, 9)$ by $(7, \text{Same-Unit}, 9)$. This process makes the tree structure of sentence 5 single-rooted (Figure 4). Note that if an input dependency graph structure is a tree, even after post-editing all the multi-root lists of the input tree, the result remains a tree structure. This post-editing reduces the number of non-projective dependency

Label	Li14	Hirao13	M-Hirao13
Attribution	3070	3182	3176
Background	937	1176	1064
Cause	692	731	729
Comparison	300	200	246
Condition	328	344	338
Contrast	1130	838	892
Elaboration	7902	10358	9242
Enablement	568	609	603
Evaluation	419	596	501
Explanation	986	1527	1255
Joint	1990	42	593
Manner-Means	226	272	266
Root	385	385	385
Same-Unit	1404	62	1092
Span	1	0	1
Summary	223	332	289
Temporal	530	271	355
TextualOrganization	157	137	121
Topic-Change	205	401	344
Topic-Comment	336	326	297

Table 1: Rhetorical label frequencies in automatically created discourse dependency corpora.

edges, even though the structure might continue to be non-projective.

5 Experiments

5.1 Analysis of Dependency Structures

5.1.1 Dependency Label Distributions

Our experiments are based on data from the RST Discourse Treebank (RST-DTB) (Carlson et al., 2003)[5], which consists of 385 Wall Street Journal articles. Following previous studies on RST-DTB, we used 18 coarse rhetorical labels. We converted all 385 RST-DTs to DDTs using the methods introduced in Section 4. Table 1 compares three distributions of 18 rhetorical labels and 2 special non-rhetorical labels: "Span"[6] and "Root". M-Hirao13 denotes a modified version of the Hirao13 dependency format by *post-editing*.

Here, we focus on the three underlined labels. Even though the DDTs produced by the Hirao13 method contain more edges labeled as "Elaboration", the number of "Joint" and "Same-Unit" labels, which are assigned to some multinuclear relations, decreases considerably. This is because for each EDU, Algorithm 4 in the Hirao13 method finds a Satellite covering the EDU through multin-

Property	Li14	Hirao13	M-Hirao13
max path len.	10.2	8.4	8.6
nodes (depth 2)	6.5	9.6	8.6
nodes (depth 3)	14.3	22.1	20.3
nodes (depth 4)	23.3	35.0	33.3
gap degree 0	385	113	247
gap degree 1	0	260	137
gap degree 2	0	12	1
projective	385	113	247
well-nested	385	385	385

Table 2: Experimental results on average maximum path length, number of nodes within depth x, and number of dependency structures that satisfy the property described in Kuhlmann and Nivre (2006).

uclear relations and most Satellites have the "Elaboration" label.

In practice, we should refine such "Elaboration" labels by encoding in them the information of multinuclear relations that appear on the path from the EDU to the Satellite. However, this encoding scheme has a trade-off; increasing the amount of information encoded in an edge label reduces the accuracy of the label prediction by automatic parsers. In future work, we will investigate what label encoding scheme strikes the best balance in the trade-off.

5.1.2 Complexity of Dependency Structures

This section investigates the complexity of the dependency structures produced by each conversion method. Table 2 shows the average maximum path length from an artificial root to a leaf EDU and the number of nodes where depth $x \in \mathbb{N}$. The results clearly show that Hirao13 produces more broad and shallow dependency tree structures than Li14.

Table 2 also displays how large a portion of the dependency structures is allowed under *projectivity*, *gap degree*, and *well-nestedness* constraints. In the dependency parsing community, it is well-known that these three constraints create a good balance between expressivity and complexity in dependency analysis. These constraints were formally defined (Kuhlmann and Nivre, 2006)[7], and refer to that work for details.

All of the DDTs produced by the Li14 method are projective. Projectivity is the most popular constraint for sentence-level dependency pars-

---

[5]https://catalog.ldc.upenn.edu/LDC2002T07

[6]In RST theory, a "Span" label may not be assigned to any dependency edges. We suspect that the illegal "Span" label in Table 1 might have been caused by an annotation error in a subtree from e-7 to e-9 of the wsj-1189 file.

[7]Unlike Kuhlmann and Nivre (2006), when calculating the statistics in Table 2, we add an edge $(0, Root, i)$ for every real root EDU e-i ($i \geq 1$) of the DDT.

		UAS	LAS
	Li14	66.6	48.3
MST (Dep)	Hirao13	55.0	43.1
	M-Hirao13	60.5	42.8
	Li14	64.7	49.0
HILDA (RST)	Hirao13	57.1	46.2
	M-Hirao13	62.4	49.2

Table 3: Dependency unlabeled and labeled attachment scores (UAS and LAS) for MST dependency and HILDA RST parsers.

ing since it offers cubic-time dynamic programming algorithms for dependency parsing (Eisner, 1996; Eisner and Satta, 1999; Gómez-Rodrıguez et al., 2008). A higher gap degree means that the dependency trees have more complex non-projective structures. Both the Hirao13 and M-Hirao13 methods produce many non-projective dependency edges, but most of the DDTs have at most 1 gap degree and all are well-nested. The well-nested dependency structures of the low gap degree also allow efficient dynamic programming solutions with polynominal time complexity to dependency parsing (Gómez-Rodrıguez et al., 2009).

5.2   Impact on Automatic Parsing Accuracy

The conversion methods introduce different complexities in DDTs. This section investigates which formats are more accurately analyzed by automatic discourse parsers. For evaluation, we implemented a maximum spanning tree algorithm for discourse dependency parsing, which was recently proposed (Muller et al., 2012; Li et al., 2014; Yoshida et al., 2014). To compare discourse dependency parsing with standard RST parsing, we also implemented the HILDA RST parser (Hernault et al., 2010), which achieved 82.6/66.6/54.2 points for a standard set of RST-style evaluation measures, i.e., Span, Nuclearity and Relation (Marcu, 2000).

We used a standard split of DDTs automatically converted from RST-DTB: 347 DDTs as the training set and 38 as the test set.

Table 3 shows the evaluation results of dependency parsing. The lower the complexity of the DDT format, the higher is the dependency unlabeled attachment score. Post-editing the Hirao13 DDTs improves the dependency attachment scores because the intra-sentential discourse analysis is more accurate than the inter-sentential one. In all the DDT formats, the labeled attachment scores

are considerably worse that the unlabeled scores.

Compared with the HILDA parser, the Hirao13 and M-Hirao13 DDTs by the MST parser are less accurate than those by the RST parser, probably because unlike word dependency parsing, the features defined over the EDUs are too sparse to describe complex non-projective dependency relations.

5.3   Impact on Text Summarization

Hirao et al. (2013) proposed a state-of-the-art single text summarization method based on trimming unlabeled DDTs. That can be formulated by the *Tree Knapsack Problem* (TKP), which they solved with integer linear programming. To examine which dependency structures produced by the three conversion schemes are more suitable to the task, we performed text summarization experiments with the TKP method.

The 30 Wall Street Journal articles have a human-made reference summary, which we used for our evaluations. Table 4 shows the ROUGE scores for the 30 gold-standard and auto-parse DDTs. The auto-parse DDTs were obtained by the MST and HILDA parsers, which were trained with 325 articles and whose hyper parameters were tuned with 30 articles.

Hirao13 achieved the best results when we employed the gold DDTs, although the differences between Hirao13 and the other methods were not large. On the other hand, Hirao13 and M-Hirao13 obtained good results when we employed automatic parse trees. The gains against Li14 are large. It is remarkable that the performance with MST's DDTs closely approached that of the gold DDTs. These results imply that the auto parse trees obtained from Hirao13 have broad and shallow hierarchies because important EDUs, which must be included in a summary, can be easily extracted by TKP. Thus, the DDTs converted by the Hirao13 rule have better tree structures for a single document summarization even though the structures are complex and difficult to parse. This is a significant advantage over Li's conversion rule.

6   Summary

We evaluated two different RST-DT-to-DDT conversion schemes from various perspectives. Experimental results show that even though the Hirao13 DDT format produces more complex dependency structures, it is more useful for text summa-

	Conv.	R-1 w/s.	R-1 wo/s.	R-2 w/s.	R-2 wo/s.
	Li14	.347	.321	.096	.098
Gold	Hirao13	**.349**	**.333**	**.109**	**.117**
	M-Hirao13	.344	.322	.106	.098
	Li14	.328	.292	.096	.086
MST (Dep)	Hirao13	**.341**	**.307**	.106	**.111**
	M-Hirao13	**.341**	.303	**.107**	**.111**
	Li14	.315	.281	.083	.086
HILDA (RST)	Hirao13	**.326**	**.294**	**.087**	**.093**
	M-Hirao13	.315	.285	.084	.089

Table 4: ROUGE-N scores for text summarization on gold and auto-parse DDTs ($N = 1, 2$).

rization. While studies developing discourse parsing have focused on improving parser accuracies, our experimental results identified the importance of extrinsic evaluations over intrinsic evaluations. In future work, we will further compare the methods by extrinsic evaluation metrics using discourse relation labels.

Acknowledgments

The authors would like to thank the anonymous reviewers for their valuable comments and suggestions to improve the quality of the paper. This work was supported in part by JSPS KAKENHI Grant Numbers JP26730126 and JP26280079.

References

Stergos Afantenos et al. 2012. An empirical resource for discovering cognitive principles of discourse organisation: the annodis corpus. In *Proceedings of the 12th International Conference on Language Resources and Evaluation*.

Nicholas Asher and Alex Lascarides. 2003. *Logics of Conversation*. Cambridge University Press.

Lynn Carlson, Daniel Marcu, and Mary Ellen Okurowski. 2003. *Building a discourse-tagged corpus in the framework of rhetorical structure theory*. Springer.

Michael Collins. 1999. *Head-driven statistical models for natural language parsing*. Ph.D. thesis, Stanford University.

Dan Cristea, Nancy Ide, and Laurent Romary. 1998. Veins theory: A model of global discourse cohesion and coherence. In *Proceedings of the 17th International Conference on Computational linguistics-Volume 1*, pages 281–285.

Laurence Danlos et al. 2008. Strong generative capacity of rst, sdrt and discourse dependency dags. pages 69–95.

Marie-Catherine De Marneffe and Christopher D Manning. 2008. The stanford typed dependencies representation. In *Coling 2008: Proceedings of the workshop on Cross-Framework and Cross-Domain Parser Evaluation*, pages 1–8.

Markus Egg and Gisela Redeker. 2010. How complex is discourse structure? In *Proceedings of the 7th International Conference on Language Resources and Evaluation*.

Jason Eisner and Giorgio Satta. 1999. Efficient parsing for bilexical context-free grammars and head automaton grammars. In *Proceedings of the 37th annual meeting of the Association for Computational Linguistics on Computational Linguistics*, pages 457–464. Association for Computational Linguistics.

Jason M Eisner. 1996. Three new probabilistic models for dependency parsing: An exploration. In *Proceedings of the 16th international conference on Computational linguistics*, pages 340–345.

Vanessa Wei Feng and Graeme Hirst. 2012. Text-level discourse parsing with rich linguistic features. In *Proceedings of the 50th Annual Meeting of the Association for Computational Linguistics: Long Papers-Volume 1*, pages 60–68.

Katja Filippova and Michael Strube. 2008. Dependency tree based sentence compression. In *Proceedings of the Fifth International Natural Language Generation Conference*, pages 25–32.

Carlos Gómez-Rodrıguez, John Carroll, and David Weir. 2008. A deductive approach to dependency parsing. In *Proceedings of the 46th Annual Meeting of the Association for Computational Linguistics: Human Language Technologies (ACL08: HLT)*, pages 968–976.

Carlos Gómez-Rodrıguez, David Weir, and John Carroll. 2009. Parsing mildly non-projective dependency structures. In *Proceedings of the 12th Conference of the European Chapter of the ACL*, pages 291–299.

Hugo Hernault, Helmut Prendinger, Mitsuru Ishizuka, et al. 2010. Hilda: a discourse parser using support vector machine classification. *Dialogue & Discourse*, 1(3).

Tsutomu Hirao, Yasuhisa Yoshida, Masaaki Nishino, Norihito Yasuda, and Masaaki Nagata. 2013. Single-document summarization as a tree knapsack problem. In *Proceedings of the Conference on Empirical Methods in Natural Language Processing*, pages 1515–1520.

Richard Johansson and Pierre Nugues. 2007. Extended constituent-to-dependency conversion for english. In *16th Nordic Conference of Computational Linguistics*, pages 105–112.

Shafiq R Joty, Giuseppe Carenini, Raymond T Ng, and Yashar Mehdad. 2013. Combining intra-and multi-sentential rhetorical parsing for document-level discourse analysis. In *Proceedings of the 51st Annual Meeting of the Association for Computational Linguistics*, volume 1, pages 486–496.

Sandra Kübler, Ryan McDonald, and Joakim Nivre. 2009. Dependency parsing. *Synthesis Lectures on Human Language Technologies*, 1(1):1–127.

Marco Kuhlmann and Joakim Nivre. 2006. Mildly non-projective dependency structures. In *Proceedings of the 21st International Conference on Computational Linguistics and 44th Annual Meeting of the Association for Computational Linguistics*, pages 507–514.

Alan Lee, Rashmi Prasad, Aravind Joshi, Nikhil Dinesh, and Bonnie Webber. 2006. Complexity of dependencies in discourse: Are dependencies in discourse more complex than in syntax. In *Proceedings of the 5th International Workshop on Treebanks and Linguistic Theories, Prague, Czech Republic, December*.

Sujian Li, Liang Wang, Ziqiang Cao, and Wenjie Li. 2014. Text-level discourse dependency parsing. In *Proceedings of the 52nd Annual Meeting of the Association for Computational Linguistics*, volume 1, pages 25–35.

David M Magerman. 1994. *Natural language parsing as statistical pattern recognition*. Ph.D. thesis, University of Pennsylvania.

William Mann and Sandra Thompson. 1988. Rhetorical structure theory: Towards a functional theory of text organization. *Text*, 8(3):243–281.

Daniel Marcu. 2000. *The theory and practice of discourse parsing and summarization*. MIT press.

Philippe Muller, Stergos Afantenos, Pascal Denis, and Nicholas Asher. 2012. Constrained decoding for text-level discourse parsing. pages 1883–1899. Proceedings of the 24th International Conference on Computational Linguistics.

Rashmi Prasad, Nikhil Dinesh, Alan Lee, Eleni Miltsakaki, Livio Robaldo, Aravind K Joshi, and Bonnie L Webber. 2008. The penn discourse treebank 2.0. In *Proceedings of the 6th International Conference on Language Resources and Evaluation*.

Kenji Sagae. 2009. Analysis of discourse structure with syntactic dependencies and data-driven shift-reduce parsing. In *Proceedings of the 11th International Conference on Parsing Technologies*, pages 81–84. Association for Computational Linguistics.

Radu Soricut and Daniel Marcu. 2003. Sentence level discourse parsing using syntactic and lexical information. In *Proceedings of the 2003 Conference of the North American Chapter of the Association for Computational Linguistics on Human Language Technology-Volume 1*, pages 149–156.

Antonine Venant, Nicholas Asher, Philippe Muller, Pascal Denis, and Stergos Afantenos. 2013. Expressivity and comparison of models of discourse structure. In *Proceedings of the SIGDIAL*, pages 2–11.

Florian Wolf and Edward Gibson. 2005. Representing discourse coherence: A corpus-based study. *Computational Linguistics*, 31(2):249–287.

Hiroyasu Yamada and Yuji Matsumoto. 2003. Statistical dependency analysis with support vector machines. In *Proceedings of the 8th International Workshop on Parsing Technologies*, volume 3.

Yasuhisa Yoshida, Jun Suzuki, Tsutomu Hirao, and Masaaki Nagata. 2014. Dependency-based discourse parser for single-document summarization. In *Proceedings of the Conference on Empirical Methods in Natural Language Processing*, pages 1834–1839.

The Role of Discourse Units in Near-Extractive Summarization

Junyi Jessy Li
University of Pennsylvania
ljunyi@seas.upenn.edu

Kapil Thadani, Amanda Stent
Yahoo Research
{thadani,stent}@yahoo-inc.com

Abstract

Although human-written summaries of documents tend to involve significant edits to the source text, most automated summarizers are extractive and select sentences verbatim. In this work we examine how *elementary discourse units* (EDUs) from Rhetorical Structure Theory can be used to extend extractive summarizers to produce a wider range of human-like summaries. Our analysis demonstrates that EDU segmentation is effective in preserving human-labeled summarization concepts within sentences and also aligns with near-extractive summaries constructed by news editors. Finally, we show that using EDUs as units of content selection instead of sentences leads to stronger summarization performance in near-extractive scenarios, especially under tight budgets.

1 Introduction

Document summarization has a wide variety of practical applications and is consequently a focus of much NLP research. When a human summarizes a document, they often edit its constituent sentences in order to succinctly capture the document's meaning. For instance, Jing and McKeown (2000) observed that summary authors trimmed extraneous content, combined sentences, replaced phrases or clauses with more general or specific variants, etc. These *abstractive* summaries thus involve sentences which deviate from those of the source document in structure or content.

In contrast, automated approaches to summarization generally produce *extractive* summaries by selecting complete sentences from the source document (Nenkova and McKeown, 2011) in order to ensure that the output is grammatical.

Extractive summarization techniques, which are widely used in practical applications, therefore address a substantially simpler problem than human summarization.

This leads to a natural question: can extractive summarization techniques be used to produce more human-like summaries? We hypothesize that automated methods can generate a wider range of summaries by extracting over sub-sentential units of meaning from the source documents rather than whole sentences. Specifically, in this paper we investigate whether *elementary discourse units* (EDUs) from Rhetorical Structure Theory (Mann and Thompson, 1988) comprise viable textual units for summarization. Our focus is on recovering salient summary content under ROUGE (Lin, 2004) while the composition of EDUs into fluent output sentences is left to future work.

We investigate this hypothesis in two complementary ways: by studying the compatibility of EDUs with human-labeled summarization units from pyramid evaluations (Nenkova et al., 2007) and by assessing their utility in reconstructing real-world document previews chosen by news editors in the New York Times corpus (Sandhaus, 2008). The contributions of this work include:

- A demonstration that EDU segmentation preserves human-identified conceptual units in the context of document summarization.

- New, large datasets proposed for research into extractive and compressive summarization of news articles.

- A study of the lexical omissions made by news editors in real-world compressive summarization.

- A comparative analysis of supervised single-document summarization over full sentences and over a range of budgets in extractive and near-extractive scenarios.

Proceedings of the SIGDIAL 2016 Conference, pages 137–147,
Los Angeles, USA, 13-15 September 2016. ©2016 Association for Computational Linguistics

2   Background and related work

Discourse structure in summarization   Rhetorical Structure Theory (RST) (Mann and Thompson, 1988) represents the discourse in a document in the form of a tree (Figure 1). The leaf nodes of RST trees are *elementary discourse units* (EDUs) which are a segmentation of sentences into independent clauses, including dependencies such as clausal subjects and complements. The more central units to each RST relation are *nuclei* while the more peripheral are *satellites*. Prior work in document compression (Daumé and Marcu, 2002) and single-document summarization (Marcu, 1999; Louis et al., 2010; Hirao et al., 2013; Kikuchi et al., 2014; Yoshida et al., 2014) has shown that the structure of discourse trees, especially the *nuclearity* of non-terminal discourse relations in the tree, is valuable for content selection in summarization.

The Penn Discourse Treebank (PDTB) (Prasad et al., 2008) on the other hand is theory-neutral and does not define a recursive structure for the entire document like RST. Discourse relations are lexically bound to explicit discourse connectives within a sentence or exist between adjacent sentences if there is no connective. Each relation is realized in two text arguments, which are similar to EDUs. However, unlike EDUs, PDTB relation arguments have flexibility in size, ordering and arrangement and do not form a complete *segmentation* of the text. They are therefore not easily interpretable as textual units that can be combined to form sentences and summaries.

In this paper, we focus on EDUs and explore their viability as basic units for summarization. We did not use PDTB-style arguments to make sure each part of a document belongs to a textual unit and that the units are strictly adjacent to each other. EDU segmentation, typically addressed as a tagging problem early in discourse parsing systems, has seen accuracy and speed improvements in recent years (Hernault et al., 2010; Joty et al., 2015). It is now practical to segment document sentences into EDUs at scale as a preprocessing step for automated summarization.

Textual units in summarization.   In extractive summarization, sentences are typically chosen as units to assemble output summaries because of their presumed grammaticality (Nenkova and McKeown, 2011). Finer-grained units such as

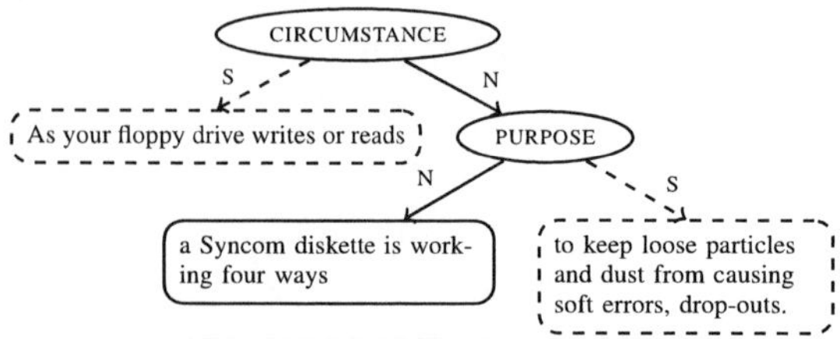

Figure 1: A RST discourse tree with EDUs as leaf nodes (example from Mann and Thompson (1988)).

n-grams are frequently used for quantifying content salience and redundancy prior to summarization over sentences (Filatova and Hatzivassiloglou, 2004; Thadani and McKeown, 2008; Gillick and Favre, 2009; Lin and Bilmes, 2011; Cao et al., 2015). In contrast, when the task at hand is more abstractive, the units are more fine-grained, e.g., n-grams and phrases in abstractive summarization (Kikuchi et al., 2014; Liu et al., 2015; Bing et al., 2015), n-grams and human-annotated concept units in summarization evaluation (Lin, 2004; Hovy et al., 2006). Recently, subject-verb-object triplets were used to automatically identify concept units (Yang et al., 2016) and in abstractive summarization (Li, 2015); however, this requires semantic processing while EDU segmentation is presently more accurate and scalable.

Here, we explore EDUs as a middle ground between fine-grained lexical units and full sentences. While EDUs have been used in prior work to directly assemble output summaries (Marcu, 1999; Hirao et al., 2013; Yoshida et al., 2014), the focus was on using discourse structure as features for sentence ranking, while our work is the first to examine the utility of EDUs themselves.

Datasets.   In this work, we address *single-document* summarization. Standard datasets for the task were created for the Document Understanding Conference (DUC) in 2001 and 2002. The datasets for each year were composed of about 600 documents accompanied by 100-word abstractive summaries. In addition, the RST Discourse Treebank (Carlson et al., 2003) contains abstractive summaries for 30 documents, which have been used for evaluation in RST-driven summarization (Hirao et al., 2013; Kikuchi et al., 2014; Yoshida et al., 2014).

In contrast, we propose the use of datasets de-

Figure 2: An EDU-segmented sentence with three human-labeled concepts (SCU contributors).

rived from the New York Times (NYT) corpus[1] that are orders of magnitude larger than the DUC dataset, featuring thousands of article summaries with varying degrees of extractiveness. Although the summaries in this dataset typically contain fewer than 100 words and are sometimes intended to serve as a teaser for the article rather than a distillation of its content, they were nevertheless created by professional editors for a highly-trafficked news website. Prior work has also demonstrated the utility of this corpus for summarization (Hong et al., 2015; Nye and Nenkova, 2015). This dataset therefore enables the study of summarization in a realistic setting.

Compressive summarization. To explore the utility of EDUs in summarization, we examine *near*-extractive summaries in the NYT corpus which are drawn from sentences in the document but omit at least one word or phrase from them. This setting is also explored in the summarization literature for techniques which combine extractive sentence selection with sentence compression (Clarke and Lapata, 2007; Berg-Kirkpatrick et al., 2011; Woodsend and Lapata, 2012; Almeida and Martins, 2013; Kikuchi et al., 2014). These approaches are typically evaluated against abstractive summaries and have not been studied with a natural compressive dataset such as the ones proposed here. We do not address techniques to generate compressive summaries in this work but instead attempt to quantify how the omitted content in a summary relates to its EDU segmentation.

3 EDUs as Concept Units in Summaries

We first investigate whether EDUs from an RST parse of the document can serve as a middle ground between abstract units of information and the sentences in which they are realized. Specifically, given a dataset containing human-labeled concepts in each article, we examine their correspondence with the EDUs extracted automatically from the article in terms of both lexical coverage and content salience.

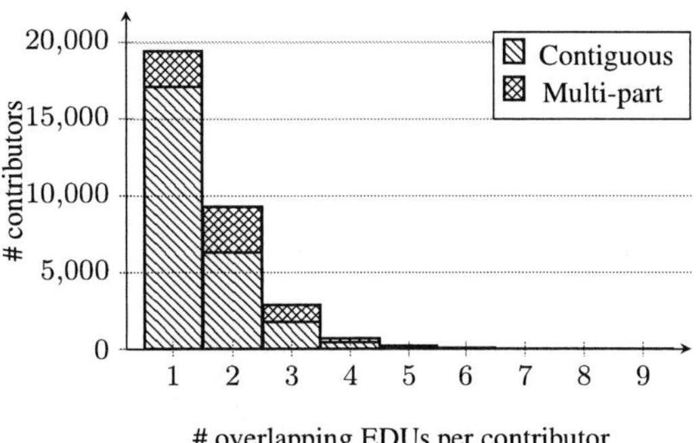

Figure 3: Number of EDUs which overlap with each SCU contributor (single or multi-part) in the DUC/TAC reference summary datasets.

3.1 Data and settings

In the DUC 2005–2007 and TAC 2008–2011 shared tasks on multi-document summarization, evaluations are conducted under the *pyramid* method—a technique which quantifies the semantic content of reference summaries and uses it as the basis of comparison for system-generated summaries (Nenkova et al., 2007). For this, human annotators must identify *summary content units* (SCUs) across reference summaries for a single topic. Each SCU has one or more *contributors* from different reference summaries which express the concept in text. Of the 32,535 contributors in the DUC and TAC data, 79% form contiguous text spans while the rest involve two or more non-contiguous parts within a sentence.

Our primary goal in this section is to investigate the degree to which EDUs correspond to SCUs. For this purpose, we treat each reference summary as an independent article and its SCU contributors as concept annotations. We parse the summaries using the RST parser of Feng and Hirst (2014a) to recover an EDU segmentation, specifically version 2.01 of the parser which shows superior EDU segmentation performance to other discourse parsers (Feng and Hirst, 2014b). An example of an EDU-segmented sentence with its human-labeled concepts is shown in Figure 2.

---

[1]Available from the LDC at `https://catalog.ldc.upenn.edu/LDC2008T19`

[The American Bookseller Association represents private bookstore owners] [and sponsors Book Expo, an annual convention.]

[Napster claimed protection under the Millenium Copyright Act] [because they had no control over users' actions.]

Figure 4: Examples of sentences in which human-labeled concepts (indicated by connected lines) span EDUs (in square brackets).

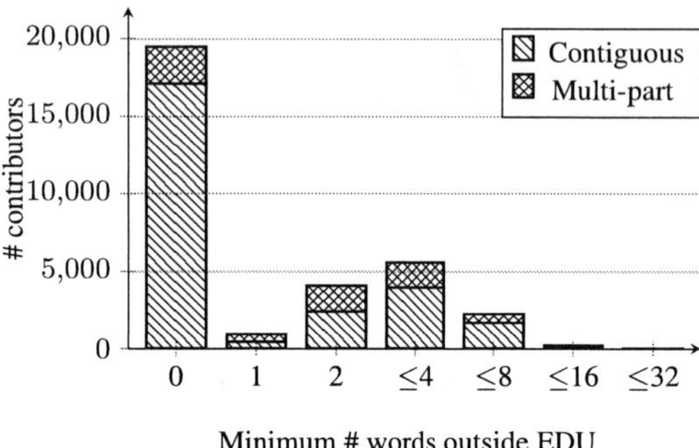

Figure 5: Number of words in SCU contributors which remain uncovered by a single EDU in the DUC/TAC reference summary datasets.

3.2   Concept coverage

Figure 3 indicates the number of EDUs that overlap by one or more tokens with each SCU contributor in the data. Most concepts (62%) are covered by a single EDU. This is more pronounced for concepts which are realized in a contiguous text span (69%), while multi-part concepts are unsurprisingly more likely to overlap with two EDUs. On average, concepts overlap with 1.56 EDUs while EDUs overlap with 1.77 concepts, significantly fewer than the average number of concepts contained in whole sentences (2.18).

Because we consider an overlap of one token to be sufficient to associate an EDU with an SCU contributor, we also examine in Figure 5 the number of non-punctuation contributor words that would need to be deleted for each concept to be covered by a single EDU. The vast majority of SCU contributors are covered by a single EDU, while the remainder typically have 2–4 words uncovered. Fewer than 8% of concepts were observed to have more than 4 words outside their corresponding EDU.

In Figure 4 we show typical examples of sentences with concepts which cross EDU boundaries. A major source for breached boundaries lies within heads of clauses. For instance, the first example contains two verb phrases in separate EDUs which each mark a concept, but their shared head "American Bookseller Association" can be in only one EDU. Errors are also often caused by overly broad SCUs which contain too much content. In the second example, the second EDU holds a causal relation with the first EDU and is thus a a satellite to the discourse relation, whereas the whole relation is combined into a single SCU contributor. These cases can potentially be resolved by taking into account the discourse relation and nuclearity status of the involved EDUs.

3.3   Salience via discourse structure

In addition to coverage of SCU contributors, we would like to see the extent to which EDUs are *meaningful* with respect to summarization concepts. One of the most intriguing aspects of EDUs is that they are not merely textual units but rather units in a discourse tree from which relative concept importance can be derived. In pyramid evaluations, the salience of an SCU is determined by the number of distinct contributors it has across all reference summaries for a topic, and thus each SCU in our dataset has an implicit weight indicating its importance. We therefore investigate the relationship between *inter*-document concept salience using these SCU weights and an *intra*-document counterpart from the EDUs in the discourse tree.

To calculate salience over EDUs, we use the scoring mechanism in Marcu (1999). Intuitively, each EDU which is a nucleus of a discourse relation (as opposed to a satellite) can be promoted one level up in the discourse tree. The score weights each EDU according to the depth that it can be promoted up to: the closer to the root, the more important the EDU is. For this analysis, we impute the discourse salience of a contributor by averaging the Marcu (1999) scores (normalized by tree depth) of the EDUs it overlaps with.

Table 1 shows the mean of these scores over all contributors with a particular SCU weight. In each group with weight w, the average EDU-derived

SCU weight	1	2	3	$\geq$4
Proportion of SCUs (%)	54.3	21.6	13.0	11.2
Mean Marcu (1999) score	0.64	0.66	0.68	0.72

Table 1: Average salience scores of EDUs overlapping with SCU contributors, stratified by SCU weight. Differences between scores for each group are statistically significant under the Wilcoxon rank-sum test ($p < 0.05$).

salience score is significantly higher ($p < 0.05$) compared to the group with weight $w - 1$. That is, the more important a SCU is *across* these documents, the more important its corresponding EDUs are *within* the discourse of each document. We infer that the human authors of these summaries make structural decisions to highlight important concepts, and that these choices are reflected in the derived discourse structure.

With a large fraction of concepts observed to be contained within EDUs, we find compelling evidence to support the notion of EDUs as operational units of summarization. Moreover, we find evidence that the RST discourse structure which typically accompanies EDU segmentation also provides a strong signal of salience, though further experimentation along these lines is left to future work. We now investigate the utility of EDUs in a practical news summarization task using a large dataset.

4 Near-extractive summarization

In order to investigate the viability of discourse units in a practical setting, we use the New York Times Annotated Corpus (Sandhaus, 2008) which contains over 1.8 million articles published between 1987 and 2007 as well as their metadata. We mine this corpus to recover *near-extractive* summaries of articles which reveal how human editors selectively omit information from article sentences in order to preview the article for potential readers. This presents a middle ground between purely extractive and fully abstractive summarization which is useful to study the role of subsentential units in content selection.

4.1 Datasets

The NYT dataset contains editor-produced *online lead paragraphs*[2] which accompany 284,980 arti-

cles featured prominently on the NYT homepage from 2001 onwards. They are explicitly intended for presentation to readers and usually consist of one or more complete sentences which serve as a brief summary or teaser for the full article.[3]

We ensure that these online lead paragraphs— henceforth *online summaries*—are composed of complete sentences by filtering out cases which contain no verbs, omit sentence-terminating punctuation or are all-uppercase, respectively indicating summaries which are caption-like, truncated or merely topic/location descriptors. We also exclude articles with frequently repeated titles, first sentences and summaries which we observe to be template-like and thus not indicative of editorial input. Finally, we preprocess the remaining 244,267 summaries by stripping HTML artifacts and structured prefixes (e.g., bureau locations), normalizing Unicode symbols and fixing whitespace inserted within or deleted between tokens. We have released our data preparation code[4] to facilitate future research on the NYT corpus.

Three mutually exclusive datasets[5] are drawn from the processed document collection:

- EX-SENT: 38,921 fully extractive instances in which each summary sentence is drawn whole from the article when ignoring case, punctuation and whitespace.

- NX-SPAN: 15,646 near-extractive instances where one or more summary sentences form a contiguous span of tokens within an article sentence, and the remaining fit the definition above.

- NX-SUBSEQ: 25,381 near-extractive instances where one or more summary sentences form a non-contiguous token subsequence within an article sentence, and the remaining fit either of the definitions above.

The remaining 164,319 instances contain fully abstractive summaries with sentences that cannot be unambiguously mapped to those in the articles; these are not considered in the remainder of this

---

[2]Despite the name, these are typically not the same as the leading sentence or paragraph of the article.

[3]Note that this differs from the *abstracts* used in prior summarization research (Yang and Nenkova, 2014; Hong et al., 2015; Nye and Nenkova, 2015). We observe that abstracts appear to serve more as high-level structured descriptions of articles (e.g., referring to type of the article and NYT sections, using present-tense and collapsed sentences) rather than narrative summaries intended for presentation to readers.

[4]https://github.com/grimpil/nyt-summ

[5]The NYT document IDs for these datasets are available at http://www.cs.columbia.edu/~kapil/datasets/docids_nytsumm.tgz

NX-SPAN (contiguous)	**Summary:** Now that their season is over, the New York Yankees are likely to shop for new players over the winter. What they really should look for are new fans. **Doc EDUs:** [Now that their season is over,] [the New York Yankees are likely to shop for new players over the winter,] [*and may even*] [*seek a new manager*] [*to take over from the estimable Joseph Paul Torre.*] [What they really should look for are new fans.]
NX-SUBSEQ (non-contiguous)	**Summary:** The country's appetite for real estate propelled sales of newly built homes to a record pace in April, adding to concerns that the housing market may be in overdrive. **Doc EDUs:** [The country's avid appetite for real estate propelled sales of newly built homes to a record pace in April,] [*the Commerce Department reported yesterday,*] [*helping to raise prices*] [*and* adding to concerns] [that the housing market may be in overdrive.]

Table 2: Examples of reference summaries from NX-SPAN and NX-SUBSEQ alongside their source sentences from the article, segmented into EDUs. Tokens omitted by the summary are italicized.

paper but left to future work. Examples of summaries from the two near-extractive datasets are presented in Table 2 along with EDU-segmented source sentences from the corresponding articles.

4.2 Summary coverage

In order for our hypothesis that EDUs are good units for summarization to hold, we would expect the omitted text in these summaries to line up closely with the EDU segmentation of the source sentences. In particular, we expect to empirically observe that the number of of token edits required to recover reference summaries from source document EDUs is small.

For each type of unit—sentence and EDU—and every instance in NX-SPAN and NX-SUBSEQ, we align units derived from the original article with corresponding units from the online summary using Jaccard similarity, which is fairly reliable as the summaries are near-extractive. This procedure for deriving the set of input units matching output units is a necessary first step in training supervised summarization systems. Following this, we inspect the number of tokens that need to be deleted or added for each unit from the original article to match its counterpart in the summary. Distributions of the units in NX-SPAN and NX-SUBSEQ with respect to the number of tokens that need to be deleted or added are shown in Figure 6 and the average counts are presented in Table 3.

We observe that the number of deleted tokens as well as the proportion of units requiring token deletions is dramatically smaller when considering EDUs as summarization units. Token deletions are more frequent in summaries from NX-SUBSEQ in which deletions do not have to be continuous. Since EDUs in the summary may be erroneously aligned to different portions of the document, extraneous tokens may also be introduced; however, we observe these are relatively rare (3%

Dataset	Unit	# deleted	# added
NX-SPAN	Sent	11.47	0.00
	EDU	1.24	0.39
NX-SUBSEQ	Sent	11.95	0.00
	EDU	1.94	0.77

Table 3: Average #tokens deleted and added from each type of unit in NX-SPAN and NX-SUBSEQ.

for NX-SPAN and 10% for NX-SUBSEQ). No extraneous tokens are observed for sentence units as both datasets are near-extractive.

We further analyze the types of tokens that are involved in the deletion process when using sentences and EDUs as base units. Figure 7 shows for each dataset the average numbers of deleted tokens grouped by their universal part-of-speech tags (Petrov et al., 2012). We observe that the number of deleted content words drops from 6.83–7.33 in the case of sentences to 0.54–0.92 for EDUs, making them easier to convert into reference summaries. For instance, spurious verbs frequently need to be removed from sentences in both datasets but this is relatively rare for EDUs.

5 Using EDUs for summarization

In this section, we compare EDUs with sentences as base units of selection in extractive and near-extractive single-document summarization. Crucially, we consider summarization under varying summary budget constraints in order to analyze whether EDU-based summarization is versatile enough to compete with typical sentence-based summarization when budgets are generous. Because our goal is to focus on the viability of summarization units for content selection, we evaluated system-generated summaries using ROUGE (Lin, 2004). Recovering readable sentences from EDU-based summaries remains a goal for future work.

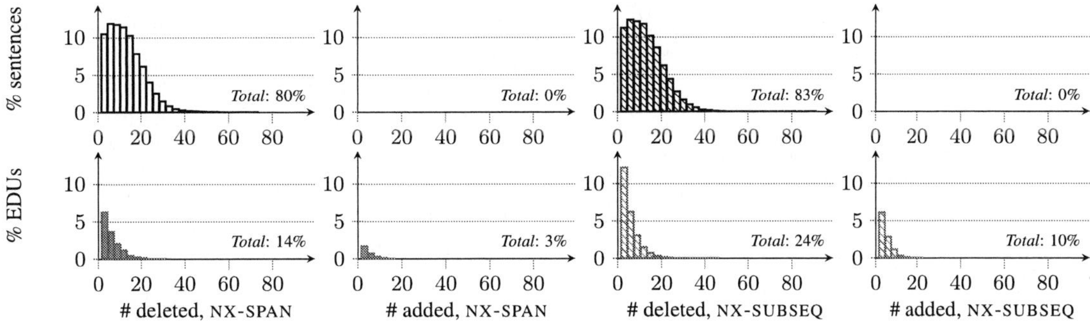

Figure 6: Proportion of source sentences and EDUs with the number of tokens deleted and added to recover summaries from NX-SPAN and NX-SUBSEQ. Cases with zero tokens added/deleted are omitted.

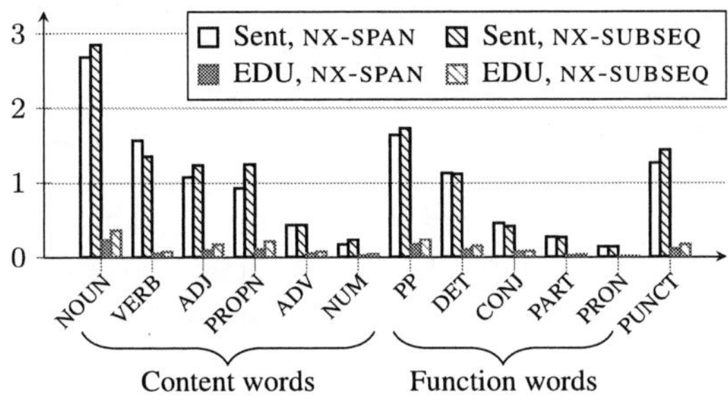

Figure 7: Average number of deleted tokens per instance in NX-SPAN and NX-SUBSEQ.

| | EDU | | Sentence | |
Dataset	Lead	Greedy	Lead	Greedy
EX-SENT	0.65	**0.67**	0.55	**0.58**
NX-SPAN	0.46	**0.48**	0.32	**0.36**
NX-SUBSEQ	0.54	**0.56**	0.37	**0.40**

Table 4: ROUGE-1 of lead sentences vs. the supervised summarizer under a 200-char budget.

Summarization framework. We adopt a supervised structured prediction approach to extractive single-document summarization. Summaries are produced through greedy search-based inference with features defined over units in the document as well as over units and partial summaries, resulting in a feature-based generalization of Carbonell and Goldstein (1998).[6] In order to focus on the role of summarization units, we work with a simple standard model using features that are *neutral* to the benefits and/or drawbacks of either sentences or EDUs:[7]

- Position of the unit
- Position of the unit in the paragraph
- Position of the paragraph containing the unit
- TF-IDF-weighted cosine similarity of the summary with the unit added and the document centroid;
- Whether the unit is adjacent to the previous unit added
- Whether the sentence containing the unit is adjacent to the sentence containing the previous unit added

Feature weights are estimated using the structured

perceptron (Collins, 2002) with parameter averaging for generalization. As inference is carried out via search, we employ a *max-violation* update policy (Huang and Feyong, 2012) to improve convergence speed and performance.

Data and settings. We use the extractive and near-extractive subsets from the NYT corpus described in Section 4.1 to train and evaluate our summarizer. To aid replicability for benchmarking, we partition all datasets by date rather than random sampling. Articles published in 2006–2007 are assigned to a held-out test partition while articles prior to 2005 are used for training, leaving articles from 2005 for a development partition.

The mean and standard deviation of summary lengths (specifically the number of characters) from our three NYT datasets are: EX-SENT 194.0 ± 92.6, NX-SPAN 134.6 ± 31.3, NX-SUBSEQ 143.3 ± 27.9. Summarization budgets are chosen to cover this range and set to 100, 150, 200, 250 and 300 characters. The lower bound (100 characters) is approximately one standard deviation below the mean across all three datasets, while the upper bound (300 characters) is approximately one standard deviation above the mean for EX-SENT, which features the longest summaries.

Comparison with lead. To validate this summarization framework, we first compare trained sum-

---

[6] We also experimented with beam search but did not observe improvements, as was also found in prior work (McDonald, 2007).

[7] For example, we do not use features related to nuclearity, discourse relation labels or discourse tree structure.

Budget	ROUGE-1		ROUGE-2		ROUGE-4	
	EDU	Sent	EDU	Sent	EDU	Sent
EX-SENT						
300	**0.80**	0.78	0.70	**0.71**	0.59	**0.71**
250	**0.75**	0.69	**0.64**	0.62	0.54	**0.61**
200	**0.67**	0.58	**0.56**	0.49	0.47	**0.48**
150	**0.54**	0.41	**0.43**	0.32	**0.35**	0.31
100	**0.35**	0.21	**0.26**	0.13	**0.20**	0.12
NX-SPAN						
300	**0.61**	0.58	**0.45**	0.44	0.37	**0.42**
250	**0.56**	0.50	**0.41**	0.36	0.33	**0.34**
200	**0.48**	0.36	**0.33**	0.20	**0.27**	0.18
150	**0.38**	0.22	**0.25**	0.08	**0.19**	0.06
100	**0.24**	0.14	**0.13**	0.04	**0.09**	0.03
NX-SUBSEQ						
300	**0.70**	0.69	0.53	**0.55**	0.38	**0.46**
250	**0.66**	0.59	**0.49**	0.44	0.35	**0.37**
200	**0.56**	0.40	**0.40**	0.24	**0.28**	0.20
150	**0.43**	0.22	**0.28**	0.08	**0.19**	0.05
100	**0.29**	0.14	**0.17**	0.04	**0.11**	0.02

Table 5: ROUGE results for EDU- and sentence-based summarization.

marizers against a standard summarization baseline which selects the leading sentence(s) of the document until the budget is exhausted. This evaluation uses a budget of 200 characters, which is about the average length of an extractive summary in our data.[8] ROUGE-1 results are shown in Table 4. Across all datasets and unit settings, the greedy summarizer consistently outperforms the lead baseline, indicating that the datasets involve non-trivial summarization problems.

Results. ROUGE results for all three datasets are shown in Table 5. For all budgets, scores are notably higher for EX-SENT which involves unambiguous alignment of reference units. ROUGE performance is also consistently higher for NX-SUBSEQ over NX-SPAN despite its higher token deletion rates (cf. Table 3), likely owing to a larger training dataset. All scores improve with bigger budgets as ROUGE is a recall-oriented measure.

We observe that EDUs outperform sentences across all datasets and budgets under ROUGE-1, on budgets within 250 characters under ROUGE-2 as well as budgets within 200 characters under ROUGE-4. Interestingly, EDU-based summarization remains competitive even on EX-SENT. The exceptionally strong performance of EDUs under tight budgets confirms our intuition that summarizers are better able to select salient informa-

---

[8]We experimented with all other aforementioned budgets with consistent results.

tion when working with smaller units. Sentences only hold a material advantage over EDUs when summarization budgets are generous enough to accommodate the more content-dense—and thus longer—source sentences. In our near-extractive datasets, this requires a budget greater than one standard deviation over the average size of reference summaries.

Analysis. Table 6 contains examples of reference summaries along with system-generated summaries produced using EDUs and sentences under a 200-character budget. All examples illustrate a common scenario in which an important source sentence is not selected by the sentence-based summarizer. Yet this is not because the model is unable to capture content salience, as the same features can recover salient EDUs. In each case, the source sentence behind the reference summary is barred from inclusion because of the summarization budget. By breaking these sentences into EDUs, the summarizer has the flexibility to select salient fragments of these sentences.

In addition, we observe a clear correspondence between EDU boundaries and the concepts which human editors selected for inclusion, regardless of whether they appear contiguously (Example B) or not (Example C). The variable length of EDUs is also helpful in keeping interdependent text whole. For instance in Example A, the third segment is 13 tokens long but belongs to a single EDU as it contains only one independent clause. This coherence is likely to be lost when working with smaller sub-sentential units such as n-grams.

6 Discussion and Future Work

In order to compare summarization units fairly, we used a simple model without utilizing the discourse structure of the document. However, the use of discourse trees has yielded promising results in summarization (Hirao et al., 2013; Yoshida et al., 2014). With larger training datasets such as the ones proposed here, an EDU-based summarizer will likely benefit from rich features over discourse relations. For instance, we observed in Section 3.3 that the Marcu (1999) measure can identify EDU importance, and furthermore a consideration of discourse relations across units is likely to encourage coherence in the resulting summary, potentially preventing the inclusion of unimportant and incongruous units.

Our results also highlight a need for future work

(A) **Ref:** Manager Willie Randolph did not see what the big deal was. All he did before last night's game against San Diego at Shea Stadium was drop Mike Piazza in the batting order to sixth from fifth and promote David Wright to fifth from sixth. But the swap led to a barrage of questions from reporters.
EDU: [Manager Willie Randolph did not see what the big deal was.] [All] [he did before last night 's game against San Diego at Shea Stadium] [was drop Mike Piazza in the batting order to sixth from fifth]
Sent: Manager Willie Randolph did not see what the big deal was. But the swap led to a barrage of questions from reporters. Was Piazza being demoted permanently? How had Piazza and Wright handled the moves?

(B) **Ref:** Big, cheap and somewhere in Manhattan. Those were the starting criteria for Kelli Grant, who was desperate to escape a long bus commute between Midtown and southern New Jersey.
EDU: [Big, cheap] [and somewhere in Manhattan.] [Those were the starting criteria for Kelli Grant,] [and for her boyfriend, James Darling,] [to be with her.]
Sent: Big, cheap and somewhere in Manhattan. At that early, uninformed stage, big meant two bedrooms, they hoped. Cheap meant up to $1,500 a month.

(C) **Ref:** The plan, which rivals the scope of Battery Park City, would rezone a 175-block area of Greenpoint and Williamsburg.
EDU: [The plan,] [which rivals the ambition and scope of the creation of Battery Park City,] [would rezone a 175-block area of Greenpoint and Williamsburg, two neighborhoods]...[and led to intense pressure]
Sent: The plan, which is expected to be approved by the full City Council next week, imposes some novel requirements for developers seeking to build the housing.

Table 6: Examples of NYT reference and system-generated summaries using EDUs and sentences from (A) EX-SENT, (B) NX-SPAN, (C) NX-SUBSEQ. An "..." separates EDUs from different source sentences.

in composing EDUs to form fluent sentences. As suggested by the coverage analysis in Section 3.2, it is very likely that this can be accomplished robustly. For instance, Daumé and Marcu (2002) demonstrated that an EDU-based document compression system can improve over sentence extraction in both grammaticality and coherence.

7 Conclusion

In this work, we explore the potential of elementary discourse units (EDUs) from Rhetorical Structure Theory in extending extractive summarization techniques to produce a wider range of human-like summaries. We first demonstrate that EDU segmentation is effective in preserving concepts extracted from a document. We also analyze summaries in the New York Times corpus whose content is extracted from parts of their original sentences. When recovering the summaries using EDUs, the amount of extraneous information in the form of content words is dramatically reduced compared to their original sentences. Finally, we demonstrate that using EDUs as units of content selection instead of sentences leads to stronger summarization performance on these near-extractive datasets under standard evaluation measures, particularly when summarization budgets are tight.

References

Miguel Almeida and André F. T. Martins. 2013. Fast and robust compressive summarization with dual decomposition and multi-task learning. In *Proceedings of the ACL*.

Taylor Berg-Kirkpatrick, Dan Gillick, and Dan Klein. 2011. Jointly learning to extract and compress. In *Proceedings of ACL-HLT*.

Lidong Bing, Piji Li, Yi Liao, Wai Lam, Weiwei Guo, and Rebecca Passonneau. 2015. Abstractive multi-document summarization via phrase selection and merging. In *Proceedings of the ACL*.

Ziqiang Cao, Furu Wei, Li Dong, Sujian Li, and Ming Zhou. 2015. Ranking with recursive neural networks and its application to multi-document summarization. In *Proceedings of AAAI*.

Jaime Carbonell and Jade Goldstein. 1998. The use of MMR, diversity-based reranking for reordering documents and producing summaries. In *Proceedings of SIGIR*.

Lynn Carlson, Daniel Marcu, and Mary Ellen Okurowski. 2003. Building a discourse-tagged corpus in the framework of rhetorical structure theory. In *Current and New Directions in Discourse and Dialogue*, volume 22 of *Text, Speech and Language Technology*, pages 85–112. Springer Netherlands.

James Clarke and Mirella Lapata. 2007. Modelling compression with discourse constraints. In *Proceedings of EMNLP-CoNLL*.

Michael Collins. 2002. Discriminative training methods for hidden markov models: Theory and experiments with perceptron algorithms. In *Proceedings of EMNLP*.

Hal Daumé, III and Daniel Marcu. 2002. A noisy-channel model for document compression. In *Proceedings of the ACL*.

Vanessa Wei Feng and Graeme Hirst. 2014a. A linear-time bottom-up discourse parser with constraints and post-editing. In *Proceedings of the ACL*.

Vanessa Wei Feng and Graeme Hirst. 2014b. Two-pass discourse segmentation with pairing and global features. *CoRR*, abs/1407.8215.

Elena Filatova and Vasileios Hatzivassiloglou. 2004. A formal model for information selection in multi-sentence text extraction. In *Proceedings of COLING*.

Dan Gillick and Benoit Favre. 2009. A scalable global model for summarization. In *Proceedings of the Workshop on Integer Linear Programming for Natural Langauge Processing*.

Hugo Hernault, Helmut Prendinger, David A duVerle, Mitsuru Ishizuka, et al. 2010. HILDA: a discourse parser using support vector machine classification. *Dialogue and Discourse*, 1(3):1–33.

Tsutomu Hirao, Yasuhisa Yoshida, Masaaki Nishino, Norihito Yasuda, and Masaaki Nagata. 2013. Single-document summarization as a tree knapsack problem. In *Proceedings of EMNLP*.

Kai Hong, Mitchell Marcus, and Ani Nenkova. 2015. System combination for multi-document summarization. In *Proceedings of EMNLP*.

Eduard Hovy, Chin-Yew Lin, Liang Zhou, and Junichi Fukumoto. 2006. Automated summarization evaluation with basic elements. In *Proceedings of LREC*.

Liang Huang and Suphan Feyong. 2012. Structured perceptron with inexact search. In *Proceedings of NAACL-HLT*.

Hongyan Jing and Kathleen R. McKeown. 2000. Cut and paste based text summarization. In *Proceedings of NAACL*.

Shafiq Joty, Giuseppe Carenini, and Raymond T. Ng. 2015. Codra: A novel discriminative framework for rhetorical analysis. *Computational Linguistics*, 41(3):385–435.

Yuta Kikuchi, Tsutomu Hirao, Hiroya Takamura, Manabu Okumura, and Masaaki Nagata. 2014. Single document summarization based on nested tree structure. In *Proceedings of the ACL*.

Wei Li. 2015. Abstractive multi-document summarization with semantic information extraction. In *Proceedings of EMNLP*.

Hui Lin and Jeff Bilmes. 2011. A class of submodular functions for document summarization. In *Proceedings of ACL*.

Chin-Yew Lin. 2004. ROUGE: A package for automatic evaluation of summaries. In *Text Summarization Branches Out: Proceedings of the ACL 2004 Workshop*.

Fei Liu, Jeffrey Flanigan, Sam Thomson, Norman Sadeh, and Noah A. Smith. 2015. Toward abstractive summarization using semantic representations. In *Proceedings of NAACL*.

Annie Louis, Aravind Joshi, and Ani Nenkova. 2010. Discourse indicators for content selection in summarization. In *Proceedings of SIGDIAL*.

William C Mann and Sandra A Thompson. 1988. Rhetorical structure theory: Toward a functional theory of text organization. *Text-Interdisciplinary Journal for the Study of Discourse*, 8(3):243–281.

Daniel Marcu. 1999. Discourse trees are good indicators of importance in text. *Advances in automatic text summarization*, pages 123–136.

Ryan McDonald. 2007. A study of global inference algorithms in multi-document summarization. In *Proceedings of ECIR*.

Ani Nenkova and Kathleen McKeown. 2011. Automatic summarization. *Foundations and Trends in Information Retrieval*, 5(2–3):103–233.

Ani Nenkova, Rebecca Passonneau, and Kathleen McKeown. 2007. The Pyramid method: Incorporating human content selection variation in summarization evaluation. *ACM Transactions on Speech and Language Processing*, 4(2), May.

Benjamin Nye and Ani Nenkova. 2015. Identification and characterization of newsworthy verbs in world news. In *Proceedings of NAACL*.

Slav Petrov, Dipanjan Das, and Ryan McDonald. 2012. A universal part-of-speech tagset. In *Proceedings of LREC*.

Rashmi Prasad, Nikhil Dinesh, Alan Lee, Eleni Miltsakaki, Livio Robaldo, Aravind Joshi, and Bonnie Webber. 2008. The Penn Discourse TreeBank 2.0. In *Proceedings of the Language Resources and Evaluation Conference*.

Evan Sandhaus. 2008. The New York Times Annotated Corpus LDC2008T19. *Linguistic Data Consortium, Philadelphia*.

Kapil Thadani and Kathleen McKeown. 2008. A framework for identifying textual redundancy. In *Proceedings of COLING*.

Kristian Woodsend and Mirella Lapata. 2012. Multiple aspect summarization using integer linear programming. In *Proceedings of EMNLP*.

Yinfei Yang and Ani Nenkova. 2014. Detecting information-dense texts in multiple news domains. In *Proceedings of AAAI*.

Qian Yang, Rebecca J Passonneau, and Gerard de Melo. 2016. PEAK: Pyramid evaluation via automated knowledge extraction. In *Proceedings of AAAI*.

Yasuhisa Yoshida, Jun Suzuki, Tsutomu Hirao, and
Masaaki Nagata. 2014. Dependency-based dis-
course parser for single-document summarization.
In *Proceedings of EMNLP*.

Initiations and Interruptions in a Spoken Dialog System

Leah Nicolich-Henkin and **Carolyn P. Rosé** and **Alan W Black**
Carnegie Mellon University
5000 Forbes Ave
Pittsburgh, PA 15213
`{leah.nh, cprose, awb}@cs.cmu.edu`

Abstract

Choosing an appropriate way for a spoken dialog system to initiate a conversation is a challenging problem, and, if done incorrectly, can negatively affect people's performance on other important tasks. We describe the results of a study in which participants play a game and are interrupted by spoken notifications in different styles. We compare people's perceptions of the notification styles, as well as their effect on task performance. The different notifications include manipulations of pre-notifications and information about the urgency of the task. We find that pre-notifications help people respond significantly faster to urgent tasks, and that 43% of people, more than in any other category, prefer a notification style in which the notification begins by stating the urgency of the task.

1 Introduction

As spoken dialog systems have improved, they have become an increasingly prominent part of our everyday lives. It is now common to interact with systems that not only perform a single, task-based function (e.g. booking an airplane flight (Bohus and Rudnicky, 2009)), but rather act as personified assistants across a range of domains, including answering questions, managing communication, and organizing schedules, as Apple Siri and Microsoft Cortana do. In particular, some dialog systems have taken up residence in our homes, acting as personal assistants, like Amazon Echo, or as the embodiment of a network of smart home devices (Oulasvirta et al., 2007). Most research has assumed that these systems are entirely user-initiated—that the system will always be respond-

ing to questions and requests from a person, rather than making its own. However, as these interactions become more natural and human-like, there are many situations in which the system will also have reason to initiate the dialog: for example, to notify someone about a time-sensitive event like taking medicine, or to start a conversation about planning dinner. In this paper we study how different wordings of initiations can change people's perceptions of the notifications and make it easier for them to manage interruptions. We find that pre-notifications and additional explicit information about urgency improve interruption management and are preferred by users. However, we also find that there is a large range of user preferences, and in particular people with greater working memory capacity have distinctly different preferences.

Allowing a system to begin a conversation raises questions about how the dialog can and should be initiated. Ideally, the system should be aware of the context of the users: where they are physically located, and what activities or interactions they are already engaged in. If it is acting as a single voice for multiple devices within the home, those devices may have competing goals, and it must decide which takes priority. Additionally, different people may have different preferences for how they want to interact with the system, including frequency, wording, and modality of interruptions, which the system should be able to accommodate. It is important that the system should not only be technically functional, but also be enjoyable to use. By taking these competing factors into consideration, it will provide a better user experience.

The factors mentioned above create a large and complex set of choices and possibilities. For the purposes of this paper we studied two variables—pre-notifications and urgency—that

148

Proceedings of the SIGDIAL 2016 Conference, pages 148–156,
Los Angeles, USA, 13-15 September 2016. ©2016 Association for Computational Linguistics

provide the potential to make very simple changes to a system which nonetheless have a large impact on people's preferences for and perception of notifications. As a language-based technology, a dialog system is uniquely situated to use linguistic strategies to accommodate different users and situations, so we focused specifically on changing the wording of the notifications to give increased amounts of warning and information at the cost of simplicity and directness.

The first variable we looked at was pre-notification. This was inspired by considering how people initiate conversations with each other. Schegloff (1968) introduces the idea that any two-person conversation typically begins with a "summons," which serves to propose the start of a conversation. The "summons" is followed by an "answer" from the other person, acknowledging participation in the conversation. Our first hypothesis is that by having the dialog system begin with a summons-style pre-notification it will feel more natural, so participants will find the interruption less annoying, and it will disrupt their task performance less.

Next, we consider how the urgency of a task affects performance and preference. A number of studies have found that people are more receptive to being interrupted if the notification is urgent (Vastenburg et al., 2008; Paul et al., 2011; Paul et al., 2015). Our second hypothesis is that participants will benefit even more from the pre-notification if it is not a generic phrase, but rather indicates the urgency of the task itself. This will allow participants to prepare themselves to complete the task as quickly as possible when necessary, but let them know that they can take their time when appropriate.

2 Related Work

There have been studies on the effects of wording in dialog systems and on different ways of providing notifications, but none of these studies have combined them to examine how linguistic style choices in a dialog system interact with and change people's perceptions of notifications.

Looking at the effects of wording in a spoken dialog system, Torrey et al. (2013) studied a system that helped people make cupcakes and found that using hedges and discourse markers made the system seem less commanding and more friendly. However, they focused on an in-progress dialog, rather than initiations and interruptions.

Interruptions, taking the form of notifications, have both benefits and risks. They can be extremely useful when reminding people of important tasks or appointments, and are particularly beneficial to people dealing with memory problems (McGee-Lennon et al., 2011). However, the danger of interruptions is that they decrease performance on the user's primary task by disrupting concentration, and, depending on the perceived worth of the notification, may also annoy or frustrate the user. Warnock et al. (2011) and Paul et al. (2015) find that all notifications cause errors in the task that is being interrupted. The ability to focus on a task and remember items despite interruptions is associated with the cognitive load of the task, which determines how much memory it requires; the working memory of the person, which measures how many items they can remember at once; and executive attention, which regulates which items they focus on (Engle, 2002). Because working memory is essential to interruption management, in this study we compare performance and perceptions across participants with different working memory capacities.

One way to address the problem of notification interruptions is by detecting natural breaking points, and interrupting during them (Hudson et al., 2003; Fogarty et al., 2005; Okoshi et al., 2015). However, this is a challenging task that relies on full knowledge or detection of the user's activities, and that may also raise privacy concerns. Changing only the delivery of the alert to make it less disruptive has a much lower barrier to entry and can be applied to a wide range of systems being designed to interact with users through dialog.

Certain types of notifications are less disruptive than others. McGee-Lennon et al. (2007) compare beeps, musical patterns, and speech-based notifications, finding that people perform slightly better with speech notifications, and that different people prefer different modalities of notification. Warnock et al. (2011) go further, also looking at notifications based on text, pictures, colors, iconic sounds, touch, and smell, where different variations must be associated with different tasks. However, although both the studies have speech as a notification option, they use only a single phrase type and do not consider the effect that different styles of speech may have on either performance or preference.

Style	Urgent notification	Non-urgent notification
base	The bathtub is overflowing.	The bathtub is dirty.
pre	Excuse me...the bathtub is overflowing.	Excuse me...the bathtub is dirty.
verbose	Urgent task...the bathtub is overflowing.	Whenever is convenient...the bathtub is dirty.

Table 1: Example notifications in each style and urgency level

A method of mitigating the negative effects of notifications is to first send a "pre-alert," as described by Andrews et al. (2009). They find that a pre-alert increases the speed with which the primary task is resumed after the interruption, and negates its disruptive effect. However, the types of alerts they compared were all non-linguistic, being either visual or consisting of a single tone.

Research has shown the benefits of pre-notifications, the relevance of urgency, the utility of language-based notifications, and the importance of wording choice to perceptions of a dialog system. These are all closely related concepts; however, unlike previous work, we incorporate all of them into a set of notifications which can be tested for their effect on users.

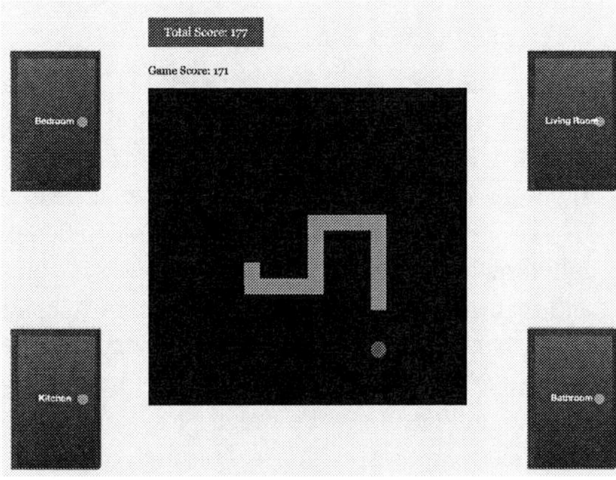

Figure 1: Screenshot of primary task screen

Figure 2: Screenshot of secondary task "Kitchen" screen

3 Experiment

As discussed above, there are many factors that can influence the perception and effect of notifications. To look at a well-defined space, we chose to study three factors: the urgency of the task, the presence of a pre-notification, and the prominence of urgency level in the notification. Participants played a browser-based game that involved going back and forth between primary and secondary tasks based on spoken notifications. By framing the activity as a game and giving players points for both types of tasks, players were encouraged to balance doing well in the game with responding to notifications. This models the real-world situation of balancing multiple tasks, some of which are prompted by a dialog system. The primary task took the form of a game of *Snake*, shown in Figure 1, and described in more detail in Section 3.2.2. In the secondary task, participants were periodically notified to go complete "household tasks." For example, in one task participants are told that the "toast is burning," and they must go click on the toast in the kitchen shown in Figure 2. Each participant went through three rounds with a different combination of variables in each round, so that we were able to both measure performance differences and get feedback on participants' perceptions of the different notifications. Examples of different notification types, described in more detail below, are displayed in Table 1.

3.1 Participants

The participants in the experiment were recruited using the Amazon Mechanical Turk crowdsourcing pool. We required participants to be located in an English-speaking country (US, Australia, Canada, Great Britain, or New Zealand), and to have a 95% or higher HIT approval rate. Additionally, participants had to sign a consent form stating they were at least 18 years old.

We conducted 206 sessions. Of those, we discarded the data of 31 because of issues including bugs in the game, people repeating the study, and people making no effort to play the game or complete tasks. We sampled the remaining data to create a data set balanced between the 18 conditions described in Section 3.2.5, leaving a total of 144 participants in the study. Of these participants, 57.64% were male, and 41.67% were female. Their ages ranged from 20-69, with a mean of 34.31.

3.2 Procedure

The study procedure consisted of the following steps:

1. Forward digit span task
2. Primary task tutorial
3. *Snake* baseline session
4. Secondary task tutorial
5. Experimental manipulation (3 rounds)

3.2.1 Forward Digit Span task

Participants started by completing the Forward Digit Span task (Hunt et al., 1973), which we used as a metric for working memory, and is associated with attention. Working memory is closely related to people's ability to deal with interruptions, leading us to hypothesize that it would help distinguish different user groups with regard to their ability to manage interruptions. In the test, digits were presented visually to the participant at one-second intervals. Each digit was visible for half a second and was followed by a pause of another half second before the next digit was displayed. At the end of each sequence, the participants entered the sequence, as they remembered it, into a text box. Participants were presented with two different sequences of equal length, beginning with length 3. If they got at least one of the two correct, the sequence length was increased by one. When they got both wrong, the task ended and the longest length at which they got at least one of the two correct was considered the participant's "digit span score." The participants' scores had a mean of 7.37 and a standard deviation of 1.83.

3.2.2 Primary task tutorial

Following the digit span task, participants were given a brief tutorial on the primary task. This involved playing the computer game *Snake*, in which a player maneuvers a "snake" graphic around a box, trying to make it hit, or "eat," circles, without hitting the sides or itself. With each circle the snake eats, the player gets points equal to the length of the snake, and the snake gets longer, thus giving a greater reward to the more difficult

situation of having a longer snake. Participants got a one-minute tutorial, presented by the same voice as used in the notifications, to familiarize them both with the game controls and the notification voice.

3.2.3 Snake baseline session

Participants played the game uninterrupted for one minute to get a baseline measurement of their skill at the game.

3.2.4 Secondary task tutorial

Next, participants were given a tutorial in the secondary task. Each task requires that the participants navigate to a different "room" in the house by clicking on a labeled door icon. This leads them to a different screen (e.g. the kitchen shown in Figure 2), where they must click on an item in the room, such as the television or the stove. Some tasks are urgent (they must be accomplished within 10 seconds), while others can be completed at any time during the game. Completing each of these tasks gives the participants 20 game points, incentivizing them to complete the task despite its potential disruption to the game.

3.2.5 Experimental manipulation

Each of the three rounds consisted of the participant playing *Snake* for 2 minutes, and being interrupted twice at 30 second intervals with notifications for secondary tasks. This simulated a person engaged in some activity in their home (represented by *Snake*) who is then interrupted by a spoken dialog notification system. To test our hypotheses that pre-notifications and additional urgency information would both be beneficial, in each round participants were given one of the three notification styles listed in Table 1.

The experiment comprises three independent variables. The first is notification style, with 3 different values, as discussed above. Second is urgency level, with two different values: urgent and non-urgent. Finally, room/task has three values: bedroom, bathroom, and kitchen. To control for the effects of different orders and combinations of variables, we conducted a 3 (notification style) × 3 (room/tasks) × 2 (urgency level) manipulation, with notification style and room/tasks as within-subject factors, and urgency as a between-subject (per-task) factor. In particular, we counterbalanced notification style and room/tasks using a 3 × 3 Latin Square, where each cell contained two tasks in the same room, delivered with the same notification style, creating 3 separate conditions. Each participant experienced both urgency levels. However, we maintained a consistent urgency level within each room for each participant. We accomplished this by constructing all six possible sequences of three assignments of urgency level such that both urgency levels were in the sequence at least once. We then crossed the three conditions from the Latin Square with the six possible orderings of the between-subject factor. Thus, in total, there were 18 experimental settings.

The six types of notifications were designed to operationalize the variables of pre-notification, urgency level, and urgency information. In the first, *base*, the participant is given just the content of the notification (e.g. "The toast is burning"). In the second, *pre*, the participant is given a simple pre-notification ("Excuse me") followed by a pause, and then the content of the notification. In both the first and second conditions, the participant must determine based on the content of the notification whether it is urgent or not. In the third condition, *verbose* , the participant is given a pre-notification specifying the urgency of the notification (either "Urgent task" or "Whenever is convenient"), followed by a pause, and then the content of the notification. Each task object has an urgent and non-urgent version. These variations are represented in Table 1. To help participants identify separate notification types, each round was associated with a different room, including two unique tasks. This room/task pair was an additional manipulated variable.

3.3 Outcomes

In order to compare the notification types, for each notification type we measured how well the participant did in the primary task interrupted by those notifications, the number of secondary tasks completed, and the amount of time it took to complete tasks. In addition, we measured baseline performance on the primary task as a metric of individual skill.

In addition to quantitative measures, at the end of the study we also asked participants about their preferences. After participants completed the task, they were asked to identify the room associated with the notifications they liked the most, and the one associated with the notifications they liked the least. They were also instructed to give more de-

tailed feedback about their preferences.

4 Results

In this section, we compare the outcomes of the study to our two hypotheses: first, that participants would perform better and prefer a system that begins with a pre-notification, and second, that participants would benefit even more from the pre-notification if it indicates the urgency of the task. To evaluate these interactions, we look first at performance on the primary task, second at performance on the secondary task, and finally at stated preference for different notification styles.

To answer the question of whether different types of notifications effect primary task performance, we analyzed the game score and number of game deaths, shown in Table 2. The gameplay was highly variable between individuals, so we compared game scores (Mean: 166.04, Standard deviation: 166.35) and number of game deaths (Mean: 7.16, Standard deviation: 5.31) using a repeated measures ANOVA across different notification styles. We also ranked each individual's rounds from one to three, and performed a chi-square test between notification style and rank. However, the only significant indicator of performance was the order of the rounds, with performance improving as people played more ($F(1, 143) = 23.80$, $p<.001$).

To answer the question of whether different types of notifications effect secondary task management, we analyzed the amount of time it took to complete tasks (Mean: 7547ms, Standard deviation: 7006ms) in different conditions, shown in Table 3. We found that whether the task was urgent or not has a significant effect on the completion time, validating our urgency manipulation ($F(1,422)=96.39$, $p<.0001$). For non-urgent tasks, the notification style did not appear to have an effect on completion time, but for urgent tasks it was highly significant ($F(2,208)=16.57$, $p<.0001$). A Tukey post-hoc test reveals that performance in *pre* and *verbose*, both of which have a pre-notification aspect to them, is virtually identical, but *base* is significantly slower. This shows that the presence of a pre-notification, regardless of the type, helps users manage interruptions to complete urgent tasks faster.

To answer the question of what effect different notification styles had on participants' perception of and preference for notifications, we per-

Table 2: Primary task performance

	F	df	P	
Game score by notification style	0.10	2,286	p = .905	
Game deaths by notification style	0.03	2,286	p = .972	
Game score by round order	23.80	1,143	p < .001	***

	χ^2	df	N	P
Rank of round by notification style	9.08	4	432	p = 0.059

Table 3: Secondary task completion times in different conditions

	F	df	P	
Urgent vs. non-urgent tasks	96.39	1,422	p < .0001	***
Non-urgent tasks with different notification styles	1.38	2,210	p = .254	
Urgent tasks with different notification styles	16.57	2,208	p < .0001	***

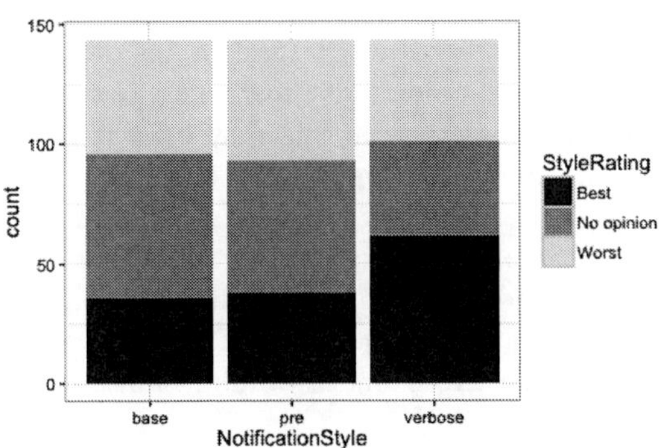

Figure 3: Preferences by Notification Style

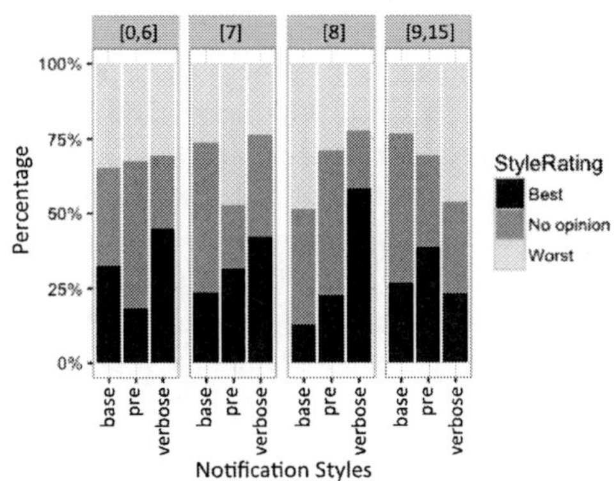

Figure 4: Preferences by Notification Style and Digit Span

formed a series of chi-square tests comparing different manipulations with the number of people who rated each best, worst, or not at all, as shown in Table 4, Here, the notification style was significant (χ^2(4, N=432)=14.61, p<.01), with the breakdown shown in Figure 3. A plurality of people liked *verbose* the most, with *base* and *pre* rated about the same. In looking at potential causes of variation, we also examined interactions between different components of the manipulation: the urgency of the task, the room containing the objects people clicked on in the task, and the order it was presented. Participants rated non-urgent tasks better, and also those in the bedroom worse (an unintentional effect of varying the tasks for different rounds was that the bedroom tasks were more difficult than others), but overall there were no significant interactions between these factors and notification style, displaying a stable main effect. The pre-notification and added urgency information were considered preferable across conditions.

These results show that having a pre-notification did not help participants on their main task, but it did help them complete urgent tasks more quickly, which is desirable. Adding urgency-related information to the pre-notification, as in the *verbose* style, did not affect task performance, but was a clear favorite across all different conditions.

Nonetheless, not all people liked the *verbose* style most, which raises the question of what factors determine a person's preferences. For the purpose of this study, we also looked at how three personal characteristics interact with notification preferences, shown in Table 5. Age and gender did not show a significant pattern, but digit span did. As depicted in Figure 4, across all groups there was a preference for the *verbose* style, except among people with the highest digit span scores.

Table 4: Interactions between round manipulation and preference distribution

Manipulated Variables	χ^2	df	N	P	
Notification style	14.61	4	432	p < .01	**
Urgency	18.95	2	432	p < .001	***
Room/task	13.26	4	432	p < .05	*
Order	2.11	4	432	p = .716	

Table 5: Interactions between personal characteristics and preference distribution

Personal Characteristics	χ^2	df	N	P	
Age (quartiles)	24.78	12	432	p = .016	
Gender	4.04	8	432	p = .854	
Digit span (quartiles)	28.99	12	432	p < .005	**

This group instead disliked *verbose* the most, and showed a slight preference for the *pre* style (χ^2 (12, N=432)=28.88, p<.005). As such, we can distinguish them as a distinct user group, with a different focus and different priorities. Given the difference in their preferences on notification style, we attempt to identify other factors that distinguish them as a group. However, we compared them to the rest of the participants using age, gender, baseline score, number of game deaths, and all the different round manipulation preferences, and they are not significantly different in any way.

To gain insight into user preferences, in addition to ranking their preferences, participants provided written comments about their favorite and least favorite rounds. We examined these to better understand what components of the round influenced their choice, and what they liked and disliked about the notifications themselves. The comments reflect what we see in the preference trends. Of the 270 comments, 23% focus only on the notification itself, while 35% focus only on the content and visual appearance of the rooms, 23% focus only on the urgency of the task, and 19% focus on other aspects of the system. When we include comments that mention multiple components of the study, 30% talk about the notification itself, while 37% talk about the room, and 30% talk about urgency. This includes a large amount of overlap, especially between notification and urgency, which are closely associated with each other.

Even though only 30% of people specifically mentioned the notification, of that 30%, the breakdown of urgencies and rooms they preferred mirrored that of the participants as a whole, suggesting that despite what people mentioned in their comments, everyone was motivated by similar factors. People who commented on notification style were most likely to say they liked *base* because it was simple and straightforward, but often complained that it didn't give them a pre-notification. For *pre*, some people said they liked it because it was polite, but even more people complained that the "excuse me" was "creepy", "annoying", or "unnecessary". Finally, for *verbose*, many people commented that it helped them to distinguish between different urgencies, but the most common complaint was the tone or wording of the message.

5 Discussion

Our hypothesis that pre-notifications would help people's performance was supported, but only in one condition, that of the urgent secondary task. This suggests that having a pre-notification does not help people manage interruptions to a primary task. However, it might be the case that the primary task, playing *Snake*, was ultimately not ideal for this evaluation because interruptions in general did not have as much of a negative impact on people's performance as we originally thought. Although participants were given a practice round, if they had a full round without any notifications at all, it would been easier for us to directly measure the performance effect of notifications, rather than just comparing different styles. Additionally, the best predictor of an individual's performance on any given round was the order of the round; in other words, people improved significantly at the game over the course of the study. Had game performance remained approximately the same over time, we might have seen a stronger effect of notification style.

Looking at preferences, we find that people who

scored higher on a test of working memory, as measured by digit span score, generally view the *verbose* style less favorably. The question remains, however, of what other factors determine people's preferences. For the purposes of this study we only looked at a few personal qualities, most of which were not good predictors of preference. If we gain more insight into people's traits, for example through additional demographics and basic personality questions, we may find other factors that affect their preferences.

The most interesting part of the extended feedback was that people frequently commented on the tone of the notification, either praising it for being "calm" and "friendly," or criticizing it for being "demanding" and "creepy." Additionally, we often assume that politeness is a positive, but in one case someone complained that the *verbose* notification was "too kind." We focused on the information contained in the notification, but subtle changes to wording or inflection can result in big changes in how language is perceived.

One shortcoming of this study was that it looked at people interacting with a system over a very short period of time. People's impressions of notifications may change over time as they become accustomed to the system. As they become used to being interrupted, the notifications may be less startling, but as people learn to predict what the system will say, they may value concise phrasing over added information. Our study lays a groundwork for what aspects of interruption people care about, but before making conclusions for use in a real-world system, it would be important to look at how people adjust and settle into patterns.

6   Conclusion

In general, the *verbose* style was both most preferred and best for people's performance. This suggests that people prefer a pre-notification before hearing the task, which enables them to know the urgency of the task and thus the type of reactions expected, and to prepare for the task. However, it's also important to note that many people did *not* like *verbose* the most, and even thought it was the worst. In particular, the difference in preference based on digit span score reveals that different types of people may have significantly different opinions. As we consider the design of spoken dialog systems, we should consider not only whether pre-notifications and urgency information can make interruptions more helpful and palatable, but also how we can accommodate a range of users. The conclusion we draw, then, is not that systems should contain urgency pre-notifications, but rather that they should have flexibility for different people to experiment with a range of initiation styles to choose the one they personally like the best.

Acknowledgments

This work is supported by Bosch Research and Technology Center North America.

References

Alyssa E Andrews, Raj M Ratwani, and J Gregory Trafton. 2009. The effect of alert type to an interruption on primary task resumption. In *Proceedings of the HFES Annual Meeting 2009*. Citeseer.

Dan Bohus and Alexander I Rudnicky. 2009. The ravenclaw dialog management framework: Architecture and systems. *Computer Speech & Language*, 23(3):332–361.

Randall W Engle. 2002. Working memory capacity as executive attention. *Current directions in psychological science*, 11(1):19–23.

James Fogarty, Scott E Hudson, Christopher G Atkeson, Daniel Avrahami, Jodi Forlizzi, Sara Kiesler, Johnny C Lee, and Jie Yang. 2005. Predicting human interruptibility with sensors. *ACM Transactions on Computer-Human Interaction (TOCHI)*, 12(1):119–146.

Scott Hudson, James Fogarty, Christopher Atkeson, Daniel Avrahami, Jodi Forlizzi, Sara Kiesler, Johnny Lee, and Jie Yang. 2003. Predicting human interruptibility with sensors: a wizard of oz feasibility study. In *Proceedings of the SIGCHI conference on Human factors in computing systems*, pages 257–264. ACM.

Earl Hunt, Nancy Frost, and Clifford Lunneborg. 1973. Individual differences in cognition: A new approach to intelligence. *The psychology of learning and motivation*, 7:87–122.

Marilyn R McGee-Lennon, Maria Wolters, and Tony McBryan. 2007. Audio reminders in the home environment.

Marilyn Rose McGee-Lennon, Maria Klara Wolters, and Stephen Brewster. 2011. User-centred multimodal reminders for assistive living. In *Proceedings of the SIGCHI Conference on Human Factors in Computing Systems*, pages 2105–2114. ACM.

Tadashi Okoshi, Julian Ramos, Hiroki Nozaki, Jin Nakazawa, Anind K Dey, and Hideyuki Tokuda.

2015. Reducing users' perceived mental effort due to interruptive notifications in multi-device mobile environments. In *Proceedings of the 2015 ACM International Joint Conference on Pervasive and Ubiquitous Computing*, pages 475–486. ACM.

Antti Oulasvirta, K-P Engelbrecht, Anthony Jameson, and Sebastian Moller. 2007. Communication failures in the speech-based control of smart home systems. In *Intelligent Environments, 2007. IE 07. 3rd IET International Conference on*, pages 135–143. IET.

Celeste Lyn Paul, Anita Komlodi, and Wayne Lutters. 2011. Again?!! the emotional experience of social notification interruptions. In *Human-Computer Interaction–INTERACT 2011*, pages 471–478. Springer.

Celeste Lyn Paul, Anita Komlodi, and Wayne Lutters. 2015. Interruptive notifications in support of task management. *International Journal of Human-Computer Studies*, 79:20–34.

Emanuel A Schegloff. 1968. Sequencing in conversational openings. *American anthropologist*, 70(6):1075–1095.

Cristen Torrey, Susan Fussell, and Sara Kiesler. 2013. How a robot should give advice. In *Proceedings of the 8th ACM/IEEE international conference on Human-robot interaction*, pages 275–282. IEEE Press.

Martijn H Vastenburg, David V Keyson, and Huib De Ridder. 2008. Considerate home notification systems: a field study of acceptability of notifications in the home. *Personal and Ubiquitous Computing*, 12(8):555–566.

David Warnock, Marilyn R McGee-Lennon, and Stephen Brewster. 2011. The impact of unwanted multimodal notifications. In *Proceedings of the 13th international conference on multimodal interfaces*, pages 177–184. ACM.

Analyzing Post-dialogue Comments by Speakers
– How Do Humans Personalize Their Utterances in Dialogue? –

Toru Hirano[*] **Ryuichiro Higashinaka** **Yoshihiro Matsuo**
NTT Media Intelligence Laboratories, Nippon Telegraph and Telephone Corporation
1-1 Hikarinooka, Yokosuka-Shi, Kanagawa, 239-0847, Japan
`{hirano.tohru,higashinaka.ryuichiro,matsuo.yoshihiro}@lab.ntt.co.jp`

Abstract

We have been studying methods to personalize system utterances for users in casual conversations. We know that personalization is important, but no well-established way to personalize system utterances for users has been proposed. In this paper, we report the results of our experiment that examined how humans personalize utterances when speaking to each other in casual conversations. In particular, we elicited post-dialogue comments from speakers and analyzed the comments to determine what they thought about the dialogues while they engaged in them. In addition, by analyzing the effectiveness of their thoughts, we found that dialogue strategies for personalization related to "topic elaboration", "topic changing" and "tempo" significantly increased the satisfaction with regard to the dialogues.

1 Introduction

Recent research on dialogue agents has focused on casual conversations or chats (Bickmore and Picard, 2005; Ritter et al., 2011; Wong et al., 2012; Meguro et al., 2014; Higashinaka et al., 2014) because chat-oriented conversational agents are useful for entertainment or counseling purposes. For chat-oriented conversational agents, it is important to personalize their utterances to increase user satisfaction (Sugo and Hagiwara, 2014). Several methods to personalize system utterances using user information extracted from dialogues have been proposed (Sugo and Hagiwara, 2014; Kim et al., 2014; Kobyashi and Hagiwara, 2016). Although we know that personalization is important,

no well-established way to personalize system utterances for users has been proposed.

In this paper, we report the results of our experiment that examined how humans personalize their utterances when speaking to each other in casual conversations. In particular, to analyze what speakers aimed to convey in dialogues (called **dialogue strategy**), we collected post-dialogue comments by interviewing speakers individually about what they thought about the dialogues after a one-to-one text-based chat. In the interview, we recorded what the speaker said and later made a transcript of the recorded voice for analysis. We manually analyzed the post-dialogue comments to break the dialogue strategies for personalization down into patterns.

In the experiment, we extracted 252 dialogue strategies for personalization from 2,498 utterances. Then, we broke them down into 39 unified dialogue strategies with 10 categories. In addition, by analyzing the effectiveness of the dialogue strategies in relation to the satisfaction of speakers with regard to the dialogues, we found that using the dialogue strategies in the "topic elaboration", "topic changing", and "tempo" categories of chat-oriented conversational agents would be expected to increase user satisfaction.

2 Related Work

ELIZA (Weizenbaum, 1966) and ALICE (Wallace, 2004) are chat-oriented conversational agents that have the capability to personalize system utterances for users. For example, these agents can use the user's name or show that they remember the user's preferences by filling slots of utterance templates with user information extracted from previous utterances.

There are several studies on personalizing system utterances using user information extracted

---

[*]Presently, the author is with Nippon Telegraph and Telephone East Corporation.

Proceedings of the SIGDIAL 2016 Conference, pages 157–165,
Los Angeles, USA, 13-15 September 2016. ©2016 Association for Computational Linguistics

from dialogues (Sugo and Hagiwara, 2014; Kim et al., 2014; Kobyashi and Hagiwara, 2016). They used the same approach as that of ELIZA and AL-ICE to show that the agents remember user information. In addition, they selected system utterances that had the most similar vectors to the user's interest, which were represented by word vectors of previous utterances. This way is often used in information search (Shen et al., 2005; Qiu and Cho, 2006) and recommendation (Ardissono et al., 2004; Jiang et al., 2011).

Some commercial chat-oriented conversational agents have a function for personalizing system utterances for a user. For instance, an application called "Caraf"[1] operates simultaneously with car navigation systems and preferentially guides the registered user in accordance with his/her favorite brands for banks, gas stations, convenience stores, and so on. A dialogue API called "TrueTALK"[2] provides information related to the user's likes and tastes, e.g. it provides concert information for the user's favorite singers when the user says "I have free time". A social robot called "Jibo"[3] can learn the user's preferences to personalize system utterances by selecting topics related to the user's preferences.

From these studies, it can be seen that there have been many attempts to personalize system utterances. However, as far as we know, there is no thorough research about ways to personalize utterances in dialogues.

3 Collecting Post-dialogue Comments

3.1 Procedure

To analyze dialogue strategies of speakers, we collected *post-dialogue comments* by interviewing experimental participants individually about what they thought about the dialogue after a one-to-one *text-based chat*. In the interview, to elicit spontaneous comments from the speakers, what the speaker said was recorded and was later manually transcribed. After the interview, each participant filled out a *questionnaire about satisfaction*.

For experimental participants, we recruited 4 advanced-level speakers of text-based chat, who use text-based chat on business, and 30 normal

---

[1]http://www.fujitsu-ten.co.jp/eclipse/product/wifi/carafl/index.html

[2]http://www.jetrun.co.jp/curation/truetalk_lp.html

[3]https://www.jibo.com/

	Total	Average
Text-based chat	2,457	27.3
Post-dialogue comments	4,986	55.4

Table 1: Number of utterances for 90 dialogues.

speakers who are good at typing and are open to having a conversation with a stranger. The male-female ratio of the experimental participants is 1:1, and most of the participants were in their 20s or 30s. They were paid for their participation.

Text-based Chat

30 normal speakers took part in 3 dialogue sessions each, talking to one of the 4 advanced-level speakers, who was the same gender as the normal speaker. The normal speaker always talked to the same advanced-level speaker.

Normal and advanced-level speakers performed text-based chat in different rooms. In preparation, to get used to the chat operation, the participants first performed an example dialogue session with the experiment manager.

Each dialogue session lasted for ten minutes. The participants were instructed to enjoy the chat with their partner.

Post-dialogue Comments

Just after text-based chat, we collected the post-dialogue comments by interviewing participants separately about what they thought about each of the utterances in the dialogue. We recorded the interview and later manually transcribed it and aligned it to utterances in the text-based chat.

Each interview session lasted for seven minutes. Normal and advanced-level speakers were interviewed in different rooms. At the beginning of each interview session, the participants were given the instruction by text to comment about each utterance in the dialogue they had just engaged in by considering the following points.

- What did you think when you saw your partner's utterance/reaction?

- What intention did you have when you replied to your partner's utterance?

Questionnaire about Satisfaction

After the interview, each participant filled out a questionnaire about satisfaction asking for his/her

No.	Speaker: Utterance
1	A: Do you like driving cars?
2	B: Yes, I do. Do you drive a car?
3	A: I don't have a driving license. My world would probably expand if I could drive a car!
4	B: Taking trains or airplanes expands your world more than driving a car.
5	A: As I recall, my friend from Gunma told me about the number of cars per capita in Gunma.
6	B: Yup, yup! it's an obscure area.
…	…
10	B: In fact, I am living in an inconvenient place now, too.
11	A: Really?
12	B: On the outskirts of Kanagawa.
…	…

Table 2: Example of text-based chat.

subjective evaluation of the dialogue on a five-point Likert scale, where 1 is "very dissatisfied", 2 is "somewhat dissatisfied", 3 is "neither satisfied nor dissatisfied", 4 is "somewhat satisfied", and 5 is "very satisfied".

3.2 Collected Data

In total, we collected 2,457 utterances (27.3 utterances per dialogue) in text-based chat and 4,986 utterances (55.4 utterances per dialogue) in post-dialogue comments for 90 dialogues as shown in Table 1.

Table 2 and Table 3 show examples of collected text-based chat and post-dialogue comments. "Target" in Table 3 means the corresponding ID (we call target) of the utterance in the text-based chat. For example, from the post-dialogue comment "She remembered that I said I am from Gunma and she said the number of cars per capita in Gunma..." whose target is 5, it can be seen that the partner selected a topic related to both current topics: "car" and the speaker's hometown. Also, from the post-dialogue comment whose target is 11 and 12, it can be seen that the speakers decided to talk about specific things, which is easy for the partners to understand.

Figure 1 shows 180 (90 dialogues × 2 participants) answers to a questionnaire about satisfaction, and the average score was 3.87 points.

Target	Post-dialogue comments
1	In line 1, a question related to the topic of the previous dialogue session has been asked!
2, 3	It is my favorite topic. But, just in case, I asked if she likes driving cars in line 2. In line 3, she replied that she does not drive a car, and I was disappointed.
5	**She remembered that I said I am from Gunma, and she said that the number of cars per capita in Gunma...** I became excited!
…	…
11, 12	In line 11, it is thoughtful of her to be surprised, and in line 12, **to be more specific, I said** "On the outskirts of Kanagawa".
12	Therefore, I think it was **easy to understand**, and it became easy to imagine.
…	…

Table 3: Example of post-dialogue comments by speaker B.

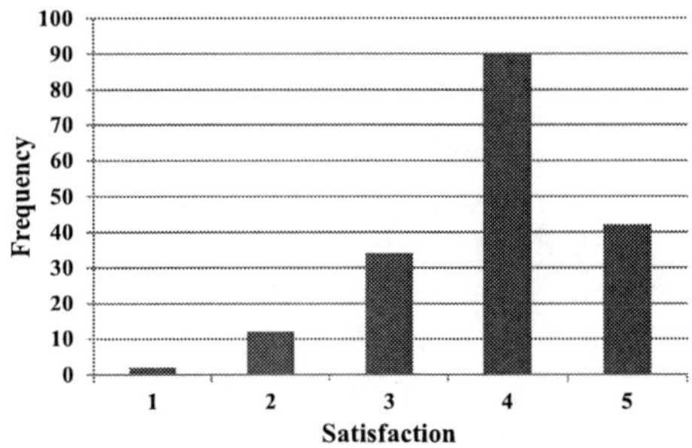

Figure 1: Satisfaction of participants.

4 Analyzing Post-dialogue Comments

4.1 Analysis Procedure

We analyzed the post-dialogue comments for what speakers thought about the dialogues while they engaged in them. The analysis was done as follows: Step 1) we read the post-dialogue comments and manually extracted the dialogue strategies for personalizing the utterances, Step 2) we annotated the extracted dialogue strategies with categories, and Step 3) we unified similar dialogue strategies within each category. In the analysis, we focused

Category	Description
Topic Changing	Strategies about when or how to change topics.
Topic Selection	Strategies about selecting next topic when changing topics.
Topic Elaboration	Strategies about elaborating on current topic.
Topic General	Strategies related to overall topics in dialogues.
Attitude	Strategies about stating one's opinions and interests.
Expression	Strategies about expressions in utterances.
Tempo	Strategies about tempo of dialogues.
Role	Strategies about roles, speakers or listeners, in dialogues.
Discourse	Strategies about flows in discourses.
Others	Other strategies.

Table 4: Categories of dialogue strategies and their descriptions.

on the comments; the content of the text-based chat was not used.

In this paper, we used 2,498 utterances of post-dialogue comments for 45 dialogues. To analyze inter-annotator agreements, two annotators individually performed the following three steps.

Step 1: Extracting Dialogue Strategies from Post-dialogue Comments

The annotators were instructed to read utterances in post-dialogue comments and find what speakers thought about personalization. When the annotators found such a thought, they annotated the utterances with a summarized text (i.e., dialogue strategy) of the thinking behind the utterances, such as "using the partner's name" or "talking about topics related to the partner's hobby". Otherwise, they annotated the utterances with "no".

For instance, from the example of post-dialogue comments shown in Table 3, the dialogue strategies "selecting topics related to both the current and previous hometown of the partner" and "bringing up a specific topic" would be extracted. The former strategy would let the partner talk about a familiar topic, and the latter would let the partner easily imagine the topic.

Step 2: Annotating Dialogue Strategies with Categories

To annotate dialogue strategies with categories, we manually defined the 10 categories shown in Table 4 by summarizing the dialogue strategies extracted at Step 1.

There are 4 categories related to topics, such as "topic changing", which consists of strategies about when or how to change topics, and "topic selection", which consists of strategies about se-

lecting the next topic when changing topics. Apart from the categories related to "topics", there are 6 categories, such as "attitude", which consists of strategies about stating one's opinions and interests, and "role", which consists of strategies about speakers or listeners in dialogues.

The annotators were instructed to annotate dialogue strategies extracted at Step 1 with one category from the ten categories shown in Table 4. For instance, the dialogue strategies "selecting topics related to both the current and previous hometown of the partner" and "bringing up a specific topic" would be annotated with the "topic elaboration" and "topic general" categories, respectively.

Step 3: Unifying Similar Dialogue Strategies within Each Category

In dialogue strategies annotated with the same category at Step 2, there may be some strategies that are similar to each other. Therefore, we combine similar dialogue strategies.

The annotators were instructed to unify similar dialogue strategies by generalizing them even though they have different details. For example, the dialogue strategies "talking about topics related to partner's hobby" and "talking about topics related to partner's hometown" would be unified to "talking about topics related to partner's information".

The unified dialogue strategies induced individually by the two annotators were later compared by the two annotators to see if they correspond to each other. If similar unified dialogue strategies were found, they were given the same identifiers for matching.

4.2 Results

Inter-annotator Agreement

From 2,498 utterances, annotator A extracted 252 dialogue strategies for personalization. The dialogue strategies were unified into 39 kinds of dialogue strategies. Annotator B extracted 303 dialogue strategies and the dialogue strategies were unified into 41 kinds of dialogue strategies. Both annotators annotated 211 utterances with dialogue strategies and 2,154 utterances with no specific strategy at Step 1. At Step 2, both annotators annotated 187 dialogue strategies with the same categories. At Step 3, we found that 156 dialogue strategies out of the 187 dialogue strategies were under the same unified dialogue strategies.

As for the agreement of the extracted dialogue strategies, *precision* is 51.5% (156/303), *recall* is 61.9% (156/252), and *F-measure* is 0.56. These values indicate how annotator B extracts the same unified dialogue strategies as annotator A and are calculated by the following formulae:

$$Precision = \frac{C}{B},$$
$$Recall = \frac{C}{A},$$
$$F\text{-}measure = \frac{2 \cdot precision \cdot recall}{precision + recall},$$

where C represents the number of dialogue strategies annotated with the same unified dialogue strategy by both annotators, A represents the total number of extracted dialogue strategies by annotator A, and B represents the total number of extracted dialogue strategies by annotator B.

The *accuracy* of the inter-annotator agreement of annotating 2,498 utterances in post-dialogue comments with unified dialogue strategies, that is the results of Step 1 + 2 + 3, is 92.4% (Cohen's $\kappa = 0.64$) (Cohen, 1960). Here, the accuracy is calculated by the following formula:

$$Accuracy = \frac{M}{T}$$

where M represents the number of utterances that are annotated with the same unified dialogue strategies or "no" by both annotators, and T represents the total number of utterances used for the analysis. Because κ is more than 0.6, we can say the agreement is substantial. Table 5 shows the inter-annotator agreement for each step in the annotation.

	Accuracy	κ
Step 1	94.7 (2,365/2,498)	0.73
Step 1 + 2	93.7 (2,341/2,498)	0.69
Step 1 + 2 + 3	92.4 (2,310/2,498)	0.64

Table 5: Inter-annotator agreement of 2,498 utterances in post-dialogue comments.

Dialogue Strategies for Personalization

Table 6 shows the results of annotator A; there are 39 kinds of dialogue strategies with annotated categories. It also shows the frequency of each unified dialogue strategy. Note that almost all the dialogue strategies for personalization presented here have not been used in any previous studies. Here, we explain some of the dialogue strategies for personalization in detail.

From this table, we can see that the most frequent dialogue strategies were "telling partner that I am interested in the current topic, too" and "showing empathy for the opinion of the partner" in the "attitude" category, which consists of dialogue strategies for letting the partner talk comfortably in a dialogue. Dialogue strategies in the "attitude" category are mainly used by the conversational participants when they were listening, and there are strategies, such as giving back-channel feedback and showing that I am impressed with the story of the partner, that can be performed by giving praise to the partner.

One of the second most frequent dialogue strategies was "bringing up a specific topic" in the "topic general" category, which is a dialogue strategy for letting the partner speak easily by providing topics that are easy to imagine. For instance, providing a specific topic, "Tigers", would let the partner speak more easily than an unspecific topic such as "baseball". In this "topic general" category, there is also a strategy "bringing up several specific topics", which is similar to the previous strategy "bringing up a specific topic". This strategy has another purpose, which is to increase the probability that the partner would be interested in one of the topics by providing several specific topics.

With a frequency equal to the dialogue strategy "bringing up a specific topic", we can see the dialogue strategy "selecting topics related to partner information" in the "topic selection" category, which is a dialogue strategy for letting the partners

Category	Dialogue Strategy	Frequency
Topic Changing	Changing topics when partner does not know about current topic.	5
	Changing topics when only I talked a lot.	3
	Changing topics when my replies seemed to be unexpected.	1
	Changing topics when partner paused for long time in dialogue.	1
	Changing topics by talking about next topic in current conversation.	1
Topic Selection	Selecting topics related to partner's information.	22
	Selecting topics related to inferred partner information.	11
	Selecting topics related to common experiences with partner.	4
	Asking question that partner asked me before.	2
	Selecting topics of similar experiences to one partner talked about.	2
Topic Elaboration	Selecting topics related to both current topic and partner information.	5
	Selecting topics related to both current topic and inferred partner info.	2
	Asking about past experiences of topic after talking about present one.	1
Topic General	Bringing up specific topic.	22
	Bringing up several specific topics.	13
	Not talking about too local topics.	8
	Bringing up topic that seems to be common topic.	6
	Bringing up topic in way that makes partner ask questions.	3
	Answering only questions that partner would ask again.	2
	Answering question and bringing up conversable topic.	2
	Asking questions that seem to be easy for partner to answer.	1
Attitude	Telling partner that I am interested in current topic, too.	24
	Showing empathy for partner.	24
	Showing that I am impressed with story of partner.	6
	Giving back-channel feedback.	2
	Not saying anything negative.	1
Expression	Using emotional terms.	16
	Using friendly and frank expressions.	10
	Using expressions that partner used.	2
	Using partner's name.	2
	Using terms for sharing feelings.	1
	Exaggerating story.	1
Tempo	Keeping dialogue fast-paced.	14
	Keeping pace with tempo of partner.	7
Role	Both participants in the conversation speaking one after another.	7
	Changing roles, speaker or listener, depending on partner.	5
Discourse	Talking about partner after talking about myself.	10
Others	Asking open questions because partner likes talking a lot.	2
	Asking "why" questions.	1

Table 6: Unified dialogue strategies to personalize utterances in dialogue extracted by annotator A.

speak easily by providing topics related to the partner. Also, we can see the strategy of selecting the topic by using information of the partner inferred from the dialogues and not selecting a totally new topic when changing topics in the dialogue. These strategies are the ones used in the related work. In this category, there is the other dialogue strategy of selecting topics related to common experiences with the partner.

There are dialogue strategies about elaborating on the current topic in the "topic elaboration" category. In this category, the most frequent strategy was "selecting topics related to both the current topic and partner information". For example, as a simple way to elaborate on the topic "car", we can select topics about "car parts", such as tire or handle, or "automakers", such as Toyota or Honda, as elaboration topics. However, this strategy selects "car life in the countryside" by considering where the partners are from and which topics are familiar to the partner.

As moderately high frequency dialogue strategies, there were strategies using "emotional terms" and "friendly and frank expressions" in the "expression" category. These dialogue strategies are to let the partner feel comfortable by using expressions for talking with one's friends or families. In this category, there are other strategies such as not only "using the partner's name", which is used in related work, but also "using the expressions that the partner used" to take advantage of being close to the partners.

Effectiveness of Category of Dialogue Strategies for Satisfaction of Participants

We analyzed the effectiveness of the category of dialogue strategies in relation to the satisfaction of participants with regard to the dialogues. For each category of dialogue strategy, we split the dialogues into two classes. One is the dialogues whose utterances in post-dialogue comments are annotated with a category, and the other is those whose utterances in post-dialogue comments are not annotated with that category. Then, we calculated the average satisfaction score of the dialogues in the two classes. For the statistical significance test, we used two-tailed tests with Welch's t-test (Welch, 1947).

Table 7 shows the results. The satisfaction of dialogues annotated with the category "topic elaboration", "topic changing", and "tempo" are significantly higher than that of other categories.

Category	Annotated	Not annotated
Topic Changing	4.20*	3.79
Topic Selection	3.90	3.85
Topic Elaboration	4.29**	3.80
Topic General	3.92	3.80
Attitude	3.90	3.84
Expression	3.89	3.87
Tempo	4.19*	3.71
Role	3.90	3.84
Discourse	3.75	3.90
Others	3.25	3.91

Table 7: Average satisfaction scores of dialogues whose utterances are annotated or not annotated with category. Superscript $*$ next to annotated scores indicates that score is statistically better than not annotated score. $**$ means $p < 0.01$; $*$ means $p < 0.05$. For statistical test, we used two-tailed Welch's t-test.

The "topic elaboration" and "tempo" categories increased the satisfaction score by 0.48 points and the "topic changing" category by 0.41 points. This means that the personalization using the dialogue strategies in these categories would be expected to increase the user satisfaction.

4.3 Discussion

By analyzing the post-dialogue comments, extracting dialogue strategies for personalization and breaking them down into patterns worked to some extent. In particular, the extracted dialogue strategies were not only the ones in the "topic selection" category, which have been used in related work, but also the ones in the other categories. In addition, by analyzing the effectiveness of the dialogue strategies in relation to the satisfaction of speakers with regard to dialogues, we found that using the dialogue strategies in the "topic elaboration", "topic changing", and "tempo" categories with conversational agents would be expected to increase the user satisfaction.

However, some issues remain about the coverage of dialogue strategies for personalization because the dialogue strategy "showing that the agent remembers user information directly", which is used in related work (e.g. saying "As I recall, you like driving a car, don't you?"), was not extracted in our analysis. In this paper, we

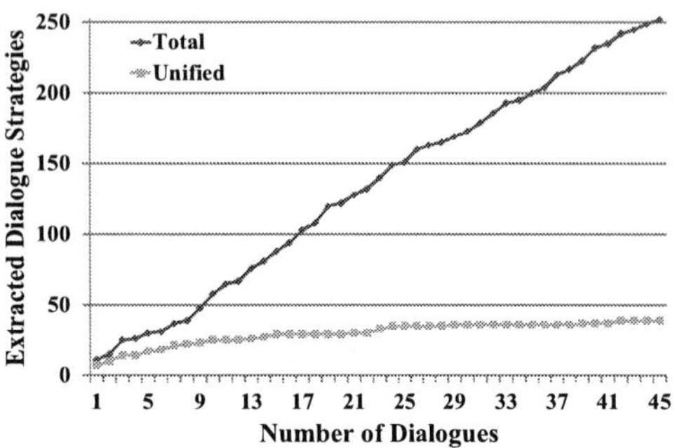

Figure 2: Number of extracted dialogue strategies.

collected all the post-dialogue comments within a day, so dialogue strategies that appear in the long term were not extracted.

It is difficult to collect new dialogue strategies for personalization efficiently by increasing the number of the post-dialogue comments because the increasing rate of unified dialogue strategies are rather low as shown in Figure 2, which shows the number of extracted total and unified dialogue strategies extracted from the post-dialogue comments.

From these points, to collect the post-dialogue comments, the periods of collecting data, such as within a few days, weeks or months, and devising a new means for collecting dialogue strategies should be considered.

5 Summary and Future Work

In this paper, we reported the results of our experiment that examined how humans personalize utterances when speaking to each other in casual conversations. In particular, we solicited post-dialogue comments from speakers and analyzed the comments to find out what they thought about the dialogues while they engaged in them.

In the experiment, we extracted 252 dialogue strategies for personalization from 2,498 utterances. Then, we broke them down into 39 unified dialogue strategies with 10 categories. In addition, we found that using the dialogue strategies in the "topic elaboration", "topic changing", and "tempo" categories of chat-oriented conversational agents would be expected to increase user satisfaction.

As future work, we would like to implement the dialogue strategies extracted in the analysis, especially the dialogue strategies in the above three categories, on chat-oriented dialogue systems to check if they actually increase user satisfaction.

References

Liliana Ardissono, Cristina Gena, Pietro Torasso, Fabio Bellifemine, Angelo Difino, and Barbara Negro. 2004. User modeling and recommendation techniques for personalized electronic program guides. In *Personalized Digital Television - Targeting Programs to Individual Viewers*, volume 6 of *Human - Computer Interaction Series*, pages 3–26.

Timothy W. Bickmore and Rosalind W. Picard. 2005. Establishing and maintaining long-term human-computer relationships. *ACM Transactions on Computer-Human Interaction*, 12(2):293–327.

J. Cohen. 1960. A coefficient of agreement for nominal scales. *Educational and Psychological Measurement*, 20(1):37–46.

Ryuichiro Higashinaka, Kenji Imamura, Toyomi Meguro, Chiaki Miyazaki, Nozomi Kobayashi, Hiroaki Sugiyama, Toru Hirano, Toshiro Makino, and Yoshihiro Matsuo. 2014. Towards an open domain conversational system fully based on natural language processing. In *Proceedings of the 25th International Conference on Computational Linguistics*, pages 928–939.

Yechun Jiang, Jianxun Liu, Mingdong Tang, and Xiaoqing Liu. 2011. An effective web service recommendation method based on personalized collaborative filtering. In *Proceedings of the 2011 IEEE International Conference on Web Services*, pages 211–218.

Yonghee Kim, Jeesoo Bang, Junhwi Choi, Seonghan Ryu, Sangjun Koo, and Gary Geunbae Lee. 2014. Acquisition and use of long-term memory for personalized dialog systems. In *Proceedings of the 2014 Workshop on Multimodal Analyses enabling Artificial Agents in Human-Machine Interaction*.

Shunya Kobyashi and Masafumi Hagiwara. 2016. Non-task-oriented dialogue system considering user's preference and human relations (in Japanese). *Transactions of the Japanese Society for Artificial Intelligence*, 31(1):DSF-A_1–10.

Toyomi Meguro, Yasuhiro Minami, Ryuichiro Higashinaka, and Kohji Dohsaka. 2014. Learning to control listening-oriented dialogue using partially observable markov decision processes. *ACM Transactions on Speech and Language Processing*, 10(4):15:1–15:20.

Feng Qiu and Junghoo Cho. 2006. Automatic identification of user interest for personalized search. In *Proceedings of the 15th International Conference on World Wide Web*, pages 727–736.

Alan Ritter, Colin Cherry, and William B. Dolan. 2011. Data-driven response generation in social media. In *Proceedings of the Conference on Empirical Methods in Natural Language*, pages 583–593.

Xuehua Shen, Bin Tan, and ChengXiang Zhai. 2005. Implicit user modeling for personalized search. In *Proceedings of the 14th ACM International Conference on Information and Knowledge Management*, pages 824–831.

Kensuke Sugo and Masafumi Hagiwara. 2014. A dialogue system with knowledge acquisition ability from user's utterance (in Japanese). *Transactions of Japan Society of Kansei Engineering*, 13(4):519–526.

Richard S. Wallace. 2004. *The Anatomy of A.L.I.C.E.* ALICE Artificial Intelligence Foundation, Inc.

Joseph Weizenbaum. 1966. ELIZA — a computer program for the study of natural language communication between man and machine. *Communications of the Association for Computing Machinery*, 9:36–45.

B. L. Welch. 1947. The generalization of 'student's' problem when several different population variances are involved. *Biometrika*, 34(1/2):28–35.

Wilson Wong, Lawrence Cavedon, John Thangarajah, and Lin Padgham. 2012. Strategies for mixed-initiative conversation management using question-answer pairs. In *Proceedings of the 24th International Conference on Computational Linguistics*, pages 2821–2834.

On the Contribution of Discourse Structure on Text Complexity Assessment

Elnaz Davoodi
Concordia University
Department of Computer Science
and Software Engineering
Montréal, Québec, Canada H3G 2W1
e_davoo@encs.concordia.ca

Leila Kosseim
Concordia University
Department of Computer Science
and Software Engineering
Montréal, Québec, Canada H3G 2W1
kosseim@encs.concordia.ca

Abstract

This paper investigates the influence of discourse features on text complexity assessment. To do so, we created two data sets based on the Penn Discourse Treebank and the Simple English Wikipedia corpora and compared the influence of coherence, cohesion, surface, lexical and syntactic features to assess text complexity.

Results show that with both data sets coherence features are more correlated to text complexity than the other types of features. In addition, feature selection revealed that with both data sets the top most discriminating feature is a coherence feature.

1 Introduction

Measuring text complexity is a crucial step in automatic text simplification where various aspects of a text need to be simplified in order to make it more accessible (Siddharthan, 2014). Despite much research on identifying and resolving lexical and syntactic complexity (e.g. Kauchak (2013), Rello et al. (2013), Bott et al. (2012), Carroll et al. (1998), Barlacchi and Tonelli (2013), Štajner et al. (2013)), discourse-level complexity remain understudied (Siddharthan, 2006; Siddharthan, 2003). Current approaches to text complexity assessment consider a text as a bag of words or a bag of syntactic constituents; which is not powerful enough to take into account deeper textual aspects such as flow of ideas, inconsistencies, etc. that can influence text complexity.

For example, according to Williams et al. (2003), Example 1.a below is more complex than Example 1.b even though both sentences use exactly the same nouns and verbs.

Example 1.a. *Although many people find speed reading hard, if you practice reading, your skills will improve.*

Example 1.b. *Many people find speed reading hard. But your skills will improve if you practice reading.*

Apart from the choice of words or the way these words form syntactically sound constituents, the way these constituents are linked to each other can influence its complexity. In other words, discourse information plays an important role in text complexity assessment.

The goal of this paper is to analyse the influence of discourse-level features for the task of automatic text complexity assessment and compare their influence to more traditional linguistic and surface features used for this task.

2 Background

A reader may find a text easy to read, cohesive, coherent, grammatically and lexically sound or on the other hand may find it complex, hard to follow, grammatically heavy or full of uncommon words. Focusing only on textual characteristics and ignoring the influence of the readers, Siddharthan (2014) defines *text complexity* as a metric to measure linguistic complexities at different levels of analysis: 1) lexical (e.g. the use of less frequent, uncommon and even obsolete words), 2) syntactic (e.g. the extortionate or improper use of passive sentences and embedded clauses), and 3) discourse (e.g. vague or weak connections between text segments).

Text complexity should be distinguished from *text readability*. Whereas text complexity is reader-independent, text readability is reader-centric. According to Dale and Chall (1949), the readability of a text is defined by its complexity as well as characteristics of the readers, such as their background, education, expertise, level of in-

Proceedings of the SIGDIAL 2016 Conference, pages 166–174,
Los Angeles, USA, 13-15 September 2016. ©2016 Association for Computational Linguistics

terest in the material and external elements such as typographical features (e.g. text font size, highlights, etc.). It is crucial that a reader have access to a text with the appropriate readability level (e.g. Collins-Thompson (2014), Williams et al. (2003)). An article which would be perceived as easy to read by a more educated or an expert reader may be hard to follow for a reader with a lower educational level.

Traditionally, the level of complexity of a text has mostly been correlated with surface features such as word length (the number of characters or number of syllables per word) or sentence length. One of the most well-known readability indexes, the Flesch-Kincaid index (Kincaid et al., 1975), measures a text's complexity level and maps it to an educational level. Traditional complexity measures (e.g. (Chall, 1958; Klare and others, 1963; Zakaluk and Samuels, 1988)) mostly consider a text as a bag of words or bag of sentences and rely on the complexity of a text's building blocks (e.g. words or phrases). This perspective does not take discourse properties into account. Webber and Joshi (2012) define discourse using fours aspects: *position of constitutes*, *order*, *context* and *adjacency*. Such discourse information plays an important role in text complexity assessment. Traditional methods do not consider the flow of information in terms of word ordering, phrase adjacency and connection between text segments; all of which can make a text hard to follow, non-coherent and more complex.

More recently, some efforts have been made to improve text complexity assessment by considering richer linguistic features. For example, Schwarm and Ostendorf (2005) and Callan and Eskenazi (2007) used language models to predict readability level by using different language models (e.g. a language model for children using children's book, a language model for more advanced readers using scientific papers, etc.).

Discourse features can refer to text cohesion and coherence. Text cohesion refers to the grammatical and lexical links which connect linguistic entities together; whereas text coherence refers to the connection between ideas. Several theories have been developed to model both cohesion (e.g. centering theory (Grosz et al., 1995)) and coherence (e.g. Rhetorical Structure Theory (Mann and Thompson, 1987), DLTAG (Webber, 2004)). Pitler and Nenkova (2008) examined a set of cohesion features based on an entity-based approach (Barzilay and Lapata, 2008) and pointed out that these features were not significantly correlated with text complexity level. However to our knowledge, the influence of coherence on text complexity has not been studied.

3 Complexity Assessment Model

The goal of this study is to evaluate the influence of coherence features for text complexity assessment. To do so, we have considered various classes of linguistic features and build a pairwise classification model to compare the complexity of pairs of texts using each class of feature. For example, given the pair of sentences of Example 1.a and 1.b (see Section 1), the classifier will indicate if 1.a is simpler or more complex than 1.b.

3.1 Data Sets

To perform the experiments, we created two different data sets using standard corpora. The first data set was created from the Penn Discourse Treebank (PDTB) (Prasad et al., 2008); while, the other was created from the Simple English Wikipedia (SEW) corpus (Coster and Kauchak, 2011). These two data sets are described below and summarized in Table 1.

3.1.1 The PDTB-based Data Set

Since we aimed to analyze the contribution of different features, we needed a corpus with different complexity levels where features were already annotated or could automatically be tagged. Surface, lexical, syntactic and cohesion features can be easily extracted; however, coherence features are more difficult to extract. Standard resources typically used in computational complexity analysis such as the Simple English Wikipedia (Coster and Kauchak, 2011), Common Core Appendix B[1] and Weebit (Vajjala and Meurers, 2012) are not annotated with coherence information; hence these features would have to be induced automatically using a discourse parser (e.g. Lin et al. (2014), Laali et al. (2015)).

In order to have better quality discourse annotations, we used the data set generated by Pitler and Nenkova (2009). This data set contains 30 articles from the PDTB (Prasad et al., 2008) which are annotated manually with both complexity level and discourse information. The complexity level

---

[1]https://www.engageny.org

	PDTB-based Data Set	**SEW-based Data Set**
Source	Penn Discourse Treebank Corpus	Simple English Wikipedia Corpus
# of pairs of articles	378	1988
# of positive pairs	194	944
# of negative pairs	184	944
Discourse Annotation	Manually Annotated	Extracted using End-to-End parser (Lin et al., 2014)

Table 1: Summary of the two data sets.

of the articles is indicated on a scale of 1.0 (easy) to 5.0 (difficult). Using this set of articles, we built a data set containing pairs of articles whose complexity levels differed by least n points. In order to have a balanced data set, we set $n = 0.7$. As a result, our data set consists of 378 instances with 194 positive instances (i.e. same complexity level where the difference between the complexity scores is smaller or equal to 0.7) and 184 negative instances (i.e. different complexity levels where the difference between complexity scores is larger than 0.7). Then, each pair of articles is represented as a feature vector where the value of each feature is the difference between the values of the corresponding feature in each article. For example, for a given pair of articles $< a_1, a_2 >$, the corresponding feature vector will be:

$$V_{a_1,a_2} = < F_1^{a_1} - F_1^{a_2}, F_2^{a_1} - F_2^{a_2}, ..., F_n^{a_1} - F_n^{a_2} >$$

where V_{a_1,a_2} represents the feature vector of a given pair of articles $< a_1, a_2 >$, $F_i^{a_1}$ corresponds to the value of the ith feature for article a_1 and $F_i^{a_2}$ corresponds to the value of the ith feature for article a_2 and n is the total number of features (in our case $n = 14$ (see Section 3.2)).

Because the Pitler and Nenkova (2009) data set is a subset of the PDTB, it is also annotated with discourse structure. The annotation framework of the PDTB is based on the DLTAG framework (Webber, 2004). In this framework, 100 discourse markers (e.g. *because, since, although,* etc.) are treated as predicates that take two arguments: Arg1 and Arg2, where Arg2 is the argument that contains the discourse marker. The PDTB annotates both explicit and implicit discourse relations. Explicit relations are explicitly signalled with a discourse marker. On the other hand implicit relations do not use an explicit discourse marker; however the reader still can infer the relation connecting the arguments. Example 2.a taken from Prasad et al. (2008) shows an explicit relation which is changed to an implicit one

in Example 2.b by removing the discourse marker *because*.

Example 2.a. *If the light is red, stop* <u>*because*</u> *otherwise you will get a ticket.*

Example 2.b. *If the light is red, stop. Otherwise you will get a ticket.*

In addition to labeling discourse relation realizations (i.e. explicit or implicit) and discourse markers (e.g. *because, since,* etc.), the PDTB also annotates the sense of each relation using three levels of granularity. At the top level, four classes of senses are used: TEMPORAL, CONTINGENCY, COMPARISON and EXPANSION. Each class is expanded into 16 second level senses; themselves subdivided into 23 third-level senses. In our work, we considered the 16 relations at the second-level of the PDTB relation inventory[2].

3.1.2 The SEW-based Data Set

In order to validate our results, we created a larger data set but this time with induced discourse information. To do so, a subset of the Simple English Wikipedia (SEW) corpus (Coster and Kauchak, 2011) was randomly chosen to build pairs of articles. The SEW corpus contains two sections that are 1) article-aligned and 2) sentence-aligned. We used the article-aligned section which contains around 60K aligned pairs of regular and simple articles. Since this corpus is not manually annotated with discourse information, we used the End-to-End parser (Lin et al., 2014) to annotate it. In total, we created 1988 pairs of articles consisting of 994 positive and 994 negative instances. Similarly to the PDTB-based data set, each positive instance represents a pair of articles at the same complexity level (i.e. either both complex or both simple).

---

[2]These are: Asynchronous, Synchronous, Cause, Pragmatic Cause, Condition, Pragmatic Condition, Contrast, Pragmatic Contrast, Concession, Pragmatic Concession, Conjunction, Instantiation, Restatement, Alternative, Exception, List.

On the other hand, for each negative instance, we chose a pair of aligned articles from the SEW corpus (i.e. a pair of aligned articles containing one article taken from Wikipedia and its simpler version taken from SEW).

3.2 Features for Predicting Text Complexity

To predict text complexity, we have considered 16 individual features grouped into five classes. These are summarized in Table 2 and described below.

3.2.1 Coherence Features

For a well written text to be coherent, utterances need to be connected logically and semantically using discourse relations. We considered coherence features in order to measure the association between this class of features and text complexity levels. Our coherence features include:

F1. Pairs of <realization, discourse relations> (e.g. <explicit, contrast>).

F2. Pairs of <discourse relations, discourse markers>, where applicable (e.g. <contrast, but>).

F3. Triplets of <discourse relations, realizations, discourse markers>, where applicable (e.g. <contrast, explicit, but>).

F4. Frequency of discourse relations.

Each article was considered as a bag of discourse properties. Then for features *F1*, *F2* and *F3*, the log score of the probability of each article is calculated using Formulas (1) and (2). Considering a particular discourse feature (e.g. pairs of <discourse relations, discourse markers>), each article may contain a combination of n occurrences of this feature with k different feature values. The probability of observing such article is calculated using the multinomial probability mass function as shown in Formula (2). In order prevent arithmetic underflow and be more computationally efficient, we used the log likelihood of this probability mass function as shown in Formula (1).

$$log\_score(P) = log(P(n)) + log(n!) + \sum_{i=1}^{k}(x_i log(p_i) - log(x_i!)) \quad (1)$$

$$P = P(n)\frac{n!}{x_1!...x_k!}P_1...P_k \quad (2)$$

$P(n)$ is the probability of an article with n instances of the feature we are considering, x_i is the number of times a feature has its ith value and P_i is the probability of a feature to have its ith value based on all the articles of the PDTB. For example, for the feature *F1* (i.e. pair of <realization, discourse relation>), consider an article containing <explicit, contrast>, <implicit, causality> and <explicit, contrast>. In this case, n is the total number of *F1* features we have in the article (i.e. $n = 3$), and $P(n)$ is the probability of an article to have 3 such features across all PDTB articles. In addition, $x_1 = 2$ because we have two <explicit, contrast> pairs and P_1 is the probability of observing the pair <explicit, contrast> over all possible pairs of <realization, discourse relation>. Similarly, $x_2 = 1$ and P_2 is the probability of observing <implicit, causality> pair over all possible pairs of <realization, discourse relation>.

3.2.2 Cohesion Features

Cohesion is an important property of well-written texts (Grosz et al., 1995; Barzilay and Lapata, 2008). Addressing an entity for the first time in a text is different from further mentions to the entity. Proper use of referencing influences the ease of following a text and subsequently its complexity. Pronoun resolution can affect text cohesion in the way that it prevents repetition. Also, according to Halliday and Hasan (1976), definite description is an important characteristic of well-written texts. Thus, in order to measure the influence of cohesion on text complexity, we considered the following cohesive devices.

F5. Average number of pronouns per sentence.

F6. Average number of definite articles per sentence.

3.2.3 Surface Features

Surface features have traditionally been used in readability measures such as (Kincaid et al., 1975) to measure readability level. Pitler and Nenkova (2009) showed that the only significant surface feature correlated with text complexity level was the length of the text. As a consequence, we investigated the influence of surface features by considering the following three surface features:

F7. Text length as measured by the number of words.

F8. Average number of characters per word.

F9. Average number of words per sentence.

Class of Features	Index	Feature Set
Coherence features	F1	Log_score of <realization-discourse relation>
	F2	Log_score of <discourse relation-discourse marker>
	F3	Log_score of <realization-discourse relation-discourse marker>
	F4	Discourse relation frequency
Cohesion features	F5	Average # of pronouns per sentence
	F6	Average # of definite articles per sentence
Surface features	F7	Text length
	F8	Average # of characters per word
	F9	Average # of words per sentence
Lexical features	F10	Average # of word overlaps per sentence
	F11	Average # of synonyms of words in WordNet
	F12	Average # of frequency of words in Google Ngram corpus
Syntactic features	F13	Average # of verb phrases per sentence
	F14	Average # of noun phrases per sentence
	F15	Average # of subordinate clauses per sentence
	F16	Average height of syntactic parse tree

Table 2: List of features in each class.

3.2.4 Lexical Features

In order to capture the influence of lexical choices across complexity levels, we considered the following three lexical features:

F10. Average number of word overlaps per sentence.

F11. Average number of synonyms of words in WordNet.

F12. Average frequency of words in the Google N-gram (Web1T) corpus.

The lexical complexity of a text can be influenced by the number of words that are used in consecutive sentences. This means that if some words are used repetitively rather than introducing new words in the following sentences, the text should be simpler. This is captured by feature *F10*: "*Average # of word overlaps per sentence*" which calculates the average number of word overlaps in all consecutive sentences.

In addition, the number of synonyms of a word can be correlated to its complexity level. To account for this feature, *F11*: "Average # of synonyms of words in WordNet" is introduced to capture the complexity of the words (Miller, 1995). Moreover, the frequency of a word can be an indicator of its simplicity. Also, feature *F12*: "*Average # of frequency of words in Google N-gram corpus*" is used based on the assumption that simpler words are more frequently used. In order to measure the frequency of each word, we used the Google N-gram corpus (Michel et al., 2011). Thus, pairs of articles at the same complexity level tend to have similar lexical features compared to pairs of articles at different complexity levels.

3.2.5 Syntactic Features

According to Kate et al. (2010), syntactic structures seem to affect text complexity level. As Barzilay and Lapata (2008) note, more noun phrases make texts more complex and harder to understand. In addition, Bailin and Grafstein (2001) pointed out that the use of multiple verb phrases in a sentence can make the communicative goal of a text more clear as explicit discourse markers will be used to connect them; however it can also make a text harder to understand for less educated adults or children. The Schwarm and Ostendorf (2005) readability assessment model was built based on a trigram language model, syntactic and surface features. Based on these previous work, we used the same syntactic features which includes:

F13. Average number of verb phrases per sentence.

F14. Average number of noun phrases per sentence.

15. Average number of subordinate clauses per sentence.

F16. Average height of syntactic parse tree.

These features were determined using the Stanford parser (Toutanova et al., 2003).

3.3 Results and Analysis

In order to investigate the influence of each class of feature to assess the complexity level of a given pair of articles, we built several Random Forest classifiers and experimented with various subsets of features. Table 3 shows the accuracy of the

Feature set	No. features	SEW-based Data Set	p-value	Stat. Sign	PDTB Data Set	p-value	Stat. Sign
Baseline	N/A	50.00%	N/A	N/A	51.23%	N/A	N/A
All features	16	**94.96%**	N/A	N/A	**69.04%**	N/A	N/A
Coherence only	4	**93.76%**	0.15	=	**64.02%**	0.45	=
Cohesion only	2	66.09%	0.00	⇓	57.93%	0.01	⇓
Surface only	3	83.45%	0.00	⇓	51.32%	0.00	⇓
Lexical only	3	78.20%	0.00	⇓	46.29%	0.00	⇓
Syntactic only	4	79.32%	0.00	⇓	62.16%	0.24	=
All-Coherence	12	**86.70%**	0.00	⇓	**62.43%**	0.08	⇓
All-Cohesion	14	95.32%	0.44	=	68.25%	0.76	=
All-Surface	13	95.10%	0.43	=	68.25%	0.61	=
All-Lexical	13	95.42%	0.38	=	64.81%	0.57	=
All-Syntactic	12	94.30%	0.31	=	66.40%	0.67	=

Table 3: Accuracy of Random Forest models built using different subset of features.

various classifiers on our data sets (see Section 3.1) using 10-fold cross-validation. In order to test the statistical significance of the results, we conducted a two-sample t-test (with a confidence level of 90%) comparing the models built using each feature set to the model trained using all features. A statistically significant decrease (⇓) or no difference (=) is specified in the column labeled Stat. Sign.

Our baseline is to consider no feature and simply assign the class label of the majority class. As indicated in Table 3, the baseline is about 50% for both data sets. When all features are used, the accuracy of the classifier trained on the SEW-based data set is 94.96% and the one trained on the PDTB-based data set is 69.04%.

Considering only one class of features, the models trained using coherence features on both data sets outperformed the others (93.76% and 64.02%) and their accuracy are statistically as high as using all features together. However one must also note that there is a significant difference between the number of features (4 for coherence only vs. 16 for all features). Indeed, in both data sets, cohesion features are more useful than lexical features and less than syntactic features.

Furthermore, it is interesting to note that surface features seem to be more discriminating in the SEW articles rather than in PDTB articles; however, viceversa is true about cohesion features. In addition, the decrease in the accuracy of all classifiers trained on the SEW using only one feature except coherence features is statistically significant. The same is true about the models trained on the PDTB with the only difference being the one trained using only syntactic features which performs as well as the one trained using all the features (62.16% vs. 69.04%).

The last section of Table 3 shows the classification results when excluding only one class of features. In this case, removing coherence features leads to a more significant drop in performance compared to the other classes of features. The classifier trained using all features except the coherence features achieves an accuracy of 86.70% and 62.43% on the SEW and PDTB corpus respectively. This decrease in both models is statistically significant; however the changes in the accuracy of other classifiers trained using all features excluding only one class is not statistically significant.

3.4 Feature Selection

In any classification problem, feature selection is useful to identify the most discriminating features and reduce the dimensionality and model complexity by removing the least discriminating ones. In this classification problem, we built several classifiers using different subsets of features; however, identifying how well a feature can discriminate the classes would be helpful in building a more efficient model with fewer number of features.

Using our pairwise classifier built with all the features, we ranked the features by their information gain. Table 4 shows all the features used in the two models using all the features trained on the PDTB-based data set and the SEW-based data set.

As can be seen in Table 4, coherence features are among the most discriminating features on the PDTB-based data set as they hold the top three positions. Also, the most discriminating feature on the SEW-based data set is a coherence feature. We investigated the power of only the top feature in both data sets by classifying the data using only this single feature and evaluated using 10-

Index	SEW-based Data Set	Index	PDTB-based Data Set
F2	Log_score of <discourse relation-marker>	*F1*	Log_score of <realization-discourse relation>
F9	Average # of words per sentence	*F3*	Log_score of <realization-relation-marker>
F14	Average # of noun phrases per sentence	*F4*	Discourse relation frequency
F7	Text length	*F5*	Average # of pronouns per sentence
F16	Average height of syntactic parse tree	*F9*	Average # of words per sentence
F13	Average # of verb phrases per sentence	*F2*	Log_score of <discourse relation-marker>
F15	Average # of subordinate clauses per sentence	*F7*	Text length
F10	Average # of word overlaps per sentence	*F8*	Average # of characters per word
F8	Average # of characters per word	*F12*	Average frequency of words in Web1T corpus
F4	Discourse relation frequency	*F11*	Average # of synonyms of words in WordNet
F6	Average # of definite articles per sentence	*F6*	Average # of definite articles per sentence
F11	Average # of synonyms of words in WordNet	*F10*	Average # of word overlaps per sentence
F3	Log_score of <realization-relation-marker>	*F15*	Average # of subordinate clauses per sentence
F1	Log_score of <realization-discourse relation>	*F14*	Average # of noun phrases per sentence
F12	Average frequency of words in Web1T corpus	*F13*	Average # of verb phrases per sentence
F5	Average # of pronouns per sentence	*F16*	Average height of syntactic parse tree

Table 4: Features ranked by information gain

fold cross-validation. Using only *F1*: "*log_score of <realization, discourse relation>*" to classify the PDTB-based data set, we achieved an accuracy of 56.34%. This feature on its own outperformed the individual class of surface features and lexical features and performed as well as combining the features of the two classes (four features). It also performed almost as well as the two cohesion features (*F5*, *F6*). In addition, using only the feature *F2*: "*log_score of <discourse relation, discourse marker>*" on the SEW corpus resulted in an accuracy of 77.26% which is much higher than the accuracy of the classifier built using the class of cohesion and almost as good as lexical features.

4   Conclusion

In this paper we investigated the influence of various classes of features in pairwise text complexity assessment on two data sets created from standard corpora. The combination of 16 features, grouped into five classes of surface, lexical, syntactic, cohesion and coherence features resulted in the highest accuracy. However the use of only 4 coherence features performed statistically as well as using all features on both data sets.

In addition, removing only one class of features from the combination of all the features did not affect the accuracy; except for coherence features. Removing the class of coherence features from the combination of all features led to a statistically significant decrease in accuracy. Thus, we can conclude a strong correlation between text coherence and text complexity. This correlation is weaker for other classes of features.

Acknowledgement

The authors would like to thank the anonymous reviewers for their feedback on the paper. This work was financially supported by NSERC.

References

Alan Bailin and Ann Grafstein. 2001. The linguistic assumptions underlying readability formulae: A critique. *Language & Communication*, 21(3):285–301.

Gianni Barlacchi and Sara Tonelli. 2013. Ernesta: A sentence simplification tool for children's stories in Italian. In *Proceeding of Computational Linguistics and Intelligent Text Processing (CICLing-2013)*, pages 476–487.

Regina Barzilay and Mirella Lapata. 2008. Modeling local coherence: An entity-based approach. *Computational Linguistics*, 34(1):1–34.

Stefan Bott, Luz Rello, Biljana Drndarevic, and Horacio Saggion. 2012. Can Spanish be simpler? LexSiS: Lexical simplification for Spanish. In *Proceesing of Coling*, pages 357–374.

Jamie Callan and Maxine Eskenazi. 2007. Combining lexical and grammatical features to improve readability measures for first and second language texts. In *Proceedings of NAACL HLT*, pages 460–467.

John Carroll, Guido Minnen, Yvonne Canning, Siobhan Devlin, and John Tait. 1998. Practical simplification of English newspaper text to assist aphasic readers. In *Proceedings of the AAAI-98 Workshop on Integrating Artificial Intelligence and Assistive Technology*, pages 7–10.

Jeanne Sternlicht Chall. 1958. *Readability: An appraisal of research and application*. Number 34. Ohio State University Columbus.

Kevyn Collins-Thompson. 2014. Computational assessment of text readability: A survey of current and future research. *ITL-International Journal of Applied Linguistics*, 165(2):97–135.

William Coster and David Kauchak. 2011. Simple English Wikipedia: A new text simplification task. In *Proceedings of the 49th Annual Meeting of the Association for Computational Linguistics: Human Language Technologies (ACL-HLT): Short papers-Volume 2*, pages 665–669, Portland, Oregon, June.

Edgar Dale and Jeanne S Chall. 1949. The concept of readability. *Elementary English*, 26(1):19–26.

Barbara J Grosz, Scott Weinstein, and Aravind K Joshi. 1995. Centering: A framework for modeling the local coherence of discourse. *Computational linguistics*, 21(2):203–225.

Michael AK Halliday and Ruqaiya Hasan. 1976. Cohesion in English. *English, Longman, London*.

Rohit J Kate, Xiaoqiang Luo, Siddharth Patwardhan, Martin Franz, Radu Florian, Raymond J Mooney, Salim Roukos, and Chris Welty. 2010. Learning to predict readability using diverse linguistic features. In *Proceedings of the 23rd International Conference on Computational Linguistics*, pages 546–554.

David Kauchak. 2013. Improving text simplification language modeling using unsimplified text data. In *Proceeding of ACL (Volume 1: Long Papers)*, pages 1537–1546.

J. Peter Kincaid, Robert P. Fishburne Jr, Richard L. Rogers, and Brad S. Chissom. 1975. Derivation of new readability formulas (automated readability index, fFog count and Flesch reading ease formula) for navy enlisted personnel. Technical report, DTIC Document.

George Roger Klare et al. 1963. *Measurement of readability*. Iowa State University Press.

Majid Laali, Elnaz Davoodi, and Leila Kosseim. 2015. The CLaC Discourse Parser at CoNLL-2015. In *Proceedings of the 19th Conference on Computational Natural Language Learning: Shared Task, CoNLL*, pages 56–60, Beijing, China.

Ziheng Lin, Hwee Tou Ng, and Min-Yen Kan. 2014. A PDTB-styled end-to-end discourse parser. *Natural Language Engineering*, 20(2):151–184.

William C Mann and Sandra A Thompson. 1987. Rhetorical structure theory: A framework for the analysis of texts. Technical report, IPRA Papers in Pragmatics 1.

Jean-Baptiste Michel, Yuan Kui Shen, Aviva Presser Aiden, Adrian Veres, Matthew K Gray, Joseph P Pickett, Dale Hoiberg, Dan Clancy, Peter Norvig, Jon Orwant, et al. 2011. Quantitative analysis of culture using millions of digitized books. *Science*, 331(6014):176–182.

George A Miller. 1995. Wordnet: a lexical database for english. *Communications of the ACM*, 38(11):39–41.

Emily Pitler and Ani Nenkova. 2008. Revisiting readability: A unified framework for predicting text quality. In *Proceedings of the Conference on Empirical Methods in Natural Language Processing (EMNLP)*, pages 186–195, Honolulu, October.

Emily Pitler and Ani Nenkova. 2009. Using syntax to disambiguate explicit discourse connectives in text. In *Proceedings of the ACL-IJCNLP 2009 Conference Short Papers*, pages 13–16, Suntec, Singapore.

Rashmi Prasad, Nikhil Dinesh, Alan Lee, Eleni Miltsakaki, Livio Robaldo, Aravind Joshi, and Bonnie L. Webber. 2008. The Penn discourse treebank 2.0. In *Proceedings of the 6th International Conference on Language Resources and Evaluation (LREC)*, Marrakesh, Morocco, June.

Luz Rello, Ricardo Baeza-Yates, Laura Dempere-Marco, and Horacio Saggion. 2013. Frequent words improve readability and short words improve understandability for people with dyslexia. In *Human-Computer Interaction–INTERACT 2013*, pages 203–219.

Sarah E Schwarm and Mari Ostendorf. 2005. Reading level assessment using support vector machines and statistical language models. In *Proceedings of the 43rd Annual Meeting on Association for Computational Linguistics (ACL)*, pages 523–530, Ann Arbor, June.

Advaith Siddharthan. 2003. Preserving discourse structure when simplifying text. In *Proceedings of the European Natural Language Generation Workshop (ENLG), 11th Conference of the European Chapter of the Association for Computational Linguistics (EACL'03)*, pages 103–110.

Advaith Siddharthan. 2006. Syntactic simplification and text cohesion. *Research on Language & Computation*, 4(1):77–109.

Advaith Siddharthan. 2014. A survey of research on text simplification. *ITL-International Journal of Applied Linguistics*, 165(2):259–298.

Sanja Štajner, Biljana Drndarevic, and Horacio Saggion. 2013. Corpus-based sentence deletion and split decisions for Spanish text simplification. *Computación y Sistemas*, 17(2):251–262.

Kristina Toutanova, Dan Klein, Christopher D Manning, and Yoram Singer. 2003. Feature-rich part-of-speech tagging with a cyclic dependency network. In *Proceedings of the 2003 Conference of the North American Chapter of the Association for Computational Linguistics on Human Language Technology-Volume 1*, pages 173–180.

Sowmya Vajjala and Detmar Meurers. 2012. On improving the accuracy of readability classification using insights from second language acquisition. In *Proceedings of the Seventh Workshop on Building Educational Applications Using NLP*, pages 163–173.

Bonnie Webber and Aravind Joshi. 2012. Discourse structure and computation: past, present and future. In *Proceedings of the ACL-2012 Special Workshop on Rediscovering 50 Years of Discoveries*, pages 42–54.

Bonnie Webber. 2004. D-LTAG: Extending lexicalized tag to discourse. *Cognitive Science*, 28(5):751–779.

Sandra Williams, Ehud Reiter, and Liesl Osman. 2003. Experiments with discourse-level choices and readability. In *Proceedings of the 9th European Workshop on Natural Language Generation (ENLG-2003)*, pages 127–134, Budapest, Hungary, April.

Beverly L Zakaluk and S Jay Samuels. 1988. *Readability: Its Past, Present, and Future.* International Reading Association.

Syntactic parsing of chat language in contact center conversation corpus

Alexis Nasr[1], Geraldine Damnati[2], Aleksandra Guerraz[2], Frederic Bechet[1]
(1) Aix Marseille Universite - CNRS-LIF, Marseille, France
(2) Orange Labs - Lannion, France

Abstract

Chat language is often referred to as *Computer-mediated communication (CMC)*. Most of the previous studies on chat language has been dedicated to collecting "*chat room*" data as it is the kind of data which is the most accessible on the WEB. This kind of data falls under the *informal register* whereas we are interested in this paper in understanding the mechanisms of a more formal kind of CMC: dialog chat in contact centers. The particularities of this type of dialogs and the type of language used by customers and agents is the focus of this paper towards understanding this new kind of CMC data. The challenges for processing chat data comes from the fact that Natural Language Processing tools such as syntactic parsers and part of speech taggers are typically trained on mismatched conditions, we describe in this study the impact of such a mismatch for a syntactic parsing task.

1   Introduction

Chat language received attention in recent years as part of the general *social media* galaxy. More precisely it is often referred to as *Computer-mediated communication (CMC)*.

This term refers to any human communication that occurs through the use of two or more electronic devices such as instant messaging, email or chat rooms. According to (Jonsson, 1997), who conducted an early work on data gathered through the Internet Relay Chat protocol and through emails: *"eletronic discourse is neither writing nor speech, but rather written speech or spoken writing, or something unique"*.

Recent projects in Europe, such as the CoM-eRe (Chanier et al., 2014) or the STAC (Asher, 2011) project gathered collections of CMC data in several languages in order to study this new kind of language. Most of the effort has been dedicated to "*chat room*" data as it is the kind of data which is the most accessible on the WEB. (Achille, 2005) constituted a corpus in French. (Forsyth and Martell, 2007) and (Shaikh et al., 2010) describe similar corpora in English. (Cadilhac et al., 2013) have studied the relational structure of such conversations through a deep discursive analysis of chat sessions in an online video game.

This kind of data falls under the *informal register* whereas we are interested in this paper in understanding the mechanisms of a more formal kind of CMC: dialog chat in contact centers. This study is realized in the context of the DATCHA project, a collaborative project funded by the French National Research Agency, which aims at performing unsupervised knowledge extraction from very large databases of WEB chat conversations between operators and clients in customer contact centers. As the proportion of online chat interaction is constantly growing in companies' Customer Relationship Management (CRM), it is important to study such data in order to increase the scope of Business Analytics. Furthermore, uch corpora can help us build automatic human-machine online dialog systems. Among the few works that have been published on contact center chat conversations, (Dickey et al., 2007) propose a study from the perspective of the strategies adopted by agents in favor of mutual comprehension, with a focus on discontinuity phenomena, trying to understand the reasons why miscomprehension can arise. (Wu et al., 2012) propose a typology of communication modes between customers and agents through a study on a conversa-

Proceedings of the SIGDIAL 2016 Conference, pages 175–184,
Los Angeles, USA, 13-15 September 2016. ©2016 Association for Computational Linguistics

tion interface. In this paper we are interested in evaluating syntactic parsing on such data, with a particular focus on the impact of language deviations.

After a description of the data and the domain in section 2, we introduce the issue of syntactic parsing in this particular context in section 3. Then a detailed analysis of language deviations observed in chat conversations is proposed in section 4. Finaly, experiments of part of speech (pos hereafter) tagging and syntactic parsing are presented in section 5.

2 Chat language in contact centers

In the book entitled *"Digital textuality"* (Trimarco, 2014), the author points out that *"[. . .] it would be more accurate to examine Computer Mediated Communication not so much by genre (such as e-mail, discussion forum, etc. . .) as in terms of communities"*. The importance of relation between participants is also pointed out in (Kucukyilmaz et al., 2008). The authors insist on the fact that chat messages are targeted for a particular individual and that the writing style of a user not only varies with his personal traits, but also heavily depends on the identity of the receiver (corresponding to the notion of sociolinguistic awareness). Customer-agent chat conversations could be considered as being closer to customer-agent phone conversations than to chat-room informal conversations. However the media induces intrinsic differences between Digital talk and phone conversations. The two main differences described in (Trimarco, 2014) are related to turn taking and synchronicity issues on the one side, and the use of semiotic resources such as punctuation or emoticons on the other.

In the case of assistance contact centers, customers engage a chat conversation in order to solve a technical problem or to ask for information about their contract. The corpus used in this study has been collected from Orange (the main French telecom operator) online assistance for Orange TV customers who contact the assistance for technical problems or information on their offers. In certain cases, the conversation follows a linear progress (as the example given in Figure 1) and in some other cases, the agent can perform some actions (such as line tests) that take some time or the client can be asked to do some operations on his installation which also imply latencies in the conversation flow. In all cases, a chat conversation is logged: the timestamps at the beginning of each line corresponds to the moment when the participant (agent or customer) presses the Enter key, i.e. the moment when the message becomes visible for the other participant.

A conversation is a succession of messages, where several consecutive messages can be posted by the same participant. The temporal information only concerns the moment when the message is sent and there is no clear evidence on when writing starts. There is no editing overlap in the Conversation Interface as the messages appear sequentially but it can happen that participants write simultaneously and that a message is written while the writer is not aware of the preceding message.

As one can see in the example in Figure 1, chat conversations are dissimilar from edited written text in that they contain typos, agrammaticalities and other informal writing phenomena. They are similar to speech in that a dialog with a focused goal is taking place, and participants take turns for solving that goal, using dialogic idiomatic terms which are not found in typical written text. They differ from speech in that there are no disfluencies, and that the text of a single turn can be repaired before being sent. We argue that these differences must be considered as relevant as the two differences pointed out by (Trimarco, 2014).

All these properties along with the particular type of language used by customers and agents is the focus of this paper towards understanding this new kind of CMC data. The challenges for processing chat comes from the fact that analysis tools such as syntactic parsers and pos taggers are typically trained on mismatched conditions, we describe in this study the impact of such a mismatch for these two tasks.

3 Syntactic parsing of chat language

An accurate analysis of human-human conversation should have access to a representation of the text content that goes beyond surfacic analyses such as keyword search.

In the DATCHA project, we perform syntactic parsing as well as semantic analysis of the textual data in order to produce high-level features that will be used to evaluate human behaviors. Our target is not perfect and complete syntax and semantic analysis of the data, but rather to reach a level allowing to qualify and compare conversations.

[12:04:20]		Vous êtes en relation avec AGENT.
[12:04:29]	AGENT	Bonjour, je suis AGENT, que puis-je pour vous ?
[12:05:05]	CUST	mes enfant ont perdu la carte dans le modem et je nai plus de tele comment dois je faire?
[12:05:27]	AGENT	Pouvez vous me confirmer votre numéro de ligne fixe
[12:05:56]	CUST	NUMTEL
[12:07:04]	AGENT	Si je comprend bien vous avez perdu la carte de votre décodeur.
[12:07:27]	CUST	oui ces bien sa
[12:07:47]	CUST	code erreure S03
[12:09:09]	AGENT	Pas de souci, je vais vous envoyer une autre carte à votre domicile.
[12:09:38]	CUST	est ce que je peux venir la chercher aujourdui
[12:10:36]	AGENT	Vous ne pouvez pas récupérer une carte depuis une boutique Orange car ils peuvent seulement faire un échange.
[12:11:33]	CUST	ok merci de me lenvoyer au plus vite vous avez bien mes coordonnée
[12:11:57]	AGENT	Oui je les bien sur votre dossier.
[12:12:51]	CUST	ok tres bien dici 48h au plus tard 72h pour la carte
[12:14:06]	AGENT	Vous la recevrez selon les délais postaux à l'adresse figurant sur votre dossier.
[12:14:25]	CUST	ok tres bien en vous remerciant a bientot
[12:15:20]	AGENT	Je vous en prie.
[12:15:29]	AGENT	Avant de nous quitter avez-vous d'autres questions ?
[12:17:23]	CUST	non merci

		You're in contact with AGENT
	AGENT	Hello, I'm AGENT, how can I help you?
	CUST	my children have lost the card in the modem and I don't have tv anymore what can I do?
	AGENT	Can you confirm your line number?
	CUST	NUMTEL
	AGENT	If I understand correctly you lost your decoder card
	CUST	Yes that's right
	CUST	error code S03
	AGENT	No problem, I will send you another card to your home address.
	CUST	can I come and get it today
	AGENT	You can't get a card from an Orange store because they can only proceed to exchanges.
	CUST	ok thank you for sending it as soon as possible you have my coordinates
	AGENT	Yes I have them in your record.
	CUST	ok fine within 48h maximum 72h for the card
	AGENT	You will receive it according to delivery time at the address in your record.
	CUST	ok fine thank you
	AGENT	You're welcome
	AGENT	Before you go, do you any other question?
	CUST	no thank you

Figure 1: Example of conversation in the TV assistance domain, in its original forme (above) and a translation without errors (below)

We believe that the current models used in the fields of syntactic and semantic parsing are mature enough to go beyond normative data that we find in benchmark corpora and process text that comes from CRM chat. The experience we gathered on parsing speech transcriptions in the framework of the DECODA (Bazillon et al., 2012) and OR-FEO (Nasr et al., 2014) projects showed that current parsing techniques can be successfully used to parse disfluent speech transcriptions.

Syntactic parsing of non canonical textual input in the context of human-human conversations has been mainly studied in the context of textual transcription of spontaneous speech. In such data, the variation with respect to canonical written text comes mainly from syntactic structures that are specific to spontaneous speech, as well as disfluencies, such as filled pauses, repetitions and false starts. Our input has some of the specificities of spontaneous speech but adds new ones. More precisely, we find in our data syntactic structures found in speech (such as a loose integration of micro syntactic units into macro structures), and for obvious reasons we do not find other features that are characteristic to speech, such as repetitions and restarts. On the other hand, we find in our data many orthographic errors. The following example, taken in our corpus, illustrates the specific nature of our data:

ces deja se que **j** ai fait les **pile** je les **est mit tou a l** heure **elle** sont **neuve**

All words highlighted can be considered as erroneous either lexically or syntactically. This sentence could be paraphrased by:

c'est déjà ce que j'ai fait, les piles je les ai mises tout à l'heure, elles sont neuves

Such an utterance features an interesting mixture of oral and written characteristics: the syntax is close to oral, but there are no repetitions nor false starts. Orthographic errors are numerous and some of them are challenging for a syntactic parser.

We present in this paper a detailed analysis of the impact of all these phenomena on syntactic parsing. Other types of social media data have been studied in the literature. In particular tweets have received lately more attention. (Ritter et al., 2011) for example provide a detailed evaluation of a pos tagger on tweets, with the final objec-tive of performing Named Entity detection. They showed that the performances of a classical tagger trained on generic news data drop when applied to tweets and that adaptation with in-domain data helps increasing these performances. More recently (Kong et al., 2014) described a dependency parser for tweets. However, to the best of our knowledge, no such study has been published on social media data from formal on line web conversations.

4 A study on orthographic errors in agent/customer chat dialogs

Chat conversations are unique from several perspectives. In (Damnati et al., 2016), we conducted a study comparing contact center chat conversations and phone conversations, both in the domain of technical assistance for Orange customers. The comparative analysis showed significant differences in terms of interaction flow. If chat conversations were on average twice as long in terms of effective duration, phone conversations contain on average four times more turns than chat conversations. This can be explained by several factors: chat is not an exclusive activity and latencies are more easily accepted than in an oral conversation. Chat utterances are formulated in a more direct style. Additionally, the fact that an utterance is visible on the screen and remains visible, reduces misunderstanding and the need for reformulation turns in an interaction. Regarding the language itself, both media induce specific noise that make it difficult for automatic Natural Language Understanding systems to process them. Phone conversations are prone to spontaneous speech effects such as disfluencies, and the need to perform Automatic Speech Recognition generates additional noise. When processing online chat conversations, these issues disappear. However the written utterances themselves can contain errors, be it orthographic and grammatical errors or typographic deviations due to high speed typing, poor orthographic skills and inattention.

In this study we focus on a corpus of 91 chat conversations that have been fully annotated with correct orthographic form, lemma and pos tags. The annotator was advised to correct misspelled words but she/he was not allowed to modify the content of a message (adding a missing word or suppressing an irrelevant word). In order to compare the original chat conversations with

	Customer	Agent	Full
#words	11798	23073	34871
SER	10.5%	1.5%	4.5%
MER	41.3%	15.7%	27.2%

Table 1: Language deviation error rates

the corrected ones, punctuation, apostrophe and case have been normalized. The manually corrected messages have then been aligned with the original messages thanks to an automatic alignment tools using the classical Levenshtein distance, with all types of errors having the same weight. A post-processing step was added after applying the alignment tool, in order to detect agglutinations or splits. An *agglutination* is detected when a deletion follows a substitution (`[en->entrain] [train->]`) becomes (`[en train->entrain]`). Conversely, a *split* is detected when an insertion follows a substitution (`[télécommande ->télé] [->commande]`) becomes (`[télécommande ->télé commande]`). Instead of being counted as two errors, agglutinations and splits are counted as one substitution. The evaluation is given in terms of Substitution Error Rate (SER) which is the amount of substitutions related to the total amount of words, and the Message Error Rate (MER) which is the amount of messages which contain at least one Substitution related to the total number of messages. As we are interested in the impact of language deviations on syntactic parsing of the messages, the latter rate should also be looked at carefully.

As can be seen in table 1, the overall proportion of misspelled words is not very high (4.5%). However, 27.2% of the turns contain at least one misspelled word. The number of words written by agents is almost twice as large as the number of words produced by Customers. In fact Agents have access to predefined utterances that they can use in various situations. They are also encouraged to formulate polite sentences that tend to increase the length of their messages, while Customers usually adopt a more direct and concise style. Consequently, Agents account for more in the overall SER and MER evaluation, artificially lowering these rates. In fact, as would be expected, Agents make much less mistakes and the distribution of their errors among conversations is quite balanced with a low standard deviation. The sit-

uation is different for Customers where both SER and MER have a high standard deviation (respectively 8.7% and 21.5%). The proportion of misspelled words depends on each Customer's linguistic skills and/or attention when typing.

In order to further study the impact of errors on Syntactic Analysis modules, we propose, as a preliminary study, to evaluate into more details the various types of substitutions encountered in the corpus. We make a distinction between the following types of deviations:

- `DIACR` *diacritic* errors are common in French as accents can be omitted, added or even substituted (à `->a`, très `->trés`, énergie `->énérgie`).

- `APOST` for missing or misplaced *apostrophe*.

- `AGGLU` for *agglutinations* of two words into one.

- `SPLIT` for a word split into two words.

- `INFL` for *inflection* errors. Morpho-syntactic inflection in French is error prone as it is common that different inflected forms of a same word are homophones (`question ->questions`). Among these errors, it is very common (Véronis and Guimier de Neef, 2006) to find past participles replaced by infinitives for verbs that end with er (`j'ai changé -> j'ai changer`).

- `SWITCH` two letters are switched.

- `SUB1C` one character substituted.

- `DEL1C` one character missing.

- `INS1C` one character inserted.

- `OTHER` for all the other errors.

These types of errors are automatically evaluated in this order and are exclusive (*e.g.* `DEL1C` corresponds to words which have one missing character and are not of any preceding type).

Table 2 presents the proportion of each type of error observed in the corpus. As can be seen, diacritic deviations are predominant. On the overall, the second source of deviations is the use of erroneous inflection for a same word. It represents a higher proportion for Agents than for Customers.

Erroneous use of apostrophes is frequent for Customers but almost never occurs for Agents. Agglutinations are more frequent than splits, and constitue more than 11% of deviations for Agents.

	Customer	Agent	Full
DIACR	44.3%	34.5%	42.2%
APOST	12.0%	0.9%	9.6%
AGGLU	6.4%	11.2%	7.4%
SPLIT	1.7%	3.2%	2.0%
INFL	11.5%	25.0%	14.4%
SWITCH	0.7%	3.2%	1.3%
SUB1C	5.8%	4.3%	5.5%
DEL1C	7.4%	5.4%	6.9%
INS1C	3.4%	5.7%	3.9%
OTHER	6.8%	6.6%	6.8%

Table 2: Proportion (in %) of the different types of language deviations

Table 3 presents the repartition of language deviations by pos category. Observing this distribution can give hints on the problems that can be encountered for pos tagging and syntactic parsing. As one can see, function words are generally less error prone than content words. Apart from present participles that are always well written, only proper names and imperative verbs have an SER below the overall SER of 4.5%. But these categories are not highly represented in our data. All other content word categories have an SER above the overall SER. The most error prone category is past participle verbs, which are, as already mentioned, often confused with the infinitive form and which are also prone to inflection errors.

5 Evaluation and Results

5.1 Corpus description

In order to evaluate the impact of errors on pos tagging and parsing, the corpus has been split into two sub-corpora (DEV and TEST]) of similar sizes.

Conversations have been extracted from logs in a chronological way, meaning that they are representative of real conditions, with a variety of call motives and situations. Hence splitting the corpus into two parts by following the chronological order reduces the risk of over-fitting between the DEV corpus and the TEST corpus.

Table 4 illustrates the lexical composition of the DEV corpus, with a comparison between the original forms and the corresponding manually

pos	prop.	SER
VER:ppre pres. participle	0.3%	0.0%
DET determiner	13.2%	1.3%
NAM proper name	1.7%	1.5%
INT interjection	2.1%	1.5%
PRO:REL relative pronoun	0.8%	1.6%
KON conjunction	4.6%	1.8%
NUM numeral	2.0%	2.4%
VER:imp verb imperative	0.9%	3.1%
PRP preposition	11.9%	3.5%
VER:inf verb infinitive	5.1%	4.6%
PRO pronoun	13.7%	5.2%
ADV adverb	6.9%	5.6%
VER verb	10.9%	5.8%
ADJ adjective	3.9%	6.7%
NOM name	19.6%	6.7%
ABR abbreviation	0.2%	10.0%
VER:pper past participle	2.2%	16.9%

Table 3: Language deviation by pos: proportion of each pos in the corpus and corresponding Substitution Error Rate

corrected version. All conversations have been anonymized and personal information has been replaced by a specific label (one label for Customer names, one for Agent names, one for phone numbers and another one for addresses). Hence, the entities concerned by this anonymization step do not account for lexical variety. It is interesting to notice that the number of different words on the Full corpus drops from 2381 when computed on the raw corpus to 2173 (15.3% relative) when computed on the corrected corpus. The proportion of words occurring just once is also reduced when computed over the manually corrected tokens. The statistics of the TEST corpus are comparable. However, the lexical intersection of both corpora is not very high as 10.3% of word occurrences in the TEST corpus are not observed in the DEV corpus (9.1% for Agents and 19.8% for Customers). When computing these rates over the manually corrected tokens, the overall percentage goes down to 9.0% (8.6% for Agents and 17.3% for Customers). These last figures remain high and show that the lexical diversity, if enhanced by scripting errors is already inherent to the data and the domain, with a variety of situations encountered by Customers. Adapting our pos tagger on the DEV corpus is a reasonable experimental approach as the preceding observations exclude the

	DEV original			DEV corrected		
	Customer	Agent	Full	Customer	Agent	Full
#words	5439	11328	16767	5425	11325	17338
diff. words	1431	1468	2381	1301	1414	2173
1 occ. words	879	652	1205	764	599	1020
	(61.4%)	(44.4%)	(50.6%)	(58.7%)	(42.4%)	(46.9%)

Table 4: Description of the DEV corpus in terms of number of words, different words and words occurring only once. Figures vary because of splits and agglutinations.

risk of over-fitting bias at the lexical level.

5.2 Tagging

The pos tagger used for our experiments is a standard Conditional Random Fields (CRF) (Lafferty et al., 2001) tagger which obtains state-of-the-art results on traditional benchmarks. We use a coarse tagset made of 18 different parts of speech.

Three different taggers based on the same architecture are evaluated, the first one, T_F, is trained on the French Treebank (Abeillé et al., 2003), which is composed of newspaper articles. The second one, T_D, is trained on our DEV corpus and the third one, T_{FD} on the union of the French Treebank and our DEV corpus.

Taggers are usually evaluated with an accuracy metric, which is based on the comparison, for every token, of its tag in the output of the tagger (the hypothesis) and its tag in the human annotated corpus (the reference). In our case, the number of tokens in the reference and the hypothesis is not the same, due to agglutinations and splits. In order to account for these phenomena in the evaluation metric, we define conventions that are depicted in Table 5: in case of an agglutination, the tag of the agglutinated token t in the hypothesis is compared to the tag of the first token in the reference (see left part of table 5, where the two tags compared are in bold face). In case of a split, the tag of the first token in the hypothesis is compared to the tag of the token in the reference (see right part of the table).

	tok.	T_F	T_{FD}	T_D
Cust.	Corr.	91.13	93.26	94.36
	Orig.	86.59	88.83	90.38
Agent	Corr.	91.01	96.60	97.30
	Orig.	90.23	95.51	96.50

Table 6: Pos accuracy of the three taggers computed on the original (Orig.) and the corrected (Corr.) versions of the TEST corpus, for Customers and Agents parts of the corpus.

The taggers have been evaluated on the TEST corpus. The results are displayed in Table 6 which shows several interesting phenomena.

First, the three taggers obtain significantly different results. T_F, which is trained on the French Treebank, obtains the lowest results: 86.59% accuracy on the customer part of the corpus and 90.23% on the agent part. Adding to the French Treebank the DEV corpus has a benefic impact on the results, accuracy reaches respectively 88.83% and 95.51%. The best results are obtained by T_D with 90.38% and 96.50% accuracy, despites the small size of the DEV corpus, on which it is trained.

Second, as could be expected, the results are systematically higher on the corrected versions of the corpora. The results are around 4.5 points higher on the customer side and around 1 point higher on the agent side. These figures constitute the upper bound of the tagging accuracy that can be expected if the corpus is automatically corrected prior to tagging.

Third, the results are higher on the agent side, this was also expected from the analysis of the errors in both parts of the corpus (see Table 1).

Tables 7 and 8 give a finer view of the influence of errors on the pos tagging accuracy for tagger T_D. Each line of the table corresponds to the status of a token. If the token is correct, the status is CORR, otherwise it corresponds to one label of the

agglutination				split			
REF		HYP		REF		HYP	
tok	tag	tok	tag	tok	tag	tok	tag
A	$\mathbf{T_A}$	AB	$\mathbf{T_{AB}}$	AB	$\mathbf{T_{AB}}$	A	$\mathbf{T_A}$
B	T_B					B	T_B

Table 5: Conventions defined when computing the accuracy of the tagger for a token. Tags in bold face are compared

status	occ.	corr.	acc.	contrib.
CORR	5916	5547	93.76	59.23
DIACR	201	120	59.70	13.00
AGGLU	76	23	30.26	8.51
SUB1C	46	13	28.26	5.30
INFL	67	45	67.16	3.53
DEL1C	43	22	51.16	3.37
OTHER	40	23	57.50	2.73
INS1C	20	12	60.00	1.28
APOST	47	40	85.11	1.12
SPLIT	6	3	50.00	0.48
SWITCH	2	2	100.00	0.00

Table 7: Influence of token errors on pos tagging, computed on the customer side of the TEST corpus.

status	occ.	corr.	acc.	contrib.
CORR	12883	12517	97.16	79.91
DIACR	61	36	59.02	5.46
INFL	46	25	54.35	4.59
AGGLU	32	18	56.25	3.06
OTHER	11	3	27.27	1.75
SPLIT	8	4	50.00	0.87
DEL1C	10	6	60.00	0.87
SUB1C	8	4	50.00	0.87
INS1C	9	8	88.89	0.22
SWITCH	4	4	100.00	0.00

Table 8: Influence of token errors on pos tagging, computed on the agent side of the TEST corpus.

error types of Table 2. The second column corresponds to the number of occurrences of tokens that fall under this category. The third column is the number of tokens of this status that were correctly tagged, column four is the accuracy for this status and column five, the contribution to the error rate.

Table 7 shows that misspelled tokens are responsible for roughly 40% of the tagging errors. Among errors, the DIACR type has the highest influence on the pos accuracy, it corresponds to 13% of the errors, followed by agglutination. Table 8 shows that erroneous tokens account for 20% of the errors on the agent side. And the first cause of token deviation that provokes tagging errors is DIACR.

5.3 Parsing

The parser used in our experiment is a transition based parser (Yamada and Matsumoto, 2003; Nivre, 2003). It is a dependency parser that takes as input tokens with their pos tag and selects for every token a syntactic governor (which is another token of the sentence) and a syntactic label. The prediction is based on several features that combine lexical information and pos tags. Orthographic errors have therefore a double impact on the parsing process: through the errors they provoke on the pos tagging process and the errors they provoke directly on the parsing process. The parser was trained on the French Treebank. Contrary to taggers, a single parser was used for our experiments since we do not have hand corrected syntactic annotation of the DATCHA corpus.

In order to evaluate the parser, we have parsed our DEV corpus with corrected tokens and gold pos tags and considered the syntactic structures produced to be our reference. The results that are given below should therefore be taken with caution. Their absolute value is not reliable (it is probably over estimated) but they can be compared with one another.

The metric used to evaluate the output of the parser is the Labeled Attachement Score (LAS) which is the ratio of tokens for which the correct governor along with the correct syntactic label have been predicted. The conventions of Table 5 defined for the tagger were also used for evaluating the parser.

Three series of parsing experiments were conducted, the first one takes as input the tokens as they appear in the raw corpus and the pos tags predicted with our best tagger (T_D). These experiments correspond to the most realistic situation, with original tokens and predicted pos tags. The second series of experiments takes as input the corrected tokens and the predicted pos tags. Its purpose is to estimate an upper bound of the parsing accuracy when using an orthographic corrector prior to tagging and parsing. The third experiment takes as input raw tokens and gold pos tags. It corresponds to an artificial situation, its purpose is to evaluate the influence of orthographic errors on parsing, independently of tagging errors.

Table 9 shows that the influence of orthographic errors on parsing is limited, most parsing errors are due to pos tagging errors.

The table also shows that the difference in parsing accuracy between the customer part of the corpus and the agent part is higher than what it was for tagging. This can be explained by the fact that,

	tok.	pos acc.	LAS
	O	90.38	73.47
Cust.	C	94.36	81.30
	O	100	94.68
	O	96.50	82.12
Agent	C	97.30	86.43
	O	100	95.74

Table 9: LAS of the parser output for three types of input: original tokens (O) and predicted pos tags, corrected tokens (C) and predicted pos tags and original tokens and gold pos tags, computed on the TEST corpus for the customer and the agent parts of the corpus.

from the syntactic point of view, agent utterances are probably closer to the data on which the parser has been trained (journalistic data) than customer utterances.

6 Conclusion

We study in this paper orthographic mistakes that occur in data collected in contact centers. A typology of mistakes is proposed and their influence on part of speech tagging and syntactic parsing is studied. We also show that taggers and parsers trained on standard journalistic corpora yield poor results on such data and that the addition of a limited amount of annotated data can significantly improve the performances of such tools.

Acknowledgments

This work has been funded by the French Agence Nationale pour la Recherche, through the project DATCHA (ANR-15-CE23-0003)

References

Anne Abeillé, Lionel Clément, and François Toussenel. 2003. Building a treebank for french. In *Treebanks*, pages 165–187. Springer.

Falaise Achille. 2005. Constitution d'un corpus de français tchaté. In *Rencontre des tudiants Chercheurs en Informatique pour le Traitement Automatique des Langues (RECITAL)*, Dourdan, France.

Nicholas Asher, 2011. *Strategic Conversation*. Institut de Recherche en Informatique de Toulouse, Université Paul Sabatier, France. https://www.irit.fr/STAC/.

Thierry Bazillon, Melanie Deplano, Frederic Bechet, Alexis Nasr, and Benoit Favre. 2012. Syntactic annotation of spontaneous speech: application to call-center conversation data. In *Proceedings of LREC*, Istambul.

Anais Cadilhac, Nicholas Asher, Farah Benamara, and Alex Lascarides. 2013. Grounding strategic conversation: Using negotiation dialogues to predict trades in a win-lose game. In *EMNLP*, pages 357–368.

Thierry Chanier, Céline Poudat, Benoit Sagot, Georges Antoniadis, Ciara R Wigham, Linda Hriba, Julien Longhi, and Djamé Seddah. 2014. The comere corpus for french: structuring and annotating heterogeneous cmc genres. *JLCL-Journal for Language Technology and Computational Linguistics*, 29(2):1–30.

Géraldine Damnati, Aleksandra Guerraz, and Delphine Charlet. 2016. Web chat conversations from contact centers: a descriptive study. In *International Conference on Language Resources and Evaluation (LREC)*.

Michael H Dickey, Gary Burnett, Katherine M Chudoba, and Michelle M Kazmer. 2007. Do you read me? perspective making and perspective taking in chat communities. *Journal of the Association for Information Systems*, 8(1):47.

Eric N Forsyth and Craig H Martell. 2007. Lexical and discourse analysis of online chat dialog. In *Semantic Computing, 2007. ICSC 2007. International Conference on*, pages 19–26. IEEE.

Ewa Jonsson. 1997. Electronic discourse: On speech and writing on the internet.

Lingpeng Kong, Nathan Schneider, Swabha Swayamdipta, Archna Bhatia, Chris Dyer, and Noah A Smith. 2014. A dependency parser for tweets. In *Proceedings of EMNLP*.

T. Kucukyilmaz, Cambazoglu B. B., C. Aykanat, and F. Can. 2008. Chat mining: Predicting user and message attributes in computer-mediated communication. *Information Processing and Management*, 44:1448–1466.

John Lafferty, Andrew McCallum, and Fernando CN Pereira. 2001. Conditional random fields: Probabilistic models for segmenting and labeling sequence data.

Alexis Nasr, Frederic Bechet, Benoit Favre, Thierry Bazillon, Jose Deulofeu, and Andre Valli. 2014. Automatically enriching spoken corpora with syntactic information for linguistic studies. In *International Conference on Language Resources and Evaluation (LREC)*.

Joakim Nivre. 2003. An efficient algorithm for projective dependency parsing. In *Proceedings of the 8th International Workshop on Parsing Technologies (IWPT*. Citeseer.

Alan Ritter, Sam Clark, Oren Etzioni, et al. 2011.
Named entity recognition in tweets: an experimental
study. In *Proceedings of the Conference on Empirical Methods in Natural Language Processing*, pages
1524–1534. Association for Computational Linguistics.

Samira Shaikh, Tomek Strzalkowski, George Aaron
Broadwell, Jennifer Stromer-Galley, Sarah M Taylor, and Nick Webb. 2010. Mpc: A multi-party chat
corpus for modeling social phenomena in discourse.
In *LREC*.

Paola Trimarco. 2014. *Digital Textuality*. Palgrave
Macmillan.

Jean Véronis and Emilie Guimier de Neef. 2006. Le
traitement des nouvelles formes de communication
écrite. *Compréhension automatique des langues et
interaction*, pages 227–248.

Min Wu, Arin Bhowmick, and Joseph Goldberg. 2012.
Adding structured data in unstructured web chat
conversation. In *Proceedings of the 25th annual
ACM symposium on User interface software and
technology*, pages 75–82. ACM.

Hiroyasu Yamada and Yuji Matsumoto. 2003. Statistical dependency analysis with support vector machines. In *Proceedings of IWPT*, volume 3, pages
195–206.

A Context-aware Natural Language Generator for Dialogue Systems

Ondřej Dušek and **Filip Jurčíček**
Charles University in Prague, Faculty of Mathematics and Physics
Institute of Formal and Applied Linguistics
Malostranské náměstí 25, CZ-11800 Prague, Czech Republic
{odusek,jurcicek}@ufal.mff.cuni.cz

Abstract

We present a novel natural language generation system for spoken dialogue systems capable of entraining (adapting) to users' way of speaking, providing contextually appropriate responses. The generator is based on recurrent neural networks and the sequence-to-sequence approach. It is fully trainable from data which include preceding context along with responses to be generated. We show that the context-aware generator yields significant improvements over the baseline in both automatic metrics and a human pairwise preference test.

1 Introduction

In a conversation, speakers are influenced by previous utterances of their counterparts and tend to adapt (align, entrain) their way of speaking to each other, reusing lexical items as well as syntactic structure (Reitter et al., 2006). Entrainment occurs naturally and subconsciously, facilitates successful conversations (Friedberg et al., 2012; Nenkova et al., 2008), and forms a natural source of variation in dialogues. In spoken dialogue systems (SDS), users were reported to entrain to system prompts (Parent and Eskenazi, 2010).

The function of natural language generation (NLG) components in task-oriented SDS typically is to produce a natural language sentence from a *dialogue act* (DA) (Young et al., 2010) representing an action, such as *inform* or *request*, along with one or more attributes (*slots*) and their values (see Fig. 1). NLG is an important component of SDS which has a great impact on the perceived naturalness of the system; its quality can also influence the overall task success (Stoyanchev and Stent, 2009; Lopes et al., 2013). However, typical

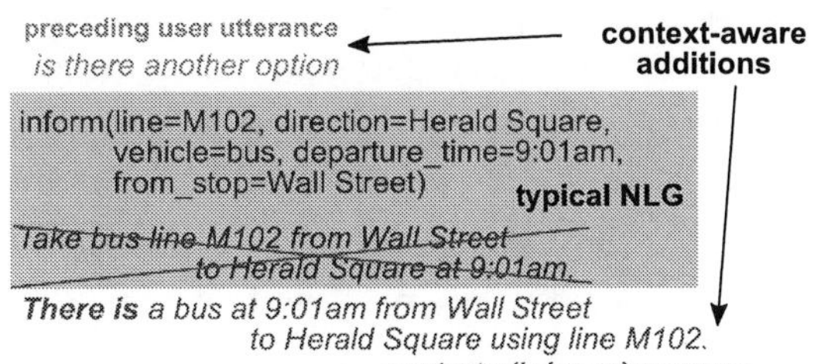

Figure 1: An example of NLG input and output, with context-aware additions.

NLG systems in SDS only take the input DA into account and have no way of adapting to the user's way of speaking. To avoid repetition and add variation into the outputs, they typically alternate between a handful of preset variants (Jurčíček et al., 2014) or use overgeneration and random sampling from a k-best list of outputs (Wen et al., 2015b). There have been several attempts at introducing entrainment into NLG in SDS, but they are limited to rule-based systems (see Section 4).

We present a novel, fully trainable context-aware NLG system for SDS that is able to entrain to the user and provides naturally variable outputs because generation is conditioned not only on the input DA, but also on the preceding user utterance (see Fig. 1). Our system is an extension of Dušek and Jurčíček (2016b)'s generator based on sequence-to-sequence (seq2seq) models with attention (Bahdanau et al., 2015). It is, to our knowledge, the first fully trainable entrainment-enabled NLG system for SDS. We also present our first results on the dataset of Dušek and Jurčíček (2016a), which includes the preceding user utterance along with each data instance (i.e., pair of input meaning representation and output sentence), and we show that our context-aware system outperforms the baseline in both automatic metrics and a human pairwise preference test.

Proceedings of the SIGDIAL 2016 Conference, pages 185–190,
Los Angeles, USA, 13-15 September 2016. ©2016 Association for Computational Linguistics

In the following, we first present the architecture of our generator (see Section 2), then give an account of our experiments in Section 3. We include a brief survey of related work in Section 4. Section 5 contains concluding remarks and plans for future work.

2 Our generator

Our seq2seq generator is an improved version of Dušek and Jurčíček (2016b)'s generator, which itself is based on the seq2seq model with attention (Bahdanau et al., 2015, see Fig. 2) as implemented in the TensorFlow framework (Abadi et al., 2015).[1] We first describe the base model in Section 2.1, then list our context-aware improvements in Section 2.2.

2.1 Baseline Seq2seq NLG with Attention

The generation has two stages: The first, *encoder stage* uses a recurrent neural network (RNN) composed of long-short-term memory (LSTM) cells (Hochreiter and Schmidhuber, 1997; Graves, 2013) to encode a sequence of input tokens[2] $\mathbf{x} = \{x_1, \ldots, x_n\}$ into a sequence of hidden states $\mathbf{h} = \{h_1, \ldots, h_n\}$:

$$h_t = \mathrm{lstm}(x_t, h_{t-1}) \qquad (1)$$

The second, *decoder stage* then uses the hidden states $\mathbf{h}$ to generate the output sequence $\mathbf{y} = \{y_1, \ldots, y_m\}$. Its main component is a second LSTM-based RNN, which works over its own internal state s_t and the previous output token y_{t-1}:

$$s_t = \mathrm{lstm}((y_{t-1} \circ c_t)W_S, s_{t-1}) \qquad (2)$$

It is initialized by the last hidden encoder state ($s_0 = h_n$) and a special starting symbol. The generated output token y_t is selected from a softmax distribution:

$$p(y_t|y_{t-1}\ldots, \mathbf{x}) = \mathrm{softmax}((s_t \circ c_t)W_Y) \qquad (3)$$

In (2) and (3), c_t represents the *attention model* – a sum over all encoder hidden states, weighted by a feed-forward network with one tanh hidden layer; W_S and W_Y are linear projection matrices and "∘" denotes concatenation.

DAs are represented as sequences on the encoder input: a triple of the structure "DA type, slot, value" is created for each slot in the DA and the triples are concatenated (see Fig. 2).[3] The generator supports greedy decoding as well as beam search which keeps track of top k most probable output sequences at each time step (Sutskever et al., 2014; Bahdanau et al., 2015).

The generator further features a simple content classification reranker to penalize irrelevant or missing information on the output. It uses an LSTM-based RNN to encode the generator outputs token-by-token into a fixed-size vector. This is then fed to a sigmoid classification layer that outputs a 1-hot vector indicating the presence of all possible DA types, slots, and values. The vectors for all k-best generator outputs are then compared to the input DA and the number of missing and irrelevant elements is used to rerank them.

2.2 Making the Generator Context-aware

We implemented three different modifications to our generator that make its output dependent on the preceding context:[4]

Prepending context. The preceding user utterance is simply prepended to the DA and fed into the encoder (see Fig. 2). The dictionary for context utterances is distinct from the DA tokens dictionary.

Context encoder. We add another, separate encoder for the context utterances. The hidden states of both encoders are concatenated, and the decoder then works with double-sized vectors both on the input and in the attention model (see Fig. 2).

n-gram match reranker. We added a second reranker for the k-best outputs of the generator that promotes outputs that have a word or phrase overlap with the context utterance. We use geometric mean of modified n-gram precisions (with $n \in \{1, 2\}$) as a measure of context overlap, i.e., BLEU-2 (Papineni et al., 2002) without brevity penalty. The log probability l of an output sequence on the generator k-best list is updated as follows:

$$l = l + w \cdot \sqrt{p_1 p_2} \qquad (4)$$

---

[1] See (Dušek and Jurčíček, 2016b) and (Bahdanau et al., 2015) for a more formal description of the base model.

[2] Embeddings are used (Bengio et al., 2003), i.e., x_t and y_t are vector representations of the input and output tokens.

[3] While the sequence encoding may not necessarily be the best way to obtain a vector representation of DA, it was shown to work well (Dušek and Jurčíček, 2016b).

[4] For simplicity, we kept close to the basic seq2seq architecture of the generator; other possibilities for encoding the context, such as convolution and/or max-pooling, are possible.

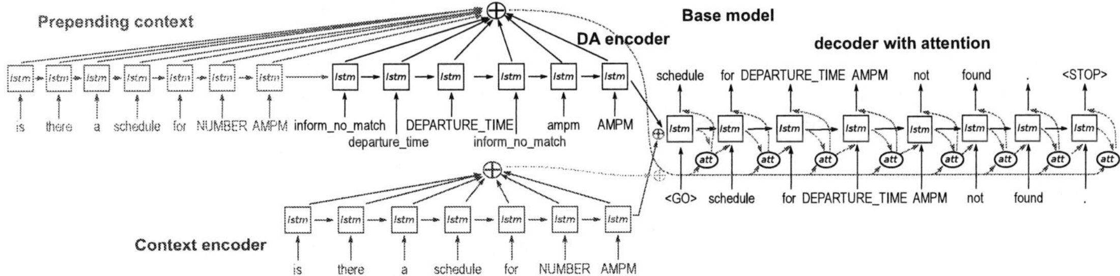

Figure 2: The base Seq2seq generator (black) with our improvements: prepending context (green) and separate context encoder (blue).

Setup	BLEU	NIST
Baseline (context not used)	66.41	7.037
n-gram match reranker	68.68	7.577
Prepending context	63.87	6.456
+ n-gram match reranker	69.26	7.772
Context encoder	63.08	6.818
+ n-gram match reranker	69.17	7.596

Table 1: BLEU and NIST scores of different generator setups on the test data.

In (4), p_1 and p_2 are modified unigram and bigram precisions of the output sequence against the context, and w is a preset weight. We believe that any reasonable measure of contextual match would be viable here, and we opted for modified n-gram precisions because of simple computation, well-defined range, and the relation to the de facto standard BLEU metric.[5] We only use unigrams and bigrams to promote especially the reuse of single words or short phrases.

In addition, we combine the n-gram match reranker with both of the two former approaches.

We used gold-standard transcriptions of the immediately preceding user utterance in our experiments in order to test the context-aware capabilities of our system in a stand-alone setting; in a live SDS, 1-best speech recognition hypotheses and longer user utterance history can be used with no modifications to the architecture.

3 Experiments

We experiment on the publicly available dataset of Dušek and Jurčíček (2016a)[6] for NLG in the pub-

lic transport information domain, which includes preceding context along with each pair of input DA and target natural language sentence. It contains over 5,500 utterances, i.e., three paraphrases for each of the over 1,800 combinations of input DA and context user utterance. The data concern bus and subway connections on Manhattan, and comprise four DA types (*iconfirm*, *inform*, *inform_no_match*, *request*). They are delexicalized for generation to avoid sparsity, i.e., stop names, vehicles, times, etc., are replaced by placeholders (Wen et al., 2015a). We applied a 3:1:1 split of the set into training, development, and test data. We use the three paraphrases as separate instances in training data, but they serve as three references for a single generated output in validation and evaluation.

We test the three context-aware setups described in Section 2.2 and their combinations, and we compare them against the baseline non-context-aware seq2seq generator. Same as Dušek and Jurčíček (2016b), we train the seq2seq models by minimizing cross-entropy on the training set using the Adam optimizer (Kingma and Ba, 2015), and we measure BLEU on the development set after each pass over the training data, selecting the best-performing parameters.[7] The content classification reranker is trained in a similar fashion, measuring misclassification on both training and development set after each pass.[8] We use 5 dif-

---

[5] We do not use brevity penalty as we do not want to demote shorter output sequences. However, adding it to the formula in our preliminary experiments yielded similar results to the ones presented here.

[6] The dataset is released at `http://hdl.handle.net/11234/1-1675`; we used a more recent version from GitHub (`https://github.com/UFAL-DSG/alex_`

`context_nlg_dataset`), which contains several small fixes.

[7] Based on our preliminary experiments on development data, we use embedding size 50, LSTM cell size 128, learning rate 0.0005, and batch size 20. Training is run for at least 50 and up to 1000 passes, with early stopping if the top 10 validation BLEU scores do not change for 100 passes.

[8] We use the same settings except for the number of passes over the training data, which is at least 20 and 100 at most. For validation, development set is given 10 times more importance than the training set.

ferent random initializations of the networks and average the results.

Decoding is run with a beam size of 20 and the penalty weight for content classification reranker set to 100. We set the n-gram match reranker weight based on experiments on development data.[9]

3.1 Evaluation Using Automatic Metrics

Table 1 lists our results on the test data in terms of the BLEU and NIST metrics (Papineni et al., 2002; Doddington, 2002). We can see that while the n-gram match reranker brings a BLEU score improvement, using context prepending or separate encoder results in scores lower than the baseline.[10] However, using the n-gram match reranker together with context prepending or separate encoder brings significant improvements of about 2.8 BLEU points in both cases, better than using the n-gram match reranker alone.[11] We believe that adding the context information into the decoder does increase the chances of contextually appropriate outputs appearing on the decoder k-best lists, but it also introduces a lot more uncertainty and therefore, the appropriate outputs may not end on top of the list based on decoder scores alone. The n-gram match reranker is then able to promote the relevant outputs to the top of the k-best list. However, if the generator itself does not have access to context information, the n-gram match reranker has a smaller effect as contextually appropriate outputs may not appear on the k-best lists at all. A closer look at the generated outputs confirms that entrainment is present in sentences generated by the context-aware setups (see Fig. 2).

In addition to BLEU and NIST scores, we measured the slot error rate ERR (Wen et al., 2015b), i.e., the proportion of missing or superfluous slot placeholders in the delexicalized generated outputs. For all our setups, ERR stayed around 3%.

3.2 Human Evaluation

We evaluated the best-performing setting based on BLEU/NIST scores, i.e., prepending context with n-gram match reranker, in a blind pairwise preference test with untrained judges recruited on the CrowdFlower crowdsourcing platform.[12] The judges were given the context and the system output for the baseline and the context-aware system, and they were asked to pick the variant that sounds more natural. We used a random sample of 1,000 pairs of different system outputs over all 5 random initializations of the networks, and collected 3 judgments for each of them. The judges preferred the context-aware system output in 52.5% cases, significantly more than the baseline.[13]

We examined the judgments in more detail and found three probable causes for the rather small difference between the setups. First, both setups' outputs fit the context relatively well in many cases and the judges tend to prefer the overall more frequent variant (e.g., for the context "starting from Park Place", the output "Where do you want to go?" is preferred over "Where are you going to?"). Second, the context-aware setup often selects a shorter response that fits the context well (e.g., "Is there an option at 10:00 am?" is confirmed simply with "At 10:00 am."), but the judges seem to prefer the more eloquent variant. And third, both setups occasionally produce non-fluent outputs, which introduces a certain amount of noise.

4   Related Work

Our system is an evolutionary improvement over the LSTM seq2seq system of Dušek and Jurčíček (2016b) and as such, it is most related in terms of architecture to other recent RNN-based approaches to NLG, which are not context-aware: RNN generation with a convolutional reranker by Wen et al. (2015a) and an improved LSTM-based version (Wen et al., 2015b), as well as the LSTM encoder-aligner-decoder NLG system of Mei et al. (2015). The recent end-to-end trainable SDS of Wen et al. (2016) does have an implicit access to previous context, but the authors do not focus on its influence on the generated responses.

There have been several attempts at modelling entrainment in dialogue (Brockmann et al., 2005; Reitter et al., 2006; Buschmeier et al., 2010) and even successful implementations of entrainment models in NLG systems for SDS, where entrainment caused an increase in perceived naturalness of the system responses (Hu et al., 2014) or increased naturalness and task success (Lopes et al.,

---

[9]w is set to 5 when the n-gram match reranker is run by itself or combined with the separate encoder, 10 if combined with prepending context.

[10]In our experiments on development data, all three methods brought a mild BLEU improvement.

[11]Statistical significance at 99% level has been assessed using pairwise bootstrap resampling (Koehn, 2004).

[12]http://crowdflower.com

[13]The result is statistically significant at 99% level according to the pairwise bootstrap resampling test.

Context	is there a later option
Input DA	iconfirm(alternative=next)
Baseline	Next connection.
n-gram match reranker	You want a later connection.
Prepending context + n-gram match reranker	You want a later connection.
Context encoder + n-gram match reranker	You want a later option.
Context	i need to find a bus connection
Input DA	inform_no_match(vehicle=bus)
Baseline	No bus found, sorry.
n-gram match reranker	I did not find a bus route.
Prepending context + n-gram match reranker	I'm sorry, I cannot find a bus connection.
Context encoder + n-gram match reranker	I'm sorry, I cannot find a bus connection.
Context	i rather take the bus
Input DA	inform(vehicle=bus, departure_time=8:01am, direction=Cathedral Parkway, from_stop=Bowling Green, line=M15)
Baseline	At 8:01am by bus line M15 from Bowling Green to Cathedral Parkway.
n-gram match reranker	At 8:01am by bus line M15 from Bowling Green to Cathedral Parkway.
Prepending context + n-gram match reranker	You can take the M15 bus from Bowling Green to Cathedral Parkway at 8:01am.
Context encoder + n-gram match reranker	At 8:01am by bus line M15 from Bowling Green to Cathedral Parkway.

Table 2: Example outputs of the different setups of our generator (with entrainment highlighted)

2013; Lopes et al., 2015). However, all of the previous approaches are completely or partially rule-based. Most of them attempt to model entrainment explicitly, focus on specific entrainment phenomena only, and/or require manually selected lists of variant expressions, while our system learns synonyms and entrainment rules implicitly from the corpus. A direct comparison with previous entrainment-capable NLG systems for SDS is not possible in our stand-alone setting since their rules involve the history of the whole dialogue whereas we focus on the preceding utterance in our experiments.

5   Conclusions and Further Work

We presented an improvement to our natural language generator based on the sequence-to-sequence approach (Dušek and Jurčíček, 2016b), allowing it to exploit preceding context user utterances to adapt (entrain) to the user's way of speaking and provide more contextually accurate and less repetitive responses. We used two different ways of feeding previous context into the generator and a reranker based on n-gram match against the context. Evaluation on our context-aware dataset (Dušek and Jurčíček, 2016a) showed a significant BLEU score improvement for the combination of the two approaches, which was confirmed in a subsequent human pairwise preference test. Our generator is available on GitHub at the following URL:

https://github.com/UFAL-DSG/tgen

In future work, we plan on improving the n-gram matching metric to allow fuzzy matching (e.g., capturing different forms of the same word), experimenting with more ways of incorporating context into the generator, controlling the output eloquence and fluency, and most importantly, evaluating our generator in a live dialogue system. We also intend to evaluate the generator with automatic speech recognition hypotheses as context and modify it to allow n-best hypotheses as contexts. Using our system in a live SDS will also allow a comparison against previous handcrafted entrainment-capable NLG systems.

Acknowledgments

This work was funded by the Ministry of Education, Youth and Sports of the Czech Republic under the grant agreement LK11221 and core research funding, SVV project 260 333, and GAUK grant 2058214 of Charles University in Prague. It used language resources stored and distributed by the LINDAT/CLARIN project of the Ministry of Education, Youth and Sports of the Czech Republic (project LM2015071). The authors would like to thank Ondřej Plátek and Miroslav Vodolán for helpful comments.

References

M. Abadi, A. Agarwal, P. Barham, E. Brevdo, Z. Chen, C. Citro, G. S. Corrado, A. Davis, J. Dean, M. Devin, S. Ghemawat, I. Goodfellow, A. Harp, G. Irving, M. Isard, Y. Jia, R. Jozefowicz, L. Kaiser, M. Kudlur, J. Levenberg, D. Mané, R. Monga, S. Moore, D. Murray, C. Olah, M. Schuster, J. Shlens, B. Steiner, I. Sutskever, K. Talwar, P. Tucker, V. Vanhoucke, V. Vasudevan, F. Viégas, O. Vinyals, P. Warden, M. Wattenberg, M. Wicke, Y. Yu, and X. Zheng. 2015. TensorFlow: Large-scale machine learning on heterogeneous systems. Software available from tensorflow.org.

D. Bahdanau, K. Cho, and Y. Bengio. 2015. Neural machine translation by jointly learning to align and translate. In *International Conference on Learning Representations*. arXiv:1409.0473.

Y. Bengio, R. Ducharme, P. Vincent, and C. Jauvin. 2003. A neural probabilistic language model. *Journal of Machine Learning Research*, 3:1137–1155.

C. Brockmann, A. Isard, J. Oberlander, and M. White. 2005. Modelling alignment for affective dialogue. In *Workshop on Adapting the Interaction Style to Affective Factors at the 10th International Conference on User Modeling*.

H. Buschmeier, K. Bergmann, and S. Kopp. 2010. Modelling and evaluation of lexical and syntactic alignment with a priming-based microplanner. In *Empirical Methods in Natural Language Generation*, number 5790 in Lecture Notes in Computer Science, pages 85–104. Springer.

G. Doddington. 2002. Automatic evaluation of machine translation quality using N-gram co-occurrence statistics. In *Proceedings of the Second International Conference on Human Language Technology Research*, pages 138–145.

O. Dušek and F. Jurčíček. 2016a. A context-aware natural language generation dataset for dialogue systems. In *Workshop on Collecting and Generating Resources for Chatbots and Conversational Agents - Development and Evaluation*, pages 6–9.

O. Dušek and F. Jurčíček. 2016b. Sequence-to-sequence generation for spoken dialogue via deep syntax trees and strings. *arXiv:1606.05491*. To appear in Proceedings of ACL.

H. Friedberg, D. Litman, and S. B. F. Paletz. 2012. Lexical entrainment and success in student engineering groups. In *Proc. of SLT*, pages 404–409.

A. Graves. 2013. Generating sequences with recurrent neural networks. *arXiv:1308.0850*.

S. Hochreiter and J. Schmidhuber. 1997. Long short-term memory. *Neural computation*, 9(8):1735–1780.

Z. Hu, G. Halberg, C. Jimenez, and M. Walker. 2014. Entrainment in pedestrian direction giving: How many kinds of entrainment. In *Proc. of IWSDS*, pages 90–101.

F. Jurčíček, O. Dušek, O. Plátek, and L. Žilka. 2014. Alex: A statistical dialogue systems framework. In *Proc. of Text, Speech and Dialogue*, pages 587–594.

D. Kingma and J. Ba. 2015. Adam: A method for stochastic optimization. In *International Conference on Learning Representations*. arXiv:1412.6980.

P. Koehn. 2004. Statistical significance tests for machine translation evaluation. In *Proceedings of EMNLP*, pages 388–395.

J. Lopes, M. Eskenazi, and I. Trancoso. 2013. Automated two-way entrainment to improve spoken dialog system performance. In *Proc. of ICASSP*, pages 8372–8376.

J. Lopes, M. Eskenazi, and I. Trancoso. 2015. From rule-based to data-driven lexical entrainment models in spoken dialog systems. *Computer Speech & Language*, 31(1):87–112.

H. Mei, M. Bansal, and M. R. Walter. 2015. What to talk about and how? selective generation using LSTMs with coarse-to-fine alignment. *arXiv:1509.00838*.

A. Nenkova, A. Gravano, and J. Hirschberg. 2008. High frequency word entrainment in spoken dialogue. In *Proc. of ACL-HLT*, pages 169–172.

K. Papineni, S. Roukos, T. Ward, and W.-J. Zhu. 2002. BLEU: A method for automatic evaluation of machine translation. In *Proc. of ACL*, pages 311–318.

G. Parent and M. Eskenazi. 2010. Lexical entrainment of real users in the Let's Go spoken dialog system. In *Proc. of Interspeech*, pages 3018–3021.

D. Reitter, F. Keller, and J. D. Moore. 2006. Computational modelling of structural priming in dialogue. In *Proc. of NAACL-HLT: Short Papers*, pages 121–124.

S. Stoyanchev and A. Stent. 2009. Lexical and syntactic priming and their impact in deployed spoken dialog systems. In *Proc. of NAACL-HLT*, pages 189–192.

I. Sutskever, O. Vinyals, and Q. VV Le. 2014. Sequence to sequence learning with neural networks. In *Advances in Neural Information Processing Systems*, pages 3104–3112. arXiv:1409.3215.

T.-H. Wen, M. Gasic, D. Kim, N. Mrksic, P.-H. Su, D. Vandyke, and S. Young. 2015a. Stochastic language generation in dialogue using recurrent neural networks with convolutional sentence reranking. In *Proc. of SIGDIAL*, pages 275–284.

T.-H. Wen, M. Gasic, N. Mrkšić, P.-H. Su, D. Vandyke, and S. Young. 2015b. Semantically conditioned LSTM-based natural language generation for spoken dialogue systems. In *Proc. of EMNLP*, pages 1711–1721.

T.-H. Wen, M. Gašić, N. Mrkšić, L. M. Rojas-Barahona, P.-H. Su, S. Ultes, D. Vandyke, and S. Young. 2016. A network-based end-to-end trainable task-oriented dialogue system. *arXiv:1604.04562*.

S. Young, M. Gašić, S. Keizer, F. Mairesse, J. Schatzmann, B. Thomson, and K. Yu. 2010. The hidden information state model: A practical framework for POMDP-based spoken dialogue management. *Computer Speech & Language*, 24(2):150–174.

Identifying Teacher Questions Using
Automatic Speech Recognition in Classrooms

Nathaniel Blanchard[1], Patrick J. Donnelly[1], Andrew M. Olney[2], Borhan Samei[2],
Brooke Ward[3], Xiaoyi Sun[3], Sean Kelly[4], Martin Nystrand[3], & Sidney K. D'Mello[1]

[1]University of Notre Dame; [2]University of Memphis;
[3]University of Wisconsin-Madison; [4]University of Pittsburgh

384 Fitzpatrick Hall

Notre Dame, IN 46646, USA

`nblancha|sdmello@nd.edu`

Abstract

We investigate automatic question detection from recordings of teacher speech collected in live classrooms. Our corpus contains audio recordings of 37 class sessions taught by 11 teachers. We automatically segment teacher speech into utterances using an amplitude envelope thresholding approach followed by filtering non-speech via automatic speech recognition (ASR). We manually code the segmented utterances as containing a teacher question or not based on an empirically-validated scheme for coding classroom discourse. We compute domain-independent natural language processing (NLP) features from transcripts generated by three ASR engines (AT&T, Bing Speech, and Azure Speech). Our teacher-independent supervised machine learning model detects questions with an overall weighted F_1 score of 0.59, a 51% improvement over chance. Furthermore, the proportion of automatically-detected questions per class session strongly correlates (Pearson's r = 0.85) with human-coded question rates. We consider our results to reflect a substantial (37%) improvement over the state-of-the-art in automatic question detection from naturalistic audio. We conclude by discussing applications of our work for teachers, researchers, and other stakeholders.

1 Introduction

Questions are powerful tools that can inspire thought and inquiry at deeper levels of comprehension (Graesser and Person, 1994; Beck et al., 1996). There is a large body of work supporting a positive relationship between the use of *certain types of questions* with increased student engagement and achievement (Applebee et al., 2003; Kelly, 2007). But not all questions are the same. Questions that solicit surface-level facts (called test questions) are far less predictive of achievement compared to more open-ended (or dialogic) questions (Nystrand and Gamoran, 1991; Gamoran and Nystrand, 1991; Applebee et al., 2003; Nystrand, 2006).

Fortunately, providing teachers with training and feedback on their use of instructional practices (including question-asking) can help them adopt techniques known to be associated with student achievement (Juzwik et al., 2013). However, automatic computational methods are required to analyze classroom instruction on a large scale. Although there are well-known coding schemes for manual coding of questions in classroom environments (Nystrand et al., 2003; Stivers and Enfield, 2010) research on *automatically* identifying these questions in live classrooms is in its infancy and is the focus of this work.

1.1 Related Work

To keep scope manageable, we limit our review of previous work to question detection from automatic speech recognition (ASR) since the use of ASR transcriptions, rather than human transcriptions, is germane to the present problem.

Boakye et al. (2009) trained models to detect questions in office meetings. The authors used the ICSI Meeting Recorder Dialog Act (MRDA) corpus, a set of 75 hour-long meetings recorded with headset and lapel microphones. Their ASR system achieved a word error rate (WER), a measure of edit distance comparing the hypothesis to the original transcript, of 0.38 on the corpus. They trained an AdaBoost classifier to detect questions from word, part-of-speech, and parse tree features derived from the ASR transcriptions, achieving F_1 scores of 0.52, 0.35, and 0.50, respectively, and 0.50 combined. Adding contextual and acoustic features slightly improved the F_1 score to 0.54,

Proceedings of the SIGDIAL 2016 Conference, pages 191–201,
Los Angeles, USA, 13-15 September 2016. ©2016 Association for Computational Linguistics

suggesting the importance of linguistic (as opposed to contextual or acoustic) information for question detection.

Stolcke et al. (2000) built a dialogue act tagger on the conversational Switchboard corpus using ASR transcripts (WER 0.41). A Bayesian model, trained on likelihoods of word trigrams from ASR transcriptions, detected 42 dialogue acts with an accuracy of 65% (chance level 35%; human agreement 84%). Dialogue acts such as statements, questions, apologies, or agreement were among those tagged. Limiting the models to consider only the highest-confidence transcription (the 1-best ASR transcript) resulted in a 62% accuracy with the bigram discourse model. Additionally, the authors noted a 21% decrease in classification error when human transcripts were used instead.

Stolcke et al. (2000) also attempted to leverage prosody to distinguish yes-no questions from statements, dialogue acts which may be ambiguous based on transcripts alone. On a selected subset of their corpus containing an equal proportion of questions and statements they achieved an accuracy of 75% using transcripts (chance 50%). Adding prosodic features increased their accuracy to 80%.

Orosanu and Jouvet (2015) investigated discrimination between statements and questions from ASR transcriptions from three French-language corpora. Their training set consisted of 10,077 statements and 10,077 questions, and their testing set consisted of 7,005 statements and 831 questions. Using human transcriptions, the models classified 73% of questions and 78% of statements correctly. When the authors tested the same model against ASR transcriptions, they observed a 3% reduction in classification accuracy. The authors also compared their datasets based on differences in speaking styles. One corpus consisted of unscripted, spontaneous speech from news broadcasts (classification accuracy 70%; WER 22%), while the other contained scripted dialogue from radio and TV channels (classification accuracy 73%; WER 28%).

All the aforementioned studies have used manually-defined sentence boundaries. However, a fully-automatic system for question detection would need to detect sentence boundaries without manual input. Orosanu and Jouvet (2015) simulated imperfect sentence boundary detection using a semi-automatic method. They substituted sentence boundaries defined by human-annotated punctuation with boundaries based on silence in the audio. When punctuation aligned with silence, the boundaries were left unchanged from the manually-defined boundaries. This semi-automatic approach to segmentation resulted in a 3% increase in classification errors.

Finally, in preliminary precursor to this work, we explored the potential for question detection in classrooms from automatically-segmented utterances that were transcribed by humans (Blanchard et al., 2016). We used 1,000 random utterances from our current corpus which we manually transcribed and coded as containing a question or not (see Section 2.3). Using leave-one-speaker-out cross-validation, we achieved an overall-weighted F_1 score of 0.66, with an F_1 of 0.53 for the question class. That work showed that question detection was possible from noisy classroom audio, albeit with human transcriptions.

1.2 Challenges, Contributions, and Novelty

We describe a novel question detection scenario in which we automatically identify teacher questions using ASR transcriptions of teacher speech in a real-world classroom environment. We have previously identified numerous constraints that need to be satisfied in order to facilitate question detection at scale. Such a system must be affordable, cannot be disruptive to either the teacher or the students, and must maintain student privacy, which precludes recording or filming individual students. Therefore, we primarily rely on a low-cost, wireless headset microphone for recording teachers as they move about the classroom freely. This approach accommodates various seating arrangements, classroom sizes, and room layouts, and attempts to minimize ambient classroom noise, muffled speech, or classroom interruptions, all factors that reflect the reality of real-world environments.

There are a number of challenges with this work. For one, teacher questions in a classroom differ from traditional question-asking scenarios (e.g., meetings, informal conversations) where the goal of a question is to elicit information and the questioner usually does not know the answer ahead of time. In contrast, rather than information-seeking, the key goal of teacher questions is to assess knowledge and to prime thought and discussion (Nystrand et al., 2003), thereby introducing difficulties in coding questions themselves.

We note that ASR on classroom speech is particularly challenging given the noisy environment that includes classroom disruptions, accidental microphone contact, and sounds from students, chairs, and desks. Previous work on this data yielded WERs ranging from 0.34 to 0.60 (D'Mello et al., 2015), suggesting that we have to contend with rather inaccurate transcripts.

In addition, previous work reviewed in Section 1.1 has focused on human-segmented speech, which is untenable for a fully-automated system. Therefore, our approach uses an automated approach to segment speech, which itself is an imperfect process.

This imperfect pipeline ranging from question coding to ASR to utterance segmentation accurately illustrates the difficulties of detecting questions in real-world environments. Nevertheless, we make several novel contributions while addressing these challenges. First, we implement fully automated methods to process teacher audio into segmented utterances from which we obtain ASR transcriptions. Second, we combine transcriptions from multiple ASR engines to offset the inevitable errors associated with automatically segmenting and transcribing teacher audio. Third, we restrict our feature set to domain-independent natural language features that are more likely to generalize across different school subjects. Finally, we use leave-one-teacher-out cross-validation so that our models generalize across teachers rather than optimizing for individual teachers.

The remainder of the paper is organized as follows. First, we discuss our data collection methods, data pre-processing, feature extraction approach, and our classification models in Section 2. In Section 3, we present our experiments and review key results. We next discuss the implications of our findings and conclude with our future research directions in Section 4.

2 Method

2.1 Data Collection

Data was collected at six rural Wisconsin middle schools during literature, language arts, and civics classes taught by 11 different teachers (three male; eight female). Class sessions lasted between 30 and 90 minutes, depending on the school. A total of 37 classroom sessions were recorded and live-coded on 17 separate days over a period of a year, totaling 32:05 hours of audio.

Each teacher wore a wireless microphone to capture their speech. Based on previous work (D'Mello et al., 2015), a Samson 77 Airline wireless microphone was chosen for its portability, noise-canceling properties, and low-cost. The teacher's speech was captured and saved as a 16 kHz, 16-bit single channel audio file.

2.2 Teacher Utterance Extraction

Teacher speech was segmented into utterances using a two-step voice activity detection (VAD) algorithm (Blanchard et al., 2015). First, the amplitude envelope of the teacher's low-pass filtered speech was passed through a threshold function in 20-millisecond increments. Where the amplitude envelope was above threshold, the teacher was considered to be speaking. Any time speech was detected, that speech was considered part of a *potential utterance*, meaning there was no minimum threshold for how short a potential utterance could be. Potential utterances were coded as complete when no speech was detected for 1,000 milliseconds (1 second).

The thresholds were set low to ensure capture of all speech, but this also caused a high rate of false alarms in the form of non-speech utterances. These false alarms were filtered from the set of potential utterances with the Bing ASR engine (Microsoft, 2014). If the ASR engine rejected a potential utterance then it was determined to not contain any speech. Additionally, any utterances less than 125 milliseconds was removed, as this speech was not considered meaningful.

We empirically validated the effectiveness of this utterance detection approach by manual coding a random subset of 1,000 potential utterances as either containing speech or not. We achieved high levels of both precision (96.3%) and recall (98.6%) and an F_1 score of 0.97. We applied this approach to the full corpus to extract 10,080 utterances from the 37 classroom recordings.

2.3 Question Coding

One limitation of automatically segmented speech is that each utterance may contain multiple questions, or conversely, a question may be spread across multiple utterances (Komatani et al., 2015). This occurs partly because we use both a static amplitude envelope threshold and a constant pause length to segment utterances rather than learning specific thresholds for each teacher. However, the use of a single threshold increases generalizability to new teachers. Regardless of method, voice activity detection is not a fully-solved problem and any method is expected to yield some errors.

To address this, we manually coded the 10,080 extracted utterances as "containing a question" or "not containing a question" rather than "question" or "statement." The distinction, though subtle, indicated that a question phrase that is embedded within a large utterance would be coded as "containing a question." Conversely, we also ensured that if a question spans adjacent utterances then each utterance would be coded as "containing a question." We also do not distinguish among different questions types in this initial work.

Our definition of "question" follows coding schemes that are uniquely designed to analyze questions in classroom discourse (Nystrand et al., 2003). Questions are utterances in which the teacher solicits information from a student either procedurally (e.g., *"Is everyone ready?"*), rhetorically (e.g., *"Oh good idea James why don't we just have recess instead of class today"*), or for knowledge assessment/information solicitation purposes (e.g., *"What is the capital of Indiana, Michael?"*). Likewise, the teacher calling on a different student to answer the same question (e.g., *"Nope. Shelby?"*) would also be considered a question, although in some coding schemes, the previous example would be classified as "Turn Eliciting" (Allwood et al., 2007). We do not consider certain cases questions, such as when the teacher calls on a student for other reasons (e.g., to discipline them) or when the teacher reads from a novel in which a character asked a question.

The coders were seven research assistants and researchers whose native language was English. The coders first engaged in a training task by labeling a common evaluation set of 100 utterances. These 100 utterances were manually selected to exemplify difficult cases. Once coding of the evaluation set was completed, the expert coder, who had considerable expertise with classroom discourse and who initially selected and coded the evaluation set, reviewed the codes. Coders were required to achieve a minimal level of agreement with the expert coder (Cohen's kappa, $\kappa = 0.80$). If the agreement was lower than 0.80, then errors were discussed with the coders.

After this training task was completed, the coders coded a subset of utterances from the complete dataset. Coders listened to the utterances in temporal order and assigned a code (question or not) to each based on the words spoken by the teacher, the teachers' tone (e.g., prosody, inflection), and the context of the previous utterance. Coders could also flag an utterance for review by a primary coder, although this was rare. In all, 36% of the 10,080 utterances were coded as containing questions. A random subset of 117 utterances from the full dataset were selected and coded by the expert coder. Overall the coders and the primary coder obtained an agreement of $\kappa = 0.85$.

2.4 Automatic Speech Recognition (ASR)

We used the Bing and AT&T Watson ASR systems (Microsoft, 2014; Goffin et al., 2005), based on evaluation in previous work (Blanchard, 2015; D'Mello et al., 2015). For both of these systems, individual utterances were submitted to the engine for transcription. We also considered the Azure Speech API (Microsoft, 2016) which processes a full-length classroom recording to produce a set of time-stamped words, from which we reconstructed the individual utterances.

We evaluated the performance of the ASR engines on a random subset of 1,000 utterances. We considered two metrics: word error rate (WER), which accounts for word order between ASR and human transcripts, and simple word overlap (SWO), a metric that does not consider word order. WER was computed by summing the number of substitutions, deletions, and insertions required to transform the human transcript into the computer transcript, divided by the number of words in the human transcript. SWO was computed by dividing the number of words that appear in both the human and computer transcripts by the number of words in the human transcript. Table 1 presents the WER and SWO for the three ASR systems, where we note moderate accuracy given the complexity of the task in that we are processing conversational speech recorded in a noisy naturalistic environment.

Table 1. ASR word error rate and simple word overlap averaged by teacher for 1,000 utterances, with standard deviations shown in parentheses.

ASR	WER	SWO
Bing Speech	0.45 (0.10)	0.55 (0.06)
AT&T Watson	0.63 (0.11)	0.42 (0.11)
Azure Speech	0.49 (0.07)	0.64 (0.16)

2.5 Model Building

We trained supervised classification models to predict if utterances contained a question or not (as defined in Section 2.3).

Feature extraction. In this work we focused on a small set of domain-general features rather than word specific models, such as n-grams or parse trees. Because we sampled many different teachers and classes, the topics covered vary significantly between class sessions, and a content-heavy approach would likely overfit to specific topics. This decision helps emphasize generalizability across topics as our models are intended to be applicable to class sessions that discuss topics not covered in the training set.

Features (N = 37) were generated using the ASR transcripts for each utterance obtained from Bing Speech, AT&T Watson, and Azure Speech engines. Of these, 34 features were obtained by processing each utterance with the Brill Tagger (Brill, 1992) and analyzing each token (Olney et al., 2003). Features included the presence or absence of certain words (e.g., *what, why, how)*, categories of words (e.g., definition, comparison), or part-of-speech tags (e.g., presence of nouns, presence of adjectives). These features were previously used to detect domain-independent question properties from human-transcribed questions (Samei et al., 2014). We supplemented these features with three additional features: proper nouns (e.g., student names), pronouns associated with uptake (teacher questions that incorporate student responses), and pronouns not associated with uptake, as recommended by a domain expert on teacher questions.

We extracted all 37 NLP features for each ASR transcription, yielding three feature sets. We also created a fourth set of NLP features that combined the features from the individual ASRs. For this set, each feature value was taken as the proportion of each features' appearances in the three ASR outputs. For example, if a feature was present in an utterance as transcribed by Bing and AT&T, but not Azure, then the feature's value would be 0.67.

Oversampling. We supplemented our imbalanced training data with synthetic instances (for the minority question class) generated with the Synthetic Minority Over-sampling Technique (SMOTE) algorithm (Chawla et al., 2011). Class distributions in the testing set were preserved.

Classification and validation. We considered the following classifiers: logistic regression, random forest, J48 decision tree, J48 with Bagging, Bayesian network, k-nearest neighbor (k = 7, 9, and 11), and J48 decision tree, using implementations from the WEKA toolkit (Hall et al., 2009). For each classifier, we tested with and without wrapping the classifiers with MetaCost, a cost-sensitive procedure for imbalanced datasets that assigned a higher penalty (weights of 2 or 4) to misclassification of the question class.

Classification models were validated using a leave-one-teacher-out cross-validation technique, in which models were built on data from 10 teachers (training set) and validated on the held-out teacher (testing set). The process was repeated until each teacher was included in the testing set.

This cross-validation technique tests the potential of our models to generalize to unseen teachers both in terms of acoustic variability and in terms of variability in question asking.

3 Results

3.1 Classification Accuracy

In Table 2 we present the best performing classification model for each ASR and their combination based on the F_1 score for the question class (target metric). Table 2 includes the F_1 score for the question class, the F_1 score for the non-question class, and the overall weighted F_1 score. The best-performing individual ASR models were each Bayesian networks. The combined model was built with J48 with Bagging and with MetaCost (miss weight of 2). We show the confusion matrix for this model in Table 3.

Table 2. Results of best models for question detection.

Model	F_1 Question	F_1 Not-Question	F_1 Overall
AT&T	0.52	0.68	0.63
Azure	0.53	0.67	0.63
Bing	0.54	0.67	0.63
Combined	**0.59**	**0.74**	**0.69**

Table 3. Confusion matrix of combined ASR model for Question (Q) and Utterances (U).

n	Actual	Predicted	
		Q	U
3586	Q	2273	1313
6494	U	1946	4548

Overall, these results show a general consistency between the models using individual ASR transcriptions, which imply the relative success of each despite the differences in WER. Furthermore, we note that the combination of three ASR transcriptions resulted in improved performance compared to models built using individual ASR transcriptions. Using the combined model, we achieved slightly higher recall (0.63) than precision (0.57) for identifying questions.

We also compared our results to a chance model that assigned the question label at the same rate (42%) as our model, but did so randomly across 10,000 iterations. We consider this approach to computing chance to be more informative than a naïve minority baseline model (as the class of interest is the minority class) that would yield perfect recall but negligible precision. The chance model had a mean recall of 0.42 and precision of 0.36 for the question class. From these averages, we calculated the chance F_1 score for questions (0.39). Our combined model achieved an F_1 score of 0.59 for the question class, which represents a 51% improvement over chance.

3.2 Feature Analysis

We explored the utility of the individual features using forward stepwise feature selection (Draper et al., 1966). For each individual ASR engine we identified the features selected in all folds of the teacher-level cross-validation procedure. We found four of the features were used in all three of the ASR models: *how*, *what*, *why*, and *wh-* (any word that starts with "*wh-*", including *who* and *where*). The selection of these features across the different ASR feature sets is perhaps unsurprising, but these results confirm that identifying question words are paramount for detecting questions regardless of the specific ASR engine.

3.3 Consistency Across Class-Sessions

The models were trained using leave-one-teacher-out cross-validation, but we perform additional post-hoc analyses exploring the model's accuracy across the 37 individual class sessions. This analysis allows an investigation of the stability of our model for individual class sessions, which will be essential for generalizability to future class sessions and topics.

Question Rate Analysis. Some applications only require an overall indication of the rate of question asking rather than identifying individual questions. To analyze the use of our model to these applications, we compared the proportion of predicted to actual questions for each class session (see Figure 1). There was a mean absolute difference of 0.08 (SD = 0.06) in the predicted proportion of questions compared to the true proportion (Pearson's r = 0.85). This small difference and strong correlation indicates that even though there are misclassifications at the level of individual utterances, the error rate is ameliorated at the session level, indicating the model performs well at correctly predicting the proportion of questions in a class session.

Performance Across Class-Sessions. Figure 2 presents a histogram of F_1 scores for the question class by class session. We note that model accuracy was evenly spread across class sessions rather than being concentrated on the tails (which would indicate a skewed distribution). In particular, 25% of the class sessions scored below 0.47

and 25% of the sessions scored above 0.66, yielding an interquartile range of 0.47 to 0.66. Encouragingly, the poorest performing class session still yielded an F_1 score of 0.33 while the best class session had a score of 0.84.

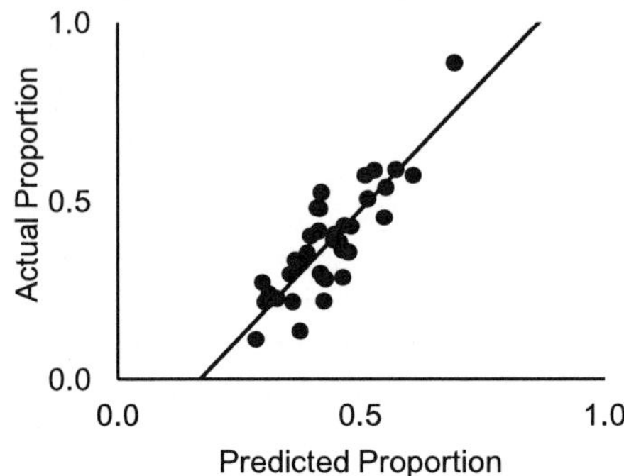

Figure 1. Proportion of predicted to actual questions in each class session.

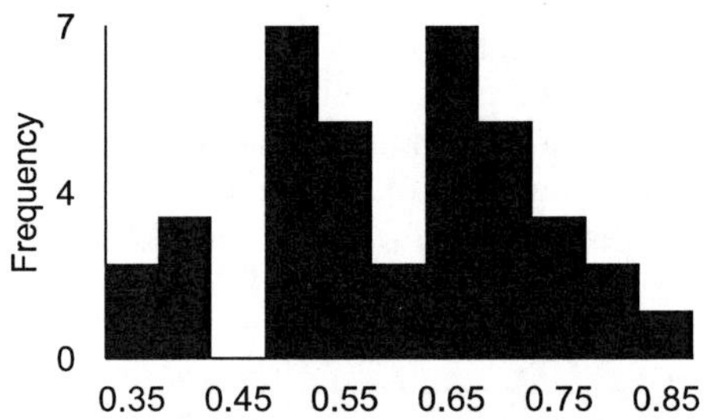

Figure 2. Histogram of F_1 scores for the question class by class-session.

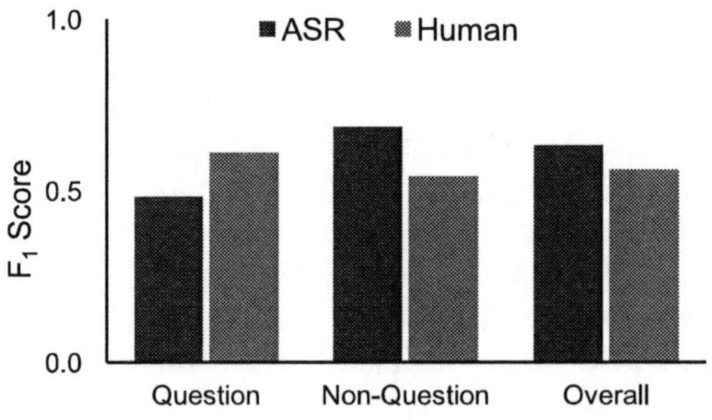

Figure 3. Models (ASR vs. human) built on 1,000 utterance subset.

3.4 Effects of ASR Errors

We explored how our models were affected by ASR errors. We built models on the subset of 1,000 utterances that we manually transcribed to evaluate WER and SWO of the ASRs in Section 2.4. Specifically, we retrained the J48 classifier reported in Section 3.1 on this data subset, using the combination of features from the three individual ASRs, comparing it to the same model built

Table 4. Confusion matrix showing a comparison of the ASR and Human models.

Actual		Predicted			
		Human Q	Human Q	Human NQ	Human NQ
Priors		ASR Q	ASR NQ	ASR Q	ASR NQ
0.30	Q	**0.15**	*0.07*	*0.03*	**0.05**
0.70	NQ	**0.18**	*0.16*	*0.09*	**0.28**

Note: Q indicates a question and NQ indicates a non-question. Bolded numbers indicate both models agreed while italicized numbers indicate disagreement.

using features extracted from the human transcriptions. The results of leave-one-teacher-out cross-validation are shown in Figure 3.

We must note that direct comparisons of models built on this subset of 1,000 instances with those built on the full data set (Section 3.1) are improper due to significantly fewer training instances in the former. In general, the human model achieved a higher F_1 for the question class compared to the combined ASR model, while the ASR model has a higher F_1 for the non-question class. We also note the tendency of the human model to over-predict questions, potentially resulting from the use of the MetaCost wrapper.

We further compared the predictions of the human and ASR models and observed that both models agreed in classifying utterances, either correctly or incorrectly, as questions and non-questions 65% of the time (see Table 4). They differed 35% of the time, disagreeing 25% of the time for non-questions and 10% of the time for questions. We note that, when the models disagreed, the human model was more likely to classify a non-question as a question (16%) compared to the ASR (9%), presumably due to its tendency to over-predict questions as noted above.

3.5 Analysis of Classification Errors

We selected a random sample of 100 incorrectly classified utterances using the human transcription model (so as to eliminate ASR errors as a potential explanation) to study possible causes of errors. We identified 44 utterances with common error patterns, whereas the cause of the error could not be easy discerned for the remaining 56 incorrectly classified utterances.

Out of the 44 errors, 24 were misses (questions predicted as non-questions). In 5 of these 24 misses, the question was only one part of the utterance (e.g., *"If I could just get this thing to open I'd be fine. Can you do it?"*). The remaining 19 errors yielded examples of question types that may be problematic for our model. These include calling on individual students (e.g., *"Sam?"*), rhetorical questions (e.g., *"musical practice,*

right?"), implicit questions requiring clues from previous context (e.g., *"why did she say that?"*), fill-in-the-blank questions (e.g., *"Madagascar and _______?"*), and students being directed to speak, rather than being asked a traditional question (e.g., *"tell us about it"*).

Additionally, there were 20 false alarms (non-questions incorrectly classified as questions). Nine of these non-questions were offhand/casual statements made by teachers (*"I don't know if you guys should call him that or not"* said jokingly) while interacting with student, indicative of the difficulty of classifying questions in contexts with informal dialogue. Five short utterances may have been classified incorrectly because of limited context (e.g., *"good."* vs. *"good?"*, *"okay."* vs. *"okay?"*). Three misclassifications involved teachers reading directly from a book, (e.g., quoting a passage from a novel in which a character asks a question). Additionally, there was one aborted statement and one aborted question, in which the teacher started to say something but changed course mid-sentence (e.g., *"No wh- ... put that away!"*). Finally, in another case, the teacher paused midsentence, resulting in a very short utterance that left the full intent of the statement to the next utterance (e.g., *"Juliet reversed course, the nurse..."*). This last example highlights the difficulties of classifying questions with imperfect sentence boundaries (see Section 2.3) as is the case with our data. In general, 15 of the 20 false alarms were associated with changes in speaking style from traditional teacher speech in classrooms.

4 General Discussion

The importance of teacher questions in classrooms is widely acknowledged in both policy (e.g., Common Core State Standards for Speaking and Listening (2010)) and research (Nystrand and Gamoran, 1991; Applebee et al., 2003; Nystrand et al., 2003). Teacher questions play a central role in student engagement and achievement, suggesting that automating the detection of questions might have important consequences for both research on effective instructional strategies and on teacher professional development. Thus, our current work centers on a fully-automated process for predicting teacher questions in a noisy real-world classroom environment, using only a full-length audio recording of teacher speech.

4.1 Main Findings

We present encouraging results with our automated processes, consisting of VAD to automatically segment teacher speech, ASR transcriptions, NLP features, and machine learning. In particular, our question detection models excel in aggregation of utterances: the detected proportion of questions per class strongly correlates with the proportion of actual questions in the classroom (Pearson's r = 0.85). In addition, our models provided promising results in the detection of individual questions, although further refinement is needed. Both types of analysis are useful in providing formative feedback to teachers, at coarse- and fine-grained levels, respectively.

A key contribution of our work over previous research is that our models were trained and tested on automatically-, and thus imperfectly-, segmented utterances. This extends the work of (Orosanu and Jouvet, 2015) which artificially explored perturbations of a subset of utterance boundaries using the automatic detection of silence within human-segmented spoken sentences. To our knowledge, our work is the first to detect spoken questions using a fully automated process. Our best model achieved an overall F_1 score of 0.69 and an F_1 score of 0.59 for the question class. This represents a substantial 37% improvement in question detection accuracy over a recent state-of-the-art model (Boakye et al., 2009) that reported an overall F_1 of 0.50; the authors do not report F_1 for the question class so the comparison is based on the overall F_1.

We validated our models using leave-one-teacher-out cross-validation, demonstrating generalizability of our approach across teachers in this dataset. Furthermore, we analyzed model performance by class session, finding our model was consistent across class sessions, an encouraging result supporting our goals of domain-independent question detection.

We also explored the differences between models using ASR transcriptions and using human transcriptions. Overall, the results were quite comparable suggesting that imperfect ASR need not be a barrier against automated question detection in live classrooms.

4.2 Limitations and Future Work

This study is not without limitations. We designed our approach to avoid overfitting to specific classes, teachers, or schools. However, all of our recordings were collected in Wisconsin, a state that uses the Common Core standard. It is possible that the Common Core may impose aspects of a particular style of teaching that our models may overfit. Similarly, although we used speaker-independent ASR and teacher-independent validation techniques to improve generalizability to new teachers, our sample of teachers are from a single region with traditional Midwestern accents and dialects. Therefore, broader generalizability across the U.S. and beyond remains to be seen.

We acknowledge that our method for teacher utterance segmentation may potentially be improved using proposed techniques in related works. Komatani et al. (2015) has explored detecting and merging utterances segmented mid-sentence, allowing analysis to take place on a full sentence, rather than a fragment, which may improve question detection by merging instances in which questions were split. An alternative approach would be to automatically detect sentence boundaries within utterances, and extract features from each detected sentence.

Our analysis of errors in Section 3.5 suggests that acoustic and contextual features may be needed to capture difficulty to classify questions. Additionally, related work on question detection (see Section 1.1) suggested that acoustic, contextual, and temporal features (Boakye et al., 2009) may aid in the detection of questions. We will explore this in future work to determine if features capturing these properties will help improve our models for this task. Likewise, we will also explore temporal models, such as conditional random fields and bi-directional long-short-term neural networks, which might better capture questions in the larger context of the classroom dialogue. This temporal analysis may help find sequences of consecutive questions, such as those present in question-and-answer sessions or in classroom discussions.

Further, Raghu et al. (2015) has explored using context to identify non-sentential utterances (NSUs), defined as utterances that are not full sentences but convey complete meaning in context. The identification of NSUs may improve our model's ability to differentiate between difficult cases (e.g., calling on students, saying a student's name for discipline).

In addition to addressing these limitations by collecting a more representative corpus and computing additional features, there are several other directions for future work. Specifically, we will focus on classifying question properties defined by Nystrand and Gameron (2003). While we have explored these properties in previous work (Samei et al., 2014; Samei et al., 2015), that work used perfectly-segmented and human-transcribed question text. We will continue this work using our fully-automatic approach that employs automatic segmentation and ASR transcriptions.

4.3   Concluding Remarks

We took steps towards fully-automated detection of teacher questions in noisy real-world classroom environments. The present contribution is one component of a broader effort to automate the collection and coding of classroom discourse. The automated system is intended to catalyze research in this area and to generate personalized formative feedback to teachers, which enables reflection and improvement of their pedagogy, ultimately leading to increased student engagement and achievement.

5   Acknowledgements

This research was supported by the Institute of Education Sciences (IES) (R305A130030). Any opinions, findings and conclusions, or recommendations expressed in this paper are those of the author and do not represent the views of the IES.

References

Jens Allwood, Loredana Cerrato, Kristiina Jokinen, Costanza Navarretta, and Patrizia Paggio. 2007. The MUMIN coding scheme for the annotation of feedback, turn management and sequencing phenomena. *Language Resources and Evaluation*, 41(3–4):273–287.

Arthur N Applebee, Judith A Langer, Martin Nystrand, and Adam Gamoran. 2003. Discussion-based approaches to developing understanding: Classroom instruction and student performance in middle and high school English. *American Educational Research Journal*, 40(3):685–730.

Isabel L. Beck, Margaret G. McKeown, Cheryl Sandora, Linda Kucan, and Jo Worthy. 1996. Questioning the author: A yearlong classroom implementation to engage students with text. *The Elementary School Journal*:385–414.

Nathaniel Blanchard, Patrick J Donnelly, Andrew M Olney, Borhan Samei, Brooke Ward, Xiaoyi Sun, Sean Kelly, Martin Nystrand, and Sidney K. D'Mello. 2016. Automatic detection of teacher questions from audio in live classrooms. In *Proceedings of the 9th International Conference on Educational Data Mining (EDM 2016),* pages 288–291. International Educational Data Mining Society.

Nathaniel Blanchard, Michael Brady, Andrew Olney, Marci Glaus, Xiaoyi Sun, Martin Nystrand, Borhan Samei, Sean Kelly, and Sidney K. D'Mello. 2015. A Study of automatic speech recognition in noisy classroom environments for automated dialog analysis. In *Proceedings of the 8th International Conference on Educational Data Mining (EDM 2015)*, pages 23-33. International Educational Data Mining Society.

Nathaniel Blanchard, Sidney D'Mello, Martin Nystrand, and Andrew M. Olney. 2015. Automatic classification of question & answer discourse segments from teacher's speech in classrooms. In *Proceedings of the 8th International Conference on Educational Data Mining (EDM 2015),* pages 282–288. International Educational Data Mining Society.

Kofi Boakye, Benoit Favre, and Dilek Hakkani-Tür. 2009. Any questions? Automatic question detection in meetings. In *Proceedings of the IEEE Workshop on Automatic Speech Recognition & Understanding, (ASRU),* pages 485–489. IEEE.

Eric Brill. 1992. A simple rule-based part of speech tagger. In *Proceedings of the Workshop on Speech and Natural Language,* pages 112–116. Association for Computational Linguistics.

Nitesh V. Chawla, Kevin W. Bowyer, Lawrence O. Hall, and W. Philip Kegelmeyer. 2011. SMOTE: synthetic minority over-sampling technique. *Journal of Artificial Intelligence Research,* 16:321–357.

Sidney K D'Mello, Andrew M Olney, Nathan Blanchard, Borhan Samei, Xiaoyi Sun, Brooke Ward, and Sean Kelly. 2015. Multimodal capture of teacher-student interactions for automated dialogic analysis in live classrooms. In *Proceedings* of the 2015 International Conference on Multimodal Interaction, pages 557–566. ACM.

Norman Richard Draper, Harry Smith, and Elizabeth Pownell. 1966. *Applied regression analysis.* Wiley New York.

Adam Gamoran and Martin Nystrand. 1991. Background and instructional effects on achievement in eighth-grade English and social studies. *Journal of Research on Adolescence*, 1(3):277–300.

Vincent Goffin, Cyril Allauzen, Enrico Bocchieri, Dilek Hakkani-Tür, Andrej Ljolje, Sarangarajan Parthasarathy, Mazin G. Rahim, Giuseppe Riccardi, and Murat Saraclar. 2005. The AT&T WATSON Speech Recognizer. In *Proceedings of the International Conference on Acoustics, Speech, and Signal Processing (ICASSP),* pages 1033–1036. IEEE.

Arthur C. Graesser and Natalie K. Person. 1994. Question asking during tutoring. *American Educational Research Journal*, 31(1):104–137.

Mark Hall, Eibe Frank, Geoffrey Holmes, Bernhard Pfahringer, Peter Reutemann, and Ian H. Witten. 2009. The WEKA Data Mining Software: An Update. *ACM SIGKDD Explorations Newsletter*, 11(1):10–18.

Mary M Juzwik, Carlin Borsheim-Black, Samantha Caughlan, and Anne Heintz. 2013. *Inspiring dialogue: Talking to learn in the English classroom.* Teachers College Press.

Sean Kelly. 2007. Classroom discourse and the distribution of student engagement. *Social Psychology of Education*, 10(3):331–352.

Kazunori Komatani, Naoki Hotta, Satoshi Sato, and Mikio Nakano. 2015. User adaptive restoration for incorrectly segmented utterances in spoken dialogue systems. In *16th Annual Meeting of the Special Interest Group on Discourse and Dialogue*, page 393.

Microsoft. 2014. The Bing Speech Recognition Control. Technical report.

Microsoft. 2016. Azure Speech API. Technical report.

Martin Nystrand. 2006. Research on the role of classroom discourse as it affects reading comprehension. *Research in the Teaching of English*:392–412.

Martin Nystrand and Adam Gamoran. 1991. Instructional discourse, student engagement, and literature achievement. *Research in the Teaching of English*:261–290.

Martin Nystrand, Lawrence L Wu, Adam Gamoran, Susie Zeiser, and Daniel A Long. 2003. Questions in time: Investigating the structure and dynamics of unfolding classroom discourse. *Discourse Processes*, 35(2):135–198.

Andrew Olney, Max Louwerse, Eric Matthews, Johanna Marineau, Heather Hite-Mitchell, and Arthur Graesser. 2003. Utterance classification in AutoTutor. In *Proceedings of the HLT-NAACL 03 Workshop on Building Educational Applications using Natural Language Processing-Volume 2*, pages 1–8. Association for Computational Linguistics.

Luiza Orosanu and Denis Jouvet. 2015. Detection of sentence modality on French automatic speech-to-text transcriptions. In *Proceedings of the International Conference on Natural Language and Speech Processing*.

Dinesh Raghu, Sathish Indurthi, Jitendra Ajmera, and Sachindra Joshi. 2015. A statistical approach for non-sentential utterance resolution for interactive QA system. In *Proceedings of the 16th Annual Meeting of the Special Interest Group on Discourse and Dialogue*, page 335.

Mickael Rouvier, Grégor Dupuy, Paul Gay, Elie Khoury, Teva Merlin, and Sylvain Meignier. 2013. An open-source state-of-the-art toolbox for broadcast news diarization. Technical report.

Borhan Samei, Andrew Olney, Sean Kelly, Martin Nystrand, Sidney D'Mello, Nathan Blanchard, Xiaoyi Sun, Marci Glaus, and Art Graesser. 2014. Domain independent assessment of dialogic properties of classroom discourse. In *Proceedings of the 7th International Conference on Educational Data Mining (EDM 2014)* pages 233-236. International Educational Data Mining Society.

Borhan Samei, Andrew M Olney, Sean Kelly, Martin Nystrand, Sidney D'Mello, Nathan Blanchard, and Art Graesser. 2015. Modeling classroom discourse: Do models that predict dialogic instruction properties generalize across populations? *Proceedings of the 8th International Conference on Educational Data Mining (EDM 2015),* pages 444-447. International Educational Data Mining Society.

Tanya Stivers and Nick J. Enfield. 2010. A coding scheme for question–response sequences in conversation. *Journal of Pragmatics*, 42(10):2620–2626.

Andreas Stolcke, Noah Coccaro, Rebecca Bates, Paul Taylor, Carol Van Ess-Dykema, Klaus Ries, Elizabeth Shriberg, Daniel Jurafsky, Rachel Martin, and Marie Meteer. 2000. Dialogue act modeling for automatic tagging and recognition of conversational speech. *Computational Linguistics*, 26(3):339–373.

A Framework for the Automatic Inference
of Stochastic Turn-Taking Styles

Kornel Laskowski

Carnegie Mellon University, Pittsburgh PA, USA

Voci Technologies, Inc., Pittsburgh PA, USA

Abstract

Conversant-independent stochastic turn-taking (STT) models generally benefit from additional training data. However, conversants are patently not identical in turn-taking style: recent research has shown that conversant-specific models can be used to refractively detect some conversants in unseen conversations. The current work explores an unsupervised framework for studying turn-taking style variability. First, within a verification framework using an information-theoretic model distance, sides cluster by conversant more often than not. Second, multi-dimensional scaling onto low-dimensional subspaces appears capable of preserving distance. These observations suggest that, for many speakers, turn-taking style as characterized by time-independent STT models is a stable attribute, which may be correlated with other stable speaker attributes such as personality. The exploratory techniques presented stand to benefit speaker diarization technology, dialogue agent design, and automated psychological diagnosis.

1 Introduction

Turn-taking is an inherent characteristic of spoken conversation. Among models of turn-taking (Jaffe et al., 1967; Brady, 1969; Wilson et al., 1984; J. Dabbs and Ruback, 1987; Laskowski, 2010; Laskowski et al., 2011b), those labeled "stochastic turn-taking models" (Wilson et al., 1984) offer a particular advantage: they are independent of the meaning of just what a "turn" might be. This is felicitous, since researchers are in disagreement over the definition. Instead, stochastic turn-taking

(STT) models provide a probability that a specific participant speaks at instant t, conditioned on what that participant and her interlocutors were doing at specific prior instants. Whether her speaking constitutes something that might be called a "turn" is not germane to the applicability of STT models.

In their most commonly studied form (Jaffe et al., 1967; Brady, 1969; Laskowski, 2010), STT models condition their estimates on a history that consists exclusively of binary speech/non-speech variables; the extension to more complex characterizations of the past have been studied (Laskowski, 2012) but comprise the minority. In this binary-feature mode of operation, STT models ablate from conversations the overwhelming majority of the overt information contained in them, including topic, choice of words, language spoken, intonation, stress, voice quality, and voice itself, leaving only speaker-attributed chronograms (Chapple, 1949) of binary-valued behavior. This is a strength particular to STT models: they are language-, topic-, and text- agnostic, and therefore stand to form a universal framework for comparison of conversational behavior, where other methods would need to be extended to cross language, topic, and speech usage boundaries.

Given the paucity of information contained in chronograms, however, it is surprising that they have been efficiently exploited in the supervised tasks of conversation-type inference, participant-role inference, social status inference, and even identity inference. The current article aims to extend understanding of STT models in an unsupervised way, by starting from a theoretically sound distance metric between models of individual, interlocutor-contextualized conversation sides. In the space induced by these distances, experiments and analyses are performed which aim to answer a fundamental question: *Do people behave self-consistently, across disparate longitudinal obser-*

Proceedings of the SIGDIAL 2016 Conference, pages 202–211,
Los Angeles, USA, 13-15 September 2016. ©2016 Association for Computational Linguistics

vations, in terms of their turn-taking preferences? (Self-consistency *within* conversations was studied indirectly in (Laskowski et al., 2011b).) To provide an answer, between-person scatter is compared to within-person scatter, and accounts are sought for both types of variability. The findings reveal that models of persons are in fact self-consistent on average, and that, therefore, both (1) the persons they model are self-consistent, and (2) the modeling framework presented here is capable of capturing that self-consistency, while simultaneously differentiating among persons. The work has important implications for social psychology, diarization technology, and dialogue system design.

2 Data

The data used in this work was drawn from the ICSI Meeting Corpus (Janin et al., 2003), which consists of 75 multi-party meetings involving naturally occurring, spontaneous speech. It has been claimed that the meetings would have taken place even if they were not being recorded.

DATASET as defined here is limited to all 29 of the Bmr meetings, i.e. those held by the group of 15 researchers working on the Meeting Recorder project at ICSI. Not all 15 persons participated in every meeting; each of the 29 meetings was attended by an average of 6.8 persons. The total number of conversation *sides* in DATASET is 197. The distribution of sides per participant is shown in Figure 1.

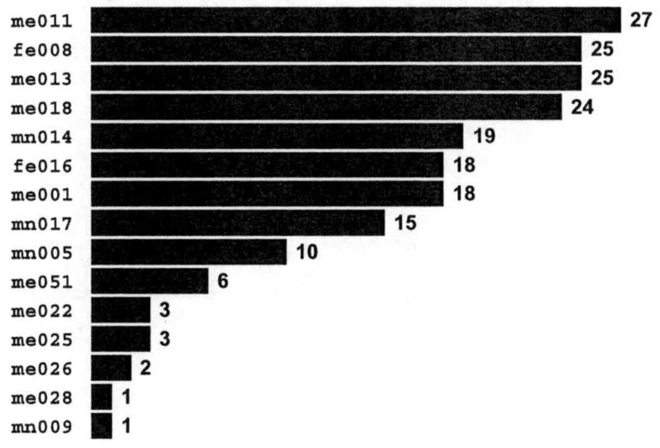

Figure 1: The number of sides in DATASET contributed by each of its 15 participants.

Each meeting in the ICSI Meeting Corpus contains an interval of time (at the beginning or end of the meeting) marked as `Digits`, used for microphone calibration. This interval was excluded for the current purposes, as it does not involve conversation. Each recording was left with between 22.8 and 74.5 minutes of data, with an average of 48.4 minutes.

3 Methodology

3.1 Chronograms

From each meeting C in DATASET, a speech/non-speech chronogram (Chapple, 1949) was constructed, designated by $\mathbf{Q}$. $\mathbf{Q}$ is a matrix whose entries are one of $\{\square, \blacksquare\}$, or equivalently $\{0, 1\}$, designating non-speech or speech respectively. Rows represent the K persons participating in the meeting, while columns represent 100-ms time frames covering its temporal support. The average $\mathbf{Q}$ in DATASET thus contained $K = 7$ rows and $T = 29K$ columns.

The cell in row k and columnt t of every $\mathbf{Q}$ was populated, by a value of $\square$ or $\blacksquare$, by inspecting the forced alignments to the manually transcribed speech attributed to the kth speaker of the corresponding meeting. The transcriptions, attributions, and alignments had been made available by ICSI in (Shriberg et al., 2004). A frame increment of 100 ms was chosen as in (Laskowski et al., 2011b) and (Laskowski et al., 2011a); this is shorter than the average syllable duration, ensuring that no speech is missed, but longer than the frame step of the recognizer used by ICSI for the forced alignment. This makes the models developed in the current work robust to imprecision in word start and end times.

3.2 Stochastic Turn-Taking Models

The models used in the current work are probabilistic generative models that, given a chronogram $\mathbf{Q} \in \{\square, \blacksquare\}^{K \times T}$, provide the probability that its kth participant will speak during its tth frame. Participants are most commonly (Jaffe et al., 1967; Brady, 1969; Laskowski et al., 2011b) treated as conditionally independent (or "single-source" in the terminology of (Jaffe et al., 1967)); namely, the probability of speaking at frame t for participant k is independent of what the other $K - 1$ participants do at frame t, but it is conditioned on the joint K-participant history. The history duration, in number of most-recent contiguous frames, is denoted henceforth by τ.

In multi-party conversation, the number K of participants varies from conversation to conversation, leading to a context of variable size. To eliminate this complication, when constructing or accessing the model describing the kth row of chronogram $\mathbf{Q}$, the remaining $K - 1$ rows (representing the kth participant's interlocutors) are collapsed via an inclusive-OR operation, to provide a single "all interlocutors" row. This results in a conditioning history of τ frames of the kth participant, and τ frames of context describing whether any of the kth participant's interlocutors were speaking at instant $t - \tau$ (Laskowski et al., 2011b).

The above method yields a history duration which is independent of K, and lends itself easily to N-gram modeling. The elements of the conditioning history are marshalled into a one-dimensional order, and counts are accumulated as elsewhere for N-grams. This results in a maximum-likelihood (ML) model $p_A(q|h)$ for a sequence denoted A, with $q \in \{\Box, \blacksquare\}$ and h the conditioning history. In (Laskowski et al., 2011b), such models were interpolated with lower-order (smaller-τ) models (Jelinek and Mercer, 1980), yielding smoothed models $\tilde{p}_A(q|h)$. In the absence of smoothing, as in the current work, the order of the elements of the $(2 \times \tau)$-length history is unimportant, provided it is fixed.

3.3 Supervised Modeling

In supervised modeling, a model A is constructed from one or more conversation sides attributed to the same speaker, and then that model is applied to a conversation side B whose speaker is unknown. In this case, a commonly used score between generative model A and sequence B is the *average negative log-likelihood* of the sequence given the model, which is also known as the *conditional cross entropy*:

$$H(p_B(q|h)\|\tilde{p}_A(q|h))$$
$$= -\sum_{h,q} p_B(h,q)\log\tilde{p}_A(q|h) , \quad (1)$$

where $p_B(h,q)$ are the ML joint probabilities observed in sequence B. Equation 1 is often normalized by subtracting the *conditional entropy* (Cover and Thomas, 1991),

$$H(p_B(q|h))$$
$$= -\sum_{h,q} p_B(h,q)\log p_B(q|h) . \quad (2)$$

yielding the *conditional relative entropy* or *conditional Kullback-Leibler divergence* (Cover and

Thomas, 1991):

$$D_{KL}(p_B(q|h)\|\tilde{p}_A(q|h))$$
$$= \sum_{h,q} p_B(h,q)\log\frac{p_B(q|h)}{\tilde{p}_A(q|h)} . \quad (3)$$

For example, in the context of stochastic turn-taking models, Equation 1 was successfully used with zero-normalization of scores (Laskowski, 2014).

3.4 Unsupervised Modeling

In the unsupervised case, a score does not normally compare a sequence B to a model A, but rather a sequence A to a sequence B (or, alternately, a model trained on sequence A to a model trained on sequence B). Because of this symmetry, it is desirable for the score itself to be symmetric; the conditional Kullback-Leibler divergence in Equation 3 does not exhibit this quality and, additionally, is unbounded. It is therefore customary to compute the conditional Jensen-Shannon divergence (Lin, 1991), which for two equal-weight conditional probability models p_A and p_B is given by

$$D_{JS}(p_A(q|h)\|p_B(q|h))$$
$$\equiv \frac{1}{2}D_{KL}(p_B(q|h)\|p(q|h))$$
$$+ \frac{1}{2}D_{KL}(p_A(q|h)\|p(q|h)) . \quad (4)$$

Here, $p(q|h)$ is the "joint-source" (ie. A and B) model; (El-Yaniv et al., 1997) showed that for models of conditional probability, its form is

$$p(q|h) = \lambda_A(h) \cdot p_A(q|h)$$
$$+ \lambda_B(h) \cdot p_B(q|h) , \quad (5)$$

namely that it is the linear interpolation of the two single-source models, with weights given by their relative probabilities of the occurrence of the context h:

$$\lambda_A(h) = \frac{p_A(h)}{p_A(h) + p_B(h)} \quad (6)$$
$$\lambda_B(h) = \frac{p_B(h)}{p_A(h) + p_B(h)} . \quad (7)$$

The *Jensen-Shannon distance*, a score which is both bounded and symmetric, is given by

$$d_{A,B} \equiv \sqrt{D_{JS}(p_A(q|h)\|p_B(q|h))} . \quad (8)$$

Table 1: Leave-one-out (LOO) modified-KNN classification accuracies, using Jensen-Shannon distances between STT models of individual conversation sides in DATASET. K specifies the maximal number of neighbors; τ is the number of 100-ms frames of conditioning history. Each frame contains 2 bits of information: whether the modeled-side participant was speaking, and whether any of that participant's interlocutors were speaking.

K	τ							
	1	2	3	4	5	6	7	8
1	0.37	0.44	0.56	0.54	0.47	0.37	0.18	0.09
3	0.36	0.53	0.51	0.55	0.48	0.37	0.16	0.09
5	0.40	0.53	0.59	0.58	0.49	0.34	0.15	0.07
7	0.40	0.54	0.59	0.57	0.49	0.33	0.16	0.07
9	0.41	0.54	0.57	0.57	0.50	0.33	0.13	0.07
11	0.43	0.55	0.59	0.57	0.52	0.33	0.15	0.08
13	0.43	0.54	*0.60*	0.57	0.54	0.34	0.15	0.09
15	0.45	0.54	*0.60*	0.58	0.54	0.35	0.18	0.10
17	0.45	0.54	0.59	0.59	0.55	0.36	0.20	0.13
19	0.45	0.55	*0.60*	0.58	0.54	0.38	0.21	0.13
25	0.44	0.53	0.57	0.57	0.53	0.38	0.21	0.13

3.5 Modified Nearest-Neighbor Classification

A central goal of the current work is the determination of whether two sequences, produced by the same person in different conversations, are more proximate than are two sequences produced by two different persons. One answer to this question can be provided by classifying sequences based on their proximity, of which the formalization is known as K-nearest neighbor classification (Fix and Hodges, 1951). The input to the algorithm is a symmetric, zero-diagonal distance matrix D, whose entries are pair-wise distances.

Here, a modified version of the algorithm is employed. If the speaker g of the side being classified is known to have produced only $N_g - 1$ other sides in the collection of sides under study, then K is limited to $N_g - 1$ for that classification trial. The use of such side information may be perceived as unfair; however, the aim is diagnostic, and no effort has been made in the current work to normalize the distances in D for local density differences. In addition, it makes little sense to penalize an analysis for those trials whose speakers produced no other sides in DATASET (cf. Section 2). The results of such a diagnostic test can be usefully compared to the outcome of random guessing under the same circumstances.

An alternative approach, consisting of applying clustering to the distance matrix, was also tried; the results yielded similar (albeit more difficult to disentangle) results and are not presented due to space constraints.

3.6 Multidimensional Scaling

Finally, multidimensional scaling (MDS; cf. (Borg and Groenen, 2005) for example) was applied in an attempt to embed models in a low-dimensional space and to facilitate visual analysis. The experiments used the `smacofSym()` function (de Leeuw and Mair, 2009) implementation in R.

4 Results

For a given $\tau \in [1, 2, 3, \ldots, 8]$, each conversation side q_n of the $N = 197$ sides in DATASET was used to train a side-specific maximum likelihood (ML) model θ_n. The distance between every pair of models was then computed using Equation 8, leading to a symmetric, zero-diagonal distance matrix $D \in \mathbb{R}_+^{197 \times 197}$.

4.1 Diagnostic Classification

D was then used within the modified K-nearest neighbor participant-identity classification framework described in Section 3.5. The achieved accuracies are shown in Table 1.

As can be seen, the highest accuracies are obtained for $\tau \in [2, 3, 4, 5]$ with $K > 7$, with an absolute maximum from among those explored of 60%, at $\tau = 3$ and $K = 15$. This is considerably in excess of 11%, the accuracy

Table 2: LOO modified-KNN classification accuracies, using distances computed following multidimensional scaling (MDS) of the distances between STT models of individual conversation sides in DATASET, to 5 dimensions. Compare to Table 1.

K	τ							
	1	2	3	4	5	6	7	8
1	0.37	0.47	0.49	0.56	0.59	0.54	0.55	0.47
3	0.39	0.49	0.57	0.58	0.62	0.61	0.58	0.48
5	0.39	0.46	0.61	0.62	0.65	0.62	0.60	0.52
7	0.40	0.48	0.59	0.63	0.66	0.61	0.59	0.53
9	0.43	0.51	0.58	0.63	0.66	0.62	0.56	0.54
11	0.43	0.49	0.58	0.62	0.68	0.61	0.59	0.53
13	0.43	0.49	0.58	0.63	0.68	0.60	0.60	0.52
15	0.45	0.51	0.57	0.64	0.69	0.61	0.59	0.52
17	0.44	0.52	0.60	0.66	*0.70*	0.63	0.59	0.54
19	0.45	0.53	0.60	0.65	0.69	0.62	0.58	0.54
25	0.44	0.53	0.59	0.65	0.68	0.63	0.59	0.53

achieved by random guessing with the DATASET priors. This result corroborates the findings in (Laskowski, 2014), that participant identities can frequently be inferred from STT models; the difference with (Laskowski, 2014) is that in the latter work, models were trained on same-person *sets* of sides in a training portion of the data, rather than on individual sides, and that the asymmetric conditional cross entropy (Equation 2, with zero-normalization) was used rather than Jensen-Shannon divergence (Equation 4).

4.2 Diagnostic Classification after Scaling

The computed pair-wise Jensen-Shannon distances lie in a space of unknown effective dimensionality; the determination of that effective dimensionality is one of the implicit aims of the current work. To this end, the distances were embedded in a fixed-dimensionality subspace, using multidimensional scaling (MDS) as described in Section 3.6. All 19306 pair-wise distances comprising D were then re-computed from the MDS-derived positions, and the diagnostic experiment of Section 4.1 was repeated. The results for a 5-dimensional subspace are shown in Table 2.

As can be seen, relative to Table 1, MDS to 5 dimensions actually increases the attainable classification accuracy, to 70% at $\tau = 5$ and $K = 17$. This suggests that there is considerable noise in the distance estimates, and that scaling effectively collapses some of that variability. The accuracy-maximizing number of dimensions, whose identification is beyond the scope of the current work,

is expected to be specific to any particular data set. However, it is notable that for DATASET this "elimination of unwanted variance" occurs for the higher-complexity ($\tau > 2$) models; distances computed using these are more likely to be noisy that those computed using simpler models, for fixed conversation-side durations. Since the $\tau = 8$ context contains the $\tau = 5$ context, this suggests that the duration of the conversations studied here, between 22.8 and 74.5 minutes, may be insufficient to infer robust long-conditioning-history models.

Similar experiments were performed after MDS scaling to each of $\{4, 3, 2, 1\}$ dimensions. The results are not shown due to space constraints. A summary of the maximum achieved accuracy in each case is depicted in Figure 2.

The figure shows that with each reduction of dimensionality of the embedding subspace, by one additional dimension, the maximum achievable accuracy falls by an increasing amount. Although for a one-dimensional subspace the accuracy of 35% is still considerably above chance (11%), it is already (just) less than halfway to the accuracy achieved without scaling (60%).

At 3 dimensions, the accuracy of 58% is almost the same as that achieved without scaling; it occurs at $\tau = 6$ and $K = 17$ (not shown). This suggests that the relative magnitudes of the distances are preserved in a continuous small-dimensional space, and may have implications for understanding what STT models actually learn. For example, each of the dimensions may be strongly correlated

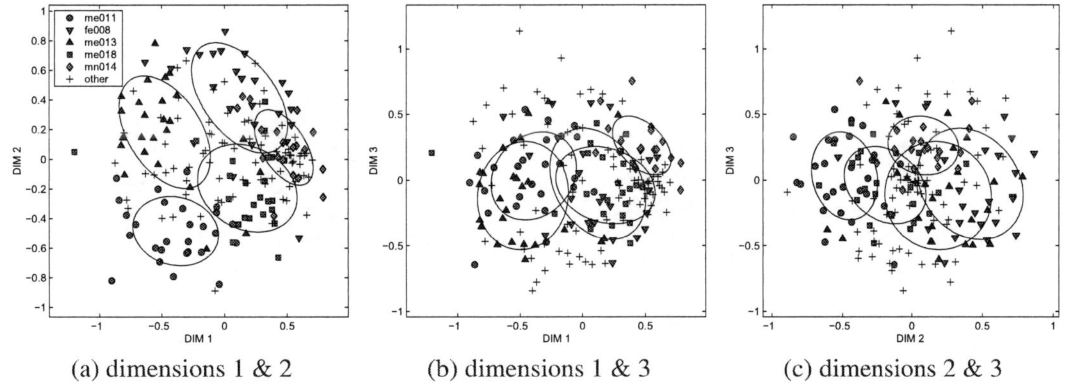

<table>
<tr><td>(a) dimensions 1 & 2</td><td>(b) dimensions 1 & 3</td><td>(c) dimensions 2 & 3</td></tr>
</table>

Figure 3: Positions of 197 models, each of one conversation side in DATASET, as inferred using a Jensen-Shannon distance matrix and multidimensional scaling (MDS) to 3 dimensions. Sides produced by the five most frequently-occurring persons (cf. Section 2) are identified explicitly, together with ellipses representing projections of the corresponding 50% error ellipsoid.

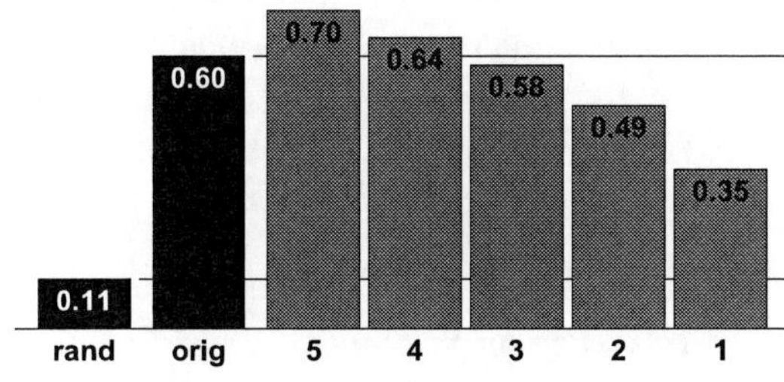

Figure 2: Maximum achieved LOO modified-KNN classification accuracies, using distances computed following MDS down to $[5, 4, 3, 2, 1]$ dimensions of the distances between STT models of individual conversation sides in DATASET. The accuracies are compared to the maximum accuracy achieved using unscaled distances ("orig") and random guessing with actual LOO priors ("rand").

with an independently measurable human trait or role trait. In that case, such traits could be used to index STT models, for both generation and recognition purposes in multi-party conversational settings.

4.3 Model Subspace Visualization

It is serendipitous that, for the data set under investigation, three dimensions suffice to yield a good approximation of the accuracy achievable without scaling. A three-dimensional space is considerably easier to inspect visually, and to understand, than are higher-dimensional spaces. Figure 3 shows the MDS-derived locations, two di-

mensions at a time. The 197 datapoints, representing models of individual conversation sides, are seen to comprise a cloud with heterogenous, locally clumpy density. The determinant of the total scatter matrix, given these inferred positions, is 2.74×10^3.

The determinants of the between-class scatter matrix and the within-class scatter matrix, given the model positions shown in Figure 3, are 3.29×10^3 and 2.86×10^3, respectively. It appears from these numbers that the variability between different-person sides is on average larger than the variability between same-person sides, which in turn suggests that people exhibit low variability — even across longitudinal spans of many months — relative to what differentiates them from others.

5 Discussion

5.1 Intra-Person Variability

It is relevant to try to determine whether the variability observed among models of the same person are due to actual variability of behavior or to measurement error. One source of measurement error could be the relative duration of conversations, leading to unequally (under)trained models. Figure 4 depicts the five most frequent participants in DATASET, at the same positions as in Figure 3(a), with marker size indicative of the duration of observation.

It can be seen that, broadly, shorter-duration conversations yield models which lie at the periphery of the error ellipses. This indicates that — were conversations longer or models more par-

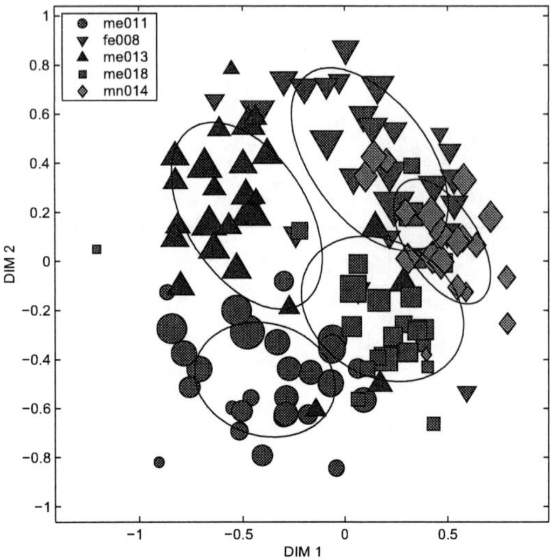
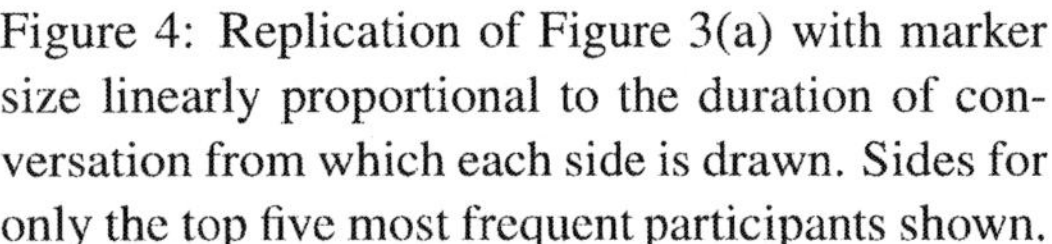
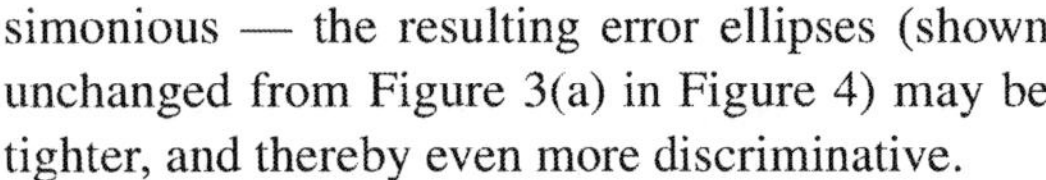
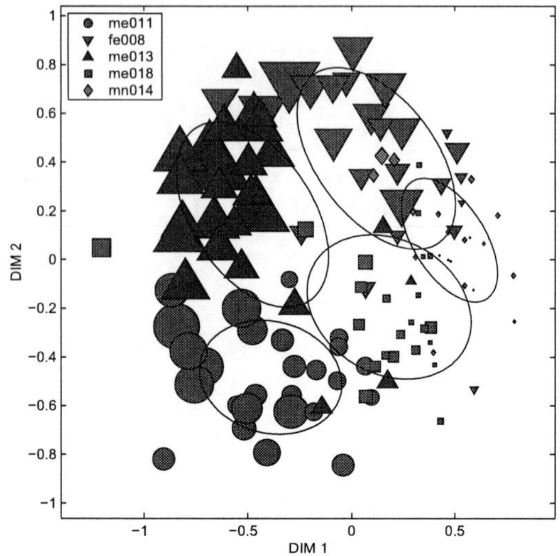

Figure 4: Replication of Figure 3(a) with marker size linearly proportional to the duration of conversation from which each side is drawn. Sides for only the top five most frequent participants shown.

Figure 5: Replication of Figure 3(a) with marker size linearly proportional to the amount of speech observed for each side. Sides for only the top five most frequent participants shown.

simonious — the resulting error ellipses (shown unchanged from Figure 3(a) in Figure 4) may be tighter, and thereby even more discriminative.

A second potential source of intra-person variability may be not just the duration of observation (i.e. the duration of conversation), but how talkative a person is during a specific conversation. Although the models employed here make no mathematical distinction between speaking and not speaking, in multi-party turn-taking the average participant speaks for only a minority of time, making speaking (versus not speaking) a distinctively marked behavior. Figure 5 is like Figure 4, but marker size is indicative of the amount of speech observed for each side.

Figure 5 shows that points lying in the bottom right of the figure represent low quantities of speech per side, globally. This appears to be true for individual speakers separately, particularly for the top three most frequent participants (and me013 most markedly). Since the ellipses appear cigar-shaped, fanning out from the bottom right, these observations suggest that when given the opportunity to speak a lot, participant models "move" to the upper left where they may be even further apart. They also suggest that a quantity encoded in the plane of the first and second MDS dimensions ("DIM1" and "DIM2" in the figure) is the proportion of speech produced by each person,

or their "talkativity".

5.2 Inter-Person Variability

A source of established (Laskowski et al., 2008) variability in turn-taking models trained using the ICSI Meeting Corpus is the relative seniority of participants within a group. (Laskowski et al., 2008) used the self-reported Education level. Figure 6 retains the topology shown in Figure 3(a), but markers represent the educational level of individual participants in DATASET. It can be seen that students (Undergrad and Grad) occupy exclusively the lower half in the diagram, while Postdoc and Professor are found predominantly in the upper half, but in separate clusters. Persons of type PhD exhibit no such leanings.

Figure 6 suggests that education level is indeed discriminated by the STT-model topology inferred via MDS. (Laskowski et al., 2008) observed that despite the fact that persons of type Professor spoke a lot, they appeared to avoid overlap with persons of type Undergrad. Such tendencies are most likely the result of social roles within the organization, and not of educational level per se, but role and education level are probably very correlated in an academic setting. It may be tentatively concluded that the ("DIM 1","DIM 2") plane also encodes, in addition to each person's "talkativity" (cf. Subsection 5.1), their tendency to initiate and terminate talk in overlap.

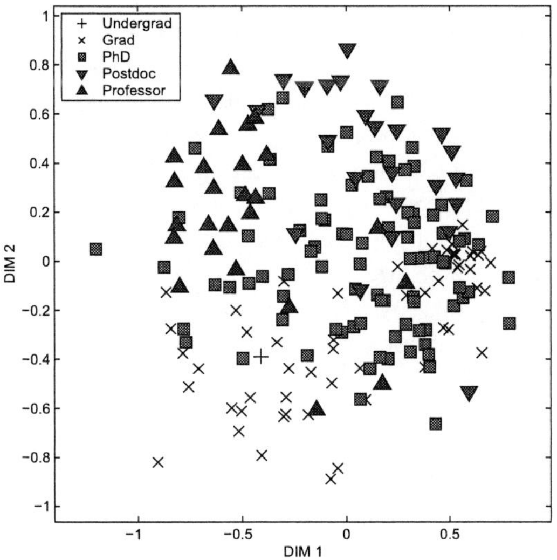

Figure 6: Replication of Figure 3(a) with marker shape denoting the self-reported education level of each side.

It should be noted that, unlike the measurement of intra-person variability, the measurement of inter-person variability is likely a function of the size of the group of people studied. As described in Section 2, the group considered here consists of 15 individuals, some of which participated in only a handful of conversations. For larger groups, it can be expected that — if models represent interaction styles — inter-person variability under a fixed model order and a fixed observation duration will decrease, since nothing a priori prevents multiple individuals from interacting using the same or similar-enough style. Since intra-person variability is independent of the number of other persons considered, it is expected to remain constant under group resizing. The ratio of the inter-person variability to the intra-person variability is therefore likely to decrease with increasingly larger group sizes, when the model complexity and observational duration remain constant.

5.3 Training Speaker-Independent Models

That within-person SST-model variability can be smaller than between-person variability, as discovered in the dataset used in the current study, has important consequences for training broad STT models, intended to be applicable to a wide variety of domains and conversational interaction styles. The results presented indicate that including more training data, without careful consideration of its interaction-style content, may bias the model towards the styles present in the training data and therefore away from the styles in test data — since they *can* be so different. In this sense, the results corroborate earlier, similar findings for domain and topic variability in language modeling within automatic speech recognition.

5.4 Potential Impact and Applications

Over and above the immediate recommendations for the training of STT models, the results obtained in the current study may have several consequences for at least three research areas.

An understanding of the contexts in which participants to conversation choose to vocalize can usefully inform the construction of speaker diarization systems. Current state-of-the-art diarization technology, as used in the transcription of far-field recordings of multi-party meetings, over-segments the temporal support of the recorded track and then performs agglomerative hierarchical clustering using spectral or voice-print similarity. The prior knowledge used in these systems consists of minimal duration constraints on intervals of single-party talk, as well as the assumption that each instant is associated with exactly one participant speaking. The detection of overlap (or of simultaneous vocalization by more than one speaker), where performed, is generally treated as a post-processing step. Information regarding consistent, participant-specific tendencies in the temporal deployment of talk — the subject of the current study — do not currently feature in any way in the assumptions or priors of today's diarization systems.

Second, dialogue system design can benefit from the results presented, particularly those systems which are conversational and whose behavior is intended to be more natural than that of simple human-query-driven information portals. The confirmation that humans exhibit self-consistency in their temporal deployment of speech, which also makes them different from other people, means that the detection of their style and an orientation to it will result in better predictions, requiring fewer resolutions. If that orientation is perceivable to the human user, the system may appear to the user as more human itself. An additional dimension of human-likeness may be inadvertently communicated by the system if it has its own, self-consistent and differentiable style, which is syntonic with its designed conversational role.

Finally, the results in this study have bearing on the design of diagnostic tools for social psychology, the domain for which STT models were originally invented (Chapple, 1949; Jaffe et al., 1967). (Chapple, 1949) was concerned with the measurement of conversational traits correlated with work performance, whereas (Jaffe et al., 1967) treated clinical settings. A considerable amount of research in this area had been conducted in the 1970s and 1980s, primarily in the detection of traits or conditions. However, the models were first-order Markovian (corresponding to $\tau = 1$ in the current work) and often relying on analysis frames as small as 20 ms. The findings presented here indicate that useful speaker-discriminating information is contained as far back as 500 ms (with frames of 100 ms and $\tau = 5$, cf. Subsection 4.2), even when models are trained on single conversations which are as short as 22 minutes long. The obtained results may warrant a re-opening of earlier investigations into diagnostic tools for the health industry.

6   Conclusions

That people exhibit a degree of consistency in their conversational behavior agrees with common sense, and should not be particularly surprising. A number of earlier works have successfully correlated identity with turn-taking preferences (Jurafsky et al., 2009; Grothendieck et al., 2011). What the analyses in the current work show — and which is surprising — is that this consistency is present even in the very shallow representation implicit in the so-called stochastic turn-taking models. In this representation, words, boundaries, durations, and prosody are markedly absent; only the frame-level occurrence of party-attributed speech activity is captured, and a definition of "turn" is neither needed nor used. Specifically, results indicate that, for conversations whose duration is 40-minutes on average, longitudinally speaker-discriminative models can be learned for a conditioning history which is only 10 bits long: whether the modeled speaker, and *any* of their interlocutors, were speaking in each of the 5 most recent 100-ms frames. The current study has shown that under these conditions, for groups of 15 people like the ICSI Bmr group, the inferred models exhibit greater between-person variabil-

ity than within-person variability. The conversants under study appear to have behaved self-consistently, across disparate longitudinal observations, in terms of their turn-taking preferences.

The current experiments also demonstrated that a conversation-side embedding in *three* dimensions approximately recovers the Jensen-Shannon distances between 10-bit-context STT models. In this embedding, between-person variability was shown to be smaller for longer conversations, implying that over time people can be observed to converge on interaction styles which are even more self-consistent. Although it is premature to unambiguously ascribe meaning to each of the three dimensions obtained using the ICSI Bmr data, jointly they appear to encode: (1) the proportion of conversation-time spent talking; (2) the inclination to initiate and terminate overlap with others; and (3) role-specific behaviors exhibited by members of a hierarchy (with — in the current work — positions within that hierarchy closely correlated with self-reported education level).

The presented work suggests the possibility of inference of speaker-characterizing conversational interaction styles, as well as the indexing of such interaction styles by points in an embedding space consisting of only a few continuous dimensions. It has immediate bearing on the training of intentionally broad, speaker-independent STT models. Finally, the work has the potential to usefully impact the design of speaker diarization algorithms for multi-human conversation settings, of human-like conversational dialogue systems, and of diagnostic software for the health industry.

7   Acknowledgments

This work was funded in part by the Riksbankens Jubileumsfond (RJ) project *Samtalets Prosodi*. Computing resources at Carnegie Mellon University were made accessible courtesy of Qin Jin and Florian Metze.

References

I. Borg and P. Groenen. 2005. *Modern Multidimensional Scaling: Theory and Applications*. Springer.

P. Brady. 1969. A model for generating on-off speech patterns in two-way conversation. *The Bell System Technical Manual*, 48(9):2445–2472.

E. Chapple. 1949. The Interaction Chronograph: Its evolution and present application. *Personnel*, 25(4):295–307.

T. Cover and J. Thomas, 1991. *Elements of Information Theory*, chapter Entropy, Relative Entropy and Mutual Information (Chapter 2), pages 12–49. John Wiley & Sons, Inc.

J. de Leeuw and P. Mair. 2009. Multidimensional scaling using majorization: SMACOF in R. *Journal of Statistical Software*, 31(3):1–30.

R. El-Yaniv, S. Fine, and N. Tishby. 1997. Agnostic classification of Markovian sequences. In *Proc. Advances in Neural Information Processing Systems (NIPS) 10*, pages 465–471, Denver CO, USA.

E. Fix and J. Hodges. 1951. Discriminatory analysis, nonparametric discrimination: Consistency properties. Technical report, USAF School of Aviation Medicine, Randolph Field TX, USA.

J. Grothendieck, A. Gorin, and N. Borges. 2011. Social correlates of turn-taking style. *Comput. Speech Lang.*, 25(4):789–801, October.

Jr. J. Dabbs and R. Ruback. 1987. Dimensions of group process: Amount and structure of vocal interaction. *Advances in Experimental Social Psychology*, 20:123–169.

J. Jaffe, S. Feldstein, and L. Cassotta. 1967. Markovian models of dialogic time patterns. *Nature*, 216:93–94.

A. Janin, D. Baron, J. Edwards, D. Ellis, D. Gelbart, N. Morgan, B. Peskin, T. Pfau, E. Shriberg, A. Stolcke, and C. Wooters. 2003. The ICSI Meeting Corpus. In *Proc. 28th IEEE International Conference on Acoustics, Speech, and Signal Processing (ICASSP)*, pages 364–367, Hong Kong, China.

F. Jelinek and R. Mercer. 1980. Interpolated estimation of Markov source parameters from sparse data. In *Proc. Workshop on Pattern Recognition in Practice*, Amsterdam, The Netherlands.

D. Jurafsky, R. Ranganath, and D. McFarland. 2009. Extracting social meaning: Identifying interactional style in spoken conversation. In *Proc. Annual Conference of the North American Chapter of the Association for Computational Linguistics*, pages 638–646, Boulder CO, USA.

K. Laskowski, M. Ostendorf, and T. Schultz. 2008. Modeling vocal interaction for text-independent participant characterization in multi-party conversation. In *Proc. 9th ISCA/ACL SIGdial Workshop on Discourse and Dialogue*, Columbus OH, USA.

K. Laskowski, J. Edlund, and M. Heldner. 2011a. Incremental learning and forgetting in stochastic turn-taking models. In *Proc. 12th Annual Conference of the International Speech Communication Association (INTERSPEECH)*, pages 2065–2068, Firenze, Italy.

K. Laskowski, J. Edlund, and M. Heldner. 2011b. A single-port non-parametric model of turn-taking in multi-party conversation. In *Proc. 36th IEEE International Conference on Acoustics, Speech, and Signal Processing (ICASSP)*, pages 5600–5603, Praha, Czech Republic.

K. Laskowski. 2010. Modeling norms of turn-taking in multi-party conversation. In *Proc. 48th Annual Meeting of the Association for Computational Linguistics (ACL)*, pages 999–1008, Uppsala, Sweden.

K. Laskowski. 2012. Exploiting loudness dynamics in stochastic models of turn-taking. In *Proc. 4th IEEE Workshop on Spoken Language Technology (SLT)*, pages 79–84, Miami FL, USA.

K. Laskowski. 2014. On the conversant-specificity of stochastic turn-taking models. In *Proc. 15th Annual Conference of the International Speech Communication Association (INTERSPEECH)*, pages 2026–2030, Singapore.

J. Lin. 1991. Divergence measrures based on the Shannon entropy. *IEEE Trans. Information Theory*, 37(1):145–151.

E. Shriberg, R. Dhillon, S. Bhagat, J. Ang, and H. Carvey. 2004. The ICSI Meeting Recorder Dialog Act (MRDA) Corpus. In *Proc. 5th ISCA/ACL SIGdial Workshop on Discourse and Dialogue*, pages 97–100, Cambridge MA, USA.

T. Wilson, J. Wiemann, and D. Zimmerman. 1984. Models of turn-taking in conversational interaction. *Journal of Language and Social Psychology*, 3(3):159–183.

Talking with ERICA, an autonomous android

Koji Inoue, Pierrick Milhorat, Divesh Lala, Tianyu Zhao, and Tatsuya Kawahara
Graduate school of informatics, Kyoto University, Japan

Abstract

We demonstrate dialogues with an autonomous android ERICA, who has an appearance like a human being. Currently, ERICA plays two social roles: a laboratory guide and a counselor. It is designed to follow the protocols of human dialogue to make the user comfortable: (1) having a chat before the main talk, (2) proactively asking questions, and (3) conveying proper feedbacks. The combination of the human-like appearance and the appropriate behaviors according to her social roles allows for symbiotic human-robot interaction.

1 Introduction

Dialogue systems deployed in various devices such as smartphones and robots have been widely used to assist users in daily life. Although they can reply to users for what they are asked, their behaviors are mechanical and the primary objective of dialogue is efficiency (Wilcock and Jokinen, 2015; Skantze and Johansson, 2015). Users need to adapt their behaviors such as their utterance style for the systems, and thus the observed users' behaviors are different from those in human communication.

In the current ERATO project, an autonomous android ERICA with the appearance of human being is developed. Our goal is to make her behave like a human being and naturally interact with human beings by tightly integrating verbal and non-verbal information. For the moment, we make ERICA play a specific social role according to the conversational situation. Figure 1 illustrates some prospective social roles which could be covered by ERICA. The roles are plotted on the two axes that are in the trade-off relation: roles of speaking and

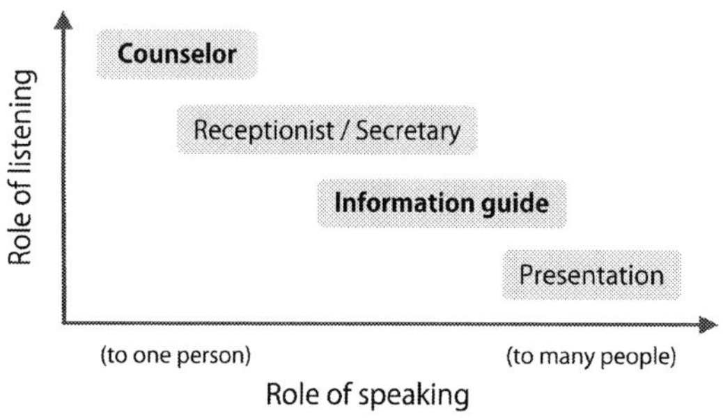

Figure 1: Social roles covered by ERICA

listening. In the long term, ERICA is expected to replace these human beings with comparable performance.

In this demonstration, ERICA plays two social roles: a laboratory guide and a counselor. The scenarios assume that the user meets ERICA for the first time where the user might be nervous. The highlight in the current demonstration is ERICA trying to make the user comfortable by doing the following:

1. Have a personal chat before the main talk to ease their nervousness (ice-breaking)
2. Occasionally make questions from ERICA toward the user when the user does not say anything (ERICA does not only respond to what is asked by the user)
3. Convey proper feedbacks to express that ERICA attentively listens to the user's talk and encourage the user to talk more

ERICA is enhanced by a multi-modal sensing system which consists of a microphone array and a depth camera to realize robust and smooth interaction.

Proceedings of the SIGDIAL 2016 Conference, pages 212–215,
Los Angeles, USA, 13-15 September 2016. ©2016 Association for Computational Linguistics

Figure 2: Android ERICA

2 Android ERICA

An image of ERICA is shown in Figure 2. ERICA is a 23 year-old woman. Her design concept is to contain both the friendliness as an android and a sense of existence as a human being. The appearance of her face and body is artificially produced in reference to characteristics of beautiful ladies.

ERICA mounts 19 active joints inside to move her face, head, shoulder, and back. It is planned to install more motors on her to move her arms and legs in the future. Even now, the flexibility of her face has diversity (including eyebrow, eyelids, lip, eyeballs, and tongue), which enables her to show various facial expressions. ERICA is therefore able to generate not only verbal responses but also non-verbal behaviors such as facial expression, eye-gaze, and nodding, which are used to convey a variety of her emotions.

3 Social roles played by ERICA

In this demonstration, we show the following two scenarios of different social roles played by ERICA.

3.1 Laboratory guide

In the first scenario, ERICA introduces research topics in our laboratory when a guest (user) visits there. We assume that the user meets ERICA for the first time. When people meet each other for the first time, it is common that they have a chat like a self-introduction to know each other well and ease the tension, called ice-breaking, so that they are able to establish rapport, which will result in better communication afterward. ERICA follows this protocol.

In the chatting phase, We provided 31 personal topics that ERICA and the user can discuss, such as their hometowns and hobbies, which will be useful for knowing each other. At first after a greeting, ERICA prompts the user to ask a ques-tion regarding herself. The uttered question is matched against the topic database by a language understanding module which is implemented by a two-step search, a keyword matching and a vector space model. After her reply, she occasionally makes a follow-up question which is related to the current topic. Here, we measure a pause as a cue which triggers this follow-up question. When the user replies to the follow-up question, ERICA says an assessment reply. The dialogue continues with either a new question from the user or a further follow-up question from ERICA. A dialogue example is as follows. Note that **U** and **E** correspond to utterances from the user and ERICA, respectively.

U1 What is your hobby?
E1 My hobbies are watching movies, sports, and cartoons.
(pause)
E2 Do you have the same hobbies as me? (follow-up question)
U2 Yes, I also like watching movies.
E3 Wow, I am happy to hear that. (assessment reply)

Other than questions, the user might say a statement in the chatting dialogue. To deal with this, if no topic is selected in the above matching, ERICA tries to detect a focus word from the user utterance, which is new information in the dialogue, and makes the following feedbacks using the detected focus word.

Partial repeats Simply repeat the focus word, or a phrase containing the focus word

Questions for elaboration Ask a question to elaborate the focus word

Formulaic responses Fixed phrases (e.g. "Oh really!")

Backchannels Short responses suggesting that ERICA is listening to the user (e.g. "okay")

The focus word detection is realized by a CRF-based classification (Yoshino and Kawahara, 2015). A dialogue example is as follows.

U1 I ate a hot dog yesterday.
E1 Hot dog? (partial repeat)
U2 Yeah, I went to a hot dog shop with my family.
E2 Where is the hot dog shop? (question for elaboration)
U3 It is near the central station.

213

E3 Oh really! (formulaic responses)

Once they have gone through a certain number of topics or the user says a specific key-phrase such as "Tell me about your research topics", the dialogue is switched to the laboratory guide phase. In this phase, ERICA presents several research topics, and the user can choose one of them based on his/her interest. This is designed as information navigation (Yoshino and Kawahara, 2015) and implemented by a finite state model. According to the topic selected by the user, ERICA briefly talks about the topic and asks the user if she can continue the topic in detail or not.

3.2 Counselor

Another social role played by ERICA is as a counselor of the user. In recent years, dialogue systems have been actively studied in the field of counseling and diagnoses (DeVault et al., 2014). Compared with them, ERICA can generate more realistic behaviors (not virtual) which could elicit more natural reactions from the interlocutor. The important role for counselors is to attentively listen to the user and give appropriate feedbacks to encourage the user to talk more. One of the listener's feedbacks are backchannels which are a short utterance such as "okay" and "wow." To generate appropriate backchannels, we need to predict the timing and form of the backchannel depending on the user utterance. Backchannel forms have a variety of different functions: one is to encourage the user to keep talking (called "continuer"), and the other is to show reaction to the user utterance (called "assessment") (Clancy et al., 1996).

In this demonstration, ERICA predicts the timing and form of the backchannel using prosodic information extracted from the user utterance. Here, we deal with four types of backchannels: three continuers and one assessment. Prediction of timing and the form is done by a logistic regression model trained with a corpus of counseling dialogue (Yamaguchi et al., 2016). For practical use, we recorded many backchannel voices varied in forms and levels, and choose the appropriate sample in real time. A dialogue example is as follows.

U1 It is nice weather today.
E1 *Un.* (continuer)
U2 It is the best day to play football outside.
E2 *Un, un.* (continuer, stronger than the previous one)

U3 I really like to play football.
    (no backchannel)
U4 I play it with my colleagues every day after work.
E3 *He-!* (assessment)

4 System

In this section, we describe a multi-modal interactive system for ERICA. Figure 3 illustrates its entire configuration. The input sensors consist of a microphone array and a depth camera. These sensors are located around ERICA, not on the android, which increases the degree of freedom of sensor arrangement.

4.1 Speech localization and recognition with microphone array

The microphone array captures multi-channel audio signals and identifies which direction the acoustic signal comes from. Here we use a 16-channel microphone array and adopt the MUltiple SIgnal Classification (MUSIC) method (Schmidt, 1986) to calculate the sound source direction. Afterwards, the input speech is enhanced by using the delay-and-sum beamforming. From the enhanced speech, we calculate prosodic information including fundamental frequency (F0) and power.

The automatic speech recognition (ASR) in ERICA is done by using the enhanced speech. Distant speech recognition elicits more natural human behavior because the user is able to use their arms and hands to show gestures. To realize the distant speech recognition, the enhanced speech is processed by a denoising auto encoder (DAE) to suppress reverberation components and signal distortion. Afterwards, the output speech signal of the DAE is decoded by an acoustic model based on a deep neural network (DNN). The DAE and DNN are trained by using multi-condition speech data so that it is robust against various types of the acoustic environment. It is also necessary for the above processes to be performed in real time.

4.2 Speaker tracking with depth camera

To realize smooth interaction, it is essential for the system to correctly identify who talks to whom and if the user is giving his/her attention toward ERICA (Yu et al., 2015). In this demonstration, we track the user's location and head orientation in the 3D space by using the Kinect v2 sensor. The user localization enables ERICA to spot if there is

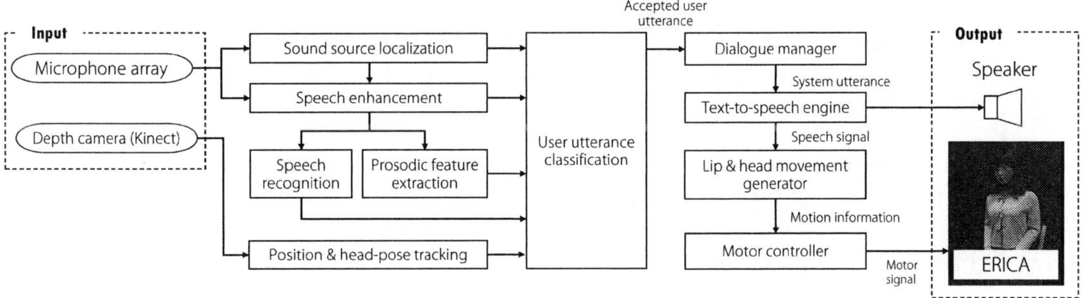

Figure 3: System architecture

a person who wants to interact with her. ERICA identifies if the user is speaking to her by the head orientation. This enables ERICA not to respond to the talking between people, for example when a person introduces ERICA to a guest standing in front of ERICA. ERICA accepts user utterances when the following are met: the user is standing in front of ERICA and looking at ERICA's face, and the sound source is coming from the direction of the user. This function is needed when we conduct a demonstration to many people such as open laboratory events.

4.3 Text-to-speech for ERICA

The speech of ERICA is generated by a text-to-speech engine developed for ERICA. It is based on the unit-selection framework from a database of many conversational-style utterances. It also contains many formulaic expressions and backchannels with a variety of prosodic patterns. At the same time, lip and head movements of ERICA are generated based on the prosodic information of the synthesized speech signals (Ishi et al., 2012; Sakai et al., 2015).

5 Conclusion

We demonstrate dialogues with ERICA who plays the two social roles. The human-like appearance of the android and the appropriate behaviors according to her social roles are combined to realize symbiotic human-robot interaction which is close to human-human interaction.

Acknowledgements

This work was supported by JST ERATO Ishiguro Symbiotic Human-Robot Interaction Project and JSPS KAKENHI Grant Number 15J07337.

References

P. Clancy, S. Thompson, R. Suzuki, and H. Tao. 1996. The conversational use of reactive tokens in English, Japanese, and Mandarin. *Journal of pragmatics*, 26(3):355–387.

D. DeVault, R. Artstein, G. Benn, T. Dey, E. Fast, et al. 2014. SimSensei kiosk: A virtual human interviewer for healthcare decision support. In *Proc. Autonomous Agents and Multi-Agent Systems*, number 1, pages 1061–1068.

C. Ishi, H. Ishiguro, and N. Hagita. 2012. Evaluation of formant-based lip motion generation in tele-operated humanoid robots. In *Proc. IROS*, pages 2377–2382.

K. Sakai, C. Ishi, T. Minaot, and H. Ishiguro. 2015. Online speech-driven head motion generating system and evaluation on a tele-operated robot. In *Proc. ROMAN*, pages 529–534.

R. Schmidt. 1986. Multiple emitter location and signal parameter estimation. *IEEE Trans. Antennas and Propagation*, 34(3):276–280.

G. Skantze and M. Johansson. 2015. Modelling situated human-robot interaction using IrisTK. In *Proc. SIGDIAL*, pages 165–167.

G. Wilcock and K. Jokinen. 2015. Multilingual WikiTalk: Wikipedia-based talking robots that switch languages. In *Proc. SIGDIAL*, pages 162–164.

T. Yamaguchi, K. Inoue, K. Yoshino, K. Takanashi, N. Ward, and T. Kawahara. 2016. Analysis and prediction of morphological patterns of backchannels for attentive listening agents. In *Proc. IWSDS*.

K. Yoshino and T. Kawahara. 2015. Conversational system for information navigation based on POMDP with user focus tracking. *Computer Speech and Language*, 34(1):275–291.

Z. Yu, D. Bohus, and E. Horvitz. 2015. Incremental coordination: Attention-centric speech production in a physically situated conversational agent. In *Proc. SIGDIAL*, pages 402–406.

Rapid Prototyping of Form-driven Dialogue Systems
Using an Open-source Framework

Svetlana Stoyanchev
Interactions Corporation
New York, USA
sstoyanchev@interactions.com

Pierre Lison
Language Technology Group
University of Oslo, Norway
plison@ifi.uio.no

Srinivas Bangalore
Interactions Corporation
Murray Hill, USA
sbangalore@interactions.com

Abstract

Most human-machine communication for information access through speech, text and graphical interfaces are mediated by *forms* – i.e. lists of named fields. However, deploying form-filling dialogue systems still remains a challenging task due to the effort and skill required to author such systems. We describe an extension to the OpenDial framework that enables the rapid creation of functional dialogue systems by non-experts. The dialogue designer specifies the slots and their types as input and the tool generates a domain specification that drives a slot-filling dialogue system. The presented approach provides several benefits compared to traditional techniques based on flowcharts, such as the use of probabilistic reasoning and flexible grounding strategies.

1 Introduction

Dialogue systems research has witnessed the emergence of several important innovations in the last two decades, such as the development of information-state architectures (Larsson and Traum, 2000), the use of probabilistic reasoning to handle multiple state hypotheses (Young et al., 2013), the application of reinforcement learning to automatically derive dialogue policies from real or simulated interactions (Lemon and Pietquin, 2012), and the introduction of incremental processing methods to allow for more natural conversational behaviours (Schlangen et al., 2010). However, few of these innovations have so far made their way into dialogue systems deployed in commercial environments (Paek and Pieraccini, 2008; Williams, 2009). Indeed, the bulk of currently deployed dialogue systems continue

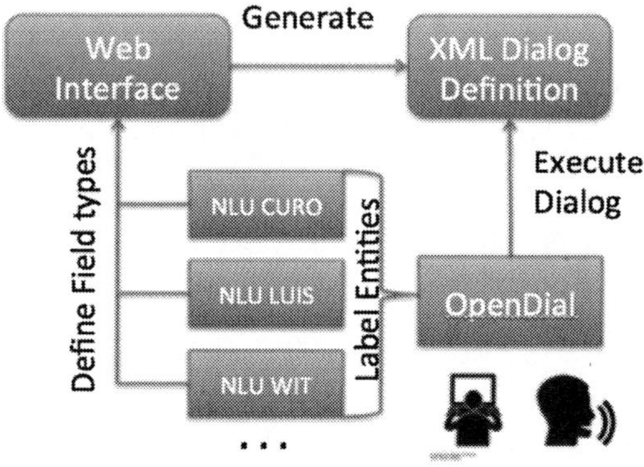

Figure 1: Architecture overview.

to rely on traditional hand-crafted finite-state or rule-based approaches to dialogue management using commercial or proprietary tools generating VoiceXML. The key reasons for this *status quo* are the need for the dialogue designer to (1) retain control over the system's behaviour, (2) ensure the system can scale to large numbers of users, and (3) easily author and edit the system's internal models. These features supersede their shortcomings. While authoring a system-initiative dialogue is quick and easy to maintain, authoring a user-initiative dialogue system in VoiceXML often results in large interdependent code bases that are increasingly difficult to maintain. Furthermore, these dialogue systems cannot capture multiple state hypotheses nor optimise the dialogue by learning from previous interactions.

Meanwhile, various dialogue authoring frameworks have been developed in academia to facilitate the development of dialogue systems by authoring state update rules (Bohus and Rudnicky, 2009; P. Lison, 2015). In particular, OpenDial, an open source dialogue system framework based on a information-state architecture, allows system developers to easily specify and edit dialogue be-

Proceedings of the SIGDIAL 2016 Conference, pages 216–219,
Los Angeles, USA, 13-15 September 2016. ©2016 Association for Computational Linguistics

haviours, which is a crucial requirement for commercial conversational applications. However, designing and maintaining dialogue systems using these tools remains a challenge.

In order to address this challenge and lower the entry barrier for authoring dialogue systems, we demonstrate a web-based tool that allows a user to create a form-filling dialogue system automatically by simply specifying a form template. The architecture of the system is shown in Figure 1. The dialogue designer using the authoring tool specifies a form template – as a list of slots associated with their corresponding semantic types – as input. The tool compiles the form template into a specification to drive the dialogue management framework, OpenDial. Natural language understanding is provided through the use of cloud-based APIs. The authoring tool satisfies the requirements of maintaining control of the dialogue flow with the use of probabilistic modelling techniques, thus allowing simple authoring of mixed-initiative slot-filling dialogue systems.

Our target audience includes both researchers and industry practitioners. A fully-functional spoken interface to a system, such as hotel reservation, airline booking, or mortgage calculator, can be generated using the tool by a non-expert in dialogue systems. The generated domain specification can be further edited by the system developers in order to integrate more advanced functionality such as escalated per-field prompts or customized language generation.

The rest of this paper is structured as follows. The next section presents the web-based tool, the generated OpenDial domain file, and the software bridges to external NLU services. Section 3 describes a preliminary evaluation, while Section 4 relates the system to previous work.

2 System

We rely on OpenDial as underlying framework (P. Lison, 2015) for dialogue management. OpenDial has been previously used for human–robot interactions, in-car driving assistants, and intelligent tutoring systems (Lison and Kennington, 2016). It is also a popular platform for teaching advanced courses on spoken dialogue systems.

2.1 Form-to-System Generation

We created a web-based tool that generates an (XML-encoded) OpenDial dialogue domain from a form specification. The web tool allows the dialogue designer to configure any number of form fields by specifying a field name, a corresponding semantic type, a natural language question for eliciting the field value, an implicit confirmation sentence, and a optional set of constraints between the slots. Figure 2 illustrates the interface for defining a form for hotel reservations with four fields: *location, arrival, duration,* and *departure.* Fields can also be marked as "optional", and can be mutually exclusive with other fields (for instance, the "duration" of a hotel stay and its "end date"). It should be noted that the *NL Question* and *NL Implicit Confirmation* can reference the values of previous slots, such as e.g. "When are you arriving in *location*". This enables the dialogue designer to implement implicit grounding strategies. When the form is submitted, the authoring tool generates the corresponding domain file.

2.2 Domain file

OpenDial stores domain-specific information in a *domain file*, which is encoded in XML. The domain file specifies the following information:

- The initial dialogue state.

- A collection of domain models, which are themselves composed of probabilistic rules.

- General configuration settings, such as settings for the cloud-based NLU.

The dialogue state is represented as a Bayesian Network, allowing for explicit capture of uncertainty. For slot-filling tasks, the state variables capture the values for each slot, the recent dialogue history, a list of slots that are already filled and grounded, and a (possibly empty) set of mutual exclusivity constraints between slots. This dialogue state is regularly updated based on user inputs and subsequent system responses.

The probabilistic rules are expressed as *if-then-else* blocks associating logical conditions to probabilistic effects (see (P. Lison, 2015) for more details). The domain file generated by the web-based tool is composed of about fifteen rules responsible for (1) updating the slot values given the user inputs, (2) selecting the most appropriate system actions based on the current state, and (3) mapping these high-level actions to concrete system responses. The (probability and utility) parameters of these rules are initially fixed to reasonable

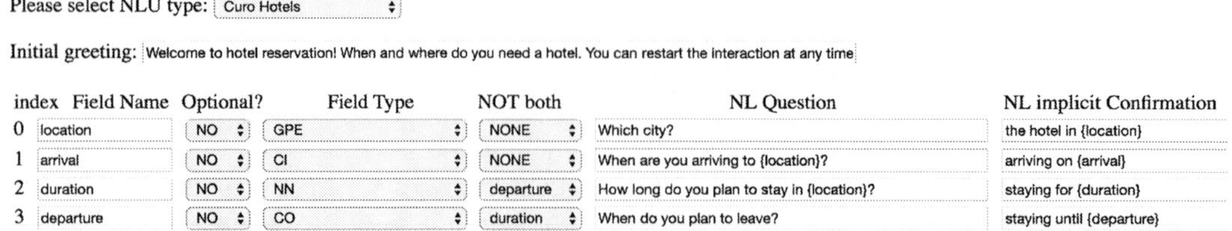

index	Field Name	Optional?	Field Type	NOT both	NL Question	NL implicit Confirmation
0	location	NO	GPE	NONE	Which city?	the hotel in {location}
1	arrival	NO	CI	NONE	When are you arriving to {location}?	arriving on {arrival}
2	duration	NO	NN	departure	How long do you plan to stay in {location}?	staying for {duration}
3	departure	NO	CO	duration	When do you plan to leave?	staying until {departure}

Figure 2: Form for generating a dialogue with hotel information domain.

defaults, but the user is free to modify the values of these parameters (or estimate them from data if such interaction data is available).

The generated dialogue domain allows for mixed-initiative interactions where a user can choose any order and combination of fields for filling the form, including a single turn (Figure 3a) or in multiple turns (Figure 3b). In addition, the dialogue manager includes correction and grounding capabilities (Figure 3c). The user may interact with the system using either text inputs or speech (using third-party APIs such as Nuance or Curo for speech recognition and synthesis).

2.3 Natural Language Understanding (NLU)

In slot-filling applications, the main objective of natural language understanding is to label the user utterance with (application-specific) semantic entities. The entities identified through NLU can then be exploited by the dialogue manager to fill the fields of the form which in turn drives the next response. The mapping between NLU labels and state variables is established through the field types specified in the form (Figure 2).

We extend OpenDial to access cloud-based NLU services through HTTP endpoints. When a user selects an *NLU type* from the list of supported services, the values in the *Field Type* drop-down boxes for each field are populated with the NL labels in the selected NLU module. To add support for a given NLU service, we create a corresponding OpenDial module configured with the service's HTTP endpoint and session parameters. This module processes the output *json* file returned from the HTTP request to the service and extracts assigned semantic labels.

We have implemented NLU modules for publicly available cloud services from Microsoft and Facebook[1] and for a proprietary Curo NLU. This enables dialogue designers with a range of alter-

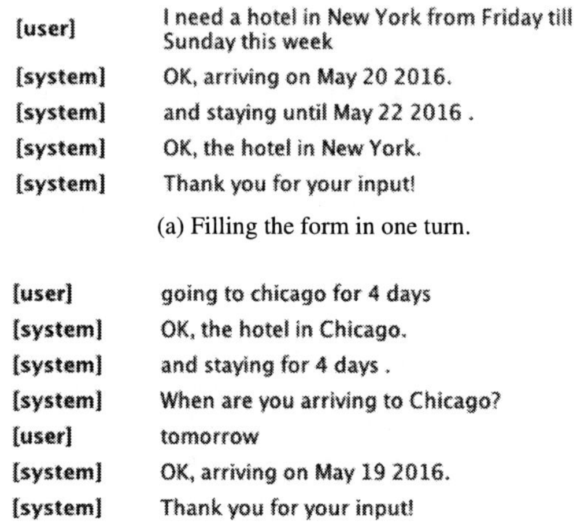

(a) Filling the form in one turn.

(b) Filling the form with multiple turns.

(c) User correction and grounding.

Figure 3: Dialogue Examples in the hotel reservations domain.

native NLU solutions, from using the already supported cloud NLU services to implementing their own NLU module in OpenDial.

3 Evaluation

For a preliminary evaluation, we asked five researchers from the lab to use the web interface and generate a dialogue system using pre-loaded hotel reservation form, evaluate it by running opendial as end-users, and explore the web interface by creating new systems. All of the participants were able to generate a hotel reservation form-filling in-

---

[1] https://www.luis.ai/, https://wit.ai

terface successfully. The participants were asked to fill out the hotel reservation form using multiple dialogue paths. On average the participants attempted four distinct dialogue paths and successfully completing three of them. All of the participants agreed that the tool *provides an effective method of generating a voice interface for a form* and four of the participants indicated that they would use it for generating spoken interfaces in the future (one was neutral).

4   Related Work

Several web-based NLU services have been recently launched by companies such as wit.ai (now part of Facebook), Microsoft, Nuance and api.ai [2]. These services provide cloud-based solutions for creating NLU for systems with simple web-based interfaces and active learning capabilities. Some of these tools have now been extended with basic dialogue management functionalities. These platforms can be employed by novices with no programming or speech experience to author and deploy spoken interfaces.

Similar to these commercial solutions, the presented authoring tool aims at lowering the entry barrier for dialogue developers wishing to quickly create functioning dialogue systems. Our solution is intended for both dialogue system researchers and commercial companies that still predominantly use VoiceXML-based platforms and have restrictions on transferring customer data to third-party services. We hope that both target audiences will benefit from the ability to deploy the system on a proprietary server, with full control over the dialogue flow, easy access to third-party ASR, NLU and TTS components, and ability to perform probabilistic reasoning and optimize dialogue policies from data.

5   Conclusions and Future Work

We have presented a web-based authoring tool to facilitate the creation of slot-filling dialogue systems. Based on a simple form template, the tool generates an XML domain file that specifies the system behavior, while intent recognition is delegated to a cloud service, either third-party or proprietary. We aim at bridging the gap between spoken dialogue research and conversational systems

deployed in the industry by providing an open-sourced tool that combines simple authoring, full control of the dialogue flow with the ability to optimize from historical interaction data.

As future work, we wish to extend the tool to handle multiple forms and design an interface for describing system behaviors in a multi-form system. We also intend to use the system for research on clarification strategies and evaluating benefits of joint ASR and NLU processing in dialogue.

References

D. Bohus and A. Rudnicky. 2009. The RavenClaw dialog management framework: Architecture and systems. *Computer Speech & Language*, 23(3):332–361.

S. Larsson and D. R. Traum. 2000. Information state and dialogue management in the TRINDI dialogue move engine toolkit. *Natural Language Engineering*, 6(3-4):323–340.

O. Lemon and O. Pietquin. 2012. *Data-Driven Methods for Adaptive Spoken Dialogue Systems: Computational Learning for Conversational Interfaces*. Springer.

P. Lison and C. Kennington. 2016. OpenDial: A toolkit for developing spoken dialogue systems with probabilistic rules. In *Proceedings of the 54th Annual Meeting of the Association for Computational Linguistics (System Demonstrations)*, Berlin, Germany.

P. Lison. 2015. A hybrid approach to dialogue management based on probabilistic rules. *Computer Speech & Language*, 34(1):232 – 255.

T. Paek and R. Pieraccini. 2008. Automating spoken dialogue management design using machine learning: An industry perspective. *Speech Communications*, 50(8-9):716–729.

D. Schlangen, T. Baumann, H. Buschmeier, O. Buß, S. Kopp, G. Skantze, and R. Yaghoubzadeh. 2010. Middleware for Incremental Processing in Conversational Agents. In *Proceedings of the 11th SIGDIAL meeting on Discourse and Dialogue*.

J. D. Williams. 2009. Spoken dialogue systems: challenges, and opportunities for research (invited talk). In *Proc IEEE Workshop on Automatic Speech Recognition and Understanding (ASRU)*, Merano, Italy.

S. Young, M. Gačić, B. Thomson, and J. D. Williams. 2013. POMDP-based statistical spoken dialog systems: A review. *Proceedings of the IEEE*, 101(5):1160–1179.

---

[2]http://wit.ai, https://www.luis.ai, https://api.ai, https://developer.nuance.com/mix.

LVCSR System on a Hybrid GPU-CPU Embedded Platform for Real-Time Dialog Applications

Alexei V. Ivanov
Educational Testing Service
90 New Montgomery St.
San Francisco, CA, USA
alexei_v_ivanov@ieee.org

Patrick L. Lange
Educational Testing Service
90 New Montgomery St.
San Francisco, CA, USA
plange@ets.org

David Suendermann-Oeft
Educational Testing Service
90 New Montgomery St.
San Francisco, CA, USA
suendermann-oeft@ets.org

Abstract

We present the implementation of a large-vocabulary continuous speech recognition (LVCSR) system on NVIDIA's Tegra K1 hyprid GPU-CPU embedded platform. The system is trained on a standard 1000-hour corpus, LibriSpeech, features a trigram WFST-based language model, and achieves state-of-the-art recognition accuracy. The fact that the system is real-time-able and consumes less than 7.5 watts peak makes the system perfectly suitable for fast, but precise, offline spoken dialog applications, such as in robotics, portable gaming devices, or in-car systems.

1 Introduction

Many of nowadays' spoken dialog systems are distributed systems whose major components, such as speech recognition, spoken language understanding, and dialog managers, are located in the cloud (Suendermann, 2011). For example, interactive voice response (IVR) systems are often connected to conventional telephony networks and handle a substantial portion of customer service interactions for numerous organizations and enterprises. One of the advantages of cloud-based systems is the strong computational power such systems can have which is believed to be critical for some of the components to produce an adequate performance (see for example recent advances in commercial speech recognition systems (Hannun et al., 2014)).

Despite their advantages, cloud-based spoken dialog systems have several limitations. E.g. they not only real-time-able speech recognizers, which poses a number of additional constraints to the implementation of the system (Ivanov et al., 2016), but, first and foremost, they require a high-speed, high-reliability, and high-fidelity connection to the client device. If this precondition is not met, spoken dialog systems cease to be what they promise to be: dialog systems. Slow, clunky, and intermittent connections may be acceptable with pseudo-dialog applications such as the ones typical in virtual assistants (Suendermann-Oeft, 2013), but they are not suited for realistic conversational applications such as in customer care (Acomb et al., 2007), virtual tutoring (Litman and Silliman, 2004), or command and control. Even more importantly, there are numerous applications for spoken dialog systems which require operation in offline mode altogether, for example in moving vehicles (Pellom et al., 2001), with robots in adverse conditions (Toptsis et al., 2004), in certain medical devices (Williams et al., 2011), or with portable video game consoles and toys (Sporka et al., 2006).

Maintaining a cloud application server farm, capable of supporting the mass service comes at a recurring operational cost, which limits the range of possible revenue models with which the spoken dialog system can be offered. A way to solve this problem is to transfer the necessary hardware to the client device and let the customer naturally cover the processing power costs. Thus, reduction of the complexity of the involved technology and reducing its power consumption become critical figures of merit according to which the portable systems such as robots, portable game consoles, and toys are going to compete.

Further advantages of using a low-footprint highly accurate real-time able speech recognizer over cloud-based recognition include

- no need for complex load balancing, instance management, or distributed, redundant server architectures;

- lower energy footprint due to the elimination of server and communication hardware

Proceedings of the SIGDIAL 2016 Conference, pages 220–223,
Los Angeles, USA, 13-15 September 2016. ©2016 Association for Computational Linguistics

needed to run cloud-based speech recognition jobs;

- no privacy concern since the data remains on the local hardware (which can be important for applications in medical, intelligence, defense, legal, or financial domains, among others);

- straight-forward user adaptation directly on the client hardware without the need to maintain potentially millions of customer profiles in the cloud;

- reduced network activity resulting in lower operation costs and improved bandwidth for other concurrent tasks requiring network communication, especially for wireless applications;

- enhanced options for voice activity detection since the speech recognizer can be constantly running, while constant streaming of audio from a client to the cloud is not feasible.

In Section 2 we present a large vocabulary speech recognition system architecture designed for NVIDIA's Tegra K1 hybrid GPU-CPU embedded System-on-a-Chip (SoC). We show that its recognition accuracy performs on par with state-of-the-art systems while maintaining low power consumption and real-time ability in Section 3.

2   System Description

Research has shown that an interaction with a dialog application becomes overly tiresome for the human interlocutor when the system's response does not occur promptly (Fried and Edmondson, 2006; Wennerstrom and Siege, 2003; Shigemitsu, 2005). Speech recognition is only the first of many steps in producing the system's response. Therefore, it is crucial that the recognition output can be produced at the rate of speech or as close to that as possible. While compromising recognition accuracy for a better real-time factor (xRT) is trivial, maintaining the state-of-the-art performance within the real-time constraints is challenging (Ivanov et al., 2016).

Building on top of our results described in (Ivanov et al., 2015) we implemented a highly parallel real-time speech recognition inference engine with rapid speaker adaptation that is model-level compatible with the Kaldi toolkit (Povey et

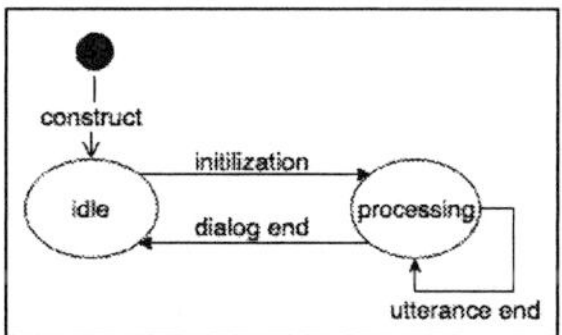

Figure 1: State diagram

al., 2011). It maintains the state-of-the-art accuracy while doing real-time online recognition with the NVIDIA's Tegra K1 hybrid GPU-CPU embedded platform. The recent studies (Morbini et al., 2013; Gaida et al., 2014) confirm state-of-the-art level of the Kaldi model-generation pipelines.

Figures 1, 2 and 3 show the ASR architecture we designed. The interaction with the ASR system follows the Client-Server architecture. Figure 1 depicts the states the server transitions through from the client's perspective. After start-up of the ASR system, it stays in an idle state until a client opens a session with the server. This session is implemented as a web-socket connection. If the ASR system is used as a component within a dialog application, this session stays open until the full conversation with the human user is finished. When the server receives a new session, it transitions into the processing state, in which it immediately processes the incoming audio on a per-chunk basis. Finalizing recognition of a single utterance within the dialog is triggered by an "end of the utterance" signal. The upstream dialog system component receives the recognition result either on a per utterance basis or as a partial feedback up until the current position in the utterance. Ability to interactively produce the intermediate recognition results is an essential feature of the dialog-oriented speech recognizer as it allows us to start interpretation of the user input even before its completion. The recognition session is stopped when the client closes the web-socket connection. Then, the server transitions back into the idle state.

In the processing state, the data flows through the ASR system as shown in Figure 2. We grouped the individual steps in the employed ASR pipeline, namely: audio data acquisition, feature extraction, i-Vector computation, acoustic probability computation, decoding, backtracking and propagating the result back to the client, represented as blocks within the figure into the modules that run in a single thread. The modules are connected to each other via the ring buffers represented as wide ar-

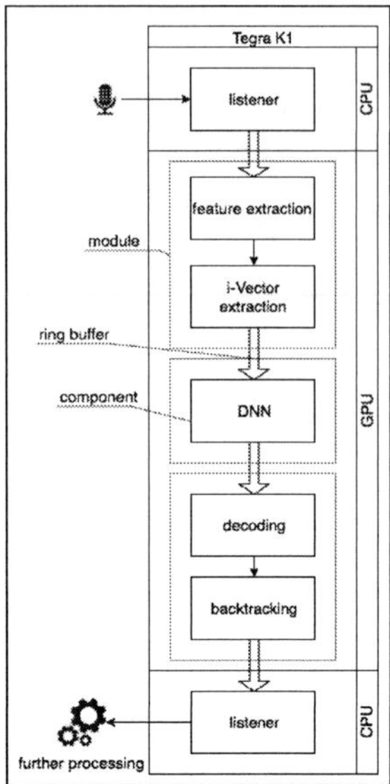

Figure 2: Data flow diagram

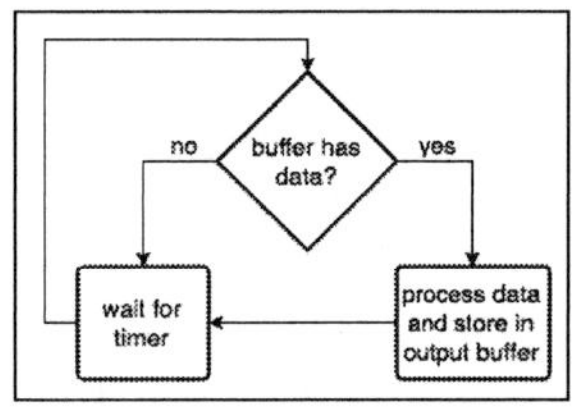

Figure 3: Component diagram

rows. Each module operates as shown in Figure 3. Every x seconds, the module checks if the input ring buffer contains a new data chunk, processes the chunk, stores it in the output ring buffer and repeats.

In Figure 2, the backtracking component is grouped together with the decoding component and executed in each processing cycle. This setup allows the ASR system to generate a partial result for each input chunk. A possible alternative to this strategy is to trigger the backtracking by the 'end of utterance' signal and only compute the resulting lattice once. This would additionally save computation time and is useful when there is no need for partial results during the recognition process.

The components running in modules placed on the GPU part of the chip have been especially implemented to utilize the parallel computing advantages of GPUs. Processing speedup with GPUs is achieved via committing larger areas of the die for solving the single task. Compared to CPUs graphical processing units (GPUs) allow for an easier

processing resource management. The GPU chip lacks extensive control logic making it potentially more efficient. The downside is increase of the programming effort.

3 Experiments

In order to verify our design we have used a set of the models, generated by the standard Kaldi model-generating recipe for the LibriSpeech acoustic corpus (Panayotov et al., 2015). Specifically, we have used the Deep Neural Network – Weighted Finite State Transducer (DNN-WFST) hybrid with i-vector acoustic adaptation. The acoustic model is implemented as the 8-layer p-norm DNN with approximately 14.22 million free parameters stored as single precision floating point numbers. For language modeling we have taken a version of the standard LibriSpeech tri-gram model pruned with the threshold of $3e{-}7$. There are approximately 200 thousands uni-grams, 1 million bi-grams and 34 thousands tri-grams. The resulting WFST has the complexity of about 10 millions nodes and 25 millions arcs. The i-vector is evaluated from a separately trained Universal Background Gaussian-Mixture Model (UBM-GMM) with 512 Gaussians. The final i-vector has 100 components. The standard Kaldi MFCC features are used.

The evaluation has been performed with the standard LibriSpeech test sets, namely: "DC" - 2703 clean development recordings ($\approx$ 5h. 24 min.); "DN" - 2864 noisy development recordings ($\approx$ 5h. 8 min.); "TC" - 2620 clean test recordings ($\approx$ 5h. 25 min.); "TN" - 2939 noisy test recordings ($\approx$ 5h. 21 min.). The evaluation is performed as the single-pass recognition with online acoustic adaptation within the speaker-specific utterance sets in order to simulate operation of the speech recognizer in short single-user dialogues.

We compare performance of our Tegra-based speech engine with the reference implementation of the Kaldi online2-wav-nnet2-latgen-faster decoder that is running on a system powered by the Intel Core i7-4930K CPU at 3.40GHz clock frequency. All operating parameters (the pruning beam widths, model mixing coefficients, etc.) are kept the same between the reference and the presented system. Table 1 summarizes accuracy and real-time factors of the compared systems. There was a minor random WER difference between the GPU and CPU implementations, similar to what was reported in the earlier publications (Ivanov et

Tasks	WER, %	CPU 1/xRT	TK1 1/xRT
DC	≈ 7.2	1.11	1.20
DN	≈ 19.6	0.97	1.02
TC	≈ 7.8	1.11	1.15
TN	≈ 19.4	0.95	1.01

Table 1: Accuracy and speed of compared recognizers. WER – word error rate; "CPU 1/xRT" – the inverse of the real-time factor (i.e. the processing-production speed ratio) for the reference system; 'TK1 1/xRT' – inverse real-time factor for the presented system. Power consumption is 150W for the "CPU" and 7.5W for the "TK1" systems. The Tegra system hardware cost is approximately 10 times smaller.

al., 2015). The WER figures reported in the table reflect the average expected performance level.

4 Conclusions

We have demonstrated the possibility to achieve the state-of-the-art accuracy with a dialog-oriented real-time able speech recognition inference engine running on a low-power consumer-grade SoC. The presented system implements a single-pass recognizer with online speaker-adaptation which is essential in dialogs. The system is immediately usable to support rich dialog experience with the guaranteed low latency locally-run dialog systems that take advantage of the complex large vocabulary continuous speech recognition models.

References

K. Acomb, J. Bloom, K. Dayanidhi, P. Hunter, P. Krogh, E. Levin, and R. Pieraccini. 2007. Technical Support Dialog Systems: Issues, Problems, and Solutions. In *Proc. of the HLT-NAACL*, Rochester, USA.

J. Fried and R. Edmondson. 2006. How Customer Perceived Latency Measures Success In Voice Self-Service. *Business Communications Review*, 36(3).

C. Gaida, P. L. Lange, R. Petrick, P. Proba, A. Malatawy, and D. Suendermann-Oeft. 2014. Comparing Open-Source Speech Recognition Toolkits. Technical report, DHBW Stuttgart, Stuttgart, Germany.

A. Hannun, C. Case, J. Casper, B. Catanzaro, G. Diamos, E. Elsen, R. Prenger, S. Satheesh, S. Sengupta, A. Coates, and A. Ng. 2014. Deep speech: Scaling up end-to-end speech recognition. In *in Proc: of the ICSLP*, ArXiv, 1412(5567).

A. V. Ivanov, P. L. Lange, and D. Suendermann-Oeft. 2015. Fast and power efficient hardware-accelerated cloud-based asr for remote dialog applications. In *in Proc. of ASRU'2015*, Scottsdale, AZ, USA.

A. V. Ivanov, P. L. Lange, D. Suendermann-Oeft, V. Ramanarayanan, Y. Qian, Z. Yu, and J. Tao. 2016. Speed vs. accuracy: Designing an optimal asr system for spontaneous non-native speech in a real-time application. In *Proc. of the IWSDS*, Saariselk, Finland.

D. Litman and S. Silliman. 2004. ITSPOKE: An Intelligent Tutoring Spoken Dialogue System. In *in Proc: of the HLT-NAACL*, Boston, USA.

F. Morbini, K. Audhkhasi, K. Sagae, R. Artstein, D. Can, P. Georgiou, S. Narayanan, A. Leuski, and D. Traum. 2013. Which ASR should I choose for my dialogue system. In *Proc. of the SIGDIAL*, Metz, France.

V. Panayotov, G. Chen, D. Povey, and S. Khudanpur. 2015. LibriSpeech: an ASR corpus based on public domain audio books. In *in Proc. of the IEEE ICASSP*, Brisbane, Australia.

B. Pellom, W. Ward, J. Hansen, R. Cole, K. Hacioglu, J. Zhang, X. Yu, and S. Pradhan. 2001. University of Colorado Dialog Systems for Travel and Navigation. In *in Proc: of the HLT*, San Diego, USA.

D. Povey, A. Ghoshal, G. Boulianne, L. Burget, O. Glembek, N. Goel, M. Hannemann, P. Motlicek, Y. Qian, P. Schwarz, J. Silovsky, G. Stemmer, and K. Vesely. 2011. The Kaldi Speech Recognition Toolkit. In *Proc. of the ASRU*, Hawaii, USA.

Y. Shigemitsu. 2005. Different Interpretations of Pauses in Natural Conversation - Japanese, Chinese and Americans. *Academic Report*, 27(2).

A. Sporka, S. Kurniawan, M. Mahmud, and P. Slavik. 2006. Non-speech input and speech recognition for real-time control of computer games. In *in Proc: of the Assets*, Portland, USA.

D. Suendermann-Oeft. 2013. Modern conversational agents. In J. Jähnert and C. Förster, editors, *Technologien fuer digitale Innovationen: Interdisziplinaere Beitraege zur Informationsverarbeitung*. Springer VS, Wiesbaden, Germany.

D. Suendermann. 2011. *Advances in Commercial Deployment of Spoken Dialog Systems*. Springer, New York, USA.

I. Toptsis, S. Li, B. Wrede, and G. Fink. 2004. A multimodal dialog system for a mobile robot. In *in Proc: of the ICSLP*, Jeju, South Korea.

A. Wennerstrom and A. F. Siege. 2003. Keeping the Floor in Multiparty Conversations: Intonation, Syntax, and Pause. *Discourse Processes*, 36(2).

J. Williams, S. Witt-Ehsani, A. Liska, and D. Suendermann. 2011. Speech Recognition in a Multi-Modal Health Care Application: Two Sides of the Coin. In *Proc. of the AVIxD/IxDA Workshop*, New York, USA.

Socially-Aware Animated Intelligent Personal Assistant Agent

Yoichi Matsuyama, Arjun Bhardwaj, Ran Zhao,
Oscar J. Romero, Sushma Anand Akoju and Justine Cassell
ArticuLab, Carnegie Mellon University, Pittsburgh, PA 15213 USA
`{yoichim, ranzhao, justine}@cs.cmu.edu`
`{arjunb1, oscarr, sakoju}@andrew.cmu.edu`

Abstract

SARA (Socially-Aware Robot Assistant) is an embodied intelligent personal assistant that analyses the user's visual (head and face movement), vocal (acoustic features) and verbal (conversational strategies) behaviours to estimate its rapport level with the user, and uses its own appropriate visual, vocal and verbal behaviors to achieve task and social goals. The presented agent aids conference attendees by eliciting their preferences through building rapport, and then making informed personalized recommendations about sessions to attend and people to meet.

1 Introduction

Currently major tech companies envision intelligent personal assistants, such as Apple Siri, Microsoft Cortana, and Amazon Alexa as the front ends to their services. However those assistants really play little other role than to query, with voice input and output - they fulfill very few of the functions that a human assistant might. In this demo, we present SARA, the Socially-Aware Robot Assistant, represented by a humanoid animated character on a computer screen, which achieves similar functionality, but through multimodal interaction, and with a focus on building a social relationship with users. Currently SARA is the front end to an event app. The animated character engages its users in a conversation to elicit their goals and preferences and uses them to recommend relevant conference sessions to attend and people to meet. During this process, the system monitors the use of specific conversational strategies (such as self-disclosure, praise, reference to shared experience, etc.) by the human user and uses this input, as well as acoustic and nonverbal input, to estimate the level of rapport between the user and system. The system then employs conversational strategies shown in our prior work to raise the level of rapport with the human user, or to maintain it at the same level if it is already high (Zhao et al., 2014), (Zhao et al., 2016b). The goal is to use rapport to elicit personal information from the user that can be used to improve the helpfulness and personalization of system responses.

2 SARA's Computational Architecture

SARA is therefore designed to build interpersonal closeness over the course of a conversation through understanding and generation visual, vocal, and verbal behaviors. The current system leverages prior work on the dynamics of rapport (Zhao et al., 2014), and the initial consideration of the computational architecture of a rapport building agent (Papangelis et al., 2014). Figure 1 shows the overview of the architecture. All modules of the system are built on top of the Virtual Human Toolkit (Hartholt et al., 2013). Main modules of our architecture are described below.

2.1 Visual and Vocal Input Analysis

Microsoft's Cognitive Services API converts speech to text, which is then fed to Microsoft's LUIS (Language Understanding Intelligent Service) to identify user intents. In the demo, as the train data of this specific domain is still limited, a Wizard of Oz GUI will be served as backup in the case of speech recognition and natural language understanding errors. OpenSmile (Eyben et al., 2010) extracts acoustic features from the audio signal, including fundamental frequency (F0), loudness (SMA), jitter and shimmer, which then serve as input to the rapport estimator and the conversational strategy classifier modules. Open-Face (Baltrušaitis et al., 2016)) detects 3D facial landmarks, head pose, gaze and Action Units, and

Proceedings of the SIGDIAL 2016 Conference, pages 224–227,
Los Angeles, USA, 13-15 September 2016. ©2016 Association for Computational Linguistics

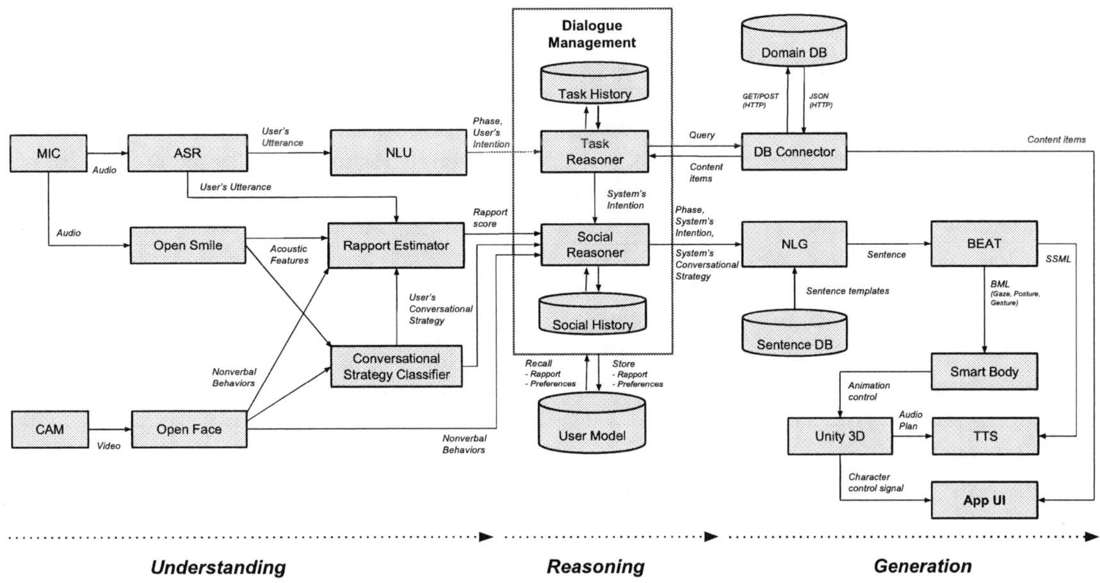

Figure 1: SARA Architecture

these also serve as input to the rapport estimator (smiles, for example, have been shown in the corpus we trained the estimator on to have a strong impact on rapport (Zhao et al., 2016b)).

2.2 Conversational Strategy Classifier

We implemented a multimodal conversational strategy classifier to automatically recognize particular styles and strategies of talking that contribute to building, maintaining or sometimes destroying a budding relationship. These include: self-disclosure (SD), elicit self-disclosure (QE), reference to shared experience (RSD), praise (PR), and violation of social norms (VSN). By analyzing rich contextual features drawn from verbal, visual and vocal modalities of the speaker and interlocutor in both the current and previous turns, we can successfully recognize these dialogue phenomena in user input with an accuracy of over 80% and with a kappa of over 60% (Zhao et al., 2016a).

2.3 Rapport Estimator

We also implemented an automatic multimodal rapport estimator, based on the framework of temporal association rule learning (Guillame-Bert and Crowley, 2012), to perform a fine-grained investigation into how sequences of interlocutor behaviors lead to (are followed by) increases and decreases in interpersonal rapport.The behaviors analyzed include visual behaviors such as eye gaze and smiles and verbal conversational strategies

such as SD, RSE, VSN, PR and BC. The rapport forecasting model involves two-step fusion of learned temporal associated rules: in the first step, the goal is to learn the weighted contribution (vote) of each temporal association rule in predicting the presence/absence of a certain rapport state (via seven random-forest classifiers); in the second step, the goal is to learn the weight corresponding to each of the binary classifiers for the rapport states, in order to predict the absolute continuous value of rapport (via linear regression) model (Zhao et al., 2016b). Ground truth comes from annotations of rapport in videos of peer tutoring sessions divided into 30 second slices which are then randomized (see (Zhao et al., 2014) for details).

2.4 Dialogue Management

The dialogue manager is composed of a task reasoner that focuses on obtaining information to fulfill the user's goals, and a social reasoner that chooses ways of talking that are intended to build rapport in the service of better achieving the user's goals. A task and social history, and a user model, also play a role in dialogue management, but will not be further discussed here.

2.4.1 Task Reasoner

The Task Reasoner is predicated on the system maintaining initiative to the extent possible. It is implemented as a finite state machine whose transitions are determined by different kinds of triggering events or conditions such as: user's intents (extracted by the NLU), past and current state of the dialogue (stored by the task history) and other contextual information (e.g., how many sessions the agent has recommended so far). Task Reasoner's output can be either a query to the domain database or a system intent that will serve as input to the Social Reasoner and hence the NLG modules. In order to handle those cases where the user takes the initiative, the module allows a specific set of user intents to cause the system to transition from its current state to a state which can appropriately handle the user's request. The task Reasoner use a statistical discriminative state tracking approach to update the dialogue state and deal with error handling, sub-dialog,s and grounding acknowledgements, similar to the implementation of the Alex framework (Jurčíček et al., 2014).

2.4.2 Social Reasoner

The Social Reasoner is designed as a network of interacting nodes where decision-making emerges from the dynamics of competence and collaboration relationships among those nodes. That is, it is implemented as a Behavior Network as originally proposed by (Maes, 1989) and extended by (Romero, 2011). Such a network is ideal here as it can efficiently make both short-term decisions (real-time or reactive reasoning) and long-term decisions (deliberative reasoning and planning). The network's structure relies on observations extracted from data-driven models (in this case the collected data referenced above). Each node (behavior) corresponds to a specific conversational strategy (e.g., SD, PR, QE, etc.) and links between nodes denote either inhibitory or excitatory relationships which are labeled as precondition and post-condition premises. As preconditions, each node defines a set of possible system intents (generated by the Task Reasoner, e.g., "self_introduction", "start_goal_elicitation", etc.), rapport levels (high, medium or low), user conversational strategies (SD, VSN, PR, etc.), visuals (e.g., smile, head nod, eye gaze, etc.), and system's conversational strategy history (e.g., system has performed VSN three times in a row). Post-conditions are the expected user's state (e.g., rapport score increases, user smiles, etc.) after performing the current conversational strategy, and what conversational strategy should be performed next. For instance, when a conversation starts (i.e., during the greeting phase) the most likely

sequence of nodes could be: [ASN, SD, PR, SD ...VSN ...] i.e., initially the system establishes a cordial and respectful communication with user (ASN), then it uses SD as an icebreaking strategy, followed by PR to encourage the user to also perform SD. After some interaction, if the rapport level is high, a VSN is performed. The Social Reasoner is adaptive enough to respond to unexpected user's actions by tailoring a reactive plan that emerges *implicitly* from the forward and backward spreading activation dynamics and as result of tuning the network's parameters which determine reasoner's functionality (more oriented to goals vs. current state, or more adaptive vs. biased to ongoing plans, or more thoughtful vs. faster.).

2.5 NLG and Behavior Generation

On the basis of the output of the dialogue manager (which includes the current conversational phase, system intent, and desired conversational strategy) sentence and behavior plans are generated. The Natural Language Generator (NLG) selects syntactic templates associated with the selected conversational strategy from the sentence database and then fills them in with content from database queries performed by the task reasoner. The generated sentence plan is sent to BEAT, a non-verbal behavior generator (Cassell et al., 2004), which tailors a behavior plan (including relevant hand gestures, eye gaze, head nods, etc.) and outputs the plan as BML (Behavior Markup Language), which is a part of the Virtual Human Toolkit (Hartholt et al., 2013). This plan is then sent to SmartBody, which renders the required non-verbal behaviours.

3 Dialogue examples

SARA was demoed at the World Economic Forum in Tianjin China in June 2016 where it served as the front end to the event app. Over 100 participants interacted with SARA to get advice on sessions to attend and people to meet. The system operated with a Wizard of Oz GUI serving as backup in the case of recognition (speech recognition and natural language understanding), task reasoning errors, and network disruptions. Table 1 shows an extract from an actual interaction with the system, annotated with the outputs of the different modules as the system works to meet social and task goals.

Table 1: Extract from an actual interaction

Turn	Speaker	Utterance	Intent	Strategy
1	System	I'm here to be your personal assistant and help you get the most out of the conference, but to be honest, I'm a little nervous. This is my first time here, is it yours as well?	introduce, do_attendance_elicitation	SD, QE
2	User	Actually, this is my first time here as well.	first_time_attending	SD
3	System	I'm finding it overwhelming. I bet you are too.	feedback_attendance_ elicitation_first_time	SD, QE
4	User	Ya, there's just so much going on. But i'm getting a hang of it.	positive_confirmation	SD
5	System	Great. Now, If you wouldn't mind sharing your goals for attending the world economic forum this year, I can try to help you achieve them.	do_goal_elicitation	ASN
6	User	Well, I'm here to meet people who are passionate about the use of technology in education, and to know more about the latest developments in the field.	recommend_people, rec- ommend_sessions	None
7	System	Great. Good goals. Can you tell me a little bit about your work so I understand your interests better?	feedback_goals, do_interest_elicitation	ASN
8	User	I am the founder of a non profit educational startup which helps deliver quality education to the remote areas.	like {startup, education}	None
9	System	Very Interesting. Let's start by finding some interesting people for you to meet that are relevant to your interests. This is my favorite part. Let me look this up. One moment.	feedback_interest_elicita- tion, do_person_recomm- endation	ASN, SD
10	User	Sure	positive_confirmation	None
11	System	I think you would enjoy meeting this attendee. On the screen are some more details. Well? What do you think?	outcome_person_recom- mendation, end_person_ recommendation	ASN, VSN

4 Conclusion and Future Work

We have described the design and first implementation of an end-to-end socially-aware embodied intelligent personal assistant. The next step is to evaluate the validity of our approach by using the data collected at the World Economic Forum to assess whether rapport does increase over the conversation. Subsequent implementations will, among other goals, improve the ability of the system to collect data about the user and employ it in subsequent conversations, as well as the generativity of the NLG module, and social appropriateness of nonverbal behaviors generated by BEAT. We hope that data collected at SIGDIAL will help us to work towards these goals.

References

Tadas Baltrušaitis, Peter Robinson, and Louis-Philippe Morency. 2016. Openface: an open source facial behavior analysis toolkit. In *Proceedings of the IEEE Winter Conference on Applications of Computer Vision (WACV)*.

Justine Cassell, Hannes Högni Vilhjálmsson, and Timothy Bickmore. 2004. Beat: the behavior expression animation toolkit. In *Life-Like Characters*, pages 163–185. Springer.

Florian Eyben, Martin Wöllmer, and Björn Schuller. 2010. Opensmile: the munich versatile and fast open-source audio feature extractor. In *Proceedings of the international conference on Multimedia*, pages 1459–1462. ACM.

Mathieu Guillame-Bert and James L. Crowley. 2012. Learning temporal association rules on symbolic time sequences. pages 159–174.

A Hartholt, D Traum, SC Marsella, A Shapiro, G Stratou, A Leuski, LP Morency, and J Gratch. 2013. All together now: Introducing the virtual human toolkit. In *Int. Conf. on Intelligent Virtual Humans*.

Filip Jurčíček, Ondřej Dušek, Ondřej Plátek, and Lukáš Žilka. 2014. Alex: A statistical dialogue systems framework. In *Text, Speech and Dialogue: 17th International Conference, TSD*, pages 587–594.

Pattie Maes. 1989. How to do the right thing. *Connection Science*, 1(3):291–323.

Alexandros Papangelis, Ran Zhao, and Justine Cassell. 2014. Towards a computational architecture of dyadic rapport management for virtual agents. In *Intelligent Virtual Agents*, pages 320–324.

Oscar J. Romero. 2011. An evolutionary behavioral model for decision making. *Adaptive Behavior*, 19(6):451–475.

Ran Zhao, Alexandros Papangelis, and Justine Cassell. 2014. Towards a dyadic computational model of rapport management for human-virtual agent interaction. In *Intelligent Virtual Agents*, pages 514–527.

Ran Zhao, Tanmay Sinha, Alan Black, and Justine Cassell. 2016a. Automatic recognition of conversational strategies in the service of a socially-aware dialog system. In *17th Annual SIGdial Meeting on Discourse and Dialogue*.

Ran Zhao, Tanmay Sinha, Alan Black, and Justine Cassell. 2016b. Socially-aware virtual agents: Automatically assessing dyadic rapport from temporal patterns of behavior. In *16th International Conference on Intelligent Virtual Agents*.

Selection method of an appropriate response
in chat-oriented dialogue systems

Hideaki Mori
Kyoto Institute of Technology
/ Matsugasaki Sakyo-ku
Kyoto 6068585 Japan
`mori@ii.is.kit.ac.jp`

Masahiro Araki
Kyoto Institute of Technology
/ Matsugasaki Sakyo-ku
Kyoto 6068585 Japan
`araki@kit.ac.jp`

Abstract

Chat functionality is currently considered an important factor in spoken dialogue systems. In this paper, we explore the architecture of a chat-oriented dialogue system that can continue a long conversation with users and can be used for a long time. To achieve this goal, we propose a method combining various types of response generation modules, such as a statistical model-based module, a rule-based module, and a topic transition-oriented module. The core of this architecture is a method for selecting the most appropriate response based on a breakdown index and a willingness index.

1 Introduction

In recent years, there have been some research and development case studies on open-domain chat dialogue systems. The merit of chat functionality in a dialogue system is to encourage the daily use of the system so as to accustom the user to the speech interface. Moreover, chat dialogue functionality can give a user a sense of closeness to the system, especially for novice users of the speech interface. Considering this situation, the requirements of a chat dialogue system are (1) to maintain a longer dialogue without a breakdown of the conversation and (2) to maintain the long duration of use. We call the property of the first requirement as "continuous" and that of the second as "long-term." The aim of this paper is to propose a framework for realizing a continuous and long-term chat-oriented dialogue system.

In previous research studies on chat dialogue systems, the central theme of these studies is how to generate an appropriate and natural response to the user's utterance (Higashinaka et al., 2014),

(Xiang et al., 2014). There was little effort to realize both continuous and long-term features in chat-oriented dialogue systems.

The chat dialogue system's robustness to respond to any user utterance is a key functionality that must be implemented to make it continuous. Therefore, a statistical response generation method is used in recent chat-oriented dialogue systems. Moreover, appropriateness and naturalness of the response are required. To realize these functionalities, Higashinaka et al. proposed a method for evaluating the coherence of the system utterance to judge the latter's appropriateness(Higashinaka et al., 2014).

On the other hand, a chat system with a long-term feature should have the ability to keep the user interested and not bored. For example, it should be able to provide a new topic in a chat based on the recent news or seasonal event. It should also be able to develop a current topic for the dialogue by bringing up related topics. In general, it is difficult to realize such a topic shift in a statistical method. The rule-based method or a hybrid of rule and statistics is appropriate for implementing such functionalities.

Because of this difference in methods in implementing a suitable functionality for a continuous and long-term chat dialogue system, it is difficult to realize the aforementioned functionalities in one response generation module. Such module could be complex and difficult to maintain. Therefore, it is reasonable to implement the elemental functionalities in separate modules and combine them to generate one plausible response for the purpose of the continuous and long-term chat dialogue.

In this paper, we propose a framework for chat-oriented dialogue systems that can continue a long conversation with users and that can be used for a long-term. To achieve this goal, we pro-

Proceedings of the SIGDIAL 2016 Conference, pages 228–231,
Los Angeles, USA, 13-15 September 2016. ©2016 Association for Computational Linguistics

pose a combination method of various types of response generation modules, such as a statistical model-based module, rule-based module, and topic transition-oriented module. The core of this architecture is a selection method of the most appropriate response based on the breakdown index and willingness index.

The rest of the paper is organized as follows. In Section 2, we explain the architecture of combining multiple response generation modules. In Section 3, we describe a selection method of the most appropriate response from several hypotheses. In Section 4, the demo description shows the details of the demonstration system. Finally, we conclude the paper in Section 5.

2 Response generation method

To realize a continuous chat dialogue, the system needs to be robust to various user utterances. Statistical methods (Sugiyama et al., 2013) (Banchs and Li, 2012) are popular in realizing the robust response generation. These methods can also generate a high-quality response in terms of appropriateness and naturalness. On the flip side of this strength, the system response tends to be confined to the expectations and, sometimes, the user considers it boring. As a result, the appropriateness and naturalness are not necessarily connected with the long-term use of the system.

Occasional and sometimes unexpected topic shift could make the chat interesting, but it requires a different response generation algorithm aiming for an appropriate and natural response.

Keeping the interest of the user in the chat system for a long-term requires changing the behavior of the system. If the system's utterance is gradually matching the user's preference, the user can feel a sense of closeness to the system. Such behavior is difficult to implement using the statistical method only. Some type of control by handwritten rule is required to begin the conversation with a new topic from the system side. In addition, the functionality of delivering the news filtered by the user's preference can encourage the daily use of the system. Such dialogue does not require robust dialogue management. The simple pattern is beneficial for both the user and the system.

As a result, the requirement of a continuous and long-term chat dialogue system is "to generate an appropriate and natural response as a majority behavior, but sometimes the system may generate an unexpected but interesting response and, sometimes, may start the chat by following the user's preference and recent news/topics." It is natural to divide the aforementioned, sometimes conflicting, functionality into individual specific modules and select the most plausible response among the candidates. Figure 1 shows our proposed architecture for realizing multiple response generations and the selection method. In the architecture, we used the following three chat dialogue systems:

- Rule-based system: This chat system is based on the ELIZA type system (Weizenbaum, 1966).

- Statistical model-based system: This one uses the NTT chat dialogue API (Yoshimura, 2014).

- Topic transition-oriented system: This one is implemented with a sequence-to-sequence model (Sutskever et al., 2014). First, the system extracts topics from user utterances and generates the nearest topic utterance in the word embedded space made by Word2Vec (Mikolov et al., 2013). By doing this, the chat system aims to generate a response that has related but unexpected contents.

The rule-based system can reply naturally when the rules match the user utterance appropriately, but it does not have a wide coverage. The statistical model-based system can respond to various topics, but sometimes it replies inappropriately. The topic transition-oriented system tends to generate unnatural responses, but sometimes it can generate appropriate ones and stimulate the user's willingness to chat effectively. We try to realize a continuous and long-term chat-oriented dialogue system by using the good aspects of these modules.

3 Evaluation method of the system response

As a result of the requirements discussed in Section 2, we created the following two evaluation indices:

Breakdown Index (BI):
 This index determines how natural the system utterance is.

Willingness Index (WI):
 This one determines how the user's willingness is stimulated.

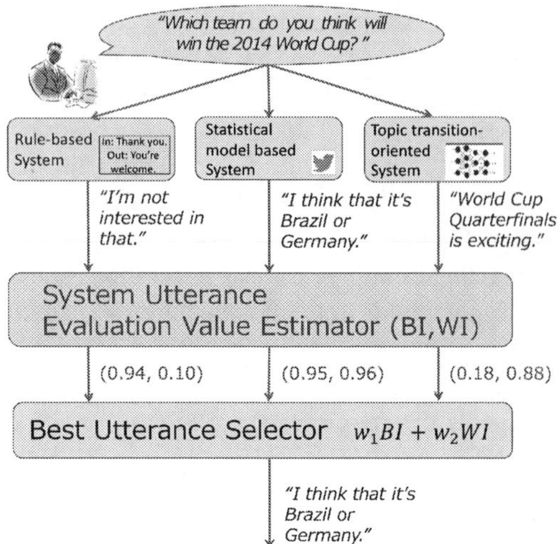

Figure 1: Proposed architecture for realizing multiple response generation modules, and the selection method.

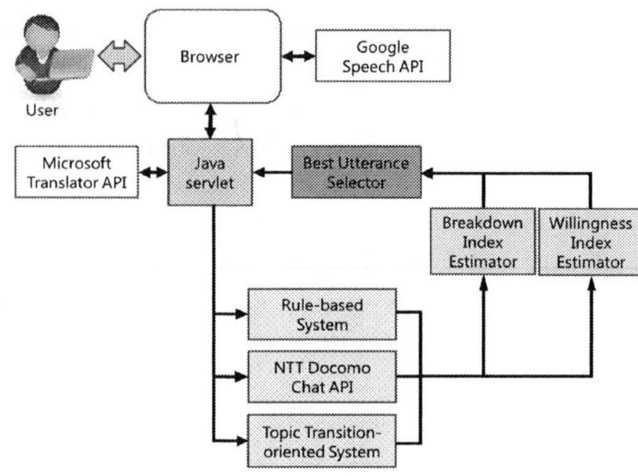

Figure 2: Architecture of the demonstration system.

To create an estimator for the BI, we used a chat-oriented dialogue corpus collected by the dialogue task group of Project Next NLP, Japan[1]. We collected training data from this corpus based on bag-of-words (unigram) from 1000 utterances (10 * 100 dialogues), which have breakdown annotations by 24 participants for each utterance, and used a linear-kernel support vector machine (SVM) as the regressor for the target value.

To create an estimator for the WI, we calculated the similarity between user-system utterance and tweet-reply pair, and use the similarity as the WI. According to the online research[2] to Japanese user (1,496 people) who use Twitter one day a week or more, the top three purposes of using Twitter are "collecting infomation about their own hobbies", "as a pleasure", and "communicating with their friends and family". Thus, Japanese users mainly use Twitter for pleasure and communicating with familier person. Therefore We calculating similarity by using twitter copus as WI.

The method of calculating WI shows as follows. First, we applied NFKC (Normalization Form Compatibility Composition) to the sentences and removed inappropriate tweets such as tweets from bots. We collected about 205k tweet pairs and built the model based on the Paragraph Vector model (Le and Mikolov, 2014). Paragraph Vector is an unsupervised algorithm that learns fixed-length feature representations from variable-length pieces of texts, such as sentences, paragraphs, and documents. We used the Paragraph Vector model for vectorizing sentences and estimated the semantic similarity by calculating the cosine similarity. We get 10-best tweets which similar to user utterance, calculate similarity between the reply and system utterance, and use the maximum value as WI.

Finally, the proposed system calculates the weighted sum of BI and WI, and selects the utterance that has the highest weighted sum as a final output. The weight is set to optimize the system output by using development test set.

4 Demo description

Our chat-oriented dialogue system was implemented based on the proposed method described in Sections 2 and 3. Figure 2 shows the architecture of the demonstration system. This system aims to select the most appropriate response by considering its naturalness and willingness. The proposed chat-oriented dialogue system works on a Japanese sentence only. Therefore, the demonstration system translates Japanese sentences to English ones using the Microsoft Translator API and shows the dialogue in both Japanese and English.

5 Conclusion

In this work, we propose a selection method of the most appropriate response by considering its naturalness and willingness. Both a breakdown index

---

[1]https://sites.google.com/site/projectnextnlp/english-page

[2]http://www.opt.ne.jp/news/pr/detail/id=2341

and a willingness index, which are related to continuous and long-term functionality, respectively, contribute to deciding what a good utterance is in a chat dialogue. In future work, we plan to conduct an experimental evaluation on the continuous and long-term use of the chat dialogue system.

References

Rafael E Banchs and Haizhou Li. 2012. IRIS: a chat-oriented dialogue system based on the vector space model. In *Proceedings of the ACL 2012 System Demonstrations*, pages 37–42. Association for Computational Linguistics.

Ryuichiro Higashinaka, Toyomi Meguro, Kenji Imamura, Hiroaki Sugiyama, Toshiro Makino, and Yoshihiro Matsuo. 2014. Evaluating coherence in open domain conversational systems. In *INTERSPEECH*, pages 130–134.

Quoc V. Le and Tomas Mikolov. 2014. Distributed Representations of Sentences and Documents. http://arxiv.org/abs/1405.4053. Mon, 02 Jun 2014 08:30:36 +0200.

Tomas Mikolov, Kai Chen, Greg Corrado, and Jeffrey Dean. 2013. Efficient estimation of word representations in vector space. *ICLR Workshop*.

Hiroaki Sugiyama, Toyomi Meguro, Ryuichiro Higashinaka, and Yasuhiro Minami. 2013. Open-domain utterance generation for conversational dialogue systems using web-scale dependency structures. In *The 14th annual SIGdial Meeting on Discourse and Dialogue*, pages 334–338.

Ilya Sutskever, Oriol Vinyals, and Quoc V Le. 2014. Sequence to sequence learning with neural networks. In *Advances in neural information processing systems*, pages 3104–3112.

Joseph Weizenbaum. 1966. ELIZA—a computer program for the study of natural language communication between man and machine. *Communications of the ACM*, 9(1):36–45.

Yang Xiang, Yaoyun Zhang, Xiaoqiang Zhou, Xiaolong Wang, and Yang Qin. 2014. Problematic Situation Analysis and Automatic Recognition for Chinese Online Conversational System. *CLP 2014*, page 43.

Takeshi Yoshimura. 2014. Casual Conversation Technology Achieving Natural Dialog with Computers.

Real-Time Understanding of Complex Discriminative Scene Descriptions

Ramesh Manuvinakurike[1], Casey Kennington[3*], David DeVault[1] and David Schlangen[2]
[1]USC Institute for Creative Technologies / Los Angeles, USA
[2]DSG / CITEC / Bielefeld University / Bielefeld, Germany
[3]Boise State University / Boise, USA
[1]`last@ict.usc.edu`, [2]`first.last@uni-bielefeld.de`
[3]`first.last@cs.boisestate.edu`

Abstract

Real-world scenes typically have complex structure, and utterances about them consequently do as well. We devise and evaluate a model that processes descriptions of complex configurations of geometric shapes and can identify the described scenes among a set of candidates, including similar distractors. The model works with raw images of scenes, and by design can work word-by-word incrementally. Hence, it can be used in highly-responsive interactive and situated settings. Using a corpus of descriptions from game-play between human subjects (who found this to be a challenging task), we show that reconstruction of description structure in our system contributes to task success and supports the performance of the word-based model of grounded semantics that we use.

1 Introduction

In this paper, we present and evaluate a language processing pipeline that enables an automated system to detect and understand complex referential language about visual objects depicted on a screen. This is an important practical capability for present and future interactive spoken dialogue systems. There is a trend toward increasing deployment of spoken dialogue systems for smartphones, tablets, automobiles, TVs, and other settings where information and options are presented on-screen along with an interactive speech channel in which visual items can be discussed (Celikyilmaz et al., 2014). Similarly, for future systems such as smartphones, quadcopters, or self-driving cars that are equipped with cameras, users

____
* The work was done while at Bielefeld University.

may wish to discuss objects visible to the system in camera images or video streams.

A challenge in enabling such capabilities for a broad range of applications is that human speakers draw on a diverse set of perceptual and language skills to communicate about objects in situated visual contexts. Consider the example in Figure 1, drawn from the corpus of RDG-Pento games (discussed further in Section 2). In this example, a human in the *director* role describes the visual scene highlighted in red (the *target image*) to another human in the *matcher role*. The scene description is provided in one continuous stream of speech, but it includes three functional segments each providing different referential information: [*this one is kind of a uh a blue T*] [*and a wooden w sort of*] [*the T is kind of malformed*]. The first and third of these three segments refer to the object at the top left of the target image, while the middle segment refers to the object at bottom right. An ability to detect the individual segments of language that carry information about individual referents is an important part of deciphering a scene description like this. Beyond detection, actually understanding these referential segments in context seems to require perceptual knowledge of vocabulary for colors, shapes, materials and hedged descriptions like *kind of a blue T*. In other game scenarios, it's important to understand plural references like *two brown crosses* and relational expressions like *this one has the L on top of the T*.

A variety of vocabulary knowledge is needed, as different speakers may describe individual objects in very different ways (the object described as *kind of a blue T* may also be called *a blue odd-shaped piece* or *a facebook*). When many scenes are described by the same pair of speakers, the pair tends to entrain or align to each other's vocabulary (Garrod and Anderson, 1987), for example by settling on *facebook* as a shorthand description for this ob-

Proceedings of the SIGDIAL 2016 Conference, pages 232–241,
Los Angeles, USA, 13-15 September 2016. ©2016 Association for Computational Linguistics

ject type. Finally, to understand a full scene description, the matcher needs to combine all the evidence from multiple referential segments involving a group of objects to identify the target image.

In this paper, we define and evaluate a language processing pipeline that allows many of these perceptual and language skills to be integrated into an automated system for understanding complex scene descriptions. We take the challenging visual reference game RDG-Pento, shown in Figure 1, as our testbed, and we evaluate both human-human and automated system performance in a corpus study. No prior work we are aware of has put forth techniques for grounded understanding of the kinds of noisy, complex, spoken descriptions of visual scenes that can occur in such interactive dialogue settings. This work describes and evaluates an initial approach to this complex problem, and it demonstrates the critical importance of segmentation and entrainment to achieving strong understanding performance. This approach extends the prior work (Kennington and Schlangen, 2015; Han et al., 2015) that assumed either that referential language from users has been pre-segmented, or that visual scenes are given not as raw images but as clean semantic representations, or that visual scenes are simple enough to be described with a one-off referring expression or caption. Our work makes none of these assumptions.

Our automated pipeline, discussed in Section 3, includes components for learning perceptually grounded word meanings, segmenting a stream of speech, identifying the type of referential language in each speech segment, resolving the references in each type of segment, and aggregating evidence across segments to select the most likely target image. Our technical approach enables all of these components to be trained in a supervised manner from annotated, in-domain, human-human reference data. Our quantitative evaluation, presented in Section 4, looks at the performance of the individual components as well as the overall pipeline, and quantifies the strong importance of segmentation, segment type identification, and speaker-specific vocabulary entrainment for improving performance in this task.

2 The RDG-Pento Game

The RDG-Pento (Rapid Dialogue Game-Pentomino) game is a two player collaborative game. RDG-Pento is a variant of the RDG-Image

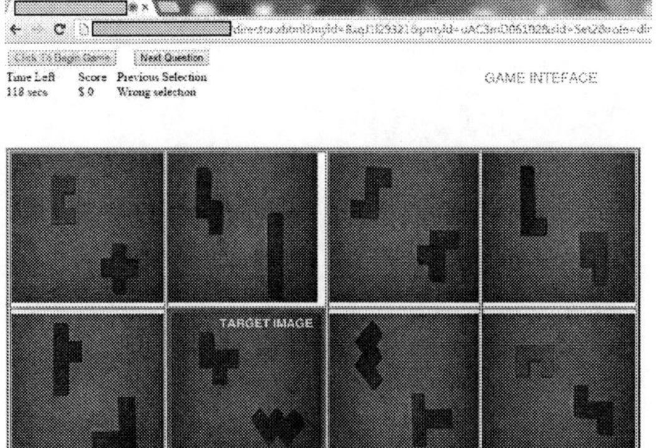

Director: this one is kind of a uh a blue T and a wooden w sort of the T is kind of malformed
Matcher: okay got it

Figure 1: In the game, the director is describing the image highlighted in red (the *target image*) to the matcher, who tries to identify this image from among the 8 possible images. The figure shows the game interface as seen by the director including a transcript of the director's speech.

game described by Manuvinakurike and DeVault (2015). As in RDG-Image, both players see 8 images on their screen in a 2X4 grid as shown in Figure 1. One person is assigned the role of director and the other person that of matcher. The director's screen has a single *target image* (TI) highlighted with a red border. The goal of the director is to uniquely describe the TI for the matcher to identify among the distractor images. The 8 images are shown in a different order on the director and matcher screens, so that the TI cannot be identified by grid position. The players can speak freely until the matcher makes a selection. Once the matcher indicates a selection, the director can advance the game. Over time, the gameplay gets progressively more challenging as the images tend to contain more objects that are similar in shape and color. The task is complex by design.

In RDG-Pento, the individual images are taken from a real-world, tabletop scene containing an arrangement of between one and six physical Pentomino objects. Individual images with varying numbers of objects are illustrated in Figure 2. The 8 images at any one time always contain the same number of objects; the number of objects increases as the game progresses. Players play for 5 rounds,

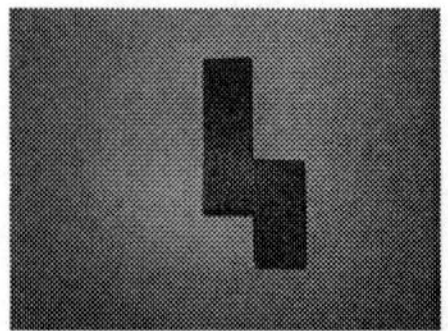

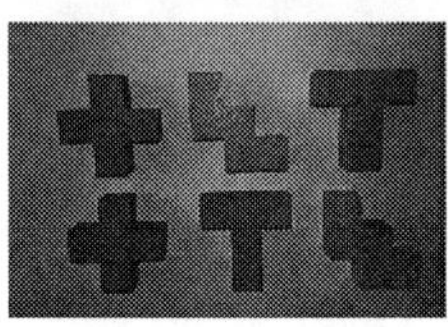

Figure 2: Example scene descriptions for three TIs

alternating roles. Each round has a time limit (about 200 seconds) that creates time pressure for the players, and the time remaining ticks down in a countdown timer.

Data Set The corpus used here was collected using a web framework for crowd-sourced data collection called Pair Me Up (PMU) (Manuvinakurike and DeVault, 2015). To create this corpus, 42 pairs of native English-speakers located in the U.S. and Canada were recruited using AMT. Game play and audio data were captured for each pair of speakers (who were not colocated and communicated entirely through their web browsers), and the resulting audio data was transcribed and annotated. 16 pairs completed all 5 game rounds, while the remaining crowd-sourced pairs completed only part of the game for various reasons. As our focus is on understanding individual scene descriptions, our data set here includes data from the 16 complete games as well as partial games. A more complete description and analysis of the corpus can be found in Zarrieß et al. (2016).

Data Annotation We annotated the transcribed director and matcher speech through a process of segmentation, segment type labeling, and referent identification. The segment types are shown in Table 1, and example annotations are provided in Figure 2. The annotation is carried out on each *tar-*

Segment type	Label	Examples
Singular	SIN	this is a green t, plus sign
Multiple objects	MUL	two Zs at top, they're all green
Relation	REL	above, in a diagonal
Others	OT	that was tough, lets start

Table 1: Segment types, labels, and examples

get image subdialogue in which the director and matcher discuss an individual target image. The segmentation and labeling steps create a complete partition of each speaker's speech into sequences of words with a related semantic function in our framework.[1]

Sequences of words that ascribe properties to a single object are joined under the SIN label. Our SIN segment type is not a simple syntactic concept like "singular NP referring expression". The SIN type includes not only simple singular NPs like *the blue s* but also clauses like *it's the blue s* and conjoined clauses like *it's like a harry potter and it's like maroon* (Figure 1). The individuation criterion for SIN is that a SIN segment must ascribe properties only to a single object; as such it may contain word sequences of various syntactic types.

Sequences of words such as *the two crosses* that ascribe properties to multiple objects are joined into a segment under the MUL label.

Sequences of words that describe a geometric relation between objects are segmented and given a REL label. These are generally prepositional expressions, and include both single-word prepositions (*underneath*, *below*) and multi-word complex prepositions (Quirk et al., 1985) which include multiple orthographic words ("next to", "left of" etc.). The REL segments generally describe geometric relations between objects referred to in SIN and MUL segments. An example would be *[MUL two crosses] [REL above] [MUL two Ts]*.

All other word sequences are assigned the type Others and given an OT label. This segment type includes acknowledgments, confirmations, feedback, and laughter, among other dialogue act types not addressed in this work.

For each segment of type SIN, MUL, or REL, the correct referent object or objects within the target image are also annotated.

In the data set, there are a total of 4132 *target*

---

[1]The annotation scheme was developed iteratively while keeping the reference resolution task and the WAC model (see Section 3.3.1) in mind. The annotation was done by an expert annotator.

image speaker transcripts in which either the director or the matcher's transcribed speech for a target image is annotated. There are 8030 annotated segments (5451 director segments and 2579 matcher segments). There are 1372 word types and 55,238 word tokens.

3 Language Processing Pipeline

In this section, we present our language processing pipeline for segmentation and understanding of complex scene descriptions. The modules, decision-making, and information flow for the pipeline are visualized in Figure 3. The pipeline modules include a Segmenter (Section 3.1), a Segment Type Classifier (Section 3.2), and a Reference Resolver (Section 3.3).

In this paper, we focus on how our pipeline could be used to automate the role of the matcher in the RDG-Pento game. We consider the task of selecting the correct target image based on a human director's transcribed speech drawn from our RDG-Pento corpus. The pipeline is designed however for eventual real-time operation using incremental ASR results, so that in the future it can be incorporated into a real-time interactive dialogue system. We view it as a crucial design constraint on our pipeline modules that the resolution process must take place *incrementally*; i.e., processing must not be deferred until the end of the user's speech. This is because humans resolve (i.e., comprehend) speech as it unfolds (Tanenhaus, 1995; Spivey et al., 2002), and incremental processing (i.e., processing word by word) is important to developing an efficient and natural speech channel for interactive systems (Skantze and Schlangen, 2009; Paetzel et al., 2015; DeVault et al., 2009; Aist et al., 2007). In the current study, we have therefore provided the human director's correctly transcribed speech as input to our pipeline on a word-by-word basis, as visualized in Figure 3.

3.1 Segmenter

The segmenter module is tasked with identifying the boundary points between segments. In our pipeline, this task is performed independently of the determination of segment types, which is handled by a separate classifier (Section 3.2).

Our approach to segmentation is similar to Celikyilmaz et al. (2014) which used CRFs for a similar task. Our pipeline currently uses linear-chain CRFs to find the segment boundaries (im-

plemented with Mallet (McCallum, 2002)). Using a CRF trained on the annotated RDG-Pento data set, we identify the most likely sequence of word-level boundary tags, where each tag indicates if the current word ends the previous segment or not.[2] An example segmentation is shown in Figure 3, where the word sequence *weird L to the top left of* is segmented into two segments, *[weird L]* and *[to the top left of]*. The features provided to the CRF include unigrams[3], the speaker's role, part-of-speech (POS) tags obtained using the Stanford POS tagger (Toutanova et al., 2003), and information about the scene such as the number of objects.

3.2 Segment Type Classifier

The segment type classifier assigns each detected segment with one of the type labels in Table 1 (SIN, MUL, REL, OT). This label informs the Reference Resolver module in how to proceed with the resolution process, as explained below.

The segment type labeler is an SVM classifier implemented in LIBSVM (Chang and Lin, 2011). Features used include word unigrams, word POS, user role, number of objects in the TI, and the top-level syntactic category of the segment as obtained from the Stanford parser (Klein and Manning, 2003). Figure 3 shows two examples of output from the segment type classifier, which assigns SIN to *[weird L]* and REL to *[to the top left of]*.

3.3 Reference Resolver

We introduce some notation to help explain the operation of the reference resolver (RR) module. When a scene description is to be resolved, there is a visual context in the game which we encode as a context set $\mathcal{C} = I_1, ..., I_8$ containing the eight visible images (see Figure 1). Each image I_k contains n objects $\{o_1^k, ..., o_n^k\}$, where n is fixed per context set, but varies across context sets from $n = 1$ to $n = 6$. The set of all objects in all images is $\mathcal{O} = \{o_l^k\}$, with $0 < k \le 8, 0 < l \le n$.

When the RR is invoked, the director has spoken some sequence of words which has been segmented by earlier modules into one or more segments $S_j = w_{1:m_j}$, and where each segment has been assigned a segment type $\text{type}(S_j) \in \{\text{SIN}, \text{MUL}, \text{REL}, \text{OT}\}$. For exam-

---

[2]We currently adopt this two-tag approach rather than BIO tagging as our tag-set provides a complete partition of each speaker's speech.

[3]Words of low frequency (i.e., <5) are replaced with a fixed symbol.

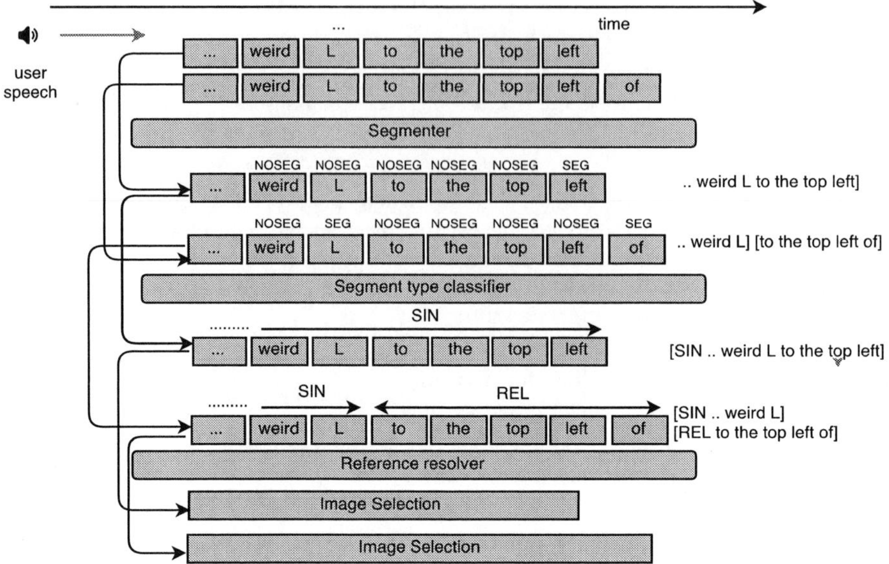

Figure 3: Information flow during processing of an utterance. The modules operate incrementally, word-by-word; as shown here, this can lead to revisions of decisions.

ple, $S_1 = \langle \text{weird}, \text{L} \rangle$, $S_2 = \langle \text{to}, \text{the}, \text{top}, \text{left}, \text{of} \rangle$ and $\text{type}(S_1) = \text{SIN}$, $\text{type}(S_2) = \text{REL}$.

The RR then tries to understand the individual words, typed segments, and the full scene description in terms of the visible objects o_l^k and the images I_k in the context set. We describe how words, segments, and scene descriptions are understood in the following three sections.

3.3.1 Understanding words

We understand individual words using the Words-as-Classifiers (WAC) model of Kennington and Schlangen (2015). In this model, a classifier is trained for each word w_p in the vocabulary. The model constructs a function from the perceptual features of a given object to a judgment about how well those features "fit" together with the word being understood. Such a function can be learned using a logistic regression classifier, separately for each word.

The inputs to the classifier are the low-level continuous features that represent the object (RGB values, HSV values, number of detected edges, x/y coordinates and radial distance from the center) extracted using OpenCV.[4] These classifiers are learned from instances of language use, i.e., by observing referring expressions paired with the ob-

ject referred to. Crucially, once learned, these word classifiers can be applied to any number of objects in a scene.

We trained a WAC model for each of the (non-relational) words in our RDG-Pento corpus, using the annotated correct referent information for our segmented data. After training, words can be applied to objects to yield a score:

$$score(w_p, o_l^k) = w_p(o_l^k) \tag{1}$$

(Technically, the score is the response of the classifier associated with word w_p applied to the feature representation of object o_l^k.)

Note that relational expressions are trained slightly differently than non-relational words. Examples of relational expressions include *underneath*, *below*, *next to*, *left of*, *right of*, *above*, and *diagonal*. A WAC classifier is trained for each full relational expression e_q (treated as a single token), and the 'fit' for a relational expression's classifier is a fit for a *pair* of objects: (The features used for such a classifier are comparative features, such as the euclidean distance between the two objects, as well as x and y distances.)

$$score_{rel}(e_q, o_{l_1}^k, o_{l_2}^k) = e_q(o_{l_1}^k, o_{l_2}^k) \tag{2}$$

There are about 300 of these expressions in RDG-Pento. *[SIN x] [REL r] [SIN y]* is resolved as

---

[4] http://opencv.org

r(x,y), so x and y are jointly constrained. See Kennington and Schlangen (2015) for details on this training.

3.3.2 Understanding segments

Consider an arbitrary segment $S_j = w_{1:m_j}$ such as $S_1 = \langle \text{weird}, \text{L} \rangle$. For a segment (SIN or MUL), we attempt to understand the segment as referring to some object or set of objects. To do so, we combine the word-level scores for all the words in the segment to yield a segment-level score[5] for each object o_l^k:

$$score(S_j, o_l^k) = score(w_1, o_l^k) \odot \; \ldots \; \odot \\ score(w_{m_j}, o_l^k) \tag{3}$$

Each segment $S_j = w_{1:m_j}$ hence induces an order R_j on the object set $\mathcal{O}$, through the scores assigned to each object o_l^k. With these ranked scores, we look at the type of segment to compute a final score $score_k^*(S_j)$ for each image I_k. For SIN segments, $score_k^*(S_j)$ is the score of the top-scoring object in I_k. For MUL segments with a cardinality of two (e.g., *two red crosses*), $score_k^*(S_j)$ is the sum of the scores of the top two objects in I_k, and so on.

Obtaining the final score $score_k^*(S_j)$ for REL segments is done in a similar manner with some minor differences. Because REL segments express a relation between *pairs* of objects (referred to in neighboring segments), a score for the relational expression in S_j can be computed for any pair of distinct objects $o_{l_1}^k$ and $o_{l_2}^k$ in image I_k using Eq. (2). We let $score_k^*(S_j)$ equal the score computed for the top-scoring objects $o_{l_1}^k$ and $o_{l_2}^k$ of the neighboring segments.

3.3.3 Understanding scene descriptions

In general, a scene description consists of segments $S_1, ..., S_z$. Composition takes segments $S_1, ..., S_z$ and produces a ranking over images. For this particular task, we make the following assumption: in each segment, the speaker is attempting to refer to a specific object (or set of objects), which from our perspective as matcher could be in any of the images. A good candidate I_k for the target image will have high scoring objects, all drawn from the same image, for all the segments $S_1, ..., S_z$.

We therefore obtain a final score for each image as shown in Eq. (4):

---

[5]The composition operator $\odot$ is left-associative and hence incremental. In this paper, word-level scores are composed by multiplying them.

Label	Precision	Recall	F-Score
SEG	0.85	0.74	0.79
NOSEG	0.93	0.97	0.95

Table 2: Segmenter performance

Label	Precision	Recall	F-score	% of segments
SIN	0.91	0.96	0.93	57
REL	0.97	0.85	0.91	6
MUL	0.86	0.60	0.71	3
OT	0.96	0.97	0.96	34

Table 3: Segment type classifier performance

$$score(I_k) = \sum_{j=1}^{z} score_k^*(S_j) \tag{4}$$

The image I_k^* selected by our pipeline for a full scene description is then given by:

$$I_k^* = \underset{k}{\arg\max} \, score(I_k) \tag{5}$$

4 Experiments & Evaluations

We first evaluate the segmenter and segment type classifier as individual modules. We then evaluate the entire processing pipeline and explore the impact of several factors on pipeline performance.

4.1 Segmenter Evaluation

Task & Data We used the annotated RDG-Pento data to perform a "hold-one-dialogue-pair-out" cross-validation of the segmenter. The task is to segment each speaker's speech for each target image by tagging each word using the tags SEG and NOSEG. The SEG tag here indicates the last word in the current segment. Figure 3 gives an example of the tagging.

Results The results are presented in Table 2. These results show that the segmenter is working with some success, with precision 0.85 and recall 0.74 for the SEG tag indicating a word boundary. Note that occasional errors in segment boundaries may not be overly problematic for the overall pipeline, as what we ultimately care most about is accurate target image selection. We evaluate the overall pipeline below (Section 4.3).

4.2 Segment Type Classifier Evaluation

Task & Data We used the annotated RDG-Pento data to perform a hold-one-pair-out cross-validation of the segment type classifier, training a

SVM classifier to predict labels SIN, MUL, REL, and OT using the features described in Section 3.2.

Results The results are given in Table 3. We also report the percentage of segments that have each label in the corpus. The segment type classifier performs well on most of the class labels. Of slight concern is the low-frequency MUL label. One factor here is that people use number words like *two* not just to refer to multiple objects, but also to describe individual objects, e.g., *the two red crosses* (a MUL segment) vs. *the one with two sides* (a SIN segment).

4.3 Pipeline Evaluation

We evaluated our pipeline under varied conditions to understand how well it works when segmentation is not performed at all, when the segmentation and type classifier modules produce perfect output (using oracle annotations), and when entrainment to a specific speaker is possible. We evaluate our pipeline on the accuracy of the task of image retrieval given a scene description from our data set.

4.3.1 Three baselines

We compare against a weak random baseline (1/8 = 0.125) as well as a rather strong one, namely the accuracies of the human-human pairs in the RDG-Pento corpus. As Table 4 shows, in the simplest case, with only one object per image, the average human success rate is 85%, but this decreases to 60% when there are four objects/image. It then increases to 68% when 6 objects are present, possibly due to the use of a more structured description ordering in the six object scenes. We leave further analysis of the human strategies for future work. These numbers show that the game is challenging for humans.

We also include in Table 4 a simple Naive Bayes classification approach as an alternative to our entire pipeline. In our study, there were only 40 possible image sets that were fixed in advance. For each possible image set, a different Naive Bayes classifier is trained using Weka (Hall et al., 2009) in a hold-one-pair-out cross-validation. The eight images are treated as atomic classes to be predicted, and unigram features drawn from the union of all (unsegmented) director speech are used to predict the target image. This method is broadly comparable to the NLU model used in (Paetzel et al., 2015) to achieve high performance in resolving references to pictures of single objects. As can

be seen, the accuracy for this method is as high as 43% for single object TIs in the RDG-Pento data set, but the accuracy rapidly falls to near the random baseline as the number of objects/image increases. This weak performance for a classifier without segmentation confirms the importance of segmenting complex descriptions into references to individual objects in the RDG-Pento game.

4.3.2 Five versions of the pipeline

Table 4 includes results for 5 versions of our pipeline. The versions differ in terms of which segment boundaries and segment type labels are used, and in the type of cross-validation performed. A first version (I) explores how well the pipeline works if unsegmented scene descriptions are provided and a SIN label is assumed to cover the entire scene description. This model is broadly comparable to the Naive Bayes baseline, but substitutes a WAC-based NLU component. The evaluation of version (I) uses a hold-one-pair-out (HOPO) cross-validation, where all modules are trained on every pair except for the one being used for testing. A second version (II) uses automatically determined segment boundaries and segment type labels, in a HOPO cross-validation, and represents our pipeline as described in Section 3. A third version (III) substitutes in human-annotated or "oracle" segment boundaries and type labels, allowing us to observe the performance loss associated with imperfect segmentation and type labeling in our pipeline. The fourth and fifth versions of the pipeline switch to a hold-one-episode-out (HOEO) cross-validation, where only the specific scene description ("episode") being tested is held out from training. When compared with a HOPO cross-validation, the HOEO setup allows us to investigate the value of learning from and entraining to the specific speaker's vocabulary and speech patterns (such as calling the purple object in Figure 2 a "harry potter").

4.3.3 Results

Table 4 summarizes the image retrieval accuracies for our three baselines and five versions of our pipeline. We discuss here some observations from these results. First, in comparing pipeline versions (I) and (II), we observe that the use of automated segmentation and a segment type classifier in (II) leads to a substantial increase in accuracy of 5-20% ($p<0.001$)[6] depending on the

---

[6]wilcoxon rank sum test

	#objects per TI				
	1	2	3	4	6
Random baseline	0.13	0.13	0.13	0.13	0.13
Naive Bayes baseline	0.43	0.20	0.14	0.14	0.13
Seg+lab X-validation					
(I) None HOPO	0.47	0.20	0.24	0.13	0.15
(II) Auto HOPO	0.52	0.40	0.31	0.24	0.23
(III) Oracle HOPO	0.54	0.42	0.32	0.30	0.26
(IV) Auto HOEO	0.60	0.46	0.37	0.25	0.23
(V) Oracle HOEO	0.64	0.50	0.41	0.34	0.44
Human-human baseline	0.85	0.73	0.66	0.60	0.68

Table 4: Image retrieval accuracies for five versions of the pipeline and three baselines.

number of objects/image. Comparing (II) and (III), we see that if our segmenter and segment type classifier could reproduce the human segment annotations perfectly, an additional improvement of 1-6% (p<0.001) accuracy would be possible. Comparing (II) to (IV), we see that exposing our pipeline training to the idiosyncratic speech and vocabulary of a given speaker would hypothetically enable an increase in accuracy of up to 8% (p<0.001). Note however that this setup cannot easily be replicated in a real-time system, as our HOEO training provides not only samples of the transcribed speech of the same speaker, but also human annotations of the segment boundaries, segment types, and correct referents for this speech (which would not generally be available for immediate use in a run-time system). Comparing (IV) to (V), we see that oracle segment boundaries and types also improve accuracies in a HOEO evaluation between 4-19% (p<0.001). Comparing our fully automated HOPO pipeline (II) to the baselines, we see that our pipeline performs considerably better than the random and Naive Bayes baselines. At the same time, there is still much room for improvement when we compare to human-human accuracy. Segmentation is harder the more objects (and hence segments) there are. Compared to HOEO, HOPO is additionally hurt by idiosyncratic vocabulary that isn't learned, so even with oracle segmentations, performance does not increase as much.

4.4 Evaluation of Object Retrieval

Table 4 shows that even when there is just one object in each of the eight images, our pipeline (II) only selects the correct image 52% of the time given the complete scene description, while humans succeed 85% of the time. We further investigated our performance at understanding de-

n	1	2	3	4	6
accuracy	1	.88	.77	.60	.66

Table 5: Accuracy for object retrieval in target images with n objects.

scriptions of individual objects by defining a constructed "object retrieval" problem. In this problem, individual SIN segments from the RDG-Pento corpus are considered one at a time, and the correct target image is provided by an oracle. The only task is to use the WAC model to select the correct referent object within the image for a single SIN segment. An example of the object retrieval problem is to select the correct referent for the SIN segment *and a wooden w sort of* in the known target image of Figure 1.

The results are shown in Table 5. We can observe that object retrieval is by itself a non-trivial problem for our WAC model, especially as the number of objects increases. This is somewhat by design in that the multiple objects present within an image are often selected to be fairly similar in their properties, and multiple objects may match ambiguous SIN segments such as *the T* or *the plus sign*. We speculate that we could gain here from factoring in positional information implicit in description strategies such as going from top left to bottom right in describing the objects.

5 Related Work

The work described in this paper directly builds off of Paetzel et al. (2015) as the same RDG game scenario was used, however reference was only made to single objects in that work. The work here also builds off of Kennington and Schlangen (2015) in the same way in that their work only focused on reference to single objects. The extension of this previous work to handle more complex scene descriptions required substantial composition on the word and segment levels. The segmentation presented here was fairly straight forward (similar in spirit to chunking as in Marcus (1995)). Composition is currently an active area in distributional semantics where word meanings are represented by high-dimensional vectors and composition amounts to some kind of vector operation (see (Milajevs et al., 2014) for a comparison of methods). An important difference is that here words and segments are composed at the denotational level (i.e., on the scores given by the

WAC model, akin to *referentially afforded concept composition* (Mcnally and Boleda, 2015)). Also related are the recent efforts in automatic image captioning and retrieval, where the task is to generate a description (a caption) for a given image or retrieve one being given a description. A frequently taken approach is to use a convolutional neural network to map the image into a dense vector, and then to condition a neural language model on this to produce an output string or using it to map the description into the same space (Vinyals et al., 2015; Devlin et al., 2015; Socher et al., 2014). See also Fang et al. (2015), which is more directly related to our model in that they use "word detectors" to propose words for image regions.

6 Conclusions & Future work

We have presented an approach to understanding complex, multi-utterance references to images containing spatially complex scenes. The approach by design works incrementally, and hence is ready to be used in an interactive system. We presented evaluations that go end-to-end from utterance input to resolution decision (but not yet taking in speech). We have shown that segmentation is a critical component for understanding complex visual scene descriptions. This work opens avenues for future explorations in various directions. Intra- and inter-segment composition (through multiplication and addition, respectively) are approached somewhat simplistically, and we want to explore the consequences of these decisions more deeply in future work. Additionally, as discussed above, there seems to be much implicit information in how speakers go from one reference to the next, which might be possible to capture in a transition model. Finally, in an online setting, there is more than just the decision "this is the referent"; one must also decide when and how to act based on the confidence in the resolution. Lastly, our results have shown that human pairs do align on their conceptual description frames (Garrod and Anderson, 1987). Whether human users would also do this with an artificial interlocutor, if it were able to do the required kind of online learning, is another exciting question for future work, enabled by the work presented here. We also plan to extend our work in the future to include descriptions which contain relations between non singular objects (Ex: [MUL two red crosses] [REL above] [SIN brown L], [MUL two red crosses] [REL on top of] [MUL two green Ts] etc.). However, such descriptions were very rare in the corpus.

Obtaining samples for training the classifiers is another issue. One source of sparsity is idiosyncratic descriptions like 'harry potter' or 'facebook'. In dialogue (our intended setting), these could be grounded through clarification requests. A more extensive solution would address metaphoric or meronymic usage ("looks like xyz"). We will explore this in future work.

Acknowledgments

This work was in part supported by the Cluster of Excellence Cognitive Interaction Technology 'CITEC' (EXC 277) at Bielefeld University, which is funded by the German Research Foundation (DFG), and the KogniHome project, funded by BMBF. This work was supported in part by the National Science Foundation under Grant No. IIS-1219253 and by the U.S. Army. Any opinions, findings, and conclusions or recommendations expressed in this material are those of the author(s) and do not necessarily reflect the views, position, or policy of the National Science Foundation or the United States Government, and no official endorsement should be inferred.

References

Gregory Aist, James Allen, Ellen Campana, Carlos Gomez Gallo, Scott Stoness, Mary Swift, and Michael K Tanenhaus. 2007. Incremental dialogue system faster than and preferred to its nonincremental counterpart. In *the 29th Annual Conference of the Cognitive Science Society*.

Asli Celikyilmaz, Zhaleh Feizollahi, Dilek Hakkani-Tur, and Ruhi Sarikaya. 2014. Resolving referring expressions in conversational dialogs for natural user interfaces. In *Proceedings of EMNLP*.

Chih-Chung Chang and Chih-Jen Lin. 2011. Libsvm: a library for support vector machines. *ACM Transactions on Intelligent Systems and Technology (TIST)*, 2(3):27.

David DeVault, Kenji Sagae, and David Traum. 2009. Can i finish?: learning when to respond to incremental interpretation results in interactive dialogue. In *Proceedings of the SIGDIAL 2009 Conference: The 10th Annual Meeting of the Special Interest Group on Discourse and Dialogue*, pages 11–20. Association for Computational Linguistics.

Jacob Devlin, Hao Cheng, Hao Fang, Saurabh Gupta, Li Deng, Xiaodong He, Geoffrey Zweig, and Margaret Mitchell. 2015. Language models for image captioning: The quirks and what works. In *Proceedings of the 53rd Annual Meeting of the Association for Computational Linguistics and the 7th International Joint Conference on Natural Language Processing (Volume 2: Short Papers)*, pages 100–105, Beijing, China, July. Association for Computational Linguistics.

Hao Fang, Saurabh Gupta, Forrest Iandola, Rupesh Srivastava, Li Deng, Piotr Dollar, Jianfeng Gao, Xiaodong He, Margaret Mitchell, John Platt, Lawrence Zitnick, and Geoffrey Zweig. 2015. From captions to visual concepts and back. In *Proceedings of CVPR*, Boston, MA, USA, June. IEEE.

Simon Garrod and Anthony Anderson. 1987. Saying what you mean in dialogue: A study in conceptual and semantic co-ordination. *Cognition*, 27:181–218.

Mark Hall, Eibe Frank, Geoffrey Holmes, Bernhard Pfahringer, Peter Reutemann, and Ian H Witten. 2009. The weka data mining software: an update. *ACM SIGKDD explorations newsletter*, 11(1):10–18.

Ting Han, Casey Kennington, and David Schlangen. 2015. Building and Applying Perceptually-Grounded Representations of Multimodal Scene Descriptions. In *Proceedings of SEMDial*, Gothenburg, Sweden.

Casey Kennington and David Schlangen. 2015. Simple learning and compositional application of perceptually grounded word meanings for incremental reference resolution. In *Proceedings of the Conference for the Association for Computational Linguistics (ACL)*.

Dan Klein and Christopher D. Manning. 2003. Accurate unlexicalized parsing. In *Proceedings of the 41st Meeting of the Association for Computational Linguistics*, pages 423–430.

Ramesh Manuvinakurike and David DeVault. 2015. Pair me up: A web framework for crowd-sourced spoken dialogue collection. In *Natural Language Dialog Systems and Intelligent Assistants*, pages 189–201. Springer.

Mitchell P Marcus. 1995. Text Chunking using Transformation-Based Learning. In *In Pro- ceedings of the Third Workshop on Very Large Cor- pora*, pages 82–94.

Andrew Kachites McCallum. 2002. Mallet: A machine learning for language toolkit. http://mallet.cs.umass.edu.

Louise Mcnally and Gemma Boleda. 2015. Conceptual vs. Referential Affordance in Concept Composition. In *Compositionality and Concepts in Linguistics and Psychology*, pages 1–20.

Dmitrijs Milajevs, Dimitri Kartsaklis, Mehrnoosh Sadrzadeh, Matthew Purver, Computer Science, and Mile End Road. 2014. Evaluating Neural Word Representations in Tensor-Based Compositional Settings. In *EMLNP*, pages 708–719.

Maike Paetzel, Ramesh Manuvinakurike, and David DeVault. 2015. "So, which one is it?" The effect of alternative incremental architectures in a high-performance game-playing agent. In *The 16th Annual Meeting of the Special Interest Group on Discourse and Dialogue (SigDial)*.

R. Quirk, S. Greenbaum, G. Leech, and J. Svartvik. 1985. *A Comprehensive grammar of the English language*. General Grammar Series. Longman.

Gabriel Skantze and David Schlangen. 2009. Incremental dialogue processing in a micro-domain. In *Proceedings of the 12th Conference of the European Chapter of the Association for Computational Linguistics*, pages 745–753. Association for Computational Linguistics.

Richard Socher, Andrej Karpathy, Quoc V Le, Christopher D Manning, and Andrew Y Ng. 2014. Grounded Compositional Semantics for Finding and Describing Images with Sentences. *Transactions of the ACL (TACL)*.

Michael J Spivey, Michael K Tanenhaus, Kathleen M Eberhard, and Julie C Sedivy. 2002. Eye movements and spoken language comprehension: Effects of visual context on syntactic ambiguity resolution. *Cognitive Psychology*, 45(4):447–481.

Michael Tanenhaus. 1995. Integration of Visual and Linguistic Information in Spoken Language Comprehension. *Science*, 268:1632–1634.

Kristina Toutanova, Dan Klein, Christopher D Manning, and Yoram Singer. 2003. Feature-rich part-of-speech tagging with a cyclic dependency network. In *Proceedings of the 2003 Conference of the North American Chapter of the Association for Computational Linguistics on Human Language Technology-Volume 1*, pages 173–180. Association for Computational Linguistics.

Oriol Vinyals, Alexander Toshev, Samy Bengio, and Dumitru Erhan. 2015. Show and tell: A neural image caption generator. In *Computer Vision and Pattern Recognition*.

Sina Zarrieß, Julian Hough, Casey Kennington, Ramesh Manuvinakurike, David DeVault, and David Schlangen. 2016. Pentoref: A corpus of spoken references in task-oriented dialogues.

Supporting Spoken Assistant Systems with a Graphical User Interface that Signals Incremental Understanding and Prediction State

Casey Kennington and **David Schlangen**
Boise State University and DSG / CITEC / Bielefeld University
caseykennington@boisestate.edu and david.schlangen@uni-bielefeld.de

Abstract

Arguably, spoken dialogue systems are most often used not in hands/eyes-busy situations, but rather in settings where a graphical display is also available, such as a mobile phone. We explore the use of a graphical output modality for signalling incremental understanding and prediction state of the dialogue system. By visualising the current dialogue state and possible continuations of it as a simple tree, and allowing interaction with that visualisation (e.g., for confirmations or corrections), the system provides both feedback on past user actions and guidance on possible future ones, and it can span the continuum from slot filling to full prediction of user intent (such as GoogleNow). We evaluate our system with real users and report that they found the system intuitive and easy to use, and that incremental and adaptive settings enable users to accomplish more tasks.

1 Introduction

Current virtual personal assistants (PAs) require users to either formulate complex intents in one utterance (e.g., "call Peter Miller on his mobile phone") or go through tedious sub-dialogues (e.g., "phone call" – *who would you like to call?* – "Peter Miller" – *I have a mobile number and a work number. Which one do you want?*). This is not how one would interact with a human assistant, where the request would be naturally structured into smaller chunks that individually get acknowledged (e.g., "Can you make a connection for me?" – *sure* – "with Peter Miller" - *uh huh* - "on his mobile" - *dialling now*). Current PAs signal ongoing understanding by displaying the state of the recognised speech (ASR) to the user, but not their semantic interpretation of it. Another type of assistant system forgoes enquiring user intent altogether and infers *likely* intents from context. GoogleNow, for example, might present traffic information to a user picking up their mobile phone at their typical commute time. These systems display their "understanding" state, but do not allow any type of interaction with it apart from dismissing the provided information.

In this work, we explore adding a graphical user interface (GUI) modality that makes it possible to see these interaction styles as extremes on a continuum, and to realise positions between these extremes and present a mixed graphical/voice enabled PA that can provide feedback of understanding to the user *incrementally* as the user's utterance unfolds–allowing users to make requests in instalments instead of fully thought-out requests. It does this by signalling ongoing understanding in an intuitive tree-like GUI that can be displayed on a mobile device. We evaluate our system by directing users to perform tasks using it under non-incremental (i.e., ASR endpointing) and incremental conditions and then compare the two conditions. We further compare a non-adaptive with an adaptive (i.e., infers likely events) version of our system. We report that the users found the interface intuitive and easy to use, and that users were able to perform tasks more efficiently with incremental as well as adaptive variants of the system.

2 Related Work

This work builds upon several threads of previous research: Chai et al. (2014) addressed misalignments in understanding (i.e., common ground (Clark and Schaefer, 1989)) between robots and humans by informing the human of the internal system state via speech. We take this idea and ap-

242

Proceedings of the SIGDIAL 2016 Conference, pages 242–251,
Los Angeles, USA, 13-15 September 2016. ©2016 Association for Computational Linguistics

ply it to a PA by displaying the internal state of
the system to the user via a GUI (explained in Section 3.5), allowing the user to determine if system
understanding has taken place–a way of providing
feedback and backchannels to the user. Dethlefs et
al. (2016) provide a good review of work that show
how backchannels facilitate grounding, feedback,
and clarifications in human spoken dialogue, and
apply an *information density* approach to determine when to backchannel using speech. Because
we don't backchannel using speech here, there is
no potential overlap between the user and the system; rather, our system can display backchannels
and ask clarifications without frustrating the user
through inadvertent overlaps.

Though different in many ways, our work is
similar in some regards to Larsson et al. (2011),
which displays information to the user and allows
the user to navigate the display itself (e.g., by saying *up* or *down* in a menu list)–functionality that
we intend to apply to our GUI in future work. Our
work is also comparable to SDS toolkits such as
IrisTK (Skantze and Moubayed, 2012) and Open-
Dial (Lison, 2015) which enable SDS designers to
visualise the internal state of their systems, though
not for end user interpretability.

Some of the work here is inspired by the *Microsoft Language Understanding Intelligent Service* (LUIS) project (Williams et al., 2015). While
our system by no means achieves the scale that
LUIS does, we offer here an additional contribution of an open source LUIS-like system (with the
important addition of the graphical interface) that
is authorable (using JSON files; we leave authoring using a web interface like that of LUIS to future work), extensible (affordances can be easily
added), incremental (in that respect going beyond
LUIS), trainable (i.e., can learn from examples,
but can still function well without examples), and
can learn through interacting (here we apply a user
model that learns during interaction).

3   System Description

This section introduces and describes our SDS,
which is modularised into four main components:
ASR, natural language understanding (NLU), dialogue management (DM), and the graphical user
interface (GUI) which, as explained below, is visualised as a right-branching tree. The overall system is represented in Figure 1. For the remainder of this section, each module is explained in

turn. As each module processes input incrementally (i.e., word for word), we first explain our
framework for incremental processing.

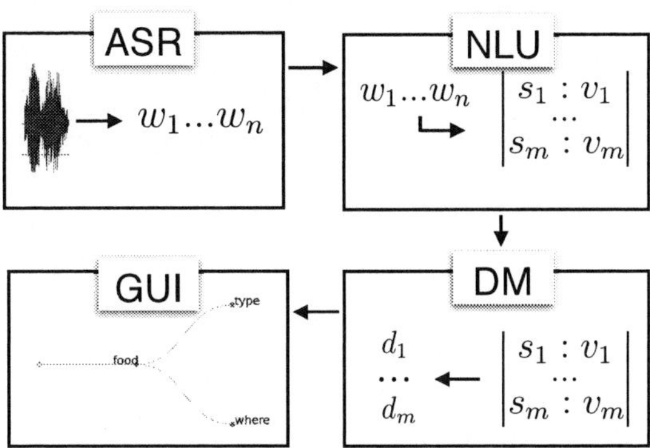

Figure 1: Overview of system made up of ASR which takes in
a speech signal and produces transcribed words, NLU, which
takes words and produces a slots in a frame, DM which takes
slots and produces a decision for each, and the GUI which
displays the state of the system.

3.1   Incremental Dialogue

An aspect of our SDS that sets it apart from others is the requirement that it process *incrementally*.
One potential concern with incremental processing is regarding informativeness: why act early
when waiting might provide additional information, resulting in better-informed decisions? The
trade off is *naturalness* as perceived by the user
who is interacting with the SDS. Indeed, it has
been shown that human users perceive incremental systems as being more natural than traditional,
turn-based systems (Aist et al., 2006; Skantze and
Schlangen, 2009; Skantze and Hjalmarsson, 1991;
Asri et al., 2014), offer a more human-like experience (Edlund et al., 2008) and are more satisfying to interact with than non-incremental systems
(Aist et al., 2007). Psycholinguistic research has
also shown that humans comprehend utterances
as they unfold and do not wait until the end of
an utterance to begin the comprehension process
(Tanenhaus et al., 1995; Spivey et al., 2002).

The trade-off between informativeness and naturalness can be reconciled when mechanisms are
in place that allow earlier decisions to be repaired.
Such mechanisms are offered by the incremental unit (IU) framework for SDS (Schlangen and
Skantze, 2011), which we apply here. Following Kennington et al. (2014), the IU framework
consists of a network of processing *modules*. A
typical module takes input, performs some kind
of processing on that data, and produces output.

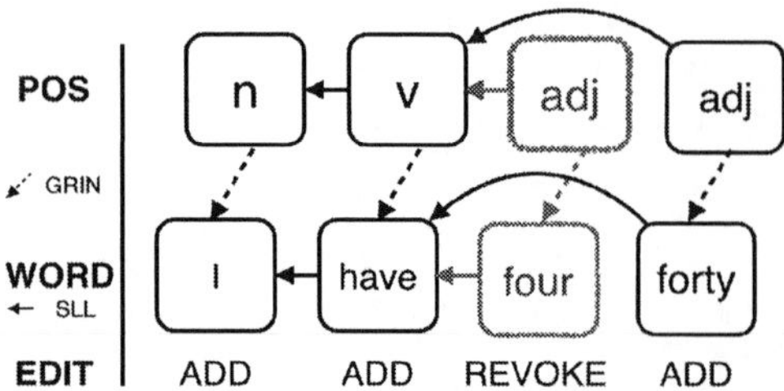

Figure 2: Example of IU network; part-of-speech tags are grounded into words, tags and words have same level links with left IU; *four* is revoked and replaced with *forty*.

The data are packaged as the payload of *incremental units* (IUs) which are passed between modules. The IUs themselves are interconnected via so-called *same level links* (SLL) and *grounded-in links* (GRIN), the former allowing the linking of IUs as a growing sequence, the latter allowing that sequence to convey what IUs directly affect it (see Figure 2 for an example of incremental ASR). Thus IUs can be *added*, but can be later *revoked* and replaced in light of new information. The IU framework can take advantage of up-to-date information, but have the potential to function in such a way that users perceive as more natural.

The modules explained in the remainder of this section are implemented as IU-modules and process incrementally. Each will now be explained.

3.2 Speech Recognition

The module that takes speech input from the user in our SDS is the ASR component. Incremental ASR must transcribe uttered speech into words which must be forthcoming from the ASR as early as possible (i.e., the ASR must not wait for end-pointing to produce output). Each module that follows must also process incrementally, acting in lock-step upon input as it is received. Incremental ASR is not new (Baumann et al., 2009) and many of the current freely-accessible ASR systems can produce output (semi-) incrementally. We opt for Google ASR for its vocabulary coverage of our evaluation language (German). Following, Baumann et al. (2016), we package output from the Google service into IUs which are passed to the NLU module, which we now explain.

3.3 Language Understanding

We approach the task of NLU as a slot-filling task (a very common approach; see Tur et al. (2012)) where an intent is complete when all slots of a *frame* are filled. The main driver of the NLU in

our SDS is the SIUM model of NLU introduced in Kennington et al. (2013). SIUM has been used in several systems which have reported substantial results in various domains, languages, and tasks (Han et al., 2015; Kennington et al., 2015; Kennington and Schlangen, 2017) Though originally a model of reference resolution, it was always intended to be used for general NLU, which we do here. The model is formalised as follows:

$$P(I|U) = \frac{1}{P(U)} P(I) \sum_{r \in R} P(U|R=r) P(R=r|I) \quad (1)$$

That is, $P(I|U)$ is the probability of the intent I (i.e., a frame slot) behind the speaker's (ongoing) utterance U. This is recovered using the mediating variable R, a set of *properties* which map between aspects of U and aspects of I. We opt for abstract properties here (e.g., the frame for `restaurant` might be filled by a certain type of cuisine intent such as `italian` which has properties like `pasta`, `mediterranean`, `vegetarian`, etc.). Properties are pre-defined by a system designer and can match words that might be uttered to describe the intent in question. For $P(R|I)$, probability is distributed uniformly over all properties that a given intent is specified to have. (If other information is available, more informative priors could be used as well.) The mapping between properties and aspects of U can be learned from data. During application, R is marginalised over, resulting in a distribution over possible intents.[1] This occurs at each word increment, where the distribution from the previous increment is combined via $P(I)$, keeping track of the distribution over time.

We further apply a simple rule to add in a-priori knowledge: if some $r \in R$ and $w \in U$ are such that $r \doteq w$ (where $\doteq$ is string equality; e.g., an intent has the property of `pasta` and the word *pasta* is uttered), then we set $C(U{=}w|R{=}r){=}1$. To allow for possible ASR confusions, we also apply $C(U{=}w|R{=}r) = 1 - ld(w,r)/max(len(w),len(r))$, where ld is the *Levenshtein distance* (but we only apply this if the calculated value is above a threshold of 0.6; i.e., the two strings are mostly similar). For all other w, $C(w|r){=}0$. This results in a distribution C, which we renormalise and blend with learned distribution to yield $P(U|R)$.

---

[1] In Kennington et al. (2013) the authors apply Bayes' Rule to allow $P(U|R)$ to produce a distribution over properties, which we adopt here.

We apply an instantiation of SIUM for each slot. The candidate slots which are processed depends on the state of the dialogue; only slots represented by visible nodes are considered, thereby reducing the possible frames that could be predicted. At each word increment, the updated slots (and their corresponding) distributions are given to the DM, which will now be explained.

3.4 Dialogue Manager

The DM plays a crucial role in our SDS: as well as determining *how* to act, the DM is called upon to decide *when* to act, effectively giving the DM the control over timing of actions rather than relying on ASR endpointing–further separating our SDS from other systems. The DM policy is based on a confidence score derived from the NLU (in this case, we used the distribution's argmax value) using thresholds for the actions (see below), set by hand (i.e., trial and error). At each word and resulting distribution from NLU, the DM needs to choose one of the following:

- `wait` – wait for more information (i.e., for the next word)

- `select` – as the NLU is confident enough, fill the slot can with the argmax from NLU

- `request` – signal a (yes/no) clarification request on the current slot and the proposed filler

- `confirm` – act on the confirmation of the user; in effect, `select` the proposed slot value

Though the thresholds are statically set, we applied OpenDial (Lison, 2015) as an IU-module to perform the task of the DM with the future goal that these values could be adjusted through reinforcement learning (which OpenDial could provide). The DM processes and makes a decision for *each slot*, with the assumption that only one slot out of all that are processed will result in an non-`wait` action (though this is not enforced).

3.5 Graphical User Interface

The goal of the GUI is to intuitively inform the user about the internal state of the ongoing understanding. One motivation for this is that the user can determine if the system understood the user's intent before providing the user with a response (e.g., a list of restaurants of a certain type); i.e., if any misunderstanding takes place, it happens before the system commits to an action and is potentially more easily repaired.

The display is a right-branching tree, where the branches directly off the root node display the affordances of the system (i.e., what domains of things it can understand and do something about). When the first tree is displayed, it represents a state of the NLU where none of the slots are filled, as in Figure 3.

When a user verbally selects a domain to ask about, the tree is adjusted to make that domain the only one displayed and

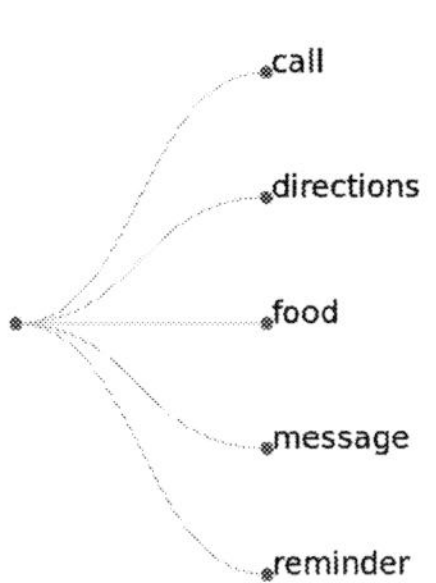

Figure 3: Example tree as branching from the root; each branch represents a system affordance (i.e., making a phone call, reminder, finding a restaurant, leaving a message, and finding a route).

the slots that are required for that domain are shown as branches. The user can then fill those slots (i.e., branches) by uttering the displayed name, or, alternatively, by uttering the item to fill the slot directly. For example, at a minimum, the user could utter the name of the domain then an item for each slot (e.g., *food Thai downtown*) or the speech could be more natural (e.g., *I'm quite hungry, I am looking for some Thai food maybe in the downtown area*). Crucially, the user can also hesitate within and between chunks, as advancement is not triggered by silence thresholding, but rather semantically. When something is uttered that falls into the `request` state of the DM as explained above, the display expands the subtree under question and marks the item with a question mark (see Figure 4). At this point, the user can utter any kind of confirmation. A positive confirmation fills the slot with the item in question. A negative confirmation retracts the question, but leaves the branch expanded. The expanded branches are displayed according to their rank as given by the NLU's probability distribution. Though a branch in the display can theoretically display an unlimited number of children, we opted to only show 7 children; if a branch had more, the final child displayed as an ellipsis.

A completed branch is collapsed, visually marking its corresponding slot as filled. At any

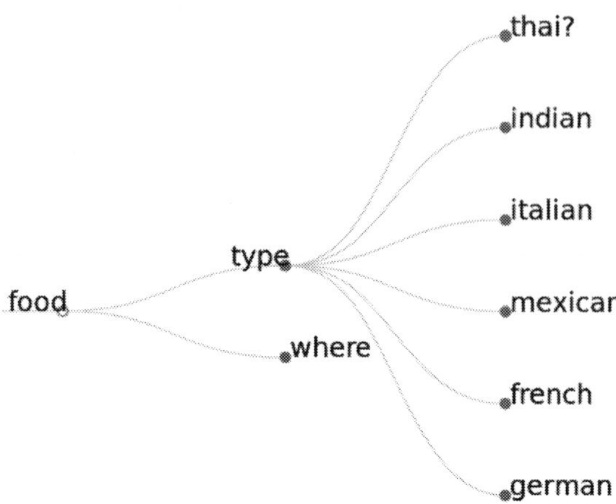

Figure 4: Example tree asking for confirmation on a specific node (in red with a question mark).

time, a user can backtrack by saying *no* (or equivalent) or start the entire interaction over from the beginning with a keyword, e.g., *restart*. To aid the user's attention, the node under question is marked in red, where completed slots are represented by outlined nodes, and filled nodes represent candidates for the current slot in question (see examples of all three in Figure 4). For cases where the system is in the `wait` state for several words (during which there is no change in the tree), the system signals activity at each word by causing the red node in question to temporarily change to white, then back to red (i.e., appearing as a blinking node to the user). Figure 5 shows a filled frame, represented as tree with one branch for each filled slot.

Figure 5: Example tree where all of the slots are filled. (i.e., `domain:food`, `location:university`, `type:thai`)

Such an interface clearly shows the internal state of the SDS and whether or not it has understood the request so far. It is designed to aid the user's attention to the slot in question, and clearly indicates the affordances that the system has. The interface is currently a read-only display that is purely speech-driven, but it could be augmented with additional functionalities, such as tapping a node for expansion or typing input that the system might not yet display. It is currently implemented as a web-based interface (using the JavaScript D3 library), allowing it to be usable as a web application on any machine or mobile device.

Adaptive Branching   The GUI as explained affords an additional straight-forward extension: in order to move our system towards adaptivity on the above-mentioned continuum, the GUI can be used to signal what the system thinks the user might say next.   This is done by expanding a branch and displaying a confirmation on that branch, signalling that the system predicts that the user will choose that particular branch. Alternatively, if the system is confident that a user will fill a slot with a particular value, that particular slot can be filled without confirmation. This is displayed as a collapsed tree branch. A system that perfectly predicts a user's intent would fill an entire tree (i.e., all slots) only requiring the user to confirm once. A more careful system would confirm at each step (such an interaction would only require the user to utter confirmations and nothing else). We applied this adaptive variant of the tree in one of our experiments explained below.

4   Experiments

In this section, we describe two experiments where we evaluated our system. It is our primary goal to show that our GUI is useful and signals understanding to the user. We also wish to show that incremental presentation of such a GUI is more effective than an endpointed system. We further want to show that an adaptive system is more effective than a non-adaptive system (though both would process incrementally). In order to best evaluate our system, we recruited participants to interact with our system in varied settings to compare endpointed (i.e., non-incremental) and non-adaptive as well as adaptive versions. We describe how the data were collected from the participants, then explain each experiment and give results.

4.1   Task & Procedure

The participants were seated at a desk and given written instructions indicating that they were to use the system to perform as many tasks as possible in the allotted time. Figure 6 shows some example tasks as they would be displayed (one at a time) to the user. A screen, tablet, and keyboard were on the desk in front of the user (see Figure 7).[2] The user was instructed to convey the task presented on the screen to the system such

---

[2]We used a Samsung 8.4 Pro tablet turned to its side to show a larger width for the tree to grow to the right. The tablet only showed the GUI; the SDS ran on a separate computer.

that the GUI on the tablet would have a completed tree (e.g., as in Figure 5). When the participant was satisfied that the system understood her intent, she was to press space bar on the keyboard which triggered a new task to be displayed on the screen and reset the tree to its start state on the tablet (as in Figure 3).

The possible task domains were *call*, which had a single slot for *name* to be filled (i.e., one out of the 22 most common German given names); *message* which had a slot for *name* and a slot for the *message* (which, when invoked, would simply fill in directly from the ASR until 1 second of silence was detected); *eat* which had slots for *type* (in this case, 6 possible types) and *location* (in this case, 6 locations based around the city of Bielefeld); *route* which had slots for *source* city and the *destination* city (which shared the same list of the top 100 most populous German cities); and *reminder* which had a slot for *message*.

Figure 6: Examples of tasks, as presented to each participant. Each icon represents a specific task domain (i.e., call, reminder, find a restaurant, leave a message, or directions).

For each task, the domain was first randomly chosen from the 5 possible domains, and then each slot value to be filled was randomly chosen (the *message* slot for the *name* and *message* domains was randomly selected from a list of 6 possible "messages", each with 2-3 words; e.g., *feed the cat*, *visit grandma*, etc.). The system kept track of which tasks were already presented to the participant. At any time after the first task, the system could choose a task that was previously presented and present it again to the participant (with a 50% chance) so the user would often see tasks that she had seen before (with the assumption that humans who use PAs often do perform similar, if not the same, tasks more than once).

The participant was told that she would interact with the system in three different phases, each for 4 minutes, and to accomplish as many tasks as possible in that time allotment. The participant was not told what the different phases were. The experiments described in Sections 4.2 and

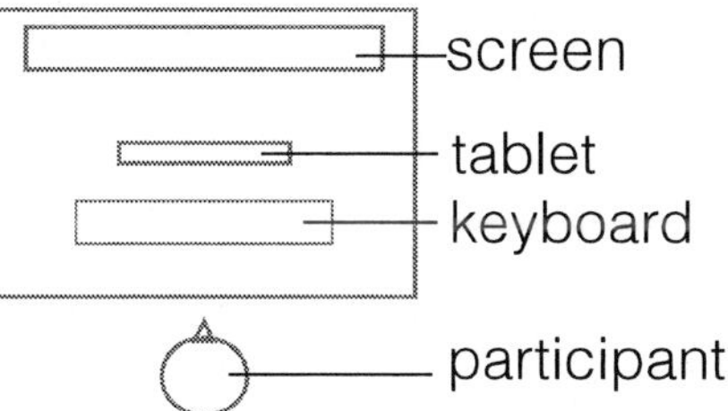

Figure 7: Bird's eye view of the experiment: the participant sat at a table with a screen, tablet, and keyboard in front of them.

4.3 respectively describe and report a comparison first between the Phase 1 and 2 (denoted as the *endpointed* and *incremental* variants of the system) in order to establish whether or not the incremental variant produced better results than the endpointed variant. We also report a comparison between Phase 2 and 3 (*incremental* and *incremental-adaptive* phases). Phase 1 and Phase 3 are not directly comparable to each other as Phase 3 is really a variant of Phase 2. Because of this, we fixed the order of the phase presentation for all participants. Each of these phases are described below. Before the participant began Phase 1, they were able to try it out for up to 4 minutes (in Phase 1 settings) and ask for help from the experimenter, allowing them to get used to the Phase 1 interface before the actual experiment began. After this trial phase, the experiment began with Phase 1.

Phase 1: Non-incremental In this phase, the system did not appear to work incrementally; i.e., the system displayed tree updates after ASR endpointing (of 1.2 seconds–a reasonable amount of time to expect a response from a commercial spoken PA). The system displayed the ongoing ASR on the tablet as it was recognised (as is often done in commercial PAs). At the end of Phase 1, a pop up window notified the user that the phase was complete. They then moved onto Phase 2.

Phase 2: Incremental In this phase, the system displayed the tree information incrementally without endpointing. The ASR was no longer displayed; only the tree provided feedback in understanding, as explained in Section 3.5.

After Phase 2, a 10-question questionnaire was displayed on the screen for the participant to fill out comparing Phase 1 and Phase 2. For each question, they had the choice of *Phase 1*, *Phase*

2, *Both*, and *Neither*. (See Appendix for full list of questions.) After completing the questionnaire, they moved onto Phase 3.

Phase 3: Incremental-adaptive In this phase, the incremental system was again presented to the participant with an added user model that "learned" about the user. If the user saw a task more than once, the user model would predict that, if the user chose that task domain again (e.g., *route*) then the system would automatically ask a clarification using the previously filled values (except for the *message* slot, which the user always had to fill). If the user saw a task more than 3 times, the system skipped asking for clarifications and filled in the domain slots completely, requiring the user only to press the space bar to confirm it was the correct one (i.e., to complete the task). An example progression might be as follows: a participant is presented with the task *route from Bielefeld to Berlin*, then the user would attempt to get the system to fill in the tree (i.e., slots) with those values. After some interaction in other domains, the user sees the same task again, and now after indicating the intent type *route*, the user must only say "yes" for each slot to confirm the system's prediction. Later, if the task is presented a third time, when entering that domain (i.e, *route*), the two slots would already be filled. If later a different route task was presented, e.g., *route from Bielefeld to Hamburg*, the system would already have the two slots filled, but the user could backtrack by saying "no, to Hamburg" which would trigger the system to fill the appropriate slot with the corrected value. Later interactions within the *route* domain would ask for a clarification on the *destination* slot since it has had several possible values given by the participant, but continue to fill the *from* slot with *Bielefeld*.

After Phase 3, the participants were presented with another questionnaire on the screen to fill out with the same questions (plus two additional questions), this time comparing Phase 2 and Phase 3. For each item, they had the choice of *Phase 2*, *Phase 3*, *Both*, and *Neither*. At the end of the three phases and questionnaires, the participants were given a final questionnaire to fill out by hand on their general impressions of the systems.

We recruited 14 participants for the evaluation. We used the Mint tools data collection framework (Kousidis et al., 2012) to log the interactions. Due to some technical issues, one of the participants did not log interactions. We collected data from 13 participants, post-Phase 2 questionnaires from 12 participants, post-Phase 3 questionnaires from all 14 participants, and general questionnaires from all 14 participants. In the experiments that follow, we report objective and subjective measures to determine the settings that produced superior results.

Metrics We report the subjective results of the participant questionnaires. We only report those items that were statistically significant (see Appendix for a full list of the questions). We further report objective measures for each system variant: total number of completed tasks, fully correct frames, average frame f-score, and average time elapsed (averages are taken over all participants for each variant; we only used the 10 participants who fully interacted with all three phases). Discussion is left to the end of this section.

4.2 Experiment 1: Endpointed vs. Incremental

In this section we report the results of the evaluation between the *endpointed* (i.e., non-incremental; Phase 1) variant vs the incremental (Phase 2) variant of our system.

Subjective Results We applied a multinomial test of significance to the results, treating all four possible answers as equally likely (with Bonferroni correction of 10). The item *The interface was useful and easy to understand* with the answer of *Both* was significant (χ^2 (4, N = 12) = 9.0, p < .005), as was *The assistant was easy and intuitive to use* also with the answer *Both* (χ^2 (4, N = 12) = 9.0, p < .005). The item *I always understood what the system wanted from me* was also answered *Both* significantly more times than other answers (χ^2 (4, N = 14) = 9.0, p < .005), similarly for *It was sometimes unclear to me if the assistant understood me* with the answer of *Both* (χ^2 (4, N = 12) = 10.0, p < .005). These responses tell us that though the participants did not report preference for either system variant, they reported a general positive impression of the GUI (in both variants). This is a nice result; the GUI could be used in either system with benefit to the users.

Objective Results The *endpointed* (Phase 1) and *incremental* (Phase 2) columns in Table 1 show the results of the objective evaluation. Though the average time per task and fscore for the endpointed variant are better than those of the

	endpointed	incr.	adaptive
tasks	105	122	124
frames	46	46	59
fscore	0.81	0.74	0.80
time	19.1	19.6	19.5

Table 1: Objective measures for Experiments 1 & 2: count of completed tasks, number of fully correct frames, average fscore (over all participants), and average elapsed time per task (over all participants).

incremental variant, the total number of tasks for the incremental variant was higher.

Manual inspection of logs indicate that participants took advantage of the system's flexibility of understanding instalments (i.e., filling frames incrementally). This is evidenced in that participants often uttered words understood by the system as being negative (e.g., *nein/no*), either as a result of an explicit confirmation request by the system (e.g., *Thai?*) or after a slot was incorrectly filled (something very easily determined through the GUI). This is a desired outcome of using our system; participants were able to repair local areas of misunderstanding as they took place instead of needing to correct an entire intent (i.e., frame). However, we cannot fully empirically measure these tendencies given our data.

4.3 Experiment 2: Incremental vs. Incremental-Adaptive

In this section we report results for the evaluation between the *incremental* (Phase 2) and *incremental-adaptive* (henceforth just *adaptive*; Phase 3) systems.

Subjective Results We applied the same significance test as Experiment 1 (with Bonferroni correction of 12). The item *The interface was useful and easy to understand* was answered with *Both* significantly (χ^2 (4, N = 14) = 10.0, p < .0042), The item *I had the feeling that the assistant attempted to learn about me* was answered with *Neither* (χ^2 (4, N = 14) = 8.0, p < .0042), though *Phase 3* was also marked (6 times). All other items were not significant. Here again we see that there is a general positive impression of the GUI under all conditions. If anyone noticed that a system variant was attempting to learn a user model at all, they noticed that it was in Phase 3, as expected.

Objective Results The *incremental* (Phase 2) and *adaptive* (Phase 3) columns in Table 1 show

the results for the objective evaluation for this experiment. There is a clear difference between the two variants, with the adaptive showing more completed tasks, more fully correct frames, and a higher average fscore (all three likely due to the fact that frames were potentially pre-filled).

4.4 Discussion

While the responses don't express any preference for a particular system variant, the overall impression of the GUI was positive. The objective measures show that there are gains to be made when the system signals understanding at a more fine-grained interval than at the utterance level, due to the higher number of completed tasks and locally-made repairs. There are further gains to be made when the system applies simple user modelling (i.e., adaptivity) by attempting to predict what the user might want to do in a chosen domain, decreasing the possibility of user error and allowing the system to accurately and quickly complete more tasks. Participants also didn't just get used to the system over time, as the average time per episode was fairly similar in all three phases.

The open-ended questionnaire sheds additional light. Most of the suggestions for improvement related to ASR misrecognition and speed (i.e., not about the system itself). Two participants suggested an ability to add "free input" or select alternatives from the tree. Two participants suggested that the system be more responsive (i.e., in `wait` states), and give more feedback (i.e., backchannels) more often. For those participants that expressed preference to the non-incremental system (Phase 1), none of them had used a speech-based PA before, whereas those that expressed preference to the incremental versions (Phases 2 and 3) use them regularly. We conjecture that people without SDS experience equate understanding with ASR, whereas those that are more familiar with PAs know that perfect ASR doesn't translate to perfect understanding–hence the need for a GUI. A potential remedy would be to display ASR with the tree, signalling understanding despite ASR errors.

5 Conclusion & Future Work

Given the results and analysis, we conclude that an intuitive presentation that signals a system's ongoing understanding benefits end users who perform simple tasks which might be performed by a PA. The GUI that we provided, using a right-branching tree, worked well; indeed, the participants who used it found it intuitive and easy to understand. There are gains to be made when the system signals understanding at finer-grained levels than just at the end of a pre-formulated utterance. There are further gains to be made when a PA attempts to learn (even a rudimentary) user model to predict what the user might want to do next. The adaptivity moves our system from one extreme of the continuum–simple slot filling–closer towards the extreme that is fully predictive, with the additional benefit of being able to easily correct mistakes in the predictions.

For future work, we intend to provide simple authoring tools for the system to make building simple PAs using our GUI easy. We want to improve the NLU and scale to larger domains.[3] We also plan on implementing this as a standalone application that could be run on a mobile device, which could actually perform the tasks. It would further be beneficial to compare the GUI with a system that responds with speech (i.e., without a GUI). Lastly, we will investigate using touch as an additional input modality to select between possible alternatives that are offered by the system.

Acknowledgements Thanks to the anonymous reviewers who provided useful comments and suggestions. Thanks also to Julian Hough for helping with experiments. We acknowledge support by the Cluster of Excellence "Cognitive Interaction Technology" (CITEC; EXC 277) at Bielefeld University, which is funded by the German Research Foundation (DFG), and the BMBF Kogni-Home project.

Appendix

The following questions were asked on both questionnaires following Phase 2 and Phase 3 (comparing the two most latest used system versions; as translated into English):

- The interface was useful and easy to understand.
- The assistant was easy and intuitive to use.
- The assistant understood what I wanted to say.
- I always understood what the system wanted from me.
- The assistant made many mistakes.
- The assistant did not respond while I spoke.

- It was sometimes unclear to me if the assistant understood me.
- The assistant responded while I spoke.
- The assistant sometimes did things that I did not expect.
- When the assistant made mistakes, it was easy for me to correct them.

In addition to the above 10 questions, the following were also asked on the questionnaire following Phase 3:

- I had the feeling that the assistant attempted to learn about me.
- I had the feeling that the assistant made incorrect guesses.

The following questions were used on the general questionnaire:

- I regularly use personal assistants such as Siri, Cortana, Google now or Amazon Echo: Yes/No
- I have never used a speech-based personal assistant: Yes/No
- What was your general impression of our personal assistants?
- Would you use one of these assistants on a smart phone or tablet if it were available? If yes, which one?
- Do you have suggestions that you think would help us improve our assistants?
- If you have used other speech-based interfaces before, do you prefer this interface?

References

Gregory Aist, James Allen, Ellen Campana, Lucian Galescu, Carlos Gallo, Scott Stoness, Mary Swift, and Michael Tanenhaus. 2006. Software architectures for incremental understanding of human speech. In *Proceedings of CSLP*, pages 1922—-1925.

Gregory Aist, James Allen, Ellen Campana, Carlos Gomez Gallo, Scott Stoness, and Mary Swift. 2007. Incremental understanding in human-computer dialogue and experimental evidence for advantages over nonincremental methods. In *Pragmatics*, volume 1, pages 149–154, Trento, Italy.

Layla El Asri, Romain Laroche, Olivier Pietquin, and Hatim Khouzaimi. 2014. NASTIA: Negotiating Appointment Setting Interface. In *Proceedings of LREC*, pages 266–271.

Timo Baumann, Michaela Atterer, and David Schlangen. 2009. Assessing and Improving the Performance of Speech Recognition for Incremental Systems. In *Proceedings of Human Language Technologies: The 2009 Annual Conference of the North American Chapter of the Association for Computational Linguistics*, pages 380–388, Boulder, USA, jun.

---

[3]Kennington and Schlangen (2017) showed that our chosen NLU approach can scale fairly well, but the GUI has some limits when applied to larger domains with thousands of items. We leave improved scaling to future work.

Timo Baumann, Casey Kennington, Julian Hough, and David Schlangen. 2016. Recognising Conversational Speech: What an Incremental ASR Should Do for a Dialogue System and How to Get There. In *Proceedings of the International Workshop Series on Spoken Dialogue Systems Technology (IWSDS) 2016*.

Joyce Y Chai, Lanbo She, Rui Fang, Spencer Ottarson, Cody Littley, Changsong Liu, and Kenneth Hanson. 2014. Collaborative effort towards common ground in situated human-robot dialogue. In *Proceedings of the 2014 ACM/IEEE international conference on Human-robot interaction*, pages 33–40, Bielefeld, Germany.

Herbert H. Clark and Edward F. Schaefer. 1989. Contributing to discourse. *Cognitive Science*, 13(2):259–294.

Nina Dethlefs, Helen Hastie, Heriberto Cuayáhuitl, Yanchao Yu, Verena Rieser, and Oliver Lemon. 2016. Information density and overlap in spoken dialogue. *Computer Speech and Language*, 37:82–97.

Jens Edlund, Joakim Gustafson, Mattias Heldner, and Anna Hjalmarsson. 2008. Towards human-like spoken dialogue systems. *Speech Communication*, 50(8-9):630–645.

Ting Han, Casey Kennington, and David Schlangen. 2015. Building and Applying Perceptually-Grounded Representations of Multimodal Scene Descriptions. In *Proceedings of SEMDial*, Gothenburg, Sweden.

Casey Kennington and David Schlangen. 2017. A Simple Generative Model of Incremental Reference Resolution in Situated Dialogue. *Comptuer Speech & Language*.

Casey Kennington, Spyros Kousidis, and David Schlangen. 2013. Interpreting Situated Dialogue Utterances: an Update Model that Uses Speech, Gaze, and Gesture Information. In *SIGdial 2013*, number August, pages 173–182.

Casey Kennington, Spyros Kousidis, and David Schlangen. 2014. InproTKs: A Toolkit for Incremental Situated Processing. In *Proceedings of the 15th Annual Meeting of the Special Interest Group on Discourse and Dialogue (SIGDIAL)*, pages 84–88, Philadelphia, PA, U.S.A. Association for Computational Linguistics.

Casey Kennington, Ryu Iida, Takenobu Tokunaga, and David Schlangen. 2015. Incrementally Tracking Reference in Human / Human Dialogue Using Linguistic and Extra-Linguistic Information. In *HLT-NAACL 2015 - Human Language Technology Conference of the North American Chapter of the Association of Computational Linguistics, Proceedings of the Main Conference*, pages 272–282, Denver, U.S.A. Association for Computational Linguistics.

Spyridon Kousidis, Thies Pfeiffer, Zofia Malisz, Petra Wagner, and David Schlangen. 2012. Evaluating a minimally invasive laboratory architecture for recording multimodal conversational data. In *Proceedings of the Interdisciplinary Workshop on Feedback Behaviors in Dialog, Interspeech Satellite Workshop*, pages 39–42.

Staffan Larsson, Alexander Berman, and Jessica Villing. 2011. Multimodal Menu-based Dialogue with Speech Cursor in DICO II +. In *Computational Linguistics*, number June, pages 92–96.

Pierre Lison. 2015. A hybrid approach to dialogue management based on probabilistic rules. *Computer Speech and Language*, 34(1):232–255.

David Schlangen and Gabriel Skantze. 2011. A General, Abstract Model of Incremental Dialogue Processing. In *Dialogue & Discourse*, volume 2, pages 83–111.

Gabriel Skantze and Anna Hjalmarsson. 1991. Towards Incremental Speech Production in Dialogue Systems. In *Word Journal Of The International Linguistic Association*, pages 1–8, Tokyo, Japan, sep.

Gabriel Skantze and Samer Al Moubayed. 2012. IrisTK : a Statechart-based Toolkit for Multi-party Face-to-face Interaction. In *ICMI*.

Gabriel Skantze and David Schlangen. 2009. Incremental dialogue processing in a micro-domain. *Proceedings of the 12th Conference of the European Chapter of the Association for Computational Linguistics on EACL 09*, (April):745–753.

Michael J. Spivey, Michael K. Tanenhaus, Kathleen M. Eberhard, and Julie C. Sedivy. 2002. Eye movements and spoken language comprehension: Effects of visual context on syntactic ambiguity resolution. *Cognitive Psychology*, 45(4):447–481.

Michael Tanenhaus, Michael Spivey-Knowlton, Kathleen Eberhard, and Julie Sedivy. 1995. Integration of visual and linguistic information in spoken language comprehension. *Science (New York, N.Y.)*, 268(5217):1632–1634.

Gokhan Tur, Li Deng, Dilek Hakkani-Tür, and Xiaodong He. 2012. Towards deeper understanding: Deep convex networks for semantic utterance classification. In *ICASSP, IEEE International Conference on Acoustics, Speech and Signal Processing - Proceedings*, pages 5045–5048. IEEE.

Jason D Williams, Eslam Kamal, Mokhtar Ashour, Hani Amr, Jessica Miller, and Geoff Zweig. 2015. Fast and easy language understanding for dialog systems with Microsoft Language Understanding Intelligent Service (LUIS). In *16th Annual Meeting of the Special Interest Group on Discourse and Dialogue. 2015.*, pages 159–161. ACL – Association for Computational Linguistics, sep.

Toward incremental dialogue act segmentation in fast-paced interactive dialogue systems

Ramesh Manuvinakurike[1], Maike Paetzel[2], Cheng Qu[1], David Schlangen[3] and David DeVault[1]
[1]USC Institute for Creative Technologies, Playa Vista, CA, USA
[2]Uppsala University, Department of Information Technology, Uppsala, Sweden
[3]Bielefeld University, Bielefeld, Germany

Abstract

In this paper, we present and evaluate an approach to incremental dialogue act (DA) segmentation and classification. Our approach utilizes prosodic, lexico-syntactic and contextual features, and achieves an encouraging level of performance in offline corpus-based evaluation as well as in simulated human-agent dialogues. Our approach uses a pipeline of sequential processing steps, and we investigate the contribution of different processing steps to DA segmentation errors. We present our results using both existing and new metrics for DA segmentation. The incremental DA segmentation capability described here may help future systems to allow more natural speech from users and enable more natural patterns of interaction.

1 Introduction

In this paper we explore the feasibility of incorporating an incremental dialogue act segmentation capability into an implemented, high-performance spoken dialogue agent that plays a time-constrained image-matching game with its users (Paetzel et al., 2015). This work is part of a longer-term research program that aims to use incremental (word-by-word) language processing techniques to enable dialogue agents to support efficient, fast-paced interactions with a natural conversational style (De-Vault et al., 2011; Ward and DeVault, 2015; Paetzel et al., 2015).

It's important to allow users to speak naturally to spoken dialogue systems. It has been understood for some time that this ultimately requires a system to be able to automatically segment a user's speech into meaningful units in real-time while they speak (Nakano et al., 1999). Still, most current systems use relatively simple and limited approaches to this segmentation problem. For example, in many systems, it's assumed that pauses in the user's speech can be used to determine the segmentation, often by treating each detected pause as indicating a dialogue act (DA) boundary (Komatani et al., 2015).

While easily implemented, such a pause-based design has several problems. First, a substantial number of spoken DAs contain internal pauses (Bell et al., 2001; Komatani et al., 2015), as in *I need a car in... 10 minutes.* Using simple pause length thresholds to join certain speech segments together for interpretation is not a very effective remedy for this problem (Nakano et al., 1999; Ferrer et al., 2003). More sophisticated approaches train algorithms to join speech across pauses (Komatani et al., 2015) or decide which pauses constitute end-of-utterances that should trigger interpretation (e.g. (Raux and Eskenazi, 2008; Ferrer et al., 2003)). This addresses the problem of DA-internal pauses, but it does not address the second problem with pause-based designs, which is that it's also common for a continuous segment of user speech to include multiple DAs *without* intervening pauses, as in *Sure that's fine can you call when you get to the gate?* A third problem is that waiting for a pause to occur before interpreting earlier speech may increase latency and erode the user experience (Skantze and Schlangen, 2009; Paetzel et al., 2015). Together, these problems suggest the need for an incremental dialogue act segmentation capability in which a continuous stream of captured user speech, including the intermittent pauses therein, is incrementally segmented into appropriate DA units for interpretation.

In this paper, we present a case study of implementing an incremental DA segmentation capability for an image-matching game called RDG-Image, illustrated in Figure 1. In this game, two players converse freely in order to identify a spe-

Proceedings of the SIGDIAL 2016 Conference, pages 252–262,
Los Angeles, USA, 13-15 September 2016. ©2016 Association for Computational Linguistics

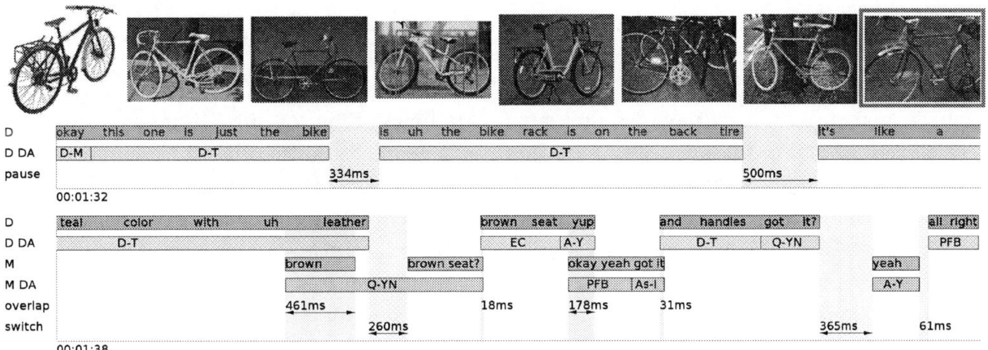

Figure 1: An example RDG-Image dialogue, where the director (D) tries to identify the target image, highlighted in red, to the matcher (M). The DAs of the director (D DA) and matcher (M DA) are indicated.

cific target image on the screen (outlined in red). When played by human players, as in Figure 1, the game creates a variety of fast-paced interaction patterns, such as question-answer exchanges. Our motivation is to eventually enable a future version of our automated RDG-Image agent (Paetzel et al., 2015) to participate in the most common interaction patterns in human-human gameplay. For example, in Figure 1, two fast-paced question-answer exchanges arise as the director D is describing the target image. In the first, the matcher M asks *brown...brown seat?* and receives an almost immediate answer *brown seat yup*. A moment later, the director continues the description with *and handles got it?*, both adding *and handles* and also asking *got it?* without an intervening pause. We believe that an important step toward automating such fast-paced exchanges is to create an ability for an automated agent to incrementally recognize the various DAs, such as yes-no questions (Q-YN), target descriptions (D-T), and yes answers (A-Y) in real-time as they are happening.

The contributions of this paper are as follows. First, we define a sequential approach to incremental DA segmentation and classification that is straightforward to implement and which achieves a useful level of performance when trained on a small annotated corpus of domain-specific DAs. Second, we explore the performance of our approach using both existing and new performance metrics for DA segmentation. Our new metrics emphasize the importance of precision and recall of specific DA types, independently of DA boundaries. These metrics are useful for evaluating DA segmenters that operate on noisy ASR output and which are intended for use in systems whose dia-

logue policies are defined in terms of the presence or absence of specific DA types, independently of their position in user speech. This is a broad class of systems. Third, while much of the prior work on DA segmentation has been corpus-based, we report here on an initial integration of our incremental DA segmenter into an implemented, high-performance agent for the RDG-Image game. Our case study suggests that incremental DA segmentation can be performed with sufficient accuracy for us to begin to extend our baseline agent's conversational abilities without significantly degrading its current performance.

2 Related Work

In this paper, we are concerned with the alignment between dialogue acts (DAs) and individual words as they are spoken within Inter-Pausal Units (IPUs) (Koiso et al., 1998) or *speech segments*. (We use the two terms interchangeably in this paper to refer to a period of continuous speech separated by pauses of a minimum duration before and after.) Beyond the work on this alignment problem mentioned in the introduction, a related line of work has looked specifically at DA segmentation and classification given an input string of words together with an audio recording to enable prosodic and timing analysis (Petukhova and Bunt, 2014; Zimmermann, 2009; Zimmermann et al., 2006; Lendvai and Geertzen, 2007; Ang et al., 2005; Nakano et al., 1999; Warnke et al., 1997). This work generally encompasses the problems of identifying DA-internal pauses as well as locating DA boundaries within speech segments. Prosody information has been shown to be helpful for accurate DA segmentation (Laskowski and Shriberg, 2010; Shriberg et al.,

2000; Warnke et al., 1997) as well as for DA classification (Stolcke et al., 2000; Fernandez and Picard, 2002). In general, DA segmentation has been found to benefit from a range of additional features such as pause durations at word boundaries, the user's dialogue tempo (Komatani et al., 2015), as well as lexical, syntactic, and semantic features. Work on system turn-taking decisions has used similar features to optimize a system's turn-taking policy during a user pause, often with classification approaches; e.g. (Sato et al., 2002; Takeuchi et al., 2004; Raux and Eskenazi, 2008). To our knowledge, very little research has looked in detail at the impact of adding incremental DA segmentation to an implemented incremental system (though see Nakano et al. (1999)).[1]

3 The RDG-Image Game and Data Set

Our work in this paper is based on the RDG-Image game (Paetzel et al., 2014), a collaborative, time constrained, fast-paced game with two players depicted in Figure 1. One player is assigned the role of director and the other the role of matcher. Both players see the same eight images on their screens (but arranged in a different order). The director's screen has a target image highlighted in red, and the director's goal is to describe the target image so that the matcher can identify it as quickly as possible. Once the matcher believes they have selected the right image, the director can request the next target. Both players score a point for each correct selection, and the game continues until a time limit is reached. The time limit is chosen to create time pressure.

3.1 Dialogue Act Annotations

We have previously collected data sets of human-human gameplay in RDG-Image both in a lab setting (Paetzel et al., 2014) and in an online, web-based version of the game (Manuvinakurike and DeVault, 2015; Paetzel et al., 2015). To support the experiments in this paper, a single annotator segmented and annotated the main game rounds from our lab-based RDG-Image corpus with a set

of DA tags.[2] The corpus includes gameplay between 64 participants (32 pairs, age: $M = 35$, $SD = 12$, gender: 55% female). 11% of all participants reported they frequently played similar games before; the other 89% had no or very rare experience with similar games. All speech was previously recorded, manually segmented into speech segments (IPUs) at pauses of 300ms or greater, and manually transcribed. The new DA segmentation and annotation steps were carried out at the same time by adding boundaries and DA labels to the transcribed speech segments from the game. The annotator used both audio and video recordings to assist with the annotation task. The annotations were performed on transcripts which were seen as segmented into IPUs.

Table 1 provides several examples of this annotation. We designed the set of DA labels to include a range of communicative functions we observed in human-human gameplay, and to encode distinctions we expected to prove useful in an automated agent for RDG-Image. Our DA label set includes Positive Feedback (PFB), Describe Target (D-T), Self-Talk (ST), Yes-No Question (Q-YN), Echo Confirmation (EC), Assert Identified (As-I), and Assert Skip (As-S). We also include a filled-pause DA (P) used for 'uh' or 'um' separated from other speech by a pause. The complete list of 18 DA labels and their distribution are included in Tables 9 and 10 in the appendix. To assess the reliability of annotation, two annotators annotated one game (2 players, 372 speech segments); we measured kappa for the presence of boundary markers ($\|$) at 0.92 and word-level kappa for DA labels at 0.83.

Summary statistics for the annotated corpus are as follows. The corpus contains 64 participants (32 pairs), 1,906 target images, 8,792 speech segments, 67,125 word tokens, 12,241 DA segments, and 4.27 hours of audio. The mean number of DAs per speech segment is 1.39. In Table 2, we summarize the distribution in number of DAs initiated per speech segment. 23% of speech segments contain the beginning of at least two DAs; this highlights the importance of being able to find the boundaries between multiple DAs inside a speech segment. Most DAs begin at the start of a speech segment (i.e. immediately after a pause), but 29% of DAs begin at the second word or later in a speech segment. 4% of DAs contain an internal pause and

---

[1] In Manuvinakurike et al. (2016), we describe a related application of incremental speech segmentation in a variant rapid dialogue game with a different corpus. In that paper, we focus on fine-grained segmentation of referential utterances that would all be labeled as D-T in this paper. The model presented here is shallower and more general, focusing on high-level DA labels.

[2] We excluded from annotation the training rounds in the corpus, where players practiced playing the game.

Example	# IPUs	# DAs	Annotation
1	1	5	PFB that's okay ‖ D-T um this castle has a ‖ ST oh gosh this is hard ‖ D-T this castle is tan ‖ D-T it's at a diagonal with a blue sky
2	1	2	D-T and it's got lemon in it ‖ Q-YN you got it
3	1	2	PFB okay ‖ D-T this is the christmas tree in front of a fireplace
4	1	2	EC fireplace ‖ As-I got it
5	2	2	D-M all right ‖ D-T this is ... this is this is the brown circle and it's not hollow
6	3	1	D-T this is a um ... tan or light brown ... box that is clear in the middle
7	3	2	D-M all right ‖ D-T he's got he's got that ... that ... first uh the first finger and the thumb pointing up
8	3	2	ST um golly ‖ DT this looks like a a a ... ginseng ... uh of some sort
9	2	4	ST oh wow ‖ D-M okay ‖ D-T this one ... looks it has gray ‖ D-T a lotta gray on this robot

Table 1: Examples of annotated DA types, DA boundaries (‖), and IPU boundaries (...). The number of IPUs and DAs in each example are indicated.

Number of DAs	0	1	2	≥ 3
% of speech segments	3	74	18	5

Table 2: The distribution in the number of DAs whose first word is within a speech segment.

thus span multiple speech segments.

4   Technical Approach

The goal for our incremental DA segmentation component is to segment the recognized speech for a speaker into individual DA segments and to assign these segments to the 18 DA classes in Table 9. We aim to do this in an incremental (word-by-word) manner, so that information about the DAs within a speech segment becomes available before the user stops or pauses their speech.

Figure 2 shows the incremental operation of our sequential pipeline for DA segmentation and classification. We use Kaldi for ASR, and we adapt the work of Plátek and Jurčíček (2014) for incremental ASR using Kaldi. The pipeline is invoked after each new partial ASR result becomes available (i.e., every 100ms), at which point all the recognized speech is resegmented and reclassified in a *restart incremental* (Schlangen and Skantze, 2011) design. The input to the pipeline includes all the recognized speech from one speaker (including multiple IPUs) for one target image subdialogue.

In our sequential pipeline, the first step is to use sequential tagging with a CRF (Conditional Random Field) (Lafferty et al., 2001) implemented in Mallet (McCallum, 2002) to perform the segmentation. The segmenter tags each word as either the beginning (B) of a new DA segment or as a continuation of the current DA segment (I).[3] Then, each

---

[3]Note that our annotation scheme completely partitions our

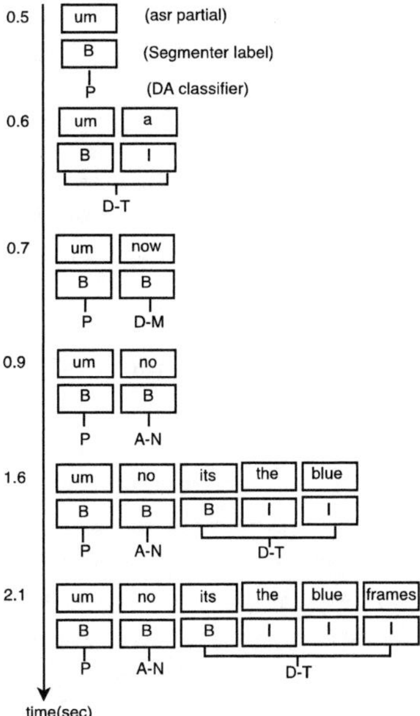

Figure 2: The operation of the pipeline on selected ASR partials (with time index in seconds).

resulting DA segment is classified into one of 18 DA labels using an SVM (Support Vector Machine) classifier implemented in Weka (Hall et al., 2009).

4.1   Features

Prosodic Features   We use word-level prosodic features similar in nature to Litman et al. (2009). The alignment between words and computed prosodic features is achieved using a forced aligner (Baumann and Schlangen, 2012) to generate word-level timing information. For each word, we first

---

data, with every word belonging to a segment and receiving a DA label. We have therefore elected not to adopt BIO (Begin-Inside-Outside) tagging.

obtain pitch and RMS values every 10ms using In-proTK (Baumann and Schlangen, 2012). Because pitch and energy features can be highly variable across users, our pitch and energy features are represented as z-scores that are normalized for the current user up to the current word. For the pitch and RMS values, we obtain the max, min, mean, variance and the co-efficients of a second degree polynomial. Pause durations at word boundaries provide an additional useful feature (Kolář et al., 2006; Zimmermann, 2009). All numeric features are discretized into bins. We currently use prosody for segmentation but not classification.[4]

Lexico-syntactic & contextual features   We use word unigrams along with the corresponding part-of-speech (POS) tags, obtained using Stanford CORENLP (Manning et al., 2014), as a feature for both the segmentation and the DA classifier. Words with a low frequency (<10) are substituted with a low frequency word symbol. The top level constituent category from a syntactic parse of the DA segment is also used.

Several contextual features are included. The role of the speaker (Director or Matcher) is included as a feature. Previously recognized DA labels from each speaker are included. Another feature is added to assist with the Echo Confirmation (EC) DA, which applies when a speaker repeats verbatim a phrase recently spoken by the other interlocutor. For this we use features to mark word-level unigrams that appeared in recent speech from the other interlocutor. Finally, a categorical feature indicates which of 18 possible image sets (e.g. bikes as in Figure 1) is under discussion; simpler images tend to have shorter segments.[5]

4.2 Discussion of Machine Learning Setup

A salient alternative to our sequential pipeline approach – also adopted for example by Ang et al. (2005) – is to use a joint classification model to solve the segmentation and classification problems simultaneously, potentially thereby improving performance on both problems (Petukhova and Bunt, 2014; Morbini and Sagae, 2011; Zimmermann, 2009; Warnke et al., 1997). We performed an initial test using a joint model and found, unlike the finding reported by Zimmermann (2009), that for

Condition	Transcripts (T)	Segment Boundaries (S)	DA labels (D)
HT-HS-HD	Human	Human	Human
HT-HS-AD	Human	Human	Automated
HT-AS-AD	Human	Automated	Automated
AT-AS-AD	ASR	Automated	Automated

Table 3: Conditions for evaluating DA segmentation and classification.

our corpus a joint approach performed markedly worse than our sequential pipeline.[6] We speculate that this is due to the relative sparsity of data on rarer DA types in our relatively small corpus. For similar reasons, we have not yet tried to use RNN-based approaches such as LSTMs, which tend to require large amounts of training data.

5 Experiment and Results

We report on two experiments. In the first experiment, we train our DA segmentation pipeline using the annotated corpus of Section 3.1 and report results on the observed DA segment boundaries (Section 5.1) and DA class labels (Section 5.2). In the second experiment, presented in Section 5.3, we report on a policy simulation that investigates the effect of our incremental DA segmentation pipeline on a baseline automated agent's performance.

For the first experiment, we use a hold-one-pair-out cross-validation setup where, for each fold, the dialogue between one pair of players is held out for testing, while automated models are trained on the other pairs. To evaluate our pipeline, we use four data conditions, summarized in Table 3, that represent increasing amounts of automation in the pipeline. These conditions allow us to better understand the sources for observed errors in segment boundaries and/or DA labels. Our notation for these conditions is a compact encoding of the data sources used to create the transcripts of user speech, the segment boundaries, and the DA labels. Our reference annotation, described in Section 3.1, is notated HT-HS-HD (human transcript, human segment boundaries, human DA labels). Example segmentations for each condition are in Table 4.

5.1 Evaluation of DA Segment Boundaries

In this evaluation, we ignore DA labels and look only at the identification of DA boundaries (notated by $\|$ in Table 4, and encoded using B and I tags in our segmenter). For this evaluation, we use human

---

[4]For the experiments reported in this paper, prosodic features were calculated offline, but they could in principle be calculated in real-time.

[5]The image set feature affects the performace of the segmenter only slightly.

[6]We used a joint CRF model similar to the BI coding of Zimmermann (2009).

Condition	# IPUs	Example	
HT-HS-HD	1	(a)	A-N um no ‖ D-T it's the blue frame ‖ D-T but it's an orange seat and an orange handle
HT-HS-AD	1	(b)	A-N um no ‖ D-T it's the blue frame ‖ D-T but it's an orange seat and an orange handle
HT-AS-AD	1	(c)	P um ‖ A-N no ‖ D-T it's the blue frame ‖ D-T but it's an orange seat ‖ D-T and an orange handle
AT-AS-AD	1	(d)	A-N on no ‖ D-T it's the blue frame ‖ D-T but it's an orange seat ‖ D-T and orange ‖ A-N no

Table 4: Examples of DA boundaries (‖) and DA labels in each condition.

Condition	Features	Accuracy	F-Score		DSER
			B tag	I tag	
1-DA-per-IPU		0.78	0.23	0.87	0.26
HT-AS-AD	Prosody (I)	0.72	0.62	0.69	0.42
HT-AS-AD	Lexico-Syntactic & Contextual (II)	0.90	0.82	0.82	0.31
HT-AS-AD	I+II	0.91	0.83	0.84	0.30
Human annotator		0.95	0.91	0.94	0.15

Table 5: Observed DA segmentation performance. These results consider only DA boundaries.

transcripts and compare the boundaries in our reference annotations (HT-HS-HD) to the boundaries inferred by our automated pipeline (HT-AS-AD).[7]

In Table 5, we present results for versions of our pipeline that use three different feature sets: only prosody features (I), only lexico-syntactic and contextual features (II), and both (I+II). We include also a simple 1-DA-per-IPU baseline that assumes each IPU is a single complete DA; it assigns the first word in each IPU a B tag and subsequent words an I tag. Finally, we also include numbers based on an independent human annotator using the subset of our annotated corpus that was annotated by two human annotators. For this subset, we use our main annotator as the reference standard and evaluate the other annotator as if their annotation were a system's hypothesis.[8]

The reported numbers include word-level accuracy of the B and I tags, F-score for each of the B and I tags, and the DA segmentation error rate (DSER) metric of Zimmermann et al. (2006). DSER measures the fraction of reference DAs whose left and right boundaries are not exactly replicated in the hypothesis. For example, in Table 4, the reference (a) contains three DAs, but only the boundaries of the second DA (*it's the blue frame*) are exactly replicated in hypothesis (c). This yields a DSER of 2/3 for this example.

We find that our automated pipeline (HT-AS-AD) with all features performs the best among the pipeline methods, with word-level accuracy of 0.91 and DSER of 0.30. Its performance how-

Condition	Metrics used for human transcripts			Alignment-based metrics	
	DER	Strict	Lenient	Levenshtein-Lenient	CER
HT-HS-AD	0.39	0.09	0.09	0.07	0.27
HT-AS-AD	0.72	0.38	0.15	0.12	0.39
AT-AS-AD				0.39	0.52

Table 6: Observed DA classification and joint segmentation+classification performance.

ever is worse than an independent human annotator, with double the DSER. This suggests there remains room for improvement at boundary identification. The 1-DA-per-IPU baseline does well on the common case of single-IPU DAs, but it fails ever to segment an IPU into multiple DAs. We use the pipeline with all features in the following sections.

5.2 Evaluation of DA Class Labels

In this evaluation, we consider DA labels assigned to recognized DA segments using several types of metrics. We summarize our results in Table 6.

Metrics used for human transcripts We first compare our reference annotations (HT-HS-HD) to the performance of our automated pipeline *when provided human transcripts as input*. For this comparison, we use three error rate metrics (Lenient, Strict, and DER) from the DA segmentation literature that are intuitively applied when the token sequence being segmented and labeled is identical (or at least isomorphic) to the annotated token sequence. Lower is better for these. The Lenient and Strict metrics (Ang et al., 2005) are based on the DA labels assigned to each individual word (by way of the label of the DA segment that contains that word). Lenient is a per-token DA label error

---

[7]We evaluate our DA segmentation performance using human transcripts, rather than ASR, as this allows a simple direct comparison of inferred DA boundaries.

[8]For comparison, the chance-corrected kappa value for word-level boundaries is 0.92; see Section 3.1.

rate that ignores DA segment boundaries.[9] In Table 6, this error rate is 0.09 when human-annotated boundaries are fed into our DA classifier (HT-HS-AD) and 0.15 when automatically-identified boundaries are used (HT-AS-AD).

Strict and DER are boundary-sensitive metrics. Strict is a per-token error rate that requires each token to receive the correct DA label and also to be part of a DA segment whose exact boundaries appear in the reference annotation. This is a much higher standard.[10] Dialogue Act Error Rate (DER) (Zimmermann et al., 2006) is the fraction of reference DAs whose left and right boundaries and label are perfectly replicated in the hypothesis. While the reported boundary-sensitive error rate numbers (0.38 and 0.72) may appear to be high, many of these boundary errors may be relatively innocuous from a system standpoint. We return to this below.

Alignment-based metrics We also report two additional metrics that are intuitively applied even when the word sequence being segmented and classified is only a noisy approximation to the word sequence that was annotated, i.e. under an ASR condition such as AT-AS-AD. The Concept Error Rate (CER) is a word error rate (WER) calculation (Chotimongkol and Rudnicky, 2001) based on a minimum edit distance alignment of the DA tags (using one DA tag per DA segment). Our fully automated pipeline (AT-AS-AD) has a CER of 0.52.

We also report an analogous word-level metric which we call 'Levenshtein-Lenient'. To our knowledge this metric has not previously been used in the literature. It replaces each word in the reference and hypothesis with the DA tag that applies to it, and then computes a WER on the DA tag sequence. It is thus a Lenient-like metric that can be applied to DA segmentation based on ASR results. Our automated pipeline (AT-AS-AD) scores 0.39.

DA multiset precision and recall metrics When ASR is used, the CER and Levenshtein-Lenient metrics give an indication of how well you are doing at replicating the ordered sequence of DA tags. But in building a system, sometimes the sequence is less of a concern, and what is desired is a breakdown in terms of precision and recall per DA tag. Many dialogue systems use policies that are triggered when a certain DA type has occurred in the user's speech (such as an agent that processes yes (A-Y) or no (A-N) answers differently, or a di-

Condition	HT-HS-AD		HT-AS-AD		AT-AS-AD	
	P	**R**	**P**	**R**	**P**	**R**
D-T	0.98	0.98	0.85	0.95	0.79	0.88
As-I	0.97	0.97	0.74	0.96	0.73	0.68
NG	0.84	0.89	0.72	0.88	0.63	0.50
PFB	0.67	0.65	0.50	0.77	0.42	0.60
ST	0.92	0.92	0.71	0.63	0.41	0.31
Q-YN	0.94	0.85	0.86	0.85	0.55	0.52
AN	0.90	0.90	0.70	0.67	0.42	0.32
A-Y	0.79	0.79	0.65	0.75	0.59	0.58

Table 7: DA multiset precision and recall metrics for a sample of higher-frequency DA tags.

rector agent for the RDG-Image game that moves on when the matcher performs As-I ("got it")). For such systems, exact DA boundaries and even the order of DAs is not of paramount importance so long as a correct DA label is produced around the time the user performs the DA.

We therefore define a more permissive measure that looks only at precision and recall of DA labels within a sample of user speech. As an example, in (a) in Table 4, there is one A-N label and two D-T labels. In (d), there are two A-N labels and 3 D-T labels. Ignoring boundaries, we can represent as a multiset the collection of DA labels in a reference A or hypothesis H, and compute standard multiset versions of precision and recall for each DA type. For reference, a formal definition of multiset precision $P(\mathrm{DA}_i)$ and recall $R(\mathrm{DA}_i)$ for DA type DA_i is provided in the appendix.

We report these numbers for our most common DA types in Table 7. Here, we continue to use the speech of one speaker during a target image subdialogue as the unit of analysis. The data show that precision and recall generally decline for all DA types as automation increases in the conditions from left to right. We do relatively well with the most frequent DA types, which are D-T and As-I. A particular challenge, even in human transcript+segment condition HT-HS-AD, is the DA tag PFB. In a manual analysis of common error types, we found that the different DA labels used for very short utterances like 'okay' (D-M, PFB, As-I) and 'yeah' (A-Y, PFB, As-I) are often confused. We believe this type of error could be reduced through a combination of improved features, collapsed DA categories, and more detailed annotation guidelines. ASR errors also often cause DA errors; see e.g. Table 4 (d).

---

[9]E.g. in Table 4 (c), the only Lenient error is at word *um*.

[10]E.g. in Table 4 (c), only the four words *it's the blue frame* would count as non-errors on the Strict standard.

	image set	total time(sec)	total points p	p/sec	NLU accuracy	avg sec/image
All DAs	Pets	984.7	182	0.18	0.77	4.15
	Zoo	921.1	203	0.22	0.79	3.60
	Cocktails	1300.3	153	0.12	0.60	5.12
	Bikes	1630.9	126	0.08	0.47	6.12
Only D-T	Pets	992.0	184	0.19	0.78	4.19
	Zoo	932.8	198	0.21	0.77	3.64
	Cocktails	1326.7	155	0.12	0.61	5.22
	Bikes	1678.4	130	0.08	0.49	6.29

Table 8: Overall performance of the eavesdropper simulation on the unsegmented data (All DAs) and the automatically segmented data (Only D-T) identified with our pipeline (AT-AS-AD).

5.3 Evaluation of Simulated Agent Dialogues

Motivation. In prior work (Paetzel et al., 2015), we developed an automated agent called Eve which plays the matcher role in the RDG-Image game and has been evaluated in a live interactive study with 125 human users. Our prior work underscored the critical importance of pervasive incremental processing in order for Eve to achieve her highest performance in terms of points scored and also the best subjective user impressions. In this second experiment, we perform an offline investigation into the potential impact on our agent's image-matching performance if we integrate the incremental DA segmentation pipeline from this paper.

We take the "fully-incremental" version of Eve from Paetzel et al. (2015) as our baseline agent in this experiment. Briefly, this version of Eve includes the same incremental ASR used in our new DA segmentation pipeline (Plátek and Jurčíček, 2014), incremental language understanding to identify the target image (Naive Bayes classification), and an incremental dialogue policy that uses parameterized rules. See Paetzel et al. (2015) for full details.

The baseline agent's design focuses on the most common DA types in our RDG-Image corpora: D-T for the director (constituting 60% of director DAs), and As-I for the matcher (constituting 46% of matcher DAs). Effectively, the baseline agent assumes every word the user says is describing the target, and uses an optimized policy to decide the right moment to commit to a selection (As-I) or ask the user to skip the image (As-S). Eve's typical interaction pattern is illustrated in Figure 3.

This experiment is narrowly focused on the impact of using the pipeline to segment out only the D-T DAs and to use only the words from detected D-Ts in the target image classifier and the agent's policy decisions. Changing the agent pipeline from using the director's full utterance towards only taking the D-T tagged words into account could po-

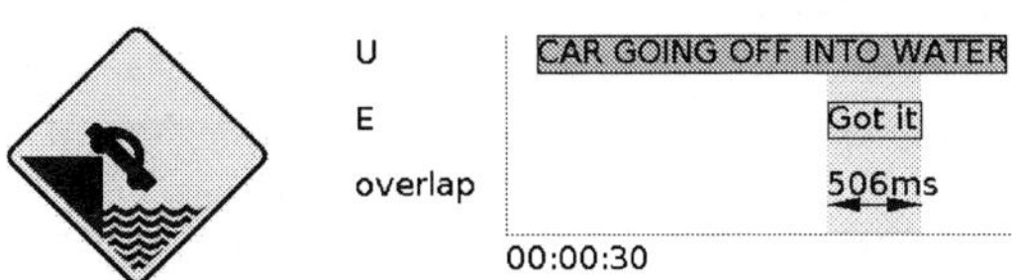

Figure 3: Eve (E) identifies a target image.

tentially have a negative impact on the baseline agent's performance. For example, for the fully automated condition AT-AS-AD in Table 7, D-T has precision 0.79 and recall 0.88. The 0.88 recall suggests that some D-T words will be lost (in false negative D-Ts) by integrating the new DA segmenter. Additionally, as shown in Figure 2, the recognized words and whether they are tagged as D-T can change dynamically as new incremental ASR results arrive, and this instability could undermine some of the advantage of segmentation. On the other hand, by excluding non-D-T text from consideration, there is a potential to decrease noise in the agent's understanding and improve the agent's accuracy or speed.

Experiment. As an initial investigation into the issues described above, we adopt the "Eavesdropper" framework for policy simulation and training detailed in Paetzel et al. (2015). In an Eavesdropper simulation, the director's speech from pre-recorded target image dialogues is provided to the agent, and the agent simulates alternative policy decisions as if it were in the matcher role. We have found that higher cross-validation performance in these offline simulations has translated to higher performance in live interactive human-agent studies (Paetzel et al., 2015).

We created a modified version of our agent that uses the fully automated pipeline (AT-AS-AD) to pass only word sequences tagged as D-T to the agent's language understanding component (a target image classifier), effectively ignoring other DA types. Tagging is performed every 100 ms on each new incremental output segment published by the

ASR. We then compare the performance of our baseline and modified agent in a cross-validation setup, using an Eavesdropper simulation to train and test the agents. We use a corpus of human-human gameplay that includes 18 image sets and game data from both the lab-based corpus of 32 games described in Section 3.1 and also the web-based corpus of an additional 98 human-human RDG-Image games described in Manuvinakurike and DeVault (2015). Each simulation yields a new trained NLU (target image classifier, based either on all text or only on D-T text) and a new optimized policy for when the agent should perform As-I vs. As-S. Within the simulations, for each target image, we compute whether the agent would score a point and how long it would spend on each image.

Table 8 summarizes the observed performance in these simulations for four sample image sets in the two agent conditions. All results are calculated based on leave-one-user-out training and a policy optimized on points per second. A Wilcoxon-Mann-Whitney Test on all 18 image sets indicated that, between the two conditions, there is no significant difference in the total time ($Z = -0.24, p = .822$), total points scored ($Z = -0.06, p = .956$), points per second ($Z = -0.06, p = .956$), average seconds per image ($Z = -0.36, p = .725$), or NLU accuracy ($Z = -0.13, p = .907$).

These encouraging results suggest that our incremental DA segmenter achieves a performance level that is sufficient for it to be integrated into our agent, enabling the incremental segmentation of other DA types without significantly compromising (or improving) the agent's current performance level. These results provide a complementary perspective on the various DA classification metrics reported in Section 5.2.

The current baseline agent (Paetzel et al., 2015) can only generate As-I and As-S dialogue acts. In future work, the fully automated pipeline presented here will enable us to expand the agent's dialogue policies to support additional patterns of interaction beyond its current skillset. For example, the agent would be better able to understand and react to a multi-DA user utterance like *and handles got it?* in Figure 1. By segmenting out and understanding the Q-YN *got it?*, the agent would be able to detect the question and answer with an A-Y like *yeah*. Overall, we believe the ability to understand the natural range of director's utterances will help the agent to create more natural interaction patterns,

which might receive a better subjective rating by the human dialogue partner and in the end might even achieve a better overall game performance, as ambiguities can be resolved quicker and the flow of communication can be more efficient.

6 Conclusion & Future Work

In this paper, we have defined and evaluated a sequential approach to incremental DA segmentation and classification. Our approach utilizes prosodic, lexico-syntactic and contextual features, and achieves an encouraging level of performance in offline analysis and in policy simulations. We have presented our results in terms of existing metrics for DA segmentation and also introduced additional metrics that may be useful to other system builders. In future work, we will continue this line of work by incorporating dialogue policies for additional DA types into the interactive agent.

Acknowledgments

We thank our reviewers. This work was supported by the National Science Foundation under Grant No. IIS-1219253 and by the U.S. Army. Any opinions, findings, and conclusions or recommendations expressed in this material are those of the author(s) and do not necessarily reflect the views, position, or policy of the National Science Foundation or the United States Government, and no official endorsement should be inferred. David Schlangen acknowledges support by the Cluster of Excellence Cognitive Interaction Technology 'CITEC' (EXC 277) at Bielefeld University, which is funded by the German Research Foundation (DFG).

Image credits. We number the images in Figure 1 from 1-8 moving left to right. Thanks to Hugger Industries (1)[11], Eric Sorenson (6)[12] and fixedgear (8)[13] for images published under CC BY-NC-SA 2.0. Thanks to Eric Parker (2)[14] and cosmo flash (4)[15] for images published under CC BY-NC 2.0, and to Richard Masonder / Cyclelicious (3)[16] (5)[17] and Florian (7)[18] for images published under CC BY-SA 2.0.

---

[11] https://www.flickr.com/photos/huggerindustries/3929138537/

[12] https://www.flickr.com/photos/ahpook/5134454805/

[13] http://www.flickr.com/photos/fixedgear/172825187/

[14] https://www.flickr.com/photos/ericparker/6050226145/

[15] http://www.flickr.com/photos/cosmoflash/9070780978/

[16] http://www.flickr.com/photos/bike/3221746720/

[17] https://www.flickr.com/photos/bike/3312575926/

[18] http://www.flickr.com/photos/fboyd/6042425285/

References

Jeremy Ang, Yang Liu, and Elizabeth Shriberg. 2005. Automatic dialog act segmentation and classification in multiparty meetings. In *ICASSP*, pages 1061–1064.

Timo Baumann and David Schlangen. 2012. The inprotk 2012 release. In *NAACL-HLT Workshop on Future Directions and Needs in the Spoken Dialog Community: Tools and Data*, pages 29–32.

Linda Bell, Johan Boye, and Joakim Gustafson. 2001. Real-time handling of fragmented utterances. In *The NAACL Workshop on Adaption in Dialogue Systems*, pages 2–8.

Ananlada Chotimongkol and Alexander I Rudnicky. 2001. N-best speech hypotheses reordering using linear regression.

David DeVault, Kenji Sagae, and David Traum. 2011. Incremental interpretation and prediction of utterance meaning for interactive dialogue. *Dialogue and Discourse*, 2(1):143–70.

Raul Fernandez and Rosalind W Picard. 2002. Dialog act classification from prosodic features using support vector machines. In *Speech Prosody 2002, International Conference*.

Luciana Ferrer, Elizabeth Shriberg, and Andreas Stolcke. 2003. A prosody-based approach to end-of-utterance detection that does not require speech. In *Proc. IEEE ICASSP*, pages 608–611.

Mark Hall, Eibe Frank, Geoffrey Holmes, Bernhard Pfahringer, Peter Reutemann, and Ian H Witten. 2009. The weka data mining software: an update. *ACM SIGKDD explorations newsletter*, 11(1):10–18.

Hanae Koiso, Yasuo Horiuchi, Syun Tutiya, Akira Ichikawa, and Yasuharu Den. 1998. An analysis of turn-taking and backchannels based on prosodic and syntactic features in japanese map task dialogs. *Language and Speech*, 41(3-4):295–321.

Jáchym Kolář, Elizabeth Shriberg, and Yang Liu. 2006. On speaker-specific prosodic models for automatic dialog act segmentation of multi-party meetings. In *Interspeech*, volume 1.

Kazunori Komatani, Naoki Hotta, Satoshi Sato, and Mikio Nakano. 2015. User adaptive restoration for incorrectly-segmented utterances in spoken dialogue systems. In *SIGDIAL*.

John D. Lafferty, Andrew McCallum, and Fernando C. N. Pereira. 2001. Conditional random fields: Probabilistic models for segmenting and labeling sequence data. In *ICML*, pages 282–289.

Kornel Laskowski and Elizabeth Shriberg. 2010. Comparing the contributions of context and prosody in text-independent dialog act recognition. In *ICASSP*, pages 5374–5377. IEEE.

Piroska Lendvai and Jeroen Geertzen. 2007. Token-based chunking of turn-internal dialogue act sequences. In *SIGDIAL*, pages 174–181.

Diane J Litman, Mihai Rotaru, and Greg Nicholas. 2009. Classifying turn-level uncertainty using word-level prosody. In *INTERSPEECH*, pages 2003–2006.

Christopher D Manning, Mihai Surdeanu, John Bauer, Jenny Finkel, Steven J Bethard, and David McClosky. 2014. The stanford corenlp natural language processing toolkit. In *ACL: System Demonstrations*, pages 55–60.

Ramesh Manuvinakurike and David DeVault, 2015. *Natural Language Dialog Systems and Intelligent Assistants*, chapter Pair Me Up: A Web Framework for Crowd-Sourced Spoken Dialogue Collection, pages 189–201.

Ramesh Manuvinakurike, Casey Kennington, David DeVault, and David Schlangen. 2016. Real-time understanding of complex discriminative scene descriptions. In *SIGDIAL*.

Andrew Kachites McCallum. 2002. Mallet: A machine learning for language toolkit. http://mallet.cs.umass.edu.

Fabrizio Morbini and Kenji Sagae. 2011. Joint identification and segmentation of domain-specific dialogue acts for conversational dialogue systems. In *Proceedings of ACL: Human Language Technologies: short papers*, pages 95–100.

Mikio Nakano, Noboru Miyazaki, Jun-ichi Hirasawa, Kohji Dohsaka, and Takeshi Kawabata. 1999. Understanding unsegmented user utterances in real-time spoken dialogue systems. In *ACL*, pages 200–207.

Maike Paetzel, David Nicolas Racca, and David DeVault. 2014. A multimodal corpus of rapid dialogue games. In *LREC*, May.

Maike Paetzel, Ramesh Manuvinakurike, and David DeVault. 2015. "So, which one is it?" The effect of alternative incremental architectures in a high-performance game-playing agent. In *SIGDIAL*.

Volha Petukhova and Harry Bunt. 2014. Incremental recognition and prediction of dialogue acts. In *Computing Meaning*, pages 235–256. Springer.

Ondřej Plátek and Filip Jurčíček. 2014. Free on-line speech recogniser based on Kaldi ASR toolkit producing word posterior lattices. In *SIGDIAL*.

Antoine Raux and Maxine Eskenazi. 2008. Optimizing endpointing thresholds using dialogue features in a spoken dialogue system. In *SIGDIAL*, pages 1–10.

Ryo Sato, Ryuichiro Higashinaka, Masafumi Tamoto, Mikio Nakano, and Kiyoaki Aikawa. 2002. Learning decision trees to determine turntaking by spoken dialogue systems. In *Proceedings of ICSLP-02*, pages 861–864.

David Schlangen and Gabriel Skantze. 2011. A general, abstract model of incremental dialogue processing. dialogue and discourse. *Dialogue and Discourse*, 2(1):83–111.

Elizabeth Shriberg, Andreas Stolcke, Dilek Hakkani-

Tür, and Gökhan Tür. 2000. Prosody-based automatic segmentation of speech into sentences and topics. *Speech communication*, 32(1):127–154.

Gabriel Skantze and David Schlangen. 2009. Incremental dialogue processing in a micro-domain. In *EACL*, pages 745–753.

Andreas Stolcke, Noah Coccaro, Rebecca Bates, Paul Taylor, Carol Van Ess-Dykema, Klaus Ries, Elizabeth Shriberg, Daniel Jurafsky, Rachel Martin, and Marie Meteer. 2000. Dialogue act modeling for automatic tagging and recognition of conversational speech. *Computational linguistics*, 26(3):339–373.

Masashi Takeuchi, Norihide Kitaoka, and Seiichi Nakagawa. 2004. Timing detection for realtime dialog systems using prosodic and linguistic information. In *Speech Prosody 2004*.

Nigel G Ward and David DeVault. 2015. Ten challenges in highly interactive dialog systems. In *AAAI 2015 Spring Symposium*.

V. Warnke, R. Kompe, H. Niemann, and E. Nth. 1997. Integrated dialog act segmentation and classification using prosodic features and language models. In *Proc. 5th Europ. Conf. on Speech, Communication, and Technology*, volume 1.

Matthias Zimmermann, Yang Liu, Elizabeth Shriberg, and Andreas Stolcke, 2006. *Second International Workshop, MLMI 2005*, chapter Toward Joint Segmentation and Classification of Dialog Acts in Multiparty Meetings, pages 187–193.

Matthias Zimmermann. 2009. Joint segmentation and classification of dialog acts using conditional random fields. In *Interspeech*.

A Appendix

Definition of multiset precision and recall Let $\mathcal{D} = \{\mathrm{DA}_1, ..., \mathrm{DA}_n\}$ be the set of possible DAs. Let $A : \mathcal{D} \to \mathbb{Z}_{\geq 0}$ be an annotated reference DA multiset and $H : \mathcal{D} \to \mathbb{Z}_{\geq 0}$ be a hypothesized DA multiset. The multiset intersection for each DA type DA_i is:

$$(A \cap H)(\mathrm{DA}_i) = \min(A(\mathrm{DA}_i), H(\mathrm{DA}_i))$$

DA-level multiset precision $P(\mathrm{DA}_i)$ and recall $R(\mathrm{DA}_i)$ are then defined as:

$$P(\mathrm{DA}_i) = (A \cap H)(\mathrm{DA}_i) \,/\, H(\mathrm{DA}_i)$$

$$R(\mathrm{DA}_i) = (A \cap H)(\mathrm{DA}_i) \,/\, A(\mathrm{DA}_i)$$

DA	Description	Example
D-T	Describe target	this is the christmas tree in front of a fireplace
As-I	Assert Identified	got it
NG	Non-game utterances	okay there i saw the light go on
PFB	Positive feedback	okay
ST	Self-talk statements	ooh this is gonna be tricky
P	Filled pause	uh
D-M	Discourse marker	alright
Q-YN	Yes-No question	is it on something white
A-Y	Yes answer	yeah
EC	Echo confirmation	the blue
As-M	Matcher assertions	it didn't let me do it
Q-C	Clarification question	bright orange eyes?
A-D	Action directive	oh oh wait hold on
A-N	No answer	no, nah
H	Hedge	i don't know what it is
Q-D	Disjunctive question	are we talking dark brown or like caramel brown
Q-Wh	Wh-question	what color's the kitty
As-S	Assert skip	i'm gonna pass on that

Table 9: The complete list of DAs in the annotated RDG-Image corpus.

DA	All	Dir	Mat	DA	All	Dir	Mat
D-T	41	60	0	EC	2	.5	6
As-I	15	0	46	As-M	2	0	4
NG	11	9	11	Q-C	2	.5	4
PFB	8	10	7	A-D	1	.3	2
ST	4	4	4	A-N	.5	.7	.2
P	4	6	2	H	.5	.7	0
D-M	3	5	.2	Q-Wh	.3	0	.5
Q-YN	3	.6	7	As-S	.1	0	.1
A-Y	2	3	1	Q-D	.4	0	1.2

Table 10: DA distribution. We report the relative percentages for each DA out of all DAs, director DAs, and matcher DAs, respectively.

Keynote: Modeling Human Communication Dynamics

Louis-Philippe Morency

Carnegie Mellon University - Language Technology Institute

Pittsburgh, PA, United States

`morency@cs.cmu.edu`

Abstract:

Human face-to-face communication is a little like a dance, in that participants continuously adjust their behaviors based on verbal and nonverbal cues from the social context. Today's computers and interactive devices are still lacking many of these human-like abilities to hold fluid and natural interactions. Leveraging recent advances in machine learning, audio-visual signal processing and computational linguistic, my research focuses on creating computational technologies able to analyze, recognize and predict human subtle communicative behaviors in social context. I formalize this new research endeavor with a Human Communication Dynamics framework, addressing four key computational challenges: behavioral dynamic, multimodal dynamic, interpersonal dynamic and societal dynamic. Central to this research effort is the introduction of new probabilistic models able to learn the temporal and fine-grained latent dependencies across behaviors, modalities and interlocutors. In this talk, I will present some of our recent achievements modeling multiple aspects of human communication dynamics, motivated by applications in healthcare (depression, PTSD, suicide, autism), education (learning analytics), business (negotiation, interpersonal skills) and social multimedia (opinion mining, social influence).

Speaker's Bio:

Louis-Philippe Morency is Assistant Professor in the Language Technology Institute at Carnegie Mellon University where he leads the Multimodal Communication and Machine Learning Laboratory (MultiComp Lab). He was formely research assistant professor in the Computer Sciences Department at University of Southern California and research scientist at USC Institute for Creative Technologies. Prof. Morency received his Ph.D. and Master degrees from MIT Computer Science and Artificial Intelligence Laboratory. His research focuses on building the computational foundations to enable computers with the abilities to analyze, recognize and predict subtle human communicative behaviors during social interactions. In particular, Prof. Morency was lead co-investigator for the multi-institution effort that created SimSensei and MultiSense, two technologies to automatically assess nonverbal behavior indicators of psychological distress. He is currently chair of the advisory committee for ACM International Conference on Multimodal Interaction and associate editor at IEEE Transactions on Affective Computing.

Proceedings of the SIGDIAL 2016 Conference, page 263,
Los Angeles, USA, 13-15 September 2016. ©2016 Association for Computational Linguistics

On the Evaluation of Dialogue Systems with Next Utterance Classification

Ryan Lowe[1], Iulian V. Serban[2], Mike Noseworthy[1], Laurent Charlin[3*], Joelle Pineau[1]

[1] School of Computer Science, McGill University
{ryan.lowe, jpineau}@cs.mcgill.ca,
michael.noseworthy@mail.mcgill.ca
[2] DIRO, Université de Montréal
iulian.vlad.serban@umontreal.ca
[3] HEC Montréal
laurent.charlin@hec.ca

Abstract

An open challenge in constructing dialogue systems is developing methods for automatically learning dialogue strategies from large amounts of unlabelled data. Recent work has proposed Next-Utterance-Classification (NUC) as a surrogate task for building dialogue systems from text data. In this paper we investigate the performance of humans on this task to validate the relevance of NUC as a method of evaluation. Our results show three main findings: (1) humans are able to correctly classify responses at a rate much better than chance, thus confirming that the task is feasible, (2) human performance levels vary across task domains (we consider 3 datasets) and expertise levels (novice vs experts), thus showing that a range of performance is possible on this type of task, (3) automated dialogue systems built using state-of-the-art machine learning methods have similar performance to the human novices, but worse than the experts, thus confirming the utility of this class of tasks for driving further research in automated dialogue systems.

1 Introduction

Significant efforts have been made in recent years to develop computational methods for learning dialogue strategies offline from large amounts of text data. One of the challenges of this line of work is to develop methods to automatically evaluate, either directly or indirectly, models that are trained in this manner (Galley et al., 2015; Schatzmann et al., 2005), without requiring human labels or

*This work was primarily done while LC was at McGill University.

human user experiments, which are time consuming and expensive. The use of automatic tasks and metrics is one key issue in scaling the development of dialogue systems from small domain-specific systems, which require significant engineering, to general conversational agents (Pietquin and Hastie, 2013).

In this paper, we consider tasks and evaluation measures for what we call 'unsupervised' dialogue systems, such as chatbots. These are in contrast to 'supervised' dialogue systems, which we define as those that explicitly incorporate some supervised signal such as task completion or user satisfaction. Unsupervised systems can be roughly separated into *response generation* systems that attempt to produce a likely response given a conversational context, and *retrieval-based* systems that attempt to select a response from a (possibly large) list of utterances in a corpus. While there has been significant work on building end-to-end response generation systems (Vinyals and Le, 2015; Shang et al., 2015; Serban et al., 2016), it has recently been shown that many of the automatic evaluation metrics used for such systems correlate poorly or not at all with human judgement of the generated responses (Liu et al., 2016).

Retrieval-based systems are of interest because they admit a natural evaluation metric, namely the recall and precision measures. First introduced for evaluating user simulations by Schatzmann et al. (2005), such a framework has gained recent prominence for the evaluation of end-to-end dialogue systems (Lowe et al., 2015a; Kadlec et al., 2015; Dodge et al., 2016). These models are trained on the *task* of selecting the correct response from a candidate list, which we call Next-Utterance-Classification (NUC, detailed in Section 3), and are evaluated using the *metric* of recall. NUC is useful for several reasons: 1) the performance (i.e. loss or error) is easy to com-

Proceedings of the SIGDIAL 2016 Conference, pages 264–269,
Los Angeles, USA, 13-15 September 2016. ©2016 Association for Computational Linguistics

pute automatically, 2) it is simple to adjust the difficulty of the task, 3) the task is interpretable and amenable to comparison with human performance, 4) it is an easier task compared to generative dialogue modeling, which is difficult for end-to-end systems (Sordoni et al., 2015; Serban et al., 2016), and 5) models trained with NUC can be converted to dialogue systems by retrieving from the full corpus (Liu et al., 2016). In this case, NUC additionally allows for making hard constraints on the allowable outputs of the system (to prevent offensive responses), and guarantees that the responses are fluent (because they were generated by humans). Thus, NUC can be thought of both as an *intermediate task* that can be used to evaluate the ability of systems to understand natural language conversations, similar to the bAbI tasks for language understanding (Weston et al., 2016), and as a *useful framework* for building chatbots. With the huge size of current dialogue datasets that contain millions of utterances (Lowe et al., 2015a; Banchs, 2012; Ritter et al., 2010) and the increasing amount of natural language data, it is conceivable that retrieval-based systems will be able to have engaging conversations with humans.

However, despite the current work with NUC, there has been no verification of whether machine and human performance differ on this task. This cannot be assumed; it is possible that no significant gap exists between the two, as is the case with many current automatic response generation metrics (Liu et al., 2016). Further, it is important to benchmark human performance on new tasks such as NUC to determine when research has outgrown their use. In this paper, we consider to what extent NUC is achievable by humans, whether human performance varies according to expertise, and whether there is room for machine performance to improve (or has reached human performance already) and we should move to more complex conversational tasks. We performed a user study on three different datasets: the SubTle Corpus of movie dialogues (Banchs, 2012), the Twitter Corpus (Ritter et al., 2010), and the Ubuntu Dialogue Corpus (Lowe et al., 2015a). Since conversations in the Ubuntu Dialogue Corpus are highly technical, we recruit 'expert' humans who are adept with the Ubuntu terminology, whom we compare with a state-of-the-art machine learning agent on all datasets. We find that there is indeed a significant separation between machine and expert hu-

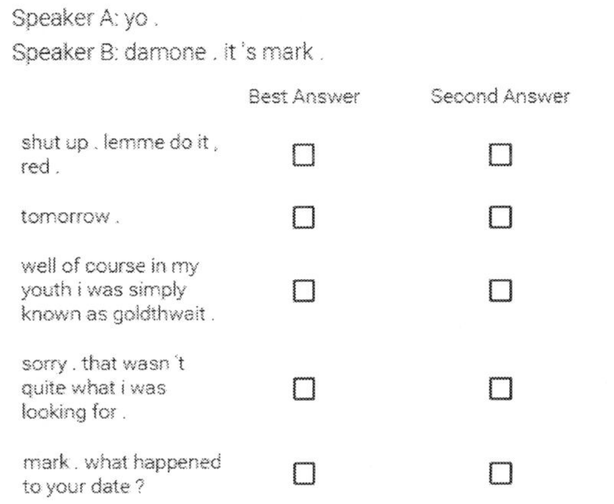

Figure 1: An example NUC question from the SubTle Corpus (Banchs, 2012).

man performance, suggesting that NUC is a useful intermediate task for measuring progress.

2 Related Work

Evaluation methods for supervised systems have been well studied. They include the PARADISE framework (Walker et al., 1997), and MeMo (Möller et al., 2006), which include a measure of task completion. A more extensive overview of these metrics can be found in (Jokinen and McTear, 2009). We focus in this paper on unsupervised dialogue systems, for which proper evaluation is an open problem.

Recent evaluation metrics for unsupervised dialogue systems include BLEU (Papineni et al., 2002) and METEOR (Banerjee and Lavie, 2005), which compare the similarity between response generated by the model, and the actual response of the participant, conditioned on some context of the conversation. Word perplexity, which computes a function of the probability of re-generating examples from the training corpus, is also used. However, such metrics have been shown to correlate very weakly with human judgement of the produced responses (Liu et al., 2016). They also suffer from several other drawbacks (Liu et al., 2016), including low scores, lack of interpretability, and inability to account for the vast space of acceptable outputs in natural conversation.

3 Technical Background on NUC

Our long-term goal is the development and deployment of artificial conversational agents. Recent deep neural architectures offer perhaps the most promising framework for tackling this problem. However training such architectures typically requires large amounts of conversation data from the target domain, and a way to automatically assess prediction errors. Next-Utterance-Classification (NUC, see Figure 1) is a *task*, which is straightforward to evaluate, designed for training and validation of dialogue systems. They are evaluated using the *metric* of Recall@k, which we define in this section.

In NUC, a model or user, when presented with the context of a conversation and a (usually small) pre-defined list of responses, must select the most appropriate response from this list. This list *includes the actual next response* of the conversation, which is the desired prediction of the model. The other entries, which act as false positives, are sampled from elsewhere in the corpus. Note that no assumptions are made regarding the number of utterances in the context: these can be fixed or sampled from arbitrary distributions. Performance on this task is easy to assess by measuring the success rate of picking the correct next response; more specifically, we measure Recall@k (R@k), which is the percentage of correct responses (i.e. the actual response of the conversation) that are found in the top k responses with the highest rankings according to the model. This task has gained some popularity recently for evaluating dialogue systems (Lowe et al., 2015a; Kadlec et al., 2015).

There are several attractive properties of this approach, as detailed in the introduction: the performance is easy to compute automatically, the task is interpretable and amenable to comparison with human performance, and it is easier than generative dialogue modeling. A particularly nice property is that one can adjust the difficulty of NUC by simply changing the number of false responses (from one response to the full corpus), or by altering the selection criteria of false responses (from randomly sampled to intentionally confusing). Indeed, as the number of false responses grows to encompass all natural language responses, the task becomes identical to response generation.

One potential limitation of the NUC approach is that, since the other candidate answers are sampled from elsewhere in the corpus, these may also represent reasonable responses given the context. Part of the contribution of this work is determining the significance of this limitation.

What is your gender?	
Male	56.5%
Female	44.5%
What is your age?	
18-20	3.4%
21-30	38.1%
31-40	33.3%
41-55	14.3%
55+	10.2%
How would you rate your fluency in English?	
Beginner	0%
Intermediate	8.2%
Advanced	6.8%
Fluent	84.4%
What is your current level of education?	
High school or less	21.1%
Bachelor's	60.5%
Master's	13.6%
Doctorate or higher	3.4%
How would you rate your knowledge of Ubuntu?	
I've never used it	70.7%
Basic	21.8%
Intermediate	5.4%
Expert	2.7%

Table 1: Data on the 145 AMT participants.

4 Survey Methodology

4.1 Corpora

We conducted our analysis on three corpora that have gained recent popularity for training dialogue systems. The SubTle Corpus (Banchs, 2012) consists of movie dialogues as extracted from subtitles, and includes turn-taking information indicating when each user has finished their turn. Unlike the larger OpenSubtitles[1] dataset, the SubTle Corpus includes turn-taking information indicating when each user has finished their turn. The Twitter Corpus (Ritter et al., 2010) contains a large number of conversations between users on the microblogging platform Twitter. Finally, the Ubuntu Dialogue Corpus contains conversations extracted from IRC chat logs (Lowe et al., 2015a). [2] For more information on these datasets, we refer the reader to a recent survey on dialogue corpora (Serban et al., 2015). We focus our attention on these as they cover a range of popular domains, and are among the largest available dialogue datasets, making them good candidates for building data-driven dialogue systems. Note that while the Ubuntu Corpus is most relevant to supervised systems, the NUC task still applies in this domain. Models that take semantic information into account (i.e., to solve the user's problem) can still be validated with NUC, as demonstrated

---

[1] http://www.opensubtitles.org
[2] http://irclogs.ubuntu.com

in Lowe et al. (2015b).

A group of 145 paid participants were recruited through Amazon Mechanical Turk (AMT), a crowdsourcing platform for obtaining human participants for various studies. Demographic data including age, level of education, and fluency of English were collected from the AMT participants, and is shown in Table 1. An additional 8 volunteers were recruited from the student population in the computer science department at the author's institution.[3] This second group, referred to as "Lab experts", had significant exposure to technical terms prominent in the Ubuntu dataset; we hypothesized that this was an advantage in selecting responses for that corpus.

4.2 Task description

Each participant was asked to answer either 30 or 40 questions (mean=31.9). To ensure a sufficient diversity of questions from each dataset, four versions of the survey with different questions were given to participants. For AMT respondents, the questions were approximately evenly distributed across the three datasets, while for the lab experts, half of the questions were related to Ubuntu and the remainder evenly split across Twitter and movies. Each question had 1 correct response, and 4 false responses drawn uniformly at random from elsewhere in the (same) corpus. An example question can be seen in Figure 1. Participants had a time limit of 40 minutes.

Conversations were extracted to form NUC conversation-response pairs as described in Sec. 3. The number of utterances in the context were sampled according to the procedure in (Lowe et al., 2015a), with a maximum context length of 6 turns — this was done for both the human trials and ANN model. All conversations were preprocessed in order to anonymize the utterances. For the Twitter conversations, this was extended to replacing all user mentions (words beginning with @) throughout the utterance with a placeholder '@user' symbol, as these are often repeated in a conversation. Hashtags were not removed, as these are often used in the main body of tweets, and many tweets are illegible without them. Conversations were edited or pruned to remove offensive language according to ethical guidelines.

---

[3]None of these participants were directly involved with this research project.

4.3 ANN model

In order to compare human results with a strong artificial neural network (ANN) model, we use the dual encoder (DE) model from Lowe et al. (2015a). This model uses recurrent neural networks (RNNs) with long-short term memory (LSTM) units (Hochreiter and Schmidhuber, 1997) to encode the context c of the conversation, and a candidate response r. More precisely, at each time step, a word x_t is input into the LSTM, and its hidden state is updated according to: $h_t = f(W_h h_{t-1} + W_x x_t)$, where W are weight matrices, and $f(\cdot)$ is some non-linear activation function. After all T words have been processed, the final hidden state h_T can be considered a vector representation of the input sequence.

To determine the probability that a response r is the actual next response to some context c, the model computes a weighted dot product between the vector representations $\mathbf{c}, \mathbf{r} \in \mathbb{R}^d$ of the context and response, respectively:

$$P(r \text{ is correct response}) = \sigma(\mathbf{c}^\top M \mathbf{r})$$

where M is a matrix of learned parameters, and σ is the sigmoid function. The model is trained to minimize the cross-entropy error of context-response pairs. For training the authors randomly sample negative examples.

The DE model is close to state-of-the-art for neural network dialogue models on the Ubuntu Dialogue Corpus; we obtained further results on the Movie and Twitter corpora in order to facilitate comparison with humans. For further model implementation details, see Lowe et al. (2015a).

5 Results

As we can see from Table 1, the AMT participants are mostly young adults, fluent in English with some undergraduate education. The split across genders is approximately equal, and the majority of respondents had never used Ubuntu before.

Table 2 shows the NUC results on each corpus. The human results are separated into AMT non-experts, consisting of paid respondents who have 'Beginner' or no knowledge of Ubuntu terminology; AMT experts, who claimed to have 'Intermediate' or 'Advanced' knowledge of Ubuntu; and Lab experts, who are the non-paid respondents with Ubuntu experience and university-level computer science training. We also presents results on the same task for a state-of-the-art artificial neural

	Number of Users	Movie Corpus		Twitter Corpus		Ubuntu Corpus	
		R@1	R@2	R@1	R@2	R@1	R@2
AMT non-experts	135	$65.9 \pm 2.4\%$	$79.8 \pm 2.1\%$	$74.1 \pm 2.3\%$	$82.3 \pm 2.0\%$	$52.9 \pm 2.7\%$	$69.4 \pm 2.5\%$
AMT experts	10	—	—	—	—	$52.0 \pm 9.8\%$	$63.0 \pm 9.5\%$
Lab experts	8	$69.7 \pm 10\%$	$94.0 \pm 5.2\%^*$	$88.4 \pm 7.0\%$	$98.4 \pm 2.7\%^*$	$83.8 \pm 8.1\%$	$87.8 \pm 7.2\%$
ANN model (Lowe et al., 2015a)	machine	50.6%	74.9%	66.9%	89.6%	66.2%	83.7%

Table 2: Average results on each corpus. 'Number of Users' indicates the number of respondents for each category. 'AMT experts' and 'AMT non-experts' are combined for the Movie and Twitter corpora. 95% confidence intervals are calculated using the normal approximation, which assumes subjects answer each question independently of other examples and subjects. Starred (*) results indicate a poor approximation of the confidence interval due to high scores with small sample size, according to the rule of thumb by Brown et al. (2001).

network (ANN) dialogue model (see (Lowe et al., 2015a) for implementation details).

We first observe that subjects perform above chance level (20% for R@1) on all domains, thus the task is doable for humans. Second we observe difference in performances between the three domains. The Twitter dataset appears to have the best predictability, with a Recall@1 approximately 8% points higher than for the movie dialogues for AMT workers, and 18% higher for lab experts. Rather than attributing this to greater familiarity with Twitter than movies, it seems more likely that it is because movie utterances are often short, generic (e.g. contain few topic-related words), and lack proper context (e.g., video cues and the movie's story). Conversely, tweets are typically more specific, and successive tweets may have common hashtags.

As expected, untrained respondents scored lowest on the Ubuntu dataset, as it contains the most difficult language with often unfamiliar terminology. Further, since the domain is narrow, randomly drawn false responses could be more likely to resemble the actual next response, especially to someone unfamiliar with Ubuntu terminology. We also observe that the ANN model achieves similar performance to the paid human respondents from AMT. However, the model is still significantly behind the lab experts for Recall@1.

An interesting note is that there is very little difference between the paid AMT non-experts and AMT experts on Ubuntu. This suggests that the participants do not provide accurate self-rating of expertise, either intentionally or not. We also found that lab experts took on average approximately 50% more time to complete the survey than paid testers; this is reflected in the results,

where the lab experts score 30% higher on the Ubuntu Corpus, and even 5-10% higher on the non-technical Movie and Twitter corpora. While we included attention check questions to ensure the quality of responses,[4] this reflects poorly on the ability of crowdsourced workers to answer technical questions, even if they self-identify as being adept with the technology.

6 Discussion

Our results demonstrate that humans outperform current dialogue models on the task of Next-Utterance-Classification, indicating that there is plenty of room for improvement for these models to better understand the nature of human dialogue. While our results suggest that NUC is a useful task, it is by no means sufficient; we strongly advocate for automatically evaluating dialogue systems with as many relevant metrics as possible. Further research should be conducted into finding metrics or tasks which accurately reflect human judgement for the evaluation of dialogue systems.

Acknowledgements The authors gratefully acknowledge financial support for this work by the Samsung Advanced Institute of Technology (SAIT) and the Natural Sciences and Engineering Research Council of Canada (NSERC).

References

R. E. Banchs. 2012. Movie-dic: A movie dialogue corpus for research and development. In *Proceedings of the 50th Annual Meeting of the Association for Computational Linguistics: Short Papers - Volume 2*.

---

[4] Only the respondents who passed all attention checks were counted in the survey.

S. Banerjee and A. Lavie. 2005. METEOR: An automatic metric for mt evaluation with improved correlation with human judgments. In *ACL workshop on intrinsic and extrinsic evaluation measures for machine translation and/or summarization*.

L. D. Brown, T. T. Cai, and A. DasGupta. 2001. Interval estimation for a binomial proportion. *Statistical science*, pages 101–117.

J. Dodge, A. Gane, X. Zhang, A. Bordes, S. Chopra, A. Miller, A. Szlam, and J. Weston. 2016. Evaluating prerequisit qualities for learning end-to-end dialog systems. *International Conference on Learning Representations (ICLR)*.

M. Galley, C. Brockett, A. Sordoni, Y. Ji, M. Auli, C. Quirk, M. Mitchell, J. Gao, and B. Dolan. 2015. deltaBLEU: A discriminative metric for generation tasks with intrinsically diverse targets. In *Proceedings of the Annual Meeting of the Association for Computational Linguistics and the International Joint Conference on Natural Language Processing (Short Papers)*.

S. Hochreiter and J. Schmidhuber. 1997. Long short-term memory. *Neural computation*, 9(8):1735–1780.

K. Jokinen and M. McTear. 2009. *Spoken Dialogue Systems*. Morgan Claypool.

R. Kadlec, M. Schmid, and J. Kleindienst. 2015. Improved deep learning baselines for ubuntu corpus dialogs. *NIPS on Machine Learning for Spoken Language Understanding*.

C. Liu, R. Lowe, I. V. Serban, M. Noseworthy, L. Charlin, and J. Pineau. 2016. How not to evaluate your dialogue system: An empirical study of unsupervised evaluation metrics for dialogue response generation. *arXiv preprint arXiv:1603.08023*.

R. Lowe, N. Pow, I. Serban, and J. Pineau. 2015a. The ubuntu dialogue corpus: A large dataset for research in unstructured multi-turn dialogue systems. In *Proceedings of SIGDIAL*.

R. Lowe, N. Pow, I. V. Serban, L. Charlin, and J. Pineau. 2015b. Incorporating unstructured textual knowledge sources into neural dialogue systems. In *NIPS Workshop on Machine Learning for Spoken Language Understanding*.

S. Möller, R. Englert, K.-P. Engelbrecht, V. V. Hafner, A. Jameson, A. Oulasvirta, A. Raake, and N. Reithinger. 2006. Memo: towards automatic usability evaluation of spoken dialogue services by user error simulations. In *INTERSPEECH*.

K. Papineni, S. Roukos, T. Ward, and W. Zhu. 2002. BLEU: a method for automatic evaluation of machine translation. In *Proceedings of the 40th annual meeting on Association for Computational Linguistics (ACL)*.

O. Pietquin and H. Hastie. 2013. A survey on metrics for the evaluation of user simulations. *The Knowledge Engineering Review*.

A. Ritter, C. Cherry, and B. Dolan. 2010. Unsupervised modeling of twitter conversations. In *North American Chapter of the Association for Computational Linguistics (NAACL)*.

J. Schatzmann, K. Georgila, and S. Young. 2005. Quantitative evaluation of user simulation techniques for spoken dialogue systems. In *Proceedings of SIGDIAL*.

I. V. Serban, R. Lowe, L. Charlin, and J. Pineau. 2015. A survey of available corpora for building data-driven dialogue systems. *arXiv preprint arXiv:1512.05742*.

I. V. Serban, A. Sordoni, Y. Bengio, A. C. Courville, and J. Pineau. 2016. Building end-to-end dialogue systems using generative hierarchical neural network models. In *Association for the Advancement of Artificial Intelligence (AAAI), 2016*, pages 3776–3784.

L. Shang, Z. Lu, and H. Li. 2015. Neural responding machine for short-text conversation. *arXiv preprint arXiv:1503.02364*.

A. Sordoni, M. Galley, M. Auli, C. Brockett, Y. Ji, M. Mitchell, J. Nie, J. Gao, and B. Dolan. 2015. A neural network approach to context-sensitive generation of conversational responses. In *Conference of the North American Chapter of the Association for Computational Linguistics (NAACL-HLT 2015)*.

O. Vinyals and Q. Le. 2015. A neural conversational model. *ICML Deep Learning Workshop*.

M. A. Walker, D. J. Litman, C. A. Kamm, and A. Abella. 1997. Paradise: A framework for evaluating spoken dialogue agents. In *Proceedings of the eighth conference on European chapter of the Association for Computational Linguistics*, pages 271–280. Association for Computational Linguistics.

J. Weston, A. Bordes, S. Chopra, and T. Mikolov. 2016. Towards ai-complete question answering: A set of prerequisite toy tasks. *International Conference on Learning Representations (ICLR)*.

Towards Using Conversations with Spoken Dialogue Systems in the Automated Assessment of Non-Native Speakers of English

Diane Litman

University of Pittsburgh
Pittsburgh, PA 15260 USA
`dlitman@pitt.edu`

Steve Young, Mark Gales, Kate Knill, Karen Ottewell, Rogier van Dalen and David Vandyke

University of Cambridge
Cambridge, CB2 1PZ, UK
`{sjy11,mjfg100,kmk1001,ko201,`
`rcv25,djv27}@cam.ac.uk`

Abstract

Existing speaking tests only require non-native speakers to engage in dialogue when the assessment is done by humans. This paper examines the viability of using off-the-shelf systems for spoken dialogue and for speech grading to automate the holistic scoring of the conversational speech of non-native speakers of English.

1 Introduction

Speaking tests for assessing non-native speakers of English (NNSE) often include tasks involving interactive dialogue between a human examiner and a candidate. An IELTS[1] example is shown in Figure 1. In contrast, most automated spoken assessment systems target only the non-interactive portions of existing speaking tests, e.g., the task of responding to a stimulus in TOEFL[2] (Wang et al., 2013) or BULATS[3] (van Dalen et al., 2015).

This gap between the current state of manual and automated testing provides an opportunity for spoken dialogue systems (SDS) research. First, as illustrated by Figure 1, human-human testing dialogues share some features with existing computer-human dialogues, e.g., examiners use standardized topic-based scripts and utterance phrasing. Second, automatic assessment of spontaneous (but non-conversational) speech is an active research area (Chen et al., 2009; Chen and Zechner, 2011; Wang et al., 2013; Bhat et al., 2014; van Dalen et al., 2015; Shashidhar et al., 2015), which work in SDS-based assessment

E: Do you work or are you a student
C: I'm a student in university er
E: And what subject are you studying

Figure 1: Testing dialogue excerpt between an IELTS human examiner (E) and a candidate (C) (Seedhouse et al., 2014).

should be able to build on. Third, there is increasing interest in building automated systems not to replace human examiners during testing, but to help candidates prepare for human testing. Similarly to systems for writing (Burstein et al., 2004; Roscoe et al., 2012; Andersen et al., 2013; Foltz and Rosenstein, 2015), automation could provide unlimited self-assessment and practice opportunities. There is already some educationally-oriented SDS work in computer assisted language learning (Su et al., 2015) and physics tutoring (Forbes-Riley and Litman, 2011) to potentially build upon.

On the other hand, differences between speaking assessment and traditional SDS applications can also pose research challenges. First, currently available SDS corpora do not focus on including speech from non-native speakers, and when such speech exists it is not scored for English skill. Even if one could get an assessment company to release a scored corpus of human-human dialogues, there would likely be a mismatch with the computer-human dialogues that are our target for automatic assessment.[4] Second, there is a lack of optimal technical infrastructure. Existing SDS components such as speech recognizers will likely need modification to handle non-

---

[1]International English Language Testing System.
[2]Test of English as a Foreign Language.
[3]Business Language Testing Service.

[4]Users speak differently to Wizard-of-Oz versus automated versions of the same SDS, despite believing that both versions are fully automated (Thomason and Litman, 2013).

Proceedings of the SIGDIAL 2016 Conference, pages 270–275,
Los Angeles, USA, 13-15 September 2016. ©2016 Association for Computational Linguistics

native speech (Ivanov et al., 2015). Existing automated graders will likely need modification to process spontaneous speech produced during dialogue, rather than after a prompt such as a request to describe a visual (Evanini et al., 2014).

We make a first step at examining these issues, by using three off-the-shelf SDS to collect dialogues which are then assessed by a human expert and an existing spontaneous speech grader. Our focus is on the following research questions:

RQ1: Will different corpus creation methods[5] influence the English skill level of the SDS users we are able to recruit for data collection purposes?

RQ2: Can an expert human grader assess speakers conversing with an SDS?

RQ3: Can an automated grader for spontaneous (but prompted) speech assess SDS speech?

Our preliminary results suggest that while SDS-based speech assessment shows promise, much work remains to be done.

2 Related Work

While SDS have been used to assess and tutor native English speakers in areas ranging from science subjects to foreign languages, SDS have generally not been used to interactively assess the speech of NNSE. Even when language-learning SDS have enabled a system's behavior to vary based on the speaker's prior responses(s), the skills being assessed (e.g., pronunciation (Su et al., 2015)) typically do not involve prior dialogue context.

In one notable exception, a trialogue-based system was developed to conversationally assess young English language learners (Evanini et al., 2014; Mitchell et al., 2014). Similarly to our research, a major goal was to examine whether standard SDS components could yield reliable conversational assessments compared to humans. A small pilot evaluation suggested the viability of a proof-of-concept trialogue system. Our work differs in that we develop a dialogue rather than a

trialogue system, focus on adults rather than children, and use an international scoring standard rather than task completion to assess English skill.

3 Computer Dialogues with NNSE

The first step of our research involved creating corpora of dialogues between non-native speakers of English and state-of-the-art spoken dialogue systems, which were then used by an expert to manually assess NNSE speaking skills. Our methods for collecting and annotating three corpora, each involving a different SDS and a different user recruitment method, are described below.

3.1 Corpora Creation

The **Laptop (L)** corpus contains conversations with users who were instructed to find laptops with certain characteristics. The SDS was produced by Cambridge University (Vandyke et al., 2015), while users were recruited via Amazon Mechanical Turk (AMT) and interacted with the SDS over the phone. To increase the likelihood of attracting non-native speakers, an AMT Location qualification restricted the types of workers who could converse with the system. We originally required workers to be from India[6], but due to call connection issues, we changed the restriction to require workers to *not* be from the United States, the United Kingdom, or Australia. In pilot studies without such qualification restrictions, primarily native speakers responded to the AMT task even though we specified that workers must be non-native speakers of English only.

The **Restaurant (R)** corpus contains conversations with users who were instructed to find Michigan restaurants with certain characteristics. The SDS used to collect this corpus was produced by VocalIQ[7] (Mrkšić et al., 2015). Users were again recruited via AMT, but interacted with this SDS via microphone using the Chrome browser. Rather than using a location qualification, the title of the AMT task was given only in Hindi.

The **Bus (B)** corpus contains conversations with users who were instructed to find bus routes in Pittsburgh. Although the SDS was again produced by Cambridge University, the dialogues were pre-

---

[5]As explained in Section 3.1, this paper compares three corpora that were created in three different ways: via Amazon Mechanical Turk with worker qualification restrictions, via Amazon Mechanical Turk with non-English task titles, and via a Spoken Dialogue Challenge with SDS users from participant sites.

[6]The speech recognizer used in the off-the-shelf grader described in Section 4.1 was trained on speakers with Gujarti as their first language. The grader itself, however, was trained on data from Polish, Vietnamese, Arabic, Dutch, French, and Thai first-language speakers (van Dalen et al., 2015).

[7]Thanks to Blaise Thompson for providing the system.

		Assessed											Not	All
	n	A1	A2	B1	B1B2	B2	B2C1	C1	C1C2	C2	Turns / Dial.	Wds. / Turn	n	n
L	21			1		4	6	7	2	1	11.48	3.9	4	25
R	14				2	8	3	1			6.36	5.5	6	20
B	20					1	2	10	6	1	13.65	2.6	2	22
C	55			1	2	13	11	18	8	2	10.96	3.6	12	67

Table 1: Human CEFR dialogue assessments, average # of user turns per dialogue, and average number of recognized words per turn, across corpora. L = Laptop, R=Restaurant, B=Bus, C=Combined.

viously collected as part of the first Spoken Dialogue Challenge (SDC) (Black et al., 2011). However, our **Bus** corpus includes only a subset of the available SDC dialogues, namely non-native dialogues from the control condition. As in our AMT corpus collections, callers in the control condition received a scenario to solve over a web interface. Furthermore, callers in the control condition were spoken dialogue researchers from around the world. Whether a caller was a non-native speaker was in fact annotated in the SDC corpus download.

Since our **Bus** corpus contained 22 dialogues[8], we used AMT to collect similar numbers of dialogues with the other SDS. After removing problematic dialogues where the AMT task was completed but there was no caller speech or the caller turned out to be a native speaker, our final **Combined (C)** corpus contained 67 dialogues, distributed as shown in the "All" column of Table 1.

3.2 Manual Speaking Skill Assessment

Once the corpora were collected, the speaking skill of the human in each dialogue was manually assessed using the Common European Framework of Reference for Languages (CEFR, 2001).[9] The CEFR is an international standard for benchmarking language ability using an ordered scale of 6 levels: A1, A2, B1, B2, C1, C2. A1 represents beginning skill while C2 represents mastery.

Assessment was done by a human expert while listening to logged SDS audio files. Speech recognition output was also made available. Since an expert in CEFR performed the assessment[10], dialogues were only scored by this single assessor. Sometimes the assessor assigned two adjacent lev-

els to a speaker. To support a later comparison with the unique numerical score produced by the automatic grader discussed in Section 4.1, dual assessments were mapped to a new intermediate level placed between the original levels in the ordered scale. For example, if the expert rated a speaker as both "B1" and "B2", we replaced those two levels with the single level "B1B2."

The A1-C2 columns of the "Assessed" section of Table 1 show the expert assessment results for each corpus. The average number of user turns per assessed dialogue ("Turns/Dial.") and the average number of recognized words[11] per user turn ("Wds./Turn") are also shown. With respect to RQ1, comparing the CEFR level distributions across rows suggests that different user recruitment methods do indeed yield different skill levels. Using AMT (the Laptop and Restaurant corpora) yielded more mid-level English speakers than the SDC method (the Bus corpus).[12] However, speakers in all three corpora are still biased towards the higher CEFR skill levels.

With respect to RQ2, not all dialogues could be assessed by the expert (as shown by the "Not" Assessed column of Table 1), often due to poor audio quality. Even for those dialogues that the expert was able to assess, human assessment was often felt to be difficult. When the SDS worked well, there was not very much user speech for making the assessment. When the SDS worked poorly, the dialogues became unnatural and speakers had to curtail potential demonstrations of fluency such as producing long sentences. Finally, only the Laptop and Bus systems recorded both sides of the conversation. Although the text for the Restaurant

---

[8]Only 22 of the 75 control callers were non-natives.

[9]The scores produced by the automatic grader described in Section 4.1 come with a mapping to CEFR.

[10]The Director of Academic Development and Training for International Students at Cambridge's Language Centre.

[11]The output of the speech recognizer for each SDS was used as only the SDC Bus download has transcriptions.

[12]A statistical analysis demonstrating that the Restaurant scores are significantly lower will be presented in Section 4.2, after the CEFR labels are transformed to a numeric scale.

Corpus		Mean (SD) Grades		Correlation	
	n	Human	Auto	R	p
L	21	24.2 (3.1)	17.1 (1.9)	.41	.07
R	14	21.5 (2.0)	11.6 (3.1)	.69	.01
B	15	25.9 (1.9)	17.1 (1.7)	-.11	.69
C	50	24.0 (3.0)	15.6 (3.3)	.59	.01

Table 2: Mean (standard deviation) of human and automated grades, along with Pearson's correlations between the human and automated individual dialogue grades, within each corpus.

system's prompts was made available, assessment was felt to be more difficult with only user speech.

4 Automated Assessment

After creating the SDS corpora with gold-standard speaker assessments (Section 3), we evaluated whether speech from such SDS interactions could be evaluated using an existing automated grader developed for prompted (non-dialogue) spontaneous speech (van Dalen et al., 2015).

4.1 The GP-BULATS Grader

The GP-BULATS automated grader (van Dalen et al., 2015) is based on a Gaussian process. The input is a set of audio features (fundamental frequency and energy statistics) extracted from speech, and fluency features (counts and properties of silences, disfluencies, words, and phones) extracted from a time-aligned speech recognition hypothesis. The output is a 0–30 score, plus a measure of prediction uncertainty. The grader was trained using data from Cambridge English's BULATS corpus of learner speech. Each of 994 learners was associated with an overall human-assigned grade between 0 and 30, and the audio from all sections of the learner's BULATS test was used to extract the predictive features. The speech recognizer for the fluency features was also trained on BULATS data. When evaluated on BULATS test data from 226 additional speakers, the Pearson's correlation between the overall grades produced by humans and by GP-BULATS was 0.83.

4.2 Applying GP-BULATS to SDS Speech

We transformed the expert CEFR ability labels (Table 1) to the grader's 0-30 scale, using a binning previously developed for GP-BULATS. The mean grades along with standard deviations are shown in the "Human" column of Table 2.[13] A one-way ANOVA with post-hoc Bonferroni tests shows that the Restaurant scores are significantly lower than in the other two corpora ($p \leq .01$).

For automatic dialogue scoring by GP-BULATS (trained prior to our SDS research as described above), the audio from every user utterance in a dialogue was used for feature extraction. The scoring results are shown in the "Auto" column of Table 2. Note that in all three corpora, GP-BULATS underscores the speakers.

The "R" and "p" columns of Table 2 show the Pearson's correlation between the human and the GP-BULATS grades, and the associated p-values (two-tailed tests). With respect to RQ3, there is a positive correlation for the corpora collected via AMT (statistically significant for Restaurant, and a trend for Laptop), as well as for the Combined corpus. Although the SDS R values are lower than the 0.83 GP-BULATS value, the moderate positive correlations are encouraging given the much smaller SDS test sets, as well as the training/testing data mismatch resulting from using off-the-shelf systems. The SDS used to collect our dialogues were not designed for non-native speakers, and the GP-BULATS system used to grade our dialogues was not designed for interactive speech.

Further work is needed to shed light on why the Bus corpus yielded a non-significant correlation. As noted in Section 3.2, shorter turns made human annotation more difficult. The Bus corpus had the fewest words per turn (Table 1), which perhaps made automated grading more difficult. The Bus user recruitment did not target Indian first languages, which could have impacted GP-BULATS speech recognition. Transcription is needed to examine recognition versus grader performance.

5 Discussion and Future Work

This paper presented first steps towards an automated, SDS-based method for holistically assessing conversational speech. Our proof-of-concept research demonstrated the feasibility of 1) using existing SDS to collect dialogues with NNSE, 2) human-assessing CEFR levels in such SDS speech, and 3) using an automated grader designed for prompted but non-interactive speech to yield scores that can positively correlate with humans.

---

[13]GP-BULATS was unable to grade 5 Bus dialogues. For example, if no words were recognized, fluency features such as the average length of words could not be computed. There are thus differing "n" values in Tables 1 and 2.

Much work remains to be done. A larger and more diverse speaker pool (in terms of first-languages and proficiency levels) is needed to generalize our findings. To create a public SDS corpus with gold-standard English skill assessments, work is needed in how to recruit speakers with such diverse skills, and how to change existing SDS systems to facilitate human scoring. Further examination of our research questions via controlled experimentation is also needed (e.g., for RQ1, comparing different corpus creation methods while keeping the SDS constant). Finally, we would like to investigate the grading impact of using optimized rather than off-the-shelf systems.

Acknowledgments

This work was supported by a Derek Brewer Visiting Fellow Award from Emmanuel College at the University of Cambridge and by a UK Royal Academy of Engineering Distinguished Visiting Fellowship Award. We thank the Cambridge Dialogue Systems Group, the ALTA Institute and Cambridge English for their support during this research. We also thank Carrie Demmans Epp, Kate Forbes-Riley and the reviewers for helpful feedback on earlier drafts of this paper.

References

Øistein E. Andersen, Helen Yannakoudakis, Fiona Barker, and Tim Parish. 2013. Developing and testing a self-assessment and tutoring system. In *Proceedings 8th Workshop on Innovative Use of NLP for Building Educational Applications*, pages 32–41.

Suma Bhat, Huichao Xue, and Su-Youn Yoon. 2014. Shallow analysis based assessment of syntactic complexity for automated speech scoring. In *Proceedings 52nd Annual Meeting of the Association for Computational Linguistics*, pages 1305–1315.

Alan W. Black, Susanne Burger, Alistair Conkie, Helen Hastie, Simon Keizer, Oliver Lemon, Nicolas Merigaud, Gabriel Parent, Gabriel Schubiner, Blaise Thomson, Jason D. Williams, Kai Yu, Steve Young, and Maxine Eskenazi. 2011. Spoken dialog challenge 2010: Comparison of live and control test results. In *Proceedings of SIGDIAL*, pages 2–7.

Jill Burstein, Martin Chodorow, and Claudia Leacock. 2004. Automated essay evaluation: The criterion online writing service. *Ai Magazine*, 25(3):27.

CEFR. 2001. Common European framework of reference for languages: Learning, teaching, assessment. Cambridge University Press.

Miao Chen and Klaus Zechner. 2011. Computing and evaluating syntactic complexity features for automated scoring of spontaneous non-native speech. In *Proceedings 49th Annual Meeting of the Association for Computational Linguistics: Human Language Technologies*, pages 722–731.

Lei Chen, Klaus Zechner, and Xiaoming Xi. 2009. Improved pronunciation features for construct-driven assessment of non-native spontaneous speech. In *Proceedings Human Language Technologies: Annual Conference of the North American Chapter of the Association for Computational Linguistics*, pages 442–449.

Keelan Evanini, Youngsoon So, Jidong Tao, D Zapata, Christine Luce, Laura Battistini, and Xinhao Wang. 2014. Performance of a trialogue-based prototype system for english language assessment for young learners. In *Proceedings Interspeech Workshop on Child Computer Interaction*.

Peter W Foltz and Mark Rosenstein. 2015. Analysis of a large-scale formative writing assessment system with automated feedback. In *Proceedings 2nd ACM Conference on Learning at Scale*, pages 339–342.

Kate Forbes-Riley and Diane Litman. 2011. Benefits and challenges of real-time uncertainty detection and adaptation in a spoken dialogue computer tutor. *Speech Communication*, 53(9):1115–1136.

Alexei V Ivanov, Vikram Ramanarayanan, David Suendermann-Oeft, Melissa Lopez, Keelan Evanini, and Jidong Tao. 2015. Automated speech recognition technology for dialogue interaction with non-native interlocutors. In *16th Annual Meeting of the Special Interest Group on Discourse and Dialogue*, page 134.

Christopher M Mitchell, Keelan Evanini, and Klaus Zechner. 2014. A trialogue-based spoken dialogue system for assessment of english language learners. In *Proceedings International Workshop on Spoken Dialogue Systems*.

Nikola Mrkšić, Diarmuid Ó Séaghdha, Blaise Thomson, Milica Gasic, Pei-Hao Su, David Vandyke, Tsung-Hsien Wen, and Steve Young. 2015. Multi-domain dialog state tracking using recurrent neural networks. In *Proceedings 53rd Annual Meeting of the Association for Computational Linguistics and 7th International Joint Conference on Natural Language Processing*, pages 794–799.

Rod D Roscoe, Danica Kugler, Scott A Crossley, Jennifer L Weston, and Danielle S McNamara. 2012. Developing pedagogically-guided threshold algorithms for intelligent automated essay feedback. In *FLAIRS Conference*.

Paul Seedhouse, Andrew Harris, Rola Naeb, Eda Üstünel, et al. 2014. Relationship between speaking features and band descriptors: A mixed methods study, the. *IELTS Research Reports Online Series*, page 30.

Vinay Shashidhar, Nishant Pandey, and Varun Aggarwal. 2015. Automatic spontaneous speech grading: A novel feature derivation technique using the crowd. In *Proceedings 53rd Annual Meeting of the Association for Computational Linguistics and 7th International Joint Conference on Natural Language Processing*, pages 1085–1094.

Pei-Hao Su, Chuan-Hsun Wu, and Lin-Shan Lee. 2015. A recursive dialogue game for personalized computer-aided pronunciation training. *IEEE/ACM Trans. Audio, Speech and Lang. Proc.*, 23(1):127–141.

Jesse Thomason and Diane Litman. 2013. Differences in user responses to a wizard-of-oz versus automated system. In *Proceedings of NAACL-HLT*, pages 796–801.

Rogier C. van Dalen, Kate M. Knill, and Mark J. F. Gales. 2015. Automatically grading learners' English using a Gaussian process. In *Proceedings Sixth Workshop on Speech and Language Technology in Education (SLaTE)*, pages 7–12.

David Vandyke, Pei-Hao Su, Milica Gašić, Nikola Mrkšić, Tsung-Hsien Wen, and Steve Young. 2015. Multi-domain dialogue success classifiers for policy training. In *ASRU*.

Xinhao Wang, Keelan Evanini, and Klaus Zechner. 2013. Coherence modeling for the automated assessment of spontaneous spoken responses. In *Proceedings Conference of the North American Chapter of the Association for Computational Linguistics: Human Language Technologies*, pages 814–819.

Measuring the Similarity of Sentential Arguments in Dialog

Amita Misra, Brian Ecker, and Marilyn A. Walker
University of California Santa Cruz
Natural Language and Dialog Systems Lab
1156 N. High. SOE-3
Santa Cruz, California, 95064, USA
`amitamisra|becker|maw@soe.ucsc.edu`

Abstract

When people converse about social or political topics, similar arguments are often paraphrased by different speakers, across many different conversations. Debate websites produce curated summaries of arguments on such topics; these summaries typically consist of lists of sentences that represent frequently paraphrased propositions, or labels capturing the essence of one particular aspect of an argument, e.g. `Morality` or `Second Amendment`. We call these frequently paraphrased propositions ARGUMENT FACETS. Like these curated sites, our goal is to induce and identify argument facets across multiple conversations, and produce summaries. However, we aim to do this automatically. We frame the problem as consisting of two steps: we first extract sentences that express an argument from raw social media dialogs, and then rank the extracted arguments in terms of their similarity to one another. Sets of similar arguments are used to represent argument facets. We show here that we can predict ARGUMENT FACET SIMILARITY with a correlation averaging 0.63 compared to a human topline averaging 0.68 over three debate topics, easily beating several reasonable baselines.

1 Introduction

When people converse about social or political topics, similar arguments are often paraphrased by different speakers, across many different conversations. For example, consider the dialog excerpts in Fig. 1 from the 89K sentences about gun control in the IAC 2.0 corpus of online dialogs (Abbott et al., 2016). Each of the sentences **S1** to **S6** provide

different linguistic realizations of the same proposition namely that *Criminals will have guns even if gun ownership is illegal.*

S1: To inact a law that makes a crime of illegal gun ownership has no effect on criminal ownership of guns..
S2: Gun free zones are zones where criminals will have guns because criminals will not obey the laws about gun free zones.
S3: Gun control laws do not stop criminals from getting guns.
S4: Gun control laws will not work because criminals do not obey gun control laws!
S5: Gun control laws only control the guns in the hands of people who follow laws.
S6: Gun laws and bans are put in place that only affect good law abiding free citizens.

Figure 1: Paraphrases of the *Criminals will have guns* facet from multiple conversations.

Debate websites, such as Idebate and ProCon produce curated summaries of arguments on the gun control topic, as well as many other topics.[1][2] These summaries typically consist of lists, e.g. Fig. 2 lists eight different aspects of the gun control argument from Idebate. Such manually curated summaries identify different linguistic realizations of the same argument to induce a set of common, repeated, aspects of arguments, what we call ARGUMENT FACETS. For example, a curator might identify sentences **S1** to **S6** in Fig. 1 with a label to represent the facet that *Criminals will have guns even if gun ownership is illegal.*

Like these curated sites, we also aim to induce and identify facets of an argument across multiple conversations, and produce summaries of all the different facets. However our aim is to do this automatically, and over time. In order to simplify the problem, we focus on SENTENTIAL ARGUMENTS, single sentences that clearly express

---

[1]See `http://debatepedia.idebate.org/en/index.php/Debate:_Gun_control,`
[2]See `http://gun-control.procon.org/`

Proceedings of the SIGDIAL 2016 Conference, pages 276–287,
Los Angeles, USA, 13-15 September 2016. ©2016 Association for Computational Linguistics

Pro Arguments
A1: The only function of a gun is to kill.
A2: The legal ownership of guns by ordinary citizens inevitably leads to many accidental deaths.
A3: Sports shooting desensitizes people to the lethal nature of firearms.
A4: Gun ownership increases the risk of suicide.

Con Arguments
A5: Gun ownership is an integral facet of the right to self defense.
A6: Gun ownership increases national security within democratic states.
A7: Sports shooting is a safe activity.
A8: Effective gun control is not achievable in democratic states with a tradition of civilian gun owership.

Figure 2: The eight facets for Gun Control on IDebate, a curated debate site.

a particular argument facet in dialog. We aim to use SENTENTIAL ARGUMENTS to produce extractive summaries of online dialogs about current social and political topics. This paper extends our previous work which frames our goal as consisting of two tasks (Misra et al., 2015; Swanson et al., 2015).

- **Task1: Argument Extraction**: How can we extract sentences from dialog that clearly express a particular argument facet?
- **Task2: Argument Facet Similarity**: How can we recognize that two sentential arguments are semantically similar, i.e. that they are different linguistic realizations of the same facet of the argument?

Task1 is needed because social media dialogs consist of many sentences that either do not express an argument, or cannot be understood out of context. Thus sentences that are useful for inducing argument facets must first be automatically identified. Our previous work on Argument Extraction achieved good results, (Swanson et al., 2015), and is extended here (Sec. 2).

Task2 takes pairs of sentences from Task1 as input and then learns a regressor that can predict Argument Facet Similarity (henceforth **AFS**). Related work on argument mining (discussed in more detail in Sec. 4) defines a finite set of facets for each topic, similar to those from Idebate in Fig. 2.[3] Previous work then labels posts or sentences using these facets, and trains a classifier to return a facet label (Conrad et al., 2012; Hasan and Ng, 2014; Boltuzic and Šnajder, 2014; Naderi and Hirst, 2015), *inter alia*. However, this simplification may not work in the long term, both because the sentential realizations of argument facets are propositional, and hence graded, and because

facets evolve over time, and hence cannot be represented by a finite list.

In our previous work on AFS, we developed an AFS regressor for predicting the similarity of **human-generated labels** for summaries of dialogic arguments (Misra et al., 2015). We collected 5 human summaries of each dialog, and then used the Pyramid tool and scheme to annotate sentences from these summaries as contributors to (paraphrases of) a particular facet (Nenkova and Passonneau, 2004). The Pyramid tool requires the annotator to provide a human readable label for a collection of contributors that realize the same propositional content. The AFS regressor operated on pairs of human-generated labels from Pyramid summaries of different dialogs about the same topic. In this case, facet identification is done by the human summarizers, and collections of similar labels represent an argument facet. We believe this is a much easier task than the one we attempt here of training an AFS regressor on automatically extracted raw sentences from social media dialogs. The contributions of this paper are:

- We develop a new corpus of sentential arguments with gold-standard labels for AFS.
- We analyze and improve our argument extractor, by testing it on a much larger dataset. We develop a larger gold standard corpus for ARGUMENT QUALITY (AQ).
- We develop a regressor that can predict AFS on extracted sentential arguments with a correlation averaging **0.63** compared to a human topline of **0.68** for three debate topics.[4]

2 Corpora and Problem Definition

Many existing websites summarize the frequent, and repeated, facets of arguments about current topics, that are linguistically realized in different ways, across many different social media and debate forums. For example, Fig. 2 illustrates the eight facets for gun control on IDebate. Fig. 3 illustrates a different type of summary, for the death penalty topic, from ProCon, where the argument facets are called out as the "Top Ten Pros and Cons" and given labels such as `Morality`, `Constitutionality` and `Race`. See the top of Fig. 3. The bottom of Fig. 3 shows how each facet is then elaborated by a paragraph for both its Pro and Con side: due to space we only show the summary for the `Morality` facet here.

These summaries are curated, thus one would

---

[3]See also the facets in Fig. 3 below from `ProCon.org`.

[4]Both the AQ and the AFS pair corpora are available at `nlds.soe.ucsc.edu`.

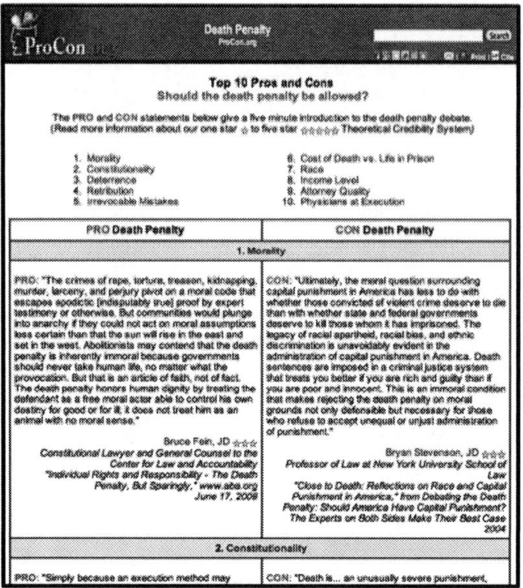

Figure 3: Facets of the death penalty debate as curated on ProCon.org

Topic	Original	Rescored	Sampled	AQ #N (%)
GC	89,722	63,025	2140	1887 (88%)
DP	17,904	11,435	1986	1520 (77%)
GM	51,543	40,306	2062	1745 (85%)

Table 1: Sentence count in each domain. Sampled bin range > 0.55 and number of sentential arguments (high AQ) after annotation. GC=Gun Control, DP=Death Penalty, GM=Gay Marriage.

not expect that different sites would call out the exact same facets, or even that the same type of labels would be used for a specific facet. As we can see, ProCon (Fig. 3) uses one word or phrasal labels, while IDebate (Fig. 2) describes each facet with a sentence. Moreover, these curated summaries are not produced for a particular topic once-and-for-all: the curators often reorganize their summaries, drawing out different facets, or combining previously distinct facets under a single new heading. We hypothesize that this happens because new facets arise over time. For example, it is plausible that for the gay marriage topic, the facet that *Gay marriage is a civil rights issue* came to the fore only in the last ten years.

Our long-term aim is to produce summaries similar to these curated summaries, but automatically, and over time, so that as new argument facets arise for a particular topic, we can identify them. We begin with three debate topics, gun control (38102 posts), gay marriage (22425 posts) and death penalty (5283 posts), from the Internet Argument Corpus 2.0 (Abbott et al., 2016). We first need to create a large sample of high quality sentential arguments (**Task1** above) and then create a large sample of paired sentential arguments in order to train the model for AFS (**Task2** above).

2.1 Argument Quality Data

We extracted all the sentences for all of the posts in each topic to first create a large corpus of topic-sorted sentences. See Table 1.

We started with the Argument Quality (**AQ**) re-

gressor from Swanson et al. (2015), which gives a score to each sentence. The AQ score is intended to reflect how easily the speaker's argument can be understood from the sentence without any context. Easily understandable sentences are assumed to be prime candidates for producing extractive summaries. In Swanson et al. (2015), the annotators rated AQ using a continuous slider ranging from hard (0.0) to easy to interpret (1.0). We refined the Mechanical Turk task to elicit new training data for AQ as summarized in Table 1. Fig. 8 in the appendix shows the HIT we used to collect new AQ labels for sentences, as described below.

We expected to to apply Swanson's AQ regressor to our sample completely "out of the box". However, we first discovered that many sentences given high AQ scores were very similar, while we need a sample that realizes many **diverse** facets. We then discovered that some extracted sentential arguments were not actually high quality. We hypothesized that the diversity issue arose primarily because Swanson's dataset was filtered using high PMI n-grams. We also hypothesized that the quality issue had not surfaced because Swanson's sample was primarily selected from sentences marked with the discourse connectives *but, first, if,* and *so*. Our sample (Original column of Table 1) is much larger and was not similarly filtered.

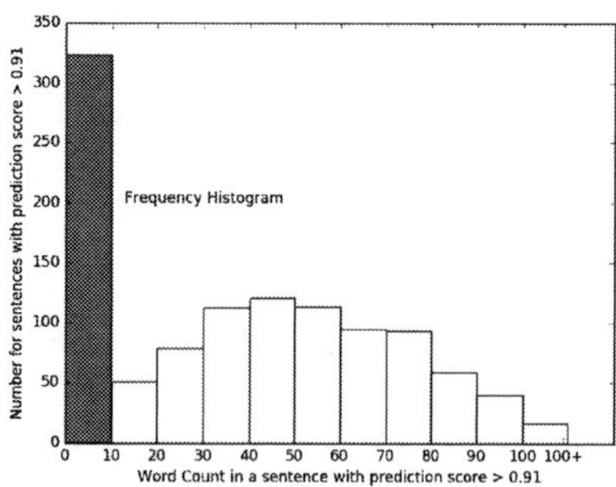

Figure 4: Word count distribution for argument quality prediction scores > 0.91 for Swanson's original model.

Fig. 4 plots the distribution of word counts for sentences from our sample that were given an AQ score > 0.91 by Swanson's trained AQ regressor. The first bin shows that many sentences with less than 10 words are predicted to be high quality, but many of these sentences in our data consisted of only a few elongated words (e.g. HA-HAHAHA...). The upper part of the distribution shows a large number of sentences with more than 70 words with a predicted AQ > 0.91. We discovered that most of these long sentences are multiple sentences without punctuation. We thus refined the AQ model by removing duplicate sentences, and rescoring sentences without a verb and with less than 4 dictionary words to AQ $= 0$. We then restricted our sampling to sentences between 10 and 40 tokens, to eliminate run-on sentences and sentences without much propositional content. We did not retrain the regressor, rather we resampled and rescored the corpus. See the Rescored column of Table 1. After removing the two tails in Fig. 4, the distribution of word counts is almost uniform across bins of sentences from length 10 to 40.

As noted above, the sample in Swanson et al. (2015) was filtered using PMI, and PMI contributes to AQ. Thus, to end up with a diverse set of sentences representing many facets of each topic, we decided to sample sentences with lower AQ scores than Swanson had used. We binned the sentences based on predicted AQ score and extracted random samples across bins ranging from .55–1.0, in increments of .10. Then we extracted a smaller sample and collected new AQ annotations for gay marriage and death penalty on Mechanical Turk, using the definitions in Fig. 8 (in the appendix). See the Sampled column of Table 1. We pre-selected three annotators using a qualifier that included detailed instructions and sample annotations. A score of 3 was mapped to a yes and scores of 1 or 2 mapped to a no. We simplified the task slightly in the HIT for gun control, where five annotators were instructed to select a yes label if the sentence clearly expressed an argument (score 3), or a no label otherwise (score 1 or 2).

We then calculated the probability that the sentences in each bin were high quality arguments using the resulting AQ gold standard labels, and found that a threshhold of predicted AQ > 0.55 maintained both diversity and quality. See Fig. 9 in the appendix. Table 1 summarizes the results of each stage of the process of producing the new AQ corpus of 6188 sentences (Sampled and then annotated). The last column of Table 1 shows that gold standard labels agree with the rescored AQ regressor between 77% and 88% of the time.

2.2 Argument Facet Similarity Data

The goal of **Task2** is to define a similarity metric and train a regression model that takes as input two sentential arguments and returns a scalar value that predicts their similarity(AFS). The model must reflect the fact that similarity is graded, e.g. the same argument facet may be repeated with different levels of explicit detail. For example, sentence A1 in Fig. 2 is similar to the more complete argument, *Given the fact that guns are weapons—things designed to kill—they should not be in the hands of the public*, which expresses both the premise and conclusion. Sentence A1 leaves it up to the reader to infer the (obvious) conclusion.

S7: Since there are gun deaths in countries that have banned guns, the gun bans did not work.
S8: It is legal to own weapons in this country, they are just tightly controlled, and as a result we have far less gun crime (particularly where it's not related to organised crime).
S9: My point was that the theory that more gun control leaves people defenseless does not explain the lower murder rates in other developed nations.

Figure 5: Paraphrases of the *Gun ownership does not lead to higher crime* facet of the Gun Control topic across different conversations.

Our approach to **Task2** draws strongly on recent work on semantic textual similarity (STS) (Agirre et al., 2013; Dolan and Brockett, 2005; Mihalcea et al., 2006). STS measures the degree of semantic similarity between a pair of sentences with values that range from 0 to 5. Inspired by the scale used for STS, we first define what a facet is, and then define the values of the AFS scale as shown in Fig. 10 in the appendix (repeated from Misra et al. (2015) for convenience). We distinguish AFS from STS because: (1) our data are so different: STS data consists of descriptive sentences whereas our sentences are argumentative excerpts from dialogs; and (2) our definition of facet allows for sentences that express opposite stance to be realizations of the same facet (AFS $= 3$) in Fig. 10.

Related work has primarily used entailment or semantic equivalence to define argument similarity (Habernal and Gurevych, 2015; Boltuzic and Šnajder, 2015; Boltuzic and Šnajder, 2015; Habernal et al., 2014). We believe the definition of AFS given in Fig. 10 will be more useful in the long run than semantic equivalence or entailment, because two arguments can only be contradictory if they are about the same facet. For example, consider that sentential argument **S7** in Fig. 5 is anti gun-control, while sentences **S8** and **S9** are pro gun-control. Our annotation guidelines label them with the same facet, in a similar way to how the curated summaries on ProCon provides both a Pro and Con side for each facet. See Fig. 3.

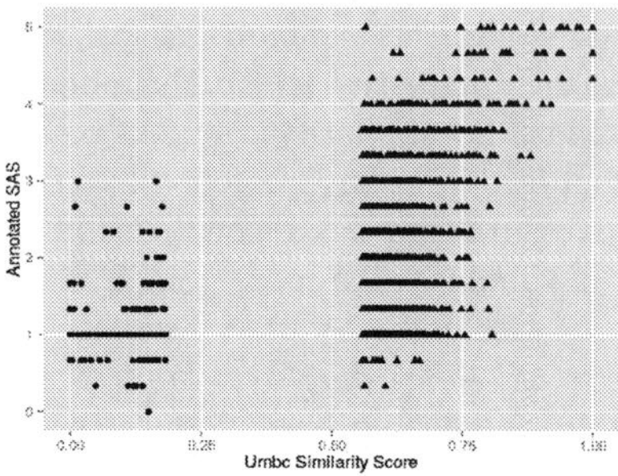

Figure 6: The distribution of AFS scores as a function of UMBC STS scores for gun control sentences.

In order to efficiently collect annotations for AFS, we want to produce training data pairs that are more likely than chance to be the same facet (scores 3 and above as defined in Fig. 10). Similar arguments are rare with an all-pairs matching protocol, e.g. in ComArg approximately 67% of the annotations are "not a match" (Boltuzic and Šnajder, 2014). Also, we found that Turkers are confused when asked to annotate similarity and then given a set of sentence pairs that are almost all highly dissimilar. Annotations also cost money. We therefore used UMBC STS (Han et al., 2013) to score all potential pairs.[5] To foreshadow, the plot in Fig. 6 shows that this pre-scoring works: (1) the lower quadrant of the plot shows that STS $< .20$ corresponds to the lower range of scores for AFS; and (2) the lower half of the left hand side shows that we still get many arguments that are low AFS (values below 3) in our training data.

We selected 2000 pairs in each topic, based on their UMBC similarity scores, which resulted in lowest UMBC scores of 0.58 for GM, 0.56 for GC and 0.58 for DP. To ensure a pool of diverse arguments, a particular sentence can appear in at most ten pairs. MT workers took a qualification test with definitions and instructions as shown in Fig. 10. Sentential arguments with sample AFS annotations were part of the qualifier. The 6000 pairs were made available to our three most reliable pre-qualified workers. The last row of Table 3 reports the human topline for the task, i.e. the average pairwise r across all three workers. Interestingly, the Gay marriage topic ($r = 0.60$) is more difficult for human annotators than either Death Penalty ($r = 0.74$) or Gun Control ($r = 0.69$).

3 Argument Facet Similarity

Given the data collected above, we defined a supervised machine learning experiment with AFS as our dependent variable. We developed a number of baselines using off the shelf tools. Features are grouped into sets and discussed in detail below.

3.1 Feature Sets

NGRAM cosine. Our primary baseline is an ngram overlap feature. For each argument, we extract the unigrams, bigrams and trigrams, and then calculate the cosine similarity between two texts represented as vectors of their ngram counts.

Rouge. Rouge is a family of metrics for comparing the similarity of two summaries (Lin, 2004), which measures overlapping units such as continuous and skip ngrams, common subsequences, and word pairs. We use all the rouge f-scores from the pyrouge package. Our analysis shows that rouge_s*_f_score correlates most highly with AFS.[6]

UMBC STS. We consider STS, a measure of the semantic similarity of two texts (Agirre et al., 2012), as another baseline, using the UMBC STS tool. Fig. 6 illustrates that in general, STS is rough approximation of AFS. It is possible that our selection of data for pairs for annotation using UMBC STS either improves or reduces its performance.

Google Word2Vec. Word embeddings from word2vec (Mikolov et al., 2013) are popular for expressing semantic relationships between words, but using word embeddings to express entire sentences often requires some compromises. In particular, averaging word2vec embeddings for each word may lose too much information in long sentences. Previous work on argument mining has developed methods using word2vec that are effective for clustering similar arguments (Habernal and Gurevych, 2015; Boltuzic and Šnajder, 2015) Other research creates embeddings at the sentence level using more advanced techniques such as Paragraph Vectors (Le and Mikolov, 2014).

We take a more direct approach in which we use the word embeddings directly as features. For each sentential argument in the pair, we create a 300-dimensional vector by filtering for stopwords and punctuation and then averaging the word embeddings from Google's word2vec model for the remaining words.[7] Each dimension of the 600 dimensional concatenated averaged vector is used directly as a feature. In our experiments, this

---

[5]This is an off-the-shelf STS tool from University of Maryland Baltimore County available at swoogle.umbc.edu/SimService/.

[6]https://pypi.python.org/pypi/pyrouge/
[7]https://code.google.com/archive/p/word2vec/

concatenation method greatly outperforms cosine similarity (Table 2, Table 3). Sec. 3.3 discusses properties of word embeddings that may yield these performance differences.

Custom Word2Vec. We also create our own 300-dimensional embeddings for our dialogic domain using the Gensim library (Řehůřek and Sojka, 2010), with default settings, and a very large corpus of user-generated dialogic content. This includes the corpus described in Sec. 2 (929, 206 forum posts), an internal corpus of 1, 688, 639 tweets on various topics, and a corpus of 53, 851, 542 posts from Reddit.[8]

LIWC category and Dependency Overlap. Both dependency structures and the Linguistics Inquiry Word Count (LIWC) tool have been useful in previous work (Pennebaker et al., 2001; Somasundaran and Wiebe, 2009; Hasan and Ng, 2013). We develop a novel feature set that combines LIWC category and dependency overlap, aiming to capture a generalized notion of concept overlap between two arguments, i.e. to capture the hypothesis that classes of content words such as affective processes or emotion types are indicative of a shared facet across pairs of arguments.

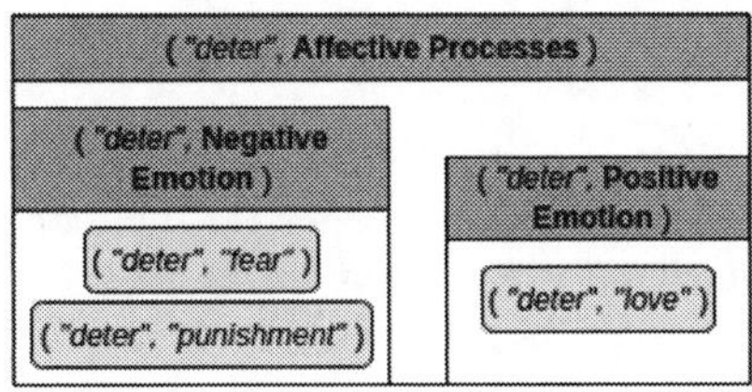

Figure 7: LIWC Generalized Dep. tuples

We create partially generalized LIWC dependency features and count overlap normalized by sentence length across pairs, building on previous work (Joshi and Penstein-Rosé, 2009). Stanford dependency features (Manning et al., 2014) are generalized by leaving one dependency element lexicalized, replacing the other word in the dependency relation with its LIWC category and by removing the actual dependency type (nsubj, dobj, etc.) from the triple. This creates a tuple of (*"governor token", LIWC category of dependent token*). We call these simplified LIWC dependencies.

Fig. 7 illustrates the generalization process for three LIWC simplified dependencies, *("deter", "fear"), ("deter", "punishment"),* and *("deter", "love")*. Because LIWC is a hierarchical lexicon,

two dependencies may share many generalizations or only a few. Here, the tuples with dependent tokens *fear* and *punishment* are more closely related because their shared generalization include both *Negative Emotion* and *Affective Processes*, but the tuples with dependent tokens *fear* and *love* have a less similar relationship, because they only share the *Affective Processes* generalization.

3.2 Machine Learning Regression Results

We randomly selected 90% of our annotated pairs to use for nested 10-fold cross-validation, setting aside 10% for qualitative analysis of predicted vs. gold-standard scores. We use Ridge Regression (RR) with l2-norm regularization and Support Vector Regression (SVR) with an RBF kernel from scikit-learn (Pedregosa et al., 2011). Performance evaluation uses two standard measures, Correlation Coefficient (r) and Root Mean Squared Error (RMSE). A separate inner cross-validation within each fold of the outer cross-validation is used to perform a grid search to determine the hyperparameters for that outer fold. The outer cross-validation reports the scoring metrics.

Simple Ablation Models. We first evaluate simple models based on a single feature using both RR and SVR. Table 2, Rows 1, 2, and 3 show the baseline results: UMBC Semantic Textual Similarity (STS), Ngram Cosine, and Rouge. Surprisingly, the UMBC STS measure does not perform as well as Ngram Cosine for Death Penalty and Gay Marriage. LIWC dependencies (Row 4) perform similarly to Rouge (Row 3) across topics. Cosine similarity for the custom word2vec model (Row 5) performs about as well or better than ngrams across topics, but cosine similarity using the Google model (Row 6) performs worse than ngrams for all topics except Death Penalty. Interestingly our custom Word2Vec models perform significantly better than the Google word2vec models for Gun Control and Gay Marriage, with both much higher r and lower RMSE, while performing identically for Death Penalty.

Feature Combination Models. Table 3 shows the results of testing feature combinations to learn which ones are complementary. Since SVR consistently performs better than RR, we use SVR only. Significance is calculated using paired t-tests between the RMSE values across folds. We paired Ngrams separately with LIWC and ROUGE to evaluate if the combination is significant. Ngram+Rouge (Row 1) is significantly better than Ngram for Gun Control and Death Penalty ($p < .01$), and Gay Marriage ($p = .03$).

---

[8]One month sample `https://www.reddit.com/r/datasets/comments/3bxlg7/i_have_every_publicly_available_reddit_comment`

ID	Features	Gun Control				Gay Marriage				Death Penalty			
		RR		SVR		RR		SVR		RR		SVR	
		r	RMSE	r	RMSE	r	RMSE	r	RMSE	r	RMSE	r	RMSE
1	UMBC	0.49	0.90	0.50	0.90	0.16	0.90	0.21	0.90	0.21	1.16	0.20	1.20
2	Ngram	0.46	0.91	0.46	0.92	0.24	0.88	0.24	0.91	0.23	1.16	0.24	1.18
3	Rouge	0.52	0.88	0.57	0.86	0.22	0.89	0.26	0.90	0.39	1.10	**0.40**	**1.11**
4	LIWC dependencies	0.50	0.89	**0.59**	**0.85**	**0.27**	**0.88**	0.26	0.90	0.34	1.12	0.40	1.12
5	CustomW2Vec Cosine	0.47	0.91	0.52	0.89	0.22	0.89	0.25	0.90	0.29	1.14	0.30	1.16
6	GoogleW2Vec Cosine	0.40	0.94	0.47	0.93	0.16	0.90	0.20	0.92	0.29	1.14	0.30	1.16

Table 2: Results for predicting AFS with individual features using Ridge Regression (RR) and Support Vector Regression (SVR) with 10-fold Cross-Validation on the 1800 training items for each topic.

ID	Feature Combinations with SVR	Gun Control		Gay Marriage		Death Penalty	
		r	RMSE	r	RMSE	r	RMSE
1	Ngram- Rouge	0.59	0.85	0.29	0.89	0.40	1.11
2	Ngram- LIWC dependencies	0.61	0.83	0.34	0.88	0.43	1.10
3	Ngram- LIWC dependencies- Rouge	0.64	0.80	0.38	0.86	0.49	1.05
4	Ngram- LIWC dependencies- Rouge-UMBC	0.65	0.79	0.40	0.86	0.50	1.05
5	CustomW2Vec Concatenated vectors	0.71	0.72	0.48	0.80	0.56	0.99
6	GoogleW2Vec Concatenated vectors	0.71	0.72	0.50	0.79	0.57	0.98
7	Ngram- LIWC dependencies- Rouge- UMBC- CustomW2Vec Concatenated vectors	0.73	0.70	0.54	0.77	0.62	0.93
8	Ngram- LIWC dependencies- Rouge- UMBC- GoogleW2Vec Concatenated vectors	**0.73**	**0.70**	**0.54**	**0.77**	**0.63**	**0.92**
9	**HUMAN TOPLINE**	0.69		0.60		0.74	

Table 3: Results for feature combinations for predicting AFS, using Support Vector Regression (SVR) with 10-fold Cross-Validation on the 1800 training items for each topic.

Ngram+LIWC (Row 2) is significantly better than Ngram for Gun Control, and Death Penalty ($p <$ .01). Thus both Rouge and LIWC provide complementary information to Ngrams.

Our best result using our hand-engineered features is a combination of LIWC, Rouge, and Ngrams (Row 3). Interestingly, adding UMBC STS (Row 4) gives a small but significant improvement ($p < 0.01$ for gun control; $p = 0.07$ for gay marriage). Thus we take Ngrams, LIWC, Rouge, and UMBC STS (Row 4) as our best hand-engineered model across all topics with a correlation of 0.65 for gun control, 0.50 for death penalty and 0.40 for gay marriage. This combination is significantly better than the baselines for Ngram baseline ($p <$ .01), UMBC STS ($p <=$ .02) and Rouge ($p <$ .01) for all three topics.

We then further combine the hand-engineered features (Row 4) with the Google Word2Vec features (Row 6), creating the model in Row 8. A paired t-test between RMSE values from each cross-validation fold for each model (Row 4 vs. Row 8 and Row 6 vs. Row 8) shows that the our hand-engineered features are complementary to Word2Vec, and their combination yields a model significantly better than either model alone ($p <$

.01). We note that although the custom word2vec model performs much better for gun control and gay marriage when using cosine, it actually performs slightly but significantly ($p = $ .05) worse when using concatenation with hand-engineered features. This may simply be due to the size of the training data, i.e. the Google model used nearly twice as much training data, while our domain-specific word2vec model achieves comparable performance to the Google model with much less training data.

3.3 Analysis and Discussion

Although it is common to translate word embeddings into single features or reduced feature sets for similarity through the use of clustering (Habernal and Gurevych, 2015) or cosine similarity (Boltuzic and Šnajder, 2015), we show that it is possible to improve results by directly combining word embeddings with hand-engineered features. In our task, sentences were limited to a maximum of 40 tokens in order to encourage single-facet sentences, but this may have provided an additional benefit by allowing us to average word embeddings while still preserving useful signal.

Our results also demonstrate that using concate-

ID	Argument 1	Argument 2	STS	Ngram	Rouge	LIWC dep	W2Vec	AFS	MT AFS
GC1	You say that gun control must not be effective because the study's conclusions about gun control were inconclusive.	You're right that gun control isn't about guns, however, but 'control' is a secondary matter, a means to an end.	1.82	2.56	2.22	1.53	**1.40**	1.5	**1**
DP2	I don't feel as strongly about the death penalty as I feel about the abortion rights debate since I can relate to the desire for vengeance that people feel.	Well I, as creator of this debate, think that there should not be a death penalty.	1.82	2.38	2.07	**1.29**	1.44	1.24	**1.33**
GC3	They do not have the expressed, enumerated power to pass any law regarding guns in the constitution.	Which passed the law requireing "smart guns", if they ever become available (right now they do not exist).	1.74	1.83	2.67	1.50	1.82	**1.88**	**2.0**
GM4	Technically though marriage is not discrimination, because gays are still allowed to marry the opposite sex.	Everyone has the right to marry someone of the opposite sex, and with gay marriage, everyone will have the right to marry someone of the same AND opposite sex.	1.76	2.09	1.68	2.00	**2.23**	2.06	**2.33**
GM5	If the state wants to offer legal protections and benefits to straight married couples, it cannot constitutionally refuse equal protections to gay ones.	Same-sex couples are denied over 1,000 benefits, rights, and protections that federal law affords to married, heterosexual couples, as well as hundreds of such protections at the state level.	1.77	1.91	1.77	2.66	**3.56**	3.72	**3.33**
DP6	In addition, it is evident that the death penalty does not deter murder rates.	BUT it is not apparent that death penalty lower crime rate.	2.03	2.31	3.71	2.21	3.84	**3.95**	**4.0**
DP7	Living in jail for life costs less money then the death penalty.	Morality aside, no evidence of deterrence aside, the death penalty costs more than life imprisonment.	1.84	2.43	2.56	**3.23**	2.90	2.90	**4.33**

Table 4: Illustrative Argument pairs, along with the predicted scores from individual feature sets, predicted(**AFS**) and the Mechanical Turk human topline (**MT AFS**). The best performing feature set is shown in bold. GC=Gun Control, DP=Death Penalty, GM=Gay Marriage.

nation for learning similarity with vector representations works much better than the common practice of reducing a pair of vectors to a single score using cosine similarity. Previous work (Li et al., 2015; Pennington et al., 2014) also shows that all dimensions are not equally useful predictors for a specific task. For sentiment classification, Li et al. (2015) find that "too large a dimensionality leads many dimensions to be non-functional ... causing two sentences of opposite sentiment to differ only in a few dimensions." This may also be the situation for the 300-dimensional embeddings used for AFS. Hence, when using concatenation, single dimensions can be weighted to adjust for non-functional dimensions, but using cosine makes this per-dimension weighting impossible. This might explain why our custom word2vec model outperforms the Google model when using cosine as compared to concatenation, i.e. more dimensions are informative in the custom model, but overall, the Google model provides more complementary information when non-functional dimensions are accounted for. More analysis is needed to fully support this claim.

To qualitatively illustrate some of the differences between our final AFS regressor model (Row 8 of Table 3) and several baselines, we apply the model to a set-aside 200 pairs per topic. Table 4 shows examples selected to highlight the strengths of AFS prediction for different models as compared to the AFS gold standard scores.

MT AFS values near 1 indicate same topic but no similarity. Rows GC1 and DP2 talk about totally different facets and only share the same topic (AFS = 1). Rouge and Ngram features based on word overlap predict scores that are too high. In contrast, LIWC dependencies and word2vec based on concept and semantic overlap are more accurate. MT values near 3 indicate same facet but somewhat different arguments. Arguments in row GM4 talk about marriage rights to all, and there is some overlap in these arguments beyond simply being the same topic, however the speakers are on opposite stance sides. Both of the arguments in row GM5 (MT AFS of 3.3) reference the same facet of the financial and legal benefits available to married couples, but Arg2 is more specific. Both Word2vec and our trained AFS model can recognize the similarity in the concepts in the two arguments and make good predictions.

MT values above 4 indicate two arguments that are the same facet and very similar. Row DP6 gets a high Rouge overlap score and Word2vec relates 'lower crime rate' as semantically similar to 'deter murder rates' thus yielding an accurately high AFS score. DP7 is an example where LIWC dependencies perform better as compared to other features, because it focuses in on the dependency between the death penalty and cost, but none of the models do well at predicting the MT AFS score. One issue here may be that, despite our attempts to sample pairs with more representatives of high AFS, there is just less training data available for this part of the distribution. Hence all the regressors will be conservative at predicting the highest values. We hope in future work to improve our AFS regressor by finding additional methods for populating the training data with more highly similar pairs.

4   Related Work

There are many theories of argumentation that might be applicable for our task (Jackson and Jacobs, 1980; Reed and Rowe, 2004; Walton et al., 2008; Gilbert, 1997; Toulmin, 1958; Dung, 1995), but one definition of argument structure may not work for every NLP task. Social media arguments are often informal, and do not necessarily follow logical rules or schemas of argumentation (Stab and Gurevych, 2014; Peldszus and Stede, 2013; Ghosh et al., 2014; Habernal et al., 2014; Goudas et al., 2014; Cabrio and Villata, 2012).

Moreover, in social media, segments of text that are argumentative must first be identified, as in our **Task1**. Habernal and Gurevych (2016) train a classifier to recognize text segments that are argumentative, but much previous work does Task1 manually. Goudas et al. (2014) annotate 16,000 sentences from social media documents and consider 760 of them to be argumentative. Hasan and Ng (2014) also manually identify argumentative sentences, while Boltuzic and Šnajder (2014) treat the whole post as argumentative, after manually removing "spam" posts. Biran and Rambow (2011) automatically identify justifications as a structural component of an argument.

Other work groups semantically-similar classes of **reasons** or **frames** that underlie a particular speaker's stance, what we call ARGUMENT FACETS. One approach categorizes sentences or posts using topic-specific argument labels, which are functionally similar to our facets as discussed above (Conrad et al., 2012; Hasan and Ng, 2014; Boltuzic and Šnajder, 2014; Naderi and Hirst, 2015). For example, Fig. 2 lists facets **A1** to **A8** for Gun Control from the IDebate website; Boltuzic and Šnajder (2015) use this list to label posts. They apply unsupervised clustering using a semantic textual similarity tool, but evaluate clusters using their hand-labelled argument tags. Our method instead explicitly models graded similarity of sentential arguments.

5   Conclusion and Future Work

We present a method for scoring argument facet similarity in online debates using a combination of hand-engineered and unsupervised features with a correlation averaging 0.63 compared to a human top line averaging 0.68. Our approach differs from similar work that finds and groups the "reasons" underlying a speakers stance, because our models are based on the belief that it is not possible to define a finite set of discrete facets for a topic. A qualitative analysis of our results, illustrated by Table 4, suggests that treating facet discovery as a similarity problem is productive, i.e. examination of particular pairs suggests facets about legal and financial benefits for same-sex couples, the claim that the death penalty does not actually affect murder rates, and an assertion that "they", implying "congress", do not have the express, enumerated power to pass legislation restricting guns.

Previous work shows that metrics used for evaluating machine translation quality perform well on paraphrase recognition tasks (Madnani et al., 2012). In our experiments, ROUGE performed very well, suggesting that other machine translation metrics such as Terp and Meteor may be useful (Snover et al., 2009; Lavie and Denkowski, 2009). We will explore this in future work.

In future, we will use our AFS regressor to cluster and group similar arguments and produce *argument facet summaries* as a final output of our pipeline. Habernal and Gurevych (2015) apply clustering in argument mining by averaging word embeddings from posts and sentences from debate portals, clustering the resulting averaged vectors, and then computing distance measures from clusters to unseen sentences ("classification units") as features. Cosine similarity between weighted and summed vector representations is also a common approach, and Boltuzic and Šnajder (2015) show word2vec cosine similarity beats bag-of-words and STS baselines when used with clustering for argument identification.

Finally, our AQ extractor treats all posts on a topic equally, operating on a set of concatenated posts. We will explore other sampling methods to ensure that the AQ extractor does not eliminate arguments made by less articulate citizens, by e.g. enforcing that *"Every speaker in a debate contributes at least one argument"*. We will also sample by stance-side, so that summaries can be organized using "Pro" and "Con", as in curated summaries. Our final goal is to combine quality-based argument extraction, our AFS model, stance, post and author level information, so that our summaries represent the diversity of views on a topic, a quality not always guaranteed by summarization techniques, human or machine.

Acknowledgments

This work was supported by NSF CISE RI 1302668. Thanks to Keshav Mathur and the three anonymous reviewers for helpful comments.

References

Robert Abbott, Brian Ecker, Pranav Anand, and Marilyn Walker. 2016. Internet argument corpus 2.0: An sql schema for dialogic social media and the corpora to go with it. In *Language Resources and Evaluation Conference, LREC2016*.

Eneko Agirre, Mona Diab, Daniel Cer, and Aitor Gonzalez-Agirre. 2012. Semeval-2012 task 6: A pilot on semantic textual similarity. In *Proc. of the First Joint Conference on Lexical and Computational Semantics*, volume 1, pages 385–393.

Eneko Agirre, Daniel Cer, Mona Diab, Aitor Gonzalez-Agirre, and Weiwei Guo. 2013. Sem 2013 shared task: Semantic textual similarity, including a pilot on typed-similarity. In *In* SEM 2013: The Second Joint Conference on Lexical and Computational Semantics*.

Oram Biran and Owen Rambow. 2011. Identifying justifications in written dialogs. In *2011 Fifth IEEE International Conference on Semantic Computing (ICSC)*, pages 162–168.

Filip Boltuzic and Jan Šnajder. 2014. Back up your stance: Recognizing arguments in online discussions. In *Proc. of the First Workshop on Argumentation Mining*, pages 49–58.

Filip Boltuzic and Jan Šnajder. 2015. Identifying prominent arguments in online debates using semantic textual similarity. In *Proc. of the Second Workshop on Argumentation Mining*.

Elena Cabrio and Serena Villata. 2012. Combining textual entailment and argumentation theory for supporting online debates interactions. In *Proc. of the 50th Annual Meeting of the Association for Computational Linguistics (Volume 2: Short Papers)*, pages 208–212.

Alexander Conrad, Janyce Wiebe, et al. 2012. Recognizing arguing subjectivity and argument tags. In *Proc. of the Workshop on Extra-Propositional Aspects of Meaning in Computational Linguistics*, pages 80–88.

William B Dolan and Chris Brockett. 2005. Automatically constructing a corpus of sentential paraphrases. In *Proc. of IWP*.

P.M. Dung. 1995. On the acceptability of arguments and its fundamental role in nonmonotonic reasoning, logic programming and n-person games* 1. *Artificial intelligence*, 77(2):321–357.

Debanjan Ghosh, Smaranda Muresan, Nina Wacholder, Mark Aakhus, and Matthew Mitsui. 2014. Analyzing argumentative discourse units in online interactions. *ACL 2014*, page 39.

Michael A. Gilbert. 1997. Coalescent argumentation.

Theodosis Goudas, Christos Louizos, Georgios Petasis, and Vangelis Karkaletsis. 2014. Argument extraction from news, blogs, and social media. In *Artificial Intelligence: Methods and Applications*, pages 287–299. Springer.

Ivan Habernal and Iryna Gurevych. 2015. Exploiting debate portals for semi-supervised argumentation mining in user-generated web discourse. In *Proc. of the 2015 Conference on Empirical Methods in Natural Language Processing (EMNLP)*, pages 2127–2137.

Ivan Habernal and Iryna Gurevych. 2016. Argumentation mining in user-generated web discourse. *CoRR*, abs/1601.02403.

Ivan Habernal, Judith Eckle-Kohler, and Iryna Gurevych. 2014. Argumentation mining on the web from information seeking perspective. In *Proc. of the Workshop on Frontiers and Connections between Argumentation Theory and Natural Language Processing*, pages 26–39.

Lushan Han, Abhay Kashyap, Tim Finin, James Mayfield, and Jonathan Weese. 2013. Umbc ebiquity-core: Semantic textual similarity systems. In *Proceedings of the Second Joint Conference on Lexical and Computational Semantics*, pages 44–52.

Kazi Saidul Hasan and Vincent Ng. 2013. Frame semantics for stance classification. In *CoNLL*, pages 124–132.

Kazi Saidul Hasan and Vincent Ng. 2014. Why are you taking this stance? identifying and classifying reasons in ideological debates. In *Proc. of the Conference on Empirical Methods in Natural Language Processing*.

Sally Jackson and Scott Jacobs. 1980. Structure of conversational argument: Pragmatic bases for the enthymeme. *Quarterly Journal of Speech*, 66(3):251–265.

M. Joshi and C. Penstein-Rosé. 2009. Generalizing dependency features for opinion mining. In *Proc. of the ACL-IJCNLP 2009 Conference Short Papers*, pages 313–316.

Alon Lavie and Michael J. Denkowski. 2009. The meteor metric for automatic evaluation of machine translation. *Machine Translation*, 23(2-3):105–115, September.

Quoc Le and Tomas Mikolov. 2014. Distributed representations of sentences and documents. In Tony Jebara and Eric P. Xing, editors, *Proc. of the 31st International Conference on Machine Learning (ICML-14)*, pages 1188–1196.

Jiwei Li, Xinlei Chen, Eduard Hovy, and Dan Jurafsky. 2015. Visualizing and understanding neural models in nlp. *arXiv preprint arXiv:1506.01066*.

C.-Y. Lin. 2004. Rouge: A package for automatic evaluation of summaries rouge: A package for automatic evaluation of summaries. In *Proc. of the Workshop on Text Summarization Branches Out (WAS 2004)*.

Nitin Madnani, Joel Tetreault, and Martin Chodorow. 2012. Re-examining machine translation metrics for paraphrase identification. In *Proceedings of the 2012 Conference of the North American Chapter of the Association for Computational Linguistics: Human Language Technologies*, NAACL HLT '12, pages 182–190, Stroudsburg, PA, USA. Association for Computational Linguistics.

Christopher D. Manning, Mihai Surdeanu, John Bauer, Jenny Finkel, Steven J. Bethard, and David McClosky. 2014. The Stanford CoreNLP natural language processing toolkit. In *Proc. of 52nd Annual Meeting of the Association for Computational Linguistics: System Demonstrations*, pages 55–60.

Rada Mihalcea, Courtney Corley, and Carlo Strapparava. 2006. Corpus-based and knowledge-based measures of text semantic similarity. In *AAAI*, volume 6, pages 775–780.

Tomas Mikolov, Ilya Sutskever, Kai Chen, Greg S Corrado, and Jeff Dean. 2013. Distributed representations of words and phrases and their compositionality. In *Advances in Neural Information Processing Systems*, pages 3111–3119.

Amita Misra, Pranav Anand, Jean E. Fox Tree, and Marilyn Walker. 2015. Using summarization to discover argument facets in dialog. In *Proc. of the 2015 Conference of the North American Chapter of the Association for Computational Linguistics: Human Language Technologies*.

Nona Naderi and Graeme Hirst. 2015. Argumentation mining in parliamentary discourse. In *CMNA 2015: 15th workshop on Computational Models of Natural Argument*.

Ani Nenkova and Rebecca Passonneau. 2004. Evaluating content selection in summarization: The pyramid method. In *Proc. of Joint Annual Meeting of Human Language Technology and the North American chapter of the Association for Computational Linguistics (HLT/NAACL)*, 6.

F. Pedregosa, G. Varoquaux, A. Gramfort, V. Michel, B. Thirion, O. Grisel, M. Blondel, P. Prettenhofer, R. Weiss, V. Dubourg, J. Vanderplas, A. Passos, D. Cournapeau, M. Brucher, M. Perrot, and E. Duchesnay. 2011. Scikit-learn: Machine learning in Python. *Journal of Machine Learning Research*, 12:2825–2830.

Andreas Peldszus and Manfred Stede. 2013. Ranking the annotators: An agreement study on argumentation structure. In *Proc. of the 7th linguistic annotation workshop and interoperability with discourse*, pages 196–204.

James W. Pennebaker, L. E. Francis, and R. J. Booth, 2001. *LIWC: Linguistic Inquiry and Word Count*.

Jeffrey Pennington, Richard Socher, and Christopher D Manning. 2014. Glove: Global vectors for word representation. In *EMNLP*, volume 14, pages 1532–1543.

Chris Reed and Glenn Rowe. 2004. Araucaria: Software for argument analysis, diagramming and representation. *International Journal on Artificial Intelligence Tools*, 13(04):961–979.

Radim Řehůřek and Petr Sojka. 2010. Software Framework for Topic Modelling with Large Corpora. In *Proc. of the LREC 2010 Workshop on New Challenges for NLP Frameworks*, pages 45–50.

Matthew Snover, Nitin Madnani, Bonnie Dorr, and Richard Schwartz. 2009. Fluency, adequacy, or HTER? Exploring different human judgments with a tunable MT metric. In *Proceedings of the Fourth Workshop on Statistical Machine Translation*, pages 259–268, Athens, Greece, March. Association for Computational Linguistics.

Swapna Somasundaran and Janyce Wiebe. 2009. Recognizing stances in online debates. In *Proc. of the 47th Annual Meeting of the ACL*, pages 226–234.

Christian Stab and Iryna Gurevych. 2014. Annotating argument components and relations in persuasive essays. In *Proc. of the 25th International Conference on Computational Linguistics (COLING 2014)*, pages 1501–1510.

Reid Swanson, Brian Ecker, and Marilyn Walker. 2015. Argument mining: Extracting arguments from online dialogue. In *Proc. of the 16th Annual Meeting of the Special Interest Group on Discourse and Dialogue*, pages 217–226.

Stephen E. Toulmin. 1958. *The Uses of Argument*. Cambridge University Press.

Douglas Walton, Chris Reed, and Fabrizio Macagno. 2008. *Argumentation Schemes*. Cambridge University Press.

A Appendix

Score	Scoring Criteria
3	The phrase is clearly interpretable AND either expresses an argument, or a premise or a conclusion that can be used in an argument about a facet or a sub-issue for the topic of gay marriage.
2	The phrase is clearly interpretable BUT does not seem to be a part of an argument about a facet or a sub-issue for the topic of gay marriage.
1	The phrase cannot be interpreted as an argument.

Figure 8: Argument Quality HIT as instantiated for the topic Gay Marriage.

Figure 8 shows the definitions used in our Argument Quality HIT.

Figure 9 shows the relation between predicted AQ score and gold-standard argument quality annotations.

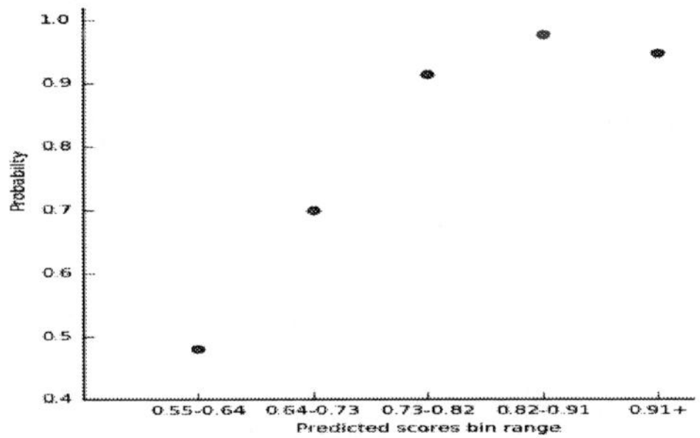

Figure 9: Probability of sentential argument for AQ score across bin for Death Penalty.

Figure 10 provides our definition of FACET and instructions for AFS annotation. This is repeated here from (Misra et al., 2015) for the reader's convenience.

Facet: A facet is a low level issue that often reoccurs in many arguments in support of the author's stance or in attacking the other author's position. There are many ways to argue for your stance on a topic. For example, in a discussion about the death penalty you may argue in favor of it by claiming that it deters crime. Alternatively, you may argue in favor of the death penalty because it gives victims of the crimes closure. On the other hand you may argue against the death penalty because some innocent people will be wrongfully executed or because it is a cruel and unusual punishment. Each of these specific points is a facet.
For two utterances to be about the same facet, it is not necessary that the authors have the same belief toward the facet. For example, one author may believe that the death penalty is a cruel and unusual punishment while the other one attacks that position. However, in order to attack that position they must be discussing the same facet.

We would like you to classify each of the following sets of pairs based on your perception of how SIMILAR the arguments are, on the following scale, examples follow.
(5) Completely equivalent, mean pretty much exactly the same thing, using different words.
(4) Mostly equivalent, but some unimportant details differ. One argument may be more specific than another or include a relatively unimportant extra fact.
(3) Roughly equivalent, but some important information differs or is missing. This includes cases where the argument is about the same FACET but the authors have different stances on that facet.
(2) Not equivalent, but share some details. For example, talking about the same entities but making different arguments (different facets)
(1) Not equivalent, but are on same topic
(0) On a different topic

Figure 10: Definitions used for Facet and AFS in MT HIT.

Investigating Fluidity for Human-Robot Interaction with Real-time, Real-world Grounding Strategies

Julian Hough and David Schlangen
Dialogue Systems Group // CITEC // Faculty of Linguistics and Literature
Bielefeld University
firstname.lastname@uni-bielefeld.de

Abstract

We present a simple real-time, real-world grounding framework, and a system which implements it in a simple robot, allowing investigation into different grounding strategies. We put particular focus on the grounding effects of non-linguistic task-related actions. We experiment with a trade-off between the fluidity of the grounding mechanism with the 'safety' of ensuring task success. The framework consists of a combination of interactive Harel statecharts and the Incremental Unit framework. We evaluate its in-robot implementation in a study with human users and find that in simple grounding situations, a model allowing greater fluidity is perceived to have better understanding of the user's speech.

1 Introduction

Developing suitable grounding mechanisms for communication in the sense of (Clark and Brennan, 1991; Clark, 1996) is an ongoing challenge for designers of robotic systems which interpret speech. If grounding is the way in which interaction participants build and align their internal representations towards shared information or 'common ground', given the vastly different internal representations of humans and robots, one might concede the title of Kruijff (2012)'s paper: 'There is no common ground in human-robot interaction'.

However despite the lack of 'real' common ground, a robot can still understand what the user means 'to a criterion sufficient for current purposes' (Clark and Brennan, 1991) at a given point in the interaction, if it is equipped with grounding mechanisms which deal with the inherent uncertainty in situated dialogue for a robot. This uncertainty lies at multiple layers, including the recognition of words, object recognition and tracking, resolving references to the objects, the recognition of the user's intentions, and the success in execution of robotic actions. Furthermore, if we are to reach beyond task completion or speed as criteria for interactive success and wish the interaction to be more 'fluid', these grounding mechanisms must operate continuously in real time as robotic actions or user utterances are in progress.

In this paper, we present a simple real-time, real-world grounding framework, and a system which implements it in a simple robot, allowing investigation into different grounding strategies. Here, we experiment with a trade-off between the fluidity of the grounding mechanism with the 'safety' of ensuring task success. The framework consists of a combination of interactive Harel statecharts (Harel, 1987) and the Incremental Unit framework (Schlangen and Skantze, 2011), and is implemented in dialogue toolkit InproTK (Baumann and Schlangen, 2012).

2 Achieving Fluid Communicative Grounding in Dialogic Robots

In this paper we are concerned with a simple pick-and-place robot with uni-modal communication abilities, which is simply its manipulation behaviour of objects– see Fig. 1 for example utterances from user U and system S's actions. While our robot does not have natural language generation (NLG) capabilities, its physical actions are first class citizens of the dialogue so it is capable of dialogic behaviour through action.

As mentioned above, while a human and robot's internal representations of a situation can differ inherently, success is possible through recovery

Proceedings of the SIGDIAL 2016 Conference, pages 288–298,
Los Angeles, USA, 13-15 September 2016. ©2016 Association for Computational Linguistics

```
A. Non-incremental grounding:

(1)   U: Put the red cross in box 2                                    right
      S:                          [moves to x] [grabs x] [moves to box 2]      [drops x]

(2)   i) U: Put the red cross in box 2                                          no, the other red cross
         S:                        [moves to x] [grabs x] [moves to box 2]

      ii) U:                                                           right
         S:[moves to x's original position][drops x][moves to y][grabs y][moves to box 2]      [drops y]

B. Incremental grounding:

(3)   U: Take the red cross            right          put it in box 2            right
      S:                        [moves to x]     [grabs x]              [moves to box 2]     [drops x]

(4)   U: Take the red cross            no the other one          right          put it in box 2            right
      S:                        [moves to x]            [moves to y]     [grabs y]              [moves to box 2]     [drops y]

C. Fluid incremental grounding, allowing concurrent user speech and robotic action:

(5)   U: Take the red cross   right     put it in box 2   right
      S:                    [moves to x][grabs x]      [moves to box 2] [drops x]

(6)   U: Take the red cross       no the other one     right   put it in box 2   right
      S:                    [moves to x(aborted)][moves to y][grabs y]      [moves to box 2] [drops y]
```

Figure 1: Grounding modes in a robotic dialogue system that manipulates real-world objects.

from misunderstanding, which has been central to dialogue systems research (Traum, 1994; Traum and Larsson, 2003), with recent work showing how this can operate incrementally (see e.g. (Buß and Schlangen, 2011; Skantze and Hjalmarsson, 2010)), and in situated dialogue domains, through simulation with virtual agents (Marge and Rudnicky, 2011; Raux and Nakano, 2010; Buschmeier and Kopp, 2012). In robotics, much of the grounding research has focussed on perspective taking and frame of reference differing between robot and human (Liu et al., 2010; Liu et al., 2012; Kollar et al., 2010).

The aspect of grounding we focus on here is the mechanisms needed for it to be done fluidly in real time. In line with results from human-human interaction where action is shown to be representative of the current state of understanding with little latency (Tanenhaus and Brown-Schmidt, 2008; McKinstry et al., 2008) and where moving in response to instructions happens *before* the end of the utterance (Hough et al., 2015), we hypothesized that the greater the fluidity, the more natural the robot's action would appear. To illustrate, in Fig. 1, we show three modes of grounding, (A) non-incremental, (B) incremental and (C) fluid. Each mode has the ability to recognize positive feedback and repair and deal with it appropriately, however (A) only allows grounding in a 'half-duplex' fashion with no overlapping speech

and robot action, and grounding can only be done once a completed semantic frame for the current user's intention has been interpreted. When the entire frame has been recognized correctly, the user waits until the robot has shown complete understanding of the user's intention through moving to the target area and awaits confirmation to drop the object there. In recovering from misunderstanding as in (2) when the user repairs the robot's action, not only must the current action be 'undone' but the new action must then also be carried out from the beginning, resulting in long periods of waiting for the user. In mode (B), grounding again happens in a half-duplex fashion, however with opportunities for grounding after shorter increments of speech and with partial information about the user's overall goal– the benefit for repair and recovery incrementally is clear in (4). In (C), the grounding again happens incrementally, however in a full-duplex way, where concurrency of speech and action is allowed and reasoned with appropriately.

To allow human-robot interaction to be more like mode (B) rather than (A), appropriate mechanisms can be designed for robots in line with computational theories of grounding (Traum, 1994; Traum and Larsson, 2003; Ginzburg, 2012), adjusting these mechanisms to work in real time rather than turn-finally, in line with recent work on incremental grounding theories (Ginzburg et al., 2014; Eshghi et al., 2015) where semantic frames can be grounded partially as an utterance progresses. To move towards fluid mode (C), this type of incremental processing not only requires incremental interpretation word-by-word, but use of the context at the exact time each word is recognized, where here, context consists in the estimation of both the user's state and the robot's current state through self-monitoring, both of which can change dynamically during the course of an utterance, or even during a word. In this setting, during a repair from the user, the robot must reason about the action currently 'under discussion' and abort it as efficiently as possible in order to switch to an action consistent with the new goal presented by the user. This self-repair of action involves an estimation of which part of the action the user is trying to repair. The same is true of the converse of repair, where positive confirmations like 'right' may need to be interpreted before the robot has shown unambiguously what its goal is to allow the fluidity in setting (C)– this requires a self-monitoring process which estimates at which point the robot has shown its goal *sufficiently* clearly to the user, during its movement and not necessarily only after its goal has become completely unambiguous.

3 Interactive Statecharts and the Incremental Unit Framework for Real-time Grounding

Our approach to modelling and implementing real-time grounding mechanisms follows work using Harel statecharts (Harel, 1987) for dialogue control in robotic dialogue systems by (Peltason and Wrede, 2010; Skantze and Al Moubayed, 2012). However here, rather than characterizing a single dialogue state which is accessed by a single dialogue manager, our statechart characterizes two independent parallel states for the user and robot, taking an agents-based approach in the sense of (Jennings, 2001).

As illustrated in the diagrams in Fig. 2 and Fig. 7 (Appendix), as per standard statecharts we utilize *states* (boxes) and *transitions* (directed edges) which are executable by *trigger events* (main edge labels) and *conditions* (edge labels within []), and, additionally triggered *actions* can be represented either within the states (the variable assignments and DO statements in the body of the boxes), or on the transition edges, after /.

We dub these *Interactive Statecharts* as the transitions in the participant states can have triggering events and conditions referring to the other interaction partner's state.

We also make use of *composite* states (or superstates) which generalize two or more substates, shown diagrammatically by a surrounding box, which modularizes, reducing the need to define the transitions for all substates, and diagrammatically reduces the number of arrows.

We also refer to variables for each agent state, which for our purposes are *UserGoal* and *RobotGoal*– these represent each agent's current private goal as estimated by the robot (i.e. this is not an omniscient world view).

Given there are mutual dependencies between the two parallel states, one could argue the statechart obscures the complexity which a Finite State Machine (FSM) characterization of the dialogue state would make explicit, and without converting them to FSMs, estimating the probability distributions for the whole composite state is less straight-forward. However, the extra expressive power makes modelling interactive situations and designing grounding mechanisms much simpler. We discuss how to deal with concurrency problems in §3.2, and discuss probabilistic state estimation in the final discussion, though it is not the main focus of this paper.

3.1 A simple concurrent grounding model

To provide a grounding mechanism for robots to achieve more fluid interaction, we characterize the user and robot as having *parallel* states (either side of the dotted line) – see Fig. 2. This allows modelling the concurrent robot and human states the robot believes they are in during the interaction without having to explicitly represent the Cartesian product of all possible dialogue states.

Fig. 2 defines the grounding states and transitions for a simple robotic dialogue system which interprets a user's speech to carry out actions. The main motivation of the model is to explore the nature of the criteria by which the robot judges both their own and their interaction partner's goals to have become publicly manifest (though not necessarily grounded) in real time, and therefore when they are *showing commitment* to them. To evaluate whether the criteria have been met we posit functions Ev for each agent's state, which is a strength-of-evidence valuation that the agent has

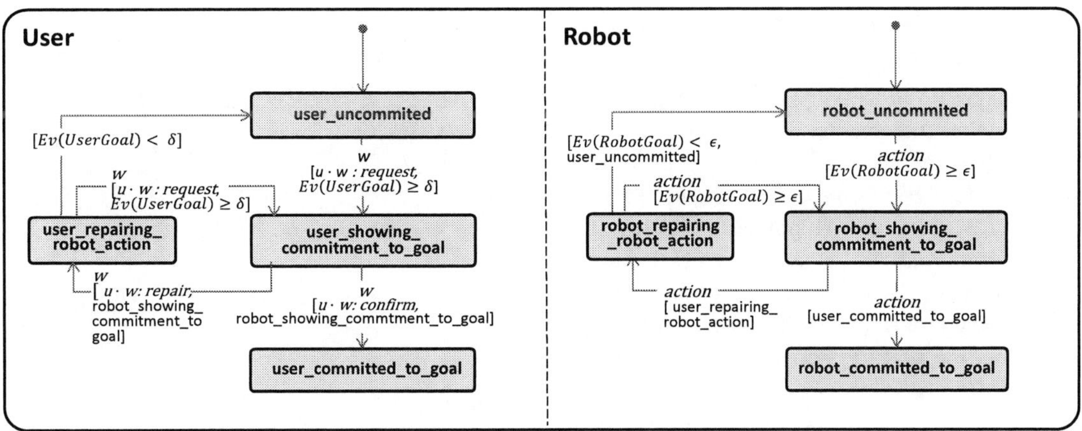

Figure 2: An Interactive Statechart as modelled by the Robot. The statechart consists of two parallel, concurrent states, one for each participant. The triggering events and conditions in the transition functions (the directed edges) can reference the other state.

displayed their goal publicly, where goals are hidden in the case of the user state and observed in the case of the robot.

As shown in Fig.7, $UserGoal$ is estimated as the most likely desired future state the user intends in the set of possible future states $States$, given the current utterance u, the robot's state $Robot$ and the current task's state $Task$, as below.

$$UserGoal := \underset{s \in States}{\arg\max} \; p(s \mid u, Robot, Task) \quad (7)$$

Note, conditioning on the current task is in line with agenda-based approaches to dialogue management (Traum and Larsson, 2003) and also in line with characterizing tasks (or games) as state machines themselves. Our future work will involve more complex task structures.

While the user's goal is being updated through new evidence, this goal can only be judged to become sufficiently mutually manifest with the robot when a certain confidence criteria has been met– here we characterize this as reaching a real-valued threshold δ. As the statechart diagram shows, once $Ev(UserGoal) \geq \delta$ then the state `user_showing_commitment_to_goal` substate can be entered, which is accessible by the Robot state machine in its transition functions to trigger the robot into `robot_showing_commitment_to_goal`. Characterizing this criteria as a threshold allows experimentation into increasing responsiveness of the robot by reducing it, and we explore this in

our implemented system– see §5 below.

Conversely, the Robot's view of its own state uses the function $Ev(RobotGoal)$ and its own threshold ϵ. Unlike the user, the robot's own state is taken to be fully observed, however it must still estimate when its own $RobotGoal$ is made public by its action, and once ϵ has been reached, the robot may enter `robot_showing_commitment_to_goal`. Once this is the case it is permissible for the user state to either commit to the goal and trigger grounding, else engage the robot in repair. The robot will be in the repairing state until the user's state has exited the `user_repairing_robot_action` state. Note that it is only possible for the user state to repair the $RobotGoal$, rather than $UserGoal$– the user can repair the latter through self-repair, but that is currently not represented as its own state.

The necessary conditions of incrementality posed by examples in Fig. 1 (B) and (C) above are met here as the increment size of the triggering events in the $User$ state is the utterance of the latest word w in current utterance u (as opposed to the latest complete utterance). The principal Natural Language Understanding (NLU) decisions are therefore to classify incrementally which type of dialogue act u is, (e.g. u : $Confirm$), whether w begins a new dialogue act or not, and estimate $UserGoal$. The statechart is then checked to see if a transition is possible from the user's current state as each word is processed, akin to incremental dialogue state tracking (Williams, 2012).

3.2 Managing Fluid Grounding with the IU framework

To manage the processing and information flow, we use the Incremental Unit (IU) framework (Schlangen and Skantze, 2011). Currently, in implemented IU framework systems such as Jindigo (Skantze and Hjalmarsson, 2010), Dy-Lan (Purver et al., 2011) and InproTK (Baumann and Schlangen, 2012), processing goes bottom-up (from sensors to actuators) and the creation of incremental units (IUs) is driven by input events to each module from bottom to top. IUs are packages of information at a pre-defined level of granularity, for instance a *wordIU* can be used to represent a single incremental ASR word hypothesis, and their creation in the output buffers of a module triggers downstream processing and creation of new IUs in modules with access to that buffer. IUs can be defined to be connected by directed edges, called *Grounded In* links, which in general take the semantics of "triggered by" from the source to the sink.

Grounded In links are useful in cases where input IU hypotheses may be *revoked* (for instance, by changing ASR hypotheses), as reasoning can be triggered about how to revoke or repair actions that are Grounded In these input IUs. Buß and Schlangen (2011) take precisely this approach with their dialogue manager DIUM, and Kennington et al. (2014) show how abandoning synthesis plans can be done gracefully at short notice.

In order to manage the grounding strategies above, we recast the IU dependencies: while the output IUs are taken as Grounded In the input IUs which triggered them, as per standard processing, in our system the reverse will also be true: consistent with the statecharts driving the behaviour, the interpretation of a user action is taken as an action in response to the robot's latest or currently ongoing robot action, consequently interpretation IUs can be grounded in action IUs– see the reversed feedback arrow in Fig. 3.

To deal with concurrency issues that this closed-loop approach has, the IU modules coordinate their behaviours by sending event instances to each other, where events here are in fact IU edit messages shared in their buffers. The edit messages consist in *ADD*s where the IU is initially created, *COMMIT*s if there is certainty they will not change their payload, and, as mentioned above *REVOKE*s may be sent if the basis for an ADDed

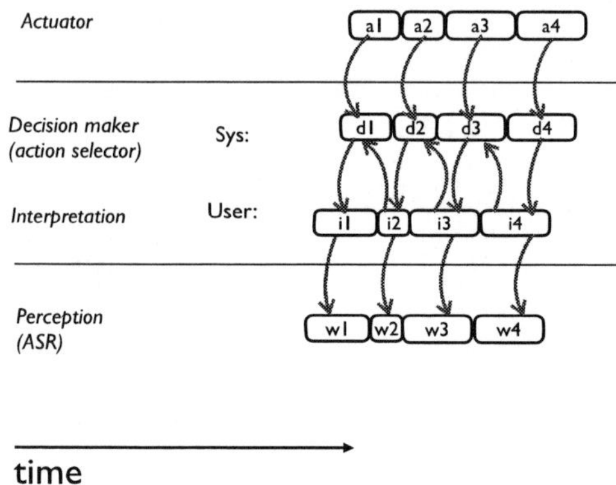

Figure 3: The addition of tight feedback over standard IU approaches helps achieve requirements of fluid interaction and situated repair interpretation. Grounded In links in blue.

IU becomes unreliable. IUs also have different temporal statuses of being either *upcoming*, *ongoing* or *completed*, a temporal logic which allows the system to reason with the status of the actions being executed or planned by the robot.

4 PentoRob: A Simple Robot for Investigating Grounding

We implement the above grounding model and incremental processing in a real-world pick-and-place robot *PentoRob*, the architecture of which can be seen in Fig. 4. The domain we use in this paper is grabbing and placing real-world Pentomino pieces at target locations, however the system is adaptable to novel objects and tasks.

Hardware For the robotic arm, we use the ShapeOko2,[1] a heavy-duty 3-axis CNC machine, which we modified with a rotatable electromagnet, whereby its movement and magnetic field is controlled via two Arduino boards. The sensors are a webcam and microphone.

4.1 System components

PentoRob was implemented in Java using the InproTK (Baumann and Schlangen, 2012) dialogue systems toolkit.[2] The modules involved are de-

---

[1] http://www.shapeoko.com/wiki/index. php/ShapeOko_2
[2] http://bitbucket.org/inpro/inprotk

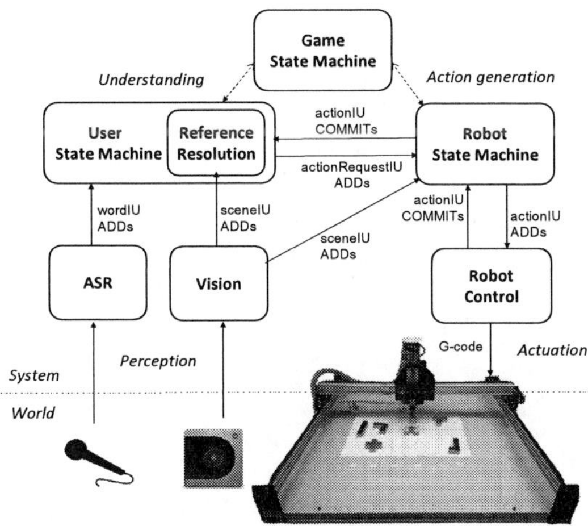

Figure 4: PentoRob's architecture.

scribed below, in terms of their input information or IUs, processing, and output IUs.

Incremental Speech Recognizer (ASR) We use Google's web-based ASR API (Schalkwyk et al., 2010) in German mode, in line with the native language of our evaluation participants. As Baumann et al. (2016) showed, while Google can produce partial results of either multiple or single words, all outputs are packaged into single *WordIUs*. Its incremental performance is not as responsive as more inherently incremental local systems such as Kaldi or Sphinx-4, however, even when trained on in-domain data, other systems cannot consistently match its Word Error Rate in our target domain in German, where it achieves 20%. Its slightly sub-optimal incremental performance did not incur great costs in terms of the grounding we focus on here.

Computer Vision (CV) We utilize OpenCV in a Python module to track objects in the camera's view. This information is relayed to InproTK from Python via the Robotics Service Bus (RSB),[3] which outputs IDs and positions of objects it detects in the scene along with their low-level features (e.g., RGB/HSV values, x,y coordinates, number of edges, etc.), converting these into *SceneIUs* which the downstream reference resolution model consumes.The Robot State Machine also uses these for reasoning about positions

of the objects it plans to grab.[4]

Reference resolution (WAC) The reference resolution component consists of a Words As Classifiers (WAC) model (Kennington and Schlangen, 2015). PentoRob's WAC model is trained on a corpus of Wizard-of-Oz Pentomino puzzle playing dialogue interactions. In off-line training, WAC learns a functional "fit" between words in the user's speech and low-level visual object features, learning a logistic regression classifier for each word. Once trained, when given the context of a novel visual scene and novel incoming words, each word classifier yields a probability given each object's features. During application, as a referring expression is uttered and recognised, each classifier for the words in the expression are applied to all objects in the scene, which after normalisation, results in a probability distribution over objects. Kennington and Schlangen (2015) report 65% accuracy on a 1-out-of-32 reference resolution task in this domain with the same features. For this paper, this accuracy can be seen as a lower bound, as the experimental setup we report below uses a maximum of 6 objects, where the performance is generally significantly better.

User State Machine We implement the principal NLU features within the User State Machine module, which constitutes the $User$ state of the Interactive Statechart. While the statechart manages the possible transitions between states, their triggering criteria require the variables of $UserGoal$, the estimated current user goal and its strength-of-evidence function Ev to be defined. In our domain we characterize $UserGoal$ as simply taking or placing most likely object in the referent set R being referred to according to WAC's output distribution given the utterance u so far, e.g. (8), and the Ev function as simply the probability value of the highest ranked object in WAC's distribution over its second highest rank as in (9).

$$UserGoal = TAKE(\arg\max_{r \in R} p(r \mid u)) \quad (8)$$

$$Ev(UserGoal) = \text{Margin}(\arg\max_{r \in R} p(r \mid u)) \quad (9)$$

As for the process which feeds incoming words into the WAC model to obtain $UserGoal$, here

---

[3] https://code.cor-lab.de/projects/rsb

[4] The objects' positions are calculated accurately from a single video stream using perspective projection.

we use a simple incremental NLU method which is sensitive to the *Robot*'s current state in addition to the *User* statechart. This is a process which first performs sub-utterance dialogue act (DA) classification, judging the utterance to be in $\{request, confirm, repair\}$ after every word. The classifier is a simple segmenter which uses key word spotting for *confirm* words and common *repair* initiating words, and also classifies a *repair* if the word indicates change in the *UserGoal* as defined in (8), else outputting the default *request*.[5] Given the DA classification, the state machine is queried to see if transitioning away from the current state is possible according to the statechart (see Fig. 7 in the Appendix)– if not it remains in the same state and treats the user's speech as irrelevant.

If a successful state change is achieved, then if *UserGoal* has changed or been instantiated in the process, a new *ActionRequestIU* is made available in its right buffer, whose payload is a frame with the dialogue act type, the action type (`take` or `place`) and optional arguments `target_piece` and `target_location`.

For dealing with repairs, as seen in Fig. 7, entering a repairing state triggers a prune of *States*, removing the evidenced *RobotGoal*. In PentoRob this is simply a pruning of the referent set R of the objects(s) in the *RobotGoal* as below:

$$R := \{x \mid p(RobotGoal \mid x) = 0\} \qquad (10)$$

This simple strategy allows *UserGoal* to be recalculated, resulting in interactions like (4) and (6) in Fig.1.

Robot State Machine The Robot's state machine gets access to its transition conditions involving the User's state machine through the ActionRequestIUs it has access to in its left buffer. As seen in Fig.7 (Appendix), when the *User* state is `showing_commitment_to_goal`, the *RobotGoal* is set to *UserGoal*, and through a simple planning function, a number of ActionIUs are cued to achieve it – it sends these as RSB messages to the PentoRob actuation module and once confirmed, again via RSB, that the action has begun, the ActionIU is *committed* and the Robot's action state is set to one of the following, with superstates in brackets:

---
[5]While a somewhat crude approach, it worked reliably enough in our test domain, and is not the focus of the paper.

```
{stationary_without_piece|
moving_without_piece|
moving_to_piece (taking) |
over_target_piece (taking) |
grabbing_piece (taking) |
stationary_with_piece (placing) |
moving_with_piece (placing) |
over_target_location (placing) |
dropping_piece (placing) }
```

For estimation of its own state, the robot state has the following function:

$$Ev(RobotGoal) = \begin{cases} 1 & \text{if over\_target\_piece,} \\ 1 & \text{if over\_target\_location,} \\ 0.5 & \text{if taking,} \\ 0.5 & \text{if placing,} \\ 0 & \text{otherwise} \end{cases} \qquad (11)$$

The simplistic function embodies the assumption that there is absolute certainty that PentoRob's goal has been demonstrated when its arm is directly over the target pieces and locations, else if it is moving to these positions, there is some evidence, else there is none.

PentoRob actuation module The module controlling the actual robotic actuation of the ShapeOKO arm is a Python module with an Arduino board G-code interface to the arm. This sends RSB feedback messages to the PentoRob control module to the effect that actions have been successful or unsuccessfully started, and with their estimated finishing time.

5 Evaluation Experiments

With the above system, we can successfully achieve all three types of grounding strategy in Fig 1. We evaluate the incremental mode (B) and fluid mode (C) in a user study with German speakers. In our first and principal study we experiment with varying the *Robot* state's ϵ grounding parameter to see whether users show preference for a more fluid model, and what effect fluidity has on task success.

The study was a within-subjects design. It had 12 participants, who played a total of 6 rounds each of a simple game with PentoRob. Users were instructed to tell the robot to pick up and place wooden Pentomino pieces onto numbered locations at the bottom of the playing board in a given order according to a photograph of final configurations showing the final location and the desired order of placement. Participants were told they could confirm or correct Pentorob's actions.

They played three rounds in progressing level of difficulty, beginning with a simple situation of 3 pieces of all differing shapes and colours arranged in a line and far apart, followed by another round with 4 pieces arranged in a non grid-like fashion, followed by a more difficult round with 6 pieces where the final two shapes to be placed were close together and the same colour. They play each round twice, once with each version of the system. The order of the conditions was changed each time. The two settings PentoRob's system operated in were as follows:

> **Incremental:** A cautious strategy whereby $\epsilon = 1$. Given (11) only allows PentoRob to enter the `robot_showing_commitment_to_goal` state when in the states `over_target_piece` or `over_target_location`, confirmations and repairs cannot be interpreted during robotic action.
>
> **Fluid:** An optimistic strategy whereby $\epsilon = 0.5$. Given (11), if PentoRob is the superstates of `taking` or `placing` then this is taken as sufficient evidence for showing commitment, and therefore confirmations or repairs can be interpreted during robotic movement.

The users rate the system after every round on a 5-point Likert scale questionnaire asking the questions (albeit in German) as shown in Fig. 5. We hypothesized that the fluid setting would be rated more favourably, due to its behaviour being closer to that observed in manipulator roles in human-human interaction. We had several objective criteria: an approximation to task success as the average time taken to place a piece in the correct location, and also as indications of the variety of dialogue behaviour the repair rate per word (i.e. words classified as belonging to a *repair* act) and the confirmation rate per word.

5.1 Results

Several rounds had to be discarded due to technical failure, leaving 24 ratings from the easier rounds (1 and 2) and 18 from the harder round 3. We found no significant differences in the overall questionnaire responses, however for the easier rounds alone, there was a significant preference for the Fluid system for the feeling that the system understood the user (Fluid mean=3.88, Incremental mean=3.18, Mann-Whitney U p <0.03). The Fluid setting was not preferred significantly in terms of ease of playing (p <0.06), and the ratings were generally positive for ratings of fun and wanting to play again but without significant differences between the two settings.

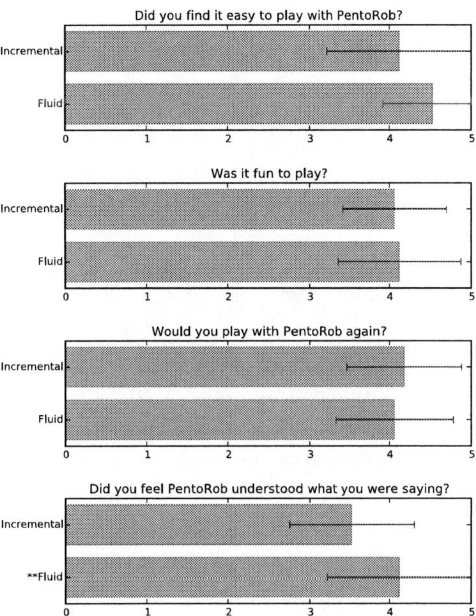

Figure 5: User ratings of the systems in the easier setting (** = Mann-Whitney U with p <0.05)

Within the objective measures in terms of task success (time per piece placed), and rates of different incremental dialogue acts, there were no significant differences between the systems, only a tendency for a higher rate of confirmation words in the fluid setting. The limiting factor of the speed of the robotic arm meant the task success was not improved, however the noticeable increase in displaying understanding was likely due to the affordance of confirming and repairing during the robotic action.

5.2 Preliminary investigation into the User's criteria for showing commitment

For a preliminary investigation into the other parameter in our grounding model, we performed a study with 4 further participants who played with a system in both the modes described above again, but this time with δ, the $User$'s judgement of showing commitment to their goal (which is a confidence threshold for WAC's reference resolution hypothesis (8)) being set much lower– 0.05, compared to 0.2 in the first study. The lower threshold results in earlier, though possibly less accurate, reference resolution and consequent movement to target pieces.

We compared this group's objective measures to a random sample of 4 participants from the first

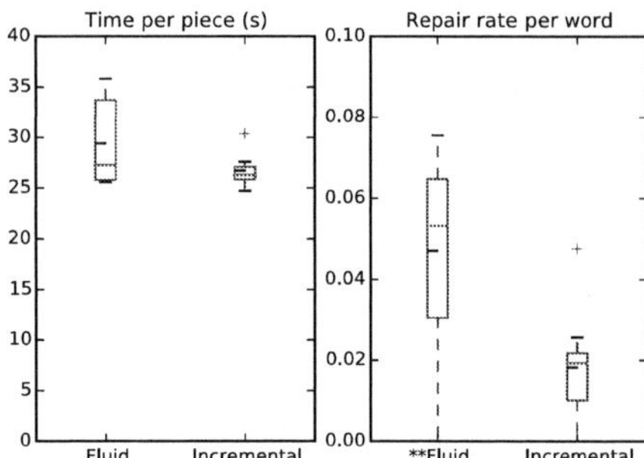

Figure 6: Preliminary result: Repair rates were significantly higher in the more fluid setting with a lower δ parameter of the grounding model whilst not affecting task success.

study, and there was a significant difference in repair rates (Fluid= 0.047 per word (st.d=0.024), Incremental=0.011 per word (st.d=0.011), T-test p <0.01) – see Fig. 6. Also, there was a tendency for higher rates of confirmation (Fluid= 0.245 per word (st.d=0.112), Incremental=0.151 per word (st.d=0.049), T-test p = 0.06). Encouragingly, the repair rates are in line with those reported in human-human similar task-oriented dialogue, with onsets occurring in 2-5% of words (Colman and Healey, 2011). However, also encouraging is that despite more time spent repairing and confirming in the more predictive system with the lower δ threshold, there was no effect on task success (e.g. see the near identical means for time taken to place each piece in Fig. 6).

5.3 Discussion

In the first experiment, the ratings results suggest the fluid setting's affordance of allowing confirmations and repairs during the robot's movement was noticed in easier rounds. More work is required to allow this effect to persist in the harder round, as severe failures in terms of task success cancelled the perception of fluidity.

The second experiment showed that the earlier movement of the robot arm to the target piece resulted in the user engaging in more repair of the movement, but this did not affect task success in terms of overall speed of completion. The degree to which the earlier demonstration of commitments to a goal during a user's speech, despite repair being required more often, can increase interactive success in more challenging reference situations will be investigated in future work.

6 Conclusion

We have presented a model of fluid, task action-based grounding, and have shown that it can be implemented in a robot that perceives and manipulates real-world objects. When general task-performance is good enough, the model leads to the perception of better understanding over a more standard incremental processing model.

There are some weaknesses with the current study. We intend to use more complex strength of evidence measures, for example for $Ev(UserGoal)$ using ASR hypotheses confidence thresholds (Williams, 2012), and having a more complex $Ev(RobotGoal)$ based on the robot's current position and velocity. We also want to explore learning and optimization for our incremental processing, with points of departure being (Paetzel et al., 2015), (Dethlefs et al., 2012), and the proposal by (Lemon and Eshghi, 2015).

The future challenge, yet potential strength, for our model is that unlike most approaches which assume a finite state Markov model for probabilistic estimation, we do not assume the Cartesian product of all possible substates needs to be modelled. The mathematics of how this can be done for a complex hierarchical model has had recent attention, for example in recent work in probabilistic Type Theory with Records (Cooper et al., 2014)– we intend to pursue such an approach in coming work.

Acknowledgments

We thank the three SigDial reviewers for their helpful comments. We thank Casey Kennington, Oliver Eickmeyer and Livia Dia for contributions to software and hardware, and Florian Steig and Gerdis Anderson for their help in running the experiments. This work was supported by the Cluster of Excellence Cognitive Interaction Technology 'CITEC' (EXC 277) at Bielefeld University, funded by the German Research Foundation (DFG), and the DFG-funded DUEL project (grant SCHL 845/5-1).

References

Timo Baumann and David Schlangen. 2012. The inprotk 2012 release. In *NAACL-HLT Workshop on Future Directions and Needs in the Spoken Dialog Community: Tools and Data*. ACL.

Timo Baumann, Casey Kennington, Julian Hough, and David Schlangen. 2016. Recognising conversational speech: What an incremental asr should do

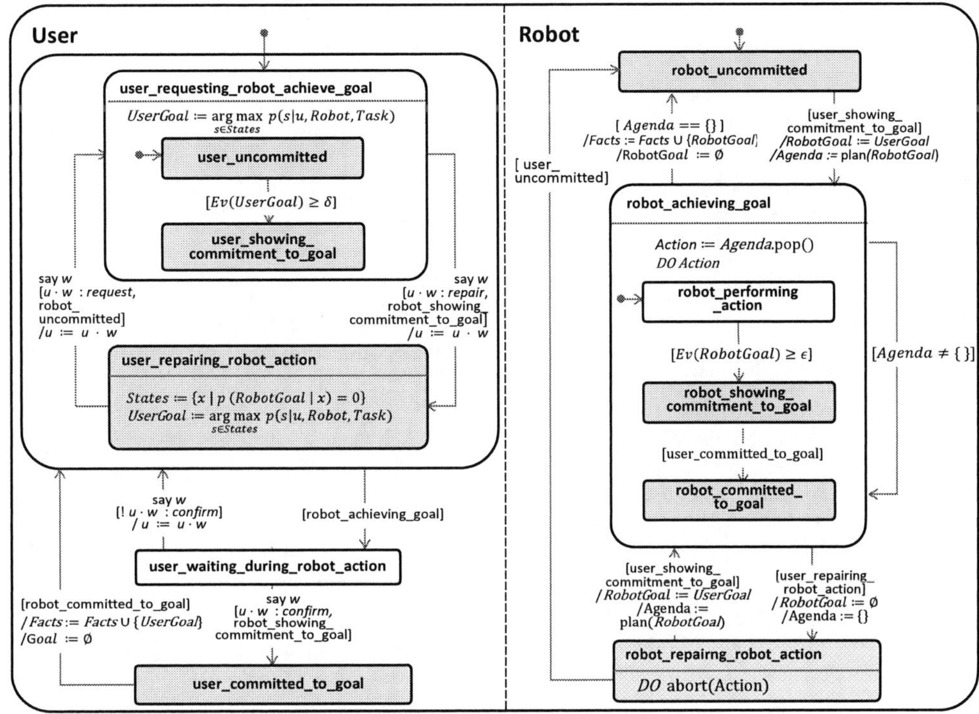

Figure 7: The full Interactive Statechart. States relevant for grounding are in grey.

for a dialogue system and how to get there. In *International Workshop on Dialogue Systems Technology (IWSDS) 2016*. Universität Hamburg.

Hendrik Buschmeier and Stefan Kopp. 2012. Using a bayesian model of the listener to unveil the dialogue information state. In *SemDial 2012: Proceedings of the 16th Workshop on the Semantics and Pragmatics of Dialogue*.

Okko Buß and David Schlangen. 2011. Dium – an incremental dialogue manager that can produce self-corrections. Proceedings of semdial 2011 (Los Angelogue).

Herbert H Clark and Susan E Brennan. 1991. Grounding in communication. *Perspectives on socially shared cognition*, 13(1991).

Herbert H Clark. 1996. *Using language*. Cambridge university press.

Marcus Colman and Patrick Healey. 2011. The distribution of repair in dialogue. In c. Hoelscher and T.F. Shipley, editors, *Proceedings of the 33rd Annual Conference of the Cognitive Science Society*, Boston, Massachussetts. Austinm TX:Cognitive Science Society.

Robin Cooper, Simon Dobnik, Shalom Lappin, and Staffan Larsson. 2014. A probabilistic rich type theory for semantic interpretation. In *Proceedings of the EACL Workshop on Type Theory and Natural Language Semantics (TTNLS)*, Gothenburg, Sweden. ACL.

Nina Dethlefs, Helen Hastie, Verena Rieser, and Oliver Lemon. 2012. Optimising incremental dialogue decisions using information density for interactive systems. In *Proceedings of the 2012 Joint Conference on Empirical Methods in Natural Language Processing and Computational Natural Language Learning*. ACL.

Arash Eshghi, Christine Howes, Eleni Gregoromichelaki, Julian Hough, and Matthew Purver. 2015. Feedback in conversation as incremental semantic update. In *Proceedings of the 11th International Conference on Computational Semantics*, London, UK. ACL.

Jonathan Ginzburg, Raquel Fernndez, and David Schlangen. 2014. Disfluencies as intra-utterance dialogue moves. *Semantics and Pragmatics*, 7(9).

Jonathan Ginzburg. 2012. *The Interactive Stance: Meaning for Conversation*. Oxford University Press.

David Harel. 1987. Statecharts: A visual formalism for complex systems. *Science of computer programming*, 8(3).

Julian Hough, Iwan de Kok, David Schlangen, and Stefan Kopp. 2015. Timing and grounding in motor skill coaching interaction: Consequences for the information state. In *Proceedings of the 19th SemDial*

Workshop on the Semantics and Pragmatics of Dialogue (goDIAL), pages 86–94.

Nicholas R Jennings. 2001. An agent-based approach for building complex software systems. *Communications of the ACM*, 44(4).

Casey Kennington and David Schlangen. 2015. Simple learning and compositional application of perceptually grounded word meanings for incremental reference resolution. Proceedings of the Conference for the Association for Computational Linguistics (ACL). ACL.

Casey Kennington, Spyros Kousidis, Timo Baumann, Hendrik Buschmeier, Stefan Kopp, and David Schlangen. 2014. Better driving and recall when in-car information presentation uses situationally-aware incremental speech output generation. In *Proceedings of the 6th International Conference on Automotive User Interfaces and Interactive Vehicular Applications*. ACM.

Thomas Kollar, Stefanie Tellex, Deb Roy, and Nicholas Roy. 2010. Toward understanding natural language directions. In *Human-Robot Interaction (HRI), 2010 5th ACM/IEEE International Conference on*. IEEE.

Geert-Jan M Kruijff. 2012. There is no common ground in human-robot interaction. In *Proceedings of SemDial 2012 (SeineDial): The 16th Workshop on the Semantics and Pragmatics of Dialogue*.

Oliver Lemon and Arash Eshghi. 2015. Deep reinforcement learning for constructing meaning by babbling. In *Interactive Meaning Construction A Workshop at IWCS 2015*.

Changsong Liu, Jacob Walker, and Joyce Y Chai. 2010. Ambiguities in spatial language understanding in situated human robot dialogue. In *AAAI Fall Symposium: Dialog with Robots*.

Changsong Liu, Rui Fang, and Joyce Y Chai. 2012. Towards mediating shared perceptual basis in situated dialogue. In *Proceedings of the 13th Annual Meeting of the Special Interest Group on Discourse and Dialogue*. ACL.

Matthew Marge and Alexander I Rudnicky. 2011. Towards overcoming miscommunication in situated dialogue by asking questions. In *AAAI Fall Symposium: Building Representations of Common Ground with Intelligent Agents*.

Chris McKinstry, Rick Dale, and Michael J Spivey. 2008. Action dynamics reveal parallel competition in decision making. *Psychological Science*, 19(1):22–24.

Maike Paetzel, Ramesh Manuvinakurike, and David DeVault. 2015. so, which one is it? the effect of alternative incremental architectures in a high-performance game-playing agent. In *16th Annual Meeting of the Special Interest Group on Discourse and Dialogue*.

Julia Peltason and Britta Wrede. 2010. Pamini: A framework for assembling mixed-initiative human-robot interaction from generic interaction patterns. In *Proceedings of the 11th Annual Meeting of the Special Interest Group on Discourse and Dialogue*. ACL.

Matthew Purver, Arash Eshghi, and Julian Hough. 2011. Incremental semantic construction in a dialogue system. In J. Bos and S. Pulman, editors, *Proceedings of the 9th IWCS*, Oxford, UK.

Antoine Raux and Mikio Nakano. 2010. The dynamics of action corrections in situated interaction. In *Proceedings of the 11th Annual Meeting of the Special Interest Group on Discourse and Dialogue*. ACL.

Johan Schalkwyk, Doug Beeferman, Françoise Beaufays, Bill Byrne, Ciprian Chelba, Mike Cohen, Maryam Kamvar, and Brian Strope. 2010. Your Word is my Command: Google Search by Voice: A Case Study. In *Advances in Speech Recognition*. Springer.

David Schlangen and Gabriel Skantze. 2011. A General, Abstract Model of Incremental Dialogue Processing. *Dialogue & Discourse*, 2(1).

Gabriel Skantze and Samer Al Moubayed. 2012. Iristk: a statechart-based toolkit for multi-party face-to-face interaction. In *Proceedings of the 14th ACM international conference on Multimodal interaction*. ACM.

Gabriel Skantze and Anna Hjalmarsson. 2010. Towards incremental speech generation in dialogue systems. In *Proceedings of the 11th Annual Meeting of SIGDIAL*. ACL.

Michael K Tanenhaus and Sarah Brown-Schmidt. 2008. Language processing in the natural world. *Philosophical Transactions of the Royal Society of London B: Biological Sciences*, 363(1493):1105–1122.

David R Traum and Staffan Larsson. 2003. The information state approach to dialogue management. In *Current and new directions in discourse and dialogue*. Springer.

David R Traum. 1994. A computational theory of grounding in natural language conversation. Technical report, DTIC Document.

Jason D Williams. 2012. A belief tracking challenge task for spoken dialog systems. In *NAACL-HLT Workshop on Future Directions and Needs in the Spoken Dialog Community: Tools and Data*. ACL.

A Supplemental Material

The full statechart is in Figure 7.

Do Characters Abuse More Than Words?

Yashar Mehdad
Yahoo! Research
Sunnyvale, CA, USA
`ymehdad@yahoo-inc.com`

Joel Tetreault
Yahoo! Research
New York, NY, USA
`tetreaul@gmail.com`

Abstract

Although word and character n-grams have been used as features in different NLP applications, no systematic comparison or analysis has shown the power of character-based features for detecting *abusive language*. In this study, we investigate the effectiveness of such features for abusive language detection in user-generated online comments, and show that such methods outperform previous state-of-the-art approaches and other strong baselines.

1 Introduction

The rise of online communities over the last ten years, in various forms such as message boards, twitter, discussion forums, etc., have allowed people from disparate backgrounds to connect in a way that would not have been possible before. However, the ease of communication online has made it possible for both anonymous and non-anonymous posters to hurl insults, bully, and threaten through the use of profanity and hate speech, all of which can be framed as "abusive language." Although detection of some of the more straightforward examples of abusive language can be handled effectively through blacklists and regular expressions, as in "*I am surprised these fuckers reported on this crap*", more complex methods are required to address the more nuanced cases, as in "*Add anotherJEW fined a bi$$ion for stealing like a lil maggot. Hang thm all.*" In that example, there are tokenization and normalization issues, as well as a conscious bastardization of words in an effort to evade blacklists or to add color to the post.

While previous work for detecting abusive language has been dominated by lexical-based approaches, we claim that morphological features play a more significant role in this task. This is based on the observation that user language evolves either consciously or unconsciously based on standards and guidelines imposed by media companies that users must adhere to, in conjunction with regular expressions and blacklists, to catch bad language and consequently remove a post. Essentially, users learn over time not to use common lexical items and words to convey certain language. Thus, characters often play an important role in the comment language. Characters, in combination with words, can act as basic phonetic, morpho-lexical and semantic units in comments such as "*kill yrslef a$$hole*". Character n-grams have been proven useful for other NLP tasks such as authorship identification (Sapkota et al., 2015), native language identification (Tetreault et al., 2013) and machine translation (Nakov and Tiedemann, 2012), but surprisingly have not been the focus in prior work for abusive language.

In this paper, we investigate the role that character n-grams play in this task by exploring their use in two different algorithms. We compare their results to two state-of-the-art approaches by evaluating on a corpus of nearly 1M comments. Briefly, our contributions are summarized as follows: **1)** character n-grams outperform word n-grams in both algorithms, and **2)** the models proposed in this work outperform the previous state-of-the-art for this dataset.

2 Related Work

Prior work in abusive language has been rather diffuse as researchers have focused on different aspects ranging from profanity detection (Sood et al., 2012) to hate speech detection (Warner and Hirschberg, 2012) to cyberbullying (Dadvar et al., 2013) and to abusive language in general (Chen et al., 2012; Djuric et al., 2015b).

The overwhelming majority of this work has

Proceedings of the SIGDIAL 2016 Conference, pages 299–303,
Los Angeles, USA, 13-15 September 2016. ©2016 Association for Computational Linguistics

focused on using supervised classification with canonical NLP features. Token n-grams are one of the most popular features across many works (Yin et al., 2009; Chen et al., 2012; Warner and Hirschberg, 2012; Xiang et al., 2012; Dadvar et al., 2013). Hand-crafted regular expressions and blacklists also feature prominently in (Yin et al., 2009; Sood et al., 2012; Xiang et al., 2012).

Other features and methodologies have also been found useful. For example, Dadvar et al. (2013) found that in the task of identifying cyberbullying in YouTube comments, a small performance improvement could be gained by including features which model the user's past behavior. Xiang et al. (2012) tackled detecting offensive tweets via semi-supervised LDA approach. Djuric et al. (2015b) use a paragraph2vec approach to classify language on user comments as abusive or clean. Nobata et al. (2016) was the first to evaluate many of the above features on a common corpus and showed an improvement over Djuric et al. (2015b). In this paper, we directly compare against the two works by using the same dataset.

3 Methodology

In general, it is not obvious how to transform comments with different lengths and characteristics to a representation that moves beyond bag of words or words/ngrams based classification approaches. For our work we employ several supervised classification methods with lexical and morphological features to measure various aspects of the user comment. A major difference of our classification phase with previous work in this area is that we use a hybrid method based on discriminative and generative classifiers. As in prior work, we constrained our work to binary classification with comments being abusive or not. Our features are divided into three main classes: tokens, characters and distributional semantics. Our motivation behind using light-weight features, instead of deeper linguistic features (e.g., part of speech tags), is two-fold: i) light-weight features are computationally much less expensive than syntactic or discourse features, and ii) it is very challenging to preprocess noisy and malformed text (i.e., comments) to extract deeper linguistic features.

We explore three different methods for abusive language detection. The first, based on distributional representation of comments (C2V), is meant to serve as a strong baseline for this task. The next two, RNNLM and NBSVM, we use as methodologies for which to explore the impact of character-based vs. token-based features.

3.1 Distributional Representation of Comments (C2V)

The ideas of distributed and distributional word and text representations has supported many applications in natural language processing successfully. The related work is largely focused on the notion of word and text representations (as in (Djuric et al., 2015a; Le and Mikolov, 2014; Mikolov et al., 2013a)), which improve previous works on modeling lexical semantics using vector space models (Mikolov et al., 2013a). More recently, the concept of embeddings has been extended beyond words to a number of text segments, including phrases (Mikolov et al., 2013b), sentences and paragraphs (Le and Mikolov, 2014) and entities (Yang et al., 2014). In order to learn vector representation we develop a comment embeddings approach akin to Le and Mikolov (2014) which is different from the one used in Djuric et al. (2015a) since our representation doesn't model the relationships between the comments (e.g., temporal). Moreover, given the similarity with a prior state-of-the-art approach (Djuric et al., 2015b), this method can also be used as a strong baseline.

In order to obtain the embeddings of comments we learn distributed representations for our comments dataset. The comments are represented as low-dimensional vectors and are jointly learned with distributed vector representations of tokens using a distributed memory model explained in Le and Mokolov (2014). In this work, we train the embeddings of the words in comments using a skip-bigram model (Mikolov et al., 2013a) with window sizes of 5 and 10 using hierarchical softmax training. We also experiment with training two low-dimensional models (100 and 300 dimensions). We limit the number of iterations to 10. For the classification phase we use the Multi-core LibLinear Library (Lee et al., 2015) logistic regression classifier over the resulting embeddings.

3.2 Recurrent Neural Network Language Model (RNNLM)

The intuition behind this model comes from the idea that if we can train a reasonably good language model over the instances for each class, then it will be straightforward to use Bayes rule to predict the class of a new comment. Language models typically require large amounts of data to achieve a decent performance, but there are currently no large-scale datasets for abuse detection. To overcome this challenge, we exploit the power of recurrent neural networks (RNNs) (Mikolov et al., 2010) which demonstrated state-of-the-art results for language models with less training data (Mikolov, 2012). Another advantage of RNNs is their potential in representing more advanced patterns (Mikolov, 2012). For example, patterns that rely on characters that could have occurred at variable comments can be encoded much more effectively with the recurrent architecture.

We train models for both classes of abusive language in comments (abuse and clean): a) token n-grams for $n = 1..5$, and b) character n-grams for $n = 1..5$ preserving the space character, to investigate our character vs. words claim. During testing, we estimate the ratio of the probability of the comment belonging to each class via Bayes rule. In this way, if the probability of a comment given the abusive language model is higher than its probability given the non-abusive language model, then the comment is classified as abusive and vice versa (Mesnil et al., 2014) and their ratio is used to calculate the AUC metric.

For the experiments we use the RNNLM toolkit developed by (Mikolov et al., 2011). We use 5% of the training set for validation and the rest for training the language model. We train one word (*word*) and two character based language models (*char$_1$* & *char$_2$*). For the *word* and *char$_1$* language models we set the size of hidden layers to 50 with 200 hashes of for direct connections and 4 steps to propagate error back (*bptt*). In order to train a better character-based language model (i.e., *char$_2$*) we increase the number of hidden layers to 200 and *bptt* set to 10. Although training a character-based RNN language model with 200 hidden layers takes much longer, our secondary goal is to measure the gains in performance with this more intensive training.

3.3 Support Vector Machine with Naive Bayes Features (NBSVM)

Naive Bayes (NB) and Support Vector Machines (SVM) have been proven to be effective approaches for NLP applications such as sentiment and text analysis. Wang and Manning (2012) showed the power of combining these two generative and discriminative classifiers where an SVM

is built over NB log-count ratios as feature values and demonstrated that this combination outperforms the standalone NB and SVM in many tasks using token n-gram features. However, to the best of our knowledge, the effect of character-based NB feature values has not been experimented.

In this work, besides using token n-grams ($n = 1..5$) features, for character level features we compute the log-ratio vector between the average character n-gram counts ($n = 1..5$) from abusive and non-abusive comments. In this way, the input to the SVM classifier is the log-ratio vector multiplied by the binary pattern for each character ngram in the comment vector. For SVM classification we use the Multi-core LibLinear Library (Lee et al., 2015) in its standard setting.

4 Evaluation

4.1 Experimental Setup

We use the same dataset employed in Djuric et al. (2015b) and Nobata et al. (2016). The labels came from a combination of in-house raters, users reactively flagging bad comments and abusive language pattern detectors. To date, this is the largest dataset available for abusive language detection. We use this dataset so as to directly compare with that prior work, and in doing so, we also adopt their evaluation methodology and employ 5-fold cross-validation and report AUC, in addition to recall, precision and F-1. As an additional baseline, we developed a token n-gram classifier with $n = 1..5$ using a logistic regression classifier.

4.2 Results

Table 1 shows the results of all experiments. The four baselines (Djuric et al. (2015), Nobata et al. (2016), token n-grams and C2V) are listed in the first seven rows, and the NBVSM and RNNLM experiments are listed under the double line. We also show the results of a method which combines the token n-grams with the features from the best performing versions of the C2V, NBSVM and RNNLM classes, using our SVM classifier ("Combination").

In terms of overall performance, all methods improved on or tied the Djuric et al. (2015b), C2V and token n-gram baselines. The top performing baseline and current state-of-the-art, Nobata et al. (2016), which consists of a comprehensive combination of a range of different features, is bested by NBSVM using solely character n-grams (77 F-

Method	Rec.	Prec.	F-1	AUC
Djuric et al.	-	-	-	80
Nobata et al.	79	77	78	91
Token n-grams	76	70	73	84
C2V d300w10*	58	77	66	85
C2V d300w5	57	76	66	84
C2V d100w10	56	75	65	82
C2V d100w5	56	76	64	82
NBSVM (word)*	60	**84**	70	89
NBSVM (char)*	72	83	**77**	**92**
RNNLM (word)*	72	59	65	82
RNNLM (char$_1$)*	**78**	60	68	85
RNNLM (char$_2$)	68	68	68	85
Combination	75	**84**	**79**	**93**

Table 1: Results on Djuric et al. (2015) data

1 and 92 AUC). This shows that a light-weight method using character level features can outperform more intricate methods for this task. Moreover, the combination of the best features (marked by * in the Table 1) outperforms all other methods in all measures save for recall. This shows that by increasing the number of relevant features we can improve precision with just a small loss in recall.

For both NBSVM and RNNLM methods, character n-grams outperform their token counterparts (7 and 3 points F-1 score respectively). As most prior work has made use of blacklists and word n-grams, this proves to be an effective method for improving performance.

Comparing the two RNNLM character-based models, using a deeper RNN model improves the precession by 8 points at the loss of 10 points in recall. This finding fits our expectations since, in general, a greater number of hidden layers is needed to achieve a good performance in a character-based language model. We can conclude that for applications which aim at higher recall for abusive language detection, lower hidden layers (e.g., 50) can provide a sufficient performance. However, it should be noted that the more intensive training done in the char$_2$ experiment does not improve upon the 68 F-1 score in char$_1$.

The C2V experiments had the worst performance of all three metrics with the best performance resulting in an F-1 score of 66 using a 300-dimensional vector and a 10 word window (d300w10) while still improving upon the previous approach using paragraph2vec (Djuric et al.,

2015b). As one would expect, decreasing the dimensionality of the embedding and the context window results in a loss of performance of as much as 18 F-1 score points (d100w5). However, based on our experiments (not included in the Table), increasing the window size over 10 causes a significant drop in performance. This is due to the fact that most of the comments are rather short (usually under ten tokens) and thus any increase in window length would have no positive impact.

Finally, we performed a manual error analysis of the cases where the character-based approaches and the token-based approaches differed. Naturally, the character-based approaches fared best in cases with irregular normalization or obfuscation of words. For instance, strings with a mixture of letters and digits (i.e., "*ni9*") were caught more readily by the character based methods. There were cases where none of the approaches and methods correctly detected the abuse, usually because the specific trigger words were rare or because the comment was nuanced.

We do note that there are many different types of online communities, and that in communities with little to no moderation, character and word n-grams may perform similarly since the writers may not feel it necessary to obfuscate their words. However, in the many communities where authors are aware of standards, the task becomes much more challenging as authors intentional obfuscate in a myriad of creative ways (Laboreiro and Oliveira, 2014).

5 Conclusions

In this paper, we have made focused contributions into the task of abusive language detection. Specifically, we showed the superiority of simple character-based approaches over the previous state-of-the-art, as well as token-based ones and two deep learning approaches. These light-weight features, when coupled with the right methods, can save system designers and practitioners from writing many regular expressions and rules as in (Sood et al., 2012; Xiang et al., 2012). For future work, we are planning to adapt C2V to the character level.

Acknowledgment

We would like to thank the anonymous reviewers for their comments. We also thank Chikashi Nobata for his contribution to this paper.

References

Ying Chen, Yilu Zhou, Sencun Zhu, and Heng Xu. 2012. Detecting offensive language in social media to protect adolescent online safety. In *Privacy, Security, Risk and Trust (PASSAT), 2012 International Conference on Social Computing (SocialCom)*, pages 71–80. IEEE.

Maral Dadvar, Dolf Trieschnigg, Roeland Ordelman, and Franciska de Jong. 2013. Improving cyberbullying detection with user context. In *Advances in Information Retrieval*, pages 693–696. Springer.

Nemanja Djuric, Hao Wu, Vladan Radosavljevic, Mihajlo Grbovic, and Narayan Bhamidipati. 2015a. Hierarchical neural language models for joint representation of streaming documents and their content. In *Proceedings of the International World Wide Web Conference (WWW)*.

Nemanja Djuric, Jing Zhou, Robin Morris, Mihajlo Grbovic, Vladan Radosavljevic, and Narayan Bhamidipati. 2015b. Hate speech detection with comment embeddings. In *Proceedings of the International World Wide Web Conference (WWW)*.

Gustavo Laboreiro and Eugénio Oliveira. 2014. What we can learn from looking at profanity. In *Computational Processing of the Portuguese Language*, pages 108–113. Springer.

Quoc Le and Tomas Mikolov. 2014. Distributed representations of sentences and documents. In Tony Jebara and Eric P. Xing, editors, *Proceedings of the 31st International Conference on Machine Learning (ICML-14)*.

Mu-Chu Lee, Wei-Lin Chiang, and Chih-Jen Lin. 2015. Fast matrix-vector multiplications for large-scale logistic regression on shared-memory systems. In Charu Aggarwal, Zhi-Hua Zhou, Alexander Tuzhilin, Hui Xiong, and Xindong Wu, editors, *ICDM*, pages 835–840. IEEE.

Grégoire Mesnil, Tomas Mikolov, Marc'Aurelio Ranzato, and Yoshua Bengio. 2014. Ensemble of generative and discriminative techniques for sentiment analysis of movie reviews. *CoRR*, abs/1412.5335.

Tomas Mikolov, Martin Karafiát, Lukás Burget, Jan Cernocký, and Sanjeev Khudanpur. 2010. Recurrent neural network based language model. In *11th Annual Conference of the International Speech Communication Association (Interspeech)*, pages 1045–1048.

Tomas Mikolov, Stefan Kombrink, Anoop Deoras, Lukar Burget, and Jan Honza Cernocky. 2011. Rnnlm - recurrent neural network language modeling toolkit. IEEE Automatic Speech Recognition and Understanding Workshop, December.

Tomas Mikolov, Kai Chen, Greg Corrado, and Jeffrey Dean. 2013a. Efficient estimation of word representations in vector space. *CoRR*, abs/1301.3781.

Tomas Mikolov, Ilya Sutskever, Kai Chen, Greg S. Corrado, and Jeff Dean. 2013b. Distributed representations of words and phrases and their compositionality. In C.J.C. Burges, L. Bottou, M. Welling, Z. Ghahramani, and K.Q. Weinberger, editors, *Advances in Neural Information Processing Systems 26*, pages 3111–3119. Curran Associates, Inc.

Tomáš Mikolov. 2012. *Statistical Language Models Based on Neural Networks*. Ph.D. thesis.

Preslav Nakov and Jörg Tiedemann. 2012. Combining word-level and character-level models for machine translation between closely-related languages. In *Proceedings of the 50th Annual Meeting of the Association for Computational Linguistics*, Jeju Island, Korea, July.

Chikashi Nobata, Joel Tetreault, Achint Thomas, Yashar Mehdad, and Yi Chang. 2016. Abusive language detection in online user content. In *Proceedings of the 25th International Conference on World Wide Web (WWW)*, pages 145–153.

Upendra Sapkota, Steven Bethard, Manuel Montes, and Thamar Solorio. 2015. Not all character n-grams are created equal: A study in authorship attribution. In *Proceedings of the NAACL-HLT '15*, Denver, Colorado, May–June.

Sara Owsley Sood, Judd Antin, and Elizabeth F Churchill. 2012. Using crowdsourcing to improve profanity detection. In *AAAI Spring Symposium: Wisdom of the Crowd*.

Joel Tetreault, Daniel Blanchard, and Aoife Cahill. 2013. A report on the first native language identification shared task. In *Proceedings of the Eighth Workshop on Innovative Use of NLP for Building Educational Applications*, Atlanta, Georgia, June.

Sida Wang and Christopher D. Manning. 2012. Baselines and bigrams: Simple, good sentiment and topic classification. In *Proceedings of the ACL '12*, pages 90–94.

William Warner and Julia Hirschberg. 2012. Detecting hate speech on the world wide web. In *Proceedings of the Second Workshop on Language in Social Media*, Montréal, Canada, June.

Guang Xiang, Bin Fan, Ling Wang, Jason Hong, and Carolyn Rose. 2012. Detecting offensive tweets via topical feature discovery over a large scale twitter corpus. In *Proceedings of CIMK '12*, pages 1980–1984.

Bishan Yang, Wen-tau Yih, Xiaodong He, Jianfeng Gao, and Li Deng. 2014. Embedding entities and relations for learning and inference in knowledge bases. *CoRR*, abs/1412.6575.

Dawei Yin, Zhenzhen Xue, Liangjie Hong, Brian D Davison, April Kontostathis, and Lynne Edwards. 2009. Detection of harassment on web 2.0. *Proceedings of the Content Analysis in the WEB*, 2:1–7.

Towards a Dialogue System that Supports Rich Visualizations of Data

Abhinav Kumar and **Jillian Aurisano** and **Barbara Di Eugenio** and **Andrew Johnson**
University of Illinois at Chicago
Chicago, IL USA
{akumar34,jauris2,bdieugen,ajohnson}@uic.edu

Alberto Gonzalez and **Jason Leigh**
University of Hawai'i at Manoa
Honolulu, HI USA
{agon,leighj}@hawaii.edu

Abstract

The goal of our research is to support full-fledged dialogue between a user and a system that transforms the user queries into visualizations. So far, we have collected a corpus where users explore data via visualizations; we have annotated the corpus for user intentions; and we have developed the core NL-to-visualization pipeline.

1 Introduction

Visualization, even in its simplest forms, remains a highly effective means for converting large volumes of raw data into insight. Still, even with the aid of robust visualization software, e.g. Tableau[1] and ManyEyes (Viegas et al., 2007), especially novices face challenges when attempting to translate their questions into appropriate visual encodings (Heer et al., 2008; Grammel et al., 2010). Ideally, users would like to tell the computer what they want to see, and have the system intelligently create the visualization. However, existing systems (Cox et al., 2001; Sun et al., 2013; Gao et al., 2015) do not offer two-way communication, or only support limited types of queries, or are not grounded in how users explore data.

Our goal is to develop Articulate 2, a full-fledged conversational interface that will automatically generate visualizations. The contributions of our work so far are: a new corpus unique in its genre;[2] and a prototype system, which is able to process a sequence of requests, create the corresponding visualizations, position them on the screen, and manage them.

2 Related Work

Much work has focused on the automatic generation of visual representations, but not via NL (Feiner, 1985; Roth et al., 1994; Mackinlay et al., 2007). Likewise, much work is devoted to multimodal interaction with visual representations (e.g. (Walker et al., 2004; Meena et al., 2014)), but not to automatically generating those visual representations. Systems like AutoBrief (Green et al., 2004) focus on producing graphics accompanied by text; or on finding the appropriate graphics to accompany existing text (Li et al., 2013).

(Cox et al., 2001; Reithinger et al., 2005) were among the first to integrate a dialogue interface into an existing information visualization system, but they support only a small range of questions. Our own Articulate (Sun et al., 2013) maps NL queries to statistical visualizations by using very simple NLP methods. When DataTone (Gao et al., 2015), the closest to our work, cannot resolve an ambiguity in an NL query, it presents the user with selection widgets to solve it. However, only one visualization is presented to the user at a given time, and previous context is lost. (Gao et al., 2015) compares DataTone to IBM Watson Analytics,[3] that allows users to interact with data via structured language queries, but does not support dialogic interaction either.

3 A new corpus

15 subjects, 8 male and 7 female, interacted with a remote Data Analysis Expert (DAE) who assists the subject in an exploratory data analysis task: analyze crime data from 2010-2014 to provide suggestions as to how to deploy police officers in four neighborhoods in Chicago. Each session consisted of multiple cycles of visualization construc-

---

[1] http://www.tableau.com/
[2] The corpus will be released at the end of the project.

[3] http://www.ibm.com/analytics/watson-analytics/

Proceedings of the SIGDIAL 2016 Conference, pages 304–309,
Los Angeles, USA, 13-15 September 2016. ©2016 Association for Computational Linguistics

DAE Communication Types	
1.	Greeting
2.	Clarification
3.	Correction
4.	Specified data not found
5.	Can do that
6.	Cannot do that
7.	Done

Table 1: DAE Communication Types

tion, interaction and interpretation, and lasted between 45 and 90 minutes.

Subjects were instructed to ask spoken questions directly to the DAE (they knew the DAE was human, but couldn't make direct contact[4]). Users viewed visualizations and limited communications from the DAE on a large, tiled-display wall. This environment allowed analysis across many different types of visualizations (heat maps, charts, line graphs) at once (see Figure 1).

Figure 1: A subject examining crime data.

The DAE viewed the subject through two high-resolution, direct video feeds, and also had a mirrored copy of the tiled-display wall on two 4K displays. The DAE generated responses to questions using Tableau, and used SAGE2 (Marrinan et al., 2014), a collaborative large-display middleware, to drive the display wall. The DAE could also communicate via a chat window, but confined herself to messages of the types specified in Table 1. Apart from greetings, and status messages (*sorry, it's taking long*) the DAE would occasionally ask for clarifications, e.g. *Did you ask for thefts or batteries*. Namely, the DAE never responded with a message, if the query could be directly visualized; neither did the DAE engage in multi-turn elicitations of the user requirements. Basically, the DAE tried to behave like a system with limited dialogue capabilities would.

Table 2 shows summary statistics for our data, that was transcribed in its entirety. So far, we

Words	Utterances	Directly Actionable Utts.
38,105	3,179	490

Table 2: Corpus size

have focused on the type of requests subjects pose. Since no appropriate coding scheme exists, we developed our own. Three coders identified the directly actionable utterances, namely, those utterances[5] which directly affect what the DAE is doing. This was achieved by leaving an utterance unlabelled or labeling it with one of 10 codes ($\kappa = 0.84$ (Cohen, 1960) on labeling an utterance or leaving it unlabeled; $\kappa = 0.74$ on the 10 codes). The ten codes derive from six different types of actionable utterances, which are further differentiated depending on the type of their argument. The six high-level labels are: requests to create new visualizations (8%, e.g. *Can I see number of crimes by day of the week?*), modifications to existing visualizations (45%, *Umm, yeah, I want to take a look closer to the metro right here, umm, a little bit eastward of Greektown*); window management instructions (12.5%, *If you want you can close these graphs as I won't be needing it anymore*); fact-based questions, whose answer doesn't necessarily require a visualization (7%, *During what time is the crime rate maximum, during the day or the night?*); requests for clarification (20.5%, *Okay, so is this statistics from all 5 years? Or is this for a particular year?*); expressing preferences (7%, *The first graph is a better way to visualize rather than these four separately*).

Three main themes have emerged from the analysis of the data. 1) Directly actionable requests cover only about 15% of what the subject is saying; the remaining 85% provides context that informs the requests (see Section 6). 2) Even the directly actionable 15% cannot be directly mapped to visualization specifications, but intermediate representations are needed. 3) An orthogonal dimension is to manage the visualizations that are generated and positioned on the screen.

So far, we have made progress on issues 2) and 3). The NL-to-visualization pipeline we describe next integrates state-of-the-art components to build a novel conversational interface. At the moment, the dialogue initiative is squarely with the user, since the system only executes the requests. However, strong foundations are in place

---

[4]In a strict Wizard-of-Oz experiment, the subjects would not have been aware that the DAE is human.

[5]What counts as an utterance was defined at transcription.

for it to become a full conversational system.

4 The NL-to-visualization pipeline

The pipeline in Figure 2 illustrates how Articulate 2 processes a spoken utterance, first by translating it into a logical form and then into a visualization specification to be processed by the Visualization Executor (VE). For create/modify visualization requests, an intermediate SQL query is also generated.

Before providing more details on the pipeline, Figure 3 presents one example comprising a sequence of four requests, which results in three visualizations. The user speaks the utterances to the system by using the Google Speech API. The first utterance asks for a heatmap of the "River North" and "Loop" neighborhoods (two downtown areas in Chicago). The system generates the visualization in the upper-left corner of the figure. In response to utterance b, Articulate 2 generates a new visualization, which is added to the first visualization (see bottom of screen in the middle); it is a line graph because the utterance requests the aggregate temporal attribute "year", as we discuss below. The third request is absent of aggregate temporal attributes, and hence the system produces a bar chart also added to the display. Finally, for the final request *d)*, the system closes the most recently generated visualization, i.e. the bar chart (this is not shown in Figure 3).

4.1 Parsing

We begin by parsing the utterance we obtain from the Google Speech API into three NLP structures. ClearNLP (Choi, 2014) is used to obtain PropBank (Palmer et al., 2005) semantic role labels (SRLs), which are then mapped to Verbnet (Kipper et al., 2008) and Wordnet using SemLink (Palmer, 2009). The Stanford Parser is used to obtain the remaining two structures, i.e. the syntactic parse tree and dependency tree. The final formulation is the conjunction $C_{predicate} \cap C_{agent} \cap C_{patient} \cap C_{det} \cap C_{mod} \cap C_{action}$. The first three clauses are extracted from the SRL. The NPs from the syntactic parse tree contain the determiners for C_{det}, adjectives for C_{mod}, and nouns as arguments for C_{action}.

4.2 Request Type Classification

A request is classified into the six actionable types mentioned earlier, for which we developed a mul-

Feature Type	Total Terms
Trigrams	3,203
Bigrams	2,311
Tagged Unigrams	784
Unigrams	584
Head word	314
Part-of-Speech	33
Chunks	15

Table 3: Feature Types

ticlass classifier. We applied popular question classification features from (Loni et al., 2011) due to the general question-based construct of the requests. Apache OpenNLP (Apache Software Foundation, 2011) was used to generate unigrams, bigrams, trigrams, chunking, and tagged unigrams, while Stanford Parser's implemented Collins rules (Collins, 2003) were used to obtain the headword. The feature vector is comprised of 7,244 total features, see Table 3. We used Weka (Hall et al., 2009) to experiment with several classifiers. We will discuss their performance in Sec. 5; currently, we use the SVM model, which performs the best.

4.3 Window Management Requests

If the classifier assigns to an utterance the window management type, a logical form along the lines described above will be generated, but no SQL query will be produced. At the moment, keyword extraction is used to determine whether the window management instruction relates to closing, opening, or repositioning; the system only supports closing the most recently created new visualization.

4.4 Create/Modify Visualization Requests

If the utterance is classified as a request to create or modify visualizations, the logical form is used to produce an SQL query. [6] SQL was partly chosen because the crime data we obtained from the City of Chicago is stored in a relational database.

Most often, in their requests users include constraints that can be conceptualized as standard *filter* and *aggregate* visualization operators. In utterance *c* in Figure 3, *assaults* can be considered as a filter, and *location* as an aggregator (*location* is meant as *office, restaurant*, etc.). We distinguish between filter and aggregate based on types stored in the KO, a small domain-dependent

---

[6]Since our system does not resolve referring expressions yet, currently all visualization requests result in a new visualization.

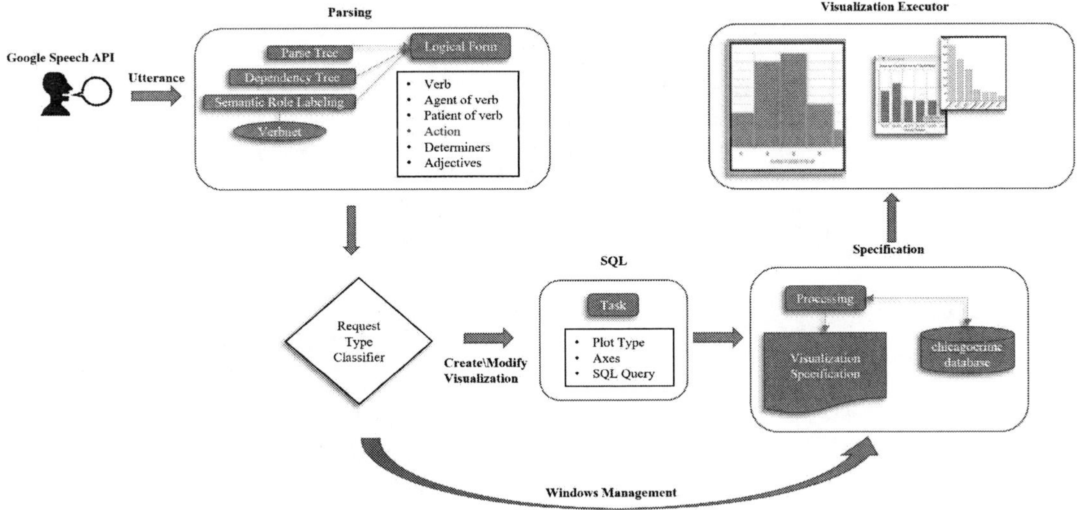

Figure 2: NL-to-Visualization Pipeline

knowledge ontology.[7] The KO contains relations, attributes, and attribute values. Filters such as "assault" are defined as attribute values in the KO, whereas aggregate objects such as "location" are attribute names. A synonym lexicon contains synonyms corresponding to each entry in the KO. SQL naturally supports these operators, since the data can be filtered using the "WHERE" clause and aggregated with the "GROUP BY" clause.

4.5 Vizualization Specification

The final transformation is from SQL to visualization specification. Overall, the specification for creating a new visualization includes the x-axis, y-axis, and plot type. Finally, the VE uses Vega (Trifacta, 2014) to plot a graphical representation of the visualization specification on SAGE2. We currently support 2-D bar charts, line graphs, and heat maps. The different representations for sentence *c)* from Figure 3 are shown here:

Logical Form: see.01(a) ∩ Action(a, Loop, assault, location) ∩ Det(a, the)

SQL: SELECT count(*) as TOTAL_CRIME, location FROM chicagocrime WHERE (neighborhood = loop) AND (crimetype = assault) GROUP BY location

Visualization Specification: {"horizontalAxis": "NON_UNIT", "horizontalGroupAxis": "location", "verticalAxis": "TOTAL_CRIME", "plotType": "BAR"}

---

[7]The system is re-configurable for different domains by updating the KO.

5 Evaluation

Since the work is in progress, a controlled user study cannot be carried out until all the components of the system are in place. We have conducted piecemeal smaller and/or informal evaluations of its components. For example, we have manually inspected the results of the pipeline on the 38 requests that concern creating new visualizations. The pipeline produces the correct SQL expression (that is, the actual SQL that a human would produce for a given request) for 31 (81.6%) of them (spoken features such as filled pauses and restarts were removed, but the requests are otherwise processed unaltered). The seven unsuccessful requests fail for various reasons, including: two are fact-based that cannot be answered yet; two require mathematical operations on the data which are not currently supported; one does not have a main verb, one does not name any attributes or values (*can I see the map* – in the future, our conversational interface will ask for clarification). For the last one, the SQL query is generated, but it is very complex and the system times out.

As concerns classifying the request type, Table 4 reports the results of the classifiers trained on the features discussed in Section 4.2. The SVM results are statistically significantly different from the Naive Bayes results (paired t-test), but indistinguishable from Random Forest or Multinomial Naive Bayes.

As concerns the whole pipeline, our prelimi-

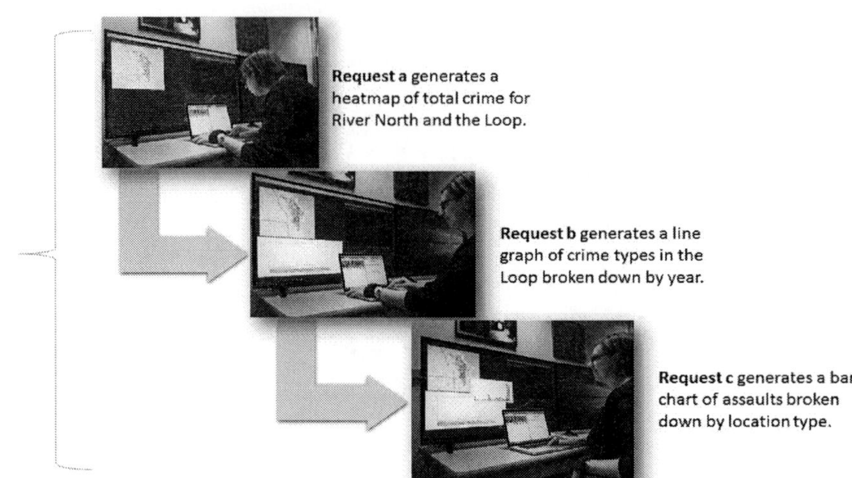

Figure 3: Incremental generation of visualizations

Classifier	Accuracy
Support Vector Machines	87.65%
Random Forest	85.60%
Multinomial Naive Bayes	85.60%
Naive Bayes	74.28%

Table 4: Request Type Classification Accuracy

nary, informal observation is that the generated visualization specifications result in accurate and appropriate visualizations. However, we have not dealt with constraints across visualizations: e.g., consistent application of colors by attribute (theft is always blue), would help users integrate information across visualizations.

6 Current Work

Annotation. We are focusing on referring expressions (see below), and on the taxonomy of abstract visualization tasks from (Brehmer and Munzner, 2013). This taxonomy, which includes *why* a task is performed, will help us analyze that 85% of the users utterances that are not directly actionable. In fact, many of those indicate the *why*, i.e. the user's goal (e.g., *"I want to identify the places with violent crimes."*).

Dialogue Manager / Referring Expressions. We are developing a Dialogue Manager (DM) and a Visualization Planner (VP) that will be in a continuous feedback loop. If the DM judges the query to be unambiguous, it will pass it to the VP. If not, the DM will generate a clarification request for the user. We will focus on referring expression resolution, necessary when the user asks for a modification to a previous visualization or wants to manipulate a particular visualization. In this domain, referring expressions can refer to graphical elements or to what those graphical elements represent (*color the short bar red* vs. *color the theft bar red*), which creates an additional dimension of coding, and an additional layer of ambiguity.

The Visualization Planner. The VP both needs to create more complex visualizations, and to manage the screen real estate when several visualizations are generated (which is the norm in our data collection, see Figure 1, and reflected in the system's output in Figure 3). The VP will determine the relationships between the visualizations on screen and make decisions about how to position them effectively. For instance, if a set of visualizations are part of a time series, they might be more effective if ordered on the display.

References

Apache Software Foundation. 2011. Apache OpenNLP. http://opennlp.apache.org.

Matthew Brehmer and Tamara Munzner. 2013. A multi-level typology of abstract visualization tasks. *IEEE Transactions on Visualization and Computer Graphics*, 19(12):2376–2385.

Jinho D. Choi. 2014. *Optimization of Natural Language Processing components for Robustness and Scalability*. Ph.D. thesis, University of Colorado Boulder.

Jacob Cohen. 1960. A coefficient of agreement for nominal scales. *Educational and Psychological Measurement*, 20:37–46.

Michael Collins. 2003. Head-driven statistical models for natural language parsing. *Computational Linguistics*, 29(4):589–637.

Kenneth Cox, Rebecca E Grinter, Stacie L Hibino, Lalita Jategaonkar Jagadeesan, and David Mantilla. 2001. A multi-modal natural language interface to an information visualization environment. *International Journal of Speech Technology*, 4(3-4):297–314.

Steven Feiner. 1985. APEX: an experiment in the automated creation of pictorial explanations. *IEEE Computer Graphics and Applications*, 5(11):29–37.

Tong Gao, Mira Dontcheva, Eytan Adar, Zhicheng Liu, and Karrie G. Karahalios. 2015. DataTone: Managing Ambiguity in Natural Language Interfaces for Data Visualization. In *Proceedings of the 28th Annual ACM Symposium on User Interface Software & Technology*, pages 489–500. ACM.

Lars Grammel, Melanie Tory, and Margaret Anne Storey. 2010. How information visualization novices construct visualizations. *IEEE Transactions on Visualization and Computer Graphics*, 16(6):943–952.

Nancy L. Green, Giuseppe Carenini, Stephan Kerpedjiev, Joe Mattis, Johanna D. Moore, and Steven F. Roth. 2004. Autobrief: an experimental system for the automatic generation of briefings in integrated text and information graphics. *Int. J. Hum.-Comput. Stud.*, 61(1):32–70.

Mark Hall, Eibe Frank, Geoffrey Holmes, Bernhard Pfahringer, Peter Reutemann, and Ian H. Witten. 2009. The WEKA data mining software: an update. *ACM SIGKDD Explorations Newsletter*, 11(1):10–18.

Jeffrey Heer, Frank Van Ham, Sheelagh Carpendale, Chris Weaver, and Petra Isenberg. 2008. Creation and collaboration: Engaging new audiences for information visualization. In *Information Visualization*, pages 92–133. Springer.

Karin Kipper, Anna Korhonen, Neville Ryant, and Martha Palmer. 2008. A large-scale classification of English verbs. *Language Resources and Evaluation*, 42(1):21–40.

Zhuo Li, Matthew Stagitis, Kathleen F. McCoy, and Sandra Carberry. 2013. Towards Finding Relevant Information Graphics: Identifying the Independent and Dependent Axis from User-Written Queries. In *Proceedings of the Twenty-Sixth International Florida Artificial Intelligence Research Society Conference (FLAIRS 13)*, pages 226–231.

Babak Loni, Gijs Van Tulder, Pascal Wiggers, David MJ Tax, and Marco Loog. 2011. Question classification by weighted combination of lexical, syntactic and semantic features. In *Text, Speech and Dialogue*, pages 243–250. Springer.

Jock D. Mackinlay, Pat Hanrahan, and Chris Stolte. 2007. Show me: Automatic presentation for visual analysis. *IEEE Transactions on Visualization and Computer Graphics*, 13(6):1137–1144.

Thomas Marrinan, Jillian Aurisano, Arthur Nishimoto, Krishna Bharadwaj, Victor Mateevitsi, Luc Renambot, Lance Long, Andrew Johnson, and Jason Leigh. 2014. Sage2: A new approach for data intensive collaboration using scalable resolution shared displays. In *Collaborative Computing: Networking, Applications and Worksharing (CollaborateCom)*, pages 177–186. IEEE.

Raveesh Meena, Gabriel Skantze, and Joakim Gustafson. 2014. Data-driven models for timing feedback responses in a Map Task dialogue system. *Computer Speech & Language*, 28(4):903–922.

Martha Palmer, Daniel Gildea, and Paul Kingsbury. 2005. The Proposition Bank: An Annotated Corpus of Semantic Roles. *Computational Linguistics*, 31(1):71–105, March.

Martha Palmer. 2009. Semlink: Linking PropBank, Verbnet and FrameNet. In *Proceedings of the Generative Lexicon Conference*, pages 9–15.

Norbert Reithinger, Dirk Fedeler, Ashwani Kumar, Christoph Lauer, Elsa Pecourt, and Laurent Romary. 2005. MIAMM - A Multimodal Dialogue System Using Haptics. In J. van Kuppevelt, L. Dybkjaer, and N. O. Bernsen, editors, *Advances in Natural Multimodal Dialogue Systems*, pages 307–332. Springer.

Steven F Roth, John Kolojejchick, Joe Mattis, and Jade Goldstein. 1994. Interactive graphic design using automatic presentation knowledge. In *Proceedings of the SIGCHI Conference on Human Factors in Computing Systems*, pages 112–117. ACM.

Yiwen Sun, Jason Leigh, Andrew Johnson, and Barbara Di Eugenio. 2013. Articulate: Creating Meaningful Visualizations from Natural Language. In Weidong Huang and Mao Lin Huang, editors, *Innovative Approaches of Data Visualization and Visual Analytics*, pages 218–235. IGI Global.

Trifacta. 2014. Vega: A Visualization Grammar. https://vega.github.io/vega/.

Fernanda B. Viegas, Martin Wattenberg, Frank Van Ham, Jesse Kriss, and Matt McKeon. 2007. ManyEyes: a Site for Visualization at Internet Scale. *IEEE Transactions on Visualization and Computer Graphics*, 13(6):1121–1128.

M.A. Walker, S.J. Whittaker, A. Stent, P. Maloor, J. Moore, M. Johnston, and G. Vasireddy. 2004. Generation and evaluation of user tailored responses in multimodal dialogue. *Cognitive Science*, 28(5):811–840.

Analyzing the Effect of Entrainment on Dialogue Acts

Masahiro Mizukami†, Koichiro Yoshino†, Graham Neubig†, David Traum‡, Satoshi Nakamura†
†Nara Institute of Science and Technology, Japan
‡USC Institute for Creative Technologies, USA
`masahiro-mi@is.naist.jp`

Abstract

Entrainment is a factor in dialogue that affects not only human-human but also human-machine interaction. While entrainment on the lexical level is well documented, less is known about how entrainment affects dialogue on a more abstract, structural level. In this paper, we investigate the effect of entrainment on dialogue acts and on lexical choice given dialogue acts, as well as how entrainment changes during a dialogue. We also define a novel measure of entrainment to measure these various types of entrainment. These results may serve as guidelines for dialogue systems that would like to entrain with users in a similar manner.

1 Introduction

Entrainment is a conversational phenomenon in which dialogue participants synchronize to each other with regards to various factors: lexical choice (Brennan and Clark, 1996), syntax (Reitter and Moore, 2007; Ward and Litman, 2007), style (Niederhoffer and Pennebaker, 2002; Danescu-Niculescu-Mizil et al., 2011), acoustic prosody (Natale, 1975; Coulston et al., 2002; Ward and Litman, 2007; Kawahara et al., 2015), pronunciation (Pardo, 2006) and turn taking (Campbell and Scherer, 2010; Beňuš et al., 2014). Previous works have reported that entrainment is correlated with dialogue success, naturalness and engagement.

However, there is much that is still unclear with regards to how entrainment affects the overall flow of the dialogue. For example, can entrainment also be observed in choice of dialog acts? Is entrainment on the lexical level more prevalent for utterances of particular dialogue acts? Does the level of entrainment increase as dialogue progresses?

If the answer to these questions is affirmative, it will be necessary to model entrainment not only on the lexical level, but also on the higher level of dialog flow. In addition, it will be necessary to adapt any entrainment features of dialogue systems to be sensitive to dialogue acts or dialogue progression. Modeling such entrainment phenomena appropriately has the potential to increase the naturalness of the conversation and open new avenues in human-machine interaction.

In this paper, we perform a study of entrainment in an attempt to answer these three questions. First, we observe the entrainment of dialogue acts, measuring whether the choice of dialogue acts synchronizes with that of the dialogue partner. For example, if one dialogue participant tends to ask questions frequently, we may hypothesize that the number of questions from the partner may also increase. Secondly, we examine lexical entrainment features given dialogue acts. It is known that dialogue acts strongly influence content of utterances, and we hypothesize that, in the same manner, dialogue acts may strongly influence the level of lexical entrainment. Finally, we examine the increase of entrainment as dialogue progresses. Previous work has discussed that entrainment can be observed throughout the whole dialogue, but it is unclear whether entrainment increases in latter parts of the dialogue. To measure this, we divide dialogues in half, and compare the entrainment of the former and latter halves.

Experimental results show that entrainment of dialogue acts does occur, indicating that it is necessary for models of dialogue to consider this fact. In addition, we find that the level of lexicon synchronization depends on dialogue acts. Finally, we confirm a tendency of entrainment increasing through the dialogue, indicating that dialogue systems may need to progressively adapt their models to the user as dialogue progresses.

Proceedings of the SIGDIAL 2016 Conference, pages 310–318,
Los Angeles, USA, 13-15 September 2016. ©2016 Association for Computational Linguistics

2 Related Works

2.1 Varieties of entrainment

As mentioned in the introduction, entrainment has been shown to occur at almost every level of human communication (Levitan, 2013), including both human-human and human-system conversation.

In human-human conversation, Kawahara et al. (2015) showed the synchrony of backchannels to the preceding utterances in attentive listening, and they investigated the relationship between morphological patterns of backchannels and the syntactic complexities of preceding utterances. Levitan et al. (2015) showed the entrainment of latency in turn taking.

In human-system conversation, Campbell and Scherer (2010) tried to predict user's turn taking behavior by considering entrainment. Fandrianto and Eskenazi (2012) modeled a dialogue strategy to increase the accuracy of speech recognition by using entrainment intentionally. Levitan (2013) unified these two works.

One of the most important questions about entrainment with respect to dialogue systems is its association with dialogue quality. Nenkova et al. (2008) proposed a score to evaluate the lexical entrainment in highly frequent words, and found that the score has high correlation with task success and engagement. This indicates that lexical entrainment has an important role in dialogue. In addition, it suggests that entrainment of lexical choice is probably affected by more detailed dialogue information, such as dialogue act.

2.2 Lexical Entrainment

The entrainment score which was proposed by Nenkova et al. (2008) is calculated by word counts in a corpus, and comparing between dialogue participants. Specifically, we calculate a uni-gram language model probability $P_{S_1}(w)$ and $P_{S_2}(w)$ based on the word frequencies of speakers S_1 and S_2, and calculate the entrainment score of word class V, $En(V)$ as:

$$En(V) = -\sum_{w \in V} |P_{S_1}(w) - P_{S_2}(w)|. \quad (1)$$

These entrainment scores have a range from -2 to 0, where higher means stronger entrainment. We calculate the average of these entrainment scores for the dialogue partner ($En_p(V)$) and non-partners ($En_{np}(V)$).

In detail, we can express this formula with word count $C_{S_1}(w)$ and $C_{S_2}(w)$, and all of words W as,

$$En(V) =$$
$$-\sum_{w \in V} \left| \frac{C_{S_1}(w)}{\sum_{w_i \in W} C_{S_1}(w_i)} - \frac{C_{S_2}(w)}{\sum_{w_i \in W} C_{S_2}(w_i)} \right|. \quad (2)$$

Nenkova et al. (2008) used following word classes as V.

25MFC: 25 Most frequent words in the corpus. The idea of using only frequent words is based on the fact that we would like to avoid the score being affected by the actual content of the utterance, and focus more on the way things are said. In addition, this filtering of highly frequent words removes any specific words (i.e. named entity, speaker's name) and words specific to the dialogue topic. This word class was highly and significantly correlated with task success in the previous work. We mainly used this word class in this paper.

25MFD: 25 Most frequent words in the dialogue. This word class was correlated with task success, like 25MFC.

ACW: Affirmative cue words (Gravano et al., 2012). This word class includes *alright, gotcha, huh, mm-hm, okay, right, uh-huh, yeah, yep, yes,* and *yup.* This class was correlated with turn-taking.

FP: Filled pauses. This word class includes *uh, um,* and *mm.* It was correlated with overlaps.

ACW and FP were pre-defined, but 25MFC and 25MFD are calculated from corpora considering frequency (V is a subset of W).

In order to use these measures to confirm whether entrainment is occurring between dialogue partners, these scores can be compared between the actual conversation partner, and an arbitrary other speaker from the database. If entrainment is actually occurring, then the score will be higher for the conversation partner than the score for the non-partner. Figure 1 shows an example of pairs used for calculation of these scores.

First, to confirm the results for previous work, we calculated the entrainment score of 25MFC using the Switchboard Corpus (Table 1). We can see that there is a difference of the entrainment score

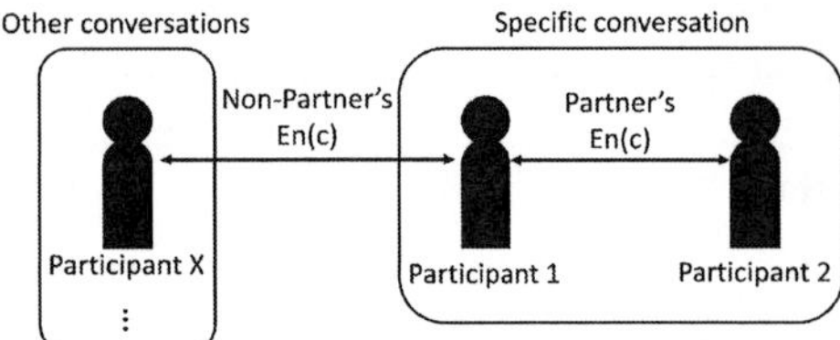

Figure 1: How to compare scores between the partner and non-partners

Table 1: The entrainment score of 25MFC

	Partner	Non-Partner
En(25MFC)	-0.211	-0.248

between "partner" who is talking the speaker and "non-partner" who is not talking with the speaker, as reported in previous work.

3 Extending the Entrainment Score

Our first contribution is an extension to the entrainment score that allows us to more accurately clarify the hypotheses that we stated in the introduction. This is necessary because the entrainment score given in Eqn. (2) does not consider the total size and variance of data to be calculated, and can be heavily influenced by data sparsity. This result in the score being biased when we compare target phenomena with different vocabulary sizes or data sizes.

For example, when considering the amount of entrainment that occurred for two different speakers, the entrainment score will tend to be higher for the more verbose speaker, regardless of the amount of entrainment that actually occurred. In addition, if we are comparing entrainment for two different sets of target phenomena, such as words and dialogue acts, the entrainment score will tend to be higher for the phenomenon that has a smaller vocabulary and thus less sparsity (in this case, dialogue acts). Thus, we propose a new "Entrainment Score Ratio" measurement that uses the rank in entrainment score, and language model smoothing to alleviate the effects of sparsity.

3.1 Entrainment Score Ratio

First, instead of using the entrainment score itself, we opt to use the relative position of the entrainment score of the partner compared to other non-partner speakers in the corpus. The entrainment score ratio is calculated according to the following procedure:

1. Calculate the entrainment score of the dialogue partner $\mathrm{En_p}(V)$. Also calculate entrainment scores of all non-partners in the corpus $\mathrm{En_{np_{1,\ldots,N}}}(V)$.

2. Compare the partner's entrainment score and all non-partners' entrainment scores.
$$\mathrm{Win}(\mathrm{En_p}(V), \mathrm{En_{np_i}}(V))$$
$$= \begin{cases} 1 & (\mathrm{En_p}(V) > \mathrm{En_{np_i}}(V)) \\ 0.5 & (\mathrm{En_p}(V) = \mathrm{En_{np_i}}(V)) \\ 0 & (\mathrm{En_p}(V) < \mathrm{En_{np_i}}(V)) \end{cases}$$

3. Calculate the ratio with which the partner's entrainment score exceeds that of the non-partners.
$$\mathrm{Ratio}(V)$$
$$= \frac{1}{|N|} \sum_{i \in N} \mathrm{Win}(\mathrm{En_p}(V), \mathrm{En_{np_i}}(V))$$

Because this score is the ratio that dialogue with the partner takes a higher entrainment score than other combinations with non-partners, it is not sensitive to the actual value of the entrainment score, but only the relative value compared to non-partners. This makes it more feasible to compare between phenomena with different vocabulary sizes, such as lexical choice and dialogue act choice. While the entrainment score for dialogue acts may be systematically higher due to its smaller vocabulary size, the relative score compared to non-partners can be expected to be approximately equal if the effect of entrainment is the same between the two classes.

3.2 Dirichlet Smoothing of Language Models

While the previous ratio score has the potential to alleviate problems due to comparing different types of phenomena, it does not help with problems caused by comparing data sets with different numbers of data points. The reason for this is that the traditional entrainment score (Nenkova et al., 2008) used uni-gram probabilities, the accuracy of which is dependent on the amount of data used to calculate the probabilities. Thus for smaller data sets, these probabilities are not well trained, and show a lower similarity when compared with those of other speakers in the corpus. In order to create a method more robust to these size differences, we introduce a method that smooths these probabilities to reduce differences between distributions of different data sizes.

Specifically, the definition of a unigram distribution of a portion of the corpus (split by speaker s, dialogue act d, part of dialogue p) using maximum likelihood estimation is,

$$P_{\text{ML},s}(w|d,p) = \frac{C_s(w_{d,p})}{\sum_{w_{d,p} \in W_{d,p}} C_s(w_{d,p})}. \quad (3)$$

When the size of data for speaker s is small, there will not be enough data to properly estimate this probability. To cope with this problem, we additively smooth the probabilities by introducing a smoothing factor α and large background language model $P_{\text{ML}}(w)$ which was trained using all of the available data:

$$P_{\text{DS},s}(w|d,p) = \frac{C_s(w_{d,p}) + \alpha P_{\text{ML}}(w)}{\sum_{w_{i,d,p} \in W_{d,p}} C_s(w_{i,d,p}) + \alpha}. \quad (4)$$

This additive smoothing is equivalent to introducing a Dirichlet distribution conditioned on $P_{\text{ML}}(w)$ as a prior probability for the small language model distribution of $P_{DS,s}(w|d,p)$ (MacKay and Peto, 1995). We choose Dirichlet smoothing because it is a simple but effective smoothing method. We determine the hyperparameter α by defining a Dirichlet process (Teh et al., 2012) prior, and maximizing the likelihood using Newton's method[1].

To verify that this method is effective, we calculated averages and variances of the standard entrainment score and the entrainment score using this proposed smoothing technique (Table 2). From the results, we can see that the entrainment score rate for partners is slightly higher with smoothing, demonstrating that the smoothed scores are as effective, or slightly more effective in identifying the actual conversational partner. In addition, the difference between variances of entrainment scores has decreased, showing that smoothing has reduced the amount of fluctuation in scores. This indicates that the smoothing works effectively to reduce the negative influence of population size when we compare distributions that have different population sizes. Because of this, for the analysis in the rest of the paper we use this smoothed entrainment score.

---

[1]The scripts for this and other calculations will be public at the link below:
`https://github.com/masahiro-mi/`
`entrainment`

4 Measured Entrainment Scores

In this section, we explain in detail the there varieties of entrainment that we examined.

4.1 Entrainment Score of Dialogue Acts

While entrainment of various phenomena has been reported in previous work, it is still not clear how entrainment affects the dialogue acts used by the conversation participants. The first thing we examine in this paper is the amount of entrainment occurring in dialogue acts, and the entrainment score of dialogue acts $\text{En}(D)$ is calculated according to the differences in distributions of dialogue acts between dialogue participants. Frequency of each dialogue act $P_{\text{DS},S_1}(d)$ and $P_{\text{DS},S_2}(d)$ of each speaker S_1, S_2 for a certain dialogue act d is used in the following equation:

$$\text{En}(D) = -\sum_{d \in D} |P_{\text{DS},S_1}(d) - P_{\text{DS},S_2}(d)|. \quad (5)$$

4.2 Lexical Entrainment Given Dialogue Acts

In the previous work, it is reported that there is an entrainment of lexical selection between dialogue participants. However, we can also hypothesize that such entrainment is more prominent for utterances with a particular dialogue act. For example, if one dialogue participant tends to say a specific backchannel frequently, the partner may change to use the same backchannel. On the other hand, when one dialogue participant has his/her own answer for a question, he/she will likely not borrow the words from the partner.

In order to examine this effect, we extended the entrainment score for lexical selection to evaluate an entrainment of lexical selection given the dialogue act of the utterance. The extended entrainment score $\text{En}(c|d)$, the score for a lexical selection given a dialogue act, is defined by using conditional language model probabilities $P_{\text{DS},S_1}(w|d)$ and $P_{\text{DS},S_2}(w|d)$ of each speaker S_1 and S_2. Specifically, we define it as follows:

$$\text{En}(V|d) = -\sum_{w \in V} |P_{\text{DS},S_1}(w|d) - P_{\text{DS},S_2}(w|d)|. \quad (6)$$

Using this measure, we clarify whether entrainment of lexicons has been affected by dialogue acts, and also which dialogue acts are more likely to be conducive to entrainment.

Table 2: The entrainment score variance with/without smoothing

	Ratio(V)	Partner		Non-Partner	
		Ave.	Var.	Ave.	Var.
w/o smoothing	0.671	-0.211	0.00537	-0.248	0.00181
w/ smoothing	0.706	-0.0983	0.00108	-0.123	0.000778

4.3 Increase of Entrainment through Dialogue

Nenkova et al. (2008) noted that the entrainment score between dialogue partners is higher than the entrainment score between non-partners in dialogue. While they reported the overall trend of the entrainment score throughout the dialogue, whether the level of entrainment changes throughout the dialog is also an important question, as it will indicate how dialogue systems must display entrainment properties to build a closer relationship with their dialogue partners. If entrainment is changing through a conversation, we can hypothesize that the entrainment score will be larger at the end of dialogue than the score at the start of dialogue.

We analyzed the extent of change in entrainment by splitting one dialogue into earlier and later parts. We calculated the entrainment score between dialogue participants in earlier/later parts of dialogue, and compared these scores.

5 Corpus

As our experimental data, we used the Switchboard Dialogue Act Corpus, which is annotated with dialogue acts according to the DAMSL standard (Discourse Annotation and Markup System of Labeling) (Jurafsky et al., 1997) for each utterance. The DAMSL has 42 types of dialogue act tags, while there were 220 tags used in the original Switchboard Corpus, Jurafsky et al. (1997) clustered the 220 tags into 42 rough-arained scale classes, and reported labeling accuracy of .80 according to the pairwise Kappa statistic.

This corpus consists of 302 male and 241 female speakers. The number of conversations is 1,155, and the number of utterances is 221,616. Each speaker is tagged with properties of sex, age, and education level.

Table 3: The entrainment score of dialogue acts

	Partner	Non-Partner	Ratio
DA	**-0.568****	-0.715	0.675

$* p < 0.10, ** p < 0.05$

6 Experimental Results

6.1 Entrainment of Dialogue Acts

First, we analyze the entrainment of dialogue acts based on the method of Section 4.1. We hypothesize that we can observe the entrainment of dialogue acts like other previously observed factors. To examine this hypothesis, we calculated the entrainment score of dialogue acts and compared between partner and non-partners. To measure the significance of these results, we calculated p-value of entrainment scores between partner and non-partner with the t-test.

Table 3 shows that there is a significant difference ($p < 0.05$) of entrainment score between partner and non-partner, with partners scoring significantly higher than non-partners. This result shows that the entrainment of dialogue acts can be observed in human-human conversation, and suggests that there may be a necessity to consider entrainment of dialogue act selection in human-machine interaction.

6.2 Lexical Entrainment given Dialogue Acts

Next, we analyze the entrainment of lexical choice given the 42 types of dialogue acts based on the method of Section 4.2. We can assume that the dialogue act affects the entrainment of lexicons, which indicates that entrainment scores are different depending on the type of the given dialogue act.

In addition, we calculate entrainment score rate and Cohen's d (Cohen, 1988) to evaluate the effect size. Cohen's d is standardized mean difference between two groups, and can calculate the amount that a particular factor effects a value while considering each group's variance. If these groups have a large difference, Cohen's d will be larger, with values less than 0.2 being considered small, values around 0.5 being medium, and values larger than 0.8 being considered large.

We show the result in Table 4, and emphasize scores that are over 0.5 in Cohen's d, and over 0.55 in Ratio(V).

We can first notice an increase of the entrainment score is more prominent given some dialogue acts. Entrainment is particularly prevalent for acts that have little actual informational content, such as greeting, backchannel, agree, answer, and repeating.

In addition, we focus on why Conventional Opening and Conventional Closing were increased in the entrainment score. This is because that Conventional Opening and Conventional Closing contain greetings ("hi", "hello") or farewells ("bye", "see you"), which show higher entrainment scores than other dialogue acts. It should be noted that this phenomenon of performing a fixed response to a particular utterance is also often called "coordination", and distinguished from entrainment. However, it is difficult to distinguish between entrainment and coordination definitely with our current measures, and devising measures to capture this distinction is future work.

On other hand, dialogue acts that express one's opinion such as Apology, Action-directive, Negative non-no answers, as well as some questions do not increase entrainment scores.

6.3 Change in Entrainment through Dialogue

In addition, we analyzed the increase of entrainment based on the method of Section 4.3. We calculated lexical entrainment scores of the earlier and later parts. "Earlier" is the entrainment score between utterances in the earlier part of dialogue, and "Later" is the entrainment score between utterances in the later part. We hypothesize that "Later" will have a higher entrainment score than "Earlier," as it is possible that dialogue participants will demonstrate more entrainment as they talk for longer and grow more comfortable with each other.

In addition, we calculate "Cross," the entrainment score between the earlier and the later parts of dialogue. We calculated this because we can also hypothesize that the effect of entrainment is delayed, and words spoken in the earlier part of the conversation may appear in the later part of the partner's utterances. Figure 2 shows the pairs used for the calculation. We show the result in Table 5.

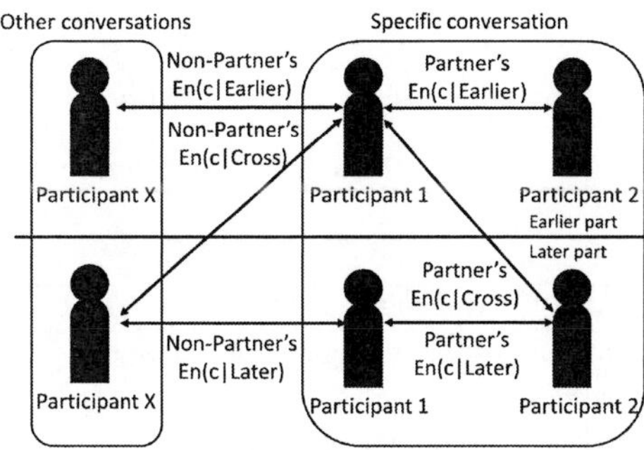

Figure 2: How we compare between earlier and later parts

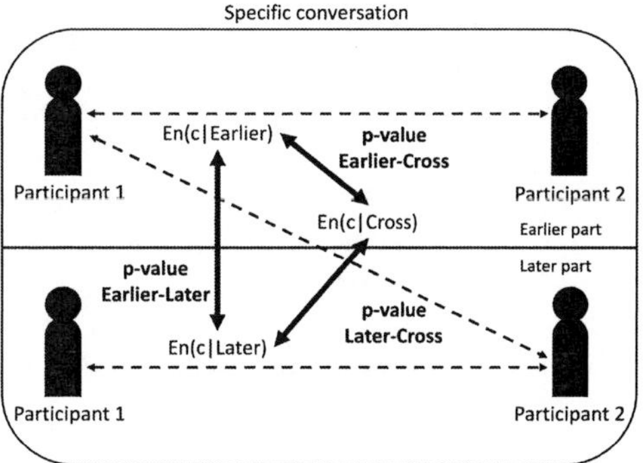

Figure 3: How to calculate p-values between each part in partner

From these results, we can see that there is a significant difference of entrainment score between partner and non-partner in all of the parts. This indicates that lexical entrainment can already be observed in the earlier part of dialogue.

In addition, we calculated p-values with the two-sided t test for partner entrainment scores between each part. Figure 2 shows an example of pairs used for calculation of p-values. We compare partner's entrainment scores between early, later, and cross, to indicate how the entrainment score changes in the partner through the dialogue. In fact, we compare three combinations of partner's entrainment scores, such as En(c|Earlier) and En(c|Later), En(c|Earlier) and En(c|Cross), and En(c|Later) and En(c|Cross). Table 6 shows that p-values of entrainment scores between each part in the partner. We find that the value of the entrainment score of the later part increased slightly over the entrainment score of the earlier part, but the increase was not significant. These results show that if there is a difference in entrainment between

Table 4: The entrainment score of lexicons given a dialogue act

		Partner $\mathrm{En_p}(V)$	Non-Partner $\mathrm{En_{np}}(V)$	Cohen's d	Ratio(V)
25MFC	Conventional-closing	**-0.0391****	-0.185	**1.50**	**0.703**
25MFC	Acknowledge (Backchannel)	**-0.201****	-0.252	**0.527**	**0.659**
25MFC	Statement-non-opinion	**-0.0930****	-0.113	0.434	**0.672**
25MFC	Statement-opinion	**-0.154****	-0.192	0.418	**0.634**
25MFC	Conventional-opening	**-0.0112****	-0.0370	0.406	0.542
25MFC	Segment (multi-utterance)	**-0.203****	-0.232	0.382	**0.618**
25MFC	Agree/Accept	**-0.279****	-0.325	0.367	**0.592**
25MFC	Appreciation	**-0.282****	-0.331	0.322	**0.564**
25MFC	Yes answers	**-0.320****	-0.375	0.274	**0.555**
25MFC	Non-verbal	**-0.104****	-0.124	0.259	**0.557**
25MFC	Abandoned or Turn-Exit, Uninterpretable	**-0.203****	-0.228	0.244	**0.592**
25MFC	Hedge	**-0.170****	-0.191	0.132	0.532
25MFC	Wh-Question	**-0.147****	-0.160	0.122	0.530
25MFC	Backchannel in question form	**-0.134****	-0.152	0.118	0.528
25MFC	No answers	**-0.199****	-0.220	0.118	0.523
25MFC	Rhetorical-Questions	**-0.0644****	-0.0754	0.102	0.522
25MFC	Response Acknowledgement	**-0.207****	-0.227	0.100	0.521
25MFC	Repeat-phrase	**-0.115****	-0.128	0.0962	0.522
25MFC	Other	-0.160	**-0.150****	0.0772	0.476
25MFC	Quotation	**-0.0817****	-0.0905	0.0749	0.517
25MFC	Collaborative Completion	**-0.0867****	-0.0929	0.0616	0.514
25MFC	Yes-No-Question	**-0.223***	-0.227	0.0490	0.512
25MFC	Hold before answer/agreement	**-0.104****	-0.112	0.0488	0.511
25MFC	Summarize/reformulate	**-0.109****	-0.114	0.0380	0.512
25MFC	Signal-non-understanding	**-0.0377****	-0.0404	0.0377	0.507
25MFC	Declarative Yes-No-Question	-0.134*	-0.138	0.0348	0.512
25MFC	Other answers	-0.0584*	-0.0620	0.0313	0.507
25MFC	Maybe/Accept-part	-0.0204	-0.0221	0.0247	0.503
25MFC	Self-talk	-0.0189	-0.0205	0.0235	0.503
25MFC	Thanking	-0.0180	-0.0195	0.0227	0.502
25MFC	Reject	-0.0670	-0.0696	0.0209	0.504
25MFC	Negative non-no answers	-0.0600	-0.0581	0.0181	0.497
25MFC	Open-Question	-0.0877	-0.0894	0.0166	0.504
25MFC	Affirmative non-yes answers	-0.134	-0.136	0.0161	0.504
25MFC	Downplayer	-0.0238	-0.0247	0.0111	0.501
25MFC	Declarative Wh-Question	-0.0147	-0.0152	0.00797	0.501
25MFC	Action-directive	-0.0935	-0.0944	0.00748	0.502
25MFC	Dispreferred answers	-0.0514	-0.0522	0.00716	0.502
25MFC	Apology	-0.0183	-0.0179	0.00667	0.500
25MFC	3rd-party-talk	-0.00969	-0.00955	0.00369	0.500
25MFC	Offers, Options Commits	-0.0204	-0.0205	0.00222	0.500
25MFC	Or-Clause	-0.0502	-0.0502	0.000816	0.500

N(Number of target speaker) = 2310, $* p < 0.10$, $** p < 0.05$

Table 5: The entrainment score for combinations of part

	Partner	Non-Partner	Rate
En(25MFC|Earlier)	**-0.106****	-0.126	0.658
En(25MFC|Cross)	**-0.106****	-0.127	0.666
En(25MFC|Later)	**-0.104****	-0.126	0.674

$* \; p < 0.10, \; ** \; p < 0.05$

Table 6: The p-values for partner's entrainment score between each part

		p-value
En(25MFC|Earlier)	En(25MFC|Later)	0.222
En(25MFC|Earlier)	En(25MFC|Cross)	0.238
En(25MFC|Later)	En(25MFC|Cross)	0.00425

earlier and later parts of the conversation, the difference is slight.

7 Conclusion

In this paper, we focused on the entrainment with respect to dialogue acts and dialogue progression, and analyzed for three phenomena: the entrainment of dialogue acts, the entrainment of lexical choice given dialogue acts, and the change in entrainment as dialogue progresses.

From the results, we found that the entrainment of dialogue acts was observed in conversation. Within dialogue systems, this has the potential to contribute to modelling of dialogue strategy, and potentially allow the system to have a closer relationship with the partner.

We also found that lexical entrainment has a different tendency depending on the dialogue act of the utterance. This has the potential to contribute to models of language generation, which can consider entrainment of each dialogue act.

Finally, we analyzed the differences of entrainment depending on the part of the dialogue. From results, we found that there is either only a slight effect, or no effect of the part of the dialogue under consideration.

In future works, we will try an analysis of the entrainment in dialogue that considers the effect of coordination.

Acknowledgement

This work is supported by JST CREST.

References

Štefan Beňuš, Agustín Gravano, Rivka Levitan, Sarah Ita Levitan, Laura Willson, and Julia Hirschberg. 2014. Entrainment, dominance and alliance in supreme court hearings. *Knowledge-Based Systems*, 71:3–14.

Susan E Brennan and Herbert H Clark. 1996. Conceptual pacts and lexical choice in conversation. *Journal of Experimental Psychology: Learning, Memory, and Cognition*, 22(6):1482.

Nick Campbell and Stefan Scherer. 2010. Comparing measures of synchrony and alignment in dialogue speech timing with respect to turn-taking activity. In *INTERSPEECH*, pages 2546–2549.

Jacob Cohen. 1988. Statistical power analysis for the behavioral sciences. 2nd edn. hillsdale, new jersey: L.

Rachel Coulston, Sharon Oviatt, and Courtney Darves. 2002. Amplitude convergence in children's conversational speech with animated personas. In *Proc. ICSLP*, volume 4, pages 2689–2692.

Cristian Danescu-Niculescu-Mizil, Michael Gamon, and Susan Dumais. 2011. Mark my words!: linguistic style accommodation in social media. In *Proceedings of the 20th international conference on World wide web*, pages 745–754. ACM.

Andrew Fandrianto and Maxine Eskenazi. 2012. Prosodic entrainment in an information-driven dialog system. In *INTERSPEECH*, pages 342–345.

Agustín Gravano, Julia Hirschberg, and Štefan Beňuš. 2012. Affirmative cue words in task-oriented dialogue. *COLING*, 38(1):1–39.

Dan Jurafsky, Elizabeth Shriberg, and Debra Biasca. 1997. Switchboard swbd-damsl shallow-discourse-function annotation coders manual. *Institute of Cognitive Science Technical Report*, pages 97–102.

Tatsuya Kawahara, Takashi Yamaguchi, Miki Uesato, Koichiro Yoshino, and Katsuya Takanashi. 2015. Synchrony in prosodic and linguistic features between backchannels and preceding utterances in attentive listening. In *APSIPA*, pages 392–395. IEEE.

Rivka Levitan, Stefan Benus, Agustın Gravano, and Julia Hirschberg. 2015. Entrainment and turn-taking in human-human dialogue. In *AAAI Spring Symposium on Turn-Taking and Coordination in Human-Machine Interaction*.

Rivka Levitan. 2013. Entrainment in spoken dialogue systems: Adopting, predicting and influencing user behavior. In *HLT-NAACL*, pages 84–90.

David JC MacKay and Linda C Bauman Peto. 1995. A hierarchical dirichlet language model. *Natural language engineering*, 1(03):289–308.

Michael Natale. 1975. Convergence of mean vocal intensity in dyadic communication as a function of social desirability. *Journal of Personality and Social Psychology*, 32(5):790.

Ani Nenkova, Agustín Gravano, and Julia Hirschberg. 2008. High frequency word entrainment in spoken dialogue. In *Proc. ACL*, pages 169–172. Association for Computational Linguistics.

Kate G Niederhoffer and James W Pennebaker. 2002. Linguistic style matching in social interaction. *Journal of Language and Social Psychology*, 21(4):337–360.

Jennifer S Pardo. 2006. On phonetic convergence during conversational interaction. *The Journal of the Acoustical Society of America*, 119(4):2382–2393.

David Reitter and Johanna D Moore. 2007. Predicting success in dialogue. In *Proc. ACL*.

Yee Whye Teh, Michael I Jordan, Matthew J Beal, and David M Blei. 2012. Hierarchical dirichlet processes. *Journal of the american statistical association*.

Arthur Ward and Diane Litman. 2007. Measuring convergence and priming in tutorial dialog. In *University of Pittsburgh*.

Towards an Entertaining Natural Language Generation System: Linguistic Peculiarities of Japanese Fictional Characters

Chiaki Miyazaki[*] **Toru Hirano**[†] **Ryuichiro Higashinaka** **Yoshihiro Matsuo**
NTT Media Intelligence Laboratories, Nippon Telegraph and Telephone Corporation
1-1 Hikarinooka, Yokosuka, Kanagawa, Japan
{miyazaki.chiaki, hirano.tohru, higashinaka.ryuichiro,
matsuo.yoshihiro}@lab.ntt.co.jp

Abstract

One of the key ways of making dialogue agents more attractive as conversation partners is characterization, as it makes the agents more friendly, human-like, and entertaining. To build such characters, utterances suitable for the characters are usually manually prepared. However, it is expensive to do this for a large number of utterances. To reduce this cost, we are developing a natural language generator that can express the linguistic styles of particular characters. To this end, we analyze the linguistic peculiarities of Japanese fictional characters (such as those in cartoons or comics and mascots), which have strong characteristics. The contributions of this study are that we (i) present comprehensive categories of linguistic peculiarities of Japanese fictional characters that cover around 90% of such characters' linguistic peculiarities and (ii) reveal the impact of each category on characterizing dialogue system utterances.

1 Introduction

One of the key ways of making dialogue agents more attractive as conversation partners is characterization, as it makes the agents more friendly, human-like, and entertaining. Especially in Japan, fictional characters (such as those in cartoons or comics and mascots) are very popular. Therefore, vividly characterized dialogue agents are strongly desired by customers.

To characterize agents, utterances suitable for them are usually manually prepared. However, it

---

[*]Presently, the author is with NTT Communications Corporation.

[†]Presently, the author is with Nippon Telegraph and Telephone East Corporation.

is expensive to do this for a large number of utterances. To reduce this cost, we have previously proposed a couple of methods for automatically converting functional expressions into those that are suitable for given personal attributes such as gender, age, and area of residence (Miyazaki et al., 2015) and closeness with a conversation partner (Miyazaki et al., 2016). However, when it comes to expressing the linguistic styles of individual fictional characters whose characteristics should be vividly expressed, these methods, which can convert only function words, i.e., which cannot convert content words such as nouns, adjectives, and verbs, do not have sufficient expressive power. As the first step in developing a natural language generator that can express the linguistic styles of fictional characters, in this work, we analyze the linguistic peculiarities of fictional characters such as those in cartoons or comics and mascots, which have strong characteristics.

The contributions of this study are that we (i) present comprehensive categories of the linguistic peculiarities of Japanese fictional characters that cover around 90% of the fictional characters' linguistic peculiarities and (ii) reveal the impact of each category on characterizing dialogue system utterances.

Note that although we use the term 'utterance', this study does not involve acoustic speech signals. We use this term to refer to a certain meaningful fragment of colloquial written language.

2 Related work

In the field of text-to-speech systems, there have been various studies on voice conversion that modifies a speaker's individuality (Yun and Ladner, 2013). However, in the field of text generation, there are not so many studies related to the characterization of dialogue agent utterances.

Proceedings of the SIGDIAL 2016 Conference, pages 319–328,
Los Angeles, USA, 13-15 September 2016. ©2016 Association for Computational Linguistics

In the field of text generation, there is a method that transforms individual characteristics in dialogue agent utterances using a method based on statistical machine translation (Mizukami et al., 2015). Other methods convert functional expressions into those that are suitable for a speaker's gender, age, and area of residence (Miyazaki et al., 2015) and closeness with a conversation partner (Miyazaki et al., 2016). However, these methods handle only function words or have difficulty in altering other expressions. In this respect, we consider these methods to be insufficient to express a particular character's linguistic style, especially when focusing on fictional characters whose individualities should be vividly expressed.

There have also been several studies on natural language generation that can adapt to speakers' personalities. In particular, a language generator called PERSONAGE that can control parameters related to speakers' Big Five personalities (Mairesse and Walker, 2007) has been proposed. There is also a method for automatically adjusting the language generation parameters of PERSONAGE by using movie scripts (Walker et al., 2011) and a method for automatically adjusting the parameters so that they suit the characters or stories of role playing games (Reed et al., 2011). However, although there is some aspect of linguistic style that is essential to expressing a particular character's style, PERSONAGE does not have any existing parameter that can manifest that linguistic reflex (Walker et al., 2011).

In the present work, we focus on the languages of fictional characters such as those in cartoons or comics and mascots. By analyzing the languages of such characters, we reveal what kind of linguistic peculiarities are needed to express a particular character's linguistic style.

3 Categories of linguistic peculiarities of fictional characters

After consulting linguistic literature and the Twitter postings of 19 fictional character bots, we have identified 13 categories of linguistic peculiarities by which the linguistic styles of most Japanese fictional characters can be characterized. The 13 categories, listed in Table 1, are made from the perspective of lexical choice, modality, syntax, phonology and pronunciation, surface options, or extra expressions just for characterization. In the rest of this section, each category of linguistic pe-

Major category		Minor category
Lexical choice	P1	personal pronouns
	P2	dialectical or distinctive wordings
Modality	P3	honorifics
	P4	sentence-end expressions (auxiliary verbs and interactional particles)
Syntax	P5	syntactic complexity
Phonology and pronunciation	P6	relaxed pronunciation
	P7	disfluency (stammer)
	P8	arbitrary phoneme replacements
Surface options	P9	word segmentation
	P10	letter type
	P11	symbols
Extras	P12	character interjections
	P13	character sentence-end particles

Table 1: Categories of linguistic peculiarities of Japanese fictional characters.

culiarities is explained in detail.

3.1 Lexical choice

We consider that lexical choice, which refers to choosing words to represent intended meanings, reflects the supposed speakers' gender, region-specific characteristics, personality, and so on. In terms of lexical choice, we utilize the following two categories.

P1: Personal pronouns

It is said that personal pronouns are one of the most important components of Japanese role language, which is character language based on social and cultural stereotypes (Kinsui, 2003). Japanese has "multiple self-referencing terms such as *watashi* 'I,' *watakushi* 'I-polite,' *boku* 'I-male self-reference,' *ore* 'I-blunt male self-reference,' and so on" (Maynard, 1997). Accordingly, if a character uses *ore* in his utterance, its reader can easily tell the character is male, the utterance is probably uttered in a casual (less formal) situation, and his personality might be rather blunt and rough. As well as the first person pronoun, there are various terms for referencing second person.

P2: Dialectical or distinctive wordings

We assume that using dialectical wordings in characters' utterances not only reinforces the region-specific characteristics of the characters but also makes the characters more friendly and less formal. It is also said that "regional dialect is a significant factor in judging personality from voice" (Markel et al., 1967).

In addition to dialects, the languages of Japanese fictional characters often involve character-specific coined words. The words are, so to speak, 'character dialect.' For example, for the character of a bear (*kuma* in Japanese), we observed that the word *ohakuma* is used instead of *ohayoo* 'good morning.'

3.2 Modality

We consider that modality, which refers to a speaker's attitude toward a proposition, reflects the supposed speakers' friendliness or closeness to their listeners, personality, and so on. As for modality, we have the following two categories.

P3: Honorifics

We consider that honorifics have a significant effect on describing speakers' friendliness or closeness to their listeners and on the speakers' social status. Depending on the social, psychological, and emotional closeness between a speaker and a listener, and whether the situation is formal or casual, Japanese has five main choices of honorific verb forms: plain-informal (*kuru* 'come'), plain-formal (*kimasu* 'come'), respectful-informal (*irassharu* 'come'), respectful-formal (*irasshaimasu* 'come'), and humble-formal (*mairimasu*) (Maynard, 1997).

Although English does not have such honorific verb forms, it does have linguistic variations corresponding to the honorifics; for example, it is said that "Americans use a variety of expressions to convey different degrees of formality, politeness, and candor" (Maynard, 1997).

P4: Sentence-end expressions

Sentence-end expressions are a key component of Japanese character language, as are personal pronouns (Kinsui, 2003). For example, there are sentence-end expressions that are dominantly used by female characters. We also consider that sentence-end expressions are closely related to speakers' personalities, since the expressions contain elements that convey speakers' attitudes.

We define a sentence-end expression as a sequence of function words that occurs at the end of a sentence. Japanese sentence-end expressions contain *interactional particles* (Maynard, 1997), which express speaker judgment and attitude toward the message and the listener. For example, *ne* (an English counterpart would be 'isn't it?') occurs at the end of utterances. In addition, Japanese sentence-end expressions contain auxiliary verbs (e.g., *mitai* 'like' and *souda* 'it seems'), which express speaker attitudes.

Some of the expressions that fall into this category have their counterparts in the parameters of PERSONAGE (Mairesse and Walker, 2007). In particular, interactional particles such as *ne* might be able to be controlled by the TAG QUESTION INSERTION parameter, and auxiliary verbs such as *mitai* and *souda* might be able to be controlled by the DOWNTONER HEDGES parameter.

3.3 Syntax

We consider that syntax, which refers to sentence structures, reflects the supposed speakers' personality and maturity. With regard to syntax, we have just one category.

P5: Syntactic complexity

Syntactic complexity is considered to be reflective of introverts, and it is also handled in PERSONAGE (Mairesse and Walker, 2007). In addition, we assume that syntactic complexity reflects the maturity of the supposed speakers. For example, the utterances of a character that is supposed to be a child would include more simple sentences than complex ones.

3.4 Phonology and pronunciation

We consider that phonology and pronunciation reflects the supposed speakers' age, gender, personality, and so on. As for phonology and pronunciation, we have three categories. What we want to handle are pronunciations reflected in written expressions.

P6: Relaxed pronunciations

Both English and Japanese have relaxed pronunciations, that is, pronunciation variants that are not normative and are usually easier and effortless ways of pronunciation. These relaxed pronunciations can often be observed as spelling variants. For example, in English, 'ya,' 'kinda', and 'hafta' can be used instead of 'you,' 'kind of', and 'have to', respectively. In Japanese, vowel alternation often occurs in adjectives; for example, alteration from *ai* to *ee*, as in *itai* to *itee* 'painful'. According to our observation, relaxed pronunciations are seen more often in the utterances of youngsters than older people and more often in males than females. We consider that relaxed pronunciations lend a blunt and rough impression to characters' utterances.

P7: Disfluency

In the utterances of some fictional characters, word fragments are often used for representing disfluent language production by the supposed speakers. For example, *ha, hai* 'Yes' and *bo, boku-wa ga, gakusei-desu* 'I am a student,' which are probably done for adding hesitant characteristics to the characters. It is also said that "including disfluencies in speech leads to lower perceived conscientiousness and openness" (Wester et al., 2015).

P8: Arbitrary phoneme replacements

In addition to relaxed pronunciation, it is often observed that arbitrary phonemes are replaced by other arbitrary phonemes, especially in character languages. For example, every consonant 'n' can be replaced by 'ny' (e.g., *nyaze nyakunyo* instead of *naze nakuno* 'Why do you cry?'). This phenomenon does not occur in actual human's utterances unless the speaker is kidding. We consider that arbitrary phoneme replacements are utilized to give a funny impression to characters' utterances and to differentiate the linguistic styles of characters.

3.5 Surface options

Since we are handling written utterances, there are some options of how an utterance is presented as a sequence of letters and symbols. We consider that surface options are utilized as an easy way of characterizing utterances and differentiating the linguistic styles of characters.

P9: Word segmentation

In normative Japanese texts, unlike English texts, words are not segmented by spaces—rather, they are written adjacently to each other. However, in characters' utterances, it is sometimes observed that words or phrases are segmented by spaces or commas. When Japanese texts are read aloud, spaces and commas are often acknowledged with slight pauses, so we think that inserting extra spaces or commas between words has the effect of giving a slow and faltering impression to the characters' utterances.

P10: Letter type

In the Japanese writing system, there are three types of letters—logographic kanji (adopted Chinese characters), syllabic hiragana, and syllabic katakana—and a combination of these three types is typically used in a sentence. Those who know a lot of rare kanji letters are often regarded as being well educated. In contrast, using too many syllabic hiragana letters in a text gives the text a very childish impression.

P11: Symbols

Symbols such as exclamation marks and emoticons are often used in Japanese texts, in the same manner as in English. We assume that symbols are commonly used as an easy way of expressing speakers' emotional states.

3.6 Extras

There are extra expressions that contribute to neither propositional meaning nor communicative function but still strongly contribute to characterization. We prepare the following two categories for such expressions.

P12: Character interjections

Some of the extra expressions occur independently or isolated from other words, as interjections do. We call such expressions 'character interjections' in this study. Onomatopoeias, which describe supposed speakers' characteristics, are often used as such expressions. For example, for the character of a sheep, *mofumofu* 'soft and fluffy' is used as a character interjection.

P13: Character sentence-end particles

There are expressions called *kyara-joshi* 'character particles' (Sadanobu, 2015), which typically occur at the end of sentences. The difference between character interjections and character particles is mainly their occurrence position. According to our observation, the word forms of the character particles are something like shortened versions of character interjections, which are often within two or three moras (e.g., *mofu* as for the character of a sheep).

4 Eval 1: Coverage of categories of linguistic peculiarities

We conducted an evaluation to assess how well our categories account for the linguistic peculiarities of Japanese fictional characters. The evaluation process is shown in Figure 1. First, we (1) collected characters' utterances. Then, we (2) annotated linguistic expressions that are peculiar to the characters, and finally, we (3) counted how

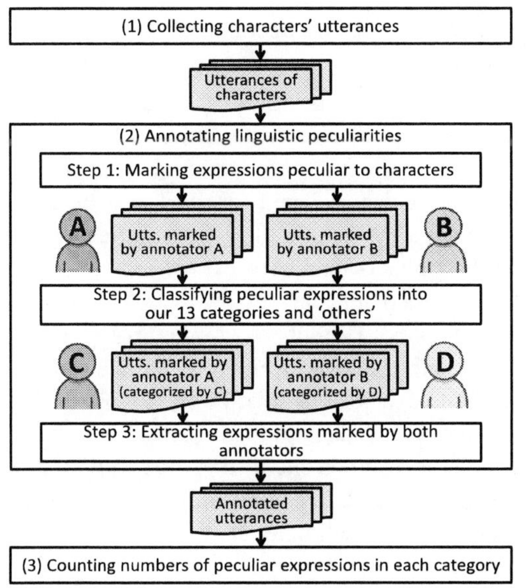

Figure 1: Process of the evaluation to assess how well our categories account for the linguistic peculiarities of Japanese fictional characters.

many expressions fall into each of our categories and how many do not fit into any category.

4.1 Collecting characters' utterances

As utterances of fictional characters, we collected the following two kinds of text.

Twitter postings We collected Twitter postings of character bots. We chose bots that are authorized by their copyright holders, as we assume these are characterized by professional writers.

Dialogue system utterances We utilize dialogue system utterances that are written by professional writers we hired. The writers are asked to create utterances that are highly probable for given characters to utter as responses to given questions. Contents and linguistic expressions of the utterances are carefully characterized by the writers in accordance with pre-defined character profiles that we created.

The characters we chose (C1–20) are shown in Table 2. These 20 characters are balanced with respect to humanity (human/non-human), animateness (animate/inanimate), gender (male/female/neuter), and maturity (adult/child or adolescent) so that we can find general and exhaustive linguistic peculiarities of various characters.

Attributes						Char.
Reality	Humanity	Animateness	Maturity	Gender	Other	ID
non-fictional	human		adult	male	celebrity	C1
				female		C2
				neuter		C3
fictional	human		child	male	student	C4
				female		C5
			adult	male	local factory owner	C6
					steward	C7
				female	local store clerk	C8
					entertainer	C9
				neuter	bar owner	C10
	non-human	animate	child	NA	bear	C11
			NA	male	dog	C12
					hawk	C13
				NA	bear	C14
					moss	C15
		inanimate	adult	male	kanji	C16
					tower	C17
			NA	NA	cocoon	C18
					jelly	C19
					tile	C20

Table 2: Characters we used and their attributes. 'NA' indicates that the value of the attribute is not specified in a character's profile. As for gender, 'neuter' refers to a character's gender being specified as neutral between male and female.

We utilized 11 fictional characters from Twitter bots (C4 and C11–20) and six fictional characters from dialogue system characters (C5–10). The reason we use dialogue system utterances along with Twitter postings is that we intend to analyze utterances that are originally designed for a dialogue system. In addition to these 17 fictional characters, we also used three non-fictional (actual human) characters for comparison (C1–3). C1 and C3 are Twitter bots that post Japanese celebrities' remarks from their TV shows or writings and C2 is the official Twitter account of a Japanese celebrity. Note that we did not use these characters in creating the categories in Section 3; that is, these characters have been prepared for evaluation purposes.

We collected 100 utterances from each character for a total of 2000 utterances. The average number of words per utterance of the characters from Twitter (C1–4 and C11–20) and the dialogue system characters (C5–10) are 25.5 and 13.3, respectively. Examples of characters' utterances are given in Table 3.

Char. ID	Example utterance
C5	アンタと？マジうけるねー anta-to? maji ukeru-ne 'With you? That's really funny, isn't it?'
C6	ええんとちゃう。おっちゃんは好きやで。 ee-n-to-chau occhan-wa suki-ya-de 'No problem. I like it.'
C7	おかえりなさいませ。 okaerinasai-mase 'Welcome back.'

Table 3: Examples of characters' utterances.

Evaluation	Annotator ID	Age	Gender	Experience with language annotation
eval 1 (step 1)	A1	30s	female	5+ years
	A2	40s	female	10+ years
	A3	50s	female	15+ years
	A4	50s	female	15+ years
eval 2	A5	20s	male	NA
	A6	20s	male	NA
	A7	30s	female	NA
	A8	30s	female	NA
	A9	30s	female	NA
	A10	40s	male	NA
	A11	40s	male	NA
	A12	50s	male	NA
	A13	50s	female	NA
	A14	50s	female	NA

Table 4: List of annotators.

4.2 Annotating linguistic peculiarities

Each of the characters' utterances was annotated with linguistic peculiarities by annotators (not the authors) who are native speakers of Japanese.

Step 1: Marking expressions peculiar to characters

For each of the 2000 utterances, we asked two annotators (a primary annotator and a secondary annotator) to mark linguistic expressions that they felt were peculiar to a character. The two annotators worked separately, i.e., without discussing or showing their work to each other. This process was performed by two of the four annotators (A1–4) shown in Table 4. These annotators correspond to annotators A and B in Figure 1.

To analyze the 'linguistic' peculiarities of fictional characters, we asked the annotators to mark peculiar surface expressions and constructions (i.e., to concentrate on 'how to say it') without taking into account the meaning or content (i.e., to ignore 'what to say') of the utterances.

Step 2: Classifying peculiar expressions into categories

For each expression marked in step 1, we asked another annotator (not one of the authors) to classify the expression into one of 14 categories, i.e., to tag the category labels to the expressions. These 14 categories include the 13 categories shown in Table 1 plus 'others' for expressions that cannot be classified into any of the 13. The annotator corresponds to annotator C or D in Figure 1. In the example shown in Figure 1, annotator C deals with the expressions marked by annotator A and annotator D deals with the expressions marked by annotator B. When classifying the expressions, annotators C and D are allowed to discuss and show their work to each other. Examples of the tagged utterances are given below.

```
<character id="C7" annotator="A2">
<u id="1"> パソコンがなければ通用し <honorific>
ません </honorific>。 </u>
(You cannot do anything without a personal computer.)
<u id="2"><pronoun> わたくし </pronoun> は子
どもたちのお世話も得意 <honorific> でございます
</honorific>。 </u>
(I am good at taking care of children.)
· · ·
</character>
```

Step 3: Extracting expressions that are agreed to be peculiar

The utterances that are marked as having peculiar expressions by the two annotators in Step 1 are compared. If the text spans of the expressions marked by the two annotators overlap, such text spans are regarded as the expressions agreed to be peculiar and are extracted.

To evaluate the agreement of the expressions marked by the two annotators, we use three measures: *recall*, *precision*, and *F-measure*. Here, we regard the task of marking expressions performed by two annotators as the secondary annotator's task of extracting the expressions marked by the primary annotator. The three measures are calculated by

$$\text{recall} = \frac{B}{P}, \quad \text{precision} = \frac{B}{S},$$

$$\text{F-measure} = \frac{2 \cdot precision \cdot recall}{precision + recall},$$

where B represents the number of expressions marked by both the primary and secondary annotators, P represents the total number of expressions

Char. ID	No. of expressions	Agreement measures		
		Rec.	Prec.	F
C1	144	0.93	0.54	0.68
C2	89	0.19	0.84	0.31
C3	251	0.81	0.70	0.75
C4	233	0.70	0.63	0.66
C5	180	0.78	0.73	0.75
C6	279	0.86	0.97	0.91
C7	160	0.81	0.88	0.84
C8	187	0.83	0.96	0.89
C9	222	0.70	0.91	0.79
C10	211	0.84	0.79	0.81
C11	715	0.78	0.77	0.78
C12	260	0.76	0.73	0.74
C13	406	0.68	0.72	0.70
C14	297	0.67	0.72	0.69
C15	163	0.65	0.74	0.69
C16	117	0.82	0.61	0.70
C17	166	0.74	0.71	0.73
C18	205	0.69	0.48	0.56
C19	459	0.86	0.83	0.85
C20	250	0.70	0.72	0.71
total	4994	**0.72**	**0.74**	**0.73**

Table 5: Number of expressions marked by both annotators and the agreement measures.

marked by the primary annotator, and S represents the total number of expressions marked by the secondary annotator.

The number of expressions that are marked by both annotators and the values of the three agreement measures are listed in Table 5. In total, 4,994 expressions were agreed to be peculiar by two annotators. The average values of recall, precision, and F-measure were 0.72, 0.74, and 0.73, respectively—sufficient for the annotators' perception of characters' linguistic peculiarities to be considered as moderately in agreement and for the extracted expressions to be reliable as characters' linguistic peculiarities.

4.3 Counting numbers of peculiar expressions in each category

We counted the number of category labels tagged to the expressions that were agreed to be peculiar in Step 3. We used 4,729 expressions that two annotators tagged with the same category (not all of the 4,994 expressions that were agreed to be peculiar). Then, we calculated the proportion of the expressions classified into each category.

4.4 Results

The results are shown in Table 6. The proportion of expressions that cannot be classified into any of our categories was just around 12%. In other words, around 88% of the linguistic peculiarities of Japanese characters are covered by our

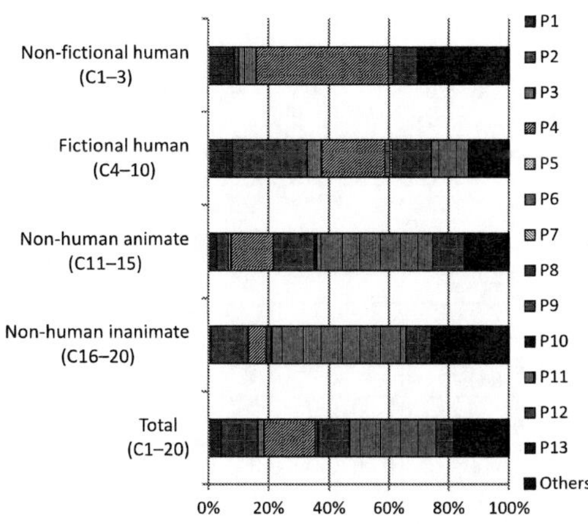

Figure 2: Proportions of expressions classified into each category shown separately by characters' attributes.

13 categories. When considering fictional characters (C4–20) only, around 90% of linguistic peculiarities are covered by our categories. However, the proportions of expressions classified into P5 (syntactic complexity), P6 (relaxed pronunciation), P7 (disfluency), P9 (word segmentation), and P10 (letter type) were less than 1%, which suggests these categories might not be as important as other categories, or might not be used as effectively as other categories. The importance (effectiveness in characterization) of each category will be discussed later in Section 5.

In Figure 2, the proportions of expressions classified into each category are shown separately by characters' attributes. The proportion of 'others' for non-fictional (actual) human characters is the largest among other characters. The proportion of 'others' is gradually lowered as fictionality is intensified, that is, as the characters become fictional, non-human, and inanimate. We think this result suggests that our 13 categories describe the linguistic peculiarities of fictional characters better than those of non-fictional humans. Actually, P8 (arbitrary phoneme replacements) should not occur so frequently in non-fictional humans' utterances because P8 is primarily for fictional characters (see details in Section 3). This came about because the annotators often confused expressions that should be classified into P6 (relaxed pronunciation) with those that should be classified into P8. The expressions classified into these two categories need to be further investigated.

	Lexical choice		Modality		Synt-ax	Phonology and pronunciation			Surface options			Extras		Othe-rs	Total
	P1	P2	P3	P4	P5	P6	P7	P8	P9	P10	P11	P12	P13		
No. of expressions	203	561	114	798	0	32	15	473	1	19	1359	281	330	543	4729
Prop. of each category	4.3%	11.9%	2.4%	16.9%	0.0%	0.7%	0.3%	10.0%	0.0%	0.4%	28.7%	5.9%	7.0%	11.5%	100.0%

Table 6: Numbers and proportions of expressions classified into each category.

Cat.	Non-fictional human			Fictional human							Non-human animate					Non-human inanimate					All
	C1	C2	C3	C4	C5	C6	C7	C8	C9	C10	C11	C12	C13	C14	C15	C16	C17	C18	C19	C20	
P1	0.02	**0.30**	**0.16**	**0.31**	0.03	0.08	0.05	**0.18**	0.02	**0.38**	0.00	**0.24**	**0.34**	0.00	0.00	0.00	0.00	0.00	0.01	0.01	**0.10**
P2	**0.17**	0.00	0.01	0.07	**0.37**	**0.12**	**0.19**	**0.36**	0.04	0.00	0.00	0.04	**0.69**	0.04	**0.77**	**0.01**	**0.48**	0.00	**0.40**	**0.17**	**0.27**
P3	**0.21**	**0.13**	0.00	0.00	0.00	0.00	**0.11**	0.00	0.09	0.00	0.00	**0.18**	0.14	0.00	**0.16**	0.00	0.04	0.00	0.00	0.00	0.03
P4	0.14	**0.53**	**0.31**	0.07	0.09	**0.14**	**0.15**	**0.20**	**0.16**	**0.34**	**0.15**	0.09	0.28	**0.19**	**0.17**	**0.01**	**0.18**	0.00	0.02	0.00	0.08
P5	0.00	0.00	0.00	0.00	0.00	0.00	0.00	0.00	0.00	0.00	0.00	0.00	0.00	0.00	0.00	0.00	0.00	0.00	0.00	0.00	0.00
P6	**0.29**	0.00	0.02	0.06	**0.11**	0.00	0.00	0.00	0.00	0.00	0.00	0.00	0.00	0.00	0.00	0.00	0.00	0.00	0.00	0.00	0.02
P7	0.00	0.00	0.00	**0.15**	0.00	0.00	0.00	0.00	0.00	0.00	0.00	0.01	0.00	0.00	0.00	0.00	0.01	0.00	0.00	0.00	0.05
P8	0.05	0.00	**0.22**	0.10	0.10	**0.19**	0.00	0.06	**0.27**	**0.09**	**0.60**	0.16	0.17	0.02	0.01	0.00	0.05	**0.06**	0.00	0.07	0.09
P9	0.00	0.00	0.00	0.07	0.00	0.00	0.00	0.00	0.00	0.00	0.00	0.00	0.00	0.00	0.00	0.00	0.00	0.00	0.00	0.00	0.01
P10	0.00	0.00	0.00	0.00	**0.21**	0.00	0.00	0.00	**0.13**	0.00	0.00	**0.17**	0.00	0.13	0.00	0.00	**0.18**	0.00	0.00	0.00	0.06
P11	0.00	0.00	0.00	**0.15**	0.03	0.00	0.00	0.00	0.10	**0.09**	0.00	0.09	**0.40**	**0.24**	0.01	**0.23**	0.15	**0.23**	**0.45**	**0.19**	0.04
P12	0.00	0.00	0.00	0.00	0.00	0.00	0.00	0.00	0.00	0.00	0.00	0.00	0.00	**0.15**	0.00	0.00	0.00	0.00	0.00	**0.20**	0.07
P13	0.00	0.00	0.00	0.00	0.00	0.00	0.00	0.00	0.03	0.00	**0.34**	0.11	0.00	0.00	0.00	**0.84**	0.00	**0.35**	**0.62**	0.00	**0.22**
other	0.45	0.16	0.01	0.20	0.25	0.12	0.23	0.13	0.04	0.07	0.10	0.20	0.17	0.44	0.06	0.10	0.06	0.06	0.07	0.02	0.04

Table 7: Correlation ratio (η) between the existence of a category and the average score of character appropriateness among ten annotators.

5 Eval 2: Relations between categories and character appropriateness

The second evaluation is for revealing the characterizing effects of each category.

5.1 Preparation: Assessing character appropriateness of utterances

For each of the 2000 utterances collected in Section 4.1, we asked ten annotators (A5–14, listed in Table 4) to assess the appropriateness of the utterances as those uttered by particular characters. The assessment was done on a five-point scale from 1 (very inappropriate; seeming like a different character's utterance) to 5 (very appropriate; expressing the character's typical linguistic characteristics).

5.2 Evaluation method

To evaluate the relationships between the categories of linguistic peculiarities and linguistic appropriateness for the given characters, we calculated the correlation ratio (η) between the existence of a category and the average score of character appropriateness among ten annotators. We consider that a high correlation ratio between the existence of a category and the score of character appropriateness tells us how effectively the category invokes humans' perceptions of the linguistic style of a particular character. We use correlation ratio because it can be applied to calculate correlation between categorical data (nominal scale) and interval scale, i.e., the categories of linguistic peculiarities and the average score of character appropriateness in this case. To be precise, the score of character appropriateness in a five-point scale is not an interval scale but an ordinal scale. However, we treat the five-point scale as an interval scale for convenience.

5.3 Results

The correlation ratios between the existence of the categories and the average scores of character appropriateness among ten annotators are shown in Table 7. The correlation ratios are shown by character and the top three η values of each character are written in bold.

When considering all characters, category P2 (dialectical or distinctive wordings) showed the best correlation ratio, P13 (character sentence-end particles) was the second, and P1 (personal pronouns) was the third. As for P2, since it ranked in the top three categories for 11 of 20 characters, we consider that using dialectical or distinctive wordings is the most general and effective way of characterizing utterances.

In addition to these top three categories across

all characters, we consider that P4 (sentence-end expressions) is an important characteristic of human characters because it ranked in the top three categories for seven of ten human characters. Although P4 did not show as high a correlation ratio as the other categories as a whole, we consider that it has a strong effect on characterizing utterances, especially for human characters.

As for non-human characters, P11 (symbols) showed a comparatively high correlation ratio in addition to the categories mentioned above. We suppose that symbols such as exclamation marks and emoticons are used as an easy and effective way of characterizing utterances, especially when handling non-human characters.

Overall, we found that most of our 13 categories of characters' linguistic peculiarities contribute to character appropriateness to some extent. In other words, most of the categories had some effect on characterizing the utterances of Japanese fictional characters.

Note that there are possibilities that the score of character appropriateness is affected by other factors than the existence of a category—such as the capability of a character creator's use of linguistic expressions that belong to our proposed categories, or a particular annotator's like or dislike of a particular category of linguistic expressions. To reduce such possibilities as much as we can, we used various characters and utilized various annotators, which are listed in Tables 2 and 4 respectively, and refrained from making conclusions of this evaluation by only looking at the result of a single character or a single annotator.

6 Conclusion and future work

With the aim of developing a natural language generator that can express a particular character's linguistic style, we analyzed the linguistic peculiarities of Japanese fictional characters. Our contributions are as follows:

- We presented comprehensive categories of the linguistic peculiarities of Japanese fictional characters.
- We revealed the relationships between our proposed categories of linguistic peculiarities and the linguistic appropriateness for the characters.

These contributions are supported by the experimental results, which show that our proposed cat-

egories cover around 90% of the linguistic peculiarities of 17 Japanese fictional characters (around 88% when we include actual human characters) and that the character appropriateness scores and the existence of our categories of linguistic peculiarities are correlated to some extent.

As future work, we intend to develop a natural language generator that can express the linguistic styles of particular characters on the basis of the 13 categories presented in this paper. To this end, we are first going to build a system that has 13 kinds of modules to convert linguistic expressions, such as a module to convert utterances without honorifics into those with honorifics (corresponds to category P3), a module to convert utterances without relaxed pronunciations into those with relaxed pronunciations (corresponds to category P6), and so on, and that can combine arbitrary kinds of modules to express various linguistic styles. After we build such a generator, we will evaluate its performance in the characterization of dialogue system utterances.

References

Satoshi Kinsui. 2003. Vaacharu nihongo: Yakuwarigo no nazo (in japanese) [Virtual Japanese: The mystery of role language]. *Iwanami Shoten*.

François Mairesse and Marilyn Walker. 2007. PERSONAGE: Personality generation for dialogue. In *Proceedings of the 45th Annual Meeting of the Association of Computational Linguistics*, pages 496–503.

Norman N Markel, Richard M Eisler, and Hayne W Reese. 1967. Judging personality from dialect. *Journal of Verbal Learning and Verbal Behavior*, 6(1):33–35.

Senko K Maynard. 1997. *Japanese communication: Language and thought in context*. University of Hawaii Press.

Chiaki Miyazaki, Toru Hirano, Ryuichiro Higashinaka, Toshiro Makino, and Yoshihiro Matsuo. 2015. Automatic conversion of sentence-end expressions for utterance characterization of dialogue systems. In *Proceedings of the 29th Pacific Asia Conference on Language, Information and Computation*, pages 307–314.

Chiaki Miyazaki, Toru Hirano, Ryuichiro Higashinaka, Toshiro Makino, Yoshihiro Matsuo, and Satoshi Sato. 2016. Probabilistic conversion of functional expressions for characterization of dialogue system utterances (in japanese). *Transactions of the Japanese Society for Artificial Intelligence*, 31(1).

Masahiro Mizukami, Graham Neubig, Sakriani Sakti, Tomoki Toda, and Satoshi Nakamura. 2015. Linguistic individuality transformation for spoken language. In *Proceedings of the 6th International Workshop On Spoken Dialogue Systems*.

Aaron A Reed, Ben Samuel, Anne Sullivan, Ricky Grant, April Grow, Justin Lazaro, Jennifer Mahal, Sri Kurniawan, Marilyn A Walker, and Noah Wardrip-Fruin. 2011. A step towards the future of role-playing games: The SpyFeet Mobile RPG Project. In *Proceedings of the 7th Conference on Artificial Intelligence and Interactive Digital Entertainment*, pages 182–188.

Toshiyuki Sadanobu. 2015. "Characters" in japanese communication and language: An overview. *Acta Linguistica Asiatica*, 5(2):9–28.

Marilyn A Walker, Ricky Grant, Jennifer Sawyer, Grace I Lin, Noah Wardrip-Fruin, and Michael Buell. 2011. Perceived or not perceived: Film character models for expressive NLG. In *Proceedings of the 4th International Conference on Interactive Digital Storytelling*, pages 109–121.

Mirjam Wester, Matthew Aylett, Marcus Tomalin, and Rasmus Dall. 2015. Artificial personality and disfluency. In *Proceedings of the 16th Annual Conference of the International Speech Communication Association*, pages 3365–3369.

Young-Sun Yun and Richard E Ladner. 2013. Bilingual voice conversion by weighted frequency warping based on formant space. In *Proceedings of the 16th International Conference on Text, Speech and Dialogue*, pages 137–144.

Reference Resolution in Situated Dialogue with Learned Semantics

Xiaolong Li
Computer & Information Science
& Engineering
University of Florida
xiaolongl@ufl.edu

Kristy Elizabeth Boyer
Computer & Information Science
& Engineering
University of Florida
keboyer@ufl.edu

Abstract

Understanding situated dialogue requires identifying referents in the environment to which the dialogue participants refer. This reference resolution problem, often in a complex environment with high ambiguity, is very challenging. We propose an approach that addresses those challenges by combining learned semantic structure of referring expressions with dialogue history into a ranking-based model. We evaluate the new technique on a corpus of human-human tutorial dialogues for computer programming. The experimental results show a substantial performance improvement over two recent state-of-the-art approaches. The proposed work makes a stride toward automated dialogue in complex problem-solving environments.

1 Introduction

The content of a situated dialogue is very closely related to the environment in which it happens (Grosz and Sidner, 1986). As dialogue systems move toward assisting users in increasingly complex tasks, these systems must understand users' language within the environment of the tasks. To achieve this goal, dialogue systems must perform reference resolution, which involves identifying the referents in the environment that the user refers to (Iida et al., 2010; Liu et al., 2014; Liu and Chai, 2015; Chai et al., 2004). Imagine a dialogue system that assists a novice student in solving a programming problem. To understand a question or statement the student poses, such as, "Should I use the 2 dimensional array?", the system must link the *referring expression* "the 2 dimensional array" to an *object*[1] in the *environment*.

This process is illustrated in Figure 1, which shows an excerpt from a corpus of tutorial dialogue situated in an introductory computer programming task in the Java programming language. The arrows link referring expressions in the situated dialogue to their referents in the environment. To identify the referent of each referring expression, it is essential to capture the semantic structure of the referring expression of the object it refers to, such as *"the 2 dimensional array"* contains two attributes, *"2 dimensional"* and *"array"*. At the same time, the dialogue history and the history of user task actions (such as editing the code) play a key role. To disambiguate the referent of *"my array"*, temporal information is needed: in this case, the referent is a variable named arra, which is an array that the student has just created.

Reference resolution in situated dialogue is challenging because of the ambiguity inherent within dialogue utterances and the complexity of the environment. Prior work has leveraged dialogue history and task history information to improve the accuracy of reference resolution (Iida et al., 2010; Iida et al., 2011; Funakoshi et al., 2012). However, these prior approaches have employed relatively simple semantic information from the referring expressions, such as a manually created lexicon, or have operated within an environment with a limited set of pre-defined objects. Besides reference resolution in situated dialogue, there is also a research direction in which machine learning models are used to learn the semantics of noun phrases in order to map noun phrases to objects in a related environment (Kennington and Schlangen, 2015; Liang et al., 2009; Naim et al., 2014; Kushman et al., 2014). However, these prior approaches operated at the granularity of single

---

[1]The word "object" has a technical meaning within the domain of object-oriented programming, which is the domain of the corpus utilized in this work. However, we follow the standard usage of "object" in situated dialogue (Iida et al., 2010), which for programming is any portion of code in the environment.

Proceedings of the SIGDIAL 2016 Conference, pages 329–338,
Los Angeles, USA, 13-15 September 2016. ©2016 Association for Computational Linguistics

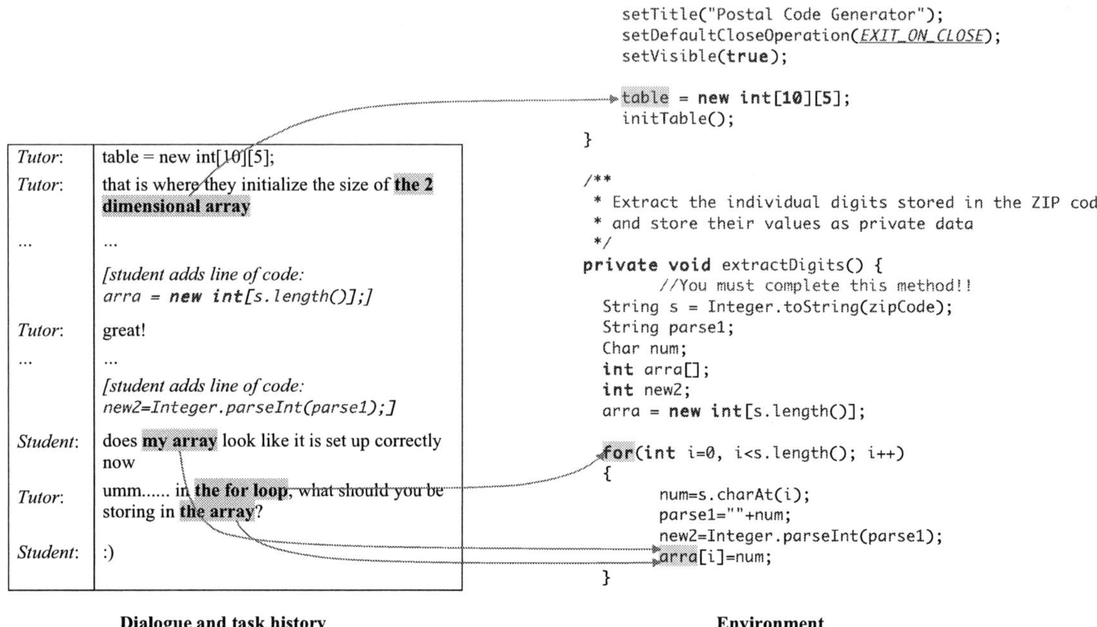

Dialogue and task history   Environment

Figure 1 Excerpt of tutorial dialogue illustrating reference resolution. Referring expressions are shown in bold italics.[2]

spoken utterances not contextualized within a dialogue history, and they too focus on environments with a limited number (and a pre-defined set) of objects. As this paper demonstrates, these prior approaches do not perform well in situated dialogues for complex problem solving, in which the user creates, modifies, and removes objects from the environment in unpredictable ways.

To tackle the problem of reference resolution in this type of situated dialogue, we propose an approach that combines semantics from a conditional-random-field-based semantic parser along with salient features from dialogue history and task history. We evaluate this approach on the JavaTutor corpus, a corpus of textual tutorial dialogue collected within an online environment for computer programming. The results show that our approach achieves substantial improvement over two existing state-of-the-art approaches, with existing approaches achieving 55.2% accuracy at best, and the new approach achieving 68.5% accuracy.

2 Related Work

The work in this paper is informed by research in coreference resolution for text as well as reference resolution in situated dialogue and multi-modal environments. This section describes related work in those areas.

The classic reference resolution problem for discourse aims to resolve coreference relationships within a given text (Martschat and Strube, 2015; McCarthy and Lehnert, 1995; Soon et al., 2001). Effective approaches for discourse cannot be directly applied to the problem of linking referring expressions to their referents in a rich situated dialogue environment, because the information embedded within the environment plays an important role in understanding the referring relationships in the situated dialogue. Our approach combines referring expressions' semantic information along with dialogue history, task history, and a representation of the environment in which the dialogue is situated.

Reference resolution in dialogue has been investigated in recent years. Some of the previous work focuses on reference resolution in a multi-modal setting (Chai et al., 2004; Liu et al., 2014; Liu et al., 2013; Krishnamurthy and Kollar, 2013; Matuszek et al., 2012). For this problem re-

---

[2]Typos and syntactic errors are shown as they appear in the original corpus.

searchers have used multimodal information, including vision, gestures, speech, and eye gaze, to contribute to the problem of reference resolution. Given that the focus of these works is on employing rich multimodal information, the research is usually conducted on a limited number of objects, and typically uses spatial relationship between objects as constraints to solve the reference resolution problem. We conduct reference resolution in an environment with a dynamic number of referents and there is no obvious spatial relationship between the objects.

More closely related work to our own involves reference resolution in dialogue situated within a collaborative game (Iida et al., 2010; Iida et al., 2011; Funakoshi et al., 2012). To link referring expressions to one of the seven gamepiece objects, they encoded dialogue history and task history, and our proposed approach leverages these features as well. However, in contrast to our complex problem-solving domain of computer programming, their domain has a small number of possible referents, so they used a manually created lexicon to extract semantic information from referring expressions. Funakoshi et al. (2012) went further, using Bayesian networks to model the relationship between referents and words used in referring expressions. That model is based on a hand-crafted concept dictionary and distribution over different referents. This approach cannot be directly applied to a dialogue with a dynamic environment because it is not possible to manually define the distribution over all possible referents beforehand, since objects in the environment are not known before they are created. So we chose Iida et al.'s work (2010) as one of the two most recent approaches to compare with.

Another closely related research direction involves reference resolution in physical environments (Kennington and Schlangen, 2015; Kushman et al., 2014; Naim et al., 2014; Liang et al., 2009). Although not within situated dialogue per se (because only one participant speaks), these lines of investigation have produced approaches that link natural language noun phrases to objects in an environment, such as a set of objects of different type and color on a table (Kennington and Schlangen, 2015) or a variable in a mathematical formula (Kushman et al., 2014). Some of these learn the mapping relationship by learning the semantics of words in the referring expressions

(Kennington and Schlangen, 2015; Liang et al., 2009) with *referring expression-referent* pairs as input. Most recently, Kennington and Schlangen (2015) used a word-as-classifier approach to learn word semantics to map referring expressions to a set of 36 Pentomino puzzle pieces on a table. We implement their word-as-classifier approach and compare it with our novel approach.

3 Reference Resolution Approach

This section describes a new approach to reference resolution in situated dialogue. It links each referring expression from the dialogue to a most likely referent object in the environment. Our approach involves three main steps. First, referring expressions from the situated dialogue are segmented and labeled according to their semantic structure. Using a semantic segmentation and labeling approach we have previously developed (Li and Boyer, 2015), we use a conditional random field (CRF) for this joint segmentation and labeling task, and the values of the labeled attributes are then extracted (Section 3.1). The result of this step is *learned semantics*, which are attributes of objects expressed within each referring expression. Then, these learned semantics are utilized within the novel approach reported in this paper. As Section 3.2 describes, dialogue and task history are used to filter the objects in the environment to build a candidate list of referents, and then as Section 3.3 describes, a ranking-based classification approach is used to select the best matching referent.

For situated dialogue we define E_t as the state of the environment at time t. E_t consists of all objects present in the environment. Importantly, the objects in the environment vary along with the dialogue: at each moment, new objects could be created ($|E_t| > |E_{t-1}|$), and existing objects could be removed ($|E_t| < |E_{t-1}|$) because of the task performed by the user.

$$E_t = \{o_i | o_i \text{ is an object in the environment at time } t\}$$

We assume that all of the objects o_i are observable in the environment. For example, in situated dialogues about programming, we can find all of the objects and extract their attributes using a source code parser. Then, reference resolution is defined as finding a best-matching o_i in E_t for referring expression RE.

3.1 Referring Expression Semantic Interpretation

In situated dialogues, a referring expression may contain rich semantic information about the referent, especially when the context of the situated dialogue is complex. Approaches such as domain-specific lexicons are limited in their ability to address this complexity, so we utilize a linear-chain CRF to parse the semantic structure of the referring expression. This more automated approach can also potentially avoid the manual labor required in creating and maintaining a lexicon.

In this approach, every object within the environment must be represented according to its attributes. We treat the set of all possible attributes of objects as a vector, and for each object o_i in the environment we instantiate and populate an attribute vector Att_Vec_i. For example, the attribute vector for a two-dimensional array in a computer program could be *[CATEGORY = 'array, DIMENSION = '2, LINE = '30, NAME = 'table, ...]*. We ultimately represent $E_t = \{o_i\}$ as the set of all attribute vectors Att_Vec_i, and for a referring expression we aim to identify Att_Vec_j, the actual referent.

Since a referring expression describes its referents either implicitly or explicitly, the attributes expressed in it should match the attributes of its referent. We segment referring expressions and label the semantics of each segment using the CRF and the result is a set of segments, each of which represents some attribute of its referent. This process is illustrated in (Figure 2 (a)). After segmenting and labeling attributes in the referring expressions, the attribute *values* are extracted from each semantic segment using regular expressions (Figure 2 (b)), e.g., value *2* is extracted from *2 dimensional* to fill in the *ARRAY_DIM* element in an empty *Att_Vec*. The result is an attribute vector that represents the referring expression.

3.2 Generating a List of Candidate Referents

Once the referring expression is represented as an object attribute vector as described above, we wish to link that vector to the closest-matching object in the environment. Each object is represented by its own attribute vector, and there may be a large number of objects in E_t. Given a referring expression R_k, we would like to trim the list to keep only those objects that are likely to be referent for R_k.

There are two desired criteria for generating the

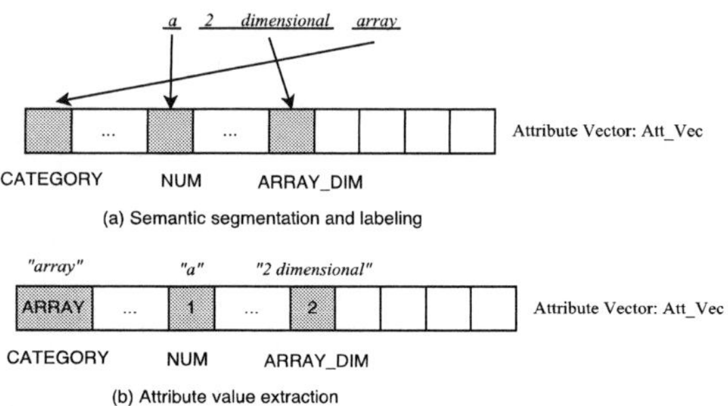

Figure 2 Semantic interpretation of referring expressions.

list of candidate referents. First, the actual referent must be in the candidate list. At the same time, the candidate list should be as short as possible. We can pare down the set of all objects in E_t by considering focus of attention in dialogue. Early approaches performed reference resolution by estimating each dialogue participant's focus of attention (Lappin and Leass, 1994; Grosz et al., 1995). According to Ariel's accessibility theory (Ariel, 1988), people tend to use more precise descriptions such as proper names in referring expressions for referents in long term memory, and use less precise descriptions such as pronouns for referents in short term memory. In a precise description, there is more semantic information, while in a more vague description like a pronoun, there is less semantic information. Thus, these two sources of information, semantics and focus of attention, work together in identifying a referent.

Our approach employs this idea in the process of candidate referent selection by tracking the focus of attention of the dialogue participants from the beginning of the dialogue through dialogue history and task history, as has been done in prior work we use for comparison within our experiments (Iida et al., 2010). We also use the learned semantics of the referring expression (represented as the referring expression's attribute vector) as filtering conditions to select candidates.

The candidate generation process consists of three steps.

1. Candidate generation from dialogue history DH.

$$DH = <O_d, T_d>$$

Here, $O_d = < o_d^1, o_d^2, ..., o_d^m >$ is a sequence of objects that were mentioned since the beginning of the dialogue. $T_d =< t_d^1, t_d^2, ..., t_d^m >$ is a sequence of timestamps when corresponding objects were mentioned. All of the objects in E_t that were ever mentioned in the dialogue history, $\{o_i | o_i \in DH \ \& \ o_i \in E_t\}$, will also be added into the candidate list.

2. Candidate generation from task history TH. Similarly, $TH =< O_b, T_b >$, which is all of the objects in E_t that were ever manipulated by the user, will be added into the candidate list.

3. Candidate generation using learned semantics, which are the referent's attributes. Given a set of attributes extracted from a referring expression, all objects in E_t with one of the same attribute values will be added into the candidate list. The attributes are considered separately to avoid the case in which a single incorrectly extracted attribute could rule out the correct referent. Table 1 shows the algorithm used in this step.

Given a referring expression R_k, whose attribute vector Att_Vec_k has been extracted.
for each element att_i **of** Att_Vec_k
   if att_i **is not null**
      for each o **in** E_t
         if $att_i == o.att_i$
            add o into candidate list C_k

Table 1 Algorithm to select candidates using learned semantics

3.3 Ranking-based classification

With the list of candidate referents in hand, we employ a ranking-based classification model to identify the most likely referent. Ranking-based models have been shown to perform well for reference resolution problems in prior work (Denis and Baldridge, 2008; Iida et al., 2010). For a given referring expression R_k and its candidate referent list $C_k = \{o_1, o_2, ..., o_{N_k}\}$, in which each o_i is an object identified as a candidate referent, we compute the probability of each candidate o_i being the true referent of R_k, $p(R_k, o_i) = f(R_k, o_i)$, where f is the classification function. (Note that our approach is classifier-agnostic. As we describe in Section 5, we experimented with several different models.) Then, the candidates are ranked by $p(R_k, o_i)$, and the object with the highest probability is taken as the referent of R_k.

4 Corpus

Human problem solving represents a highly complex domain that poses great challenges for reference resolution. We evaluate our new reference resolution approach on a corpus of human-human textual dialogue in the domain of computer programming (Boyer et al., 2011). In each dialogue, a human tutor assisted a student remotely using typed dialogue as the student completed given programming tasks in the Java programming language. The programming tasks involved array manipulation and control flow, which are challenging for students with little programming experience. Students' and tutors' view of the task were synchronized in real time. At the beginning of each problem-solving session students were provided a framework of code to fill in, which is around 200 lines initially. The corpus contains 45 tutoring sessions, 4857 utterances in total, 108 utterances for each session on average. We manually annotated the referring expressions in the dialogue and their referents in the corresponding Java code for six dialogues from the corpus (346 referring expressions). These six sessions contain 758 utterances. The dialogues focus on the details of solving the programming problems, with very little social or off-task talk. Figure 1 shows an excerpt of this dialogue.

5 Experiments & Result

To evaluate the new approach, we performed a set of experiments that compare our approach with two state-of-the-art approaches.

5.1 Semantic Parsing

The referring expressions were extracted from the tutorial dialogues and their semantic segments and labels were manually annotated. A linear-chain CRF was trained on that data and used to perform referring expression segmentation and labeling (Li and Boyer, 2015). The current paper reports the first use of that learned semantics approach for reference resolution.

Next, we proceeded to extract the attribute values, a step that our previous work did not address. For the example shown in Figure 2 (b), from the learned semantic structure, we may know that *2 dimensional* refers to the dimension of the array, the attribute *ARRAY_DIM*. (In the current domain there are 14 attributes that comprise the generic attribute vector V, such as ARRAY_DIM, NUM, and CATEGORY.) To actually extract the attribute values, we use regular expressions that capture our three types of attribute values: categorical, numeric, and strings. For example, the value type of *CATEGORY* is categorical, like *method* or *variable*. Its values are taken from a closed set. *NAME* has values that are strings. *LINE_NUMBER*'s value is numeric. For categorical attributes, we add the categorical attribute values into the semantic tag set of the CRF used for segmentation. In this way, the attribute values of categorical attributes will be generated by the CRF. For attributes with text string values, we take the whole surface string of the semantic segment as its attribute value. The accuracy of the entire semantic parsing pipeline is 93.2% using 10-fold cross-validation. The accuracy is defined as the percentage of manually labeled attribute values that were successfully extracted from referring expressions.

5.2 Candidate Referent Generation

We applied the approach described in Section 3.2 on each session to generate a list of candidate referents for each referring expression. In a program, there could be more than one appearance of the same object. We take all of the appearances of the same object to be the same, since they all refer to the same artifact in the program. The average number of generated candidates for each referring expression was 44.8. The percentage of referring expressions whose actual referents were in the generated candidate list, or '"hit rate" is 90.5%, based on manual tagging. This performance indicates that the candidate referent list generation performs well.

A referring expression could be a pronoun, such as "it" or "that", which does not contain attribute information. In previous reference resolution research, it was shown that training separate models for different kinds of referring expressions could improve performance (Denis and Baldridge, 2008). We follow this idea and split the dataset into two groups: referring expressions containing attributes, RE_{att}, (270 referring expressions), and referring expressions that do not contain attributes, RE_{non} (76 referring expressions).

The candidate generation approach performed better for the referring expressions without attributes (hit rate 94.7%), compared to referring expressions with attributes (hit rate 89.3%). Since the candidate list for referring expressions without attributes relies solely on dialogue and task history, 94.7% of those referents had been mentioned in the dialogue or manipulated by the user previously. For referring expressions with attribute information, the generation of the candidate list also used learned semantic information. Only 70.0% of those referents had been mentioned in the dialogue or manipulated by the user before.

5.3 Identifying Most Likely Referent

We applied the approach described in section 3.3 to perform reference resolution on the corpus of tutorial dialogue. The data from the six manually labeled Java tutoring sessions were split into a training set and a test set. We used leave-one-dialogue-out cross validation (which leads to six folds) for the reference resolution experiments. In each fold, annotated referring expressions from one of the tutoring sessions were taken as the test set, and data from the other five sessions were the training set. We tested logistic regression, decision tree, naive Bayes, and neural networks as classifiers to compute the $p(R_k, o_i)$ for each *(referring expression, candidate)* pair for the ranking-based model. The features provided to each classifier are shown in Table 2.

To evaluate the performance of the new approach, we compare against two other recent approaches. First, we compare against a ranking-based model that uses dialogue history and task history features (Iida et al., 2010). This model uses semantics from a domain-specific lexicon instead of a semantic parser. (As described in Section 2, their work was extended by Funakoshi et al. (2012), but that work relies upon a handcrafted probability distribution of referents to concepts, which is not feasible in our domain since it has no fixed set of possible referents.) Therefore, we compare against their 2010 approach, implementing it in a way that creates the strongest possible baseline: we built a lexicon directly from our manually labeled semantic segments. First, we split all of the semantic segments into groups by their tags. Then, for each group of segments, any token that appeared twice or more was added into the lexi-

Learned Semantic Features (SF)
SF1: whether RE has CATEGORY attribute
SF2: whether RE.CATEGORY == o.CATEGORY
SF3: whether RE has RE.NAME
SF4: whether RE.NAME == o.NAME
SF5: RE.NAME ≈ o.NAME
SF6: RE.VAR_TYPE exist
SF7: RE.VAR_TYPE == o.VAR_TYPE
SF8: RE.LINE_NUMBER exist
SF9: RE.LINE_NUMBER == o.LINE_NUMBER
SF10: RE.ARRAY_DIMENSION exist
SF11: RE.ARRAY_DIMENSION == o.ARRAY_DIMENSION
SF12: CATEGORY of o
Dialogue History (DH) Features
DH1: whether o is the latest mentioned object
DH2: whether o was mentioned in the last 30 seconds
DH3: whether o was mentioned in the last [30, 60] seconds
DH4: whether o was mentioned in the last [60, 180] seconds
DH5: whether o was mentioned in the last [180, 300] seconds
DH6: whether o was mentioned in the last [300, 600] seconds
DH7: whether o was mentioned in the last [600, infinite] seconds
DH8: whether o was never mentioned from the beginning
DH9: String matching between o and RE
Task History (TH) Features
TH1: whether o is the most recent object manipulated
TH2: whether o was manipulated in the last 30 seconds
TH3: whether o was manipulated in the last [30, 60] seconds
TH4: whether o was manipulated in the last [60, 180] seconds
TH5: whether o was manipulated in the last [180, 300] seconds
TH6: whether o was manipulated in the last [300, 600] seconds
TH7: whether o was manipulated in the last [600, infinite] seconds
TH8: whether o was never manipulated from the beginning
TH9: whether o is in the current working window

Table 2 Features used for segmentation and labeling.

con. Although the necessary data to do this would not be available in a real application of the technique, it ensures that the lexicon for the baseline condition has good coverage and creates a high baseline for our new approach to compare against. Additionally, for fairness of comparison, for each semantic feature used in our model, we extracted the same feature using the lexicon. There were three kinds of attribute values in the domain: categorical, string, and numeric (as described in Section 5.1). We extracted categorical attribute values using the appearance of tokens in the lexicon. We used regular expressions to determine whether a referring expression contains the name of a candidate referent. We also used regular expressions to extract attribute values from referring expressions, such as line number. We also provided the *Iida* baseline model (2010) with a feature to indicate string matching between referring expressions and candidate referents, since this feature was captured in our model as an attribute.

We also compared our approach against a very recent technique that leveraged a word-as-classifier approach to learn semantic compatibility between referring expressions and candidate referents (Kennington and Schlangen, 2015). To create this comparison model we used a word-as-classifier to learn the semantics of referring expressions instead of CRF. This weakly supervised approach relies on co-appearance between words and object's attributes. We then used the resulting semantic compatibility in a ranking-based model to select the most likely referent.

The three conditions for our experiment are as follows.

- *Iida Baseline Condition*: Features including dialogue history, task history, and **semantics from a handcrafted lexicon** (Iida et al., 2010).

- *Kennington Baseline Condition*: Features including dialogue history, task history, and **learned semantics from a word-as-classifier model** (Kennington and Schlangen, 2015).

- *Proposed approach*: Features including dialogue history, task history, and **learned semantics from CRF**.

Within each of these experimental conditions, we varied the classifier used to compute $p(R_k, o_i)$, testing four classifiers: logistic regression (LR), decision tree (DT), naive Bayes (NB), and neural network (NN). The neural network has one hidden layer and the best-performing number of perceptrons was 100 (we experimented between 50 and 120).

To measure the performance of the reference resolution approaches, we analyzed accuracy, defined to be the percent of referring expressions that were successfully linked to their referents. We chose accuracy for our metric following standard practice (Iida et al., 2010; Kennington and Schlangen, 2015) because it provides an overall measure of the number of (R_k, o_i) pairs that were correctly identified. For the rare cases in which one referring expression referred to multiple referents, the output referent of the algorithm was taken as correct if it selected any of the multiple referents.

The results are shown in Table 3. We focus on comparing the results on referring expressions that contain attribute information, shown in the table as REF_{ATT}. REF_{ATT} accounts for 78% of all of the cases (270 out of 346). Among the three approaches, our proposed approach outperformed both prior approaches. Compared to the Iida 2010 approach which achieved a maximum of 55.2% accuracy, our approach achieved 68.5% accuracy using a neural net classifier, and this difference is statistically significant based on the results of a Wilcoxon signed-rank test ($n = 6$; $p = 0.046$). Our approach outperformed the Kennington 2015 approach even more substantially, as its best performance was 46.3% accuracy ($p = 0.028$). Intuitively, the better performance of our model compared to the Iida approach is due to its ability to more accurately model referring expressions' semantics. Compared to a lexicon, semantic parsing finds optimal segmentation for a referring expression, while a lexicon approach extracts different attribute information from referring expressions separately. Note that our approach and the Iida 2010 approach achieved the same performance on REF_{NON} referring expressions. Since these referring expressions do not contain attribute information, these two approaches used the same set of features.

Interestingly, the model using a word-as-classifier approach to learn the semantic compatibility between referring expressions and referent's attributes performs the worst. We believe that the reason for this poor performance is mainly from the way it performs semantic compositions. It cannot learn structures in referring expressions, such as that *2 dimensional* is a segment, *dimensional* represents the type of the attribute, and *2* is the value of the attribute. The word-as-classifier

model cannot deal with this complex semantic composition.

The results reported above relied on learned semantics. We also performed experiments using manually labeled, gold-standard semantics of referring expressions. The result in Table 4 shows that ranking-based models have the potential to achieve a considerably better result, 73.6%, with more accurate semantic information. Given the 85.3% agreement between two human annotators, the model performs very well, since the semantics of whole utterances in situated dialogue also play a very important role in identifying a given referring expression's referent.

experimental condition	$f(R_k, o_i)$ classifier	accuracy	
		REF_{ATT}	REF_{NON}
Iida 2010	LR	0.500	0.440
	DT	0.537	0.453
	NB	0.466	0.413
	NN	**0.552**	0.373
Kennington 2015	**LR**	**0.4627**	0.3867
	DT	0.3769	0.3333
	NB	0.3209	0.4000
	NN	0.4216	0.4000
Our approach	LR	0.631	0.440
	DT	0.631	0.453
	NB	0.493	0.413
	NN	**0.685**	0.373

Table 3 Reference resolution results.

models	accuracy	
	REF_{ATT}	REF_{NON}
LR + SEM_gold	0.684	0.429
DT + SEM_gold	0.643	0.429
NB + SEM_gold	0.511	0.377
NN + SEM_gold	**0.736**	0.325

Table 4 Reference resolution results with gold semantic labels.

6 Conclusion

Dialogue systems need to move toward supporting users in increasingly complex tasks. To do this effectively, accurate reference resolution is crucial. We have presented a new approach that applies learned semantics to reference resolution in situated dialogue for collaborative tasks. The experiments with human-human dialogue on a collaborative programming task showed a tremendous improvement using semantic information that was learned with a CRF-based semantic parsing approach compared to the previous state-of-art approaches. The accuracy was improved substantially, from 55.2% to 68.5%.

There are several important future research directions in reference resolution for situated dialogues. First, models should incorporate more semantic information from discourse structure and utterance understanding besides semantics from referring expressions. This is illustrated by the observation that the reference resolution accuracy using gold-standard semantic information from referring expressions is still substantially lower than the agreement rate between human annotators. Another research direction that holds promise is to use an unsupervised approach to extract semantic information from referring expressions. It is hoped that this line of investigation will enable rich natural language dialogue interactions to support users in a wide variety of complex situated tasks.

Acknowledgments

The authors wish to thank the members of the LearnDialogue group at the University of Florida and North Carolina State University, particularly Joseph Wiggins, along with Wookhee Min and Adam Dalton for their helpful input. This work is supported in part by Google through a Capacity Research Award and by the National Science Foundation through grant CNS-1622438. Any opinions, findings, conclusions, or recommendations expressed in this report are those of the authors, and do not necessarily represent the official views, opinions, or policy of the National Science Foundation.

References

Ariel, Mira. 1988. Referring and Accessibility. *Journal of Linguistics*, 24, 65-87.

Björkelund, Anders and Kuhn, Jonas. 2014. Learning Structured Perceptrons for Coreference Resolution with Latent Antecedents and Non-local Features. *Proceedings of the 52nd Annual Meeting of the Association for Computational Linguistics (Volume 1: Long Papers)*, 47-57.

Boyer, Kristy Elizabeth and Ha, Eun Young and Phillips, Robert and Lester, James C.. 2011. The Impact of Task-Oriented Feature Sets on HMMs for Dialogue Modeling. *Proceedings of the 12th Annual Meeting of the Special Interest Group on Discourse and Dialogue*, 49–58.

Chai, Joyce and Hong, Pengyu and Zhou, Michelle. 2004. A Probabilistic Approach to Reference Resolution in Multimodal User Interfaces. *Proceedings of the 9th International Conference on Intelligent User Interfaces SE - IUI '04*, 70-77.

Denis, Pascal and Baldridge, Jason. 2008. Specialized Models and Reranking for Coreference Resolution. *Proceedings of the Conference on Empirical Methods in Natural Language Processing*, 660-669.

Devault, David and Kariaeva, Natalia and Kothari, Anubha and Oved, Iris and Stone, Matthew. 2005. An Information-State Approach to Collaborative Reference. *Proceedings of the ACL 2005 on Interactive Poster and Demonstration Sessions*, 1-4.

Funakoshi, Kotaro and Nakano, Mikio and Tokunaga, Takenobu and Iida, Ryu. 2012. A Unified Probabilistic Approach to Referring Expressions. *Proceedings of the 13th Annual Meeting of the Special Interest Group on Discourse and Dialogue*, 237-246.

Graesser, A C and Lu, S and Jackson, G T and Mitchell, H H and Ventura, M and Olney, A and Louwerse, M M. 2004. AutoTutor: A Tutor with Dialogue in Natural Language. *Behavior Research Methods, Instruments, & Computers*, 36, 180-192.

Grosz, B J and Weinstein, S and Joshi, A K. 1995. Centering - a Framework for Modeling the Local Coherence of Discourse. *Computational Linguistics*, 21(2), 203-225.

Grosz, Barbara J and Sidner, Candace L. 1986. Attention, Intentions, and the Structure of Discourse. *Computational Linguistics*, 175-204.

Harabagiu, Sanda M. and Räzvan C. Bunescu and Maiorano, Steven J.. 2001. Text and Knowledge Mining for Coreference Resolution. *Proceedings of the second meeting of the North American Chapter of the Association for Computational Linguistics on Language technologies. (NAACL-HLT)*, 1-8.

Heeman, Peter a. and Hirst, Graeme. 1995. Collaborating on Referring Expressions. *Computational Linguistics*, 21, 351-382.

Huwel, Sonja and Wrede, Britta. 2006. Spontaneous Speech Understanding for Robust Multimodal Human-robot Communication. *Proceedings of the COLING/ACL*, 391-398.

Iida, Ryu and Kobayashi, Shumpei and Tokunaga, Takenobu. 2010. Incorporating Extra-linguistic Information into Reference Resolution in Collaborative Task Dialogue. *Proceedings of the 48th Annual*

Meeting of the Association for Computational Linguistics, 1259-1267.

Iida, Ryu and Yasuhara, Masaaki and Tokunaga, Takenobu. 2011. Multi-modal Reference Resolution in Situated Dialogue by Integrating Linguistic and Extra-Linguistic Clues. *Proceedings of the 5th International Joint Conference on Natural Language Processing (IJCNLP 2011)*, 84-92.

Kennington, Casey and Schlangen, David. 2015. Simple Learning and Compositional Application of Perceptually Grounded Word Meanings for Incremental Reference Resolution. *Proceedings of the 53rd Annual Meeting of the Association for Computational Linguistics and the 7th International Joint Conference on Natural Language Processing*, 292-301.

Krishnamurthy, Jayant and Kollar, Thomas. 2013. Jointly Learning to Parse and Perceive: Connecting Natural Language to the Physical World. *Association for Computational Linguistics*, 193-206.

Kruijff, Geert-Jan M and Lison, Pierre and Benjamin, Trevor. 2010. Situated dialogue processing for human-robot interaction. *Cognitive Systems Monographs*, 8, 311-364.

Kushman, Nate and Artzi, Yoav and Zettlemoyer, Luke and Barzilay, Regina. 2014. Learning to Automatically Solve Algebra Word Problems. *Proceedings of the 52nd Annual Meeting of the Association for Computational Linguistics*, 271-281.

Lappin, Shalom and Leass, Herbert J.. 1994. An Algorithm for Pronominal Anaphora Resolution. *Computational Linguistics*, 535-561.

Li, Xiaolong and Boyer, Kristy Elizabeth. 2015. Semantic Grounding in Dialogue for Complex Problem Solving. *Proceedings of the Conference of the North American Chapter of the Association for Computational Linguistics and Human Language Technology (NAACL HLT)*, 841-850.

Liang, Percy and Jordan, Michael I and Klein, Dan. 2009. Learning Semantic Correspondences with Less Supervision. *Proceedings of the Joint Conference of the 47th Annual Meeting of the ACL and the 4th International Joint Conference on Natural Language Processing of the AFNLP*, 91–99.

Liu, Changsong and Chai, Joyce Y. 2015. Learning to Mediate Perceptual Differences in Situated Human-Robot Dialogue. *Proceedings of AAAI 2015*, 2288-2294.

Liu, Changsong and She, Lanbo and Fang, Rui and Chai, Joyce Y. 2014. Probabilistic Labeling for Efficient Referential Grounding Based On Collaborative Discourse. *Proceedings of the 52nd Annual Meeting of the Association for Computational Linguistics (ACL)*, 13-18.

Liu, Changsong and Fang, Rui and She, Lanbo and Chai, Joyce. 2013. Modeling Collaborative Referring for Situated Referential Grounding. *Proceedings of the 14th Annual Meeting of the Special Interest Group on Discourse and Dialogue*, 78–86.

Manning, Christopher D and Bauer, John and Finkel, Jenny and Bethard, Steven J. 2014. The Stanford CoreNLP Natural Language Processing Toolkit. *Proceedings of the 52nd Annual Meeting of the Association for Computational Linguistics: System Demonstrations*, 55-60.

Martschat, Sebastian and Strube, Michael. 2015. Latent Structures for Coreference Resolution. *Transactions of the Association for Computational Linguistics*, 3, 405-418.

Matuszek, Cynthia and FitzGerald, Nicholas and Zettlemoyer, Luke and Liefeng, Bo and Fox, Dieter. 2012. A Joint Model of Language and Perception for Grounded Attribute Learning. *Proceedings of the 29th International Conference on Machine Learning*, 1671-1678.

McCarthy, Joseph F. and Lehnert, Wendy G.. 1995. Using Decision Trees for Coreference Resolution. *Proceedings of the Fourteenth International Joint Conference on Artificial Intelligence (IJCAI)*, 1-5.

Naim, I and Song, Yc and Liu, Q and Kautz, H and Luo, J and Gildea, D. 2014. Unsupervised Alignment of Natural Language Instructions with Video Segments. *Proceedings of AAAI 2014*, 1558-1564.

Ponzetto, Simone Paolo and Strube, Michael. 2006. Exploiting Semantic Role Labeling, WordNet and Wikipedia for Coreference Resolution. *Proceedings of the Main Conference on Human Language Technology Conference of the North American Chapter of the Association of Computational Linguistics*, 192-199.

Soon, Wee Meng and Ng, Hwee Tou and Lim, Daniel Chung Yong. 2001. Incorporating Extra-linguistic Information into Reference Resolution in Collaborative Task Dialogue. *Computational Linguistics*, 27, 521-544.

VanLehn, Kurt and Jordan, P W and Rosé, C P and Bhembe, D and Bottner, M and Gaydos, A and Makatchev, M and Pappuswamy, U and Ringenberg, M and Roque, A. 2002. The Architecture of Why2-Atlas: A Coach for Qualitative Physics Essay Writing. *Proceedings of the Sixth International Conference on Intelligent Tutoring System*, 2363, 158-167.

Training an adaptive dialogue policy for interactive learning of visually grounded word meanings

Yanchao Yu
Interaction Lab
Heriot-Watt University
y.yu@hw.ac.uk

Arash Eshghi
Interaction Lab
Heriot-Watt University
a.eshghi@hw.ac.uk

Oliver Lemon
Interaction Lab
Heriot-Watt University
o.lemon@hw.ac.uk

Abstract

We present a multi-modal dialogue system for interactive learning of perceptually grounded word meanings from a human tutor. The system integrates an incremental, semantic parsing/generation framework - Dynamic Syntax and Type Theory with Records (DS-TTR) - with a set of visual classifiers that are learned throughout the interaction and which ground the meaning representations that it produces. We use this system in interaction with a simulated human tutor to study the effects of different dialogue policies and capabilities on accuracy of learned meanings, learning rates, and efforts/costs to the tutor. We show that the overall performance of the learning agent is affected by (1) who takes initiative in the dialogues; (2) the ability to express/use their confidence level about visual attributes; and (3) the ability to process elliptical and incrementally constructed dialogue turns. Ultimately, we train an adaptive dialogue policy which optimises the trade-off between classifier accuracy and tutoring costs.

1 Introduction

Identifying, classifying, and talking about objects or events in the surrounding environment are key capabilities for intelligent, goal-driven systems that interact with other agents and the external world (e.g. robots, smart spaces, and other automated systems). To this end, there has recently been a surge of interest and significant progress made on a variety of related tasks, including generation of Natural Language (NL) descriptions of images, or identifying images based on NL descriptions (Karpathy and Fei-Fei, 2014; Bruni et

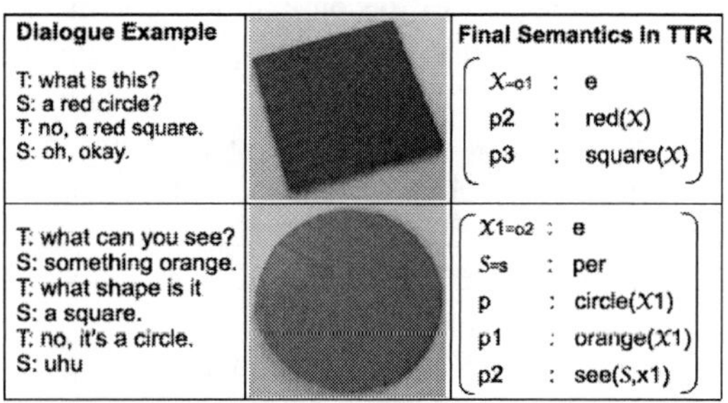

Figure 1: Example dialogues & interactively agreed semantic contents.

al., 2014; Socher et al., 2014; Farhadi et al., 2009; Silberer and Lapata, 2014; Sun et al., 2013).

Our goal is to build *interactive* systems that can learn grounded word meanings relating to their perceptions of real-world objects – this is different from previous work such as e.g. (Roy, 2002), that learn groundings from descriptions without any interaction, and more recent work using Deep Learning methods (e.g. (Socher et al., 2014)).

Most of these systems rely on training data of high quantity with no possibility of online error correction. Furthermore, they are unsuitable for robots and multimodal systems that need to continuously, and incrementally learn from the environment, and may encounter objects they haven't seen in training data. These limitations are likely to be alleviated if systems can learn concepts, as and when needed, from situated dialogue with humans. Interaction with a human tutor also enables systems to take initiative and seek the particular information they need or lack by e.g. asking questions with the highest information gain (see e.g. (Skocaj et al., 2011), and Fig. 1). For example, a robot could ask questions to learn the colour of a "square" or to request to be presented with more "red" things to improve its performance on the concept (see e.g. Fig. 1). Furthermore, such systems could allow for meaning negotiation in the

Proceedings of the SIGDIAL 2016 Conference, pages 339–349,
Los Angeles, USA, 13-15 September 2016. ©2016 Association for Computational Linguistics

form of clarification interactions with the tutor.

This setting means that the system must be *trainable from little data, compositional, adaptive, and able to handle natural human dialogue with all its glorious context-sensitivity and messiness* – for instance so that it can learn visual concepts suitable for specific tasks/domains, or even those specific to a particular user. Interactive systems that learn continuously, and over the long run from humans need to do so *incrementally, quickly,* and *with minimal effort/cost to human tutors.*

In this paper, we first outline an implemented dialogue system that integrates an incremental, semantic grammar framework, especially suited to dialogue processing – Dynamic Syntax and Type Theory with Records (DS-TTR[1] (Kempson et al., 2001; Eshghi et al., 2012)) with visual classifiers which are learned during the interaction, and which provide perceptual grounding for the basic semantic atoms in the semantic representations (Record Types in TTR) produced by the parser (see Fig. 1, Fig. 2 and section 3).

We then use this system in interaction with a simulated human tutor, to test hypotheses about how the accuracy of learned meanings, learning rates, and the overall cost/effort for the human tutor are affected by different dialogue policies and capabilities: (1) who takes **initiative** in the dialogues; (2) the agent's ability to utilise their level of **uncertainty** about an object's attributes; and (3) their ability to process **elliptical as well as incrementally constructed dialogue turns**. The results show that differences along these dimensions have significant impact both on the accuracy of the grounded word meanings that are learned, and the processing effort required by the tutors.

In section 4.3 we train an adaptive dialogue strategy that finds a better trade-off between classifier accuracy and tutor cost.

2   Related work

In this section, we will present an overview of vision and language processing systems, as well as multi-modal systems that learn to associate them. We compare them along two main dimensions: *Visual Classification methods: offline vs. online* and *the kinds of representation learned/used.*

Online vs. Offline Learning. A number of implemented systems have shown good performance on classification as well as NL-description of novel physical objects and their attributes, either using offline methods as in (Farhadi et al., 2009; Lampert et al., 2014; Socher et al., 2013; Kong et al., 2013), or through an incremental learning process, where the system's parameters are updated after each training example is presented to the system (Furao and Hasegawa, 2006; Zheng et al., 2013; Kristan and Leonardis, 2014). For the interactive learning task presented here, only the latter is appropriate, as the system is expected to learn from its interactions with a human tutor over a period of time. Shen & Hasegawa (2006) propose the SOINN-SVM model that re-trains linear SVM classifiers with data points that are clustered together with all the examples seen so far. The clustering is done incrementally, but the system needs to keep all the examples so far in memory. Kristian & Leonardis (2014), on the other hand, propose the oKDE model that continuously learns categorical knowledge about visual attributes as probability distributions over the categories (e.g. colours). However, when learning from scratch, it is unrealistic to predefine these concept groups (e.g. that red, blue, and green are colours). Systems need to learn for themselves that, e.g. colour is grounded in a specific sub-space of an object's features. For the visual classifiers, we therefore assume no such category groupings here, and instead learn individual binary classifiers for each visual attribute (see section 3.1 for details).

Distributional vs. Logical Representations. Learning to ground natural language in perception is one of the fundamental problems in Artificial Intelligence. There are two main strands of work that address this problem: (1) those that learn distributional representations using Deep Learning methods: this often works by projecting vector representations from different modalities (e.g. vision and language) into the same space in order to be able to retrieve one from the other (Socher et al., 2014; Karpathy and Li, 2015; Silberer and Lapata, 2014); (2) those that attempt to ground symbolic logical forms, obtained through semantic parsing (Tellex et al., 2014; Kollar et al., 2013; Matuszek et al., 2014) in classifiers of various entities types/events/relations in a segment of an image or a video. Perhaps one advantage of the latter over the former method, is that it is strictly compositional, i.e. the contribution of the meaning of an individual word, or semantic atom, to the whole representation is clear, whereas this is hard to say

---

[1]Download from http://dylan.sourceforge.net

about the distributional models. As noted, our work also uses the latter methodology, though it is dialogue, rather than sentence semantics that we care about. Most similar to our work is probably that of Kennington & Schlangen (2015) who learn a mapping between individual words - rather than logical atoms - and low-level visual features (e.g. colour-values) directly. The system is compositional, yet does not use a grammar (the compositions are defined by hand). Further, the groundings are learned from pairings of object references in NL and images rather than from dialogue.

What sets our approach apart from others is: a) that we use a domain-general, incremental semantic grammar with principled mechanisms for parsing and generation; b) Given the DS model of dialogue (Eshghi et al., 2015), representations are constructed jointly and interactively by the tutor and system over the course of several turns (see Fig. 1); c) perception and NL-semantics are modelled in a single logical formalism (TTR); d) we effectively induce an ontology of atomic types in TTR, which can be combined in arbitrarily complex ways for generation of complex descriptions of arbitrarily complex visual scenes (see e.g. (Dobnik et al., 2012) and compare this with (Kennington and Schlangen, 2015), who do not use a grammar and therefore do not have logical structure over grounded meanings).

3 System Architecture

We have developed a system to support an attribute-based object learning process through natural, incremental spoken dialogue interaction. The architecture of the system is shown in Fig. 2. The system has two main modules: a vision module for visual feature extraction, classification, and learning; and a dialogue system module using DS-TTR. Below we describe these components individually and then explain how they interact.

3.1 Attribute-based Classifiers used

Yu et. al (2015a; 2015b) point out that neither multi-label classification models nor 'zero-shot' learning models show acceptable performance on attribute-based learning tasks. Here, we instead use Logistic Regression SVM classifiers with Stochastic Gradient Descent (SGD) (Zhang, 2004) to incrementally learn attribute predictions.

All classifiers will output attribute-based label sets and corresponding probabilities for novel un-

seen images by predicting binary label vectors. We build visual feature representations to learn classifiers for particular attributes, as explained in the following subsections.

3.1.1 Visual Feature Representation

In contrast to previous work (Yu et al., 2015a; Yu et al., 2015b), to reduce feature noise through the learning process, we simplify the method of feature extraction consisting of two base feature categories, i.e. the colour space for colour attributes, and a 'bag of visual words' for the object shapes/class.

Colour descriptors, consisting of HSV colour space values, are extracted for each pixel and then are quantized to a $16 \times 4 \times 4$ HSV matrix. These descriptors inside the bounding box are binned into individual histograms. Meanwhile, a bag of visual words is built in PHOW descriptors using a visual dictionary (that is pre-defined with a hand-made image set). These visual words will be calculated using 2x2 blocks, a 4-pixel step size, and quantized into 1024 k-means centres. The feature extractor in the vision module presents a 1280-dimensional feature vector for a single training/test instance by stacking all quantized features, as shown in Figure 2.

3.2 Dynamic Syntax and Type Theory with Records

Dynamic Syntax (DS) a is a word-by-word incremental semantic parser/generator, based around the Dynamic Syntax (DS) grammar framework (Cann et al., 2005) especially suited to the fragmentary and highly contextual nature of dialogue. In DS, dialogue is modelled as the interactive and incremental construction of contextual and semantic representations (Eshghi et al., 2015). The contextual representations afforded by DS are of the fine-grained semantic content that is jointly negotiated/agreed upon by the interlocutors, as a result of processing questions and answers, clarification requests, corrections, acceptances, etc. We cannot go into any further detail due to lack of space, but proceed to introduce Type Theory with Records, the formalism in which the DS contextual/semantic representations are couched, but also that within which perception is modelled here.

Type Theory with Records (TTR) is an extension of standard type theory shown to be use-

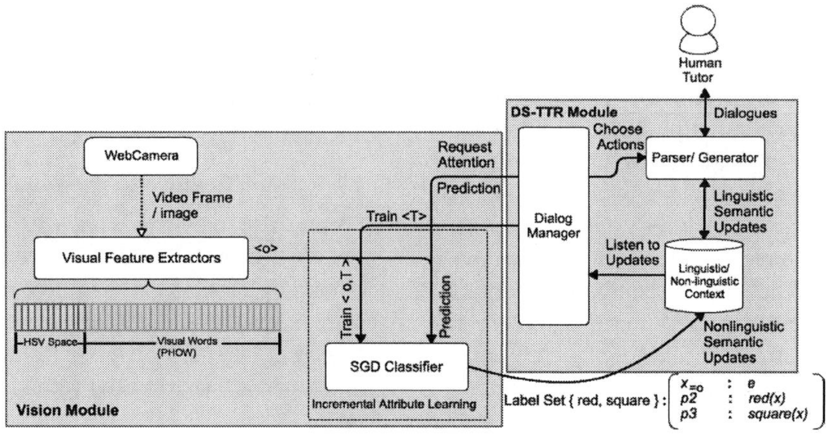

Figure 2: Architecture of the teachable system

ful in semantics and dialogue modelling (Cooper, 2005; Ginzburg, 2012). TTR is particularly well-suited to our problem here as it allows information from various modalities, including vision and language, to be represented within a single semantic framework (see e.g. Larsson (2013); Dobnik et al. (2012) who use it to model the semantics of spatial language and perceptual classification).

In TTR, logical forms are specified as *record types* (RTs), which are sequences of *fields* of the form $[\, l : T \,]$ containing a label l and a type T. RTs can be witnessed (i.e. judged true) by *records* of that type, where a record is a sequence of label-value pairs $[\, l = v \,]$. We say that $[\, l = v \,]$ is of type $[\, l : T \,]$ just in case v is of type T.

$$
R_1 : \begin{bmatrix} l_1 & : T_1 \\ l_{2=a} & : T_2 \\ l_{3=p(l_2)} & : T_3 \end{bmatrix}
\qquad
R_2 : \begin{bmatrix} l_1 & : T_1 \\ l_2 & : T_{2'} \end{bmatrix}
\qquad
R_3 : [\,]
$$

Figure 3: Example TTR record types

Fields can be *manifest*, i.e. given a singleton type e.g. $[\, l : T_a \,]$ where T_a is the type of which only a is a member; here, we write this using the syntactic sugar $[\, l_{=a} : T \,]$. Fields can also be *dependent* on fields preceding them (i.e. higher) in the record type (see Fig. 3).

The standard subtype relation $\sqsubseteq$ can be defined for record types: $R_1 \sqsubseteq R_2$ if for all fields $[\, l : T_2 \,]$ in R_2, R_1 contains $[\, l : T_1 \,]$ where $T_1 \sqsubseteq T_2$. In Figure 3, $R_1 \sqsubseteq R_2$ if $T_2 \sqsubseteq T_{2'}$, and both R_1 and R_2 are subtypes of R_3. This subtyping relation allows semantic information to be incrementally specified, i.e. record types can be indefinitely extended with more information/constraints. For us here, this is a key feature since it allows the system to en-

code *partial* knowledge about objects, and for this knowledge (e.g. object attributes) to be extended in a principled way, as and when this information becomes available.

3.3 Integration

Fig. 2 shows how the various parts of the system interact. At any point in time, the system has access to an ontology of (object) types and attributes encoded as a set of TTR Record Types, whose individual atomic symbols, such as 'red' or 'square' are grounded in the set of classifiers trained so far.

Given a set of individuated objects in a scene, encoded as a TTR Record, the system can utilise its existing ontology to output a Record Type which maximally characterises the scene (see e.g. Fig. 1). Dynamic Syntax operates over the same representations, they provide a direct interface between perceptual classification and semantic processing in dialogue: this representation acts not only as (1) the non-linguistic (here, visual) context of the dialogue for the resolution of e.g. definite reference and indexicals (see (Hough and Purver, 2014)); but also as (2) the logical database from which the system can generate utterances (descriptions), ask, or answer questions about the objects - Fig. 4 illustrates how the semantics of the answer to a question is retrieved from the visual context through *unification* (this uses the standard subtype checking operation within TTR).

Conversely, for concept learning, the DS-TTR parser incrementally produces Record Types (RT), representing the meaning jointly established by the tutor and the system so far. In this domain, this is ultimately one or more type judgements, i.e. that some scene/image/object is judged to be of a

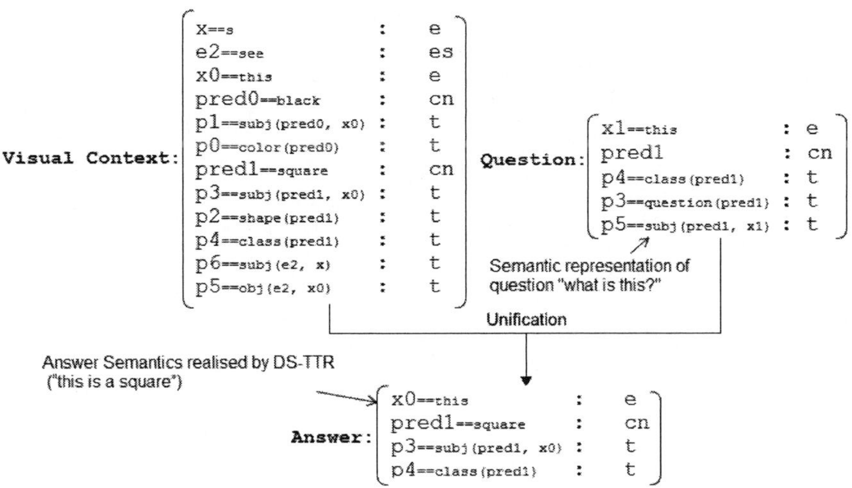

Figure 4: Question Answering by the system

particular type, e.g. in Fig. 1 that the individuated object, $o1$ is a red square. These jointly negotiated type judgements then go on to provide training instances for the classifiers. In general, the training instances are of the form, $\langle O, T \rangle$, where O is an image/scene segment (an object or TTR Record), and T, a record type. T is then decomposed into its constituent atomic types $T_1 \ldots T_n$, s.t. $\bigwedge T_i = T$ - where $\bigwedge$ is the so called *meet* operation corresponding to type conjunction. The judgements $O : T_i$ are then used directly to train the classifiers that ground the T_i.

4   Experimental Setup

As noted in the introduction, interactive systems that learn continuously, and over the long run from humans need to do so *incrementally*; *as quickly as possible*; and *with as little effort/cost to the human tutor as possible*. In addition, when learning takes place through dialogue, the dialogue needs to be as human-like/natural as possible.

In general, there are several different dialogue capabilities and policies that a concept-learning agent might adopt, and these will lead to different outcomes for the accuracy of the learned concepts/meanings, learning rates, and cost to the tutor – with trade-offs between these. Our goal in this paper is therefore an experimental study of the effect of different dialogue policies and capabilities on the overall performance of the learning agent, which, as we describe below is a measure capturing the trade-off between accuracy of learned meanings and the cost of tutoring.

Design. We use the dialogue system outlined above to carry out our main experiment with a $2 \times 2 \times 2$ factorial design, i.e. with three factors each with two levels. Together, these factors determine the learner's dialogue behaviour: (1) **Initiative** (**Learner/Tutor**): determines who takes initiative in the dialogues. When the tutor takes initiative, s/he is the one that drives the conversation forward, by asking questions to the learner (e.g. "What colour is this?" or "So this is a ....") or making a statement about the attributes of the object. On the other hand, when the learner has initiative, it makes statements, asks questions, initiates topics etc. (2) **Uncertainty** (**+UC/-UC**): determines whether the learner takes into account, in its dialogue behaviour, its own subjective confidence about the attributes of the presented object. The confidence is the probability assigned by any of its attribute classifiers of the object being a positive instance of an attribute (e.g. 'red') - see below for how a confidence threshold is used here. In +UC, the agent will not ask a question if it is confident about the answer, and it will hedge the answer to a tutor question if it is not confident, e.g. "T: What is this? L: errm, maybe a square?". In -UC, the agent always takes itself to know the attributes of the given object (as given by its currently trained classifiers), and behaves according to that assumption. (3) **Context-Dependency** (**+CD/-CD**): determines whether the learner can process (produce/parse) context-dependent expressions such as short answers and incrementally constructed turns, e.g. "T: What is this? L: a square", or "T:

<table>
<tr>
<td>L-UC-CD

L: This is red.
T: No, it is blue.
L: Okay. This is a square.
T: Yes.</td>
<td>L+UC+CD

L: What colour is this?
T: Red.
L: Okay. Is this a square?
T: No, a circle.
L: Okay.</td>
<td>L+UC-CD

L: Is this a circle?
T: No, it's a triangle.
L: Okay. Is it green?
T: Yes.</td>
<td>L-UC+CD

L: This is a square
T: No, a triangle.
L: Okay. This is red.
T: Yes.</td>
</tr>
<tr>
<td>T+UC+CD

T: This is a ...
L: Errm, a square?
T: Yes. What colour is it?
L: Red.
T: No, it's green.
L: Okay.</td>
<td>T-UC-CD

T: What (shape) is this?
L: This is a circle.
T: Yes. What colour is it?
L: it is red.
T: No, it's purple.
L: Okay.</td>
<td>T+UC-CD

T: What is this?
L: (long pause)
T: It is a square.
L: Okay.
T: What colour is it?
L: Is it blue?
T: Yes.</td>
<td>T-UC+CD

T: What is this?
L: A square.
T: Yes. What colour is it?
L: Blue.
T: No, it is green.
L: Uhu.</td>
</tr>
</table>

Figure 5: Example dialogues in different conditions

So this one is ...? L: red/a circle". This setting can be turned off/on in the DS-TTR dialogue model.

Tutor Simulation and Policy To run our experiment on a large-scale, we have hand-crafted an *Interactive Tutoring Simulator*, which simulates the behaviour of a human tutor[2]. The tutor policy is kept constant across all conditions. Its policy is that of an always *truthful*, *helpful* and *omniscient* one: it (1) has complete access to the labels of each object; and (2) always acts as the context of the dialogue dictates: answers any question asked, confirms or rejects when the learner describes an object; and (3) always corrects the learner when it describes an object erroneously.

Dependent Measures We now go on to describe the dependent measures in our experiment, i.e. that of classifier accuracy/score, tutoring cost, and the overall performance measure which combines the former two measures.

Confidence Threshold To determine when the agent takes themselves to be confident in an attribute prediction, we use confidence-score thresholds. It consists of two values, a base threshold (e.g. 0.5) and a positive threshold (e.g. 0.9).

If the confidences of all classifiers are under the base threshold (i.e. the learner has no attribute label that it is confident about), the agent will ask for information directly from the tutor via questions (e.g. "L: what is this?").

On the other hand, if one or more classifiers score above the base threshold, then the positive threshold is used to judge to what extent the agent

trusts its prediction or not. If the confidence score of a classifier is between the positive and base thresholds, the learner is not very confident about its knowledge, and will check with the tutor, e.g. "L: is this red?". However, if the confidence score of a classifier is above the positive threshold, the learner is confident enough in its knowledge not to bother verifying it with the tutor. This will lead to less effort needed from the tutor as the learner becomes more confident about its knowledge. However, since a learning agent that has high confidence about a prediction will not ask for assistance from the tutor, a low positive threshold would reduce the chances that allow the tutor to correct the learner's mistakes. We therefore tested different fixed values for the confidence threshold and this determined a fixed 0.5 base threshold and a 0.9 positive threshold were deemed to be the most appropriate values for an interactive learning process - i.e. these values preserved good classifier accuracy while not requiring much effort from the tutor - see below Section 4.3 for how an adaptive policy was learned that adjusts the agent's confidence threshold dynamically over time.

4.1 Evaluation Metrics

To test how the different dialogue capabilities and strategies affect the learning process, we consider both the cost to the tutor and the accuracy of the learned meanings, i.e. the classifiers that ground our colour and shape concepts.

Cost The cost measure reflects the effort needed by a human tutor in interacting with the system. Skocaj et. al. (2009) point out that a comprehensive teachable system should learn as autonomously as possible, rather than involving human tutor too frequently. There are several pos-

---

[2]The experiment involves hundreds of dialogues, so running this experiment with real human tutors has proven too costly at this juncture, though we plan to do this for a full evaluation of our system in the future.

Table 1: Tutoring Cost Table

C_{inf}	C_{ack}	C_{crt}	$C_{parsing}$	$C_{production}$
1	0.25	1	0.5	1

sible costs that the tutor might incur, see Table 1: C_{inf} refers to the cost of the tutor providing information on a single attribute concept (e.g. "this is red" or "this is a square"); C_{ack} is the cost for a simple confirmation (like "yes", "right") or rejection (such as "no"); C_{crt} is the cost of correction for a single concept (e.g. "no, it is blue" or "no, it is a circle"). We associate a higher cost with correction of statements than that of polar questions. This is to penalise the learning agent when it confidently makes a false statement – thereby incorporating an aspect of trust in the metric (humans will not trust systems which confidently make false statements). And finally, parsing (C_{parse}) as well as production ($C_{production}$) costs for tutor are taken into account: each single word costs 0.5 when parsed by the tutor, and 1 if generated (production costs twice as much as parsing). These exact values are based on intuition but are kept constant across the experimental conditions and therefore do not confound the results reported below.

Learning Performance As mentioned above, an efficient learner dialogue policy should consider both classification accuracy and tutor effort (Cost). We thus define an integrated measure – the *Overall Performance Ratio* (R_{perf}) – that we use to compare the learner's overall performance across the different conditions:

$$R_{perf} = \frac{\Delta Acc}{C_{tutor}}$$

i.e. the increase in accuracy per unit of the cost, or equivalently the gradient of the curve in Fig. 4c. We seek dialogue strategies that maximise this.

Dataset The dataset used here is comprised of 600 images of single, simple handmade objects with a white background (see Fig.1)[3]. There are nine attributes considered in this dataset: 6 colours (black, blue, green, orange, purple and red) and 3 shapes (circle, square and triangle), with a relative balance on the number of instances per attribute.

4.2 Evaluation and Cross-validation

In each round, the system is trained using 500 training instances, with the rest set aside for test-

ing. For each training instance, the system interacts (only through dialogue) with the simulated tutor. Each dialogue about an object ends either when both the shape and the colour of the object are discussed and agreed upon, or when the learner requests to be presented with the next image (this happens only in the Learner initiative conditions). We define a **Learning Step** as comprised of 10 such dialogues. At the end of each learning step, the system is tested using the test set (100 test instances).

This process is repeated 20 times, i.e. for 20 rounds/folds, each time with a different, random 500-100 split, thus resulting in 20 data-points for cost and accuracy after every learning step. The values reported below, including those on the plots in Fig. 6a, 6b and 6c, correspond to averages across the 20 folds.

4.3 Learning an Adaptive Policy for a Dynamic Confidence Threshold

In the experiment presented above, the learning agent's positive confidence threshold was held constant, at 0.9. However, since the confidence threshold itself becomes more reliable as the agent is exposed to more training instances, we further hypothesised that a threshold that changes dynamically over time should lead to a better trade-off between classification accuracy and cost for the tutor, i.e. a better *Overall Performance Ratio* (see above). For example, lower positive thresholds may be more appropriate at the later stages of training when the agent is already performing well with attribute classifiers which are more reliable. This leads to different dialogue behaviours, as the learner takes different decisions as it encounters more training examples.

To test this hypothesis we further trained and evaluated an adaptive policy that adjusts the learning agent's confidence threshold as it interacts with the tutor (in the +UC conditions only). This optimization used a Markov Decision Process (MDP) model and Reinforcement Learning[4], where: (1) the **state space** was determined by vari-

---

[3]All data from this paper will be made freely available.

[4]A reviewer points out that one can handle uncertainty in a more principled way, possibly with better results, using POMDPs. Another reviewer points out that the policy learned is only adapting the confidence threshold, and not the other conditions (uncertainty, initiative, context-dependency). We point out that we are addressing both of these limitations in work in progress, where we feed each classifier's outputted confidence level as a continuous feature in a (continuous space) MDP for *full dialogue control*.

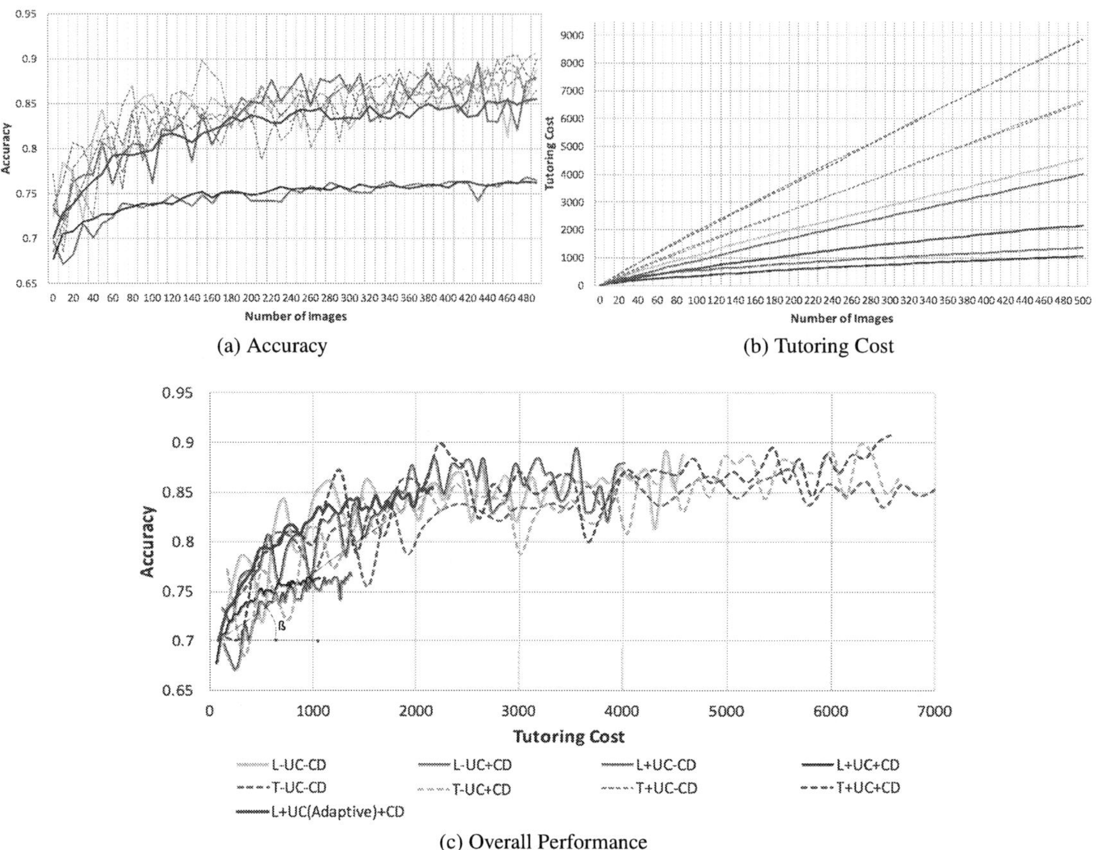

(a) Accuracy

(b) Tutoring Cost

(c) Overall Performance

Figure 6: Evolution of Learning Performance

ables for the number of training instances seen so far, and the agent's current confidence threshold (2) the **actions** were either to increase or decrease the confidence threshold by 0.05, or keep it the same; (3) the **local reward signal** was directly proportional to the agent's *Overall Performance Ratio* over the previous Learning Step (10 training instances, see above); and (4) the **SARSA algorithm** (Sutton and Barto, 1998) was chosen for learning, with each **episode** defined as a complete run through the 500 training instances.

5 Results

Fig. 5 shows example interactions between the learner and the tutor in some of the experimental conditions. Note how the system is able to deal with (parse and generate) utterance continuations as in $T+UC+CD$, short answers as in $L+UC+CD$, and polar answers as in $T + UC + CD$.

Fig. 6a and 6b plot the progression of average Accuracy and (cumulative) Tutoring Cost for each of the 8 conditions in our main experiment,

as the system interacts over time with the tutor about each of the 500 training instances. The ninth curve in red (L+UC(Adaptive)+CD) shows the same for the learning agent with a dynamic confidence threshold using the policy trained using Reinforcement Learning (section 4.3) - the latter is only compared below to the dark blue curve (L+UC+CD). As noted in passing, the vertical axes in these graphs are based on averages across the 20 folds - recall that for Accuracy the system was tested, in each fold, at every learning step, i.e. after every 10 training instances.

Fig. 6c, on the other hand, plots Accuracy against Tutoring Cost directly. Note that it is to be expected that the curves should not terminate in the same place on the x-axis since the different conditions incur different total costs for the tutor across the 500 training instances. The gradient of this curve corresponds to *increase in Accuracy per unit of the Tutoring Cost*. It is the gradient of the line drawn from the beginning to the end of each curve (*tan(β)* on Fig. 4c) that constitutes our main

346

evaluation measure of the system's overall performance in each condition, and it is this measure for which we report statistical significance results:

A between-subjects Analysis of Variance (ANOVA) shows significant main effects of Initiative ($p < 0.01; F = 448.33$), Uncertainty ($p < 0.01; F = 206.06$) and Context-Dependency ($p < 0.05; F = 4.31$) on the system's overall performance. There is also a significant Initiative×Uncertainty interaction ($p < 0.01; F = 194.31$).

Keeping all other conditions constant (L+UC+CD), there is also a significant main effect of Confidence Threshold type (Constant vs. Adaptive) on the same measure ($p < 0.01; F = 206.06$). The mean gradient of the red, adaptive curve is actually slightly lower than its constant-threshold counter-part blue curve - discussed below.

6 Discussion

Tutoring Cost As can be seen on Fig. 6b, the cumulative cost for the tutor progresses more slowly when the learner has initiative (L) and takes its confidence into account in its behaviour (+UC) - the grey, blue, and red curves. This is so because *a form of active learning* is taking place: the learner only asks a question about an attribute if it isn't confident enough already about that attribute. This also explains the slight decrease in the gradients of the curves as the agent is exposed to more and more training instances: its subjective confidence about its own predictions increases over time, and thus there is progressively less need for tutoring.

Accuracy On the other hand, the L+UC curves (grey and blue) on Fig. 6a show the slowest increase in accuracy and flatten out at about 0.76. This is because the agent's confidence score in the beginning is unreliable as the agent has only seen a few training instances: in many cases it doesn't query the tutor or have any interaction whatsoever with it and so there are informative examples that it doesn't get exposed to. In contrast to this, the L+UC(adaptive)+CD curve (red) achieves much better accuracy.

Comparing the gradients of the curves on Fig. 6c shows that the overall performance of the agent on the gradient measure is significantly better than others in the L+UC conditions (recall the significant Initiative × Uncertainty interaction). However, while the agent with an **adaptive** thresh-old (red/L+UC(adaptive)+CD) achieves slightly lower overall gradient than its constant threshold counter-part (blue/L+UC+CD), it achieves much higher Accuracy overall, and does this much faster in the first 1000 units of cost (roughly the total cost in L+UC+CD condition). We therefore conclude that the adaptive policy is more desirable. Finally, the significant main effect of **Context-Dependency** on the overall performance is explained by the fact in the +CD conditions, the agent is able to process context-dependent and incrementally constructed turns, leading to less repetition, shorter dialogues, and therefore better overall performance.

7 Conclusion and Future work

We have presented a multi-modal dialogue system that learns grounded word meanings from a human tutor, incrementally, over time, and employs a dynamic dialogue policy (optimised using Reinforcement Learning). The system integrates a semantic grammar for dialogue (DS), and a logical theory of types (TTR), with a set of visual classifiers in which the TTR semantic representations are grounded. We used this implemented system to study the effect of different dialogue policies and capabilities on the overall performance of a learning agent - a combined measure of accuracy and cost. The results show that in order to maximise its performance, the agent needs to take initiative in the dialogues, take into account its changing confidence about its predictions, and be able to process natural, human-like dialogue.

Ongoing work further uses Reinforcement Learning to learn complete, incremental dialogue policies, i.e. which choose system output at the lexical level (Eshghi and Lemon, 2014). To deal with uncertainty this system takes all the classifiers' outputted confidence levels directly as features in a continuous space MDP.

Acknowledgements

This research is supported by the EPSRC, under grant number EP/M01553X/1 (BABBLE project[5]), and by the European Union's Horizon 2020 research and innovation programme under grant agreement No. 688147 (MuMMER project[6]).

---

[5]https://sites.google.com/site/hwinteractionlab/babble

[6]http://mummer-project.eu/

References

Elia Bruni, Nam-Khanh Tran, and Marco Baroni. 2014. Multimodal distributional semantics. *J. Artif. Intell. Res.(JAIR)*, 49(1–47).

Ronnie Cann, Ruth Kempson, and Lutz Marten. 2005. *The Dynamics of Language*. Elsevier, Oxford.

Robin Cooper. 2005. Records and record types in semantic theory. *Journal of Logic and Computation*, 15(2):99–112.

Simon Dobnik, Robin Cooper, and Staffan Larsson. 2012. Modelling language, action, and perception in type theory with records. In *Proceedings of the 7th International Workshop on Constraint Solving and Language Processing (CSLPÄô12)*, pages 51–63.

Arash Eshghi and Oliver Lemon. 2014. How domain-general can we be? learning incremental dialogue systems without dialogue acts. In *Proceedings of SemDial*.

Arash Eshghi, Julian Hough, Matthew Purver, Ruth Kempson, and Eleni Gregoromichelaki. 2012. Conversational interactions: Capturing dialogue dynamics. In S. Larsson and L. Borin, editors, *From Quantification to Conversation: Festschrift for Robin Cooper on the occasion of his 65th birthday*, volume 19 of *Tributes*, pages 325–349. College Publications, London.

A. Eshghi, C. Howes, E. Gregoromichelaki, J. Hough, and M. Purver. 2015. Feedback in conversation as incremental semantic update. In *Proceedings of the 11th International Conference on Computational Semantics (IWCS 2015)*, London, UK. Association for Computational Linguisitics.

Ali Farhadi, Ian Endres, Derek Hoiem, and David Forsyth. 2009. Describing objects by their attributes. In *Proceedings of the IEEE Computer Society Conference on Computer Vision and Pattern Recognition (CVPR*.

Shen Furao and Osamu Hasegawa. 2006. An incremental network for on-line unsupervised classification and topology learning. *Neural Networks*, 19(1):90–106.

Jonathan Ginzburg. 2012. *The Interactive Stance: Meaning for Conversation*. Oxford University Press.

Julian Hough and Matthew Purver. 2014. Probabilistic type theory for incremental dialogue processing. In *Proceedings of the EACL 2014 Workshop on Type Theory and Natural Language Semantics (TTNLS)*, pages 80–88, Gothenburg, Sweden, April. Association for Computational Linguistics.

Andrej Karpathy and Li Fei-Fei. 2014. Deep visual-semantic alignments for generating image descriptions. *CoRR*, abs/1412.2306.

Andrej Karpathy and Fei-Fei Li. 2015. Deep visual-semantic alignments for generating image descriptions. In *IEEE Conference on Computer Vision and Pattern Recognition, CVPR 2015, Boston, MA, USA, June 7-12, 2015*, pages 3128–3137.

Ruth Kempson, Wilfried Meyer-Viol, and Dov Gabbay. 2001. *Dynamic Syntax: The Flow of Language Understanding*. Blackwell.

Casey Kennington and David Schlangen. 2015. Simple learning and compositional application of perceptually grounded word meanings for incremental reference resolution. In *Proceedings of the Conference for the Association for Computational Linguistics (ACL-IJCNLP)*. Association for Computational Linguistics.

Thomas Kollar, Jayant Krishnamurthy, and Grant Strimel. 2013. Toward interactive grounded language acqusition. In *Robotics: Science and Systems*.

Xiangnan Kong, Michael K. Ng, and Zhi-Hua Zhou. 2013. Transductive multilabel learning via label set propagation. *IEEE Trans. Knowl. Data Eng.*, 25(3):704–719.

Matej Kristan and Ales Leonardis. 2014. Online discriminative kernel density estimator with gaussian kernels. *IEEE Trans. Cybernetics*, 44(3):355–365.

Christoph H. Lampert, Hannes Nickisch, and Stefan Harmeling. 2014. Attribute-based classification for zero-shot visual object categorization. *IEEE Trans. Pattern Anal. Mach. Intell.*, 36(3):453–465.

Staffan Larsson. 2013. Formal semantics for perceptual classification. *Journal of logic and computation*.

Cynthia Matuszek, Liefeng Bo, Luke Zettlemoyer, and Dieter Fox. 2014. Learning from unscripted deictic gesture and language for human-robot interactions. In *Proceedings of the Twenty-Eighth AAAI Conference on Artificial Intelligence, July 27 -31, 2014, Québec City, Québec, Canada.*, pages 2556–2563.

Deb Roy. 2002. A trainable visually-grounded spoken language generation system. In *Proceedings of the International Conference of Spoken Language Processing*.

Carina Silberer and Mirella Lapata. 2014. Learning grounded meaning representations with autoencoders. In *Proceedings of the 52nd Annual Meeting of the Association for Computational Linguistics (Volume 1: Long Papers)*, volume 1, pages 721–732, Baltimore, Maryland, June. Association for Computational Linguistics.

Danijel Skocaj, Matej Kristan, Alen Vrecko, Marko Mahnic, Miroslav Janícek, Geert-Jan M. Kruijff, Marc Hanheide, Nick Hawes, Thomas Keller, Michael Zillich, and Kai Zhou. 2011. A system for interactive learning in dialogue with a tutor. In *2011 IEEE/RSJ International Conference on Intelligent*

Robots and Systems, IROS 2011, San Francisco, CA, USA, September 25-30, 2011, pages 3387–3394.

Danijel Skočaj, Matej Kristan, and Aleš Leonardis. 2009. Formalization of different learning strategies in a continuous learning framework. In *Proceedings of the Ninth International Conference on Epigenetic Robotics; Modeling Cognitive Development in Robotic Systems*, pages 153–160. Lund University Cognitive Studies.

Richard Socher, Milind Ganjoo, Christopher D. Manning, and Andrew Y. Ng. 2013. Zero-shot learning through cross-modal transfer. In *Advances in Neural Information Processing Systems 26: 27th Annual Conference on Neural Information Processing Systems*, pages 935–943, Lake Tahoe, Nevada, USA.

Richard Socher, Andrej Karpathy, Quoc V Le, Christopher D Manning, and Andrew Y Ng. 2014. Grounded compositional semantics for finding and describing images with sentences. *Transactions of the Association for Computational Linguistics*, 2:207–218.

Yuyin Sun, Liefeng Bo, and Dieter Fox. 2013. Attribute based object identification. In *Robotics and Automation (ICRA), 2013 IEEE International Conference on*, pages 2096–2103. IEEE.

Richard S. Sutton and Andrew G. Barto. 1998. *Reinforcement Learning: an Introduction*. MIT Press.

Stefanie Tellex, Pratiksha Thaker, Joshua Mason Joseph, and Nicholas Roy. 2014. Learning perceptually grounded word meanings from unaligned parallel data. *Machine Learning*, 94(2):151–167.

Yanchao Yu, Arash Eshghi, and Oliver Lemon. 2015a. Comparing attribute classifiers for interactive language grounding. In *Proceedings of the Fourth Workshop on Vision and Language*, pages 60–69, Lisbon, Portugal, September. Association for Computational Linguistics.

Yanchao Yu, Oliver Lemon, and Arash Eshghi. 2015b. Interactive learning through dialogue for multimodal language grounding. In *SemDial 2015, Proceedings of the 19th Workshop on the Semantics and Pragmatics of Dialogue, Gothenburg, Sweden, August 24-26 2015*, pages 214–215.

Tong Zhang. 2004. Solving large scale linear prediction problems using stochastic gradient descent algorithms. In *Proceedings of the twenty-first international conference on Machine learning*, page 116. ACM.

Jun Zheng, Furao Shen, Hongjun Fan, and Jinxi Zhao. 2013. An online incremental learning support vector machine for large-scale data. *Neural Computing and Applications*, 22(5):1023–1035.

Learning Fine-Grained Knowledge about Contingent Relations between Everyday Events

Elahe Rahimtoroghi, Ernesto Hernandez and **Marilyn A Walker**
Natural Language and Dialogue Systems Lab
Department of Computer Science, University of California Santa Cruz
Santa Cruz, CA 95064, USA
elahe@soe.ucsc.edu, eherna23@ucsc.edu, mawalker@ucsc.edu

Abstract

Much of the user-generated content on social media is provided by ordinary people telling stories about their daily lives. We develop and test a novel method for learning fine-grained common-sense knowledge from these stories about contingent (causal and conditional) relationships between everyday events. This type of knowledge is useful for text and story understanding, information extraction, question answering, and text summarization. We test and compare different methods for learning contingency relation, and compare what is learned from topic-sorted story collections vs. general-domain stories. Our experiments show that using topic-specific datasets enables learning finer-grained knowledge about events and results in significant improvement over the baselines. An evaluation on Amazon Mechanical Turk shows 82% of the relations between events that we learn from topic-sorted stories are judged as contingent.

1 Introduction

The original idea behind scripts as introduced by Schank was to capture knowledge about the fine-grained events of everyday experience, such as *opening a fridge* enabling *preparing food*, or the event of *getting out of bed* being triggered by *an alarm going off* (Schank and Abelson, 1977; Mooney and DeJong, 1985) This idea has motivated previous work exploring whether common-sense knowledge about events can be learned from text, however, only a few learn from data other than newswire (Hu et al., 2013; Manshadi et al., 2008; Beamer and Girju, 2009). News articles (obviously) cover newsworthy topics such

---

Camping Trip
We packed all our things on the night before Thu (24 Jul) except for frozen food. We brought a lot of things along. **We woke up** early on Thu and JS started packing the frozen marinatinated food inside the small cooler... In the end, we decided the best place to set up the tent was the squarish ground that's located on the right. Prior to setting up our tent, **we placed a tarp on the ground**. In this way, the underneaths of the tent would be kept clean. After that, **we set the tent up**.

Storm
I don't know if I would've been as calm as I was without the radio, as **the hurricane made landfall** in Galveston at 2:10AM on Saturday. As **the wind blew**, branches thudded on the roof or trees snapped, it was helpful to pinpoint the place... **A tree fell** on the garage roof, but it's minor damage compared to what could've happened. We then **started cleaning up**, despite Sugar Land implementing a curfew until 2pm; I didn't see any policemen enforcing this. Luckily my dad has a gas saw (as opposed to electric), so **we helped cut up** three of our neighbors' trees. **I did a lot of raking**, and there's so much debris in the garbage.

Figure 1: Excerpts of two stories in the blogs corpus on the topics of *Camping Trip* and *Storm*.

as *bombing, explosions, war* and *killing* so the knowledge learned is limited to those types of events.

However, much of the user-generated content on social media is provided by ordinary people telling stories about their daily lives. These stories are rich with common-sense knowledge. For example, the *Camping Trip* story in Fig. 1 contains implicit common-sense knowledge about contingent (causal and conditional) relations between camping-related events, such as *setting up a tent* and *placing a tarp*. The *Storm* story contains implicit knowledge about events such as *the hurricane made landfall, the wind blew, a tree fell*. Our aim is to learn fine-grained common-sense knowledge about contingent relations between everyday events from such stories. We show that the fine-

350

Proceedings of the SIGDIAL 2016 Conference, pages 350–359,
Los Angeles, USA, 13-15 September 2016. ©2016 Association for Computational Linguistics

grained knowledge we learn is simply not found in publicly available narrative and event schema collections (Chambers and Jurafsky, 2009; Balasubramanian et al., 2013).

Personal stories provide both advantages and disadvantages for learning common-sense knowledge about events. An advantage is that they tend to be told in chronological order (Swanson and Gordon, 2009), and temporal order between events is a strong cue to contingency (Prasad et al., 2008; Beamer and Girju, 2009). However, their structure is more similar to oral narrative than to newswire (Rahimtoroghi et al., 2014; Swanson et al., 2014). Only about a third of the sentences in a personal narrative describe actions,[1] so novel methods are needed to find useful relationships between events.

Another difference between our work and prior research is that much of the work on narrative schemas, scripts, or event schemas characterize what is learned as "collections of events that tend to co-occur". Thus what is learned is not evaluated for contingency (Chambers and Jurafsky, 2008; Chambers and Jurafsky, 2009; Manshadi et al., 2008; Nguyen et al., 2015; Balasubramanian et al., 2013; Pichotta and Mooney, 2014). Historically, work on scripts explicitly modeled causality (Lehnert, 1981; Mooney and DeJong, 1985) *inter alia*. Our work is motivated by Penn Discourse Treebank (PDTB) definition of CONTINGENCY that has two types: CAUSE and CONDITION, and is more similar to approaches that learn specific event relations such as contingency or causality (Hu et al., 2013; Do et al., 2011; Girju, 2003; Riaz and Girju, 2010; Rink et al., 2010; Chklovski and Pantel, 2004). Our contributions are as follows:

- We use a corpus of everyday events for learning common-sense knowledge focusing on the contingency relation between events. We first use a subset of the corpus including general-domain stories. Next, we produce a topic-sorted set of stories using a semi-supervised bootstrapping method to learn finer-grained knowledge. We use two different datasets to directly compare what is learned from topic-sorted stories as opposed to a general-domain story corpus (Sec. 2);

- We develop a new method for learning contingency relations between events that is tailored to the "oral narrative" nature of blog

stories. We apply Causal Potential (Beamer and Girju, 2009) to model the contingency relation between two events. We directly compare our method to several other approaches as baselines (Sec. 3). We also identify topic-indicative contingent event pairs from our topic-specific corpus that can be used as building blocks for generating coherent event chains and narrative schema for a particular theme (Sec. 4.3);

- We conduct several experiments to evaluate the quality of the event knowledge learned in our work that indicate our results are contingent and topic-related. We directly compare the common-sense knowledge we learn with the Rel-grams collection and show that what we learn is not found in available corpora (Sec. 4).

We release our contingent event pair collections for each topic for future use of other research groups [2].

2 A Corpus of Everyday Events

Our dataset is drawn from the Spinn3r corpus of millions of blog posts (Burton et al., 2009; Gordon and Swanson, 2009; Gordon et al., 2012). We hypothesize that personal stories are a valuable resource to learn common-sense knowledge about relations between everyday events and that finer-grained knowledge can be learned from topic-sorted stories (Riaz and Girju, 2010) that share a particular theme, so we construct two different sets of stories:

General-Domain Set. We created a random subset from the Spinn3r corpus from personal blog domains: *livejournal.com, wordpress.com, blogspot.com, spaces.live.com, typepad.com, travelpod.com*. This set consists of 4,200 stories not selected for any specific topic.

Topic-Specific Set. We produced a dataset by filtering the corpus using a bootstrapping method to create topic-specific sets for topics such as *going camping, being arrested, going snorkeling or scuba diving, visiting the dentist, witnessing a major storm*, and *holiday activities* associated with Thanksgiving and Christmas (see Table 1).

We apply AutoSlog-TS, a semi-supervised algorithm that learns narrative *event-patterns* to bootstrap a collection of stories on the same

---

[1] The other two thirds provide scene descriptions and descriptions of the thoughts or feelings of the narrator.

[2] https://nlds.soe.ucsc.edu/everyday_events

Topic	Events
Camping Trip	camp(), roast(dobj:marshmallow), hike(), pack(), fish(), go(dobj:camp), grill(), put(dobj:tent , prt:up), build(dobj:fire)
Storm	restore(), lose(dobj:power), rescue(), evacuate(), flood(), damage(), sustain(), survive(), watch(dobj:storm)
Christmas Holidays	open(dobj:present), wrap(), , celebrate() sing(), play(), exchange(dobj:gift), snow(), buy(), decorate(dobj:tree)
Snorkeling and Scuba Diving	see(dobj:fish), swim(), snorkel(), sail(), surface(), dive(), dart(), rent(dobj:equipment), enter(dobj:water), see(dobj:turtle)

Table 1: Some topics and examples of their indicative events.

Topic	Event-Pattern (Case Frame) Examples
Camping Trip	NP-Prep-(NP):CAMPING-IN NP-Prep-(NP):HIKE-TO (subj)-ActVB-Dobj:WENT-CAMPING NP-Prep-(NP):TENT-IN
Storm	(subj)-ActVp-Dobj:LOST-POWER (subj)-ActVp:RESTORED (subj)-AuxVp-Dobj:HAVE-DAMAGE (subj)-ActVp:EVACUATED

Table 2: Examples of narrative event-patterns (case frames) learned from corpus.

theme (Riloff, 1996). These patterns, developed for information extraction, search for the syntactic constituent with the designated word as its head. For example, consider the example in the first row of Table 2: `NP-Prep-(NP):CAMPING-IN`. This pattern looks for a *Noun Phrase (NP)* followed by a *Preposition (Prep)* where the head of the NP is CAMPING and the Prep is IN. Our algorithm consists of the following steps for each topic:

1. Hand-labeling: We manually labeled a small set ($\sim$ 200-300) of stories on the topic.

2. Generating Event-Patterns: Given hand-labeled stories on a topic (from Step 1), and a random set of stories that are not relevant to that topic, AutoSlog-TS learns a set of syntactic templates (case frame templates) that distinguish the linguistic patterns characteristic of the topic from the random set. For each pattern it generates frequency and conditional probability which indicate how strongly the pattern is associated with the topic.

Table 2 shows examples of such patterns that we have learned for two different topics. We call them *indicative event-patterns* for each topic. Table 1 shows examples of the indicative event-patterns for different topics. They are mapped to our event representation described in Sec 3, e.g., the pattern `(subj)-ActVB-Dobj:WENT-CAMPING` in Table 2 is mapped to `go(dobj:camp)`.

3. Parameter Tuning: We use the frequency and probability generated by AutoSlog-TS and apply a threshold for filtering to select a subset of indicative event-patterns strongly associated with the topic. In this step we aim to find optimal val-

ues for frequency and probability thresholds denoted as *f-threshold* and *p-threshold* respectively. We divided the hand-labeled data from Step 1 into train and development sets and designed a classifier based on our bootstrapping method: if the number of event-patterns extracted from a post is more than a certain number (*n-threshold*), it is labeled as positive and otherwise it is labeled as negative meaning that it is not related to the topic. We repeated the classification for several combinations of different values for each of the three parameters and measured the precision, recall and f-measure. We selected the optimal values for the thresholds that resulted in high precision (above 0.9) and average recall (around 0.4). We compromised on a lower recall to achieve a high precision to establish a highly accurate bootstrapping algorithm. Since bootstrapping is performed on a large set of stories, a low recall stills result in identifying enough stories per topic.

4. Bootstrapping: We use the patterns learned in previous steps as indicative event-patterns for the topic. The bootstrapping algorithm processes each story, using AutoSlog-TS to extract lexico-syntactic patterns. Then it counts the indicative event-patterns in the extracted patterns, and labels the blog as a positive instance for that topic if the count is above the n-threshold value for that topic.

The manually labeled dataset includes 361 Storm and 299 Camping Trip stories. After one round of bootstrapping the algorithm identified 971 additional Storm and 870 more Camping Trip stories. The bootstrapping method is not evaluated separately, however, the results in Sec. 4.2 indicate that using the bootstrapped data considerably improves the accuracy of the contingency model and enhances extracting topic-relevant event knowledge.

3 Learning Contingency Relation between Narrative Events

In this section we describe our representation of events in narratives and our methods for modeling contingency relationship between events.

3.1 Event Representation

In previous work different representations have been proposed for the event structure such as single verb and verb with two or more arguments. Verbs are used as a central indication of an event in a narrative. However, other entities related to the verb also play a strong role in conveying the meaning of the event. In (Pichotta and Mooney, 2014) it is shown that the multi-argument representation is richer than the previous ones and is capable of capturing interactions between multiple events. We use a representation that incorporates the *Particle* of the verb in the event structure in addition to the *Subject* and the *Direct Object* and define an event as a verb with its dependency relations as follows:

Verb Lemma (subj:Subject Lemma,
dobj:Direct Object Lemma, prt:Particle)

Table 3 shows example sentences describing an event from the Camping topic along with their event structure. The examples show how including the arguments often change the meaning of an event. In Row 1 the *direct object* and *particle* are required to completely understand the event in this sentence. Row 2 shows another example where the verb *have* cannot implicate what event is happening and the direct object *oatmeal* is needed to understand what has occurred in the story.

We parse each sentence and extract every verb lemma with its arguments using Stanford dependencies (Manning et al., 2014). For each verb, we extract the *nsubj*, *dobj*, and *prt* dependency relations if they exist, and use their lemma in the event representation. To generalize the event representations, we use the types identified by Stanford's Named Entity Recognizer and map each argument to its named entity type if available, e.g., in Row 3 of Table 3, the *Lost Valley River Campground* is represented by its type LOCATION. We use abstract types for named entities such as PERSON, ORGANIZATION, TIME and DATE. We also represent each pronoun by the abstract type PERSON, e.g. Row 5 in Table 3.

#	Sentence → Event Representation
1	but it wasn't at all frustrating *putting up the tent* and setting up the first night → put (dobj:tent, prt:up)
2	The next day *we had oatmeal* for breakfast → have (subj:PERSON, dobj:oatmeal)
3	by the time *we reached the Lost River Valley Campground*, it was already past 1 pm → reach (subj:PERSON, dobj:LOCATION)
4	then *JS set up a shelter* above the picnic table → set (subj:PERSON, dobj:shelter, prt:up)
5	once the rain stopped, *we built a campfire* using the firewoods → build (subj:PERSON, dobj:campfire)

Table 3: Event representation examples from Camping Trip topic.

3.2 Causal Potential Method

We define a *contingent event pair* as a sequence of two events (e_1, e_2) such that e_1 and e_2 are likely to occur together in the given order and e_2 is contingent upon e_1. We apply an unsupervised distributional measure called *Causal Potential* to induce the contingency relation between two events.

Causal Potential (CP) was introduced by Beamer and Girju (2009) as a way to measure the tendency of an event pair to encode a causal relation, where event pairs with high CP have a higher probability of occurring in a causal context. We calculate CP for every pair of adjacent events in each topic-specific dataset. We used a 2-skip bigram model which considers two events to be adjacent if the second event occurs within two or less events after the first one.

We use skip-2 bigram in order to capture the fact that two related events may often be separated by a non-essential event, because of the oral-narrative nature of our data (Rahimtoroghi et al., 2014). In contrast to the verbs that describe an event (e.g., *hike, climb, evacuate, drive*), some verbs describe private states such as as *belong, depend, feel, know*. We filter out clauses that tend to be associated with private states (Wiebe, 1990). A pilot evaluation showed that this improves the results.

Equation 1 shows the formula for calculating Causal Potential of a pair consisting of two events: (e_1, e_2). Here P denotes probability and $P(e_1 \rightarrow e_2)$ is the probability of e_2 occurring after e_1 in the adjacency window which is equal to 3 due to the skip-2 bigram model. $P(e_2|e_1)$ is the conditional probability of e_2 given that e_1 has been seen in the adjacency window. This is equivalent to the

353

Event-Bigram model described in Sec. 3.3.

$$CP(e_1, e_2) = log \frac{P(e_2|e_1)}{P(e_2)} + log \frac{P(e_1 \rightarrow e_2)}{P(e_2 \rightarrow e_1)} \quad (1)$$

To calculate CP, we need to compute event counts from the corpus and thus we need to define when two events are considered equal. The simplest approach is to define two events to be equal when their verb and arguments exactly match. However, with a close look at the data this approach does not seem adequate. For example, consider the following events:

go (subj:PERSON, dobj:camp)
go (subj:family, dobj:camp)
go (dobj:camp)

They encode the same action although their representations do not exactly match and differ in the subject. Our intuition is that when we count the number of events represented as `go (subj:PERSON, dobj:camp)` we should also include the count of `go (dobj:camp)`. To be able to generalize over the event structure and take into account these nuances, we consider two events to be equal if they have the same verb lemma and share at least one argument other than the subject.

3.3 Baseline Methods

Our previous work on modeling contingency relations in film scripts data compared Causal Potential to methods used in previous work: Bigram event models (Manshadi et al., 2008) and Pointwise Mutual Information (PMI) (Chambers and Jurafsky, 2008) and the evaluations showed that CP obtains better results (Hu et al., 2013). In this work, we use CP for inducing contingency relation between events and apply three other models as baselines for comparison:

Event-Unigram. This method will produce a distribution of normalized frequencies for events.

Event-Bigram. We calculate the bigram probability of every pair of adjacent events using skip-2 bigram model using the Maximum Likelihood Estimation (MLE) from our datasets:

$$P(e_2|e_1) = \frac{Count(e_1, e_2)}{Count(e_1)} \quad (2)$$

Event-SCP. We use the Symmetric Conditional Probability between event tuples (Rel-grams) used

Label	Rel-gram Tuples
Contingent & Strongly Relevant	7 %
Contingent & Somewhat Relevant	0 %
Contingent & Not Relevant	35 %
Total Contingent	42 %

Table 4: Evaluation of Rel-gram tuples on AMT.

in (Balasubramanian et al., 2013) as another baseline method. The Rel-gram model is the most relevant previous work to our method and outperforms the previous state of the art on generating narrative event schema. This metric combines bigram probability considering both directions:

$$SCP(e_1, e_2) = P(e_2|e_1) \times P(e_1|e_2) \quad (3)$$

Like Event-Bigram, we used MLE for estimating Event-SCP from the corpus.

4 Evaluation Experiments

We conducted three sets of experiments to evaluate different aspects of our work. First, we compare the content of our topic-specific event pairs to current state of the art event collections to show that the fine-grained knowledge we learned about everyday events does not exist in previous work focused on the news genre. Second, we run an automatic evaluation test, modeled after the COPA task (Roemmele et al., 2011), on a held-out test set to evaluate the event pair collections that we have extracted from both General-Domain and Topic-Specific datasets, in terms of contingency relations. We hypothesize that the contingent event pairs can be used as basic elements for generating coherent event chains and narrative schema. So, in the third part of the experiments, we extract topic-indicative contingent event pairs from our Topic-Specific dataset and run an experiment on Amazon Mechanical Turk (AMT) to evaluate the top N pairs with respect to their contingency relation and topic-relevance.

4.1 Comparison to Rel-gram Tuple Collections

We chose Rel-gram tuples (Balasubramanian et al., 2013) for comparison since it is the most relevant previous work to us: they generate pairs of relational tuples of events, called *Rel-grams* using co-occurrence statistics based on Symmetric Conditional Probability described in Sec 3.3. Additionally, the Rel-grams are publicly available through an online search interface[3] and their evaluations show that their method outperforms the previous state of the art on generating narrative event schema.

However, their work is focused on news articles and does not consider the causal relation between events for inducing event schema. We compare the content of what we learned from our topic-specific corpus to the Rel-gram tuples to show that the fine-grained type of knowledge that we learn is not found in their events collection. We also applied the co-occurrence statistics that they used on our data as a baseline (Event-SCP) for comparison to our method and present the results in Sec. 4.2.

In this experiment we compare the event pairs extracted from our Camping Trip topic to the Rel-gram tuples. The Rel-gram tuples are not sorted by topic. To find tuples relevant to Camping Trip, we used our top 10 indicative events and extracted all the Rel-gram tuples that included at least one event corresponding to one of the Camping Trip indicative events. For example, for `go(dobj:camp)`, we pulled out all the tuples that included this event from the Rel-grams collection. The indicative events for each topic were automatically generated during the bootstrapping using AutoSlog-TS (Sec. 2).

Then we applied the same sorting and filtering methods presented in the Rel-grams work and removed any tuple with frequency less than 25 and sorted the rest by the total symmetrical conditional probability. These numbers are publicly available as a part of the Rel-grams collection. We evaluated the top $N = 100$ tuples of this list using the Mechanical Turk task described later in Sec. 4.3. The evaluation results presented in Table 4 show that 42% of the Rel-gram pairs were labeled as contingent by the annotators and only 7% were both contingent and topic-relevant. We argue that this is mainly due to the limitations of the newswire data which does not contain the fine-grained everyday events that we have extracted from our corpus.

4.2 Automatic Two-Choice Test

For evaluating our contingent event pair collections we have automatically generated a set of two-choice questions along with the answers, modeled after the COPA task (Roemmele et al., 2011). We produced questions from held-out test sets for each dataset. Each question consists of

---

Topic	Dataset	# Docs
Camping Trip	Hand-labeled held-out test	107
	Hand-labeled train (Train-HL)	192
	Train-HL + Bootstrap (Train-HL-BS)	1,062
Storm	Hand-labeled held-out test	98
	Hand-labeled train (Train-HL)	263
	Train-HL + Bootstrap (Train-HL-BS)	1,234

Table 5: Number of stories in the train and test sets from topic-specific dataset.

Model	Accuracy
Event-Unigram	0.478
Event-Bigram	0.481
Event-SCP (Rel-gram)	0.477
Causal Potential	0.510

Table 6: Automatic two-choice test results for General-Domain dataset.

one event and two choices. The *question event* is one that occurs in the test data. One of the choices is an event adjacent to the question event in the document. The other choice is an event randomly selected from the list of all events occurring in the test set. The following is an example of a question from the Camping Trip test set:

> **Question event:** arrange (dobj:outdoor)
> **Choice 1:** help (dobj:trip)
> **Choice 2:** call (subj:PERSON)

In this example, `arrange (dobj:outdoor)` is followed by the event `help (dobj:trip)` in a document from the test set and `call (subj:PERSON)` was randomly generated. The model is supposed to predict which of the two choices is more likely to have a contingency relation with the event in the question. We argue that a strong contingency model should be able to choose the correct answer (the one that is adjacent to the question event) and the accuracy achieved on the test questions is an indication of the model's robustness.

For the General-Domain dataset, we split the data into train (4,000 stories) and held-out test (200 stories) sets. For each topic-specific set, we divided the hand-labeled data into a train (Train-HL) and held-out test, and created a second train set consisting of Train-HL and the data collected by bootstrapping (Train-HL-BS) as shown in Table 5. We automatically created a question for every event occurring in the test data which

---

[3]http://relgrams.cs.washington.edu:10000/relgrams

Topic	Model	Train Dataset	Accuracy
Camping Trip	Event-Unigram	Train-HL-BS	0.507
	Event-Bigram	Train-HL-BS	0.510
	Event-SCP	Train-HL-BS	0.508
	Causal Potential	Train-HL	0.631
	Causal Potential	Train-HL-BS	0.685
Storm	Event-Unigram	Train-HL-BS	0.510
	Event-Bigram	Train-HL-BS	0.523
	Event-SCP	Train-HL-BS	0.516
	Causal Potential	Train-HL	0.711
	Causal Potential	Train-HL-BS	0.887

Table 7: Automatic two-choice test results for Topic-Specific dataset.

1	go (nsubj:PERSON) → go (dobj:trail , prt:down)
2	find (nsubj:PERSON , dobj:fellow) → go (prt:back)
3	see (nsubj:PERSON , dobj:gun) → see (dobj:police)
4	come (nsubj:PERSON) → go (nsubj:PERSON)
5	go (prt:out) → find (nsubj:PERSON , dobj:sconce)
6	go (nsubj:PERSON) → see (dobj:window, prt:out)
7	go (nsubj:PERSON) → walk (dobj:bit , prt:down)
8	go (nsubj:PERSON) → go (nsubj:PERSON , dobj:rafting)

Figure 2: Examples of event pairs with high CP scores extracted from General-Domain stories.

resulted in 3,123 questions for General-Domain data, 2,058 for the Camping and 2,533 questions for the Storm topic.

For each dataset, we applied the baseline methods and Causal Potential model on the train sets to learn contingent event pairs and tested the pair collections on the questions generated from held-out test set. We extracted about 418K contingent event pairs from General-Domain train set, 437K from Storm Train-HL-BS and 630K pairs from Camping Trip Train-HL-BS set using Causal Potential model. We used our automatic test approach to evaluate these event pair collections. The results for General-Domain and Topic-Specific datasets are shown in Table 6 and Table 7 respectively.

The Causal Potential model trained on Train-HL-BS dataset achieved accuracy of 0.685 on Camping Trip and 0.887 on Storm topic which is significantly stronger than all the baselines. Our experiments indicate that having more training data collected by bootstrapping improves the accuracy of the model in predicting contingency relation between events. Additionally, the Causal Potential results on Topic-Specific dataset is significantly stronger than General-Domain narratives indicating that using a topic-sorted dataset improves learning causal knowledge about events.

Label	Camping	Storm
Contingent & Strongly Relevant	44 %	33 %
Contingent & Somewhat Relevant	8 %	20 %
Contingent & Not Relevant	30 %	24 %
Total Contingent	82 %	77 %

Table 8: Results of evaluating indicative contingent event pairs on AMT.

Fig. 2 shows some examples of event pairs with high CP scores extracted from general-Domain set. In the following section we extract topic-indicative contingent event pairs and show that Topic-Specific data enables learning of finer-grained event knowledge that pertain to a particular theme.

4.3 Topic-Indicative Contingent Event Pairs

We identify contingent event pairs that are highly indicative of a particular topic. We hypothesize that these event pairs serve as building blocks of coherent event chains and narrative schema since they encode contingency relation and correspond to a specific theme. We evaluate the pairs on Amazon Mechanical Turk (AMT).

To identify event sequences that have a strong correlation to a topic (topic-indicative pairs) we applied two filtering methods. First, we selected the frequent pairs for each topic and removed the ones that occur less than 5 times in the corpus. Second, we used the indicative event-patterns for each topic and extracted the pairs that at least included one of these patterns. Indicative event-patterns are automatically generated during the bootstrapping using AutoSlog-TS and mapped to their corresponding event representation as described in Sec. 2. Then we used the Causal Potential scores from our contingency model for ranking the topic-indicative event pairs to identify the highly contingent ones. We sorted the pairs based on the Causal Potential score and evaluated the top N pairs in this list.

Evaluations and Results. We evaluate the indicative contingent event pairs using human judgment on Amazon Mechanical Turk (AMT). Narrative schema consists of chains of events that are related in a coherent way and correspond to a common theme. Consequently, we evaluate the extracted pairs based on two main criteria:

- **Contingency:** Two events in the pair are

Topic	Label > 2 : Contingent & Strongly Topic-Relevant	Label < 1 : Not Contingent
Camping Trip	person - pack up → person - go - home person - wake up → person - pack up - backpack person - head → hike up climb → person - find - rock person - pack up - car → head out	person - pick up - cup → person - swim pack up - tent → check out - video person - play → person - pick up - sax pack up - material → switch off - projector person - pick up - photo → person - swim
Storm	wind - blow - transformer → power - go out tree - fall - eave → crush Ike - blow → knock down - limb air - push - person → person - fall out hit - location → evacuate - person	restore - community → hurricane - bend boil → tree - fall - driveway clean up - person → people - come out blow - sign → person - sit person - rock - way → bottle - fall

Table 9: Examples of event pairs evaluated on AMT.

likely to occur together in the given order and the second event is contingent upon the first one.

- **Topic Relevance:** Both events strongly correspond to the specified topic.

We have designed one task to assess both criteria since if an event pair is not contingent, it cannot be used in narrative schema for not satisfying the required coherence (even if it is topic-relevant). We asked the AMT annotators to rate each pair on a scale of 0-3 as follows:

0: The events are not contingent.
1: The events are contingent but not relevant to the specified topic.
2: The events are contingent and somewhat relevant to the specified topic.
3: The events are contingent and strongly relevant to the specified topic.

To ensure that the Amazon Mechanical Turk annotations are reliable, we designed a *Qualification Type* which requires the workers to pass a test before they can annotate our pairs. If the workers score 70% or more on the test they will qualify to do the main task. For each topic we created a Qualification test consisting of 10 event pairs from that topic that were annotated by two experts. To make the events more readable for the annotators we used the following representation:

Subject - Verb Particle - Direct Object

For example, `hike(subj:person, dobj:trail, prt:up)` is mapped to `person - hike up - trail`. For each topic we evaluated top $N = 100$ event pairs and assigned 5 workers to rate each one. We generated a gold standard label for each

pair by averaging over the scores assigned by the annotators and interpreted the average as follows:

Label >2: Contingent & strongly topic-relevant.
Label = 2: Contingent & somewhat topic-relevant.
$1 \leq$ Label < 2: Contingent & not topic-relevant.
Label < 1: Not contingent.

To assess the inter-annotator reliability we calculated kappa between each worker and the majority of the labels assigned to each pair. The average kappa was 0.73 which indicates substantial agreement. The results in Table 8 show that 52% of the Camping Trip and 53% of the Storm pairs were labeled as contingent and topic-relevant by the annotators. The results also indicate that our model is capable of identifying event pairs with strong contingency relations: 82% of the Camping Trip pairs and 77% of the Storm pairs were marked as contingent by the workers. Examples of the strongest and weakest pairs evaluated on Mechanical Turk are shown in Table 9. By comparison to Fig. 2, we can see that we can learn finer-grained type of events knowledge from topic-specific stories as compared to general-domain corpus.

5 Discussion and Conclusions

We learned fine-grained common-sense knowledge about contingent relations between everyday events from personal stories written by ordinary people. We applied a semi-supervised bootstrapping approach using event-patterns to create topic-sorted sets of stories and evaluated our methods on a set of general-domain narratives as well as two topic-specific datasets. We developed a new method for learning contingency relations between events that is tailored to the "oral narrative" nature of the blog stories. Our evaluations indicate that a method that works well on the news genre does not generate coherent results on personal stories (comparison of Event-SCP baseline with Causal Potential).

We modeled the contingency (causal and conditional) relation between the events from each dataset using Causal Potential and evaluated on the questions automatically generated from a held-out test set. The results show significant improvement over the Event-Unigram, Event-Bigram, and Event-SCP (Rel-grams method) baselines on Topic-Specific stories: 25% improvement of accuracy on Camping Trip and 41% on Storm topic compared to Bigram model. In our future work, we plan to explore existing topic-modeling algorithms to create a broader set of topic-sorted corpora for learning contingent event knowledge.

Our experiments show that most of the fine-grained contingency relations we learn from narrative events are not found in existing narrative and event schema collections induced from the newswire datasets (Rel-grams). We also extracted indicative contingent event pairs from each topic and evaluated them on Mechanical Turk. The evaluations show that 82% of the relations between events that we learn from topic-sorted stories are judged as contingent. We publicly release the extracted pairs for each topic. In future work, we plan to use the contingent event pairs as building blocks for generating coherent event chains and narrative schema on several different themes.

References

Niranjan Balasubramanian, Stephen Soderland, Mausam, and Oren Etzioni. 2013. Generating coherent event schemas at scale. In *EMNLP*, pages 1721–1731.

Brandon Beamer and Roxana Girju. 2009. Using a bigram event model to predict causal potential. In *Computational Linguistics and Intelligent Text Processing*, pages 430–441.

David M Blei. 2012. Probabilistic topic models. *Communications of the ACM*, 55(4):77–84.

Kevin Burton, Akshay Java, and Ian Soboroff. 2009. The icwsm 2009 spinn3r dataset. In *Proc. of the Annual Conference on Weblogs and Social Media (ICWSM)*.

Nathanael Chambers and Dan Jurafsky. 2008. Unsupervised learning of narrative event chains. *Proc. of ACL-08: HLT*, pages 789–797.

Nathanael Chambers and Dan Jurafsky. 2009. Unsupervised learning of narrative schemas and their participants. In *Proc. of the 47th Annual Meeting of the ACL*, pages 602–610.

Timothy Chklovski and Patrick Pantel. 2004. Verbocean: Mining the web for fine-grained semantic verb relations. In *Proc. of Conference on Empirical Methods in Natural Language Processing (EMNLP-04)*, Barcelona, Spain.

Quang Xuan Do, Yee Seng Chan, and Dan Roth. 2011. Minimally supervised event causality identification. In *Proc. of the Conference on Empirical Methods in Natural Language Processing*, pages 294–303. Association for Computational Linguistics.

Christiane Fellbaum. 1998. *WordNet: An Electronic Lexical Database*. MIT Press, Cambridge, MA.

Roxana Girju. 2003. Automatic detection of causal relations for question answering. In *Proceedings of the ACL 2003 workshop on Multilingual summarization and question answering-Volume 12*, pages 76–83. Association for Computational Linguistics.

Andrew Gordon and Reid Swanson. 2009. Identifying personal stories in millions of weblog entries. In *Third International Conference on Weblogs and Social Media, Data Challenge Workshop, San Jose, CA*.

Andrew S Gordon, Christopher Wienberg, and Sara Owsley Sood. 2012. Different strokes of different folks: Searching for health narratives in weblogs. In *Privacy, Security, Risk and Trust (PASSAT), 2012 International Conference on and 2012 International Confernece on Social Computing (SocialCom)*, pages 490–495. IEEE.

Zhichao Hu, Elahe Rahimtoroghi, Larissa Munishkina, Reid Swanson, and Marilyn A Walker. 2013. Unsupervised induction of contingent event pairs from film scenes. In *Proc. of Conference on Empirical Methods in Natural Language Processing*, pages 370–379.

Wendy G Lehnert. 1981. Plot units and narrative summarization. *Cognitive Science*, 5(4):293–331.

Christopher D Manning, Mihai Surdeanu, John Bauer, Jenny Rose Finkel, Steven Bethard, and David McClosky. 2014. The Stanford CoreNLP natural language processing toolkit. In *ACL (System Demonstrations)*, pages 55–60.

Mehdi Manshadi, Reid Swanson, and Andrew S Gordon. 2008. Learning a probabilistic model of event sequences from internet weblog stories. In *Proc. of the 21st FLAIRS Conference*.

Raymond Mooney and Gerald DeJong. 1985. Learning schemata for natural language processing. *Urbana*, 51:61801.

Kiem-Hieu Nguyen, Xavier Tannier, Olivier Ferret, and Romaric Besançon. 2015. Generative event schema induction with entity disambiguation. In *Proceedings of the 53rd annual meeting of the Association for Computational Linguistics (ACL-15)*.

Karl Pichotta and Raymond J Mooney. 2014. Statistical script learning with multi-argument events. *EACL 2014*, page 220.

R. Prasad, N. Dinesh, A. Lee, E. Miltsakaki, L. Robaldo, A. Joshi, and B. Webber. 2008. The penn discourse treebank 2.0. In *Proc. of the 6th International Conference on Language Resources and Evaluation (LREC 2008)*, pages 2961–2968.

Elahe Rahimtoroghi, Thomas Corcoran, Reid Swanson, Marilyn A. Walker, Kenji Sagae, and Andrew S. Gordon. 2014. Minimal narrative annotation schemes and their applications. In *7th Workshop on Intelligent Narrative Technologies*.

Mehwish Riaz and Roxana Girju. 2010. Another look at causality: Discovering scenario-specific contingency relationships with no supervision. In *Semantic Computing (ICSC), 2010 IEEE Fourth International Conference on*, pages 361–368.

Ellen Riloff. 1996. Automatically generating extraction patterns from untagged text. In *Proceedings of the Thirteenth National Conference on Artificial Intelligence (AAAI-96)*, pages 1044–1049.

Bryan Rink, Cosmin Adrian Bejan, and Sanda M Harabagiu. 2010. Learning textual graph patterns to detect causal event relations. In *FLAIRS Conference*.

Melissa Roemmele, Cosmin Adrian Bejan, and Andrew S Gordon. 2011. Choice of plausible alternatives: An evaluation of commonsense causal reasoning. In *AAAI Spring Symposium: Logical Formalizations of Commonsense Reasoning*.

Roger Schank and Robert Abelson. 1977. *Scripts, plans, goals and understanding*. Lawrence Erlbaum.

Reid Swanson and Andrew S. Gordon. 2009. A comparison of retrieval models for open domain story generation. In *Proc. of the AAAI 2009 Spring Symposium on Intelligent Narrative Technologies II*, Stanford, CA.

Reid Swanson, Elahe Rahimtoroghi, Thomas Corcoran, and Marilyn A Walker. 2014. Identifying narrative clause types in personal stories. In *15th Annual Meeting of the Special Interest Group on Discourse and Dialogue*, page 171.

Janyce M Wiebe. 1990. Identifying subjective characters in narrative. In *Proc. of the 13th Conference on Computational linguistics. V2*, pages 401–406.

When do we laugh?

Ye Tian[1], Chiara Mazzocconi[2] & Jonathan Ginzburg[2,3]
[1]Laboratoire Linguistique Formelle (UMR 7110)
& [2]CLILLAC-ARP (EA 3967) & [3]Laboratoire d'Excellence (LabEx)—EFL
Université Paris-Diderot, Paris, France
`tiany.03@gmail.com`

Abstract

Studies on laughter in dialogue have proposed resolving what laughter is *about* by looking at what laughter follows. This paper investigates the sequential relation between the laughter and the laughable. We propose a semantic/pragmatic account treating laughter as a gestural event anaphor referring to a laughable. Data from a French and Chinese dialogue corpus suggest a rather free time alignment between laughter and laughable. Laughter can occur (long) before, during, or (long) after the laughable. Our results challenge the assumption that what laughter follows is what it is about, and thus question claims which rely on this assumption.

1 Introduction

Studies about laughter in interaction have been mainly focused on the acoustic or perceptual features, and often observations of the events preceding to it have been the base for claims concerning what laughter is about. (Provine, 1993) made a claim that has been subsequently adopted in much of the literature: laughter is, for the most part, not related to humour, because it is found to most frequently *follow* banal comments. Similar reasoning has been adopted by several other studies on the kind of situations that elicit laughter. The deduction process in these studies rely on an important yet untested assumption: what laughter *follows* is what it is *about*. Our paper investigates this assumption. We first briefly discuss previous studies on laughter in interaction; we then argue for a semantic/pragmatic account in which we treat laughter as a gestural event anaphora referring to a *laughable*. We present a corpus study of laughables and evaluate our results against previous proposals.

1.1 Studies on what laughter is about

In (Provine, 1993), the researcher observed natural conversations, and "when an observer heard laughter, she recorded in a notebook the comment immediately preceding the laughter and if the speaker and/or the audience laughed, the gender, and the estimated age of the speaker and the audience [...]. A laugh episode was defined as the occurrence of audible laughter and included any laughter by speaker or audience that followed within an estimated 1 s of the initial laugh event. The laugh episode included the last comment by a speaker if it occurred within an estimated 1 s preceding the onset of the initial laughter. A laugh episode was terminated if an estimated 1 s passed without speaker or audience laughter, or if either the speaker or the audience spoke.". They found that "Only about 10-20% of episodes were estimated by the observers to be humorous" (Provine, 1993), and thus derived the conclusion which is now widely adopted in the literature: laughter is, for the most part, not related to humour but about social interaction. An additional conclusion based on this study is that laughter never interrupts speech but "*punctuates*" it occurring exclusively at phrase boundaries.

Similarly, (Vettin and Todt, 2004) used exclusively timing parameters – i.e., what precedes and what follows the laugh (within a threshold of 3s) – to distinguish 6 different contexts (see table 1) for laughter occurrence to support claims about situations that elicit laughter.

1.2 Weaknesses

In (Provine, 1993), the author assumed that laughter always immediately follows the laughable. Not only do the methods described above provide imprecise data (timing information was estimated during observation), it prevents the possibility of recording any data where laughter does not follow the laughable. In addition, even when the com-

Proceedings of the SIGDIAL 2016 Conference, pages 360–369,
Los Angeles, USA, 13-15 September 2016. ©2016 Association for Computational Linguistics

Conversational Parter	A participant's laughter occurring immediately (up to 3s) after a complete utterance of their conversational partner
Participant	The participant laughed immediately (up to 3s) after his/her own complete utterance
Short confirma-tion	Participan's laughter immediately (up to 3s) after a confirming 'mm', 'I see' or something comparable by himself or his conversational partner
Laughter	Participant's laughter after a conversational partner's laughter. With an interval of less than 3s
Before utterance	Participant's laughter after a short pause (at least 3s) in conversation, but immediately (up to 500ms) before an utterance by him/herself
Situation	Laughter occurring during a pause in conversation (at least 3s), not followed by any utterance. The laughter is attibuted to the general situation and not to an utterance

Table 1: Vetting and Todt, 2004 - Context classification

ment that immediately precedes laughter *is* the actual trigger for a laugh, and it is not "amusing" in itself (i.e. it is a "banal comment"), it doesn't necessarily entail that the *laughable* is not humourous. The funniness might arise from the "banal comment" in relation to the previous utterance, the context of the interaction, shared experiences between the speakers, world knowledge and cultural conventions. For example, in (1) "what's funny" resides in the implicit content that the utterance refers to. In (2), the preceding utterance is funny only in relation to the context.

(1) A: Do you remember that time?
B and A: < laughter/ >.
Laughable= the enriched denotation of 'that time'.

(2) (Context: the speakers are discussing the plan of an imagined shared apartment, and they have already planned two bathrooms).
A: I want another bathroom. B: < laughter/ >
Laughable= "I want another bathroom"

(Vettin and Todt, 2004) is methodologically more precise than (Provine, 1993), and they allow for the possibility that in addition to laughter occurring after the laughable, a laughter may precede an utterance, or occur during an exophoric situation. However, this analysis excludes laughters that occur in the middle of or overlaps with an utterance, and it uses exclusively timing parameters to determine what laughter is about (as illustrated in figure 1). For example, whether a laugh is considered to be about the preceding utterance or about the following utterance is decided purely on the difference in the length of gaps with the two utterances. Crucially, the conclusion is also drawn assuming an adjacency relationship between laughter and laughable.

2 Laughter as an event anaphor

We argue that previous studies have ignored analysing the *laughable* because they did not attempt to integrate their account with an explicit semantic/pragmatic module on the basis of which content is computed.[1] The sole recent exception to this, as far as we are aware, is the account of (Ginzburg et al., 2015), which sketches an information state–based account of the meaning and use of laughter in dialogue.

Taking this as a starting point, we argue that laughter is a gestural event anaphor, whose meaning contains two dimensions: one dimension about the *arousal* and the other about the trigger or the *laughable*. In line with (Morreall, 1983) we think that laughter effects a "positive psychological shift", and the "arousal" dimension signals the amplitude in the shift.[2] The positive psychological shift is triggered by an appraisal of an event - the laughable l, and the second dimension communicates the type of the appraisal. (Ginzburg et al., 2015) propose two basic types of meaning in the *laughable* dimension: the person laughing may express her perception of the laughable l as being *incongruous*, or just that l is enjoyable (playful). We propose that in addition, certain uses of laughter in dialogue may suggest the need for a third possible type: expressing that l is a socially close *ingroup* situation.

2.1 Formal treatment of laughter

Here we sketch a formal semantic and pragmatic treatment of laughter. On the approach developed in KoS (Ginzburg, 2012), information states comprise a private part and the dialogue gameboard that represents information arising from publicized interactions. In addition to tracking shared assumptions/visual space, Moves, and QUD, the dialogue gameboard also tracks **topoi** and **enthymemes** that conversational participants exploit during an interaction (e.g., in reasoning about rhetorical relations.). Here topoi represent general inferential patterns (e.g., *given two routes choose*

---

[1]This is not the case for some theories of humour, e.g., that due to (Raskin, 1985), who offers a reasonably explicit account of incongruity emanating from verbal content without, however, attempting to offer a theory of laughter in conversation.

[2]The amplitudes in the shift depend on both the trigger itself and on the individual current information/emotional state. It is important to point out that laughter does not signal that the speaker's current emotional state is positive, merely that there was a *shift* which was positive. The speaker could have a very negative baseline emotional state (being very sad or angry) but the recognition of the incongruity in the laughable or its enjoyment can provoke a positive shift (which could be very minor) The distinction between the overall emotional state and the direction of the shift explains why laughter can be produced when one is sad or angry.

the shortest one) represented as functions from records to record types, and enthymemes are instances of topoi (e.g., *given that the route via Walnut street is shorter than the route via Alma choose Walnut street*). An enthymeme belongs to a topos if its domain type is a subtype of the domain type of the topos.

(Ginzburg et al., 2015) posit distinct, though quite similar lexical entries for enjoyment and incongruous laughter. For reasons of space in (3) we exhibit a unified entry with two distinct contents. (3) associates an enjoyment laugh with the laugher's judgement of a proposition whose situational component l is *active* as enjoyable; for incongruity, a laugh marks a proposition whose situational component l is *active* as *incongruous*, relative to the currently maximal enthymeme under discussion. (3) makes appeal to a notion of an *active situation*. This pertains to the accessible situational antecedents of a laughter act, given that (Ginzburg et al., 2015) proposed viewing laughter as an event anaphor. However, given the existence of a significant amount of speech laughter, as we discuss below, this notion apparently needs to be rethought somewhat, viewing laughter in gestural terms. This requires interfacing the two channels, a problem we will not address here, though see (Rieser, 2015) for a recent discussion in the context of manual gesture.

(3)

$$
\begin{bmatrix}
\text{phon} : \texttt{laughterphontype} \\
\text{dgb-params} : \begin{bmatrix}
\text{spkr} : \text{Ind} \\
\text{addr} : \text{Ind} \\
\text{t} : \text{TIME} \\
\text{c1} : \text{addressing(spkr,addr,t)} \\
\text{MaxEud} = \text{e} : \text{(Rec)RecType} \\
\text{p} = \begin{bmatrix} \text{sit} = \text{l} \\ \text{sit-type} = \text{L} \end{bmatrix} : \text{prop} \\
\text{c2} : \text{ActiveSit(l)}
\end{bmatrix} \\
\text{content}_{enjoyment} = \text{Enjoy(spkr,p)} : \text{RecType} \\
\text{content}_{incongruity} = \text{Incongr(p,e,}\tau\text{)} : \text{RecType}
\end{bmatrix}
$$

The dialogue gameboard parameters utilised in the account of (Ginzburg et al., 2015) are all 'informational' or utterance related ones. However, in order to deal with notions such as arousal and psychological shift, one needs to introduce also parameters that track appraisal (see e.g.,

(Scherer, 2009)). For current purposes, we mention merely one such parameter we dub *pleasantness* that relates to the appraisal issue—in Scherer's formulation—*Is the event intrinsically pleasant or unpleasant?*. We assume that this parameter is scalar in value, with positive and negative values corresponding to varying degrees of pleasantness or unpleasantness.

This enables us to formulate conversational rules of the form 'if A laughs and pleasantness is set to k, then reset pleasantness to $k + \theta(\alpha)$', where α is a parameter corresponding to arousal.

2.2 Research questions

The study is part of a broader project where we analyse laughter using a multi-layered scheme and propose a semantic/ pragmatic account of the meaning and effects of laughter. The focus of the current study is the positioning of laughter in relation to its laughable.

Our account suggests that resolving the *laughable* is crucial for deriving the content of a laughter event. We hypothesize that laughter is not always adjacent to its laughable. Rather, the sequential distribution between laughter and laughable is somewhat free, illustrated in Figure 2. We hypothesize that laughter can occur before, during and after the laughable, and that it is possible for intervening materials to occur between a laughter event and its laughable.

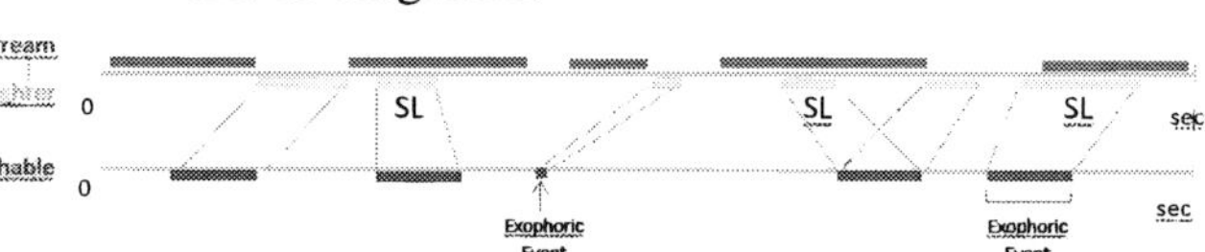

Figure 1: Temporal misalignment speech stream, laughter and laughable

In more detail, we make the following hypotheses in relation to our research questions:

Q1: Does laughter always follow its laughable?

–If not, does laughter-laughable alignment differ among different types of laughters?

We hypothesize that laughter can occur before, during or after the laughable; laughter and laughable should not have a one-to-one relationship: one laughable can be the referent of several laughter events.

–More specifically, laughter-laughable alignment may vary depending on at least the source of the laughable (self or partner) and whether it is speech laugh or laughter bouts.

Q2: Does laughter interrupt speech?

We hypothesize that laughter can occur both at utterance boundaries and at utterance-medial position.

Q3: Is laughter-laughable alignment pattern language specific?

We hypothesize that language/culture influence alignment and thus predict to find differences between, in this case, French and Chinese.

3 Material and method

3.1 Corpus

We analyzed a portion of the DUEL corpus (Hough et al., 2016a) The corpus consists of 30 dyads (10 per language)/ 24 hours of natural, face-to-face, loosely task-directed dialogue in French, Mandarin Chinese and German. Each dyad conversed in three tasks which in total lasted around 45 minutes. The three tasks used were:

1. **Dream Apartment**: the participants are told that they are to share a large open-plan apartment, and will receive a large amount of money to furnish and decorate it. They discuss the layout, furnishing and decoration decisions;

2. **Film Script**: The participants spend 15 minutes creating a scene for a film in which something embarrassing happens to the main character;

3. **Border control**: one participant plays the role of a traveller attempting to pass through the border control of an imagined country, and is interviewed by an officer. The traveller has a personal situation that disfavours him/her in this interview. The officer asks questions that are general as well as specific. In addition, the traveller happens to be a parent-in-law of the officer.

The corpus is transcribed in the target language and glossed in English. Disfluency, laughter, and exclamations are annotated. The current paper presents analysis of laughter in two dyads in French and Chinese (3 tasks x 2 pairs x 2 languages).

3.2 Audio-video coding of laughter

Coding was conducted by the first and second authors and by 2 trained, but naïve to the aim of the study, masters students: each video was observed until a laugh occurred. The coder detected the exact onset and offset in Praat (Boersma and others, 2002), and conducted a multi-layer analysis as explained shortly. A laugh was identified referring to the same criteria used in (Nwokah et al., 1994), based on the facial expression and vocalization descriptions of laughter elaborated by (Apte, 1985) and (Ekman and Friesen, 1975). Following (Urbain and Dutoit, 2011) we counted laughter offset (final laughter in-breath inhalation) as part of the laughter event itself, thus resulting in laughter timings longer than other authors (Bachorowski and Owren, 2001; Rothgänger et al., 1998).

All laughter events were categorised according to different parameters: formal and contextual aspects, semantic meaning and functions (see Table 2). The formal and contextual level analysis include whether a laughter overlaps speech (speech laugh), whether it co-occurs with or immediately follows a partner's laughter (dyadic/ antiphonal laughter), and its position in relation to the laughable. The semantic meaning level analysis include perceived arousal and whether it contains an element of incongruity could be identified by the coders. The function analysis codes the effect of laughter on the interaction, and distinguishes whether the effect is cooperative, i.e., promotes interaction (e.g. showing enjoyment, smoothing) or non-cooperative, i.e., in some way disaffects interaction (e.g., mocking or evade questions). Due to space constraints and current focus, we do not provide a detailed explanation of the multi-level laughter coding scheme, for which see (Mazzocconi et al., 2016). Reliability was assessed by having a masters student as a second coder for 10% of the material observed. Percentage agreements between the two coders for French and Chinese data averaged respectively 87% and 87.76, with an overall Krippendorff α (Krippendorff, 2012) across all tiers of 0.672 and 0.636.

For the main analysis, we include in our analysis both laughter and speech laughter (Nwokah et al., 1999). In the current study we restrict our observations about the aspects pertaining to the form, to the contextual distribution and positioning of a laugh in relation to others' laughter, the laughable and laugher's herself speech.

Form level	Speech & laughter	Speech-Laugh	A laughter produced simultaneously with speech		Nwokah et al. 1999
		Standalone laugh	A laughter not overlapping with own speech		Nwokah et al. 1994
	Temporal sequence	Isolated	A laughter not preceded by other laughter within 4s		Nwokah et al. 1994
		Dyadic/Antiphonal	Reciprocal	A laughter occurring within 4s after a laughter by a partner	Nwokah et al. 1994
			Co-active	Participants start laughing together	Smoski & Bachorowski, 2003
Semantic level	Arousal	low/medium/high	Qualitative judgment		
	Presence of incongruity	Incongruity/ No incongruity	Perception of elements unexpected in relation to the context		
Function/ Effect level	Cooperative	E.g show enjoyment, smoothing/softening, show agreement, mark funniness, benevolence induction			
	Non cooperative	E.g. offensive, mocking, threat, challenge, show disagreement/ skepticism, avoid topic, evade conversation			

Figure 2: Laughter coding parameters

3.3 Identifying laughables

We consider as the laughable the event which, after appraisal, produces a positive psychological shift in the laugher. We distinguish three different kinds of laughable types: described events, metalinguistic stimuli and exophoric events. We also mark whether they originated from the laugher him/herself or by the partner.

(4) **Described event** A: il y a (un: + un) de mes potes? idiot comme il est, qui (< p = pose > po- < /p > qui pose) un steak sur le rebord (de: + du) balcon? B:< laughter/ >. < laughspeech > ils sont bizarres tes potes < /laughspeech >

(Translation) A: There is (one + one) of my buddies, stupid as he is, who put a steak on the border of the: of the balcony B: < laughter/ >. < laughspeech > you have weird buddies < /laughspeech >

Laughable= "who put a steak on the border of the balcony": described event

(5) **Metalinguistic stimuli** B: Alors je viens pour {euh} avoir mon passeport? pour Inra:schabella? < laughter/ >

(Translation) B: So I'm here for, euh, having my passport? for Inraschabella? < laughter/ >

Laughable= "Inraschabella" (linguistic form, laugh after laugher's speech)

(6) **Exophoric event** The examiner is asking A to move the arms because of technical issues A: movement arms mimicking a robot B: < laughter/ > A: < laughter/ >

Laughable=the way A moved his arms: exophoric event

3.4 Audio-video coding of laughable

Every time a laugh was identified, coders would mark on the Praat TextGrid, based on personal inference, the laughable the laugh would refer to.

The time boundaries were marked, the content (whether verbal or not) was annotated and an index was assigned in order to map laughter (or multiple laughters) and laughable. Laughables were classified according to three main categories: described, metalinguistic and exhophoric event. Reliability of type assignment was assessed by having a masters student as a second coder for 10% of the material observed. Percentage agreements between the two coders for French and Chinese averaged 92.5% with a Krippendorff α (Krippendorff, 2012) of 0.77.

4 Results

In our data sample (summarized in Table2), laughter is very frequent, constituting 17% of the conversation duration in French and 7.2% in Chinese. Each laughable is "laughed about" more than once (1.7 times in French and 1.4 times in Chinese).

	French	Chinese
Dialogue.dur	77min	85min
mean utterance.dur	1.8sec	1.5sec
No. laughter	436	221
laughter.dur	1.9s (sd .97)	1.4s (se .53)
No. laughable	256	158
laughable.dur	2.7s (sd 1.5)	2.8s (sd 2.1)
No.laughter per laughable	1.7	1.4

Table 2: Data summary

4.1 Does laughter always follow the laughable?

To investigate the time alignment between laughter and laughable, we calculated "start of laughter minus start of laughable", "end of laughter minus end of laughable", and "start of laughter minus end of laughable". If laughter always follow the laughable, all three measurements should be above zero. This was not the case. In both Chinese and French, on average, laughter starts *during* rather than after the laughable, and finishes after the laughable. In general, laughs in Chinese are more likely to overlap with the laughable than in French. The distribution varies over a wide range. Table 3 summarizes the gaps between the boundaries of laughter and laughable, and figure 3 plots specifically the gap between the end of the laughable and the start of laughter. They show that it is common for laughs to start before, during and after the laughable. When a laugh has no overlap with its laughable, they are not always adjacent to each other (average utterance duration is under 2 seconds while the gap can be up to 10 seconds). In the following example, the first two instances of speech laugh refer to a laughable in a later utterance.

(7) 那个老师(要 他+要 求 小 诗) 用"不 约 而 同"造
句 子, 后 来 小 明< laughspeech >就 想 了 一
想< /laughspeech >, 然 后 说 呃 说 呃 这 样 吧?
< laughspeech >(我 就+小 诗)< /laughspeech >
就 想 了 想 说, 呃:呃:我 在 路 上 碰 见 一 个 美 女, 然 后 我
就 问 她, 约 吗?< laughspeech > 然 后 美 女 说, 滚,我
们 不 约 儿 童< /laughspeech >.

(Translation) B: The teacher asked Xiaoshi to make a sentence with "bu yue er tong" (coincidentally together). Xiaoshi < laughspeech > then < laughspeech/ > thought about it, and said, uh, < laughspeech > (I + Xiaoshi) < laughspeech/ > thought about it and said, uh, uh I saw a pretty girl in the street, and I asked her "shall we go for a date?", and < laughspeech > the girl said "shouldn't date children" < laughspeech/ >. *(note: "shouldn't date children" is phonologically identical to "incidentally together")*

Laughable= "the girl said 'shouldn't date children' "

Based on whether laughter occurs entirely outside or overlapping with the laughable, we grouped the laughters into 4 alignment categories: "before", "overlap", "immediately after" and "other after" (see figure 4). We found that in both languages, laughters that immediately follow (within 0.3s) the laughable constitute 30% . There are more overlapping laughters in Chinese than in French ($\chi^2(1)$=6.9, p= .008).

	Fr			Ch		
(in seconds)	mean	sd	range	mean	sd	range
start.L-start.LB	2.2	2.4	-9.4 -13.7	1.3	2.3	-19.6 - 9.6
end.L-end.LB	1.4	2.3	-12.8 - 11.6	0.5	2.6	-24.6 - 5.2
start.L-end.LB	-0.5	2.3	-13.9 - 8.4	-0.9	2.6	-25.1 - 3.0

Table 3: Time alignment of laughter ("L") and laughable ("LB")

4.2 Does laughter-laughable alignment differ among different "types" of laughables and laughters?

Our analysis mainly focuses on the distinction between self and partner produced laughables, and

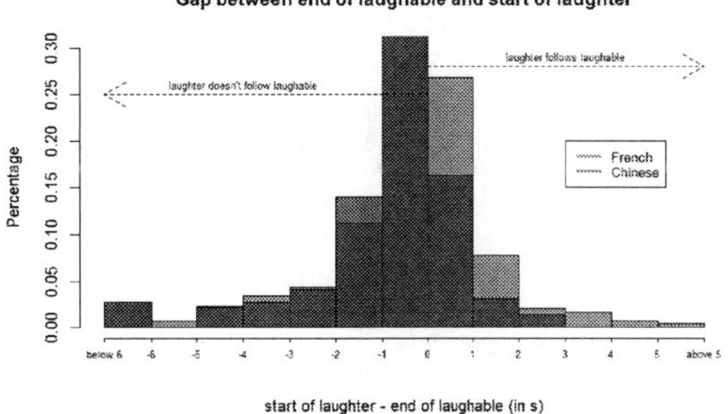

Figure 3: Gap between laughable and laughter

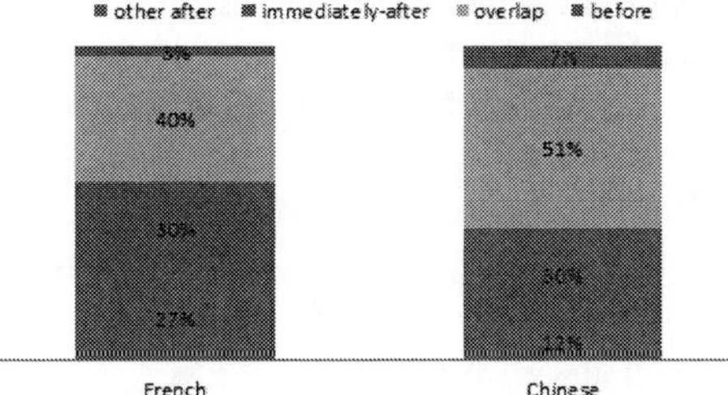

Figure 4: laughters before, after or overlapping with laughable

between speech laugh and laughter bouts, presented separately below. Due to space constraints, the effect of the rest of the tiers are not discussed.

4.2.1 Self vs. partner produced laughables

We coded whether the laughables are described events, meta-linguistic, or exophoric events. In our corpus described events are the commonest (92% in French and 89% in Chinese), followed by exophoric laughables (7% in French and 10%). Metalinguistic (1% in both languages) laughables are rare, so we grouped them with described events in the current analysis. On average, there are more self-produced than partner-produced laughables, supporting the idea that speakers laugh more often than the audience. Interestingly, 3% of the laughables are jointly produced (one person finishing the other's sentence, or both saying roughly the same thing at the same time) (see (8)). With the former two categories, we also coded whether the laughable is produced by the laugher or her partner, which allow us to compare our results with studies of "speaker" or "audience" laughter.

(8) (totally overlapping turns are italicized)

B: c'est une personne qui est aux toilettes dans < laughter > des toilettes publiques *A: < laughter > X ah: oui: oui un mec qui parle a cute'* < laughter/ > *B: dans* < laughter > *des toilettes publiques* voila sauf que l'autre il est au

365

telephone et l'autre il lui croit qu'il parle . C'est genant
< laughter/ >

(Translation) B: it is a person who is in the bathroom in < laughter > in public bathroom *A:*< laughter > *Ah yes yes a guy who is talking in the next stall* < laughter/ > *B: in* < laughter > *in public bathroom* exactly but the other is on the phone and the other thinks he is speaking with him. That's embarrassing < laughter/ >

Laughable= "exactly but the other is on the phone and the other thinks he is speaking with him"

We found that laughters about a partner-produced laughable start later than those about a self-produced laughable, but still the average starting time is before the end of the laughable. With partner-produced laughables, the average gap between the end of laughable and start of laughter is -0.02s in French and -0.3s in Chinese, while with self-produced laughables, the average gap is -0.7s in French and -1.3s in Chinese.

4.2.2 Speech laugh vs. laughter bouts

Laughter frequently overlaps with speech. 36% of laughter events in French and 47% of laughter events in Chinese contain speech laughter. Speech laughter is on average 0.3 seconds longer than stand alone laughter bouts. Speech laughs overlap with the laughable more than laughter bouts. 52% of speech laughters in French and 70% in Chinese overlap with the laughables. In comparison, 33% of laughter bouts in French and 34% in Chinese overlap with the laughable. The reason why speech laugh more often overlap with the laughables is likely to do with the difference in function between speech laugh and laughter bouts. Laughters that mark an upcoming laughable most frequently overlaps with speech, and these laughter events are also ones that tend to stretch until the middle or the end of the laughable. A more detailed analysis of the function/effect of laughter is reported in (Mazzocconi et al., 2016).

Notice that not all speech laughs overlap with the laughable, suggesting that often, laughter that co-occurs with speech is not about the co-occurring speech (47.8% in French and 30% in Chinese). In the following example, speaker B says that she'll take the bigger bedroom, and laughs. Speaker A joins the laughter but starts a new utterance.

(9) B: okay. les chambres maintenant A:alo:rs F euh: bon évidemment F euh: B: je prends la plus grande < laughter/ > A: c'est là < laughter > où il y a un problème t'vois < /laughter >

(Translation) B: okay. the bedrooms now A: well euh: well obviously euh: B: I take the bigger one < laughter/ > A: It's there < laughspeech > where there is a problem you see < /laughspeech >

Laughable= "je prends la plus grande"

4.3 Does laughter interrupt speech?

We investigated whether laughter occurs at utterance-medial positions when one party is speaking, and when the partner is speaking.

Does laughter interrupt partners' utterances? Yes. We found that 51.8% of laughter bouts in French and 56.7% of laughter bouts in Chinese start during the partner's utterances (not necessarily laughables), for example:

(10) B: pour faire un mur de son quoi < laughspeech > en fait c'est une < english > ra:ve < /english > notre appartement < /laughspeech > A: < laughter/ >

(Translation) B: to create a sound barrier which < laughspeech > in fact it is a rave, our apartment < /laughspeech > A:< laughter/ >

Laughable= "in fact it is a rave, our apartment"

Does laughter interrupt one's own utterances?

We found 14 laughter bouts (5%) in French and 12 (8.6%) in Chinese that occurred in utterance-medial positions. These proportions are statistically higher than zero: French $\chi^2(1)=12.3$, $p=.0004$; Chinese $\chi^2(1)=10.5$, $p=.001$. Most of these interruptions at not at phrase boundaries. For example:

(11) 那你之前有没有啊:.有过什么... < laughter/ > < laughter >犯罪记录吗?

(Translation) Do you have, uh, have any < laughter/ > criminal records?

Laughable= "criminal records"

5 Discussion

The aim of the current study was to deepen the little research available on the relation between laughter, laughable and speech in natural conversation, starting from the observation of their temporal sequence and alignment. We investigated three questions: whether laughter always follows, or at least is adjacent to its laughable, as is commonly assumed; whether this sequential alignment differ depending on differeht "types" of laughters; and whether laughter always punctuates speech. Our main findings are:

1. Time alignment between laughter and laughable is rather free.

   — Laughter and laughable does not have a one-to-one relationship. A laughable can be referred to by more than one laughters.

   — Contrary to popular belief, only 30% of laughters occur immediately after the laughable. Laughters frequently start during the laughable (more so with "speaker" laughter than "audience" laughter).

   — Laughters can occur long before or long after the laughable, and not be adjacent to their laughable.

   — Between 30 to 50 percent of speech laughs do not overlap with the laughable, suggesting that frequently laughs are not about the co-occurring speech.

   If looking just at laughter bouts, about 40% occur immediately after the laughable.

2. Laughter-laughable alignment may differ depending on the different "types" of laughable and laughter. Specifically, laughters about a partner-produced laughable (audience laughter) start later than those about a self-produced laughable (speaker laughter). Speech laughs occur earlier than laughter bouts, and overlaps more with the laughable.

3. Comparing Chinese and French, the majority of the patterns are similar, except that in Chinese, laughs are more likely to overlap with the laughable than in French. This provides an initial indication that while certain aspects of laughter behaviour are influenced by culture/language, generally we use laughter similarly in interaction. [3]

4. Laughter *does* interrupt speech: we often laugh when others are speaking (half of all laughter bouts) and occasionally we insert stand-alone laughters mid-sentence (less than 10%). Moreover, very frequently laughter overlaps speech (around 40% of all laughters).

The relatively free alignment between laughter and speech seems analogous at a first approximation to the relation between manual gesture and speech (Rieser, 2015). We propose to consider

---

[3]Of course a caveat to this conclusion is the small number of speakers for each language. We will expand the study with more speakers and more genres of interaction.

laughter as a verbal gesture, having an independent channel from speech, with which it communicates through an interface.

5.1 Is laughter rarely about funny stimuli?

Our results discredit the method of inferring what the laughter is about by looking at the elements that immediately precede or follow it. Therefore, previous conclusions using this method should be revisited (Provine, 1993; Provine, 1996; Provine, 2001; Provine and Emmorey, 2006; Vettin and Todt, 2004). One such conclusion is that because they follow "banal comments", laughter is mostly about not about funny stimuli. We have shown that the logic does not hold, as very often, those preceding "banal comments" are not the laughables. And even if they are, the "funniness" or incongruity may reside between the laughable and something else, e.g., the context of occurrence, world knowledge, cultural norms, experiences, informational and intentional states shared between interlocutors. For example, in the following exchange, the exchange seems rather banal, but in fact, they are laughing about the exophoric situation that they are acting.

(12) A: Oh comment allez-vous? $<$ laughter$/>$ B: ça va et toi? tu vas bien? A : très bien merci:

(Translation) A: Oh how are you? $<$ laughter$/>$ B: fine and you? are you ok? A: very well thanks

Laughable= exophoric situation (they started acting)

Exactly what proportion of laughables contain funny incongruity is a topic for further research. For now, our results questions the validity of existing proposals on this score.

5.2 Laughter Punctuating Speech?

It has been suggested (notably by Provine) that laughter bouts almost never (0.1%) disrupt phrases but punctuate them (Provine, 1993; Provine, 1996; Provine, 2001). He explains this finding on the basis of an organic constraint: laughter and speech share the same vocal apparatus and speech has "priority access". Curiously enough, Provine has always excluded speech-laughs from his investigations, without any justification. A more recent study on laughter in deaf ASL signers (Provine and Emmorey, 2006) showed that signers rarely laugh during their own utterances, where no competition for the same channel of expression is present. Provine and Emmory conclude that the punctuation effect of laughter holds even for signers, and possibly is not a simple physical constraint that determines the placement of laughter in dialogues, but due to a higher order linguistic ordered structure (Provine, 2006).

On the surface, their findings in speakers and signers are similar: speakers do not stop mid-sentence to insert a laugh, and signers do not laugh while signing a sentence. However, this "similarity" may be a difference in disguise. We have shown that speakers frequently overlap laughter and speech. If it were indeed true that signers do not laugh while signing, it raises the question why speech laughter is common for speakers but rare for signers. (Provine and Emmory, 2006) hypothesised that the placement of laughter in dialogue is controlled by a higher linguistic ordered structure, where laughter is secondary to language. Therefore, even when the two don't occur in competing channels, e.g., for signers, laughter still only occurs at phrase boundaries.

We argue for a different explanation. Assuming speech laughter data (laughter that overlaps utterances) were not excluded in the ASL study as they were in spoken dialogue studies, in deaf signers, since the laughter is perceived only visually and involves marked facial movements, it would interfere with the perception of the message conveyed by language. In sign languages, body and face movements constitute important communicative elements at all linguistic levels from phonology to morphology, semantics, syntax and prosody (Liddell, 1978; Campbell, 1999). Despite the fact that emotional facial expressions can overlap with linguistic facial movements (Dachkovsky and Sandler, 2009), a laugh, implying a significant alteration of facial configuration (see identification of a laughter episode) could be excessively disruptive for the message aimed to be conveyed. While in verbal language the laughter signal can be completely fused in the speech as a paralinguistic feature (Crystal, 1976) and used in a sophisticated manner to enrich and facilitate communication, (Nwokah et al., 1999) report that not even from an acoustic perspective is laughter secondary to speech: when co-occurring the laugh indeed does not resemble the speech spectral patterns nor does the speech resemble the laughter ones, but together they create a new idiosyncratic pattern. Laughter is fully meaningful and communicative in itself, universally across cultures, and the emotional components that it carries are not secondary to speech or trivial.

6 Conclusion and future work

Our study provides the first systematic analysis of laughables, and demonstrates the existence of a corpus, the DUEL corpus (Hough et al., 2016b) in which less than a third of the laughs immediately follow their referents. Instead, the laugh can occur before, during or after the laughable with wide time ranges. In addition, laughter *does* "interrupt" speech: we frequently start laughing in the middle of an utterance of the interlocutor or of ourselves (often speech-laugh). Our results challenge the assumption that what laughter follows is what it is about, and thus question previous claims based on this assumption.

In future work, we will study to what extent laughter-laughable alignment differs by the function/effect of laughter, and what the limit is for the "free" alignment. This work may be useful for dialogue systems which allows a computer agent to generate laughter at appropriate times depending on the type and location of the laughable.

Acknowledgments

We would like to thank three anonymous reviewers for SigDial 2016 for their very helpful comments. We acknowledge the support of the French Investissements d'Avenir-Labex EFL program (ANR-10-LABX-0083) and the Disfluency, Exclamations, and Laughter in Dialogue (DUEL) project within the *projets franco-allemand en sciences humaines et sociales* funded by the ANR and the DFG.

References

Mahadev L Apte. 1985. *Humor and laughter: An anthropological approach*. Cornell Univ Pr.

Jo-Anne Bachorowski and Michael J Owren. 2001. Not all laughs are alike: Voiced but not unvoiced laughter readily elicits positive affect. *Psychological Science*, 12(3):252–257.

Paul Boersma et al. 2002. Praat, a system for doing phonetics by computer. *Glot international*, 5(9/10):341–345.

Ruth Campbell. 1999. Categorical perception of face actions: Their role in sign language and in communicative facial displays. *The Quarterly Journal of Experimental Psychology: Section A*, 52(1):67–95.

David Crystal. 1976. *Prosodic systems and intonation in English*, volume 1. CUP Archive.

Svetlana Dachkovsky and Wendy Sandler. 2009. Visual intonation in the prosody of a sign language. *Language and Speech*, 52(2-3):287–314.

Paul Ekman and Wallace V Friesen. 1975. Unmasking the face: A guide to recognizing emotions from facial cues.

Jonathan Ginzburg, Ellen Breitholtz, Robin Cooper, Julian Hough, and Ye Tian. 2015. Understanding laughter. In *Proceedings of the 20th Amsterdam Colloquium*, University of Amsterdam.

Jonathan Ginzburg. 2012. *The Interactive Stance: Meaning for Conversation*. Oxford University Press, Oxford.

Julian Hough, Ye Tian, Laura de Ruiter, Simon Betz, David Schlangen, and Jonathan Ginzburg. 2016a. Duel: A multi-lingual multimodal dialogue corpus for disfluency, exclamations and laughter. In *10th edition of the Language Resources and Evaluation Conference*.

Julian Hough, Ye Tian, Laura de Ruiter, Simon Betz, David Schlangen, and Jonathan Ginzburg. 2016b. Duel: A multi-lingual multimodal dialogue corpus for disfluency, exclamations and laughter. In *Proceedings of LREC 2016*.

Klaus Krippendorff. 2012. *Content analysis: An introduction to its methodology*. Sage.

Scott K Liddell. 1978. Nonmanual signals and relative clauses in american sign language. *Understanding language through sign language research*, pages 59–90.

Chiara Mazzocconi, Ye Tian, and Jonathan Ginzburg. 2016. Multi-layered analysis of laughter. In *Proceedings of SemDial 2016 (JerSem), the 20th Workshop on the Semantics and Pragmatics of Dialogue*.

John Morreall. 1983. *Taking laughter seriously*. SUNY Press.

Evangeline E Nwokah, Hui-Chin Hsu, Olga Dobrowolska, and Alan Fogel. 1994. The development of laughter in mother-infant communication: Timing parameters and temporal sequences. *Infant Behavior and Development*, 17(1):23–35.

Evangeline E Nwokah, Hui-Chin Hsu, Patricia Davies, and Alan Fogel. 1999. The integration of laughter and speech in vocal communicationa dynamic systems perspective. *Journal of Speech, Language, and Hearing Research*, 42(4):880–894.

Robert R Provine and Karen Emmorey. 2006. Laughter among deaf signers. *Journal of Deaf Studies and Deaf Education*, 11(4):403–409.

Robert R. Provine. 1993. Laughter punctuates speech: Linguistic, social and gender contexts of laughter. *Ethology*, 95(4):291–298.

Robert R Provine. 1996. Laughter. *American scientist*, 84(1):38–45.

Robert R Provine. 2001. *Laughter: A scientific investigation*. Penguin.

V. Raskin. 1985. *Semantic mechanisms of humor*, volume 24. Springer.

Hannes Rieser. 2015. When hands talk to mouth. gesture and speech as autonomous communicating processes. *SEMDIAL 2015 goDIAL*, page 122.

Hartmut Rothgänger, Gertrud Hauser, Aldo Carlo Cappellini, and Assunta Guidotti. 1998. Analysis of laughter and speech sounds in italian and german students. *Naturwissenschaften*, 85(8):394–402.

Klaus R Scherer. 2009. The dynamic architecture of emotion: Evidence for the component process model. *Cognition and emotion*, 23(7):1307–1351.

Jérôme Urbain and Thierry Dutoit. 2011. A phonetic analysis of natural laughter, for use in automatic laughter processing systems. In *Affective Computing and Intelligent Interaction*, pages 397–406. Springer.

Julia Vettin and Dietmar Todt. 2004. Laughter in conversation: Features of occurrence and acoustic structure. *Journal of Nonverbal Behavior*, 28(2):93–115.

Small Talk Improves User Impressions of Interview Dialogue Systems

Takahiro Kobori[†], Mikio Nakano[‡], and Tomoaki Nakamura[†]
[†]University of Electro-Communications
1-5-1 Chofugaoka, Chofu, Tokyo 182-8585, Japan
`{t_kobori@radish, naka_t@apple}.ee.uec.ac.jp`
[‡]Honda Research Institute Japan Co., Ltd.
8-1 Honcho, Wako, Saitama 351-0188, Japan
`nakano@jp.honda-ri.com`

Abstract

This paper addresses the problem of how to build interview systems that users are willing to use. Existing interview dialogue systems are mainly focused on obtaining information from users, thus they just repeatedly ask questions. We propose a method for improving user impressions by engaging in small talk during interviews. The system performs frame-based dialogue management for interviewing and generates small talk utterances after the user answers the system's questions. Experimental results using a text-based interview dialogue system for diet recording showed the proposed method gives a better impression to users than interview dialogues without small talk. It is also found that generating too many small talk utterances makes user impressions worse because of the system's low capability of continuously generating appropriate small talk utterances.

1 Introduction

Our goal is to build dialogue systems that can obtain information from users. In this paper, we call such systems *interview dialogue systems*. An example is a dialogue system that interviews a user about what he/she ate and drank. The information obtained by the system is expected to be used for health care.

Although interviews have not been as popular as database search and reservations as applications of dialogue systems, they have commercial potential (Stent et al., 2006). Interview dialogue systems would be useful not only because they save human labor but also because users are expected to disclose their personal information to automated systems more often than to human-operated systems (Lucas et al., 2014).

We propose a method for dialogue management for such a dialogue system. Although several interview dialogue systems have been developed so far, most of them put their focus mainly on obtaining information, repeating questions and making mechanical dialogues. It might be acceptable if the user is expected to use the system only once, like a system for an opinion poll. However, such a strategy is not acceptable for systems like the one for diet recording, because users might not want to use such a system every day.

In human-human conversations, participants sometimes try to obtain information from another participant while enjoying the chat. If a system can engage in such kinds of conversation, a user may be willing to use it. However, the capability of even state-of-the-art chat systems is not good enough to chat for a long time. They sometimes cause dialogue breakdowns for various reasons (Higashinaka et al., 2015).

Our proposed dialogue management method mainly engages in an interview dialogue and sometimes inserts *small talk utterances*.[1] In this paper, a small talk utterance means an utterance that is not directly related to the task of the dialogue but makes the dialogue smoother and friendly. Examples of small talk utterances are utterances telling impression (e.g., "It sounds very nice") and self-disclosures (e.g., "That's my favorite food."). We expect that generating small talk utterances will enable users to enjoy using the system and they will want to use the system again.

Using the proposed method, we built an interview dialogue system for diet recording and con-

---

[1]We use the term *utterance* rather than *sentence* even though we deal with only text-based dialogue systems in this paper, because sentences used in those systems are more colloquial.

Proceedings of the SIGDIAL 2016 Conference, pages 370–380,
Los Angeles, USA, 13-15 September 2016. ©2016 Association for Computational Linguistics

ducted a user study to investigate the effectiveness of the small talk utterances. We found that the small talk utterances give the user a better impression but it was suggested that generating too many small talk utterances increases the possibility of generating unnatural utterances, resulting in bad impressions.

This paper is organized as follows. Section 2 surveys related work, and Section 3 proposes the method for dialogue management. Section 4 explains in detail the interview dialogue systems for diet recording as an implementation of the proposed method. Section 5 shows the experimental evaluation results before concluding the paper in Section 6.

2 Related Work

Although interviews have not been popular applications of dialogue systems, several systems have been developed so far.

One of the earliest systems is MORE (Kahn et al., 1985), which can elicit knowledge for diagnosis from human experts. It uses a number of heuristic rules to generate questions to human experts. Although the paper does not clearly state how it understands user replies, it does not seem to perform complicated language processing. Stent et al. (2006) built a spoken dialogue system for interview-based surveys for rating college courses. They showed dialogue epiphenomena can be used to learn more than the system asks. Johnston et al. (2013) built a spoken dialogue system for government and social scientific surveys. They are concerned with confirmation strategies for reducing errors in the surveys. Skantze et al. (2012) use robot behaviors for increasing the reply rate in survey interviews. All these systems focus on obtaining information from users. They are suitable to be used once but it is not clear whether users want to continuously use them.

On the contrary, *chat-oriented dialogue systems*, which can engage in small talk, have been built so that users will enjoy conversations with them (Wallace, 2008; Wilks et al., 2011; Higashinaka et al., 2014). It has been tried to combine chat-oriented dialogue systems with task-oriented dialogue systems (Traum et al., 2005; Nakano et al., 2006; Lee et al., 2006). Recent commercial dialogue systems such as Siri (Bellegarda, 2013) also have functionality for engaging in small talk.

Incorporating small talk into interview dialogue systems has been considered as well, since small talk is known to be effective in building *rapport* (Bickmore and Picard, 2005), they are expected to increase the rate that the user honestly answers the questions. For example, Conrad et al. (2015) showed that small talk in survey interviewing to increase the users' comprehension and engagement. Bickmore and Cassell (2005) also used small talk to increase trust. Unlike those studies whose aim is to obtain more information from the users, we focus on how to give better impressions to the users. In addition, while both Conrad et al. (2015) and Bickmore and Cassell (2005) conducted Wizard-of-Oz based studies, we take into account that it is inevitable for systems to generate inappropriate utterances.

3 Proposed Method

There are two possible dialogue management strategies for engaging in both interview dialogues and chat-oriented dialogues. One is to deal with chat as the primary strategy and sometimes invoke an interview dialogue to ask questions to the users. This strategy is taken by some of the previously built dialogue systems that integrate task-oriented dialogues and chat-oriented dialogues (Nakano et al., 2006; Lee et al., 2006). The other strategy is to deal with interviewing as the primary strategy and chat as the secondary strategy.

In the former approach, since the capability of the current chat-oriented dialogue systems is not good enough to always generate utterances that match the dialogue context (Higashinaka et al., 2015), engaging in chat for many turns might make the user's impression worse.

We therefore take the latter approach. Our method systematically asks questions for the interview based on frame-based (Bobrow et al., 1977; Goddeau et al., 1996), agenda-based (Bohus and Rudnicky, 2009), or other kinds of dialogue management. Then when the user replies to the system's questions, it may start small talk by choosing one of the small talk utterances stored in a database. After several turns, it goes back to the interview. When to start small talk and when to finish are determined by heuristic rules or probabilistic rules learned from a corpus. By this strategy, even if small talk does not go well, the system can go back to the interview and evolve the dialogue.

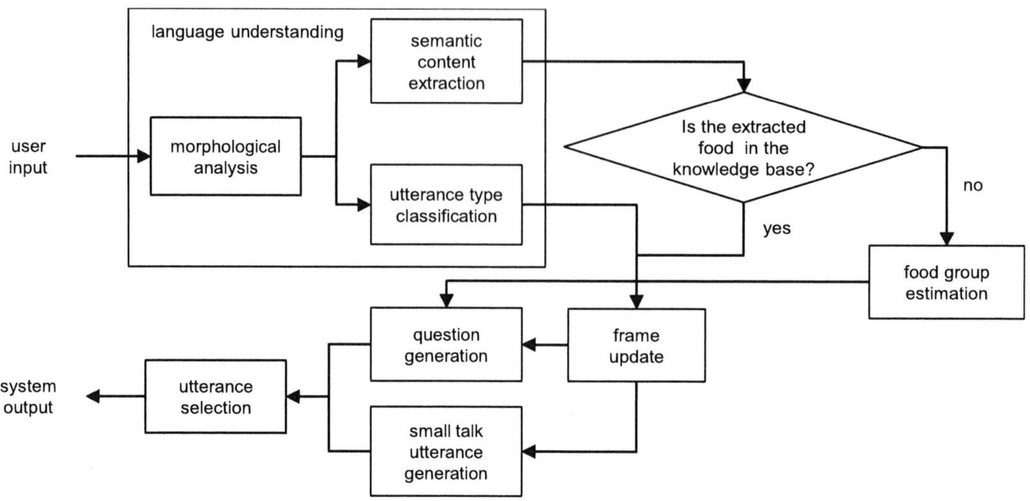

Figure 1: Architecture for the interview dialogue system for diet recording

4 Implementation: An Interview Dialogue System for Diet Recording

Based on the proposed method, we have developed a Japanese text-based interview dialogue system that asks the user what he/she ate and drank the day before. Figure 1 shows the architecture of the system.

Note that the goal of the system is to obtain rough information of what the user had each day. We assume the information is used to know the tendency of the user's dietary habits. Obtaining detailed dietary records so that it can be used for nutritional guidance is out of the scope of our research.

4.1 Knowledge Base

Our system assumes most users have meals with typical meal compositions for Japanese. For example, lunch can consist of a one-dish meal and soup, or it can consist of *shushoku* (side dish mainly containing carbohydrates), a couple of *okazu* (main or side dish containing few carbohydrates), and soup. Each kind of food can be one of these categories; for example, steamed rice and bread are *shushoku*, and sandwiches and tacos are one-dish meals. We call these categories *food groups*. The system has a knowledge base that contains a list of foods for each food group as shown in Table 1.

4.2 Understanding User Utterances

The language understanding module first performs a morphological analysis using MeCab (Kudo et

al., 2004) to segment the input text into words and get their part-of-speech information.

It then determines the type of the user utterance. The type is either *greeting*, *affirmative utterance* (including replies to system questions), or *negative utterance*. The number of types is small because, in interview dialogues, user utterances have small variations. An utterance telling the food and drink the user had is an affirmative utterance. This utterance type classification is done by LR (Logistic Regression), which uses bag-of-words features. We used LIBLINEAR (Fan et al., 2008) for the implementation of LR.

It then performs semantic content extraction, that is, obtaining five kinds of information, namely, food and drink, ingredient, food group, amount of food, and time of having food. This is done by CRF (Conditional Random Fields) using the IOB2 tagging framework (Hahn et al., 2011). For the CRF, we used commonly used features such as unigram and bigram of the surface form, original form and part of speech of the word. We used CRFsuite (Okazaki, 2007) for the implementation of CRF.

These statistical models for LR and CRF were trained on 5,630 utterances. This set was artificially created by randomly changing content words in 563 sentences manually written by developers.

4.3 Dialogue Management for Interviewing

Dialogue management for interviewing is based on a frame. Slots of the frame are compositions

Food group	Examples instances	# of instances
shushoku (side dish mainly containing carbohydrates)	steamed rice, bread, cereal	20
okazu (main or side dish containing few carbohydrates)	Hamburg steak, fried shrimp, grilled fish	106
soup	corn soup, *miso* soup	18
one-dish meal	sandwich, noodle soup, pasta, rice bowl	78
drink	orange juice, coffee	32
dessert	cake, pancake, jelly	16
confectionery	chocolate, donut	34
total		304

Table 1: Content of the knowledge base

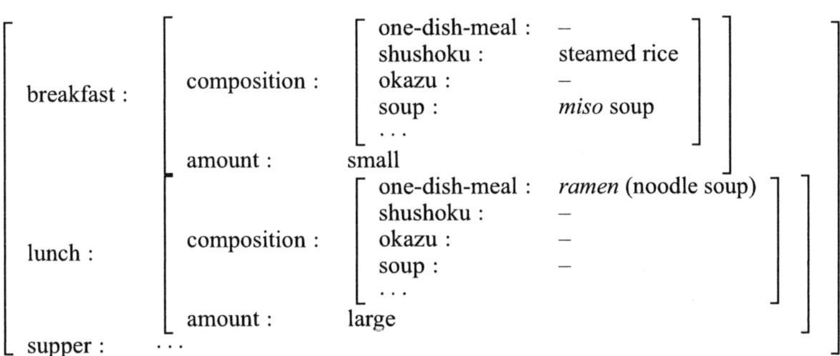

Figure 2: A snapshot of the frame

for each meal (breakfast, lunch, supper) and the amount of each food. Figure 2 shows a snapshot of the frame.

The frame is updated each time the user makes an utterance, based on its language understanding result. When there is food or drink in the understanding result, the system needs to know its group so that it can fill the appropriate slot of the frame. For example, when the user says he/she had steak for supper, the system needs to know if it is an *okazu* (main or side dish) so that it can fill the "okazu" slot of the "composition" slot of the "supper" slot. This is done using the food list in each food group in the knowledge base. If the food is not in the food and drink list, the system estimates its food group and requests confirmation from the user as will be explained in Section 4.4. Slot values can be a set of food and drink. So if the user says he/she had a steak and a salad, the *okazu* slot value is the set of "steak" and "salad".

The system-utterance selection is done with manually written rules. The system asks what the user ate and drank in order. This is because in human-human dialogues we collected in advance, participants asked what the other participant had in a particular order. In addition the system asks the user brief descriptions of the food, and then asks the composition in detail. For example, when

asking about breakfast, the system asks first "what did you have for breakfast?" and then asks detailed questions such as "what else did you have?" and "what did you have for *shushoku*?" When the frame satisfies conditions for each meal (breakfast, lunch, and supper), the system moves to asking about the next meal, and then finishes after obtaining information about all meals. In this process, constraints on slot values are considered; for example, if the *one-dish-meal* slot value is not empty, the system does not ask about *shushoku*, because people do not tend to have both one-dish meals and *shushoku* in one meal. The system's questions are not always the same; they are randomly chosen from a variety of candidate expressions.

This frame representation is not perfect in that it cannot represent meal compositions that are not typical for Japanese users. Some users may have more than three meals in one day. Augmenting the system to deal with a variety of meal composition is among our future work.

Even if the system cannot understand the user's answer perfectly, the system moves the dialogue forward so that the dialogue does not get stuck.

4.4 Acquiring Food Groups

When the recognized food is not in the database, to estimate its group, we used a method proposed

Type	#
showing empathy	26
telling impression of that the amount is large	22
telling impression of that the amount is small	50
asking a question	6
self-disclosure	2
backchannel	6
telling impression of the user's negative answer	7
reaction to individual food	323
Total	442

Table 2: The number of small talk utterance candidates for each type

S: What did you have for breakfast?
U: I had *natto-gohan* (steamed rice with fermented soybeans).
S: Is *natto-gohan* an *okazu* or *shushoku*?
U: It's a *shushoku*.

Figure 3: Example dialogue for food group acquisition

by Otsuka et al. (2013). Although they used both a model trained from a food database and Web search results, we only used the former. It estimates the group of the food as one of the seven groups in Table 1 and asks a question such as "Is *osuimono* (Japanese broth soup) soup?". This is done by logistic regression, which uses the bag of words, unigram and bigram of characters as features, the type of characters used in Japanese (*hiragana*, *katakana*, Chinese characters, and alphabet). The amount of training data consists of 863 expressions.

The system does not always ask back to the user only the top estimation result. It sometimes generates n-ary questions using n-best estimation results. For example, a binary question "Is sweet roll a confectionery or a one-dish meal?" can be asked. This is because the top estimation result is not always correct. In addition, n-ary questions are sometimes easy to understand because the user does not know the list of food groups in advance and he/she may not understand what *shushoku* really means. How many candidates are used in the question is decided based on posterior probabilities but we omit the detailed explanation because it is not really related to the main topic of this paper.

The dialogue management for acquiring the group of a food is performed separately from the management for interview dialogues; that is, when the food name that the user says is not in the database, the control moves to the food group acquisition dialogue managers, and after obtaining the food group, the control moves back to the interview dialogue manager. Figure 3 shows a translation of an example food group acquisition dialogue.

4.5 Generating Small Talk Utterances

Small talk utterances are selected from a predefined list based on the type and the content of the preceding user utterance. When the user utterance is affirmative, negative utterances are avoided as

candidates for small talk utterances. For example, the following utterances can be chosen.

It's my favorite food! (self-disclosure)
Great! (showing empathy)
Is it tasty? (asking a question)

When the user utterance is negative, utterances showing impression of the user's negative answer, such as "It lowers my spirit...", "Let's go to eat something you like!" are selected.

In addition, when a specific food is included in the preceding user utterance, small talk utterances corresponding to the food are chosen. For example, if the user utterance includes "tiramisu", utterances such as "Tiramisu means 'cheer me up' in Italian." can be chosen.

When the amount of a meal is mentioned by the user, a small talk utterance showing an impression of the amount is chosen. For example, if the user says that the amount is large (e.g., "I ate too much"), an utterance such as "Please be careful about your health!" is chosen.

We constructed the predefined list of small talk utterances by asking our colleagues and 100 people recruited through a crowdsourcing site to list them, obtaining 442 utterances in total. The number of utterances for each type is shown in Table 2.

4.6 Response Selection

The response selection module needs to select one utterance from many candidates for questions and small talk utterances. Although learning a strategy for selecting appropriate system utterances from a corpus is among our future work, the current system adopts a very simple heuristic rule. First it decides if it asks questions or generates small talk utterances. If the number of small talk utterances generated after the previous system question is smaller than N, which is set in advance, it generates a small talk utterance, and otherwise it asks

$N = 0$ (no small talk utterances)

S:	What did you have for lunch?
U:	I had *okonomiyaki* (Japanese pancake) for lunch.
S:	Did you have any other food for lunch?
U:	No, I didn't have any other food.
S:	How much did you have for lunch yesterday?
U:	I had only a small amount.

$N = 1$ (one small talk utterance)

S:	What did you have for breakfast yesterday?
U:	*Shoku-pan* (sliced bread) and corn soup.
S:	Those are good!
U:	I agree.
S:	What else did you have for breakfast yesterday?

$N = 3$ (three small talk utterances)

S:	What did you have for lunch yesterday?
U:	I had a Hamburg steak.
S:	You had a Hamburg steak, did you?
U:	Yes, it was a Hamburg steak.
S:	Do you like Hamburg steaks?
U:	Yes, I like them very much.
S:	Actually I had a Hamburg steak.
U:	Really? Was it tasty?
S:	What else did you have for lunch yesterday?

Figure 4: Example dialogues
(S means the system and U means the user)

Favored condition	Frequency
NO	67
ONE	46
TWO	107
THREE	270
TWO-CONSECUTIVE	65
THREE-CONSECUTIVE	45
Total	600

Table 3: Result of questionnaire survey on the number of small talk utterances

a question. Small talk utterances are randomly selected from the candidates but repeating the same small talk utterance within the N turns is avoided.

4.7 Example Dialogues

Figure 4 shows translations of example dialogues collected in the user study to be described in Section 5 with N being zero (no small talk utterances), one, and three. A longer example can be found in the appendix.

5 User Study

To investigate the effectiveness of the small talk utterances, we conducted a user study.

5.1 Compared Conditions

In this user study, to evaluate the effectiveness of generating small talk utterances, we compared the following three conditions:

NO-STU: The system does not generate any small talk utterances ($N = 0$ in Section 4.6. This is the baseline condition),

1-STU: The system generates one small talk utterance after the user replies to the system question for diet recording ($N = 1$), and

3-STU: The system generates three small talk utterances (three turns) after the user replies to the system question for diet recording ($N = 3$).

We have chosen these for the following reason. First, we conducted a preliminary questionnaire survey to 100 people via crowdsourcing. We showed each participant six sets of dialogues. Each set includes six dialogues each of which has one system question, the user's reply, one of the following, and another system question:

NO: nothing,

ONE: small talk containing one system turn,

TWO: small talk containing two system turns,

THREE: small talk containing three system turns,

TWO-CONSECUTIVE: one system turn having two consecutive small talk utterances and the user's reaction, and

THREE-CONSECUTIVE: one system turn having three consecutive small talk utterances and the user's reaction.

These dialogues were created by the authors based on the functionality of the implemented interview dialogue system. Each participant is asked which he/she likes the best among the six dialogues for each set. Table 3 shows the result. We found the participants liked THREE best.

We also found, however, increasing the number of small talk utterances does not give a better impression to the participants in the trial use of the system. This is probably because the second and third small talk utterances need to react to the user responses to the first small talk utterance and it is difficult to generate utterances appropriate in the context. On the contrary, the dialogues we showed in the above questionnaire survey did not include any inappropriate utterances, thus the participant must have chosen THREE.

ID	Adjective pair		
Q_1	system responses are meaningful	↔	system responses are meaningless
Q_2	fun	↔	not fun
Q_3	natural	↔	unnatural
Q_4	warm	↔	cold
Q_5	want to talk to the system again	↔	don't want to talk to the system again
Q_6	lively	↔	not lively
Q_7	simple	↔	complicated

Table 4: Survey items

We therefore used 1-STU in addition to 3-STU in the user study. We also used NO-STU which was dealt with as the baseline.

5.2 Experimental Method

We asked 100 participants recruited through a crowdsourcing site to evaluate the system with different conditions after engaging in the dialogues. We did not collect their personal profiles such as gender and age. The participants accessed the dialogue server to engage in dialogues with the system with the three conditions. The order of the conditions was random. The participants were asked to evaluate the dialogue by rating seven items on a 5-point Likert-scale after finishing the dialogue with the system with each condition. The system finished the dialogue if the number of turns reached 33. For a technical reason, the maximum number of system turns of the dialogue is 34.

When analyzing the evaluation data, we excluded those of eight participants whose dialogues were interrupted due to system problems and who repeated the same utterances many times. The average number of system turns in the dialogues with the NO-STU system, the 1-STU system, and the 3-STU system were respectively 16.5, 23.4, and 30.8.

5.3 Language Understanding Performance

We first evaluated the performance of the language understanding module. We randomly extracted 1,000 user utterances and their understanding results from the collected dialogue logs. We found that the utterance types of the 91.7% of utterances are correctly classified and the semantic contents from the 84.8% of utterances were perfectly extracted.

We also evaluated food group estimation by investigating randomly chosen 200 food group acquisition dialogues. The accuracy of the food group estimation was 84.0%, when we consider

the estimation result is correct if one of the candidates the system provided to the user was correct.

5.4 User Impressions

Figure 5 shows the user evaluation results. First, for "simplicity", NO-STU is the best, followed by 1-STU. This is reasonable because the total number of turns becomes smaller when a lower number of small talk utterances are generated.

As for the remaining survey items, we found the 1-STU got significantly higher scores for "fun", "warmth" "want-to-talk-again" and "liveliness" than NO-STU. In addition it is not worse than NO-STU for the other items. This shows small talk utterances improve the impressions of the system.

However, scores of 3-STU are better than those of NO-STU only for "warmth" and "liveliness" and not better than for any items than 1-STU, In addition the "naturalness" scores of 3-STU are significantly lower than those of NO-STU and 1-STU. We discuss this below.

5.5 Discussion

The scores for 3-STU are not good probably because, as we already discussed in Section 5.1, increasing the number of small talk utterances raises the possibility of generating unnatural system utterances. We confirmed this by manually investigating the frequency of inappropriate small talk utterances. We randomly chose five participants and checked their dialogue in 3-STU, and intuitively judged if the small talk utterances are inappropriate considering both the utterance content and the dialogue context. We found that 27 out of 33 first system utterances in the small talk (82%) were appropriate, but that only 18 of 32 (56%) second utterances and 8 of 29 (28%) third utterances were appropriate. We guess this is why 3-STU gives a worse impression to the participants.

We found that the participants are split into two groups depending on the scores for "naturalness" and "liveliness" as shown in Figure 6. Although we have not figured out the exact cause of this, we suspect this is because the expectations of the participants to the ability of the system are different. By looking at the free-form descriptions of impressions of the participants, the participants who scored low in "naturalness" wrote impressions such as "not interesting" and "can't respond well", but the participants who scored high wrote impressions such as "It's fun to think how to speak in order to be understood by the system" and "It's

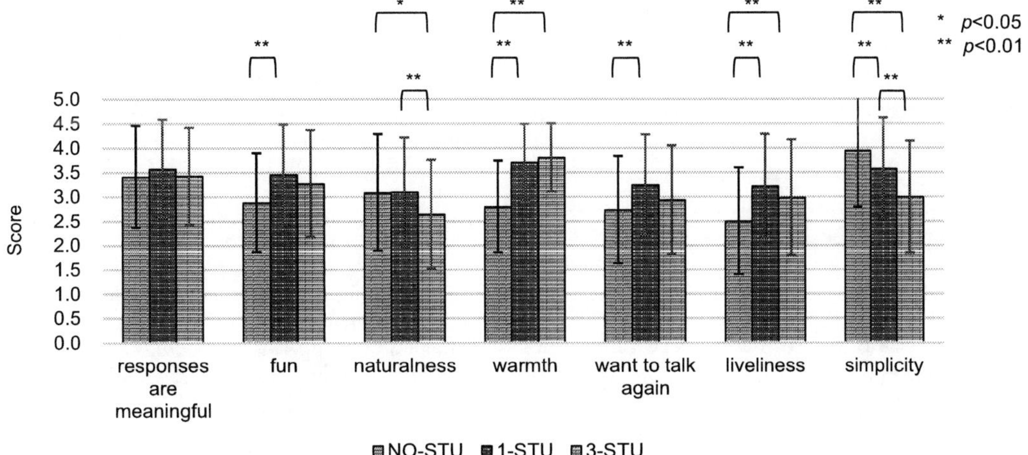

Figure 5: Averages and standard deviations (shown as error bars) of user evaluations on the system. The statistical significances are evaluated using Wilcoxon signed-rank tests.

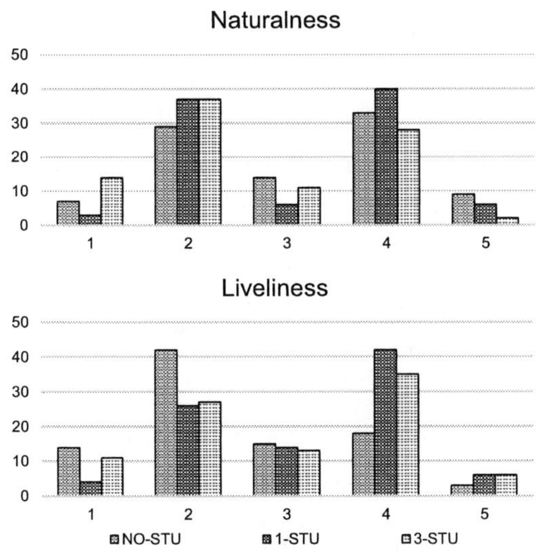

Figure 6: Distributions of "naturalness" and "liveliness" scores

fun to chat with the robot"[2]. That is, those who scored high in "naturalness" did not seem to have high expectations in the ability of the dialogue system. Based on this observation, finding a method for decreasing user expectations is expected to be effective to improve their impressions.

---

[2]The chat display shows an illustration of a robot.

6   Concluding Remarks

Interviewing is one of the promising applications of dialogue systems technology although not many studies have been conducted so far. This paper proposed to generate small talk utterances to improve user impressions of interview dialogue systems. Based on the proposal, we implemented a Japanese text-based interview dialogue system for diet recording.

The results of a user study showed that small talk utterances give a better impression to users but suggested that generating too many small talk utterances increases the possibility of generating unnatural utterances, making the users' impressions worse.

The user study presented in this paper was based on crowdsourcing. So there can be bias in user attributes such as gender and age. In addition, although our long-term goal is to build interview dialogue systems that users are willing to repeatedly use, the participants used the system only once in the user study. We are planning to conduct another user study to investigate how generating small talk utterances affects the continuous use of the system by recruiting a variety of participants.

The current system uses a fixed number of small talk utterances. We are planning to incorporate a strategy for flexibility selecting utterances from candidates for questions and small talk utterances depending on the context and user reactions. Such a strategy will be learned from the corpus that we collected in the user study described in Section 5. Furthermore, taking a deep-learning-based approach to utterance selection (Lowe et al., 2015) is one possibility if we can obtain enough training data.

Finally, we plan to investigate how well the results of this study can be applied to interview dialogue systems in other domains.

Acknowledgments

The authors would like to thank Eric Nichols for his valuable comments.

References

Jerome R. Bellegarda. 2013. Spoken language understanding for natural interaction: The Siri experience. In Joseph Mariani, Sophie Rosset, Martine Garnier-Rizet, and Laurence Devillers, editors, *Natural Interaction with Robots, Knowbots and Smartphones*, pages 3–14. Springer.

Timothy Bickmore and Justine Cassell. 2005. Social dialogue with embodied conversational agents. In Jan C. J. van Kuppevelt, Laila Dybkjar, and Niels Ole Bernsen, editors, *Advances in Natural Multimodal Dialogue Systems*, pages 23–54. Springer.

Timothy W. Bickmore and Rosalind W. Picard. 2005. Establishing and maintaining long-term human-computer relationships. *ACM Transactions on Computer-Human Interaction*, 12(2):293–327.

Daniel G. Bobrow, Ronald M. Kaplan, Martin Kay, Donald A. Norman, Henry Thompson, and Terry Winograd. 1977. GUS, a frame driven dialog system. *Artificial Intelligence*, 8(2):155–173.

Dan Bohus and Alexander I. Rudnicky. 2009. The RavenClaw dialog management framework: Architecture and systems. *Computer Speech and Language*, 23(3):332–361.

Frederick G. Conrad, Michael F. Schober, Matt Jans, Rachel A. Orlowski, Daniel Nielsen, and Rachel Levenstein. 2015. Comprehension and engagement in survey interviews with virtual agents. *Frontiers in Psychology*, 6. Article 1578.

Rong-En Fan, Kai-Wei Chang, Cho-Jui Hsieh, Xiang-Rui Wang, and Chih-Jen Lin. 2008. LIBLINEAR: A library for large linear classification. *Journal of Machine Learning Research*, 9.

D. Goddeau, H. Meng, J. Polifroni, S. Seneff, and S. Busayapongchai. 1996. A form-based dialogue manager for spoken language applications. In *Proceedings of the Fourth International Conference on Spoken Language Processing (ICSLP-96)*, pages 701–704.

Stefan Hahn, Marco Dinarelli, Christian Raymond, Fabrice Lefèvre, Patrick Lehnen, Renato De Mori, Alessandro Moschitti, Hermann Ney, and Giuseppe Riccardi. 2011. Comparing stochastic approaches to spoken language understanding in multiple languages. *IEEE Transactions on Speech and Audio Processing*, 19(6):1569–1583.

Ryuichiro Higashinaka, Kenji Imamura, Toyomi Meguro, Chiaki Miyazaki, Nozomi Kobayashi, Hiroaki Sugiyama, Toru Hirano, Toshiro Makino, and Yoshihiro Matsuo. 2014. Towards an open-domain conversational system fully based on natural language processing. In *Proceedings of the 25th International Conference on Computational Linguistics (COLING-2014)*, pages 928–939.

Ryuichiro Higashinaka, Kotaro Funakoshi, Masahiro Araki, Hiroshi Tsukahara, Yuka Kobayashi, and Masahiro Mizukami. 2015. Towards taxonomy of errors in chat-oriented dialogue systems. In *Proceedings of the 16th Annual Meeting of the Special Interest Group on Discourse and Dialogue (SIGDIAL 2015)*, pages 87–95.

Michael Johnston, Patrick Ehlen, Frederick G. Conrad, Michael F. Schober, Christopher Antoun, Stefanie Fail, Andrew Hupp, Lucas Vickers, Huiying Yan, and Chan Zhang. 2013. Spoken dialog systems for automated survey interviewing. In *Proceedings of the 15th Annual Meeting of the Special Interest Group on Discourse and Dialogue (SIGDIAL 2013)*, pages 928–939.

Gary Kahn, Steve Nowlan, and John McDermott. 1985. MORE: an intelligent knowledge acquisition tool. In *Proceedings of the 9th International Joint Conference on Artificial Intelligence (IJCAI-85)*, pages 581–584.

Taku Kudo, Kaoru Yamamoto, and Yuji Matsumoto. 2004. Applying conditional random fields to Japanese morphological analysis. In *Proceedings of the 2004 Conference on Empirical Methods in Natural Language Processing (EMNLP-2004)*, pages 230–237.

Cheongjae Lee, Sangkeun Jung, Minwoo Jeong, and Gary Geunbae Lee. 2006. Chat and goal-oriented dialog together: A unified example-based architecture for multi-domain dialog management. In *Proceedings of the 2006 IEEE Spoken Language Technology Workshop (SLT-2006)*.

Ryan Lowe, Nissan Pow, Iulian V. Serban, and Joelle Pineau. 2015. The Ubuntu dialogue corpus: A large dataset for research in unstructured multi-turn dialogue systems. In *Proceedings of the 16th Annual Meeting of the Special Interest Group on Discourse and Dialogue (SIGDIAL 2015)*, pages 285–294.

Gale M. Lucas, Jonathan Gratch, Aisha King, and Louis-Philippe Morency. 2014. It's only a computer: Virtual humans increase willingness to disclose. *Computers in Human Behavior*, 37:94–100.

Mikio Nakano, Atsushi Hoshino, Johane Takeuchi, Yuji Hasegawa, Toyotaka Torii, Kazuhiro Nakadai, Kazuhiko Kato, and Hiroshi Tsujino. 2006. A robot that can engage in both task-oriented and non-task-oriented dialogues. In *Proceedings of the 6th IEEE-RAS International Conference on Humanoid Robots (Humanoids 2006)*, pages 404–411.

Naoaki Okazaki. 2007. CRFsuite: a fast implementation of conditional random fields (CRFs). http://www.chokkan.org/software/crfsuite/.

Tsugumi Otsuka, Kazunori Komatani, Satoshi Sato, and Mikio Nakano. 2013. Generating more specific questions for acquiring attributes of unknown concepts from users. In *Proceedings of the 15th Annual Meeting of the Special Interest Group on Discourse and Dialogue (SIGDIAL 2013)*, pages 70–77.

Gabriel Skantze, Samer Al Moubayed, Joakim Gustafson, Jonas Beskow, and Bjorn Granstrom. 2012. Furhat at robotville: A robot head harvesting the thoughts of the public through multi-party dialogue. In *Proceedings of the IVA 2012 Workshop on Real-Time Conversations with Virtual Agents (RCVA 2012)*.

Amanda Stent, Svetlana Stenchikova, and Matthew Marge. 2006. Dialog systems for surveys: the rate-a-course system. In *Proceedings of the 2006 IEEE Spoken Language Technology Workshop (SLT-2006)*, pages 210–213.

David Traum, William Swartout, Stacy Marsella, and Jonathan Gratch. 2005. Fight, flight, or negotiate: Believable strategies for conversing under crisis. In *Proceedings of the International Conference on Intelligent Virtual Agents 2005 (IVA-2005)*, pages 52–64.

Richard S. Wallace. 2008. The anatomy of A.L.I.C.E. In Robert Epstein, Gary Roberts, and Grace Beber, editors, *Parsing the Turing Test: Philosophical and Methodological Issues in the Quest for the Thinking Computer*, pages 181–210. Springer.

Yorick Wilks, Roberta Catizone, Simon Worgan, Alexiei Dingli, Roger Moore, Debora Field, and Weiwei Cheng. 2011. A prototype for a conversational companion for reminiscing about images. *Computer Speech and Language*, 25(2):140–157.

Appendix: An Example Dialogue of the 1-STU system

Agent	Translation	Original utterance in Japanese*
S:	Let me start an interview. What did you have for breakfast yesterday?	Kore kara intabyû o hajime masu; Kinô no asa wa nani o tabe mashita ka?
U:	I had cereal.	Siriaru desu
S:	I want to eat it, too.	Watashi mo tabe tai desu
U:	You do.	Sô desu ka
S:	What else did you have for breakfast yesterday?	Kinô no chôshoku de hoka ni nani o tabe mashita?
U:	I didn't have any other food.	Tabete nai desu
S:	How much did you have for breakfast yesterday?	Kinô no chôshoku wa dore kurai tabe mashita ka?
U:	I had a normal amount.	Futsûryô desu
S:	How much do you think you had for breakfast yesterday?	Kinô no chôshoku no ryô wa dore kurai datta to omoi masu ka?
U:	A normal amount.	Futsû desu
S:	Sorry, I couldn't understand the answer. Please type in just "yes". [This request is for moving the dialogue forward.]	Sumimasen. Kono ôtô wa ninshiki deki masen deshita; Hai to dake nyûryoku shite kudasai.
U:	Yes.	Hai
S:	What did you have for lunch yesterday?	Kinô no chûshoku, nani o meshiagari mashita?
U:	I had *yakisoba* (Japanese stir-fried noodles).	Yakisoba desu
S:	Is *yakisoba* a one-dish meal?	Yakisoba wa ippin mono desu ka?
U:	Yes.	Hai
S:	Well, you had *yakisoba*.	Hê yakisoba dattan desu ne
U:	Yes, I did.	Sôdesu yo
S:	What else did you have for lunch yesterday?	Kinô no chûshoku de hoka ni meshiagatta mono wa ari masu ka?
U:	Nothing.	Nai desu
S:	How much do you think you had for lunch yesterday?	Kinô no chushoku no ryô wa dorekurai datta to omoi masu ka?
U:	A proper amount.	Teki ryô desu
S:	Can you tell me what you had for supper yesterday?	Kinô no yûshoku ni tabeta mono o oshiete kudasai
U:	I had curry and rice	Karê desu
S:	I want to eat it!	Tabe tai desu!
U:	I see!	Sokka!
S:	What else did you have for supper yesterday?	Kinô no yûshoku de karê igai ni meshiagatta mono wa ari masu ka?
U:	Nothing.	Naidesu
S:	Did you have a lot for supper yesterday?	Kinô no yûshoku wa gattsuri tabe mashita ka?
U:	A lot. [Semantic content extraction failed.]	Gattsuri desu
S:	How much did you have?	Dorekurai tabemashita ka?
U:	A lot.	Gattsuri desu
S:	This interview is finished. Thank you.	Kono intabyû wa shûryô desu. Arigatô gozaimasu

* Note that the user and the system used Japanese characters for interaction.

Automatic Recognition of Conversational Strategies
in the Service of a Socially-Aware Dialog System

Ran Zhao, Tanmay Sinha, Alan W Black, Justine Cassell
Language Technologies Institute, School of Computer Science
Carnegie Mellon University, Pittsburgh, PA 15213 USA
{rzhao1,tanmays,awb,justine}@cs.cmu.edu

Abstract

In this work, we focus on automatically recognizing social conversational strategies that in human conversation contribute to building, maintaining or sometimes destroying a budding relationship. These conversational strategies include self-disclosure, reference to shared experience, praise and violation of social norms. By including rich contextual features drawn from verbal, visual and vocal modalities of the speaker and interlocutor in the current and previous turn, we can successfully recognize these dialog phenomena with an accuracy of over 80% and kappa ranging from 60-80%. Our findings have been successfully integrated into an end-to-end socially aware dialog system, with implications for virtual agents that can use rapport between user and system to improve task-oriented assistance.

1 Introduction and Motivation

People pursue multiple conversational goals in dialog (Tracy and Coupland, 1990). Contributions to a conversation can be divided into those that fulfill *propositional* functions, contributing informational content to the dialog; those that fulfill *interactional* functions, managing the conversational interaction; and those that fulfill *interpersonal* functions, managing the relationship between the interlocutors (Cassell and Bickmore, 2003; Fetzer, 2013). In the category of talk that fulfills interpersonal goals are conversational strategies - units of discourse that are larger than speech acts (in fact, a single conversational strategy can span more than one turn in conversation), and that can achieve social goals.

In this paper, we propose a technique to automatically recognize conversational strategies. We demonstrate that these conversational strategies are most effectively recognized when verbal (linguistic), visual (nonverbal) and vocal (acoustic) features are all taken into account (and, in a demo paper published in this volume, we demonstrate that the results here can be effectively integrated into an end-to-end socially-aware dialog system).

As naturalistic interactions with dialog systems increasingly become a part of people's daily lives, it is important for these systems to advance their capabilities of not only conveying information and achieving smooth interaction, but also managing long-term relationships with people by building intimacy (Pecune et al., 2013) and rapport (Zhao et al., 2014), not just for the sake of companionship, but as an intrinsic part of successfully fulfilling collaborative tasks.

Rapport, or the feeling of harmony and connection with another, is an important aspect of human interaction, with powerful effects in domains such as education (Ogan et al., 2012; Sinha and Cassell, 2015a; Sinha and Cassell, 2015b) and negotiation (Drolet and Morris, 2000). The central theme of our work is to develop a dialog system that can facilitate such interpersonal rapport with users over interactions in time. Taking a step towards this goal, our prior work (Zhao et al., 2014) has developed a dyadic computational model that explains how interlocutors manage rapport through use of specific conversational strategies to fulfill the intermediate goals that lead to rapport - face management, mutual attentiveness, and coordination.

Foundational work by (Spencer-Oatey, 2008) conceptualizes the interpersonal nature of *face* as a desire to be recognized for one's social value and individual positive traits. Face-boosting strategies such as *praise* serve to create increased self-esteem in the individual and increased interper-

Proceedings of the SIGDIAL 2016 Conference, pages 381–392,
Los Angeles, USA, 13-15 September 2016. ©2016 Association for Computational Linguistics

sonal cohesiveness or rapport in the dyad (Zhao et al., 2014). (Spencer-Oatey, 2008) also posits that over time, interlocutors intend to increase *coordination* by adhering to behavior expectations, which are guided by sociocultural norms in the initial stages of interaction and by interpersonally determined norms afterwards. In these later stages, general norms may be purposely violated to accommodate the other's behavioral expectations.

Meanwhile, in the increasing trajectory of interpersonal closeness, *referring to shared experience* allows interlocutors to increase coordination by indexing common history and differentiating in-group and out-group individuals (Tajfel and Turner, 1979) (cementing the sense that the two are part of a group in ways that similar phenomena such as "referring to shared interests" do not appear to). To better learn about the other person *mutual attentiveness* plays an important role (Tickle-Degnen and Rosenthal, 1990). We have seen in our own corpora that mutual attentiveness is fulfilled by leading one's interlocutors to provide information about themselves through the strategy of *eliciting self-disclosure*. As the relationship proceeds and social distance decreases, these self-disclosures become more intimate in nature.

Motivated by this theoretical rationale and our prior empirical findings concerning the relationship between these conversational strategies and rapport (Sinha et al., 2015), in the current work, our goals are twofold: Our theoretical question is to understand the nature of conversational strategies in greater detail, by correlating them with associated observable verbal, vocal and visual cues (section 5). Our methodological question is then to use this understanding to automatically recognize these conversational strategies by leveraging statistical machine learning techniques (section 6).

We believe that the answers to these questions can contribute important insights into the nature of human dialog. By the same token, we believe this work to be crucial if we wish to develop a socially-aware dialog system that can identify conversational strategy usage in real-time, assess its impact on rapport, and then produce an appropriate next conversational strategy as a follow-up to maintain or increase rapport in the service of improving the system's ability to support the user's goals. (Papangelis et al., 2014).

2   Related Work

Below we describe related work that focuses on computational modeling of social conversational phenomena. For instance, (Wang et al., 2016) developed a model to measure self-disclosure in social networking sites by deploying emotional valence, social distance between the poster and other people and linguistic features such as those identified by the Linguistic Inquiry and Word Count program (LIWC) etc. While the features used here are quite interesting, this study relied only on the verbal aspects of talk, while we also include vocal and visual features.

Interesting prior work on quantifying social norm violation has taken a heavily data-driven focus (Danescu-Niculescu-Mizil et al., 2013b; Wang et al., 2016). For instance, (Danescu-Niculescu-Mizil et al., 2013b) trained a series of bigram language models to quantify the violation of social norms in users' posts on an online community by leveraging cross-entropy value, or the deviation of word sequences predicted by the language model and their usage by the user. Another kind of social norm violation was examined by (Riloff et al., 2013), who developed a classifier to identify a specific type of sarcasm in tweets. They utilized a bootstrapping algorithm to automatically extract lists of positive sentiment phrases and negative situation phrases from given sarcastic tweets, which were in turn leveraged to recognize sarcasm in an SVM classifier. Experimental results showed the adequacy of their approach.

(Wang et al., 2012) investigated the different social functions of language as used by friends or strangers in teen peer-tutoring dialogs. This work was able to successfully predict impoliteness and positivity in the next turn of the dialog. Their success with both annotated and automatically extracted features suggests that a dialog system will be able to employ similar analyses to signal relationships with users. Other work, such as (Danescu-Niculescu-Mizil et al., 2013a) has developed computational frameworks to automatically classify requests along a scale of politeness. Politeness strategies such as requests, gratitude and greetings, as well as their specialized lexicons, were used as features to train a classifier.

In terms of hedges or indirect language, (Prokofieva and Hirschberg, 2014) proposed a preliminary approach to automatic detection, relying on a simple lexical-based search. Machine learning methods that go beyond keyword searches are a promising extension, as they may be able to better capture language used to hedge as a function of contextual usage.

However, a common limitation of the above work is its focus on only the verbal modality, while studies have shown conversational strategies to be associated with specific kinds of nonverbal behaviors. For instance, (Kang et al., 2012) discovered that head tilts and pauses were the strongest nonverbal cues to interpersonal intimacy. Unfortunately, here too only one modality was examined. While nonverbal behavioral correlates to intimacy in self-disclosure were modeled, the verbal and vocal modalities of the conversation was ignored. Computational work has also modeled rapport using only nonverbal information (Huang et al., 2011). In what follows we describe our approach to modeling social conversational phenomena, which relies on verbal, visual and vocal content to automatically recognize conversational strategies. Our models are trained on a peer tutoring corpus, which gives us the opportunity to look at conversational strategies as they are used in both a task and social context.

3 Study Context

Reciprocal peer tutoring data was collected from 12 American English-speaking dyads (6 friends and 6 strangers; 6 boys and 6 girls), with a mean age of 13 years, who interacted for 5 hourly sessions over as many weeks (a total of 60 sessions, and 5400 minutes of data), tutoring one another in algebra (Yu et al., 2013). Each session began with a period of getting to know one another, after which the first tutoring period started, followed by another small social interlude, a second tutoring period with role reversal between the tutor and tutee, and then the final social time.

Prior work demonstrates that peer tutoring is an effective paradigm that results in student learning (Sharpley et al., 1983), making this an effective context to study dyadic interaction with a concrete task outcome. Our student-student data, in addition, demonstrates that a tremendous amount of rapport-building takes place during the task of reciprocal tutoring (Sinha and Cassell, 2015b).

4 Ground Truth

We assessed our automatic recognition of conversational strategies against this corpus annotated for those strategies (as well as other educational tutoring phenomena not discussed here). Inter-rater reliability (IRR) for the conversational strategy annotations, computed via Krippendorff's alpha, was 0.75 for self-disclosure, 0.79 for reference to shared experience, 1.0 for praise and 0.75 for social norm violation. IRR for visual behavior was 0.89 for eye gaze, 0.75 for smile count (how many smiles occur), 0.64 for smile duration and 0.99 for head nod. Below we discuss the definitions of each conversational strategy and nonverbal behavior that was annotated.

4.1 Coding Conversational Strategies

Self-Disclosure (SD): Self-disclosure refers to the conversational act of revealing aspects of oneself (personal private information) that otherwise would not be seen or known by the person being disclosed to (or would be difficult to see or know). A lot of psychological literature talks about the ways people reveal facts about themselves as ways of building relationships, but we are the first to look at the role of self-disclosure during social and task interactions by the same dyad, particularly for adolescents engaged in reciprocal peer tutoring. We coded for two sub-categories: (1) revealing the long-term aspects of oneself that one may feel are deep and true (e.g, "I love my pets"), (2) revealing one's transgressive (forbidden or socially-unacceptable) behaviors or actions, which may be a way of attempting to make the interlocutor feel better by disclosing one's flaws (e.g, "I suck at linear equations").

Referring to Shared Experience (SE): We differentiate between shared experience - an experience that the two interlocutors engage in or share with one another at the same time (such as "that facebook post Cecily posted last week was wild!") - from shared interests (such as "you like Xbox games too?). Shared experiences may index a shared community membership (even if a community of two), which can in turn build rapport. We coded for shared experiences (e.g, going to the mall together last week).

Praise (PR): We annotated both labeled praise (an expression of a positive evaluation of a specific attribute, behavior or product of the other; e.g, "great job with those negative numbers"), and unlabeled praise (a generic expression of positive evaluation, without a specific target;e.g, "Perfect").

Violation of Social Norms (VSN): Social norm violations are behaviors or actions that go against general socially acceptable and stereotypical behaviors. In a first pass, we coded whether an utterance was a social norm violation. In a second pass, if a social norm violation, we differentiated: (1) breaking the conversational rules of the experiment (e.g. off-task talk during tutoring session, insulting the experimenter or the experiment, etc); (2) face threatening acts (e.g. criticizing, teasing, or insulting, etc); (3) referring to one's own or the other person's social norm violations or general social norm violations (e.g. referring to the need to get back to focusing on work, or to the other person being verbally annoying etc). Social norms are culturally-specific, and so we judged a social norm violation by the impact it had on the listener (e.g. shock, specific reference to the behavior as a violation, etc.). Social norm violations may signal that a dyad is becoming closer, and no longer feels the need to adhere to the norms of the larger community.

4.2 Coding Visual Behaviors

Eye Gaze: Gaze for each participant was annotated individually. Front facing video for the individual participant was supplemented with a side camera view when needed. Audio was turned off so that words didn't influence the annotation. We coded (1) Gaze at the partner (gP), (2) Gaze at one's own worksheet (gO), (3) Gaze at partner's worksheet (gN), (4) Gaze elsewhere (gE).

Smile: A smile is defined by the elongation of the participant's lips and rising of their cheeks (smiles will often be asymmetric). It is often accompanied by creases at the corner of the eyes. Smiles have three parameters: rise, sustain, and decay (Hoque et al., 2011). We annotated a smile from the beginning of the rise to the end of the decay.

Head Nod: We coded temporal intervals of head nod rather than individual nod - the beginning of the head moving up and down until the moment the head came to rest.

5 Understanding Conversational Strategies

Our first objective, then, was to understand the nature of different conversational strategies (discussed in section 4) in greater detail. Towards this end, we first under-sampled the non-annotated

examples of self disclosure, shared experience, praise and social norm violation in order to create a balanced dataset of utterances. The utterances chosen to reflect the non-annotated cases were randomly selected. We made sure to have a similar average utterance length for all annotated and non-annotated cases, to prevent conflation of results due to lower or higher opportunities for detection of multimodal features. The final corpus (selected from 60 interaction sessions) comprised of 1014 self disclosure and 1014 non-self disclosure, 184 shared experience and 184 non-shared experience, 167 praise and 167 non-praise, 7470 social norm violation and 7470 non-social norm violation.

Second, we explored observable verbal and vocal behaviors of interest that could potentially be associated with different conversational strategies, assessing whether the mean value of these features were significantly higher in utterances with a particular conversational strategy label than in ones with no label (two-tailed correlated samples t-test). Bonferroni correction was used to correct the p-values with respect to the number of features, because of multiple comparisons involved. Finally, for all significant results (p <0.05), we also calculated effect size via Cohen's d to test for generalizability of results.

Third, for visual behaviors like smile, eye gaze, head nod, we binarized these features by denoting their presence (1) or absence (0) in one clause. If an individual shifts gaze during a particular spoke conversational strategy, we might have multiple types of eye gaze represented. We performed χ^2 test to see whether the appearance of visual annotations were independent of whether the utterance belonged to a particular conversational strategy or not. For all significant χ^2 test statistics, odds ratio (o) was computed to explore co-occurrence likelihood. Majority of the features discussed in the subsequent sub-sections were drawn from qualitative observations and note-taking, during and after the formulation of our coding manuals.

5.1 Verbal

We used Linguistic Inquiry and Word Count (LIWC 2015) (Pennebaker et al., 2015) to quantify verbal cues of interest that were semantically associated with a broad range of psychological constructs and could be useful in distinguishing conversational strategies. The input to LIWC were conversational transcripts that had been transcribed and segmented into syntactic clauses.

Self-disclosure: We observed personal concerns of students (sum of words identified as belonging to categories of work, leisure, home, money, religion and death etc) to be significantly higher, than in non self-disclosure utterances with a moderate effect size (d=0.44), signaling that students referred significantly more to their personal concerns during self-disclosure. Next, due to the fact that self-disclosures are often likely to comprise of emotional expressions when revealing one's likes and dislikes (Sparrevohn and Rapee, 2009), we used the LIWC dictionary to capture words representative of negative emotions (d=0.32) and positive emotion words (d=0.18). Also, to formalize the intuition that when people reveal themselves in an authentic or honest way, they are more personal, humble, and vulnerable, the standardized LIWC summary variable of Authenticity (d=1.16) was taken into account. Finally, as expected, we found self-disclosure utterances had significantly higher usage of first person singular pronouns (d=1.62).

Reference to shared experience: We looked at three LIWC categories: (1) Affiliation drive, which comprises words signaling a need to affiliate such as ally, friend, social etc (d=0.92), (2) Time Orientation words, which capture past (mostly in ROE) , present (mostly in RIE) and future focus and comprises words such as ago, did, talked, today, is, now, may, will, soon etc (d=0.95). Such words are not only used by interlocutors to index commonality within a time frame (Enfield, 2013), but also to signal an increased need for affiliation with the conversational partner, perhaps to indicate common ground(Clark, 1996), (3) First person plural such as we, us, our etc. In line with expectations, this feature had high effect size (d=0.93), since interlocutors focused on both themselves and the conversational partner.

Praise: We looked at positive emotions (d=2.55), since praise is one form of verbal persuasion that increases the interlocutor's confidence and boosts self efficacy (Bandura, 1994). Most of the praise utterances in our dataset were not very specific or directed at the tutee's performance or effort. Also, the LIWC standardized summary variable of Emotional Tone from LIWC was considered for the sake of completeness, which puts positive emotion and negative emotion dimensions into a single summary variable, such

that the higher the number, the more positive the tone (d=3.56).

Social norm violation: We looked at different categories of off-task talk from LIWC, such as social processes comprising words related to friends, family, male and female references (d=0.78), biological processes comprising words belonging to the categories of body, health etc (d=0.30) and personal concerns (d=0.24). The effect sizes across these categories ranged from moderate to low. Next, we looked at usage of swearing words like fuck, damn, shit etc and found low effect size (d=0.13) for this category in utterances of social norm violation. For the LIWC category of anger (words such as hate, annoyed etc), the effect size was moderate (d=0.27).

In our qualitative analysis of social norm violation utterances, we had discovered interactions of students to be reflective of need for power, meaning attention to or awareness of relative status in a social setting (perhaps this could be a result of putting one student in the tutor role). We formalized this intuition from the LIWC category of power drive that comprises words such as superior etc (d=0.18). Finally, based on prior work (Kacewicz et al., 2009) that found increased use of first-person plural to be a good predictor of higher status, and increased use of first-person singular to be a good predictor of lower status, we posited that when students violated social norms, they were more likely to freely make statements that involved others. However, the effect size for first-person plural usage in utterances of social norm violation was negligible (d=0.07). Table 2 in the appendix provides complete set of results.

5.2 Vocal

In our qualitative observations, we noticed the variations of both pitch and loudness when interlocutors used different conversational strategies. We were thus motivated to explore the mean difference of those low-level vocal descriptors as differentiators among the different conversational strategies. By using Open Smile (Eyben et al., 2010), we extracted two sets of basic features - for loudness features, pcm-loudness and its delta coefficient were tested; for pitch-based features, jitterLocal, jitterDDP, shimmerLocal, F0final and also their delta coefficients were tested. pcm-loudness represents the loudness as the normalised intensity raised to a power of 0.3. F0final is the smoothed fundamental frequency contour. Jitter-Local is the frame-to-frame pitch period length deviations. JitterDDP is the differential frame-to-frame jitter. ShimmerLocal is the frame-to-frame amplitude deviations between pitch periods.

Self-disclosure: We found a moderate effect size for pcm-loudness-sma-amean (d=0.26). Despite often becoming excited when disclosing things that they loved or liked, sometimes students also seemed to hesitate and spoke at a lower pitch when they revealed a transgressive act. However, the effect size for pitch was negligible. One potential reason for our results not aligning with hypothesis could be consideration of utterances with annotations of enduring states as well as transgressive acts together.

Reference to shared experience: We found a moderate negative effect size for the shimmerLocal-sma-amean (d=-0.32).

Praise: We found negative effect size for loudness (d=-0.51), meaning the speakers spoke in a lower voice when praising the interlocutor (mostly the tutee). We also found positive and moderate effect sizes for jitterLocal-sma-amean (d=0.45) and shimmerLocal-sma-amean (d=0.39).

Social norm violation: We found high effect sizes for pcm-loudness-sma-amean (d=0.72) and F0final-sma-amean (d=0.61) and interestingly, negative effect sizes for jitter (d=-0.09) and shimmer (d=-0.16). One potential reason could be that when student violate social norms, their behaviors are likely to become outliers compared to their normative behaviors. In fact, we noticed usage of "joking" tone of voice (Norrick, 2003) and pitch different than usual, to signal a social norm violation. When the content of the utterance was unaccepted by the social norms, students also tried to lower down their voice, which could be a way of hedging these violations. Table 2 in the appendix provides complete set of results.

5.3 Visual

Computing the odds ratio o involved comparing the odds of occurrence of a non-verbal behavior for a pair of categories of a second variable (whether an utterance was a specific conversational strategy or not). Overall, we found that that smile and gaze were significantly more likely to occur in utterances of self-disclosure (o(Smile)=1.67, o(gP)=2.39, o(gN)=0.498, o(gO)=0.29, o(gE)=2.8) compared to a non self-disclosure utterance. A similar

trend was observed for reference to shared experience (o(Smile)=1.75, o(gP)=3.02, o(gN)=0.58, o(gO)=0.31, o(gE)=4.19) and social norm violation (o(Smile)=3.35, o(gP)=2.75, o(gN)=0.8, o(gO)=0.47, o(gE)=1.67) utterances, compared to utterances that did not belong to these categories.

The high odds ratio for gP in these results suggests that an interlocutor was likely to gaze at their partner when using specific conversational strategies, signaling attention towards the interlocutor. The extremely high odds ratio for smiling behaviors during a social norm violation is also interesting. However, for praise utterances, we did not find all kinds of gaze and smile to be more likely to occur than non-praise utterances. Only gazing at partner (o(gP)=0.44) or their worksheet (o(gN)=4.29) or gazing elsewhere (o(gE)=0.30) were among the non-verbals that were significantly greatly present in praise utterances. Table 3 in the appendix provides complete set of results for the speaker (as discussed above) and also for the listener.

6 Machine Learning Modeling

In this section, our objective was to build a computational model for conversational strategy recognition. Towards this end, we first took each clause, or the smallest units that can express a complete proposition, as the prediction unit. Next, three sets of features were used as input. The first set f_1 comprised verbal (LIWC), vocal and visual features of the speaker, informed from the qualitative and quantitative analysis as discussed above. While LIWC features helped in categorization of words used during usage of a particular conversational strategy, they did not capture contextual usage of words within the utterance. Thus, we also added bigrams, part of speech bigrams and word-part of speech pairs from the speaker's utterance.

In addition to the speaker's behavior, we also added two sets of interlocutor behavior to capture the context around usage of a conversational strategy. The feature set f_2 comprised visual behaviors of the interlocutor (listener) in the current turn. The feature set f_3 comprised verbal (bigrams, part of speech bigrams and word-part of speech pairs), vocal and visual features of the interlocutor in the previous turn.

Finally, early fusion was applied on these multimodal features (by concatenation) and L2 regularized logistic regression with 10-fold cross validation was used as the machine learning algorithm, with rare threshold for feature extraction being set to 10 and performance evaluated using accuracy and kappa[1] measures. The following table shows our comparison with other standard machine learning algorithms such as Support Vector Machine (SVM) and Naive Bayes (NB), where we found Logistic Regression (LR) to perform better in recognition of the four conversational strategies. In next sub-section, we therefore denote the feature weights derived from logistic regression in brackets to offer interpretability of results.

Conversational Strategy	LR	SVM	NB
Self-disclosure	Acc=0.85 $\kappa = 0.7$	Acc=0.84 $\kappa = 0.68$	Acc=0.83 $\kappa = 0.65$
Shared Experience	Acc=0.84 $\kappa = 0.67$	Acc=0.82 $\kappa = 0.64$	Acc=0.79 $\kappa = 0.59$
Praise	Acc=0.91 $\kappa = 0.81$	Acc=0.90 $\kappa = 0.80$	Acc=0.88 $\kappa = 0.76$
Social Norm Violation	Acc=0.80 $\kappa = 0.61$	Acc=0.78 $\kappa = 0.55$	Acc=0.73 $\kappa = 0.47$

Table 1: Comparative Performance Evaluation using Accuracy (Acc) and Kappa (κ) for Logistic Regression (LR), Support Vector Machine (SVM) and Naive Bayes (NB)

6.1 Results and Discussion

Self-Disclosure: We could successfully identify self-disclosure from non self-disclosure utterances with an accuracy of **85%** and a kappa of **70%**. The top features from feature set f_1 predictive of speakers disclosing themselves included gazing at partner (0.44), head nodding (0.24) and not gazing at their own worksheet (-0.60) or the interlocutor's worksheet (-0.21). Head nod is a way to emphasize what one is saying (Poggi et al., 2010), while gazing at the partner signals one's attention. Higher usage of first person singular by the speaker (0.04) was also positively predictive of self-disclosure in the utterance. The top features from feature set f_2 predictive of speakers disclosing included listener behaviors such as head nodding (0.3) to communicate their attention (Schegloff, 1982), gazing elsewhere (0.12) or at the speaker (0.09) instead of gazing at their own worksheet (-0.89) or the speaker's worksheet (-0.27). The top features from feature set f_3 predictive of speakers disclosing included no smiling

(-0.30),no head nodding (-0.15) and lower loudness in voice (-0.11) from the interlocutor in the last turn.

Reference to shared experience: We achieved an accuracy of **84%** and kappa of **67%** for prediction. The top features from feature set f_1 predictive of speakers referring to shared experience included not gazing at own worksheet (-0.66), partner's worksheet (-0.40) or at the partner (-0.22), no smiling (-0.18) and having lower shimmer in voice (-0.26). Instead, words signaling affiliation drive (0.07) and time orientation (0.06) from the speaker were deployed to index shared experience. The top features from feature set f_2 predictive of speakers using shared experience included listener behaviors such as smiling (0.53) perhaps to indicate appreciation towards the content of the talk, or encourage the speaker to go on (Niewiadomski et al., 2010). Besides, the listener gazing elsewhere (0.50) or at the speaker (0.47), and neither gazing at own worksheet (-0.45) nor head nodding (-0.28) had strong predictive power. The top features from feature set f_3 predictive of speakers using shared experience included lower loudness in voice (-0.58), smiling (0.47), gazing elsewhere (0.59), at own worksheet (0.27) or at the partner (0.22) but not at partner's worksheet (-0.40) from the interlocutor in the last turn.

Praise: For praise, our computational model achieved an accuracy of **91%** and kappa of **81%**. The top features from feature set f_1 predictive of speakers using praise included gazing at partner's worksheet (0.68) indicative of directing attention to the partner's (perhaps the tutee's) work, smiling (0.51), perhaps to mitigate the potential embarassment of praise (Niewiadomski et al., 2010) and head nodding (0.35) with a positive tone of voice (0.04), perhaps to emphasize the praise. The top features from feature set f_2 predictive of speakers using praise included listener behaviors such as head nodding (0.45) for backchanneling and acknowledgement and not gazing at partner's worksheet (-1.06), elsewhere (-0.5) or at the partner (-0.49). The top features from feature set f_3 predictive of speakers using praise included smiling (0.51), lower loudness in voice (-0.91) and overlap (-0.66) from the interlocutor in the last turn.

Violation of Social Norm: We achieved an accuracy of **80%** and kappa of **61%** for prediction. The top features from feature set f_1 predictive of speakers violating social norms included smiling

---

[1]The discriminative ability over chance of a predictive model, for the target annotation, or the accuracy adjusted for chance

(0.40), gazing at partner (0.45) but not head nodding (-0.389). (Keltner and Buswell, 1997) introduced a remedial account of embarrassment, emphasizing that smiles signal awareness of a social norm being violated and serve to provoke forgiveness from the interlocutor, in addition to being a hedging indicator. (Kraut and Johnston, 1979) posited that smiling evolved from primate appeasement displays and is likely to occur when a person has violated a social norm. The top features from feature set f_2 predictive of speakers violating social norms included listener behaviors such as smiling (0.54), gazing at own worksheet (0.32) or at the partner's (0.14). The top features from feature set f_3 predictive of speakers violating social norms included high loudness (0.86) and jitter in voice (0.50), lower shimmer in voice (-0.53), gazing at own worksheet (0.49) and no head nodding (-0.31) from the interlocutor in the last turn.

6.2 Implications

We began this paper indicating our interest in better understanding conversational strategies in and of themselves, and in employing automatic recognition of conversational strategies to improve interactive systems. With respect to this first goal, because the current approach takes into account verbal, vocal and visual behaviors, it can identify regularities in social interaction processes that have not been identified by earlier work. This becomes especially important as automatic behavioral analysis increasingly develops new real-time metrics to predict other kinds of conversational strategies related to interpersonal dynamics like politeness, sarcasm etc, that are not easily captured by observer-based labeling. Similar benefits may accrue in other areas of automated human behavior understanding.

With respect to interactive systems, these findings are applicable to building virtual peer tutors in whom rapport improves learning gains as it does for human-human tutors, training military personnel and police to build rapport with the communities in which they work, and trustworthy dialog systems for clinical decision support (DeVault et al., 2013). Improved understanding of conversational strategy response pairs can help us better estimate the level of rapport at a given point in a dialog (Sinha et al., 2015; Zhao et al., 2016), which means that for the design of interactive systems, our work could help improve the capability of a natural language understanding module to capture

user's interpersonal goals, such as those of building, maintaining or destroying rapport.

More broadly, understanding of these particular ways of talking may also help us in building artificially intelligent systems that exhibit and evoke behaviors not just as conversationalists, but also as confidants to whom we can relay personal and emotional information with the expectation of acknowledgement, empathy and sympathy in response (Boden, 2010). These social strategies improve the bond between interlocutors which, in turn, can improve the efficacy of their collaboration. Efforts to experimentally generate interpersonal closeness (Aron et al., 1997) to achieve positive task and social outcomes depend on advances in moving beyond behavioral channels in isolation and leveraging the synergy and complementarity provided by multimodal human behaviors.

7 Conclusion

In this work, by performing quantitative analysis of our peer tutoring corpus followed by machine learning modeling, we learnt the discriminative power and generalizability of verbal, vocal and visual behaviors from both the speaker and listener, in distinguishing conversational strategy usage.

We found that interlocutors usually accompany the disclosure of personal information with head nods and mutual gaze. When faced with such self-disclosure listeners, on the other hand, often nod and avert their gaze . When the conversational strategy of reference to shared experience is used, speakers are less likely to smile, and more likely to avert their gaze (Cassell et al., 2007). Meanwhile, listeners smile to signal their coordination. When speakers praise their partner, they direct their gaze to the interlocutor's worksheet, smile and nod with a positive tone of voice. Meanwhile, listeners simply smile, perhaps to mitigate the embarrassment of having been praised.

Finally, speakers tend to gaze at their partner and smile when they violate a social norm, without nodding. The listener, faced with a social norm violation, is likely to smile extensively (once again, most likely to mitigate the face threat of social norm violations such as teasing or insults). Overall, these results present an interesting interplay of multimodal behaviors at work when speakers use conversational strategies to fulfil interpersonal goals in a dialog.

These results have been integrated into a real-time end-to-end socially aware dialog system

(SARA)[2] described in (Matsuyama et al., 2016) in this same volume. SARA is capable of detecting conversational strategies, relying on the conversational strategies detected in order to accurately estimate rapport between the interlocutors, reasoning about how to respond to the intentions behind those particular behaviors, and generating appropriate social responses as a way of more effectively carrying out her task duties. To our knowledge, SARA is the first socially-aware dialog system that relies on visual, verbal, and vocal cues to detect user social and task intent,and generates behaviors in those same channels to achieve her social and task goals.

8 Limitations and Future Work

We acknowledge some methodological limitations in the current work. In the current work we undersampled the negative examples in order to make a balanced dataset. For future work, we will work with corpora that have a more natural distribution and deal with the sparsity of the phenomena through machine learning methods. This will improve applicability to a real-time system where conversation strategies are likely to be less frequent than in our training dataset. Moreover, in current work, we looked at individual modalities in isolation initially, and fused them later via a simple concatenation of feature vectors. Including sequentially occurring features may better exploit correlation and dependencies between features from different modalities. As a next step, we have thus started to investigate the impact of temporal ordering of verbal and visual behaviors that lead to increased rapport (Zhao et al., 2016).

In terms of future work, one concrete example of an application area where we are beginning to apply these findings is the domain of learning technologies. While we know from research on dialog-based intelligent tutoring systems that conversations with such computer systems help students learn (Graesser, 2016), we also know that those students who are academically challenged, perhaps because under-represented in the fields they are trying to learn (Robinson et al., 2005), are most likely to need a social component to their learning interactions. Hence a major critique of existent intelligent tutoring systems is that they serve to fulfil only the task-goal of the interaction. Traditionally (DMello and Graesser, 2013), this is instantiated via an expectation and misconception

tailored dialog directed towards the portions of learning content where student under-performance is noted, and simply blended with some motivational scaffolding.

Despite significant advances in such conversational tutoring systems (Rus et al., 2013), we believe that future systems that provide intelligent support for tutoring via dialog should support the social as well as task nature of natural peer tutoring. Because learning does not happen in a cultural or social void, it is important to think about how we can leverage dialog, the natural modality of pedagogy, to foster supportive relationships that make learning challenging, engaging and meaningful [3].

We have also begun to use the social conversational strategies described here to complement the curriculum script in a traditional tutoring dialogue comprising knowledge-telling or knowledge-building utterances, shallow or deep question asking, hints and other forms of feedback. We believe this is a step towards building SCEM-sensitive (social, cognitive, emotional and motivational) tutors (Graesser et al., 2010), and towards more accurate computational models of human interaction that will need to underlie those new kinds of intelligent tutors.

Dialog systems that can recognize and use conversational strategies such as self-disclosure, reference to shared experience, and violation of social norms, are also part of a new genre of dialog system that departs from the rigid repetitive natural language generation templates of the olden days, and that can learn to speak with style. It is conceivable that contemporary corpus-based approaches to NLG that introduce stylistic variation into a dialog (Wen et al., 2015) may one day learn on the user's own conversational style, and entrain to it. In a system like that, real-time recognition of conversational strategies like that demonstrated here could play an essential role.

References

Arthur Aron, Edward Melinat, Elaine N Aron, Robert Darrin Vallone, and Renee J Bator. 1997. The experimental generation of interpersonal closeness: A procedure and some preliminary findings. *Personality and Social Psychology Bulletin*, 23(4):363–377.

Albert Bandura. 1994. *Self-efficacy*. Wiley Online Library.

---

[2] sociallyawarerobotassistant.net

[3] http://articulab.hcii.cs.cmu.edu/projects/rapt/

Margaret A Boden. 2010. Conversationalists and confidants. *Artificial Companions in Society: Perspectives on the Present and Future*, page 5.

Justine Cassell and Timothy Bickmore. 2003. Negotiated collusion: Modeling social language and its relationship effects in intelligent agents. *User Modeling and User-Adapted Interaction*, 13(1-2):89–132.

Justine Cassell, Alastair J Gill, and Paul A Tepper. 2007. Coordination in conversation and rapport. In *Proceedings of the workshop on Embodied Language Processing*, pages 41–50. ACL.

Herbert H Clark. 1996. *Using language*. Cambridge university press.

Cristian Danescu-Niculescu-Mizil, Moritz Sudhof, Dan Jurafsky, Jure Leskovec, and Christopher Potts. 2013a. A computational approach to politeness with application to social factors. *arXiv preprint arXiv:1306.6078*.

Cristian Danescu-Niculescu-Mizil, Robert West, Dan Jurafsky, Jure Leskovec, and Christopher Potts. 2013b. No country for old members: User lifecycle and linguistic change in online communities. In *Proceedings of the 22nd international conference on World Wide Web*, pages 307–318. International World Wide Web Conferences Steering Committee.

David DeVault, Kallirroi Georgila, Ron Artstein, Fabrizio Morbini, David Traum, Stefan Scherer, Albert Rizzo, and Louis-Philippe Morency. 2013. Verbal indicators of psychological distress in interactive dialogue with a virtual human. In *SIGDIAL*, Metz, France, August.

Aimee L Drolet and Michael W Morris. 2000. Rapport in conflict resolution: Accounting for how face-to-face contact fosters mutual cooperation in mixed-motive conflicts. *Journal of Experimental Social Psychology*, 36(1):26–50.

Sidney DMello and Art Graesser. 2013. Design of dialog-based intelligent tutoring systems to simulate human-to-human tutoring. In *Where Humans Meet Machines*, pages 233–269. Springer.

Nick J Enfield. 2013. Reference in conversation. *The handbook of conversation analysis*, pages 433–454.

Florian Eyben, Martin Wöllmer, and Björn Schuller. 2010. Opensmile: the munich versatile and fast open-source audio feature extractor. In *Proceedings of the international conference on Multimedia*, pages 1459–1462. ACM.

Anita Fetzer. 2013. 'no thanks': a socio-semiotic approach. *Linguistik Online*, 14(2).

Arthur C Graesser, Fazel Keshtkar, and Haiying Li. 2010. The role of natural language and discourse processing in advanced tutoring systems. In *Oxford Handbook of Language and social psychology*, pages 1–12. New York: Oxford University Press.

Arthur C Graesser. 2016. Conversations with autotutor help students learn. *International Journal of Artificial Intelligence in Education*, pages 1–9.

Mohammed Hoque, Louis-Philippe Morency, and Rosalind W Picard. 2011. Are you friendly or just polite?–analysis of smiles in spontaneous face-to-face interactions. In *Affective Computing and Intelligent Interaction*, pages 135–144. Springer.

Lixing Huang, Louis-Philippe Morency, and Jonathan Gratch. 2011. Virtual rapport 2.0. In *International Workshop on Intelligent Virtual Agents*, pages 68–79. Springer.

E Kacewicz, J. W Pennebaker, M Davis, M Jeon, and A. C Graesser. 2009. The language of social hierarchies.

Sin-Hwa Kang, Jonathan Gratch, Candy Sidner, Ron Artstein, Lixing Huang, and Louis-Philippe Morency. 2012. Towards building a virtual counselor: modeling nonverbal behavior during intimate self-disclosure. In *Proceedings of the 11th International Conference on Autonomous Agents and Multiagent Systems-Volume 1*, pages 63–70.

Dacher Keltner and Brenda N Buswell. 1997. Embarrassment: its distinct form and appeasement functions. *Psychological bulletin*, 122(3):250.

Robert E Kraut and Robert E Johnston. 1979. Social and emotional messages of smiling: An ethological approach. *Journal of personality and social psychology*, 37(9):1539.

Yoichi Matsuyama, Arjun Bhardwaj, Ran Zhao, Oscar J. Romero, Sushma Akoju, and Justine Cassell. 2016. Socially-aware animated intelligent personal assistant agent. In *17th Annual SIGdial Meeting on Discourse and Dialogue*.

Radoslaw Niewiadomski, Ken Prepin, Elisabetta Bevacqua, Magalie Ochs, and Catherine Pelachaud. 2010. Towards a smiling eca: studies on mimicry, timing and types of smiles. In *Proceedings of the 2nd international workshop on Social signal processing*, pages 65–70.

Neal R Norrick. 2003. Issues in conversational joking. *Journal of Pragmatics*, 35(9):1333–1359.

Amy Ogan, Samantha Finkelstein, Erin Walker, Ryan Carlson, and Justine Cassell. 2012. Rudeness and rapport: Insults and learning gains in peer tutoring. In *Intelligent Tutoring Systems*, pages 11–21. Springer.

Alexandros Papangelis, Ran Zhao, and Justine Cassell. 2014. Towards a computational architecture of dyadic rapport management for virtual agents. In *Intelligent Virtual Agents*, pages 320–324. Springer.

Florian Pecune, Magalie Ochs, Catherine Pelachaud, et al. 2013. A formal model of social relations for artificial companions. In *Proceedings of The European Workshop on Multi-Agent Systems (EUMAS)*.

James W Pennebaker, Ryan Boyd, Kayla Jordan, and Kate Blackburn. 2015. The development and psychometric properties of liwc2015.

Isabella Poggi, Francesca D'Errico, and Laura Vincze. 2010. Types of nods. the polysemy of a social signal. In *LREC*.

Anna Prokofieva and Julia Hirschberg. 2014. Hedging and speaker commitment. In *5th Intl. Workshop on Emotion, Social Signals, Sentiment & Linked Open Data, Reykjavik, Iceland*.

Ellen Riloff, Ashequl Qadir, Prafulla Surve, Lalindra De Silva, Nathan Gilbert, and Ruihong Huang. 2013. Sarcasm as contrast between a positive sentiment and negative situation. In *EMNLP*, pages 704–714.

Debbie R Robinson, Janet Ward Schofield, and Katrina L Steers-Wentzell. 2005. Peer and cross-age tutoring in math: Outcomes and their design implications. *Educational Psychology Review*, 17(4):327–362.

Vasile Rus, Sidney DMello, Xiangen Hu, and Arthur Graesser. 2013. Recent advances in conversational intelligent tutoring systems. *AI magazine*, 34(3):42–54.

Emanuel A Schegloff. 1982. Discourse as an interactional achievement: Some uses of uh huhand other things that come between sentences. *Analyzing discourse: Text and talk*, 71:93.

Anna M Sharpley, James W Irvine, and Christopher F Sharpley. 1983. An examination of the effectiveness of a cross-age tutoring program in mathematics for elementary school children. *American Educational Research Journal*, 20(1):103–111.

Tanmay Sinha and Justine Cassell. 2015a. Finegrained analyses of interpersonal processes and their effect on learning. In *Artificial Intelligence in Education*, pages 781–785. Springer.

Tanmay Sinha and Justine Cassell. 2015b. We click, we align, we learn: Impact of influence and convergence processes on student learning and rapport building. In *Proceedings of the 2015 Workshop on Modeling Interpersonal Synchrony, 17th ACM International Conference on Multimodal Interaction.* ACM.

Tanmay Sinha, Ran Zhao, and Justine Cassell. 2015. Exploring socio-cognitive effects of conversational strategy congruence in peer tutoring. In *Proceedings of the 2015 Workshop on Modeling Interpersonal Synchrony, 17th ACM International Conference on Multimodal Interaction. ACM.*

Roslyn M Sparrevohn and Ronald M Rapee. 2009. Self-disclosure, emotional expression and intimacy within romantic relationships of people with social phobia. *Behaviour Research and Therapy*, 47(12):1074–1078.

Helen Spencer-Oatey. 2008. Face,(im) politeness and rapport.

Henri Tajfel and John C Turner. 1979. An integrative theory of intergroup conflict. *The social psychology of intergroup relations*, 33(47):74.

Linda Tickle-Degnen and Robert Rosenthal. 1990. The nature of rapport and its nonverbal correlates. *Psychological inquiry*, 1(4):285–293.

Karen Tracy and Nikolas Coupland. 1990. Multiple goals in discourse: An overview of issues. *Journal of Language and Social Psychology*, 9(1-2):1–13.

William Yang Wang, Samantha Finkelstein, Amy Ogan, Alan W Black, and Justine Cassell. 2012. Love ya, jerkface: using sparse log-linear models to build positive (and impolite) relationships with teens. In *13th annual SIGdial meeting on discourse and dialogue*, pages 20–29. Association for Computational Linguistics.

Yi-Chia Wang, Moira Burke, and Robert Kraut. 2016. Modeling self-disclosure in social networking sites. In *Proceedings of the 19th ACM Conference on Computer-Supported Cooperative Work & Social Computing*, pages 74–85. ACM.

Tsung-Hsien Wen, Milica Gasic, Nikola Mrksic, Pei-Hao Su, David Vandyke, and Steve Young. 2015. Semantically conditioned lstm-based natural language generation for spoken dialogue systems. *arXiv preprint arXiv:1508.01745*.

Zhou Yu, David Gerritsen, Amy Ogan, Alan W Black, and Justine Cassell. 2013. Automatic prediction of friendship via multi-model dyadic features. In *14th Annual SIGdial Meeting on Discourse and Dialogue, Metz, France*.

Ran Zhao, Alexandros Papangelis, and Justine Cassell. 2014. Towards a dyadic computational model of rapport management for human-virtual agent interaction. In *Intelligent Virtual Agents*, pages 514–527. Springer.

Ran Zhao, Tanmay Sinha, Alan Black, and Justine Cassell. 2016. Socially-aware virtual agents: Automatically assessing dyadic rapport from temporal patterns of behavior. In *16th International Conference on Intelligent Virtual Agents*.

A Appendix: Complete Statistics for Understanding Conversational Strategies (Section 5)

Conversational Strategy	Verbal/Vocal(Speaker)	t-test value	Mean value	Effect Size
1. Self-Disclosure	LIWC Personal Concerns	$t(1013)=7.06$***	SD=4.13, NSD=1.58	d=0.44
	LIWC Positive Emotion	$t(1013)=2.98$*	SD=7.61, NSD=5.50	d=0.18
	LIWC Negative Emotion	$t(1013)=5.51$***	SD=5.62, NSD=2.22	d=0.32
	LIWC First Person Singular	$t(1013)=25.87$***	SD=20.12, NSD=7.77	d=1.62
	LIWC Authenticity	$t(1013)=18.59$***	SD=66.71, NSD=34.07	d=1.16
	pcm-loudness-sma-amean	$t(1013)=4.11$***	SD=0.64, NSD=0.59	d=0.26
2. Shared Experience	LIWC Affiliation Drive	$t(183)=6.22$***	SE=4.64, NSE=0.77	d=0.92
	LIWC Time Orientation	$t(183)=6.47$***	SE=24.89, NSE=15.02	d=0.95
	LIWC First Person Plural	$t(183)=6.29$***	SE=3.99, NSE=0.48	d=0.93
	shimmerLocal-sma-amean	$t(183)=-2.21$*	SE=0.18, NSE=0.194	d=0.32
3. Praise	LIWC Positive Emotion	$t(166)=16.48$***	PR=55.63, NPR=4.56	d=3.56
	LIWC Emotional Tone	$t(166)=22.96$***	PR=91.1, NPR=33.5	d=2.55
	pcm-loudness-sma-amean	$t(166)=-3.33$***	PR=0.5, NPR=0.6	d=-0.51
	jitterLocal-sma-amean	$t(166)=2.93$*	PR=0.1, NPR=0.07	d=0.45
	shimmerLocal-sma-amean	$t(166)=2.56$*	PR=0.2, NPR=0.18	d=0.39
4. Social Norm Violation	LIWC Social Processes	$t(7469)=33.98$***	VSN=17.35, NVSN=6.45	d=0.78
	LIWC Biological Processes	$t(7469)=12.95$***	VSN=4.21, NVSN=1.38	d=0.30
	LIWC Personal Concerns	$t(7469)=10.61$***	VSN=2.61, NVSN=1.33	d=0.24
	LIWC Swearing	$t(7469)=5.85$***	VSN=0.49, NVSN=0.11	d=0.13
	LIWC Anger	$t(7469)=11.64$***	VSN=1.19, NVSN=0.20	d=0.27
	LIWC Power Drive	$t(7469)=7.83$***	VSN=1.99, NVSN=1.14	d=0.18
	LIWC First Person Plural	$t(7469)=3.23$**	VSN=0.85, NVSN=0.64	d=0.07
	pcm-loudness-sma-amean	$t(7469)=31.24$***	VSN=0.69, NVSN=0.56	d=0.72
	F0final-sma-amean	$t(7469)=26.6$***	VSN=231.09, NVSN=206.99	d=0.61
	jitterLocal-sma-amean	$t(7469)=-4.09$***	VSN=0.083, NVSN=0.087	d=-0.09
	shimmerLocal-sma-amean	$t(7469)=-7.02$***	VSN=0.1818, NVSN=0.1897	d=-0.16

Table 2: Complete Statistics for presence of numeric verbal and vocal features in Self-Disclosure (SD)/Non-Self Disclosure (NSD), Shared Experience (SE)/Non-Reference to Shared Experience (NSE), Praise (PR)/Non-Praise (NPR) and Violation of Social Norms (VSN)/Non-Violation of Social Norms (NVSN). Effect size assessed via Cohen's d. Significance: ***:$p < 0.001$, **:$p < 0.01$, *:$p < 0.05$

Conversational Strategy	Visual (Speaker) - χ^2 test value - Odds Ratio	Visual (Listener) - χ^2 test value - Odds Ratio
1. Self-Disclosure	Smile - $\chi^2(1,1013)=20.67$*** - o=1.67	Smile - $\chi^2(1,1013)=18.63$*** - o=1.63
	Gaze (gP) - $\chi^2(1,1013)=93.04$*** - o=2.39	Gaze (gP) - $\chi^2(1,1013)=131.34$*** - o=2.84
	Gaze (gN) - $\chi^2(1,1013)=35.1$*** - o=0.49	Gaze (gN) - $\chi^2(1,1013)=73.23$*** - o=0.38
	Gaze (gO) - $\chi^2(1,1013)=173.88$*** - o=0.29	Gaze (gO) - $\chi^2(1,1013)=152.12$*** - o=0.31
	Gaze (gE) - $\chi^2(1,1013)=120.77$*** - o=1.8	Gaze (gE) - $\chi^2(1,1013)=78.92$*** - o=2.37
2. Shared Experience	Smile - $\chi^2(1,183)=4.73$* - o=1.75	Smile - $\chi^2(1,183)=7.53$** - o=2.07
	Gaze (gP) - $\chi^2(1,183)=25.37$*** - o=3.02	Gaze (gP) - $\chi^2(1,183)=33.36$*** - o=3.59
	Gaze (gN) - $\chi^2(1,183)=3.73$* - o=0.58	Gaze (gN) - $\chi^2(1,183)=17.68$*** - o=0.32
	Gaze (gO) - $\chi^2(1,183)=27.87$*** - o=0.31	Gaze (gO) - $\chi^2(1,183)=16.55$*** - o=0.41
	Gaze (gE) - $\chi^2(1,183)=38.13$*** - o=4.19	Gaze (gE) - $\chi^2(1,183)=32.45$*** - o=3.92
3. Praise	Gaze (gP) - $\chi^2(1,166)=9.94$*** - o=0.44	Gaze (gP) - $\chi^2(1,166)=14.22$*** - o=0.39
	Gaze (gN) - $\chi^2(1,166)=37.52$*** - o=4.29	Gaze (gN) - $\chi^2(1,166)=15.19$*** - o=0.33
	Gaze (gO) - N.S	Gaze (gO) - $\chi^2(1,166)=24.23$*** - o=3.30
	Gaze (gE) - $\chi^2(1,166)=14.44$*** - o=0.30	Gaze (gE) - $\chi^2(1,166)=9.77$** - o=0.39
4. Social Norm Violation	Smile - $\chi^2(1,7469)=871.73$*** - o=3.35	Smile - $\chi^2(1,7469)=869.29$*** - o=3.37
	Gaze (gP) - $\chi^2(1,7469)=911.89$*** - o=2.75	Gaze (gP) - $\chi^2(1,7469)=609.06$*** - o=2.27
	Gaze (gN) - $\chi^2(1,7469)=34.82$*** - o=0.8	Gaze (gN) - $\chi^2(1,7469)=239.22$*** - o=0.55
	Gaze (gO) - $\chi^2(1,7469)=515.26$*** - o=0.47	Gaze (gO) - $\chi^2(1,7469)=110.48$*** - o=0.70
	Gaze (gE) - $\chi^2(1,7469)=195.17$*** - o=1.67	Gaze (gE) - $\chi^2(1,7469)=12.38$** - o=1.14
	Head Nod - $\chi^2(1,7469)=8.06$** - o=0.77	Head Nod - $\chi^2(1,7469)=44.51$*** - o=0.56

Table 3: Complete Statistics for presence of binary non-verbal features in Self-Disclosure (SD), Shared Experience (SE), Praise (PR) and Violation of Social Norms (VSN). Odds ratio signals how much more likely is a non-verbal behavior likely to occur in conversational strategy utterances compared to non-conversational strategy utterances. Significance: ***:$p < 0.001$, **:$p < 0.01$, *:$p < 0.05$

Neural Utterance Ranking Model for Conversational Dialogue Systems

Michimasa Inaba
Hiroshima City University
3-4-1 Ozukahigashi, Asaminami-ku,
Hiroshima, Japan
inaba@hiroshima-cu.ac.jp

Kenichi Takahashi
Hiroshima City University
3-4-1 Ozukahigashi, Asaminami-ku,
Hiroshima, Japan
takahashi@hiroshima-cu.ac.jp

Abstract

In this study, we present our neural utterance ranking (NUR) model, an utterance selection model for conversational dialogue agents. The NUR model ranks candidate utterances with respect to their suitability in relation to a given context using neural networks; in addition, a dialogue system based on the model converses with humans using highly ranked utterances. Specifically, the model processes word sequences in utterances and utterance sequences in context via recurrent neural networks. Experimental results show that the proposed model ranks utterances with higher precision relative to deep learning and other existing methods. Furthermore, we construct a conversational dialogue system based on the proposed method and conduct experiments on human subjects to evaluate performance. The experimental result indicates that our system can offer a response that does not provoke a critical dialogue breakdown with a probability of 92% and a very natural response with a probability of 58%.

1 Introduction

The study of conversational dialogue systems (also known as non-task-oriented or chat-oriented dialogue systems) has a long history. To construct such systems, rule-based methods have long been used (Weizenbaum, 1966; Colby, 1981; Wallace, 2008); however, construction and maintenance costs are very high because these rules are manually created. Moreover, intuition tells us that the performance of such systems depends on the number of established rules, though reports indicate that performance did not improve much even if the number of rules was doubled (Higashinaka et al., 2015b), indicating that performance of rule-based systems is limited.

Recently, the study of statistical-based methods that use statistical processing with large volumes of web data has become increasingly active. The key benefit of this approach is that manual response creation is not necessary; thus, construction and maintenance costs are low; however, since web data contains noise, this approach has the potential to output grammatically or semantically incorrect sentences. To tackle this problem, some studies extract correct sentences as utterances for dialogue systems from web data (Inaba et al., 2014; Higashinaka et al., 2014). These studies focus solely on extraction and do not indicate how replies are generated using extracted sentences.

In our study, we propose a neural utterance ranking (NUR) model that ranks candidate utterances by their suitability in a given context using neural networks. Previously, we proposed an utterance selection model (Koshinda et al., 2015) in the framework same as that of the NUR model, which ranks utterances in order of suitability to given context. In section 4, we experimentally show that the performance of the NUR model exceeds that of our previous model.

Our proposed method processes the word sequences in utterances and utterance sequences in context via multiple recurrent neural networks (RNNs). More specifically, the RNN encodes both utterances in a given context and candidates into fixed-length vectors. Such encoding enables suitable feature extraction for ranking. Next, another RNN receives these utterance-encoded vectors in chronological order, and our proposed NUR model ranks candidates using the output of this RNN. Our model considers the order of utterances in a given context; this architecture makes it pos-

Proceedings of the SIGDIAL 2016 Conference, pages 393–403,
Los Angeles, USA, 13-15 September 2016. ©2016 Association for Computational Linguistics

sible to handle distant semantic relationships between context and candidates.

2 Related Work

Statistical-based response methods incorporate two major approaches.

The first approach is the example-based method (Murao et al., 2003), which searches a large database of previously recorded dialogue for given user input selecting an utterance identified as the most similar. Well-known dialogue systems based on this approach include Jabberwacky (De Angeli and Carpenter, 2005) which won the Loebner prize contest[a] (i.e., a conversational dialogue system competition) in 2005 and 2006. In addition, Banch and Li. proposed a model based on the vector space model (Banchs and Li, 2012) and Nio et al. constructed a dialogue system that uses movie scripts and Twitter data (Nio et al., 2014). A disadvantage of example-based methods is that it is difficult to consider context. If the implemented approach searches for user input with context in a database, it can be difficult to find a suitable context because of the diversity of contexts; in such cases, system replies become unsuitable. In contrast, our NUR model can select responses while also taking into account a flexible set of contexts.

The second statistical-based response approach is the machine translation (MT) method. Ritter et al. first introduced the MT technique into response generation (Ritter et al., 2011). They used tweet-reply pairs in Twitter data, regarding a tweet as the source language sentence and the reply as a target one in MT. In other words, the MT method translates user input into system responses. More recently, response generation using neural networks has been widely studied, most work grounded in the MT method (Cho et al., 2014; Sordoni et al., 2015; Shang et al., 2015; Vinyals and Le, 2015). A problem with this method is that it might generate utterances containing syntax errors; further, it tends to generate utterances with broad utility that frequently appear in training data, e.g., "I don't know." or "I'm OK." (Li et al., 2016).

Our proposed method is not categorized into either of the above two methods. Some hard-to-classify statistical-based response methods similar to our model have been proposed, e.g., Shibata et al. proposed a method that selects a suitable sentence extracted from webpages as a response

[a]http://www.loebner.net/Prizef/loebner-prize.html

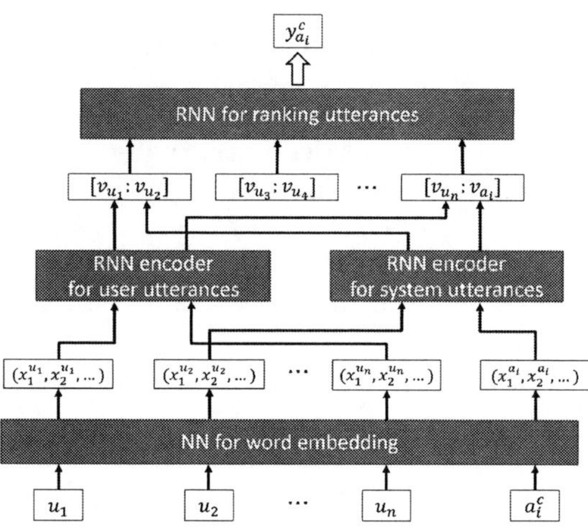

Figure 1: Neural utterance ranking model

to user input (Shibata et al., 2009). Sugiyama et al. generated responses using templates and dependency structures of sentences gathered from Twitter (Sugiyama et al., 2013). There are only few common points, although most of the hard-to-classify methods use not only dialogue data but also non-dialogue data such as webpages or normal tweets (not pairs of tweet reply) on Twitter.

3 Neural Utterance Ranking Model

For our ranking model, we first define sequences of utterances from the beginning of a dialogue to a certain point of time in context $c = (u_1, u_2, \ldots, u_l)$ Each $u_i (i = 1, 2, ..., l)$ denotes an utterance in the context, and l denotes the number of utterances. We assume here that a dialogue system and user speak alternately and last utterance u_l is given by the system. We define candidate utterance list $a_c = (a_1^c, a_2^c, \ldots, a_m^c)$ generated depending on context c, and score $t_c = (t_1^c, t_2^c, \ldots, t_m^c)$. Herein, m denotes the number of candidate utterances. We define utterance ranking to sort given candidate utterance list a_c in order of suitability to context c. The correct order is defined by score t_c with sorting based on the model's output $y_{a_c} = (y_1, y_2, \ldots, y_m)$ corresponding to a_c.

Our proposed utterance ranking model, i.e., the NUR model illustrated in in Figure 1, receives context c and candidate utterance list a_c, then outputs y_{a_c}. Details of our NUR model are described below.

3.1 Utterance Encoding

To extract information from context and candidate utterances for suitable utterance selection, our NUR model utilizes an RNN encoder.

Previous work utilized an RNN encoder for MT (Kalchbrenner and Blunsom, 2013; Bahdanau et al., 2015) and response generation in dialogue systems (Cho et al., 2014; Sordoni et al., 2015; Shang et al., 2015; Vinyals and Le, 2015). In these studies, the encoder reads as input a variable-length word sequence and outputs a fixed-length vector. Next, another RNN decodes a given fixed-length vector, producing an objective variable-length word sequence. Therefore, the encoder has learned to embed necessary information to generate objective sentences and place them into vectors. The RNN in our model does not generate sentences using this RNN decoder approach. Results of encoding are used for features to rank candidate utterances. The RNN encoder in our NUR model has a similar architecture, but the characteristics of the output vector are profoundly different, because our model learns to extract important features for utterance ranking.

Our model first converts word sequence $w = (w_1, w_2, \ldots, w_n)$ in an utterance into a distributed representation of word sequence, i.e., $x = (x_1, x_2, \ldots, x_n)$ which the RNN encoder then reads. To convert into a distributed representation here, a neural network for word embedding (as shown in Figure 1) learns via the skip-gram model (Mikolov et al., 2013). This network has two layers, i.e., an input layer that reads a one-hot-vector representing each word and a certain denominational hidden layer.

The RNN encoder has two networks, i.e., a forward and a backward network. The forward RNN reads x at the beginning of a sentence and outputs $\overrightarrow{h} = (\overrightarrow{h_1}, \overrightarrow{h_2}, \ldots, \overrightarrow{h_n})$ correspond to input sequence. The backward RNN reads x in reverse, then outputs $\overleftarrow{h} = (\overleftarrow{h_1}, \overleftarrow{h_2}, \ldots, \overleftarrow{h_n})$. By joining the outputs of these forward and backward RNNs, we acquire objective encoded utterance vector $v = [\overrightarrow{h_n}; \overleftarrow{h_n}]$; note that $[x; y]$ the concatenation of vectors x and y.

In the following experiments, we used two-layer long short-term memory (LSTM) (Hochreiter and Schmidhuber, 1997) networks as our RNN encoders. The effective features extracted from utterances for candidate ranking are different between the user and the system. Therefore, our

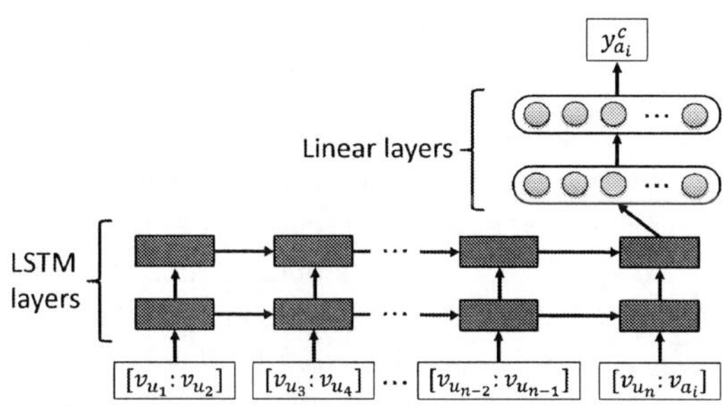

Figure 2: RNN for ranking utterances

NUR model has two RNN encoders, one for user utterances, the other for system utterances, as illustrated in Figure 1

3.2 Ranking Candidate Utterances

Another RNN is used to rank candidate utterances, as illustrated in 2. This RNN has two LSTM layers and two linear layers; further, we use rectified linear unit (ReLU) as the activation function. Thus, this RNN reads encoded utterance sequences and outputs scores.

3.2.1 Context-Candidate Vector Sequence

To select suitable responses, we not only must evaluate suitability of utterances based on the last utterance in the given context, but also must consider prior dialogue. The RNN for ranking utterances in our model reads vector sequences constructed by context and candidate utterances in chronological order, then outputs scores for the candidate in relation to the context.

Thus, context-candidate vector sequence $v_{a_i}^c$ is constructed using context vector sequence $v_c = (v_{u_1}, v_{u_2}, \ldots, v_{u_l})$, with ith candidate utterance vector v_{a_i} defined as follows:

$$
v_{a_i}^c =
\begin{cases}
([v_{u_1}; v_{u_2}], [v_{u_3}; v_{u_4}], \ldots, [v_{u_l}; v_{a_i}^c]), \\
\qquad\qquad\qquad\qquad \text{if } l \text{ is odd} \\
([0; v_{u_1}], [v_{u_2}; v_{u_3}], \ldots, [v_{u_l}; v_{a_i}^c]), \\
\qquad\qquad\qquad\qquad \text{if } l \text{ is even}
\end{cases}
$$

Here, 0 denotes the zero vector. Our model inputs user and system utterances at one time so that it can consider dialogue history in a given context along with the relevance between candidate utterances and the last response given by a user.

3.2.2 Loss Function in Learning

In cases where a neural network outputs a one-dimensional value, like our model, the mean squared error (MSE) between training data and the model's output is generally used as a loss function; however, our objective is not to model scores, but rather for ranking, thus we use the distance between rank data based on training data and that based on the model's outputs as a loss function. Several methods for modeling rank data have been proposed, including the Bradley-Terry-Luce model (Bradley and Terry, 1952; Luce, 1959), the Mallows model (Mallows, 1957) and the Plackett-Luce model (Plackett, 1975; Luce, 1959). In our study, to calculate ranking distance, we selected the Plackett-Luce model, which has been used in various ranking models, such as ListNet (Cao et al., 2007), BayesRank (Kuo et al., 2009), etc.

The Plackett-Luce model transforms a score list for ranking into a probability distribution wherein higher scores in the given list are allocated higher probabilities. Probability of score t_i^c in score list $t_c = (t_1^c, t_2^c, \ldots, t_m^c)$ ranked on the top is calculated by the Plackett-Luce model as follows:

$$p(t_i^c) = \frac{\exp(t_i^c)}{\sum_{k=1}^{m} \exp(t_k^c)}$$

Using the same equation, the output scores of our NUR model are transformed into probability distributions. We use cross-entropy between probability distributions as our loss function.

4 Experiments

We conducted experiments to verify the performance of ranking given candidate utterances and given contexts. For comparison, we also tested a few baseline methods.

4.1 Datasets

For our experiments, we used dialogue data between a conversational dialogue system and a user for both training and test data. We released a conversational dialogue system called KELDIC on Twitter (screen name: @KELDIC)[b]. KELDIC selects an appropriate response from candidates extracted by the utterance acquisition method of (Inaba et al., 2014) using ListNet(Cao et al., 2007). The utterance acquisition method extracted suitable sentences for system utterances related to given keywords from Twitter data by filtering inappropriate sentences. Details of the response algorithm of KELDIC is further described in (Koshinda et al., 2015).

We collected training and test data by first collecting pairs of context and candidate utterances that the system used for reply on Twitter. Next, annotators evaluated the suitability of each candidate utterance in relation to the given context. Here annotators must evaluate utterances that were actually used by the system on Twitter.

Evaluation criterion was based on the Dialogue Breakdown Detection Challenge (DBDC) (Higashinaka et al., 2016). Each system's utterances were annotated using one of the following three breakdown labels:

(NB) Not a breakdown It is easy to continue the conversation.

(PB) Possible breakdown It is difficult to continue the conversation smoothly.

(B) Breakdown It is difficult to continue the conversation.

Annotators evaluated dialogue data on a tool we prepared. They were first shown a context and 10 candidate utterances, including how KELDIC actually replied on Twitter, as well as labels for each candidate. We instructed them to assign at least one NB label to given candidate utterances. If there were no suitable candidates for the NB label, they could optionally add candidate utterances. If they were still not able to find a suitable response, we allowed them to skip the evaluation. We recruited annotators on crowd-sourcing site Crowd-Works[c].

In our evaluation, we regard candidates with 50% or more annotators decided as NB as correct utterances and others as incorrect.

We used 1581 data points (i.e., 1581 contexts and 17533 candidate utterances), each evaluated by three or more annotators. We choose 300 data points that contained at least one correct candidate for the given test data; the remaining 1057 data points were used for training data. Table 1 shows statistics for our data.

In learning the model, we need scores for candidate utterances to define ranking. Score y_i^c of candidate utterance a_i^c is calculated as follows:

$$y_i^c = s_{\text{NB}} \frac{n_{\text{NB}}}{N} + s_{\text{PB}} \frac{n_{\text{PB}}}{N} + s_{\text{B}} \frac{n_{\text{B}}}{N}$$

$$N = n_{\text{NB}} + n_{\text{PB}} + n_{\text{B}}$$

[b]https://twitter.com/KELDIC

[c]https://crowdworks.jp

Table 1: Statistics of the datasets

	Train	Test	All
Data	1281	300	1581
Utterances in context	1.67	2.04	1.74
Candidates per data	11.12	10.94	11.09
Words per candidate	11.17	10.70	11.08
Num of Annotators	3.97	3.88	3.95

Here, n_{NB}, n_{PB} and n_{B} denote the numbers of annotators assigned as NB, PB and B, respectively, and s_{NB}, s_{PB} and s_{B} denote scoring parameters of NB, PB and B, respectively. In our experiments, we set $(s_{\mathrm{NB}}, s_{\mathrm{PB}}, s_{\mathrm{B}}) = (10.0, -5.0, -10.0)$.

4.2 Experimental Settings

In the word-embedding neural network of our NUR model, we used 1000 embedding cells, a skip-gram window size of five, and learned via 100GB of Twitter data (Other layers were learned by 1281 data points).

In our encoding and ranking RNNs, we used LSTM layers with 1000 hidden cells in each layer. The dropout rate was set to 0.5, and the model was trained via AdaGrad (Duchi et al., 2011).

To validate our NUR model, we conducted experiments with the following two settings:.

Proposed using limited context

To verify the effectiveness of context sequence processing by the ranking RNN, this setting causes our system to only use the last user utterance as context, discarding the rest.

Proposed using MSE

To verify the effectiveness of the Plackett-Luce model, this setting causes our system to learn using the MSE of utterance scores instead of the Plackett-Luce model.

We also compared performance to the following three methods:

BoW + DNN

This method ranks candidate utterances using deep neural networks (DNNs) and bag-of-words (BoW) features. The DNN consisted of six layers, excluding input and output layers optimized by MSE. The input vector is made by concatenating three BoW vectors, i.e., candidate utterance, last user utterance in the given context, and the given context without the last user utterance. In the BoW vector,

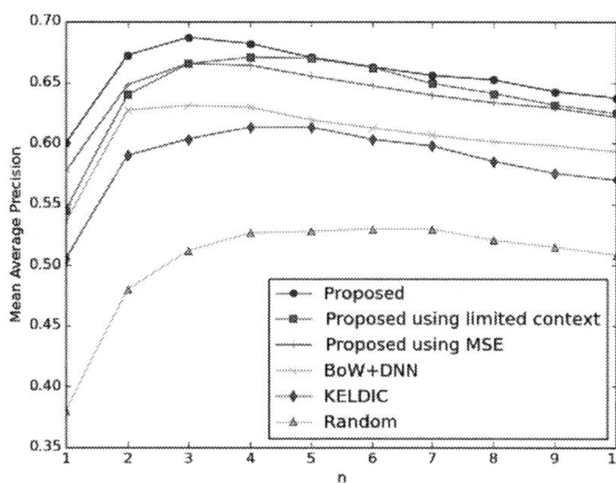

Figure 3: MAP over top n candidates

we used 6203 words that occur at least two times in the training data, thus, the input layer of the DNN has 18609 cells. Each hidden layer has 5000 cells, with ReLU as the activation function, the dropout rate set to 0.5, and the model trained by AdaGrad (Duchi et al., 2011). The score for training was the same as the model proposed in Section 4.1.

KELDIC

The second comparative approach used the output of our KELDIC system. This dialogue system ranks utterances using ListNet (Cao et al., 2007) and selects the top-ranked utterance to reply. The feature vector for ranking is generated from context and candidate utterance. It primarily utilizes n-gram pairs between utterances in context and candidates as features.

Random

This approach randomly shuffles candidates and uses them as a ranking list, thus serving as a baseline for ranking performance.

4.3 Results

To evaluate ranking performance, we used mean average precision (MAP) and mean reciprocal rank (MRR) measures. Figure 3 shows MAP results over the top n ranked candidate utterances, while Figure 4 shows MRR results. Using the MAP measure, our proposed method showed the highest performance as compared to the other methods. The proposed using limited context and MSE follow this, suggesting that utterance encoding by RNN is effective to extract features for ranking.

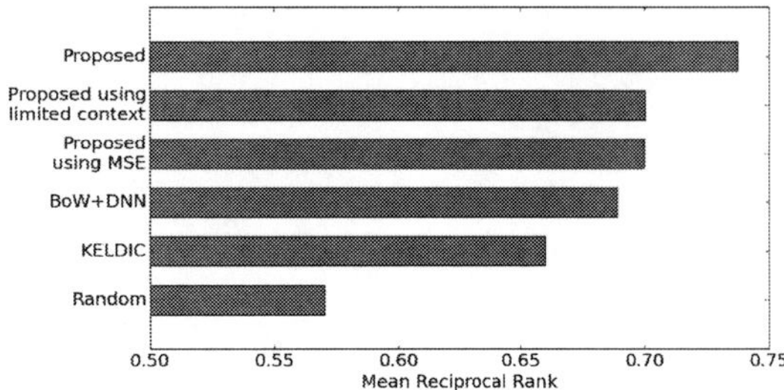

Figure 4: Mean Reciprocal Rank

BoW + DNN did not provide strong performance results, because it could not handle the order relation of utterances in context and syntax due to the use of BoW features. KELDIC showed higher performance than that of Random, but lower than that of BoW + DNN, because it also has the problem of context processing and its generalization capability is lower than that of DNNs.

Here, $n = 1$ of MAP indicates that the rate of correct utterance ranked on the top (The maximum value of $n = 1$ of MAP is 1.0 because each data points in the test data contains at least one correct candidate utterance). Since the top-ranked utterance is selected as a response in dialogue systems, it was found that our proposed method correctly replied with a probability of approximately 60%.

Results of MRR (i.e., Figure 4) showed very similar results, i.e., our proposed method ranked suitable utterances higher.

Table 2 shows an example of context in the test data and Table 3 shows candidate utterances to the context shown in Table 2, plus ranking results for the applied methods and NB rates of annotations for candidates. These results indicate that our proposed method ranked correct utterances higher and incorrect utterances lower, as desired.

5 Dialogue Experiment

In the previous section, since test data must contain correct candidate utterances, the ability of our NUR model in terms of actual dialogue is uncertain, thus we developed a conversational dialogue system based on our proposed method and conducted dialogue experiments with human subjects.

The dialogue format and rules were fully compliant with the Dialogue Breakdown Detection Challenge (DBDC) (see (Higashinaka et al., 2015a)). A dialogue is started by a system utterance, then user and the system communicate with one another. When a system speaks 11 times, the dialogue is finished. Therefore, a dialogue contains 11 system and 10 human utterances.

Our dialogue system and subjects chat on our website; we collected 120 text chat dialogues. Annotators then labeled 1200 system utterances (excluding initial greetings) using breakdown labels NB, PB, and B. We again recruited subjects and annotators via CrowdWorks.

For comparison, we used DBDC development/test data[d] collected by chatting with a system based on NTT Docomo's chat API[e] (see (Onishi and Yoshimura, 2014) . Since the DBDC system selects a suitable response from large-scale utterance data, the architecture is similar to our model and therefore suitable as a comparative system.

DBDC data has been annotated by 30 annotators using the breakdown labels and we use them without any change in this experiment. Therefore, the annotation rule is same but the annotators are different between our dialogue data and DBDC data.

5.1 Dialogue System

A conversational dialogue system based on our NUR model selects an utterance as a response from candidates generated by the acquisition method of (Inaba et al., 2014). The system extracts nouns from the last user and system utterances, generating candidate utterances related to nouns. We used approximately one billion Japanese tweets collected from January through February 2015 for utterance acquisition. Our NUR model ranked candidates, and the system used top-ranked utterances as responses. If there were less than five acquired utterances, the system retroactively extracted nouns in context one by one to acquire further candidates.

The first utterance in the beginning of a dialogue was randomly selected from 16 manually created open question utterances, such as "What is your favorite website?" or "What kind of part-time job do you have?". If the user's response does not contain any nouns or the number of acquired utterances is less than five, the system randomly selects the 16 utterances again.

5.2 Results

Table 4 shows statistics of the data, annotations, and experimental results. Dialogue data used in

[d]https://sites.google.com/site/dialoguebreakdowndetection/
[e]https://www.nttdocomo.co.jp/service/

Table 2: Example context (translated by authors)

Speaker	Utterance in context
User	大学行くモチベーションが見た目に如実に表れてる My motivation to attend college is cosmetically significant.
System	わかります。一夜が明け、仕事へのモチベーションはまずまずであるものの テンションは非常に低いよね I see. It's dawn and although I'm downhearted now, my motivation for working is not bad.
User	わかる Sure.
System	だよね！普段のテンションが高い分、落ち込んだらとことん落ち込むよ Indeed! I have high motivation on an average day, but once I get depressed, things become increasingly worse.
User	そうなんだ。落ち込むな元気出せ！ Oh, don't be so depressed and cheer up!

Table 3: Example candidate utterances with ranking results (translated by authors)

Proposed	BoW + DNN	KELDIC	NB	Candidate Utterance
1	6	3	1.00	相当なモチベーションが必要だよ It requires a considerable degree of motivation.
2	8	6	0.33	独学はモチベーションを保つのが大変だよ Self-education is difficult to keep me motivated.
3	10	2	0.00	どんなモチベーションでチャリこげばいいよね What is my motivation to pedal a bicycle?
4	1	8	0.33	勉強へのモチベーションがすごい My motivation to study is quite good.
5	9	4	0.33	モチベーションには繋がるよ It's to be a motivation.
6	4	9	0.00	ポケモンのモチベーションが皆無だよ I have no motivation to play Pokemon.
7	7	10	0.00	実習のモチベーション保つのって大変だね It's hard to stay motivated in practical training.
8	3	5	0.00 0	東方のモチベーションがすごくなってるよ My motivation to play Touhou games is quite high.
9	5	1	0.00	PC に対するモチベーション低いしやる気でない My motivation to use a PC is low, and I don't feel like doing anything.
10	2	7	0.00	モチベーション低い幹事は良くない An organizer who has low motivation is bad.

our system were annotated by 34 human annotators. Fleiss's K measure for our system's data was lower than that of the DBDC dataset, but both are low. "PB + B" indicates that PB and B are treated as a single label. The table also shows the ratio of NB, PB, and B labels. These annotation results indicate that output probabilities of PB and B utterances by our system were significantly lower, while NB was higher than that of the DBDC system ($p < 0.01$).

The Breakdown ratio (B) and (PB + B) values are calculated by the labels of majority vote in 34 (proposed) or 30 (DBDC) annotators in each system's utterance. Breakdown ratio (B) is the ratio of the B majority label to all majority labels. Breakdown ratio (PB + B) is the ratio of PB and B majority labels (treated as a single label). This indicates that our system can offer a response that does not provoke a critical dialogue breakdown with a probability of approximately 90% and a

399

Table 4: Statistics of the data and experimental results (U and S indicate statistics of user and system utterances, respectively)

	Proposed	DBDC
Dialogues	120	100
Utterances (U)	1200	1000
Utterances (S)	1320	1100
Words per utterance (U)	9.32	9.43
Words per utterance (S)	8.63	7.17
Vocabularies (U)	1684[f]	1491
Vocabularies (S)	1386[f]	1218
Annotators	34	30
NB (Not a breakdown)	57.7%	37.1%
PB (Possible breakdown)	27.0%	32.2%
B (Breakdown)	15.2 %	30.6%
Fleiss's κ (NB, PB, B)	0.26	0.20
Fleiss's κ (NB, PB+B)	0.37	0.27
Breakdown ratio (B)	0.08	0.25
Breakdown ratio (PB+B)	0.42	0.71

very natural response with a probability of 60%. Both breakdown ratios showed significant differences between our system and the DBDC system ($p < 0.001$).

Table 4 also shows the number of words per utterance and the number of vocabularies. These results are important for system evaluation, because if a system always use innocuous responses, such as "I don't know" or "That's true", it is relatively easy to avoid dialogue breakdown. By these values, we can find whether a system frequently uses innocuous responses or not; however, to increase user satisfaction with a dialogue system, it is important not only to avoid dialogue breakdown, but also to offer flexible replies. From Table 4, we also observe that the number of words per utterance and the number of vocabularies in our system were bigger than that of the DBDC system, indicating that our system infrequently used innocuous responses and had a good vocabulary for generating responses. Indeed, our system rarely used such utterances, but the DBDC system sometimes used them.

The number of words per utterance by user between both datasets was almost the same, but the number of vocabularies by user of the DBDC system was lower than that of our system. This was attributable to the DBDC system's utterances that increased the incident of dialogue breakdown.

---

[f] calculated using 100 dialogues

When the DBDC system uses such utterances, the user responds with formulaic responses, such as "What do you mean?". Since the DBDC system frequently caused dialogue breakdowns, users used formulaic replies, and as a result, the number of vocabularies decreased.

6   Conclusions

In this study, we proposed a new utterance selection method called the NUR model for conversational dialogue systems. Our model ranks candidate utterances by their suitability in given contexts using neural networks. Our proposed model encodes utterances in context and candidates into fixed-length vectors, then processes these encoded vectors in chronological order to rank utterances. Experimental results showed that our proposed model ranked utterances more accurately than that of deep learning and other existing methods. In addition, we constructed a conversational dialogue system based on our proposed method and conducted experiments to evaluate its performance via dialogue with human subjects. By comparing the dialogue system of DBDC, we found our system able to conduct conversations more naturally than DBDC.

The dialogue system used in the experiment acquired topic words from given context in a simple manner. Because of this, there are some cases that the system selects inappropriate topics and fails in changing topics. Thus, future work includes topic management. Moreover, the system is unskilled at answering questions, and it often provokes dialogue breakdown. It requires a question-answering method corresponding to conversational dialogue systems.

Acknowledgements

This study received a grant of JSPS Grants-in-aid for Scientific Research 16H05880 and a research grant from Kayamori Foundation of Informational Science Advancement.

References

Dzmitry Bahdanau, Kyunghyun Cho, and Yoshua Bengio. 2015. Neural machine translation by jointly learning to align and translate. *Proc. ICLR*.

Rafael E Banchs and Haizhou Li. 2012. Iris: a chat-oriented dialogue system based on the vector space model. In *Proceedings of the ACL 2012*, pages 37–42. Association for Computational Linguistics.

Ralph Allan Bradley and Milton E Terry. 1952. Rank analysis of incomplete block designs: I. the method of paired comparisons. *Biometrika*, 39(3/4):324–345.

Z. Cao, T. Qin, T.Y. Liu, M.F. Tsai, and H. Li. 2007. Learning to rank: from pairwise approach to listwise approach. In *Proceedings of the 24th international conference on Machine learning*, pages 129–136.

Kyunghyun Cho, Bart van Merrienboer, Caglar Gulcehre, Dzmitry Bahdanau, Fethi Bougares, Holger Schwenk, and Yoshua Bengio. 2014. Learning phrase representations using rnn encoder-decoder for statistical machine translation. *Proceedings of the 2014 Conference on Empirical Methods in Natural Language Processing (EMNLP)*, pages 1724–1734.

K.M. Colby. 1981. Modeling a paranoid mind. *Behavioral and Brain Sciences*, 4(4):515–560.

Antonella De Angeli and Rollo Carpenter. 2005. Stupid computer! abuse and social identities. In *Proceedings of the INTERACT 2005 workshop Abuse: The darker side of Human-Computer Interaction*.

John Duchi, Elad Hazan, and Yoram Singer. 2011. Adaptive subgradient methods for online learning and stochastic optimization. *The Journal of Machine Learning Research*, 12:2121–2159.

Ryuichiro Higashinaka, Nozomi Kobayashi, Toru Hirano, Chiaki Miyazaki, Toyomi Meguro, Toshiro Makino, and Yoshihiro Matsuo. 2014. Syntactic filtering and content-based retrieval of twitter sentences for the generation of system utterances in dialogue systems. *Proc. IWSDS*, pages 113–123.

Ryuichiro Higashinaka, Kotaro Funakoshi, Masahiro Araki, Hiroshi Tsukahara, Yuka Kobayashi, and Masahiro Mizukami. 2015a. Towards taxonomy of errors in chat-oriented dialogue systems. In *16th Annual Meeting of the Special Interest Group on Discourse and Dialogue*, pages 87–95.

Ryuichiro Higashinaka, Toyomi Meguro, Hiroaki Sugiyama, Toshiro Makino, and Yoshihiro Matsuo. 2015b. On the difficulty of improving hand-crafted rules in chat-oriented dialogue systems. In *2015 Asia-Pacific Signal and Information Processing Association Annual Summit and Conference (APSIPA)*, pages 1014–1018.

Ryuichiro Higashinaka, Kotaro Funakoshi, Kobayashi Yuka, and Michimasa Inaba. 2016. The dialogue breakdown detection challenge: Task description, datasets, and evaluation metrics. In *10th edition of the Language Resources and Evaluation Conference*.

Sepp Hochreiter and Jürgen Schmidhuber. 1997. Long short-term memory. *Neural computation*, 9(8):1735–1780.

Michimasa Inaba, Sayaka Kamizono, and Kenichi Takahashi. 2014. Candidate utterance acquisition method for non-task-oriented dialogue systems from twitter. *Transactions of the Japanese Society for Artificial Intelligence*, 29(1):21–31.

Nal Kalchbrenner and Phil Blunsom. 2013. Recurrent continuous translation models. *Proc. EMNLP*, 3(39):413.

Makoto Koshinda, Michimasa Inaba, and Kenichi Takahashi. 2015. Machine-learned ranking based non-task-oriented dialogue agent using twitter data. In *2015 IEEE/WIC/ACM International Conference on Web Intelligence and Intelligent Agent Technology (WI-IAT)*, volume 3, pages 5–8.

Jen-Wei Kuo, Pu-Jen Cheng, and Hsin-Min Wang. 2009. Learning to rank from bayesian decision inference. In *Proceedings of the 18th ACM conference on Information and knowledge management*, pages 827–836.

Jiwei Li, Michel Galley, Chris Brockett, Jianfeng Gao, and Bill Dolan. 2016. A diversity-promoting objective function for neural conversation models. *Proceedings of the NAACL-HLT 2016*.

R.D. Luce. 1959. *Individual choice behavior: A theoretical analysis*. Wiley, New York.

Colin L Mallows. 1957. Non-null ranking models. i. *Biometrika*, 44(1/2):114–130.

Tomas Mikolov, Ilya Sutskever, Kai Chen, Greg S Corrado, and Jeff Dean. 2013. Distributed representations of words and phrases and their compositionality. In *Advances in neural information processing systems*, pages 3111–3119.

Hiroya Murao, Nobuo Kawaguchi, Shigeki Matsubara, Yukiko Yamaguchi, and Yasuyoshi Inagaki. 2003. Example-based spoken dialogue system using woz system log. In *4th SIGdial Workshop on Discourse and Dialogue*, pages 140–148.

Lasguido Nio, Sakriani Sakti, Graham Neubig, Toda Tomoki, and Satoshi Nakamura. 2014. Utilizing human-to-human conversation examples for a multi domain chat-oriented dialog system. *IEICE TRANSACTIONS on Information and Systems*, 97(6):1497–1505.

Kanako Onishi and Takeshi Yoshimura. 2014. Casual conversation technology achieving natural dialog with computers. *NTT DOCOMO Technical Jouranl*, 15(4):16–21.

RL Plackett. 1975. The analysis of permutations. *Applied Statistics*, pages 193–202.

Alan Ritter, Colin Cherry, and William B Dolan. 2011. Data-driven response generation in social media. In *Proceedings of the conference on empirical methods in natural language processing*, pages 583–593.

Lifeng Shang, Zhengdong Lu, and Hang Li. 2015. Neural Responding Machine for Short Text Conversation. *Proceedings of the 53th Annual Meeting of Association for Computational Linguistics and the 7th International Joint Conference on Natural Language Processing*, pages 1577–1586.

Masahiro Shibata, Tomomi Nishiguchi, and Yoichi Tomiura. 2009. Dialog system for open-ended conversation using web documents. *Informatica*, 33(3).

Alessandro Sordoni, Michel Galley, Michael Auli, Chris Brockett, Yangfeng Ji, Margaret Mitchell, Jian-Yun Nie, Jianfeng Gao, and Bill Dolan. 2015. A neural network approach to context-sensitive generation of conversational responses. In *Proceedings of the NAACL-HLT 2015*, pages 196–205.

Hiroaki Sugiyama, Toyomi Meguro, Ryuichiro Higashinaka, and Yasuhiro Minami. 2013. Open-domain utterance generation for conversational dialogue systems using web-scale dependency structures. In *Proc. SIGDIAL*, pages 334–338.

Oriol Vinyals and Quoc Le. 2015. A neural conversational model. In *Proceedings of the ICML Deep Learning Workshop*, pages 1–7.

R.S. Wallace. 2008. The anatomy of A.L.I.C.E. *Parsing the Turing Test*, pages 181–210.

J. Weizenbaum. 1966. ELIZA-a computer program for the study of natural language communication between man and machine. *Communications of the ACM*, 9(1):36–45.

A Dialogue Example

Table 5 shows example dialogue between our NUR-based dialogue system and a user. In the table, NB, PB, and B indicate respective rates of each label by 34 annotators.

Table 5: Examples of dialogues by our system (translated by authors)

Speaker	NB	PB	B	Utterance
System	-	-	-	こんにちは。最近はどんな感じ？ Hello. How have you been recently?
User	-	-	-	鼻炎がひどくてたいへんだよ。 My sinus is really bothering me.
System	100.0%	0.0%	0.0%	鼻炎の人って辛すぎるよ Sinus victims feel terrible.
User	-	-	-	そうなんだよ、くしゃみと鼻水が止まらなんだ。 That's right. I can't stop sneezing and have a runny nose.
System	100.0%	0.0%	0.0%	くしゃみする時の顔ってやばすぎるよ A sneezing face looks so terrible.
User	-	-	-	なので、マスクは必須アイテムです。 So a mask is an indispensable item
System	85.3%	14.7%	0.0%	くしゃみの音が大きいのが悩みだよ My loud sound of sneezing is more worrying.
User	-	-	-	たしかに、マスクじゃ音は止められないね。 I agree that the sound can't be stopped by a mask.
System	94.1%	5.9%	0.0%	くしゃみやばいのは結構辛い Sneezing is bad for my health
User	-	-	-	鼻炎の薬飲んでみたらどうですか？ Why don't you try sinus medicine?
System	58.8%	35.3%	5.9%	鼻炎が酷すぎて辛い My sinus is too terrible.
User	-	-	-	そうだよね、ティッシュペーパーがいくらあっても足りないよね。 Sure. You never have enough tissue paper, don't you?
System	61.8%	32.4%	5.9%	お腹に不安がありすぎて迂闊に咳やくしゃみも出来ねえ Because of my concerns about my stomach, I can't cough and sneeze.
User	-	-	-	やっぱり、医者で鼻炎のおクスリを貰ったらどうですか？ Ideally, why don't you get medicine from a hospital?
System	58.8%	23.5%	17.6%	風邪っぽいのでクスリ飲むよ I seem to have a cold, so I'll take medicine.
User	-	-	-	そりゃあ、早く飲んで栄養つけて休んだ方がいいよ。 You should take that, get nutrition and get some rest.
System	73.5%	26.5%	0.0%	お腹も弱いんだよね I also have a weak stomach.
User	-	-	-	じゃあ、おかゆでも食べる？ Then would you have rice gruel?
System	91.2%	8.8%	0.0%	味がついたおかゆはおいしい Flavored rice gruel is delicious.
User	-	-	-	はい、たまごを混ぜてお塩で味付けした粥です。 Yes, this rice gruel is flavored with egg and salt.
System	20.6%	44.1%	35.3%	照り焼きチキンとたまごのサンドイッチはおいしい Chicken teriyaki and egg sandwich is delicious.

Strategy and Policy Learning for Non-Task-Oriented Conversational Systems

Zhou Yu, Ziyu Xu, Alan W Black and Alex I. Rudnicky
School of Computer Science
Carnegie Mellon University
{zhouyu,awb,air}@cs.cmu.edu, ziyux@andrew.cmu.edu

Abstract

We propose a set of generic conversational strategies to handle possible system breakdowns in non-task-oriented dialog systems. We also design policies to select these strategies according to dialog context. We combine expert knowledge and the statistical findings derived from data in designing these policies. The policy learned via reinforcement learning outperforms the random selection policy and the locally greedy policy in both simulated and real-world settings. In addition, we propose three metrics for conversation quality evaluation which consider both the local and global quality of the conversation.

1 Introduction

Non-task-oriented conversational systems do not have a stated goal to work towards. Nevertheless, they are useful for many purposes, such as keeping elderly people company and helping second language learners improve conversation and communication skills. More importantly, they can be combined with task-oriented systems to act as a transition smoother or a rapport builder for complex tasks that require user cooperation. There are a variety of methods to generate responses for non-task-oriented systems, such as machine translation (Ritter et al., 2011), retrieval-based response selection (Banchs and Li, 2012), and sequence-to-sequence recurrent neural network (Vinyals and Le, 2015). However, these systems still produce utterances that are incoherent or inappropriate from time to time. To tackle this problem, we propose a set of conversational strategies, such as switching topics, to avoid possible inappropriate responses (breakdowns). After we have a set of strategies, which strategy to perform according to

the conversational context is another critical problem to tackle. In a multi-turn conversation, the user experience will be affected if the same strategy is used repeatedly. We experimented on three policies to control which strategy to use given the context: a random selection policy that randomly selects a policy regardless of the context, a locally greedy policy that focuses on local context, and a reinforcement learning policy that considers conversation quality both locally and globally. The strategies and policies are applicable for non-task-oriented systems in general. The strategies can prevent a possible breakdown, and the probability of possible breakdowns can be calculated using different metrics according to different systems. For example, a neural network generation system (Vinyals and Le, 2015) can use the posterior probability to decide if the generated utterance is possibly causing a breakdown, thus replacing it with a designed strategy. In this paper, we implemented the strategies and policies in a keyword retrieval-based non-task-oriented system. We used the retrieval confidence as the criteria to decide whether a strategy needed to be triggered or not.

Reinforcement learning was introduced to the dialog community two decades ago (Biermann and Long, 1996) and has mainly been used in task-oriented systems (Singh et al., 1999). Researchers have proposed to design dialogue systems in the formalism of Markov decision processes (MDPs) (Levin et al., 1997) or partially observable Markov decision processes (POMDPs) (Williams and Young, 2007). In a stochastic environment, a dialog system's actions are system utterances, and the state is represented by the dialog history. The goal is to design a dialog system that takes actions to maximize some measure of system reward, such as task completion rate or dialog length. The difficulty of such modeling lies in the state representation. Representing the dialog by the entire history is often neither feasible nor

404

Proceedings of the SIGDIAL 2016 Conference, pages 404–412,
Los Angeles, USA, 13-15 September 2016. ©2016 Association for Computational Linguistics

conceptually useful, and the so-called belief state approach is not possible, since we do not even know what features are required to represent the belief state. Previous work (Walker et al., 1998) has largely dealt with this issue by imposing prior limitations on the features used to represent the approximate state. In this paper, instead of focusing on task-oriented systems, we apply reinforcement learning to design a policy to select designed conversation strategies in a non-task-oriented dialog systems. Unlike task-oriented dialog systems, non-task-oriented systems have no specific goal that guides the interaction. Consequently, evaluation metrics that are traditionally used for reward design, such as task completion rate, are no longer appropriate. The state design in reinforcement learning is even more difficult for non-task-oriented systems, as the same conversation would not occur more than once; one slightly different answer would lead to a completely different conversation; moreover there is no clear sense of when such a conversation is "complete". We simplify the state design by introducing expert knowledge, such as not repeating the same strategy in a row, as well as statistics obtained from conversational data analysis.

We implemented and deployed a non-task-oriented dialog system driven by a statistical policy to avoid possible system breakdowns using designed general conversation strategies. We evaluated the system on the Amazon Mechanical Turk platform with metrics that consider both the local and the global quality of the conversation. In addition, we also published the system source code and the collected conversations [1].

2   Related Work

Many generic conversational strategies have been proposed in previous work to avoid generating incoherent utterances in non-task-oriented conversations, such as introducing new topics (e.g. "Let's talk about favorite foods!") in (Higashinaka et al., 2014), asking the user to explain missing words (e.g. "What is SIGDIAL?") (Maria Schmidt and Waibel, 2015). In this paper, we propose a set of generic strategies that are inspired by previous work, and test their usability on human users. No researcher has investigated thoroughly on which strategy to use in different conversational contexts. Compared to task-oriented dialog systems, non-

task-oriented systems have more varied conversation history, which are thus harder to formulate as a mathematical problem. In this work, we propose a method to use statistical findings in conversational study to constrain the dialog history space and to use reinforcement learning for statistical policy learning in a non-task-oriented conversation setting.

To date, reinforcement learning is mainly used for learning dialogue policies for slot-filling task-oriented applications such as bus information search (Lee and Eskenazi, 2012), restaurant recommendations (Jurčíček et al., 2012), and sight-seeing recommendations (Misu et al., 2010). Reinforcement learning is also used for some more complex systems, such as learning negotiation policies (Georgila and Traum, 2011) and tutoring (Chi et al., 2011). Reinforcement learning is also used in question-answering systems (Misu et al., 2012). Question-answering systems are very similar to non-task-oriented systems except that they do not consider dialog context in generating responses. They have pre-existing questions that the user is expected to go through, which limits the content space of the dialog. Reinforcement learning has also been applied to a non-task-oriented system for deciding which sub-system to choose to generate a system utterance (Shibata et al., 2014). In this paper, we used reinforcement learning to learn a policy to sequentially decide which conversational strategy to use to avoid possible system breakdowns.

The question of how to evaluate conversational systems has been under discussion throughout the history of dialog system research. Task completion rate is widely used as the conversational metric for task oriented systems (Williams and Young, 2007). However, it is not applicable for non-task-oriented dialog systems which don't have a task. *Response appropriateness (coherence)* is a widely used manual annotation metric (Yu et al., 2016) for non-task-oriented systems. However, this metric only focuses on the utterance level conversational quality and is not automatically computable. Perplexity of the language model is an automatically computable metric but is hard to interpret (Vinyals and Le, 2015). In this paper, we propose three metrics: *turn-level appropriateness, conversational depth* and *information gain*, which access both the local and the global conversation quality of a non-task-oriented conversation. *Information*

---

[1]www.cmuticktock.org

gain is automatically quantifiable. We use supervised machine learning methods to built automatic detectors for *turn level appropriateness* and *conversational depth*. All three of the metrics are general enough to be applied to any non-task-oriented system.

3 Conversational Strategy Design

We implemented ten strategies in total for response generation. The system only selects among Strategy 1-5 if their trigger conditions are meet. If more than one strategy is eligible, the system selects the higher ranked strategy. The rank of the strategies, shown in the following list, is determined via expert knowledge. The system only selects among Strategy 6-10 if Strategy 1-5 cannot be selected. This rule reduces the design space of all policies. We design three different versions of the surface form for each strategy, so the user would get a slightly different version every time, thus making the system seem less robotic.

We implemented these strategies in TickTock (Yu et al., 2015). TickTock is a non-task-oriented dialog system that takes typed text as the input and produces text as output. It performs anaphora detection and candidate re-ranking with respect to history similarity to track conversation history. For a detailed system description, please refer to (Yu et al., 2016). This version of TickTock took the form of a web-API, which we put on Amazon Mechanical Turk platform to collect data from a large number of users. The system starts the conversation by proposing a topic to discuss. The topic is randomly selected from five designed topics: movies, music, politics, sports and board games. We track the topic of the conversation throughout the interaction. Each conversation has more than 10 turns. Table 1 is an example conversation of TickTock talking with a human user. We describe the ten strategies with their ranking order in the following.

1. **Match Response** (continue): In a keyword-based system, the retrieval confidence is the weighted score of all the matching keywords from the user input and the chosen utterance from the database. When the retrieval confidence score is higher than a threshold (0.3 in our experiment), we use the retrieved response as the system's output. If the system is a sequence-to-sequence neural networks system, then we select the output of the system when the posterior probability of the generated response is higher than a certain threshold.

2. **Don't Repeat** (no repeat): When users repeat themselves, the system confronts them by saying:"You already said that!".

3. **Ground on Named Entities** (named entity) A lot of raters assume that TickTock can answer factual questions, so they ask questions such as "Which state is Chicago in?" and "Are you voting for Clinton?". We use the Wikipedia knowledge base API to tackle such questions. We first perform a shallow parsing to find the named entity in the sentence, and then we search the named entity in a knowledge base, and retrieve the corresponding short description of it. Finally we design several templates to generate sentences using the obtained short description of the named entity. The resulting output can be "Are you talking about the city in Illinois?" and "Are you talking about Bill Clinton, the 42rd president of the United States, or Hillary Clinton, a candidate for the Democratic presidential nomination in the 2016 election?". This strategy is considered one type of grounding strategy in human conversations. Users feel like they are understood when this strategy is triggered correctly. In addition, we make sure we never ground the same named-entity twice in single conversation.

4. **Ground on Out of Vocabulary Words** (oov) If we find that the user utterance contains a word that is out of our vocabulary, such as "confrontational". Then TickTock will ask: "What is confrontational?". We expand our vocabulary with the new user-defined words continuously, so we will not ask for grounding on the same word twice.

5. **React to Single-word Sentence** (short answer) We found that some users type in meaningless single words such as 'd', 'dd', or equations such as '1+2='. TickTock will reply: "Can you be serious and say things in a complete sentence?" to deal with such condition.

6. **Switch Topic** (switch) TickTock proposes a new topic other than the current topic, such

as "sports" or "music". For example: "Let's talk about sports." If this strategy is executed, we will update the tracked topic to the new topic introduced.

7. **Initiate Activities** (initiation) TickTock invites the user to do an activity together. Each invitation is designed to match the topic of the current conversation. For example, the system would ask: "Do you want to see the latest Star Wars movie together?" when it is talking about movies with a user.

8. **End topics with an open question** (end): TickTock closes the current topic and asks an open question, such as " Sorry I don't know. Could you tell me something interesting?".

9. **Tell A Joke** (joke): TickTock tells a joke such as: "Politicians and diapers have one thing in common. They should both be changed regularly, and for the same reason". The jokes are designed with respect to different topics as well. The example joke is related to the topic "politics".

10. **Elicit More Information** (more): TickTock asks the user to say more about the current topic, using utterances such as " Could we talk more about that?".

4   Strategy Design

As a baseline policy, we use a random selection policy that randomly chooses among Strategies 6-10 whenever Strategies 1-5 are not applicable. In the conversations collected using the baseline, we found that the sentiment polarity of the utterance has an influence on which strategy to select. People tend to rate the *switch* strategy more favorably if there is negative sentiment in the previous utterances. For example:

TickTock: Hello, I really like politics. Let's talk about politics.
User: No, I don't like politics.
TickTock: Why is that?
User: I just don't like politics.
TickTock: OK, how about we talk about movies?

In another scenario, when all the previous three utterances are positive, the *more* strategy (e.g.

Do you want to talk more about that?) is preferred over the *switch* strategy (e.g. Do you like movies?).

We set out to find the optimum strategy given the context which is the sentiment polarity of the previous three utterances. We found all the scenarios when Strategy 6-10 are triggered, then we generate five different versions of the conversations by replacing the original used strategy with Strategies 6-10. We asked workers on Amazon Mechanical Turk to rate the strategy's appropriateness given three previous utterances. For each conversation, we collected ratings from three different raters and used the majority vote as the final rating. Then we constructed a table of a distribution of the probability of each strategy with respect to the context. We collected 10 ratings for each strategy under each context. We use the Vader (Hutto and Gilbert, 2014) sentiment predictor for automatic sentiment prediction. The output of the sentiment predictor is a label with three categories: positive (pos), negative(neg) and neutral (neu).

We found that the output of the rating task supports our hypothesis: different strategies are preferred with respect to different sentiment context. In Table 3, we show the distribution of appropriateness ratings for Strategy 6-10 in a context when all the previous utterances are positive. Users rated the *more* strategy more appropriate than the *end* strategy and the *switch* strategy. One interesting observation is that the *joke* strategy is rated poorly. We examined the cases in which it is used and found that the low appropriateness is mostly the result of being unexpected. The *initiation* strategy can be appropriate when the activity fits the previous content semantically. In another sentiment context, when there are consecutive negative utterances, the *switch* strategy and the *end* strategy are preferred. We can see that which strategy to use is heavily dependent on the immediately sentiment context of the conversation. Sentiment polarity captures some conversational level information which is a discriminating factor. We then use these findings to design the locally greedy policy. The system chooses the strategy that is rated as the most appropriate given the context. The context is the sentiment polarity of previous three utterances.

We conducted another Amazon Mechanical Turk study to test if sentiment context beyond three utterances would influence the preferred strategy. In order to reduce the work load, we

Turn	Participant	TickTock
1	I am not sure. What's on your mind?	Well, you know, I'm not sure. Let me tell you something, politicians and diapers have one thing in common. They should both be changed regularly, and for the same reason.
2	Wow. That's funny and insightful.	Uhh, I can't answer this. Can we talk about something else?
3	How about movies. Have you seen any good movies?	Of course. What do you think?
4	I love super hero movies. Have you seen Deadpool?	Are you talking about Deadpool,the animation character?
5	Yes, exactly. They made a movie of him.	That sounds really interesting.

Table 1: An example conversation with TickTock in the real-world setting

Turn	A.L.I.C.E.	TickTock
1	When do I do it?	I don't know.
2	That is interesting.	Do you want to go to my friend's party tonight?
3	Sure, just download me to your notebook or PDA and take me along.	Sounds great. Do you want to play board games together some time.
4	I like to play the Turing Game.	I don't know how to play it. Is it difficult to play?
5	Interesting gossip. It could be.	Possibly.

Table 2: An example conversation of TickTock in the simulated setting

tested one condition: the previous three utterances are all positive. We provide the complete conversation history of that dialog to the raters. We found that strategies used most recently are rated less favorably if used again. This motivates us to include information that relates to the previous strategy usage and a longer history to design policy in the reinforcement learning setting.

Strategy	App	Inter	Inapp
switch	0.1	0.3	0.6
initiation	0.2	0.4	0.4
joke	0.1	0.2	0.7
end	0.1	0.3	0.6
more	0.4	0.5	0.1

Table 3: Appropriateness rating distribution when the recent three utterances are positive.

5 Reinforcement Learning

We model the conversation process as a Markov Decision Process (MDP)-based problem, so we can use reinforcement learning to learn a conversational policy that makes sequential decisions by considering the entire context. We used Q-learning, a model-free method to learn the conversational policy for our non-task-oriented conversational system.

In reinforcement learning, the problem is defined as $(S, A, R, \gamma, \alpha)$, where S is the set of states that represents the system's environment, in this case the conversational context. A is a set of actions available per state. In our setting, the actions are strategies available. By performing an action, the agent can move from one state to another. Executing an action in a specific state provides the agent with a reward (a numerical score), $R(s, a)$. The goal of the agent is to maximize its total reward. It does this by learning which action is optimal to take for each state. The action that is optimal for each state is the action that has the highest long-term reward. This reward is a weighted sum of the expected values of the rewards of all future steps starting from the current state, where the discount factor γ is a number between 0 and 1 that trades off the importance of sooner versus later rewards. γ may also be interpreted as the likelihood to succeed (or survive) at every step. The algorithm therefore has a function that calculates the quantity of a state-action combination, $Q : S \times A \to R$. The core of the algorithm is a simple value iteration update. It assumes the old value and makes a correction based on the new information at each time step, t. See Equation (1) for details of the iteration function.

The critical part of the modeling is to design appropriate states and the corresponding reward function. We reduce the number of the states by incorporating expert knowledge and the statistical findings in our analysis. We used another chatbot, A.L.I.C.E. [2] as a user simulator in the training process. We include features: turn index, times each strategy was previously executed, and the sentiment polarity of previous three utterances. We constructed the reward table based on the statis-

[2]http://alice.pandorabots.com/

$$Q_{t+1}(s_t, a_t) \leftarrow Q_t(s_t, a_t) + \alpha_t(s_t, a_t) \cdot \left(R_{t+1} + \gamma \max_a Q_t(s_{t+1}, a) - Q_t(s_t, a_t) \right) \tag{1}$$

$$\text{Turn-level appropriateness} * 10 + \text{Conversational depth} * 100 + round(\text{Information gain}, 5) * 30 \tag{2}$$

tics collected from the previous experiment. In order to make the reward table tractable, we imposed some of the rules we constructed based on expert knowledge. For example, if certain strategies have been used before, then the reward of using it again is reduced. If the trigger condition of Strategy 1-5 is meet, the system chooses them over Strategy 6-10. This may result in some less optimum solutions, but reduces the state space and action space considerably. During the training process, we constrained the conversation to be 10 turns. The reward function is only given at the end of the conversation, it is a combination of the automatic predictions of the three metrics that consider the conversation quality both locally and globally, discussed them in detail in the next section. It took 5000 conversations for the algorithm to converge. We looked into the learned Q table and found that the policy prefers the strategy that uses less frequently if the context is fixed.

6 Evaluation Metrics

In the learning process of the reinforcement learning, we use a metric which is a combination of three metrics: *turn-level appropriateness, conversational depth* and *information gain*. *Conversational depth* and *information gain* measure the quality of the conversation across multiple turns. Since we use another chatbot as the simulator, making sure the overall conversation quality is accessed is critical. All three metrics are related to each other but cover different aspects of the conversation. We used a weighted score of the three metrics for the learning process, which is shown in Equation (2). The coefficients are chosen based on empirical heuristics. We built automatic predictors for *turn-level appropriateness* and *conversation depth* based on annotated data as well.

6.1 Turn-Level Appropriateness

Turn-level appropriateness reflects the coherence of the system's response in each conversational turn. See Table 4 for the annotation scheme. The inter-annotator agreement between the two experts is relatively high (kappa = 0.73). We collapse

the "Appropriate" and "Interpretable" labels into one class and formulate the appropriateness detection as a binary classification problem. Our designed policies and strategies intend to avoid system breakdowns (the inappropriate responses), so we built this detector to tell whether a system response is appropriate or not.

We annotated the appropriateness for 1256 turns. We balance the ratings by generating more inappropriate examples by randomly pairing two utterances. In order to reduce the variance of the detector, we use five-fold cross-validation and a Z-score normalizer to scale all the features into the same range. We use early fusion, which simply concatenates all feature vectors. We use a v-Support Vector (Chang and Lin, 2011) with a RBF Kernel to train the detector. The performance of the automatic appropriateness detector is 0.73 in accuracy while the accuracy of the majority vote is 0.5.

We use three sets of features: the strategy used in the response, the word counts of both the user's and TickTock's utterances, and the utterance similarity features. The utterance similarity features consist of a feature vector obtained from a word2vec model (Mikolov et al., 2013), the cosine similarity score between the user utterance and the system response, and the similarity scores between the user response and all the previous system responses. For the word2vec model, we trained a 100-dimension model using the collected data.

6.2 Conversational Depth

Conversational depth reflects the number of consecutive utterances that share the same topic. We design an annotation scheme (Table 5) based on the maximum number of consecutive utterances on the same topic. We annotate conversations into three categories: "Shallow", "Intermediate" and "Deep". The annotation agreement between the two experts is moderate (kappa = 0.45). Users manually labeled 100 conversations collected using TickTock. We collapse "Shallow" and "Intermediate" into one category and formulate the

Label	Definition	Example
Inappropriate (Inapp)	Not coherent with the user utterance	*Participant*: How old are you? *TickTock*: Apple.
Interpretable (Inter)	Related and can be interpreted	*Participant*: How old are you? *TickTock*: That's too big a question for me to answer.
Appropriate (App)	Coherent with the user utterance	*Participant*: How is the weather today? *TickTock*: Very good.

Table 4: Appropriateness rating scheme.

Conv. depth	Consecutive utterances
Shallow	< 6
Intermediate	$[7, 10]$
Deep	> 10

Table 5: Conversational depth annotation scheme

problem as a binary classification problem. We use the same machine learning setting as the turn level appropriateness predictor. The performance of the automatic conversational depth detector has a 72.7% accuracy, while the majority vote baseline accuracy is 63.6%. The conversational depth detector has three types of features:

1. The number of dialogue exchanges between the user and TickTock and the number of times TickTock uses the *continue*, *switch* and *end* strategy.

2. The count of a set of keywords in the conversation. The keywords are "sense", "something" and interrogative pronouns, such as "when", "who", "why", etc. "Sense" often occurs in sentence, such as "You are not making any sense" and "something" often occurs in sentence, such as "Can we talk about something else?" or "Tell me something you are interested in.". Both of them indicate a possible change of a topic. Interrogative pronouns are usually involved in questions that probe users to go deep into the current topic.

3. We convert the entire conversation into a vector using doc2vec and also include the cosine similarity scores between adjacent responses of the conversation.

6.3 Information Gain

Information gain reflects the number of unique words that are introduced into the conversation from both the system and the user. We believe that the more information the conversation has, the better the conversational quality is. This metric is calculated automatically by counting the number of unique words after the utterance is tokenized.

7 Results and Analysis

We evaluate the three policies with respect to three evaluation metrics: *turn-level appropriateness*, *conversational depth* and *information gain*. We show the results in the simulated setting in Table 6 and the real-world setting in Table 7. In the simulated setting, users are simulated using a chatbot, A.L.I.C.E.. We show an example simulated conversion in Table 2. In the real-world setting, the users are people recruited on Amazon Mechanical Turk. We collected 50 conversations for each policy. We compute *turn-level appropriateness* and *conversational depth* using automatic predictors in the simulated setting and use manual annotations in the real-world setting.

The policy learned via reinforcement learning outperforms the other two policies in all three metrics with statistical significance ($p < 0.05$)in both the simulated setting and the real-world setting. The percentage of inappropriate turns decreases when the policy considers context in selecting strategies. However, the percentage of appropriate utterances is not as high as we hoped. This is due to the fact that in some situations, no generic strategy is appropriate. For example, none of the strategies can produce an appropriate response for a content-specific question, such as "What is your favorite part of the movie?" However, the *end* strategy can produce a response, such as: "Sorry, I don't know, tell me something you are interested." This strategy is considered "Interpretable" which in turn saves the system from a breakdown. The goal of designing strategies and policies is to avoid system breakdowns, so using the *end* strategy is a good choice in such a situation. These generic strategies are designed to

Policy	Appropriateness	Conversational depth	Info gain
Random Selection	62%	32%	50.2
Locally Greedy	72%	34%	62.4
Reinforcement Learning	82%	45%	68.2

Table 6: Performance of different policies in the simulated setting

Policy	App	Inter	Inapp	Conversational depth	Info gain
Random Selection	30%	36%	32%	30%	56.3
Locally Greedy	30%	42%	27%	52%	71.7
Reinforcement Learning	34%	43%	23%	58%	73.2

Table 7: Performance of different policies in the real-world setting.

avoid system breakdowns, so some times they are not "Appropriate", but only "Interpretable".

Both the reinforcement learning policy and the locally greedy policy outperform the random selection policy with a huge margin in conversational depth. The reason is that they take context into consideration in selecting strategies, while the random selection policy uses the *switch* strategy randomly without considering the context. As a result, it cannot keep the user on the same topic for long. However, the reinforcement learning policy only outperforms the locally greedy policy with a small margin. Because there are cases when the user has very little interest in a topic, the reinforcement learning policy will switch the topic to satisfy the *turn-level appropriateness* metric, while the locally greedy policy seldom selects the *switch* strategy according to the learned statistics.

The reinforcement learning policy has the best performance in terms of information gain. We believe the improvement mostly comes from using the *more* strategy appropriately. The *more* strategy elicits more information from the user compared to other strategies in general.

In Table 2, we can see that the simulated user is not as coherent as a human user. In addition, the simulated user is less expressive than a real user, so the depth of the conversation is generally lower in the simulated setting than in the real-world setting.

8 Conclusion and Future Work

We design a set of generic conversational strategies, such as switching topics and grounding on named-entities, to handle possible system breakdowns in any non-task-oriented system. We also learn a policy that considers both the local and global context of the conversation for strategy selection using reinforcement learning methods. The policy learned by reinforcement learning outperforms the locally greedy policy and the random selection policy with respect to three evaluation metrics: turn-level appropriateness, conversational depth and information gain.

In the future, we wish to consider user's engagement in designing the strategy selection policy in order to elicit high quality responses from human users.

References

Rafael E Banchs and Haizhou Li. 2012. Iris: a chat-oriented dialogue system based on the vector space model. In *Proceedings of the ACL 2012 System Demonstrations*, pages 37–42. Association for Computational Linguistics.

Alan W Biermann and Philip M Long. 1996. The composition of messages in speech-graphics interactive systems. In *Proceedings of the 1996 International Symposium on Spoken Dialogue*, pages 97–100.

Chih-Chung Chang and Chih-Jen Lin. 2011. LIBSVM: a library for support vector machines. *ACM Transactions on Intelligent Systems and Technology (TIST)*, 2(3):27.

Min Chi, Kurt VanLehn, Diane Litman, and Pamela Jordan. 2011. Empirically evaluating the application of reinforcement learning to the induction of effective and adaptive pedagogical strategies. *User Modeling and User-Adapted Interaction*, 21(1-2):137–180.

Kallirroi Georgila and David R Traum. 2011. Reinforcement learning of argumentation dialogue policies in negotiation. In *INTERSPEECH*, pages 2073–2076.

Ryuichiro Higashinaka, Kenji Imamura, Toyomi Meguro, Chiaki Miyazaki, Nozomi Kobayashi, Hiroaki

Sugiyama, Toru Hirano, Toshiro Makino, and Yoshi-hiro Matsuo. 2014. Towards an open-domain conversational system fully based on natural language processing. In *COLING*, pages 928–939.

Clayton J Hutto and Eric Gilbert. 2014. Vader: A parsimonious rule-based model for sentiment analysis of social media text. In *Eighth International AAAI Conference on Weblogs and Social Media*.

Filip Jurčíček, Blaise Thomson, and Steve Young. 2012. Reinforcement learning for parameter estimation in statistical spoken dialogue systems. *Computer Speech & Language*, 26(3):168–192.

Sungjin Lee and Maxine Eskenazi. 2012. Pomdp-based let's go system for spoken dialog challenge. In *Spoken Language Technology Workshop (SLT), 2012 IEEE*, pages 61–66. IEEE.

Esther Levin, Roberto Pieraccini, and Wieland Eckert. 1997. Learning dialogue strategies within the markov decision process framework. In *Automatic Speech Recognition and Understanding, 1997. Proceedings., 1997 IEEE Workshop on*, pages 72–79. IEEE.

Jan Niehues Maria Schmidt and Alex Waibel. 2015. Towards an open-domain social dialog system. In *Proceedings of the 6th International Workshop Series on Spoken Dialog Systems*, pages 124–129.

Tomas Mikolov, Kai Chen, Greg Corrado, and Jeffrey Dean. 2013. Efficient estimation of word representations in vector space. *arXiv preprint arXiv:1301.3781*.

Teruhisa Misu, Komei Sugiura, Kiyonori Ohtake, Chiori Hori, Hideki Kashioka, Hisashi Kawai, and Satoshi Nakamura. 2010. Modeling spoken decision making dialogue and optimization of its dialogue strategy. In *Proceedings of the 11th Annual Meeting of the Special Interest Group on Discourse and Dialogue*, pages 221–224. Association for Computational Linguistics.

Teruhisa Misu, Kallirroi Georgila, Anton Leuski, and David Traum. 2012. Reinforcement learning of question-answering dialogue policies for virtual museum guides. In *Proceedings of the 13th Annual Meeting of the Special Interest Group on Discourse and Dialogue*, pages 84–93. Association for Computational Linguistics.

Alan Ritter, Colin Cherry, and William B Dolan. 2011. Data-driven response generation in social media. In *Proceedings of the conference on empirical methods in natural language processing*, pages 583–593. Association for Computational Linguistics.

Tomohide Shibata, Yusuke Egashira, and Sadao Kurohashi. 2014. Chat-like conversational system based on selection of reply generating module with reinforcement learning. In *Proceedings of the 5th International Workshop Series on Spoken Dialog Systems*, pages 124–129.

Satinder P Singh, Michael J Kearns, Diane J Litman, and Marilyn A Walker. 1999. Reinforcement learning for spoken dialogue systems. In *Nips*, pages 956–962.

Oriol Vinyals and Quoc Le. 2015. A neural conversational model. ICML Deep Learning Workshop 2015.

Marilyn A Walker, Jeanne C Fromer, and Shrikanth Narayanan. 1998. Learning optimal dialogue strategies: A case study of a spoken dialogue agent for email. In *Proceedings of the 36th Annual Meeting of the Association for Computational Linguistics and 17th International Conference on Computational Linguistics-Volume 2*, pages 1345–1351. Association for Computational Linguistics.

Jason D Williams and Steve Young. 2007. Partially observable markov decision processes for spoken dialog systems. *Computer Speech & Language*, 21(2):393–422.

Zhou Yu, Alexandros Papangelis, and Alexander Rudnicky. 2015. TickTock: A non-goal-oriented multimodal dialog system with engagement awareness. In *Proceedings of the AAAI Spring Symposium*.

Zhou Yu, Ziyu Xu, Alan Black, and Alexander Rudnicky. 2016. Chatbot evaluation and database expansion via crowdsourcing. In *Proceedings of the chatbot workshop of LREC*.

Author Index

Association for Computational Linguistics
209 N. Eighth Street
Stroudsburg, Pennsylvania 18360

ISBN 978-1-5108-3014-1